SCENE OF THE
Cybercrime
Computer Forensics Handbook

Debra Littlejohn Shinder

Ed Tittel Technical Editor

KEY	SERIAL NUMBER
001	JG9H7GYV83
002	R2UV7T5CVF
003	HJ9HFSCX3A
004	9MB76N679Y
005	U8NLT5R33S
006	X5L7NC4ES6
007	G8D4EB42AK
008	9BKMVC6RD7
009	SGWKP7V6FH
010	5BVFJJM39Z

PUBLISHED BY
Syngress Publishing, Inc.
800 Hingham Street
Rockland, MA 02370

Scene of the Cybercrime: Computer Forensics Handbook

Printed in the United States of America

2 3 4 5 6 7 8 9 0

ISBN: 1-931836-65-5

Technical Editor: Ed Tittel
Acquisitions Editor: Andrew Williams
Developmental Editor: Kate Glennon

Cover Designer: Michael Kavish
Page Layout and Art by: Personal Editions
Copy Editor: Darlene Bordwell
Indexer: Claire A. Splan

Distributed by Publishers Group West in the United States and Jaguar Book Group in Canada.

AAX - 3975

Acknowledgments

We would like to acknowledge the following people for their kindness and support in making this book possible.

Richard Kristof and Duncan Anderson of Global Knowledge, for their generous access to the IT industry's best courses, instructors, and training facilities.

Ralph Troupe, Rhonda St. John, and the team at Callisma for their invaluable insight into the challenges of designing, deploying and supporting world-class enterprise networks.

Karen Cross, Lance Tilford, Meaghan Cunningham, Kim Wylie, Harry Kirchner, Kevin Votel, Kent Anderson, Frida Yara, Bill Getz, Jon Mayes, John Mesjak, Peg O'Donnell, Sandra Patterson, Betty Redmond, Roy Remer, Ron Shapiro, Patricia Kelly, Andrea Tetrick, Jennifer Pascal, Doug Reil, and David Dahl of Publishers Group West for sharing their incredible marketing experience and expertise.

Jacquie Shanahan, AnnHelen Lindeholm, David Burton, Febea Marinetti, and Rosie Moss of Elsevier Science for making certain that our vision remains world-wide in scope.

Annabel Dent and Paul Barry of Elsevier Science/Harcourt Australia for all their help.

David Buckland, Wendi Wong, Marie Chieng, Lucy Chong, Leslie Lim, Audrey Gan, and Joseph Chan of Transquest Publishers for the enthusiasm with which they receive our books.

Kwon Sung June at Acorn Publishing for his support.

Jackie Gross, Gayle Voycey, Alexia Penny, Anik Robitaille, Craig Siddall, Darlene Morrow, Iolanda Miller, Jane Mackay, and Marie Skelly at Jackie Gross & Associates for all their help and enthusiasm representing our product in Canada.

Lois Fraser, Connie McMenemy, Shannon Russell and the rest of the great folks at Jaguar Book Group for their help with distribution of Syngress books in Canada.

A special welcome to the folks at Woodslane in Australia! Thank you to David Scott and everyone there as we start selling Syngress titles through Woodslane in Australia, New Zealand, Papua New Guinea, Fiji Tonga, Solomon Islands, and the Cook Islands.

Author Acknowledgments and Dedications

It may or may not take a village to raise a child, but I know for sure that it takes a whole network of people, across time and the globe, to bring a book like this one into being. An author, like a parent, feels a certain proprietary investment in the final product—but I couldn't have done it alone, and I'm glad I didn't have to.

This book is the culmination of three separate but intertwined vocations I've pursued during my life: law enforcement, computer networking (a.k.a. IT), and writing. They say that in the end, the last shall be first, and that was and is true for me. To be a professional writer was one of my first aspirations, way back in eighth grade when I scrawled my first (badly written but somewhat complete) 300-page novel on notebook paper and loaned it out to friends like a one-person library. I went on to write for and edit my high school and college newspapers, and the teachers and friends who encouraged my ambitions back then deserve the first debt of gratitude: Bobbie Ferguson, Michael Britton, and Barbara Gifford Brown—wherever you are now, thank you.

I never gave up that dream, but the kind of writing I was doing early on didn't pay the bills, so I followed in my father's footsteps into government work, and ended up falling in love with law enforcement and following that path for the third decade of my life. Without my experience as a police officer and police academy instructor, this would be just another tech book, so I want to thank some of those who made all that possible: Larry Beckett, Sarah Whitaker, Danny Price, Marty Imwalle, Mike Walker, Patt Scheckel-Hollingsworth, Lin Kirk Jones, and Neal Wilson.

I enjoyed being a cop, but as I got older, I found there was something else I enjoyed even more—and it was easier on the body and paid better, to boot. I'd been a computer hobbyist for a long time (my old VIC-20 and Commodore 64 are still here on a high shelf in the closet) and after meeting my husband online, together we set up our home network and studied together to become MCSEs. He was as tired of medicine as I was of police work, and when it came time for us to look for a new career we could share, the solution was obvious. The tech world beckoned. We did consulting for a while, and then started teaching. There were many who helped us along the way: Cash Traylor, Johnnie and Irene at Eastfield, Thomas Lee and everyone on the Saluki list, David (Darkcat) Smith and the gang at DigitalThink, Donna Gang at Technology Partners, and all our students in the MCSE programs.

Through it all, writing was still my secret passion. When the opportunity arose to author tech books, it seemed that my life had come full circle. For providing that opportunity, I have to thank the folks at Syngress and Dave Dusthimer at Cisco Press. Many people contributed to the success of my and Tom's writing careers, especially Julie, Maribeth, Kitty, Carl, our tech editors, and most of all, the readers who bought the books.

Which brings us to this book. I had a huge amount of input and assistance from many corners, all of which added value and made writing it easier and more fun: Andrew Williams, who made it possible; James Michael Stewart, without whose contributions to Chapters 8 and 9 this book would not have been finished on time; "Tech Ed" Tittel and Developmental Editor Kate Glennon, whose comments and questions kept me on my toes. I also want to thank David Rhoades of Maven Security, for the information about "click kiddies," and all the law enforcement officers who shared their experiences and cybercrime expertise, especially Wes Edens, Glen Klinkhart, Dave Pettinari, Troy Lawrence, Bryan Blake, Dean Scoville, Robert Bell, Bud Levin and Robert S. Baldygo, James Rogers, Bob Foy, Michael J. West, Tom Burns, and Ira Wilsker.

Finally (and the first shall be last), there were the friends and family members who provided encouragement all along the way. This book is dedicated to Tom (my husband, best friend, and business partner, who also wrote part of the section on name resolution in Chapter 5), Kris and Kniki (the two best kids in the world), Mom, Dad (whom I still miss every day), Jeff Tharp (one of the few friends who really *did* keep in touch after he moved away), all the Piglets (especially Bob, Lash, Dee, Robert, Shawn, bud, the Buerger King, Chief Al, MikeO and "Ms. V, Wherever You Are"), the MarketChat gang, the Storytalkers, the Writingchatters and all the rodents of unusual sizes on the CBP and related lists.

—*Debra Littlejohn Shinder*

Author

Debra Littlejohn Shinder is a former Police Sergeant and Police
Academy Instructor, turned IT professional. She and her husband, Dr.
Thomas W. Shinder, have provided network consulting services to businesses and municipalities, conducted training at colleges and technical
training centers, and spoken at seminars around the country. Deb specializes in networking and security, and she and Tom have written numerous
books, including the best selling *Configuring ISA Server 2000* (Syngress
Publishing, ISBN: 1-928994-29-6), and Deb is the sole author of
Computer Networking Essentials. Deb also is the author of over 100 articles
for print publications and electronic magazines such as *TechProGuild,
CNET, 8Wire*, and *Cramsession*. Deb is a member of the editorial board of
the Journal of Police Crisis Negotiations and the advisory board of the
Eastfield College Criminal Justice Training Center.

Technical Editor and Contributor

Ed Tittel is a 20-year veteran of the computing industry who has worked as a programmer, systems engineer, technical manager, writer, consultant, and trainer. A contributor to over 100 computer books, Ed created the Exam Cram series of certification guides. Ed also writes for numerous Web sites and magazines on certification topics including InformIT.com, *Certification* and *IT Contractor* magazines, and numerous TechTarget venues (www.searchsecurity.com, www.searchnetworking.com, www.searchWin2000.com, www.searchWebManagement.com). When he's not busy writing, researching, or teaching, Ed likes to shoot pool, consume the occasional glass of red wine, and walk his Labrador retriever, Blackie.

Contributors

James Michael Stewart (MCSE, CCNA, CISSP, TICSA, CIW Security Analyst) is a writer, researcher, and trainer who specializes in IT security and networking related certification topics. A contributor to over 75 books, Michael has most recently contributed to titles on CISSP, TICSA, Windows 2000, and Windows XP topics. Michael also teaches for NetWorld + Interop twice yearly, where he offers courses on Windows security and on Windows performance optimization and tuning. In his spare time, Michael is an avid handyman, waterskier, world traveler, and a dancin' fool (primarily the two-step).

Michael Cross (MCSE, MCP+I, CNA, Network+) is an Internet Specialist and Programmer with the Niagara Regional Police Service and has also served as their Network Administrator. Michael performs computer forensic examinations of computers involved in criminal investigations, and has consulted and assisted in cases dealing with computer-related/Internet crimes. He is responsible for designing and maintaining their Web site at www.nrps.com, and two versions of their Intranet (one used by workstations, and another accessed through patrol vehicles). He programs applications used by various units of the Police Service, has been responsible for network security and administration, and continues to assist in this regard. Michael is part of an Information Technology team that provides support to a user base of over 800 civilian and uniform users. His theory is that when the users carry guns, you tend to be more motivated in solving their problems.

Previous to working for the Niagara Regional Police Service, Michael worked as an instructor for private colleges and technical schools in London, Ontario, Canada. It was during this period that he was recruited as a writer for Syngress Publishing, and became a regular member of their writing team. Michael also owns KnightWare, a company that provides Web page design and other services. He currently resides in St. Catharines, Ontario Canada, with his lovely wife, Jennifer.

Contents

Foreword

This book, more than any other I've written up to this point in my life, was a labor of love. It allowed me to combine the knowledge and experience of two careers (over a decade in government and law enforcement, and close to another decade in the computer field, encompassing almost 20 years of working with computers as a hobbyist). When I was a working police officer, computer crime was an esoteric specialty area—investigators in small- and medium-sized agencies rarely encountered a case involving digital evidence, and the term *cybercrime* was unheard of in most police circles.

Today, all of that has changed. In fact, our whole way of life has changed over the past two decades, and many of those changes can be directly attributed to the Internet. I met my husband on the Net in 1994, when I was still a cop and he was practicing medicine. We've come a long way, baby, since then.

Today, the two of us make our livings online, as authors, consultants, and providers of online training. Ninety percent of our business is conducted via the Internet. Many of our friendships began in the virtual world, and we use e-mail to keep in touch with family members in remote locations, with whom we probably would rarely have contact otherwise. There are plenty of others out there like us, whose "real world" lives are inextricably intertwined with the time that we spend in the netherworld of cyberspace. It is inevitable, I suppose, that members of the same antisocial element of society I dealt with as a police officer would find their ways onto the Net, as well.

The more I delved into the intricacies of computers and networking in pursuit of my new profession, the more I was reminded of my old one as I realized that the commercialization and widespread use of the Internet provided opportunities for the scam artists, thieves, child pornographers, drug dealers and abusive personalities that make up every law enforcement officer's cadre of "clientele." Yet much of the law enforcement world seemed to lag behind when it came to technology. In the late

1990s, there were still many agencies across the country where cops did their reports by hand and police secretaries were the only ones in the office who had computers, which they used as nothing more than fancy word processors.

When it comes to computer crimes, the criminals got a big head start. But the law enforcement community in the twenty-first century seems to have finally awakened to the fact that resistance is futile and computers are here to stay. I've watched my former police colleagues struggle to understand this Brave New World where the once-tangible "tool of the crime" can be an ethereal series of bits and bytes, where offenses can be committed by "remote control" from hundreds or thousands of miles away, and where the rules of evidence have been turned upside down by the nature of digital communication. I also began to realize, as cybercrime became the hot topic of the day, that many of my fellow information technology professionals know a lot about programming and network administration but understand very little about the law. Hanging out in techie newsgroups and sorting through posts to police-only mailing lists, I saw a pattern emerging: the information and communication gap between law enforcement and IT was obvious from both sides of the fence. As I heard misperceptions repeated on both sides—misperceptions that made it impossible for the police and IT professionals to combine their talents and efforts against cybercriminals—I kept thinking, "Someone should write a book." So I did.

My goal in writing this book is to reach a dual audience; I hope to give other technical experts a little peek into the law enforcement world, a highly structured environment where the "letter of the law" is paramount and procedures must be followed closely lest an investigation be contaminated and all the evidence collected rendered useless. I also hope to provide law enforcement officers with an idea of some of the technical aspects of how cybercrimes are committed—and how technology can be used to track down and build a case against the criminals who commit them. I want to provide a roadmap that those on both sides of the table can use to navigate the legal and technical landscape, so that together we can understand, prevent, detect, and successfully prosecute the criminal behavior that is as much a threat to the online community as "traditional" crime is to the neighborhoods in which we live.

The first chapter, "Facing the Cybercrime Problem Head On," provides a broad overview of cybercrime: what it is (and isn't), ways in which it's different from other types of crime (and ways in which it isn't), and how we can break the larger concept of "cybercrime" down into categories that make it more manageable to discuss, legislate, enforce, and ideally, prevent. This is where you'll find statistics and formal definitions, as well as a brief introduction to some of the topics that will be covered in more detail in later chapters, such as jurisdictional issues and the nature of local, state, national, and international law regulating online behavior. The chapter ends with a proposal for educating cybercrime fighters at all levels (not only technical professionals and law enforcement officers, but also members of other parts of the criminal justice system, legislators, and the community at large) and explains how a united effort is the only way we'll ever be able to take a significant "byte" out of cybercrime.

Chapter 2, "Reviewing the History of Cybercrime," steps back to take a historical perspective. Cybercrime didn't just "appear" overnight, but there's no doubt that proportionately more criminal activity is occurring online today than in the early years of the Internet. This chapter attempts to analyze the reasons for the rising crime rate in this "place" called cyberspace, by tracing the tremendous growth of the Net from its origins in the 1960s to its present incarnation as a major commercial and sociological force that reaches all over the world. We look at how both the technology itself and the demographic makeup of the Internet have changed over the years, and how that (along with the sheer numbers of people getting online each year) has contributed to the crime problem. This chapter also addresses the ways in which the advent of new technologies makes the lives of criminals—not just our lives—easier.

Chapter 3, "Understanding the People on the Scene," breaks momentarily from the concentration on technological and legal issues to explore the human element of cybercrime. Here we delve into the fascinating new realm of *cyberpsychology*, the study of human behavior in cyberspace. First we discuss the cybercriminals: common motivations, personality types, and the differences between those who commit different types of cybercrimes. We look at the art and science of criminal profiling and how it can be applied to online lawbreakers. But we don't stop there. The criminals aren't the only ones on the scene of the cybercrime whom the investigator needs to understand. We also discuss how to apply the principles of victimology to those who fall prey to cybercriminals, and how an understanding of these principles can help to predict the criminals' behavior and aid in apprehension, along with helping to prevent others from being victimized in the future. Next, we focus on the cybercrimes investigator. Here you'll learn about the characteristics that contribute to being a good cyber-detective, and the skills that are required to do the job. Finally, we briefly discuss the role played by company executives and managers in the cases of cybercrimes that involve corporate networks, and how management personnel can provide an important service by acting as liaison between law enforcement officers and IT personnel.

Chapter 4, "Understanding Computer Basics," plunges you head first into the technical details of how computers work. We provide a "fast track" course (or for some readers, a review) of computer hardware basics, explaining the binary language used by machines to process information and communicate with one another, and we describe how software—especially the operating system—functions as the "middle man" between user and machine. Each section of this chapter includes a subsection titled "Why This Matters to the Investigator," that explains the significance of the information in terms of conducting a criminal investigation.

Chapter 5 is titled "Understanding Networking Basics" and is a natural continuation of the information in the preceding chapter. Here we focus on network communications, describing how they work and introducing you to the hardware and software components that make them possible. You learn about the function of networking hardware (hubs, switches, routers, and more) and you find out about client and server software, network file systems, and protocols. Finally, we focus more tightly on the TCP/IP protocol suite that forms the basis of communications on the Internet and on most large networks today. You'll learn about addressing, routing and name resolution, and how TCP/IP utilities can be used to gather information about the network. Once again, we provide "Why This Matters to the Investigator" sections to tie the technical details back to the work of a cybercrime fighter.

Chapter 6, "Understanding Network Intrusions and Attacks," addresses a specific type of cybercrime—the type that is generally committed by more technically savvy criminals (although you'll learn how "script kiddies" with limited knowledge and skills can also launch these attacks using tools provided by more sophisticated hackers). This chapter looks at the pre-intrusion activities that a hacker may engage in while he or she prepares to attack, and then it moves on to the methods hackers use for gaining entry to networks and/or bringing them down. We include a section on password cracking, and discuss the different types of technical exploits that use the characteristics of common applications, operating systems, and protocols to create Denial of Service and other network disruptions.

Chapter 7 is titled "Understanding Cybercrime Prevention" and it starts with an overview of computer and network security concepts. We discuss physical security and the differences between hardware-based and software-based security products, and you learn why a multi-layered security plan is essential in today's threat-intensive world and how to develop one. We get specific in this chapter, explaining how authentication, confidentiality, and data integrity can be provided using cryptographic techniques; you'll also learn about new methods of identifying network users such as smart cards and biometrics. Another important topic addressed here is firewall technology, as well as packet, circuit, and application filtering—you'll learn how these technologies protect the network. We also discuss digital certificates and the Public Key Infrastructure, and wrap it up with an overview of incident response planning and a detailed discussion of security policies and how they are developed and implemented.

Chapter 8, "Implementing System Security," gets down to the nitty-gritty about how to implement security measures in specific cases and with specific technologies and software. You learn about steps that can be taken to protect broadband connections, ways to make Web browsing safer, and how network administrators can protect Web servers from attack. Next we look at operating system security. You'll find out some of the ways that the different Microsoft operating systems (Windows 9*x*, NT and 2000) are vulnerable to hack attacks and what can be done about it. We also talk about securing UNIX and Linux-based computers, and how security issues affect the Macintosh operating systems, especially Apple's new UNIX-based OS X. Finally, we touch on mainframe security and how wireless networking can be made more secure.

Chapter 9 deals with "Implementing Cybercrime Detection Techniques." This chapter focuses on the issue central to the criminal investigation: gathering information that may be relevant to identifying and apprehending the cybercriminal and that might also serve as evidence in the criminal case. You'll learn here how to use security auditing and read log files, including firewall logs and reports. Then we discuss how to unravel the mystery of e-mail headers to develop clues that lead you back to the sender. You'll find out how to trace domain names and IP addresses, and filter through the wealth of information that is available when you use a commercial Intrusion Detection System (IDS). You'll also learn about the methods that criminals use to hide their identities and avoid detection, such as IP spoofing.

Chapter 10, "Collecting and Preserving Digital Evidence," is the "meat and potatoes" that takes the investigator all the way into the world of computer forensics. Here you learn about how to recover files and bits of data that the suspect may have thought were deleted or erased. You'll also learn about ways to access encrypted data and to find steganographic data that can be hidden, using special software, inside other files. You'll learn about all the places that data can hide on a disk, including file slack, alternate data streams, and partition gaps. You'll find out where to look for "forgotten" evidence that is often left behind in Web caches, history logs, swap files, and other locations. We'll provide step-by-step guidelines for searching and seizing computers and digital evidence, including specific tasks performed by first responders, investigators, and crime scene technicians. We'll tell you how to preserve volatile evidence (evidence that disappears when the computer is powered down) and how to use disk imaging techniques to create exact bitstream duplicates of suspect hard disks so the original can be preserved in its original state. We talk about environmental factors that can affect digital evidence, and how it should be packaged and documented. Next, we look at the legal issues surrounding search and seizure, including search warrant requirements, search without a warrant, and Fourth Amendment issues, and how the courts have applied them to computer-related cases. We also include a section on the ways in which the U.S. Patriot Act has changed the law in regard to electronic evidence.

Chapter 11, "Building the Cybercrime Case," takes you beyond the apprehension of the cybercriminal and the collection of evidence, and shows you how to put together all the information you've gathered in the course of the investigation to prove the prosecution's case. We talk first about some of the difficulties peculiar to cybercrimes, including the lack of concrete definitions and the jurisdictional dilemma. You'll learn about basic criminal justice theory and the bodies and levels of law. You'll also learn the differences between civil and criminal law and how they can sometimes overlap in computer-related cases. We discuss the "naturally adversarial" relationship that often arises between law enforcement officers and IT personnel, provide some explanations for why it occurs, and offer some suggestions to help create more cooperation between the two camps. Then we look at the investigative process, including how to evaluate evidence and how to use the standard investigative tools (information, interview/interrogation, and instrumentation) to facilitate the investigation. We outline the typical steps in an investigation, and how to define areas of responsibility so that the investigative team works most effectively. Finally, we talk about the last step in the process—testifying in a cybercrimes case. We approach this from the standpoints of both evidentiary and expert witnesses, and include some tips on understanding the trial process and dealing with the opposing attorneys' tactics.

Throughout the book, we provide several types of sidebars to supplement the main text. In addition to explanatory Notes, we include the following:

- **CyberStats** These sidebars provide statistical information related to the topic at hand.

- **Crimestoppers** These sidebars provide information about tools and techniques that can be used to help prevent or detect cybercrimes.

- **CyberLaw Review** These sidebars discuss legal aspects of the topic being discussed in the text, including related statutes and case law citations.

- **On the Scene** These are real life accounts of cybercrime investigators and advice based on experiences in the field.

You'll find a lot of citations of other sources as you go through the text. This book was intended to serve as handbook or reference, and I wanted to create something that could be used as a text for introductory cybercrimes courses (including those that I plan to teach), but I also wanted it to be readable and interesting, not a dry academic-styled textbook. I've tried to deal in concepts as well as specifics. I want readers to understand the "big picture," not just how to implement various security solutions or how to use various forensics techniques. The laws and techniques will change over the years, but the concepts that form the foundation of cybercrime fighting will remain the same.

Due to the dynamic nature of the World Wide Web, some of the online resources we cite herein may be gone or relocated by the time you read this book. Please let us know about any dead links; we will attempt to track down new sources for the same or similar information and post them on my Web site at www.sceneofthecybercrime .com and/or the publisher's Web site at www.syngress.com/solutions. You can e-mail me at debshinder@sceneofthecybercrime.com.

Finally, I wanted this to be a *friendly* book, one that could be enjoyed by "just plain folks" who are interested in computer forensics and cybercrime as well as by professionals in the law enforcement and technology fields. I hope I've accomplished that. My wish is that you will have as much fun reading it as I had writing it, and that it will make you think about the constantly evolving nature of both law and technology—just as it forced me to think (and rethink) many of my own ideas about "how things work" as I put them down in words.

Chapter 1

Facing the Cybercrime Problem Head On

Topics we'll investigate in this chapter:

- Defining Cybercrime

- Categorizing Cybercrime

- Fighting Cybercrime

☑ Summary

☑ Frequently Asked Questions

☑ Resources

Introduction

Today we live and work in a world of global connectivity. We can exchange casual conversation or conduct multimillion dollar monetary transactions with people on the other side of the planet quickly and inexpensively. The proliferation of personal computers, easy access to the Internet, and a booming market for related new communications devices have changed the way we spend our leisure time and the way we do business.

The ways in which criminals commit crimes is also changing. Universal digital accessibility opens up new opportunities for the unscrupulous. Millions of dollars are lost to computer-savvy criminals by both businesses and consumers. Worse, computers and networks can be used to harass victims or set them up for violent attacks—even to coordinate and carry out terrorist activities that threaten us all. Unfortunately, in many cases law enforcement agencies have lagged behind these criminals, lacking the technology and the trained personnel to address this new and growing threat, which has been aptly termed *cybercrime.*

Until recently, many information technology (IT) professionals lacked awareness of and interest in the cybercrime phenomenon. In many cases, law enforcement officers have lacked the tools needed to tackle the problem; old laws didn't quite fit the crimes being committed, new laws hadn't quite caught up to the reality of what was happening, and there were few court precedents to look to for guidance. Furthermore, debates over privacy issues hampered the ability of enforcement agents to gather the evidence needed to prosecute these new cases. Finally, there was a certain amount of antipathy—or at the least, distrust—between the two most important players in any effective fight against cybercrime: law enforcement agents and computer professionals. Yet close cooperation between the two is crucial if we are to control the cybercrime problem and make the Internet a safe "place" for its users.

Law enforcement personnel understand the criminal mindset and know the basics of gathering evidence and bringing offenders to justice. IT personnel understand computers and networks, how they work, and how to track down information on them. Each has half of the key to defeating the cybercriminal. This book's goal is to bring the two elements together, to show how they both can and must work together in defending against, apprehending, and prosecuting people who use modern technology to harm individuals, organizations, businesses, and society.

Quantifying the Crisis

Cybercrime: It sounds exotic, the stuff of which futuristic science fiction novels are made. However, law enforcement officers, network administrators, and others who deal with crime and/or cyberspace are discovering that the future is now, and cybercrime is a big and growing problem. For example:

- According to the Internet Fraud Complaint Center (IFCC), a partnership between the Federal Bureau of Investigation (FBI) and the National White Collar Crime Center, between May 2000 and May 2001, its first year of operation, the IFCC Web site received 30,503 complaints of Internet fraud. (The full report can be downloaded in .PDF format at www1.ifccfbi.gov/strategy/IFCC_Annual_Report.pdf.)

- According to the Computer Security Institute's *Computer Crime and Security Survey* for 2001, conducted in conjunction with the FBI's Computer Intrusion Squad, 186 responding corporations and government agencies reported total financial losses of over US\$3.5 million, due primarily to theft of proprietary information and financial fraud (see www.gocsi.com/press/20020407.html).

- According to the Cybersnitch Voluntary Online Crime Reporting System, Internet-related crimes range from desktop forgery to child pornography and include such potentially violent crimes as electronic stalking and terrorist threats. (A full list of reported cybercrimes is available at www.cybersnitch.net/csinfo/csdatabase.asp.)

- According to Meridien Research, as reported at epaynews.com (www.epaynews.com/statistics/fraud.html), the cost of Internet fraud is expected to reach between US\$5 billion and US\$15 billion by 2005.

Although almost anyone has the potential to be affected by cybercrime, two groups of people must deal with this phenomenon on an ongoing basis:

- Information technology professionals, who are most often responsible for providing the first line of defense and for discovering cybercrime when it does occur

- Law enforcement professionals, who are responsible for sorting through a bewildering array of legal, jurisdictional, and practical issues in their attempts to bring cybercriminals to justice

CyberStats...

Charting the Online Population Explosion

Nua Internet Surveys showed that as of February 2002, approximately 544 million people were online worldwide. As the global population becomes more and more "connected," the opportunities for criminals to use the Net to violate the law will expand, and cybercrime will touch more and more lives.

Although it is imperative to the success of any war against cybercrime that these two groups work together, often they are at odds because neither has a real understanding of what the other does or of the scope of their own roles in the cybercrime-fighting process.

Defining Cybercrime

You might not find the word *cybercrime* in your dictionary (ironically, it doesn't even show up in Microsoft's *Encarta World Dictionary 2001,* an online dictionary, as you can see in Figure 1.1), but a Web search for the word, using the popular Google search engine, reveals over 140,000 hits.

We might not officially know what cybercrime is, but everyone is talking about it. Even without a dictionary definition, legislators and law enforcers all over the world seem to believe of cybercrime that they "know it when they see it," as U.S. Supreme Court Justice Potter Stewart said of obscenity in 1964. Laws that address online crime are being passed in all jurisdictions, and those who make and enforce the laws are, after a slow start, springing into action to address the problem.

Police departments in the United States and the rest of the world are establishing computer crimes units, and cybercrime makes up a large proportion of the offenses investigated by these units. The National Cybercrime Training Partnership (NCTP) encompasses local, state, and federal law enforcement agencies in the United States. The International Association of Chiefs of Police (IACP) hosts an annual Law Enforcement Information Management training conference that focuses on IT security and cybercrime. The European Union has created a body called the Forum on Cybercrime, and a number of European states have signed the Council of Europe's Convention on Cybercrime treaty, which attempts to standardize European laws concerning crime on the Internet.

Figure 1.1 The word *cybercrime* doesn't appear in most dictionaries, including Microsoft's online *Encarta*.

Each organization and the authors of each piece of legislation have their own ideas of what cybercrime is—and isn't. These definitions may vary a little or a lot. To effectively discuss cybercrime in this book, however, we need a working definition. Toward that end, we start with a broad, general definition and then define specific cybercriminal offenses.

Moving from the General to the Specific

Cybercrime can be generally defined as a subcategory of computer crime. The term refers to criminal offenses committed using the Internet or another computer network as a component of the crime. Computers and networks can be involved in crimes in several different ways:

- The computer or network can be the tool of the crime (used to commit the crime)

- The computer or network can be the target of the crime (the "victim")

- The computer or network can be used for incidental purposes related to the crime (for example, to keep records of illegal drug sales)

To be enforceable, laws must be specific. It is useful to provide a general definition to be used in discussion, but criminal offenses consist of specific acts or omissions, together with a specified culpable mental state.

In many instances, specific pieces of legislation contain definitions of terms. This is necessary to avoid confusion, argument, and litigation over the applicability of a law or regulation. These definitions should be as narrow as possible, but legislators don't always do a good job of defining terms (and sometimes don't define them at all, leaving it up to law enforcement agencies to guess, until the courts ultimately make a decision).

One of the biggest criticisms of the European treaty is its overly broad definitions. For example, the definition of the term *service provider* is so vague that it could be applied to someone who sets up a two-computer home network, and the definition of *computer data,* because it refers to any representation of facts, information, or concepts in any form suitable for processing in a computer system, would include almost every possible form of communication, including handwritten documents and the spoken word (which can be processed by handwriting and speech recognition software). Likewise, the U.S. Department of Justice (DoJ) has been criticized for a definition of *computer crime* that specifies "any violation of criminal law that involved the knowledge of computer technology for its perpetration, investigation, or prosecution" (reported in the August 2002 *FBI Law Enforcement Bulletin*). Under such a definition, virtually any crime could be classified as a computer crime, simply because a detective searched a computer database as part of conducting an investigation.

These examples illustrate the difficulty of creating usable definitions of cybercrime and related terms. Later in this chapter, we will develop our own working definition of cybercrime for the purposes of this book.

Understanding the Importance of Jurisdictional Issues

Another factor that makes a hard-and-fast definition of cybercrime difficult is the jurisdictional dilemma. Laws in different jurisdictions define terms differently, and it is important for law enforcement officers who investigate cybercrime, as well as network administrators who want to become involved in prosecuting cybercrimes that are committed against their networks, to become familiar with the applicable laws. In the case of most crimes in the United States, that means getting acquainted with local ordinances and state statutes that pertain to the offense. Generally, criminal behavior is subject to the jurisdiction in which it occurs. For example, if someone assaults you, you would file charges with the local police in the city or town where the assault actually took place.

Because cybercrimes often occur in the virtual "place" we call cyberspace, it becomes more difficult to know what laws apply. In many cases, offender and victim are hundreds or thousands of miles apart and might never set foot in the same state or even the same country. Because laws can differ drastically in different geographic jurisdictions, an act that is outlawed in one location could be legal in another.

What can you do if someone in California, which has liberal obscenity laws, makes pornographic pictures available over the Internet to someone in Tennessee, where prevailing community standards—on which the state's laws are based—are much more conservative? Which state has jurisdiction? Can you successfully prosecute someone under state law for commission of a crime in a state where that person has never been? As a matter of fact, that was the subject of a landmark case, *U.S. v. Thomas and Thomas* (see the "CyberLaw Review" sidebar in this section).

CyberLaw Review...

U.S. v. Thomas and Thomas

Robert and Carleen Thomas, residents of California, were charged with violation of the obscenity laws in Tennessee when a Memphis law enforcement officer downloaded sexually explicit materials from their California bulletin board service (BBS) to a computer in Tennessee. This was the first time prosecutors had brought charges in an obscenity case in the location where the material was *downloaded* rather than where it *originated*. The accused were convicted, and they appealed; the appeals court upheld the conviction and sentences; the U.S. Supreme Court rejected their appeal.

Even if the act that was committed is illegal across jurisdictions, however, you might find that no one wants to prosecute because of the geographic nightmare involved in doing so (see the "On the Scene" sidebar in this section for an example of one officer's experience).

We discuss jurisdictional issues in much more depth and detail in Chapter 11, "Building the Cybercrime Case."

On the Scene...

Real Life Experiences

From Wes Edens,
Criminal Investigator and Computer Forensics Examiner

Here's how the typical multijurisdictional case complicates the life of a working police detective. Put yourself in this detective's shoes: Bob Smith, who lives in your jurisdiction in Oklahoma, reports that he has had some fraudulent purchases on his credit card. In addition, he has been informed that two accounts have been opened using his information via the Internet at two banks: Netbank, based in Georgia, and Wingspan, which was recently bought by Bank One.

The suspect(s) applied for a loan to buy a car in Dallas, Texas. As a result, the suspects changed Bob's address on his credit profile to 123 Somewhere Street, Dallas. This is a nonexistent address.

In the course of your investigation, you contact Netbank (Georgia) and they inform you that they do not keep Internet Protocol (IP) addresses of people opening accounts online. You obtain a copy of the online credit application. It contains all of Bob Smith's credit information, but the address is now 321 Elsewhere Street, Dallas. It is also a nonexistent address.

You contact all the companies at which purchases have been made with Bob's bogus credit cards. Half won't speak to you unless you have paperwork, and half of *those* say that the paperwork has to be from a court in the state where they are located, not where you are. Now you have to find police departments in five different states that are willing to help you generate court papers to get records. Since you have filed no charges and the victim (and presumably the suspect) do not live in their jurisdiction, most of these organizations are reluctant to get involved.

You get the paperwork from half of the companies. Of 10, only one actually has an IP address. It is an American Online (AOL) account, which means it could have been accessed from anywhere in the world, further complicating the jurisdictional nightmare, but you press on. You get a subpoena for AOL, requesting the subscriber information for that IP address at that date and time. Three weeks later, AOL informs you that they keep logs for only 21 days, so you're out of luck because the target IP date and time occurred two months ago.

Continued

You run down the 15 phone numbers used on the various suspect accounts and applications. All 15 are different. Three are in Dallas, two in Fort Worth, and the remainder are either disconnected numbers or are in a random spattering of towns across south Texas. There is no apparent connection between any of the numbers. You get the addresses used to ship the purchased items. Every address is different; three are in Dallas, two in Fort Worth. Several are either pay-by-the-week rentals or "flop houses" where people come and go as in a bus station. A couple are mail drops. You subpoena those records, only to find that all the information they contain is bogus.

You decide to visit with your boss and explain to him that you need to travel to another state for a few days to solve this US$1500 caper. He listens intently until you start mentioning going to Georgia, Maryland, and Texas. You then tell him you also have three other such cases that involve nine other states, and you'll probably have to go to all those locations, too. You can hear him laughing as he walks out the door.

You decide to go visit with the DA just for the heck of it. You explain the case thus far, and she asks: What crime was committed here? (Your answer: "Well, none that I know of for sure.") Does the suspect live here? (Probably not.) Can we show that any exchange of money or physical contact between suspect and victim took place here? (No, not really.) Do you have any idea where the suspect is? (Probably in Texas.) Were any of the purchases made in Oklahoma? (No.) Why are you conducting this investigation? (Because the victim is standing in my office.)

The DA tells you that the victim needs to report this crime to the Texas authorities. You give the victim a list of seven different agencies in Texas, one in Georgia, and one in Maryland. You tell him that he needs to contact them. He calls you back three days later and says that they want him to go to each place to fill out a crime report and he can't afford to take off two weeks and travel 2000 miles to report that he is a victim. You suggest he call the FBI, even though deep down you know that they are not going to touch a US$1500 fraud case.

You give up on that case and pick up the other three identity-theft cases that landed on your desk while you were spinning your wheels on this one. You note that all three were done entirely through the Internet and, like the first one, they all involve a multitude of states.

Differentiating Crimes That *Use* the Net from Crimes That *Depend on* the Net

In many cases, crimes that we would call cybercrimes under our general definition are really just the "same old stuff," except that a computer network is somehow involved. That is, a person could use the Internet to run a pyramid scheme or chain letter, set up clients for prostitution services, take bets for illegal gambling, or download pornographic pictures of minors. All these acts are already criminal in certain jurisdictions and could be committed without the use of the computer network. The "cyber" aspect is not a necessary element of the offense; it merely provides the means to commit the crime. The computer network gives criminals a new way to commit the same old crimes. Existing statutes that prohibit these acts can be applied to people who use a computer to commit them as well as to those who commit them without the use of a computer or network.

In other cases, the crime is unique and came into existence with the advent of the Internet. Unauthorized access is an example; while it might be likened to breaking and entering a home or business building, the elements that comprise unauthorized computer access and physical breaking and entering are different. By statutory definition, breaking and entering generally require physical entry onto a premise, an element that is not present in the cyberspace version of the crime. Thus, new statutes had to be written prohibiting this specific behavior.

CyberLaw Review...

Theft of Intangible Property

Theft of intangible property, such as computer data, poses a problem under the traditional theft statutes of many U.S. jurisdictions. A common statutory definition of theft is "unlawful appropriation of the property of another without the effective consent of the owner, with the intent to deprive the owner of the property." (This definition is taken from the Texas Penal Code, Section 31.03.)

This definition works well with tangible property; if I steal your diamond necklace or your new Dell laptop, my intent to deprive you of the use of the property is clear. However, I can "steal" your company's financial records or the first four chapters of the great American novel you're writing *without* depriving you of the property or its use at all.

Continued

If I were prosecuted under the theft statute, my defense attorney could argue that the last element of the offense wasn't met.

This is the reason new statutes had to be written to cover theft of intangible or intellectual properties, which are not objects that can be in the possession of only one person at a time.

"Traditional" intellectual property laws (copyright, trademark, and the like) are civil laws, not prosecuted in criminal court other than under special newer laws pertaining to only narrowly defined types of intellectual property such as software and music. Some federal laws prohibit theft of data, but the FBI and federal agencies have jurisdiction only in certain circumstances, such as when the data is stolen from federal government computers or when it constitutes a trade secret. In most cases, it's up to the state to prosecute. States can't bring charges under federal law, only under their state statutes. Until recently, many states didn't have statutes that covered data theft because it didn't fit under traditional theft statutes and they didn't have "theft of intellectual property" statutes.

Collecting Statistical Data on Cybercrime

Another problem with adequately defining cybercrime is the lack of concrete statistical data on these offenses. At the beginning of this chapter, we provided some statistical information gathered by agencies formed to deal with cybercrime issues. However, reporting crimes to these agencies is voluntary. This means that the figures are almost certainly much lower than the actual occurrence of network-related crimes. This is because not only do an unknown number of cybercrimes go unreported (as with all crimes), but many or most of those that *are* reported to police are not reported to the agencies that collect these statistics.

Currently it is, in fact, practically impossible to even get an accurate count of the number of cybercrimes reported to police. To understand why that's true, let's look at how crime data is reported and collected in the United States.

Understanding the Crime Reporting System

Local law enforcement agencies—municipal police departments and county sheriffs' offices—are individually responsible for keeping records of criminal complaints filed with their agencies, the offenses they investigate, and the arrests they make. There is no mandated, standardized record-keeping system; each agency can set up its own database, use one of many proprietary record-keeping software packages marketed to law enforcement, or even keep the records manually as police agencies did for years prior to the computerization of local government operations.

In an effort to provide national crime statistics, the FBI operates the Uniform Crime Reporting (UCR) program. Local law enforcement agencies complete a monthly report that is sent to the FBI. This information is consolidated and issued as reports documenting the "official" national crime statistics. The program has been in place since the 1960s; over 18,000 agencies provide data, either directly or through their state reporting systems. These statistics are made available to the media and through the FBI's Web site, as shown in Figure 1.2.

Figure 1.2 The FBI collects crime data from local law enforcement agencies and issues annual statistical reports.

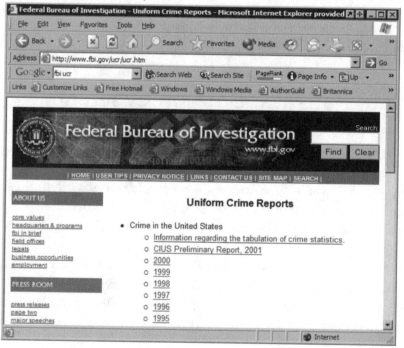

In the 1980s, the UCR program was expanded and redesigned to become an incident-based reporting system in which crimes are placed into predefined categories. The National Incident-Based Reporting System (NIBRS) specifies data to be reported directly to the FBI through data-processing systems that meet the NIBRS specifications. (Agencies that don't have the requisite equipment and resources still file the standard UCR reports.)

Categorizing Crimes for the National Reporting System

NIBRS collects more details on more categories of crime than the UCR, which provides only summaries of various crime categories. Even so, the 22 Group A offense categories and the 11 Group B offense categories for which NIBRS collects data include no category that identifies an offense as a cybercrime. (See the "CyberStats" sidebar in this section for a list of the NIBRS categories.)

CyberStats...

NIBRS Crime Categories

According to the *UCR Handbook* (NIBRS Edition, pages 1–2), offenses are categorized into the following groups. Extensive data is collected for Group A offenses, whereas only arrest data is collected for Group B offenses.

Group A Offense Categories

1. Arson
2. Assault (aggravated, simple, and assault by intimidation)
3. Bribery
4. Burglary/Breaking and Entering
5. Counterfeiting/Forgery
6. Destruction/Damage/Vandalism of Property
7. Drug/Narcotic Offenses (including drug equipment violations)
8. Embezzlement
9. Extortion/Blackmail
10. Fraud Offenses
11. Gambling Offenses
12. Homicide Offenses
13. Kidnapping/Abduction
14. Larceny/Theft (excluding motor vehicle theft)
15. Motor Vehicle Theft

Continued

16. Pornography/Obscenity

17. Prostitution Related

18. Robbery

19. Sex Offenses (forcible)

20. Sex Offenses (nonforcible)

21. Stolen Property Offenses (excluding theft)

22. Weapons Law Violations

Group B Offense Categories

1. Bad Checks

2. Curfew/Loitering/Vagrancy

3. Disorderly Conduct

4. Driving Under the Influence

5. Drunkenness

6. Family Offenses (nonviolent)

7. Liquor Law Violations

8. Voyeurism ("peeping Tom")

9. Runaway

10. Trespass

11. All Other Offenses

As you can see from the list of NIBRS offense categories shown in the sidebar, a local agency reporting a cybercrime must either find a standard category into which it fits (for example, an online con game that asked people to send money to a "charity" under false pretenses would be classified under Fraud Offenses, whereas entering a computer's files from across the Internet and stealing trade secrets would be classified as Theft) or place it into the catch-all "All Other Offenses" category. Either way, no information in the national crime reports generated from this data indicates that these offenses are cybercrimes.

Agencies that deal with cybercrime must formulate their own cybercrime-specific categories for internal record keeping in order to accurately determine the types of cybercrimes occurring in their jurisdictions. Agencies that have technically savvy officers or in-house IT specialists will be able to do this without outside help. In many cases, however, local law enforcement personnel don't have the technical expertise to understand the differences between different network–related crimes. Police officers might understand the concept of "hacking," for example, but they might not be able to differentiate between a hacker who gains unauthorized access to a network and one who disrupts the network's operations by launching a denial of service (DoS) attack against it.

This is where IT professionals can work with law enforcement to help more clearly and specifically define the elements of an offense so that it can be investigated and prosecuted properly. Agencies might need to hire outside IT security specialists as consultants and/or officers might need to receive specialized training to understand the technical elements involved in various cybercrimes.

We discuss the law enforcement-IT professional relationship in detail, along with more specifics about how the two can work together, in Chapter 11.

Toward a Working Definition of Cybercrime

Why is it so important for us to develop a standard definition of cybercrime? Unless we all use the same—or at least substantially similar—definitions, it is impossible for IT personnel, users and victims, police officers, detectives, prosecutors, and judges to discuss the offense intelligently. For that reason, too, it will continue to be impossible to collect meaningful statistics that can be used to analyze crime patterns and trends.

Crime analysis allows agencies to allocate resources more effectively and to plan their own strategies for responding to problems. It is difficult for agency heads to justify the need for additional budget items (specialized personnel, training, equipment, and the like) to appropriations committees and governing bodies without hard data to back up the requests. Standard definitions and meaningful statistical data are also needed to educate the public about the threat of cybercrime and involve communities in combating it. Crime analysis is the foundation of crime prevention; understanding the types of crime that are occurring, where and when they are happening, and who is involved is necessary in order to develop proactive prevention plans.

Even though we have no standard definitions to invoke, let's look at how cybercrime is defined by some of the most prominent authorities.

U.S. Federal and State Statutes

We have already mentioned the somewhat broad definition of computer crime adopted by the U.S. Department of Justice. Individual federal agencies (and task forces within those agencies) have their own definitions. For example, the FBI's

National Computer Crime Squad (NCCS), which is charged with investigating violations of the federal Computer Fraud and Abuse Act, lists specific categories of computer- and network-related crimes that they investigate:

- Public switched telephone network (PSTN) intrusions
- Major computer network intrusions
- Network integrity violations
- Privacy violations
- Industrial/corporate espionage
- Software piracy
- Other crimes in which computers play a major role in committing the offense

Title 18 of the U.S. Code, in Chapter 47, Section 1030, defines a number of fraudulent and related activities that can be prosecuted under federal law in connection with computers. Most pertain to crimes involving data that is protected under federal law (such as national security information), involving government agencies, involving the banking/financial system, or involving intrastate or international commerce or "protected" computers. Defining and prosecuting crimes that don't fall into these categories usually is the province of each state.

Most U.S. states have laws pertaining to computer crime. These statutes are generally enforced by state and local police and might contain their own definitions of terms. For example, the Texas Penal Code's Computer Crimes section defines only one offense, Breach of Computer Security (Texas Penal Code Section 33.02), defined as "knowingly accessing a computer, computer network, or computer system without the effective consent of the owner." The classification and penalty grade of the offense is increased according to the dollar amount of loss to the system owner or benefit to the offender.

California Penal Code (Section 502), on the other hand, defines a list of eight acts that constitute computer crime, including altering, damaging, deleting, or otherwise using computer data to execute a scheme to defraud; deceiving, extorting, or wrongfully controlling or obtaining money, property, or data; using computer services without permission; disrupting computer services; assisting another in unlawfully accessing a computer; or introducing contaminants (such as viruses) into a system or network.

Thus, the definition of computer crime under state law differs, depending on the state. Once again, the jurisdictional question rears its ugly head. If the multijurisdictional nature of cybercrime prevents us from even defining it, how can we expect to effectively prosecute it?

International Law: The United Nations Definition of Cybercrime

Cybercrime spans not only state but national boundaries as well. Perhaps we should look to international organizations to provide a standard definition of the crime.

At the Tenth United Nations Congress on the Prevention of Crime and Treatment of Offenders, in a workshop devoted to the issues of crimes related to computer networks, cybercrime was broken into two categories and defined thus:

> a. Cybercrime in a narrow sense (computer crime): Any illegal behavior directed by means of electronic operations that targets the security of computer systems and the data processed by them.

> b. Cybercrime in a broader sense (computer-related crime): Any illegal behavior committed by means of, or in relation to, a computer system or network, including such crimes as illegal possession [and] offering or distributing information by means of a computer system or network.

Of course, these definitions are complicated by the fact that an act may be illegal in one nation but not in another.

The paper goes on to give more concrete examples, including:

- Unauthorized access
- Damage to computer data or programs
- Computer sabotage
- Unauthorized interception of communications
- Computer espionage

These definitions, although not completely definitive, do give us a good starting point—one that has some international recognition and agreement—for determining just what we mean by the term *cybercrime*.

IT professionals need good definitions of cybercrime in order to know when (and what) to report to police, but law enforcement agencies *must* have statutory definitions of specific crimes in order to charge a criminal with an offense. The first step in specifically defining individual cybercrimes is to sort all the acts that can be considered cybercrimes into organized categories.

Categorizing Cybercrime

As the attempts to define it show, cybercrime is such a broad and all-encompassing term that it is all but useless in any but the most general discussion. Certainly if you called the police to report that your home was burglarized, you wouldn't start by saying that you'd been the victim of a "property crime." In order for police to have a chance of identifying the criminal or to bring charges against that person once identified, they must know the specific act that was committed.

Categorizing crimes as property crimes, crimes against persons, weapons offenses, official misconduct, and so on is useful in that it helps us organize related, specific acts into groups. That way, general statistics can be collected and law enforcement agencies can form special units to deal with related types of crimes. Furthermore, officers can specialize and thus become more expert in categories of crime.

Similarly, it's useful to define categories of cybercrime and then place specific acts (offenses) into those categories. First, we must realize that cybercrimes, depending on their nature, can be placed into existing categories already used to identify different types of crime. For example, many cybercrimes (such as embezzling funds using computer technology) could be categorized as *white-collar crimes,* generally defined as nonviolent crimes committed in the course of business activities, usually (although not always) motivated by monetary profit and often involving theft, cheating, or fraud. On the other hand, Internet child pornographers are usually classified as sex offenders (pedophiles) and regarded as violent or potentially violent criminals.

This crossover into other categories and the widely diverse acts that constitute cybercrime make it difficult to break cybercrime into its own narrower categories. However, most agencies that deal with cybercrime want to do so if only because it also helps them identify the type of suspect they're looking for. (The profile for a person who operates a child pornography site on the Internet is different from that of a person who hacks into others' computer systems, which in turn is different from that of a person who uses e-mail to run a chain letter scheme.)

We discuss the types of cybercriminals and their common characteristics in detail in Chapter 3, "Understanding the People on the Scene."

Developing Categories of Cybercrimes

There are several ways we can categorize the various cybercrimes. We can start by dividing them into two very broad categories: one, those crimes committed by violent or potentially violent criminals, and two, nonviolent crimes.

Violent or Potentially Violent Cybercrime Categories

Violent or potentially violent crimes that use computer networks are of highest priority for obvious reasons: these offenses pose a physical danger to some person or persons. Types of violent or potentially violent cybercrime include:

- Cyberterrorism
- Assault by threat
- Cyberstalking
- Child pornography

The U.S. Department of State defines terrorism as "premeditated politically motivated violence perpetrated against noncombatant targets by subnational groups or clandestine agents." *Cyberterrorism* refers to terrorism that is committed, planned, or coordinated in cyberspace—that is, via computer networks.

This category includes using e-mail for communications between coconspirators to impart information to be used in violent activities as well as recruiting terrorist group members via Web sites. More ambitiously, it could include sabotaging air traffic control computer systems to cause planes to collide or crash; infiltrating water treatment plant computer systems to cause contamination of water supplies; hacking into hospital databases and changing or deleting information that could result in incorrect, dangerous treatment of a patient or patients; or disrupting the electrical power grid, which could cause loss of air conditioning in summer and heat in winter or result in the death of persons dependent on respirators in private residences if they don't have generator backup.

Assault by threat can be committed via e-mail. This cybercrime involves placing people in fear for their lives or threatening the lives of their loved ones (an offense that is sometimes called *terroristic threat*). It could also include e-mailed bomb threats sent to businesses or governmental agencies.

Cyberstalking is a form of electronic harassment, often involving express or implied physical threats that create fear in the victim and that could escalate to real-life stalking and violent behavior.

Child pornography involves a number of aspects: people who create porno-graphic materials using minor children, those who distribute these materials, and those who access them. When computers and networks are used for any of these activities, child pornography becomes a cybercrime.

CyberLaw Review...

National Child Pornography Laws

In the United States, it is a federal crime (18 USC 2251 and 2252) to advertise or knowingly receive child pornography. The Child Pornography Prevention Act (CPPA) of 1996 expanded the definition of *child pornography* to any visual depiction of sexually explicit conduct in which the production involved the use of a minor engaging in sexually explicit behavior, even if the visual depiction only *appears to be* of a minor engaging in such conduct or is advertised or presented to convey the impression that it is of a minor engaging in such conduct. The Free Speech Coalition sued to have the law struck down as unconstitutional, and a federal appellate court did strike down the statute. In October 2001, the Supreme Court heard arguments in the case *Ashcroft v. the Free Speech Coalition* on the constitutionality of the CPPA. In April 2002, the Supreme Court ruled that the provisions of USC 2256 that prohibit "virtual child pornography" (computer-generated images of children engaging in sexual conduct) are overly broad and unconstitutional.

In the United Kingdom, under the Protection of Children Act (1978) and Section 160 of the Criminal Justice Act of 1988, it is a criminal offense for a person to possess either a photograph or a "pseudo-photograph" of a child that is considered indecent. The term *pseudo-photograph* is defined as an image made by computer graphics or that otherwise appears to be a photograph. Typically this is a photograph that is created using a graphics manipulation software program such as Adobe Photoshop to superimpose a child's head on a different body (the same type of "virtual child pornography" addressed by the U.S. Supreme Court in its April 2002 decision).

Most countries have laws addressing child pornography. For a synopsis of national laws compiled by Interpol (the International Criminal Police Organisation), see the Interpol Sexual Offenses Against Children Web site at www.interpol.int/Public/Children/SexualAbuse/NationalLaws.

Child pornography is generally considered a violent crime, even if some of the persons involved have had no physical contact with children. This is the case because sexual abuse of children is required to produce pornographic materials and because people who are interested in viewing these types of materials often do not confine their interest to pictures and fantasies but are instead practicing pedophiles, or aspire to be, in real life.

On the Scene...

Real Life Experiences

From Detective Glen Klinkhart,
Anchorage Police Department Computer Crimes Unit

Not too long ago, a friend of mine with the FBI called me with a request. He told me that he had received a transcript from an Internet Relay Chat (IRC) session, and he wanted to tell me about it. During the IRC correspondence, one of the participants had written a detailed plan about preparing the kidnap and rape of a young boy from a shopping mall. The chat indicated that the mall might be somewhere in our city. The FBI agent asked if I would be interested in reading the chat sessions logs and giving him my opinion of the situation.

When the agent arrived I took a look at the transcript and was horrified by what I read. The IRC session showed what appeared to be two people chatting online. One, called "PITH," apparently sent the FBI the computer chat logs, and the other was the suspect, known only as "Kimmo." PITH saved the chat log file and then contacted law enforcement about the incident. The chat was a chilling and frightening view into a demented mind.

The eight pages of chat noted extremely graphic, sexually explicit details, which included the very specific ways that the suspect said he would enjoy "raping" and "torturing" his victim. During the rest of the chat, the suspect, Kimmo, gave details about the specific shopping mall that he had scoped out and the general location of his cabin, north of the city. Kimmo was very specific about the sexual acts that he was going to perpetrate against his victim. It was apparent that Kimmo had been thinking and fantasizing about this attack for some time.

The FBI and our department immediately began working on the case. At one point, we had 14 agents and police detectives working on

Continued

this single investigation. We continued to track the location of our suspect by going under cover into Internet chat rooms looking for Kimmo, tracing his IP address, and using tools such as search warrants and subpoenas to gather a trail of information leading to our suspect.

The trail led to a divorced father living on the outskirts of the city. Agents began watching him and his house. Others checked into his background and learned more about how he operated. He appeared to have no criminal history; however, he was very adept at using computers. He also matched many of the details that had been communicated to PITH during the disturbing chat session.

We obtained search warrants for the suspect's house and prepared to search his office as well. On a clear, cold morning, we hit the office and the house of our suspect. Another group of officers attempted to interview the suspect.

When confronted, the suspect played it as though he didn't know what we were talking about. He denied any knowledge of the chat session between PITH and Kimmo. When presented with irrefutable evidence, including an electronic trail that led directly to his home computer, he finally admitted that he was Kimmo. He stated that he participated in the chat because he was heavily intoxicated at the time. He told investigators that he had never harmed a child and that he would never hurt anyone.

His computer systems at home and at work told another tale. On his home computer and on various computer media, we found hundreds of images of child pornography, including images of children being forced into bondage and raped. Kimmo had also developed a fondness for collecting hundreds of computer drawings depicting children having their bodies sliced, mutilated, and displayed in disturbing and gory fashion.

The suspect was arrested. He later pleaded guilty to possession and distribution of child pornography. He is currently serving his time in federal prison.

Was the suspect merely drunk when he was chatting with PITH? Would he really "never harm a child," as he told us? Would he have grabbed a kid from the mall and taken him to a cabin to be raped and tortured? We might never know for certain. I do know that for at least the next few years, this guy will not have a chance to make good on his plans, thanks to the hard work of the FBI, the U.S. Attorney's office, and our team of dedicated investigators.

Nonviolent Cybercrime Categories

Most cybercrimes are nonviolent offenses, due to the fact that a defining characteristic of the online world is the ability to interact without any physical contact. The perceived anonymity and "unreality" of virtual experiences are the elements that make cyberspace such an attractive "place" to commit crimes.

Nonviolent cybercrimes can be further divided into several subcategories:

- Cybertrespass
- Cybertheft
- Cyberfraud
- Destructive cybercrimes
- Other cybercrimes

A number of more specific criminal acts can fit into each of these categories.

Cybertrespass

In *cybertrespass* offenses, the criminal accesses a computer's or network's resources without authorization but does not misuse or damage the data there. A common example is the teenage hacker who breaks into networks just "because he (or she) can"—to hone hacking skills, to prove him- or herself to peers, or because it's a personal challenge.

Cybertrespassers enjoy "snooping," reading your personal e-mail and documents and noting what programs you have on the system, what Web sites you've visited, and so forth, but they don't do anything with the information they find. Nonetheless, cybertrespass is a crime in most jurisdictions, usually going under the name of "unauthorized access," "breach of network security" or something similar.

Law enforcement professionals need to be aware of the laws in their jurisdictions and avoid automatically dismissing a complaint of network intrusion simply because the victim can't show loss or damage. Network administrators need to be aware of this crime because under criminal statutes, a company can prosecute intruders simply for accessing the network or its computers without permission. In this regard, it might be easier to build a criminal case than a civil lawsuit, since the latter often requires proof of damages in order to recover.

Cybertheft

There are many different types of *cybertheft,* or ways of using a computer and network to steal information, money, or other valuables. Because profit is an almost universal motivator and because the ability to steal from a distance reduces the thief's risk of detection or capture, theft is one of the most popular cybercrimes. Cybertheft offenses include:

- *Embezzlement,* which involves misappropriating money or property for your own use that has been entrusted to you by someone else (for example, an employee who uses his or her legitimate access to the company's computerized payroll system to change the data so that he is paid extra, or who moves funds out of company bank accounts into his own personal account)

- *Unlawful appropriation,* which differs from embezzlement in that the criminal was never entrusted with the valuables but gains access from outside the organization and transfers funds, modifies documents giving him title to property he doesn't own, or the like

- *Corporate/industrial espionage,* in which persons inside or outside a company use the network to steal trade secrets (such as the recipe for a competitor's soft drink), financial data, confidential client lists, marketing strategies, or other information that can be used to sabotage the business or gain a competitive advantage

- *Plagiarism,* which is the theft of someone else's original writing with the intent of passing it off as one's own

- *Piracy,* which is the unauthorized copying of copyrighted software, music, movies, art, books, and so on, resulting in loss of revenue to the legitimate owner of the copyright

- *Identity theft,* in which the Internet is used to obtain a victim's personal information, such as Social Security and driver's license numbers, in order to assume that person's identity to commit criminal acts or to obtain money or property or use credit cards or bank accounts belonging to the victim

- *DNS cache poisoning,* a form of unauthorized interception in which intruders manipulate the contents of a computer's DNS cache to redirect network transmissions to their own servers

On the Scene...

Real Life Experiences

Press Release, U.S. Department of Justice
Federal agents arrested a Jacksonville, Florida, man in March 2002 for identity theft in connection with stealing personnel records of 60,000 Prudential Insurance Company employees from a computer database. The man was a former IT employee for Prudential, and he attempted to sell the database information over the Internet for the purpose of obtaining fraudulent credit cards using the stolen identities.

Network administrators should be aware that in many cases, network intrusion is much more than simply an annoyance; cybertheft costs companies millions of dollars every year. Law enforcement officers need to understand that theft does not always necessarily involve money; a company's data can also be stolen, and in most jurisdictions, there are laws (including, in some cases, federal laws) that can be used to prosecute those who "only" steal information.

Cybertheft is closely related to cyberfraud, and in some cases the two overlap. This overlap becomes apparent when you encounter cases of cyberfraud that involve misappropriation of money or other property.

Cyberfraud

Generally, *cyberfraud* involves promoting falsehoods in order to obtain something of value or benefit. Although it can be said to be a form of theft, fraud differs from theft in that in many cases, the victim knowingly and *voluntarily* gives the money or property to the criminal—but would not have done so if the criminal hadn't made a misrepresentation of some kind.

Cyberfraud includes the same types of con games and schemes that were around long before computers and networks. For example, the con artist sends an e-mail asking you to send money to help a poor child whose parents were killed in an auto accident, or promising that if you "invest" a small amount of money (by sending it to the con artist) and forward the same message to 10 friends, you'll be sent thousands of times your "investment" within 30 days. Other frauds involve misrepresenting credentials to obtain business (and often not providing the service or product promised). The Internet simply makes it easier and quicker for these con artists to operate and gives them a greatly expanded number of potential victims to target.

Fraudulent schemes, cyber-based or not, often play on victims' greed or good will. Law enforcement professionals find that these crimes can often be prosecuted under laws that have nothing to do with computer crime, such as general fraud statutes in the penal code or business code. Fraud is often aimed at individuals, but network administrators should be aware that con artists also sometimes target companies, sending their pleas for charity and "get rich quick" schemes to people in the workplace, where they can find a large audience. Such "spam" should be reported to the corporate IT department, where steps can be taken to report the abuse to the authorities and/or block mail from the con artist's address if it is a continuing problem.

On the Scene...

Real Life Experiences

Press Release, U.S. Department of Justice,
U.S. Attorney Emily M. Sweeney
A Miami, Florida, man was indicted in September 2001 of defrauding bidders through the eBay online auction site by advertising rare baseball and basketball cards, collecting payments from bidders, and then failing to send the items. He was charged under Title 18 of the U.S. Code, pled guilty, and was sentenced to five months in prison, to be followed by five months of home confinement (electronic monitoring).

Cyberfraud can take other forms; any modification of network data to obtain a benefit can constitute fraud (although some states have more specific computer crimes statutes that apply). For example, a student who hacks into a school system's computer network to change grades or a person who accesses a police database to remove his arrest record or delete speeding tickets from his driving record is committing a form of fraud.

Destructive Cybercrimes

Destructive cybercrimes include those in which network services are disrupted or data is damaged or destroyed, rather than stolen or misused. These crimes include:

- Hacking into a network and deleting data or program files

- Hacking into a Web server and "vandalizing" Web pages

- Introducing viruses, worms, and other malicious code into a network or computer

- Mounting a DoS attack that brings down the server or prevents legitimate users from accessing network resources

Each of these in some way deprives the owners and authorized users of the data and/or network of their use.

Cybervandalism can be a random act done "just for fun" by bored hackers with a malicious streak, or it might be a form of computer sabotage for profit (erasing all the files of a business competitor, for example). In some cases, cybervandalism might be performed to make a personal or political statement (as in *cybergraffiti*).

CNN.com reported on January 8, 2002, that the number of "defaced" Web sites increased more than fivefold between 2000 and 2001. Immediately following the crash landing of a U.S. spy plane in China in 2001, numerous incidents of Chinese and U.S. hackers defacing each other's Web sites were reported in a so-called "cyberwar."

The increase in cybervandalism points up the necessity of not only setting up general intrusion detection systems (IDSs) but also ensuring that known vulnerabilities in Web servers be addressed by staying up to date on the latest attack types and faithfully applying the updates and "fixes" released by vendors to patch such security holes. IT professionals need to be aware that older operating systems and applications were not designed with high security in mind, simply because the risk was not as great and security was not as well understood at the time they were released. On the other hand, new operating systems and applications could have security vulnerabilities that haven't yet been discovered. Most software vendors are quick to address security problems once they become known, but that often doesn't happen until a hacker discovers and exploits the problem.

Law enforcement officials, in many cases, need legislation that specifically addresses network intrusion in order to prosecute cybervandals because it might be difficult to fit these activities into the elements of existing vandalism laws.

Viruses and other malicious code comprise a huge problem to all Internet-connected computers. There is some confusion, even within the tech world, about the terminology used to describe malicious code. A computer *virus* is a program that causes an unwanted—and often destructive—result when it is run. A *worm* is a virus that replicates itself. A *Trojan* (or *Trojan horse)* is an apparently harmless or legitimate program inside which malicious code is hidden; it is a way to get a virus or worm into the network or computer.

Malicious code does millions of dollars' worth of damage to computer systems, and virus writers are very active, continually turning out new viruses and worms and modifying old ones so they won't be detected by antivirus (AV) software. The advent of modern e-mail programs that support Hypertext Markup Language (HTML) mail and attachments has made spreading viruses easier than ever. It's no longer necessary to break into the network to introduce malicious code—now you can simply e-mail it to one technically unsophisticated user, and it will quickly spread throughout the local area network (LAN) and beyond.

AV software such as that marketed by Symantec (Norton AntiVirus, shown in Figure 1.3) and McAfee is an essential part of every network's security plan. Whichever AV package is used, it is essential that its *virus definition files,* used to identify and red-flag known malicious code, be updated frequently.

Viruses, worms, and Trojans are discussed in much more detail in Chapter 6, "Understanding Network Intrusions and Attacks."

Figure 1.3 A good antivirus software package, updated frequently, is an essential first line of defense.

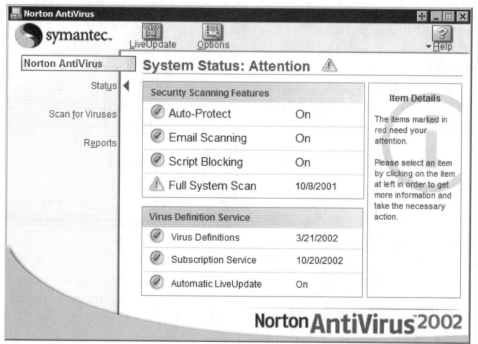

CyberStats...

The Cost of Malicious Code

Computer Economics, a California research organization that advises businesses on technology issues, published a report estimating that virus and other malicious code cost over US$13 billion worldwide in 2001. Critics question the accuracy of the figure, and any such estimate will be just that—an estimate based only on reported cases and relying on companies' assessments of the loss. But there is no question that virus attacks can cost more than just the value of the lost data. Loss in productivity during the resulting downtime, damage to the company's reputation, resultant loss of business, and other difficult-to-measure factors must also be taken into consideration. (See www.computereconomics.com/cei/press/pr92101.html for a discussion of the ramifications.)

Other Nonviolent Cybercrimes

There are many more nonviolent varieties of cybercrime. Again, many of these only incidentally use the Internet to accomplish criminal acts that have been around forever (including the world's oldest profession). Some examples include:

- Advertising/soliciting prostitution services over the Internet
- Internet gambling
- Internet drug sales (both illegal drugs and prescription drugs)
- *Cyberlaundering*, or using electronic transfers of funds to launder illegally obtained money
- *Cybercontraband*, or transferring illegal items, such as encryption technology that is banned in some jurisdictions, over the Internet

Prostitution is illegal in all U.S. states except Nevada and in many countries. The statutes in most states are written in such a way so that soliciting sexual services using the Internet falls under the law. Additionally, according to Mike Goodwin of the Electronic Frontier Foundation, in an interview entitled *Prostitution and the Internet* (published at www.bayswan.org/EFF.html), it is a federal offense to use interstate commerce to solicit "unlawful activity"; 18 USC 1952 defines "prostitution in violation of state laws" as an unlawful activity.

Nonetheless, according to the March 13, 2001, issue of the *E-Commerce Times,* high-tech hookers advertise their services extensively on the Internet, often under the guise of "escort services." Online prostitution is often closely affiliated with online pornography services, which (unless children are involved) are generally protected as speech in the United States under the First Amendment to the Constitution.

An interesting law enforcement issue is that of "cyberprostitution," which involves trading *virtual* sex for money. Because no physical contact actually takes place, these activities don't fall under most states' prostitution statutes. In 1996, the U.S. Congress passed the Communications Decency Act, which prohibited "indecent" or "patently offensive" communications on the Internet. Then, in 1997, in *Reno v. ACLU,* the Supreme Court struck down the law as unconstitutional (a violation of First Amendment free speech). It is important for law enforcement professionals to realize that the laws governing online sexual conduct and content are constantly evolving; this is an area in which it is vital to stay up to date because what's legal today could be illegal tomorrow, and vice versa.

Network professionals have other issues to consider regarding sexual content. Even if not a crime, posting or allowing sexually offensive material on a company network can result in civil lawsuits alleging sexual harassment. Employers who create a "hostile workplace" environment can be sued under Title VII of the Civil Rights Act of 1964.

Internet gambling has flourished, with online customers able to place bets in virtual casinos using credit cards. In July 2000, the U.S. House of Representatives voted on and rejected a proposed Internet Gambling Prohibition Act. However, the federal government has used the 1961 Interstate Wireline Act (18 USC 1084) to prosecute online gambling operations. This act prohibits offering or taking bets from gamblers over phone lines or through other "wired devices" (which include Internet-connected computers) unless authorized by a particular state to do so. As with many other Internet crimes, jurisdiction is a problem in prosecuting Internet gambling proprietors.

Internet gambling is another area in which laws can change quickly and vary tremendously from one jurisdiction to another. Indeed, some states themselves engage in online gambling, offering lottery sales on the Internet.

Internet drug sales comprise another big business. Both the trafficking of illegal drugs and the sale of prescription drugs by online pharmacies are growing problems. The Internet's impact on the international trafficking of illegal drugs such as opium has been studied by the United Nations and individual governments. In March 2000, the UN passed a resolution with the objective of "deterring the use of the World Wide Web for the proliferation of drug trafficking and abuse," encouraging its members to adopt a set of measures to prevent or reduce sales of illicit drugs through the Internet.

CyberLaw Review...

Offline and Online Gambling

In the United States, offline gaming is legal in some states and not in others. Some countries, such as Antigua and other Caribbean states, permit and license Internet gaming operations. Some states have enacted statutes prohibiting Internet gambling. In 2000, South Dakota passed such a law, the Act to Prohibit the Use of the Internet for Certain Gambling Activities, which makes Internet gambling a felony in that state. (The state lottery and casinos licensed in South Dakota are exempt from prosecution, however.)

Internet-based pharmacies that sell controlled substances might be legal, legitimate businesses that work much the same as traditional mail-order pharmacies, abiding by state licensing laws and processing prescriptions issued by patients' doctors. Other online pharmacies provide prescription drugs based merely on a form filled out by the "patient," which is purportedly evaluated by a physician who has never seen the "patient" and without requiring any verification of identification. Spammers bombard the mailboxes of e-mail users with unsolicited advertisements for drugs such as Viagra, diet pills, Prozac, birth control pills, and other popular prescription medicines.

In the United States, the Internet Pharmacy Consumer Protection Act was introduced by a House Committee but failed to make it to the House floor. Nonetheless, a number of existing laws are applicable to the Internet. The Controlled Substances Act and the Food, Drug and Cosmetic Act can be used to prosecute offenders under federal law, and each state has laws regarding licensing of pharmacies and requirements for prescribing and dispensing drugs. The DoJ, the Food and Drug Administration (FDA), and the Federal Trade Commission (FTC) have all cracked down on companies selling controlled substances over the Net without valid prescriptions. In addition, several state attorneys general have sued such online pharmacies to prevent them from doing business in those states. In March 2001, federal and local authorities cooperated to close down an Oklahoma-based pharmacy that allegedly sold prescription drugs illegally online. Law enforcement officials should become familiar with the many state and federal laws that regulate the sales of prescription drugs as well as those that address sales and possession of illicit drugs.

Cyberlaundering involves using the Internet to hide the origins of money that was obtained through illegal means. Money laundering is a very old crime, but the relative anonymity of the Internet has made it easier for criminals to turn "dirty money" into apparently legitimate assets or investments.

NOTE

The origin of the term *money laundering* is said to date back to the habit of the famous Chicago gangster Al Capone: hiding his profits from illegal gambling in coin-operated Laundromats.

The Internet gambling operations discussed earlier provide one way to launder money: a criminal uses the illegally obtained cash in gambling transactions. Online banking also offers opportunities for criminals, who can open accounts without meeting banking officials face to face. Money can be deposited in a secret offshore bank account or transferred electronically from one bank to another until its trail is difficult or impossible to follow. Although criminals still face the challenge of initially getting large amounts of cash deposited into the system without raising suspicions, once they do, they can move these funds around and manipulate them much more easily and quickly with the convenience of today's electronic transfers.

Cybercontraband refers to data that is illegal to possess or transfer. For example, in the United States, the International Traffic in Arms Regulations (ITAR) prohibits the export of strong cryptographic software and invokes prison and/or fines up to US$1 million for sending such software to anyone outside the United States. In 1997, a U.S. District judge ruled that the regulations were unconstitutional and violated First Amendment rights to freedom of speech. In 2000, the Clinton Administration adopted new, more relaxed encryption export regulations.

Under the Digital Millennium Copyright Act (DMCA), software that circumvents protection of copyrighted materials is illegal to make available to the public. A Russian cryptographer named Dmitri Sklyarov was arrested in Las Vegas in 2001 for "trafficking in" a software program that breaks the encryption codes created by Adobe to protect its eBook product. The charges against Sklyarov were dropped in exchange for his agreement to testify against the company he worked for, which was charged with the same offense. At this writing, the latter case is still pending. This, the first criminal case brought under this section of the DMCA, has generated a great deal of controversy, especially since the software in question is legal under the laws of Sklyarov's own country, Russia. There is much disagreement over interpretations of various sections of the DMCA; an interesting aspect is that the act does not appear to prohibit possession (or even use) of the software by end users, only the "provision" of such software to others.

CyberLaw Review...

Making Software Illegal

A bill introduced in the U.S. Senate in 2002 by Senator Fritz Hollings would prohibit creating, selling, or distributing software that does not include government-approved security standards. IT professionals have speculated that if passed, the law would make open-source operating systems such as Linux illegal. In the current national security-conscious environment and with the international focus on preventing terrorism, we can expect to see more proposed laws that would turn certain software programs or even data itself into contraband.

In the United States, most data is currently protected under the First Amendment, although there are obvious exceptions, such as child pornography (discussed earlier in this chapter). The concept of cybercontraband is a relatively new—and controversial—one. Law enforcement professionals are still feeling their way in this area, along with legislators who attempt to balance the freedoms and rights of Internet users with the desire to protect society from "harmful" information.

Prioritizing Cybercrime Enforcement

As cybercrime proliferates, it will obviously be impossible for law enforcement agencies to devote the time and effort required to investigate and prosecute every instance of Internet-related criminal activity. Establishing crime categories helps agencies prioritize enforcement duties.

Factors to consider in deciding which types of cybercrime will get top enforcement priority include:

- **Extent of harm** Cybercrimes that involve violence or potential violence against people (especially crimes against children) are normally of high priority; property crimes that result in the largest amount of monetary loss generally take precedence over crimes for which the amount of loss is less.

- **Frequency of occurrence** Cybercrimes that occur with more frequency usually result in more concerted efforts than those that seldom occur.

- **Availability of personnel** Cybercrimes that can be investigated easily by one detective might get more agency attention simply because there are not sufficient personnel resources to set up sophisticated investigations that require many investigators.

- **Training of personnel** Which cybercrimes are investigated and which aren't sometimes depends on which ones investigators have the training to handle.

- **Jurisdiction** Agencies generally prefer to focus their resources on crimes that affect local citizens. Even if the agency has legal jurisdiction, it might choose not to spend resources on cybercrimes that cross jurisdictional boundaries.

- **Difficulty of investigation** Closely related to the two preceding factors, the difficulty of the investigation and the likelihood of a successful outcome could affect which crimes get top priority.

- **Political factors** The prevailing political climate often influences an agency's priorities. If the politicians who govern the agency have a special concern about specific crimes, enforcement of those crimes is likely to take precedence.

In dealing with law enforcement officials on cybercrime cases, it is important for IT professionals to understand how these factors might cause some cybercrimes to be investigated more enthusiastically and prosecuted more vigorously than others.

Fighting Cybercrime

To successfully fight cybercrime, as with any other type of crime, we must first understand it. *Know thine enemy* is good advice, regardless of the type of war we plan to wage. The first step in developing a plan to fight cybercrime is to define it, both generally and specifically. This chapter has given you some definitions to serve as a starting point in identifying just what cybercrime is—and what it isn't.

Another important element in determining our strategy against cybercrime is to collect statistical data so that we can perform an analysis to detect patterns and trends. Without reliable statistics, it is difficult to establish effective prevention and enforcement policies.

Statistics are the basis for the next step: writing clear, enforceable laws when needed to address cybercrimes that aren't covered by existing laws.

Finally, an effective crime-fighting effort must educate all those who deal with or are touched by cybercrime: those in the criminal system community, those in the IT community, and those in the community at large.

Determining Who Will Fight Cybercrime

By necessity, the fight against cybercrime must involve more than just the police. Legislators must make appropriate laws. The IT community and the community at large must be on the lookout for signs of cybercrime and report it to the authorities—as well as taking measures to prevent becoming victims of these crimes themselves. The law enforcement community must investigate, collect evidence, and build winnable cases against cybercriminals. Jurors must weigh the evidence and make fair and reasonable determinations of guilt or innocence. Courts must assign fair and effective penalties. The corrections system must attempt to provide rehabilitation for criminals who might not fit the standard "criminal profile."

A major problem in writing, enforcing, prosecuting, and interpreting cybercrime laws is the lack of technical knowledge on the part of people charged with these duties. Legislators, in most cases, don't have a real understanding of the technical issues and what is or is not desirable—or even possible—to legislate. Police investigators are becoming more technically savvy, but in many small jurisdictions, no one in the department knows how to recover critical digital evidence. The budget might not allow for bringing in high-paid consultants or, for instance, sending a disk to a high-priced data recovery service (not to mention the fact that both of these options can create chain-of-custody issues that might ultimately prevent the recovered data from being admissible as evidence).

Prosecutors have the advantage of being able to bring in expert witnesses to explain the intricacies, but prosecutors must have a minimal grasp of the technical issues involved to know what to ask those witnesses on the stand. Juries, too, are often in over their heads when evaluating the merits of a cybercrime case. If jury members don't have enough technical understanding to determine for themselves whether the elements of an offense have been proven, they must rely on conflicting opinions presented by the attorneys and the experts without really understanding the basis of those opinions.

On the Scene…

Real Life Experiences

Here's an illustration of how technically complex cybercrime cases can present a challenge to jurors beyond that of, for example, a murder case:

In determining whether a defendant is guilty of murder, the jury will hear testimony, such as eyewitness accounts that the defendant picked up a gun, aimed it at the victim, and fired, or testimony of forensics experts who testify that the defendant's fingerprints were on the gun. The veracity of the witnesses' statements might be in question, and the defense attorney could argue that the defendant had handled the gun previously but didn't use it to kill the victim, but the basic issues are not difficult to understand. Everyone on the jury knows what a gun is, and it is pretty well established that fingerprints are unique and can be positively identified as belonging to a specific person.

In a case involving hacking into a computer network, on the other hand, jurors might hear testimony about open ports and TCP/IP exploits and how IP spoofing can be used to disguise the origin of a network transmission. These terms probably mean little to jurors whose only exposure to computers is as end users, and the finer points of network communications and security are not topics that can be easily explained in the limited amount of time that's usually available during trial testimony. If the jurors don't understand *how* the crime occurred, it will be difficult for them to decide whether a particular defendant committed it.

Judges, too, often have a lack of technical expertise that makes it difficult for them to do what courts do: interpret the laws. The fact that many computer crime laws use vague language exacerbates the problem.

Lack of technical understanding also comes into play when judges hand down sentences. In an attempt to "make the punishment fit the crime," in many jurisdictions judges exercise creativity in dealing with computer-related crimes. Rather than assigning the penalties normally associated with criminal conduct—fines and/or imprisonment—judges are imposing sentences such as probation with "no use of computers or networks" for a specific period of time. In today's world, where computers are quickly becoming ubiquitous, a strict interpretation of some sentences would prohibit a person from even using the telephone network and would make it practically impossible for that person to function—and certainly impossible for him or her to gain productive employment.

Corrections officials don't need technology expertise to deal with cyber-criminal inmates, but they are challenged by a growing population of prisoners unlike the formerly typical lower-class, undereducated criminal they are used to handling. White-collar criminals could be at special risk within a general prison population, yet providing separate facilities for them might bring complaints from politicians and pundits that they are being housed in "country clubs" and given preferential treatment. This situation could escalate to debates charging racial discrimination, since a majority of convicted cybercriminals are white—the opposite of the prison population in general.

The answer to all these dilemmas is the same: education and awareness programs. These programs must be aimed at everyone involved in the fight against cybercrime, including:

- Legislators and other politicians
- Criminal justice professionals
- IT professionals
- The community at large and the cyberspace community in particular

Educating Cybercrime Fighters

An effective cybercrime-fighting strategy requires that we educate and train everyone who will be involved in preventing, detecting, reporting, or prosecuting cybercrime. Even potential cybercriminals, with the right kind of education, could be diverted from criminal behavior.

Educating Legislators and Criminal Justice Professionals

Those who make, enforce, and carry out the law already understand the basics of legislation, investigation, and prosecution. They need training in the basics of information technology: how computers work, how networks work, what can and cannot be accomplished with computer technology, and most important, how crimes can be committed using computers and networks.

This training, to be most useful, should be targeted at the criminal justice audience rather than a repackaging of the same material, taught the same way, that is used to train IT professionals. Although much of the information might be the same, the focus and scope should be different. A cybercrime investigator doesn't need to know the details of how to install and configure an operating system. He or she *does* need to know how a hacker can exploit the default configuration settings to gain unauthorized access to the system.

The training necessary for legislators to understand the laws they propose and vote on is different from the training needed for detectives to ferret out digital evidence. The latter should receive not only theoretical but hands-on training in working with data discovery and recovery, encryption and decryption, and reading and interpreting audit files and event logs. Prosecuting attorneys need training to understand the meanings of various types of digital evidence and how to best present them at trial.

Police academies should include a block on computer crime investigation in their basic criminal investigation courses; agencies should provide more advanced computer crime training to in-service officers as a matter of course. Many good computer forensics training programs are available, but in many areas these tend to be either high-priced, short-duration seminars put on by companies in business to make a profit or in-house programs limited to larger and more urban police agencies. Enrollees primarily tend to be detectives. Few states have standard mandated curricula for computer crime training in their basic academy programs or as a required part of officers' continuing education.

In rural areas and small-town jurisdictions, few if any officers have training in computer crime investigation, although this situation is slowly changing. Again, officers who do have training are usually detectives or higher-ranking officers— yet it is the patrol officer who generally is the first responder to a crime scene. He or she is in a position to recognize and preserve (or inadvertently destroy or allow to be destroyed) valuable digital evidence.

Ideally, all members of the criminal justice system would receive some basic training in computer and network technology and forensics. However, that is an unrealistic goal in the short term. The next best solution is to establish and train units or teams that specialize in computer-related crime. If every legislative body had a committee of members who are trained in and focus on technology issues; if every police department had a computer crime investigation unit with special training and expertise; and if every district attorney's office had one or more prosecutors who are computer crimes specialists, we would be a long way toward building an effective and coordinated cybercrime-fighting mechanism.

For years law enforcement lagged behind in the adoption of computer technology within departments. Over the last decade, the law enforcement community has begun to catch up. Federal agencies such as the FBI have excellent computer forensics capabilities. Large police organizations such as the IACP and Police Futurists International (PFI) have embraced modern technology issues and provide excellent resources to agencies. Metropolitan police departments and state police agencies have recognized the importance of understanding computer technology and established special units and training programs to address computer crime issues. But law enforcement in the United States and other countries still has a long way to go before all law enforcement agencies have the technical savvy to understand and fight cybercrime.

Those agencies that are still lacking in such expertise can benefit greatly by working together with other more technically sophisticated agencies and partnering with carefully selected members of the IT community to get the training they need and develop a cybercrime-fighting plan for their jurisdictions. The Internet reaches into the most remote areas of the country and the world. Cybercrime cannot remain only the province of law enforcement in big cities; cybercriminals and their victims can be found in any jurisdiction.

Educating Information Technology Professionals

IT professionals already understand computer security and how it can be breached. The IT community needs to be educated in other areas:

- **Computer crime awareness** An understanding of what is and isn't against the law, the difference between criminal and civil law, penalty and enforcement issues.

- **How laws are made** This area includes how IT professionals can get involved at the legislative level by testifying before committees, sharing their expertise, and making their opinions known to members of their governing bodies.

- **How crimes are investigated** This area includes how IT professionals can get involved at the investigative level by assisting police, both as victims and interested parties and as consultants to law enforcement agencies.

- **How crimes are prosecuted** This area includes how IT professionals can get involved at the prosecution level as expert witnesses.

- **The basic theory and purpose behind criminal law and the justice system** This area includes why IT professionals should support laws against computer crime.

Perhaps a more controversial issue surrounds the attitude of many IT professionals toward those in law and law enforcement. Although by no means universal, an antipathy toward the government and authority figures is common in some parts of the IT community.

There are undoubtedly a number of reasons for this attitude. Technological prowess is highly valued, so skilled hackers garner a certain amount of admiration, even among many corporate IT pros. The IT industry is young, compared with other professions, and has been largely unregulated. IT professionals fear the inefficiency and increased difficulty that overregulation will impose on them in the course of doing their jobs, as they have seen happen to some other professions. Many tech people are not familiar with legal procedure, and distrust of the unknown is a common human reaction. Finally, many technical people buy into the hacker mantra that "information wants to be free" and disagree with at least some of the cybercrime laws (particularly those restricting encryption technologies and making software and music or movie copyright violations criminal offenses).

Thus, in order to actively engage the IT world in the fight against cybercrime, we face the challenge of educating IT personnel in how cybercrime laws actually work to their benefit. We won't be able to do this unless we can show IT professionals that the laws themselves are fair, that they are fairly enforced, and that they can be effectively enforced. Network administrators and other IT professionals are generally busy people. Even if they believe that cybercriminals should be brought to justice, they won't take the time to report suspected security breaches or work with law enforcement in investigations if they have no confidence in the competence or integrity of the criminal justice system.

One way IT personnel can become more familiar with and more comfortable with the legal process is through more exposure to it. Law enforcement personnel should actively solicit their help and involve them as much as possible in the fight against cybercrime, giving IT professionals a personal stake in the outcome.

Educating and Engaging the Community

Finally, we must educate the community at large, especially the subset that consists of the end users of computer and network systems. These are the people who are frequently direct victims of cybercrime and who all are ultimately indirect victims in terms of the extra costs they pay when companies they patronize are victimized and the extra taxpayer dollars they spend every year in response to computer-related crimes.

Just as neighborhood watch groups and similar programs have given citizens a way to become proactive about crime prevention in their physical localities, educational programs can be developed to teach citizens of the virtual community how to protect themselves online. These programs would teach network users about common types of cybercrime, how to recognize when they are in danger of becoming cybercrime victims, and what to do if they do encounter a cyber-criminal. In some areas, such as online scams and fraud, this type of education alone would greatly reduce the success of con artists' schemes. Organizations such as Cyberangels (www.cyberangels.com) have been created for this purpose.

Law enforcement and IT professionals need to work more closely with the community (including businesses, parents, students, teachers, librarians, and others) to build a cybercrime-fighting team that has the skills, the means, and the authority necessary to greatly reduce the instances of crime on the Internet.

Getting Creative in the Fight Against Cybercrime

The fight against cybercrime has the best chance for success if we approach it from many different angles. The legal process is just one way to fight crime. The best methods are *proactive* rather than *reactive*—that is, it's best to prevent the crime before it happens. Failing that, this section discusses some creative ways that businesses and individuals can shield themselves from some of the consequences of being victims if a cybercrime does occur.

Crimestoppers...

Cybercrime Fighting Organizations

The National Cyber Security Alliance is a cooperative effort between industry and government to foster awareness of cybersecurity through educational outreach and public awareness. More information is available at www.staysafeonline.info.

The National Infrastructure Protection Center (NIPC) was established in 1998 and is located in FBI headquarters in Washington, D.C. It combines representatives from federal, state, and local government, the military, and the private sector to protect the nation's critical infrastructures, including the Internet. More information is available at www.nipc.gov.

The International Association of Computer Investigative Specialists (IACIS) is an international volunteer nonprofit organization from local, state, and federal law enforcement agencies. IACIS provides training and education in the field of forensic computer science. More information is available at http://cops.org.

Using Peer Pressure to Fight Cybercrime

One way to reduce the incidence of Internet crime is to encourage groups to apply peer pressure to their members. If cybercriminals are shamed rather than admired, some will be less likely to engage in the criminal conduct. This method is especially effective when it comes to young people. Many teenage hackers commit network break-ins in order to impress their friends. If more technology-oriented young people were taught a code of computer ethics early—emphasizing that respect for others' property and territory in the virtual world is just as important as it is in the physical world—hackers might be no more admired by the majority of upstanding students than are the "bad kids" who steal cars or break into houses.

Certainly it's been shown that peer pressure and changes in peer group attitudes can affect behavior. To a large degree, the increasing social stigma associated with smoking has been linked with a decline in the percentage of smokers in the United States.

Of course, some people will commit crimes regardless of peer pressure, but this pressure is a valuable tool against many of those cybercriminals who are otherwise upstanding members of the community and whose criminal behavior online erroneously reflects the belief that "everyone does it."

On the Scene...

Real Life Experiences

Jorge Gonzalez, the owner of one Internet file-sharing portal, Zeropaid.com, took an innovative approach to combating the swapping of child pornography through his site. He has posted a number of bogus files on the site, which uses the popular Gnutella file-sharing program. These bogus files are identified as child porn images, although they are not. When users try to access those files, they are "busted." The user's IP address (which can be used to trace his or her identity) is recorded and posted on the site's Wall of Shame. (The Wall of Shame site was actually created by a Gnutella user who identifies himself as Lexx Nexus.) This tactic is similar to the tactics of some newspapers that print the names of people arrested for crimes such as drunk driving or prostitution. The premise is that the fear of publicity will deter some people from committing these crimes.

Using Technology to Fight Cybercrime

In the spirit of "fighting fire with fire," one of our best weapons against technology crimes is—you guessed it—technology. The computer and network security industry is hard at work, developing hardware and software to aid in preventing and detecting network intrusions. Operating system vendors are including more and more security features built into operating systems. In January 2002, Bill Gates announced that security would henceforth be the top priority in developing Microsoft products, and development teams were provided in-depth security training.

Third-party security products, from biometric authentication devices to firewall software, are available in abundance to prevent cybercriminals from invading your network or system. Monitoring and auditing packages allow IT professionals to collect detailed information to assist in detecting suspicious activities. Many of these packages include notification features that can alert network administrators immediately when a breach occurs.

Data recovery products assist law enforcement personnel in gathering evidence despite criminals' efforts to destroy it, and police can—with a search warrant—get into criminals' protected systems using the same tools that hackers use to illegitimately break into systems.

We discuss all these technologies and more in Chapter 7, "Understanding Cybercrime Prevention"; Chapter 8, "Implementing System Security"; Chapter 9, "Implementing Cybercrime Detection Techniques"; and Chapter 10, "Collecting and Preserving Digital Evidence."

Finding New Ways to Protect Against Cybercrime

It is not possible to prevent all cybercrime or to always avoid becoming a cybercrime victim. However, organizations and individuals can take steps in advance to minimize the impact that cybercrime will have on them or their organizations.

For example, *The Austin Business Journal* reported in the April 28, 2000, print edition that companies are taking out insurance policies to cover cybercrime-related damages. As the cybercrime problem grows, it is inevitable that potential victims will come up with new ways to protect themselves from financial loss.

Summary

Cybercrime is already a big problem all over the world—and it's growing fast. The law enforcement world is scrambling to catch up; legislators are passing new laws to address this new way of committing crime, and police agencies are forming special computer crime units and pushing their officers to become more technically savvy.

However, the cybercrime problem is too big and too widespread to leave to politicians and police to solve. The former often don't have the technical expertise to pass effective laws, and the latter lack sufficient training, manpower, and time—not to mention the confusing issue of jurisdiction—to tackle any but the most egregious of Internet crimes.

Cybercrime, like crime in general, is a social problem as well as a legal one. To successfully fight it, we must engage people in the IT community (many of whom might be reluctant to participate) and those in the general population who are affected, directly or indirectly, by the criminal activity that has found a friendly haven in the virtual world.

We can use a number of tactics and techniques, including the legal system, peer pressure, and existing and emerging technologies, to prevent cybercrime. Failing that, we can develop formal and informal responses that will detect cybercrime more immediately, minimizing the harm done and giving us more information about the incident, maximizing the chances of identifying and successfully prosecuting the cybercriminal.

We're all in this boat together. The only way to stop cybercrime is to work together and share our knowledge and expertise in different areas to build a Class A cybercrime-fighting team.

Frequently Asked Questions

The following Frequently Asked Questions, answered by the authors of this book, are designed to both measure your understanding of the concepts presented in this chapter and to assist you with real-life implementation of these concepts. To have your questions about this chapter answered by the author, browse to **www.syngress.com/solutions** and click on the **"Ask the Author"** form.

Q: Is the law enforcement community opposed to the use of encryption?

A: Most law enforcement professionals who specialize in cybercrime do not oppose use of encryption for legitimate communications. The Department of Justice states its official position on the www.cybercrime.gov Web site: "We do not oppose the use of encryption—just the opposite, because strong encryption can be an extraordinary tool to prevent crime. We believe that the use of strong cryptography is critical to the development of the 'Global Information Infrastructure,' or the GII. We agree that communications and data must be protected—both in transit and in storage—if the GII is to be used for personal communications, financial transactions, medical care, the development of new intellectual property, and other applications. The widespread use of unrecoverable encryption by criminals, however, poses a serious risk to public safety."

Q: Is software piracy really a big problem?

A: According to some estimates, the average purse snatcher gets only US$20 or US$30 per stolen purse, and the average strong-arm robbery (mugging) yields US$50 or less. In contrast, pirated software programs often cost from several hundred to several thousand dollars. Thus, economically, one act of software piracy is several times more "serious" than victimization by a petty thief or robber.

Q: Why, then, do many people feel that software piracy is not a serious crime?

A: There are a number of reasons. Software piracy doesn't carry the emotional, face-to-face impact that purse snatching and robbery do. Software is "intangible"; it is made up of bits and bytes of electronic data, unlike a piece of physical property. Software piracy is not "theft" in the traditional meaning of the word because it is taken by copying, not by depriving the owner of its use. Many people feel that software vendors' licensing terms are unfair, and thus piracy is somewhat justified retaliation. There is also a general feeling that because copying of software is so widespread and appears to do no harm, it's not a "real crime" (similarly to the way many people, who would never think of running a red light, feel about speeding).

Q: With all the computer and network security products currently on the market, why aren't all systems completely secured?

A: Despite all the excellent products available, the only completely secure computer is one that is turned off. In law enforcement firearms training, officers learn about "security holsters" that are designed to prevent a criminal from taking away an officer's weapon and using it against him or her. The first thing an officer who tries a security holster learns is that it is more difficult to use than a traditional, nonsecure holster and that the officer must practice diligently or he won't be able to draw his weapon quickly when it's needed. The simple truth is that the only totally secure holster is one into which the gun is permanently glued. Then it's not accessible to the bad guy, but it's not accessible to the officer, either. Computer and network security includes this same balancing act of security and accessibility, and the two factors will always be at odds. The more secure your systems, the less accessible they are, and vice versa. Because the very purpose of a computer network is accessibility, no network can ever be 100-percent secure.

References

- Internet Fraud Complaint Center (IFCC) statistical reports
  www1.ifccfbi.gov/index.asp

- Computer Security Institute *2001 Computer Crime and Security Survey*
  www.gocsi.com/prelea/000321.html

- Cybersnitch Basic Crime Report Statistics
  www.cybersnitch.net/csinfo/csdatabase.asp

- Meridien Research
  www.meridien-research.com

- National Cybercrime Training Partnership (NCTP)
  www.nctp.org

- International Association of Chiefs of Police (IACP)
  Law Enforcement Information Management Training Conference
  www.iacptechnology.org/2002LEIM.htm

- Council of Europe Convention on Cybercrime Treaty
  http://conventions.coe.int/Treaty/EN/WhatYouWant.asp?NT=185

- Tenth United Nations Congress on the Prevention of Crime and the
  Treatment of Offenders, Vienna, April 2000
  www.uncjin.org/Documents/congr10/4r3e.pdf

- Texas Penal Code, Chapter 33, Computer Crimes
  www.capitol.state.tx.us/statutes/pe/pe003300.html#pe001.33.01

- California Penal Code, Section 502, Computer Crimes
  http://caselaw.lp.findlaw.com/cacodes/pen/484-502.9.html

- *Cyberterrorism: Fact or Fancy*, Mark M. Pollitt, FBI Laboratory
  www.cs.georgetown.edu/~denning/infosec/pollitt.html

- National Center for Victims of Crime Cyberstalking
  www.ncvc.org/special/cyber_stk.htm

- Regulation of Child Pornography on the Internet resource page
  www.cyber-rights.org/reports/child.htm

- CNN.com, January 8, 2002: Report: *Cybervandalism Jumped in 2001*
  www.cnn.com/2002/TECH/internet/01/08/cybervandal.jump.idg/
  ?related

- E-Commerce Times, March 13, 2001: *New Economy, Oldest Profession*
  www.ecommercetimes.com/perl/story/8121.html

- *Understanding the Law of Internet Gambling,*
  I. Nelson Rose, Professor of Law
  www.gamblingandthelaw.com/internet_gambling.html

- *Regulation of Pharmaceuticals Online*, Amy Cassner-Sems
  www.gase.com/cyberlaw/toppage1.htm

- EduCause Current Issues: The Digital Millennium Copyright Act
  www.educause.edu/issues/dmca.html

Chapter 2

Reviewing the History of Cybercrime

Topics we'll investigate in this chapter:

- **Exploring Criminality in the Days of Standalone Computers**

- **Understanding Early Phreakers, Hackers, and Crackers**

- **How Online Services Made Cybercrime Easy**

- **Introducing the ARPANet: The Wild West of Networking**

- **Watching Crime Rise with the Commercialization of the Internet**

- **Bringing the Cybercrime Story Up to Date**

- ☑ **Summary**

- ☑ **Frequently Asked Questions**

- ☑ **Resources**

Introduction

How old is the phenomenon of cybercrime? It's safe to say that soon after the first computer networks were built, some people were looking for ways to exploit them for their own illegal purposes. The idea of theft is as old as the concept of privately owned property, and an element of almost all societies is dedicated to taking as much as possible of what isn't theirs—by whatever means they can.

As soon as it was widely recognized that computers store something of value (information), criminals saw an opportunity. But just as it's more difficult to target a robbery victim who stays locked up in his own home every day, the data on closed, standalone systems has been difficult to steal. However, when that data began to move from one computer to another over networks, like the robbery victim who travels from place to place, this data became more vulnerable. Networks provided another advantage: an entry point. Even if the information that was of value was never sent across the wire, the comings and goings of other bits of data opened up a way for intruders to sneak inside the computer, like a robber taking advantage of the victim's housemates who leave the doors unlocked on their way out.

However, cybercrime didn't spring up as a full-blown problem overnight. In the early days of computing and networking, the average criminal didn't possess either the necessary hardware or the technical expertise to seize the digital opportunity of the day. Computers were million-dollar mainframe monstrosities, and only a few of them were in existence. An aspiring cybercriminal could hardly go out and buy (or steal) a computer, and even if he did, it's unlikely that he would have known what to do with it. There were no "user-friendly" applications; working with early systems required the ability to "speak" *machine language*—that is, to communicate in the 1s and 0s of binary calculation that computers understood.

The cybercrime problem emerged and grew as computing became easier and less expensive. Today almost everyone in industrialized countries has access to computer technology; children learn to use PCs in elementary school, and people who can't afford computers of their own can use PCs in public libraries or on college campuses for free, or they can rent computer time at business centers or Internet cafés. Applications are "point and click" or even voice-activated; it no longer requires a computer science degree to perform once-complex tasks such as sending e-mail or downloading files from another machine across the Internet. Some of today's cybercriminals are talented programmers (the hacker elite), but most are not. Advanced technical abilities make it easier for cybercriminals to "do their thing" and cover their tracks, but these abilities are by no means a job requirement.

In this chapter, we take a look at these issues:

- The challenges of computer crime in the days of standalone computers
- How early network-connected criminals operated
- How members of ARPANet (predecessor of the Internet) increased the opportunities for criminal activity
- How the phenomenal growth of the commercial Internet led to the equally phenomenal rise in cybercrime
- How the advent of easy-to-use online services such as CompuServe and America Online (AOL) made online criminality even easier
- Where we are today and how the "latest and greatest" technologies have created new security vulnerabilities

First, let's go back to the 1940s, when Dr. J. Presper Eckert and Dr. John W. Mauchly devised one of the first digital computers, the Electronic Numerical Integrator and Computer (ENIAC).

Exploring Criminality in the Days of Standalone Computers

ENIAC was a behemoth, requiring more than 1500 square feet of floor space—more than many of today's "starter homes." This gigantic machine used more than 17,000 vacuum tubes and could do about 1000 calculations per second, compared with the millions of calculations per second attained by compact, inexpensive modern PCs.

ENIAC was quite an accomplishment, but the good doctors involved in its development didn't rest on their laurels. In 1949, they introduced the Binary Automatic Computer (BINAC), which stored data on a magnetic tape. Shortly thereafter, they invented the Universal Automatic Computer (UNIVAC), the first commercially marketed computer, under a grant from the U.S. government.

When the first UNIVAC was delivered to the U.S. Census Bureau in 1951, it was the size of a room and cost $1 million. The manufacturer eventually built 46 UNIVACs for government and business customers. The UNIVAC used magnetic tape, which was faster than the IBM punch card system that was its direct competitor.

> **NOTE**
>
> The first punch card tabulation machines were invented in the late 1800s by an engineer named Herman Hollerith. Like the UNIVAC, punch card technology was originally developed for the U.S. Census Bureau to use in sorting and analyzing its data. Hollerith's Tabulating Machine Company, founded in 1896, was acquired by IBM in 1924.

These early computers had some inherent security advantages: They were huge and expensive, they were standalone systems, and most of the world didn't really know what a computer was, much less how to use it.

Sharing More Than Time

It wasn't long before scientific types were enamored of computers. The Programmed Data Processor (PDP-1), developed and marketed by Digital Equipment Corporation (DEC) in the 1960s, was the first computer used for commercial time sharing (that is, the owners of the computer rented computer time to other businesses, schools, laboratories, and programmers who couldn't afford to buy computers of their own).

Because numerous people and businesses were using the same computer, the data and programs stored on it were vulnerable. Thus the first doors to hacking were opened—and despite the efforts of systems administrators, security product vendors, and law enforcement, those doors have never been closed since.

The Evolution of a Word

In the 1960s, the term *hacker* was used to refer to someone who was considered a "real programmer," who had mastered the computer systems of the day and was able to manipulate programs to do more than they were originally intended to do.

In the late1960s and early 1970s, hacking became associated with the radical underground ("yippie") movement and took on an antiestablishment flavor. Law enforcement agencies began to arrest *phreakers* for tampering with the phone system, as we discuss in more detail in the following section. In the 1980s, the FBI made some of the first high-profile arrests of computer hackers (including that of Kevin Mitnick, who became something of a "martyr to the cause" in the hacking community). Movies such as John Badham's *WarGames* in the 1980s and Iain Softley's *Hackers* in the 1990s brought into the mainstream the concept of the hacker as a brilliant and somewhat romantic figure who breaks the law (but usually for noble purposes).

NOTE

The first hackers' group came about, not surprisingly, at the Massachusetts Institute of Technology (MIT) in 1961 shortly after MIT got its first PDP-1. The group, called the Tech Model Railroad Club, was made up of members who programmed for the sheer joy of it—the essence of hacking in its original sense.

Understanding Early Phreakers, Hackers, and Crackers

Hacking in the modern sense of the word—as applied to someone who breaks into systems, usually remotely—couldn't have come into its own without the network. However, we mustn't forget that networks existed long before there were computers. In the 1940s, when the first real computers were being developed, today's huge global telephone network, the construction of which began in the late 1800s, had already been steadily growing for 60 years.

The first electronic hackers broke into the phone system to make long distance calls without having to pay for them. These telephone network hackers became known as *phreakers*. Yet another term that originated during the early years of electronic communication is *cracker*, used to describe someone who "cracks" a system's security; this term now often refers to someone who specializes in cracking passwords.

Hacking Ma Bell's Phone Network

An MIT student named Stewart Nelson, who figured out how use MIT's computer to generate the tones to access the phone company's long distance service, was one of the first known phreakers, according to the article *Hacking History—Phreaking* in the Internet/Network Security section of the About.com Web site.

Some especially talented phreakers were able to reproduce these tones merely by whistling, but most phreakers used a device called the *blue box*, which was a tone generator set to reproduce the 2600Hz frequency. Today's phone systems don't use the 2600 tone for long distance access, but there is still an active contingent of phone phreakers who take advantage of the complexities of modern systems to find new ways to exploit the telephone system technology to their benefit.

Phamous Phreakers

John Draper, a U.S. Air Force veteran and engineering technician for National Semiconductor who went by the alias of Cap'n Crunch, is generally credited with designing the original blue box after discovering that the toy whistle included in boxes of Cap'n Crunch cereal could produce the 2600Hz signal that granted access to AT&T's long distance service. Draper was arrested and served time in a California minimum-security prison for this infraction. According to legend, he held seminars while in prison, teaching other inmates how to hack the phone system. He was later arrested again in New York.

Steve Jobs and Steve Wozniak, who later founded Apple Computer, are reported by several sources (including Wozniak himself, who worked for Draper prior to meeting Jobs) to have made and sold blue boxes in the early 1970s.

NOTE

> The *2600 Magazine* and Web site, popular resources for the hacker underground, got their names from the 2600Hz phone phreaking frequency.

Phreaking on the Other Side of the Atlantic

The British phone system had its own phreakers, dating back to the time when the "Toll A" hack was discovered and exploited to make free long distance calls. Later, British phreakers constructed "bleeper boxes" that served the same purpose as the blue box in the United States but used different sets of frequencies.

A Box for Every Color Scheme

In addition to the original blue box, phreakers constructed a number of other devices to outwit the phone system. The *red box* replicates the tones that are produced when coins are deposited in a pay phone, and a *black box* allows calls placed *to* the phone to which it is attached to be made free of charge.

Not all phone phreaking was done for the purpose of circumventing long distance charges. Manipulation of the phone system was also popular with people engaged in other criminal activities, to cover their tracks when conducting illegal business over the phone. The *cheese box* was devised to connect two lines at a location in such as way as to allow bookies or drug dealers to receive calls from another remote location and go through the cheese box to disguise the number at which they were actually located.

From Phreaker to Hacker

A huge wealth of information about phreaking is available on the Web, including detailed instructions for "wannabe" phreakers. The phreaker "attitude" (disdain for large corporations such as the telephone company and a belief in the "right" of those who are clever enough to rip off these corporations) formed the basis of the later hacker subculture. Many of the first computer hackers began their criminal careers as phone phreakers.

Living on the LAN: Early Computer Network Hackers

In the 1970s, the first affordable personal computer, the Altair 8800, became available. The machine was sold as a kit that the buyer had to put together, and it didn't do much once it was built because the owner also had to write his or her own programs for it. Nevertheless, the Altair gave birth to hacking as we know it today; this device made it possible for individuals to own their own computers and learn to program.

Other relatively low-cost computers followed; the Commodore 64 was a popular "toy" that introduced many youngsters, mostly teenage boys, to the joys of programming and, later, full-fledged hacking. Radio Shack's TRS-80 (affectionately known as the *Trash 80*) and the original IBM PC brought more powerful computing to people who were eager to find new ways to exploit the systems' capabilities. But it was the PC network that really opened the floodgates for all hacking that followed.

The first computer "networks" were not actually made up of networked computers. Rather, they consisted of one computer—a mainframe—and many terminals that connected to the mainframe, ran programs on it, and accessed its files. Although these terminals were networked in one sense of the word, they were "dumb" terminals that possessed no processing power of their own. This mainframe time sharing linked multiple users and allowed them to share files and printers. It also allowed early hackers to access the files of other mainframe users.

Disadvantages of mainframe computing included the high cost of the computer and the single point of failure that it represented. If the system went down, no one on the network could do any computing, since the terminals they operated were dumb. *Minicomputers* (such as the DEC PDP and VAX and the IBM AS/400) were created as lower-cost, more compact alternatives to the full-fledged mainframe, but these machines still relied on dumb terminals and worked in essentially the same way as the older devices. Eventually, the search for a better way led to the development of smaller, less expensive computers (then called *microcomputers* and later called *personal computers,* or *PCs*) that could sit on a desktop. With each worker having a full-fledged computer on the desktop, there was much more fault tolerance than with the mainframe; if one computer went down, everyone else could keep computing.

However, workers missed some of the advantages of the mainframe environment, such as the ability to easily share files with others. "Sneakernet"—copying files to a floppy disk and physically transporting the disk to another computer—was the workaround, but that system didn't work so well when the users who wanted to share files were in different parts of the building or the files were too large to fit on a floppy. The solution was to connect the standalone desktop computers in a network, providing the resource-sharing benefits of mainframe computing with the fault tolerance of decentralized computing. Networked PCs give us, in many ways, the best of both worlds. They also give the hackers among us a way to access our information, whether we want to share it or not.

In the 1970s, researchers at Xerox's Palo Alto Research Center (PARC) developed Ethernet, which still forms the basis of most local area networks (LANs) today. DEC, Intel, and Xerox got together in 1979 to create Ethernet standards (originally called DIX after the company names) to make it easy for vendors to create compatible products. In 1983, the Institute of Electrical and Electronics Engineers (IEEE) released the 802.3 specifications based on thick coaxial cable and called 10Base5. Ethernet gave companies a way to link their computers easily and relatively inexpensively, especially after the IEEE developed and standardized a second version based on thin coax (10Base2) in 1985. Networked PCs began to emerge as a popular alternative to mainframe computing (or in some cases, an addition to it) in the 1980s.

How BBSs Fostered Criminal Behavior

In addition to networking PCs together at one location to create a LAN, PCs could be used to link to one another from remote locations using a modem and a telephone line. This led to the advent of the *bulletin board service (BBS),* a computer system equipped with one or more modems so that users can dial in and download files from it or post messages to a "board" to carry on public virtual discussions.

Ward Christensen and Randy Suess developed the software for the Computerized Bulletin Board System (CBBS) in the 1970s in Chicago. They described it in an article published in *Byte Magazine* in 1978. The system was a huge success, and BBSs sprang up all over the country.

Early hackers and phreakers seized on the BBS idea as a way to communicate with one another and share their tricks and techniques. Most boards included both the public forum and e-mail service between members of the BBS. Although many BBSs were legitimate "places" where computer hobbyists could gather and share the software they'd written themselves or discuss issues of the day, the BBS had a natural appeal to the criminal element. The BBSs spawned the first large-scale method of distributing *warez* (hacker jargon for pirated software), often computer games. Other BBSs specialized in sharing of pornographic pictures and/or stories.

Early BBSs were slow (2400-baud modems were top of the line at the time) and expensive unless you were lucky enough to live in the same locality as your cohorts or you were a phreaker who didn't pay for long distance calls. It was often difficult to get connected because most BBSs were operated out of someone's home on a limited budget, so the average systems operator, or sysop (the person who ran the BBS), didn't have a large number of modems and phone lines. While some sysops ran these systems for fun, many (especially those who dealt in pornography) charged members a monthly or annual fee to connect.

Some BBSs are still in operation today, but the popularity of these forums began to decline in the 1990s, when Internet access became commercially available at an affordable price and the graphical nature of the World Wide Web made the BBS systems with their ASCII drawings seem hopelessly outdated.

How Online Services Made Cybercrime Easy

In the early days of the commercial Internet, getting online was not necessarily an easy proposition. Unlike today's operating systems, the operating systems in use (mostly Windows 3.*x*) didn't come with the Transmission Control Protocol/ Internet Protocol (TCP/IP) stack built in; also not included was the software required to make a dialup connection to the Internet and use its applications (Winsock). The correct software had to be downloaded, complex text configuration files had to be edited, and it took a certain amount of technical savvy (not to mention patience) to put it all together and successfully log on to the Internet. In addition, users had to log on through the first commercial Internet service providers (ISPs), which were often brand-new ventures launched by a couple of nerds on a shoestring budget, working out of an apartment. These entrepreneurs generally didn't provide user-friendly setup CDs to configure the settings for you, as most ISPs do today.

There was, however, an easier way to get online: the online service. Companies such as CompuServe, Prodigy, and AOL offered access to their network "communities." Once logged onto the service, users could download software, post messages to bulletin boards, find information on a wide variety of topics, and waste amazing amounts of time in chat rooms or holding private conversations through instant messaging.

The big lure of these services was ease of use. They provided a disk that usually installed the proper software automatically and configured users' computer settings, so users didn't have to know anything about much of anything to get "connected." In their early days, the services were excruciatingly expensive by modern standards; in the 1980s it cost US$25 an *hour* to connect to CompuServe. Prices dropped in the early 1990s to around US$3 an hour, and eventually the services went to unlimited usage plans that cost less than US$20 a month.

The online services were *not,* in their early days, ISPs. Rather, they were private wide area networks (WANs) in which members interacted with each other but not with the "outside world" of the Internet—they were similar to BBSs on steroids. Later the services provided e-mail gateways so that their members could exchange e-mail with others outside the private network. They also added access to the World Wide Web. Today, most online services are also ISPs. Even though ease of use associated with regular Internet providers has increased dramatically, many "Net newbies" still find the online services easier to use. This ease of use attracts criminals (along with legitimate users) who are not particularly technically proficient.

Another benefit of the online services that attracts criminals is the anonymity they offer. Generally, if you set up an account with a regular ISP, you're assigned a user account name and an e-mail address based on that name. It's possible to get the ISP to change your account name, but it's a lot of trouble and can't be done too frequently. Services such as AOL allow users to create secondary "screen names" that they can change whenever they want, making it easier for a criminal to change identities and cover his or her tracks.

Introducing the ARPANet: the Wild West of Networking

In the beginning (or what was the beginning of today's vast global internetwork), there was the ARPANet. The ARPANet eventually begat the Internet.

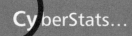

CyberStats...

The Popularity of Online Services

According to AOL's corporate Web site, as of 2002 AOL has an estimated 34 million members. AOL also now owns its former competitor, CompuServe, which claims about 3 million members. Prodigy Communications, which was the first consumer-oriented online service (founded in 1984, one year before AOL), estimates its membership at 3.6 million. Microsoft's Microsoft Network (MSN) service claims close to 9 million users.

Sputnik Inspires ARPA

Back in 1957, no one could have foreseen the communications system that today connects friends, relatives, business partners, and strangers all over the world. In 1957, President Dwight Eisenhower authorized the creation of the Advanced Research Projects Agency (ARPA) in response to the launch of the Soviet Union's first artificial Earth-orbiting satellite, Sputnik.

ARPA's first project was to develop a satellite of its own for the United States; it was not until years later that the agency began to work on computer and networking technology. In the 1960s, as the cold war with the Soviet Union continued, the government considered the possibility of nuclear war and how to maintain communications if the unthinkable occurred. This is where ARPA's involvement with computing began.

ARPA Turns Its Talents to Computer Technology

Dr. J.C.R. Licklider was appointed to run ARPA's computer technology project in 1962. He was largely responsible for building the beginnings of a wide area network connecting government/military and university sites, using redundant links so that if one node was taken out, messages could still get through by taking a different path. This network, based on packet-switching technology developed in the 1960s, was called the *ARPANet*.

The first node of the network was installed at the University of California at Los Angeles (UCLA) in 1969. Additional nodes were installed at Stanford, U.C. at Santa Barbara (UCSB), and the University of Utah, located at Salt Lake City.

Network Applications Come into Their Own

In the early 1970s, e-mail—which today is still the Internet's "killer application" in terms of popularity—was invented. Gateways were devised to connect networks using different architectures, and specifications were developed for what would become File Transfer Protocol (FTP).

By the end of the 1970s, Usenet newsgroups had been established, and the first interactive multiple-user sites, called *multiuser dungeons*, or *MUDs*, had appeared. By that time, the ARPANet had been up and running for over 10 years, although it was still limited mostly to university and government sites.

The Internetwork Continues to Expand

In the early 1980s, the TCP/IP suite was defined as the standard for communications on the ARPANet. Soon after, name servers were created to handle the translation of "friendly" computer names and paths to the IP addresses computers use to route messages to one another.

William Gibson's sci-fi novel *Neuromancer,* published in 1984, coined the term *cyberspace* as a description of the online world. At that time, no one had any idea just how crowded cyberspace would soon become.

The ARPANet of the 1980s

The worldwide network was steadily growing, but in 1986 there were still only about 5000 hosts (computers) on the Net. About this time, the National Science Foundation (NSF), which maintained the Internet backbone, established five supercomputer centers, which resulted in a dramatic increase in available connections. The next year, 1987, the number of hosts had risen to either 10,000 or 28,000 (depending on the source you consult), and a year after that, the NFSNet backbone was upgrade to 1.544Mbps (a T-1 line). By 1989, all sources agree that there were over 100,000 hosts on the network.

The Internet of the 1990s

In 1990, the ARPANet ceased to exist, and the Internet was born. In actuality, ARPA had already been split into two parts in the 1980s: Milnet (for military use, which was integrated into the Defense Data Network) and the NSFNet, which handled civilian communications. NSF upgraded the backbone again, to T-3 speed (44.736Mbps). The NSFNet grew into today's commercial Internet, and by 1992, there were over 1 million Internet hosts. In 1995, NSFNet gave the backbone services to interconnected commercial network access providers

(NAPs) and became a research network again, establishing the very high-speed Backbone Network Service (vBNS) that connected the five supercomputer centers. The commercialization of the Internet had begun.

The Worm Turns—and Security Becomes a Concern

During the early ARPANet days, security was both a major concern to the military contingent and almost a nonissue to research scientists, who were more interested in what the technology could do than in securing it)—hence the split-up of the network. The small number of nodes on the network limited the scope of the threat posted by security breaches. However, in 1988, a *worm* (a self-replicating program) was released on the Internet and attacked computers running Berkeley UNIX, spreading all across the United States, infecting thousands of computers and shutting down a large portion of the Internet. This was the wakeup call; Internet users suddenly realized that some in their midst harbored malicious intent. Many more virus attacks and hacks were to follow.

Watching Crime Rise with the Commercialization of the Internet

By 1991, e-mail users had begun to consider the possibility that their Internet communications would be intercepted. Philip Zimmermann released an encryption program called Pretty Good Privacy (PGP) that could be used to protect sensitive messages. PGP was also used by criminals to hide evidence of their crimes from police.

The first cyberbank, called First Virtual, came online in 1994, opening up vast new opportunities for hackers. Also that year, researchers began work on the "next generation" of the Internet Protocol, called IPv6. The primary purpose of the new version was to address the anticipated shortage of IP addresses using the current IPv4's 32-bit address space, but another concern addressed by the new protocol version was to be IP security.

In 1995, the U.S. Secret Service and the Drug Enforcement Agency (DEA) obtained an Internet wiretap to help build a case against suspects who were accused of producing and selling illegal cell phone cloning equipment.

In 1996, Congress became concerned about the amount of pornography that was being exchanged over the Internet and passed the Communications Decency Act (CDA), which was later declared unconstitutional. Meanwhile, a cracker was able to shut down the Public Access Networks Corporation in New York using a hack attack that was described in *2600 Magazine*. A "cancelbot" launched on

Usenet destroyed over 25,000 newsgroup messages, and in the same year, U.S. Department of Justice, Central Intelligence Agency, and Air Force computers (among others) were hacked.

In the next three years, many more government agencies and prominent companies had their systems hacked, including the U.S. Department of Commerce, UNICEF, and the *New York Times*. eBay, Microsoft, and the U.S. Senate Web sites also fell victim to hackers. The Melissa virus caused company e-mail servers to shut down. A fraudulent Web page that was designed to appear to be a Bloomberg financial news story resulted in the shares of a small tech company increasing 31 percent in response to the false "news."

As we entered the 2000s, a huge, distributed DoS attack shut down major Web sites such as Yahoo! and Amazon. Apache, RSA Security, and Western Union were hacked, the Code Red worm attacked thousands of Web servers, and the Sircam virus hit e-mail accounts all over the world.

However, malicious code and hack attacks comprised only a small portion of the overall criminal activity that in some way used or depended on the Internet. From the infamous "Nigerian letter" scam to the use of the Net to plot the September 11, 2001, terrorist attacks, crime was running rampant on the network—and still is today.

Bringing the Cybercrime Story Up to Date

The new millennium brought with it the growing popularity of new and exciting technologies, such as wireless networking and low-cost, high-speed "always on" connectivity options through Digital Subscriber Line (xDSL) and cable modem. These technologies have become available in increasing numbers of places. Unfortunately, these technologies also provide new opportunities for cybercriminals, for a number of reasons, which we explore here.

Understanding How New Technologies Create New Vulnerabilities

Most of us are much more security-conscious today than we were a decade ago, in regard to both our computers and life in general. Certainly there are more security products on the market today than there were a few years ago. Lawmakers all over the world have "cracked down" on behaviors such as unauthorized access that not long ago weren't covered by criminal statutes.

We seem to have all the most important elements for reducing the incidence of cybercrime: We have the laws ("with teeth"); we have the tools; we even have the widespread awareness that is sometimes the most difficult component of a crime prevention effort. Why, then, is cybercrime not only *not* going away, but steadily increasing?

An important reason for the increase in cybercrime is the whirlwind pace at which new technologies are being developed to make our computing experience more productive, easier, faster, and more fun. However, convenience and performance often come with a price, and that price is security.

Cybercriminals love new technologies, including:

- Broadband

- Wireless

- Mobile computing and remote access

- Sophisticated Web technologies such as Java, ActiveX, and so on

- Fancy e-mail programs that support Hypertext Markup Language (HTML) and scripting

- E-commerce and online banking

- Instant messaging

- New operating systems

Cybercriminals also love standardization. If everyone uses the same operating system, or the same Web browser, or the same e-mail client, or if all vendors adhere to the same specifications, the potential attacker has much less to learn and a much larger playing field.

Let's discuss why these new technologies and the standardization of computer and networking technologies are so dear to the heart of the cybercriminal.

Why Cybercriminals Love Broadband

Broadband technologies such as xDSL, cable modem, and satellite Internet services have made Internet users' lives easier, but they have also made it easier for hackers to invade those users' computers and networks. Because individual computers attached to broadband networks such as cable modem or DSL behave more like computers attached to a network than like individual computers that use telephone lines to dial into the Internet, it is easier to exploit the technology to gain unauthorized access. As a consequence, broadband users need to be much more security conscious than dialup Internet users.

> ## CyberStats...
>
> ### Broadband Internet Use
>
> According to *Cable Datacom News,* March 2002, the number of broadband subscribers (cable modem, DSL, satellite, and fixed wireless) in North America reached over 6.4 million in 2001. This figure still represents only 10-percent market penetration in the United States and 22-percent penetration in Canada, but total revenues are in excess of US$4.5 billion, and most experts expect this market to continue to grow each year for the foreseeable future.

The Problem with 24/7 Connectivity

A network is vulnerable to an attack from outside only when it is connected to an outside network. When most users and companies were connecting to the Internet with analog modems or dialup ISDN connections, their vulnerability to attack was limited because the system was available to outsiders only during a session. When you finished doing what you wanted to do on the Net, you disconnected and your system "disappeared" from the Internet.

Additionally, most ISPs use Dynamic Host Configuration Protocol (DHCP) to assign IP addresses to dialup users. This means that your Internet-connected computer gets a new IP address each time you hang up and reconnect.

DSL and cable are referred to as "always-on" technologies. You don't have to dial up a connection each time you want to get onto the Internet; instead, you stay connected 24 hours a day, seven days a week. This makes it quicker and easier for you to access Internet resources. It also makes it easier for you to run a server, allowing other authorized users to remotely access shared files on your system. Because your IP address generally stays the same, since you don't disconnect, these authorized clients can find your server more easily from one communication session to the next. Of course, powering the computers down breaks the connection (and "shuts the door" to potential hackers). However, today's computers are made to run continuously (and except for some peripherals such as the monitors, generally run better and last longer when they do), so many technically savvy users never turn their systems off.

The problem with 24/7 technologies is that they make it easier for *unauthorized* folks to access your system, too. Your exposure is much greater because you're "always open for business," giving a hacker more time to mount a brute-force attack to guess your password or figure out which TCP/UDP ports might be open and vulnerable. Furthermore, because your IP address stays the same, it's easier for these hackers to return to your system next time they want to do a little virtual breaking and entering.

The Problem with High-Speed Connectivity

Another advantage of broadband is the increased connectivity speed. Unlike an analog modem that's limited to 56Kbps (and practically speaking, less than that due to federal regulations and line considerations), DSL and cable companies offer high-speed downloads and often higher upload speeds as well. This means improved performance on your end—but if your service offers a high upload speed, it also means an intruder will be able to snatch your files more quickly.

Luckily, in terms of security if not usability, most broadband services are asymmetric. That means that upload and download speeds are not created equal; typically for consumer accounts, the upstream transfer rate is limited to 128Kbps by cable companies and anywhere from 128Kbps to 764Kbps by DSL providers.

> **NOTE**
>
> Most commercial ISPs limit (or *throttle)* upstream speeds in order to discourage home users from running servers (which is a violation of many cable and DSL contract terms of service).

Even with these limitations, however, upstream speed is generally at least twice that of an analog modem—a boon to hackers downloading data from your computer to their own.

The Problem with Low-Cost, 24/7, High-Speed Connectivity

The problems linked to high-speed 24/7 connectivity and high-speed data rates associated with consumer broadband technologies also exist with traditional 24/7 high-speed business solutions such as T-1. However, because most T-1 lines are connected to companies that employ IT professionals, it is more likely that security measures are in place to offset the security risk.

The problem with cable and DSL is that these technologies have brought high-speed, always-on access to home and small office users who can't afford the high cost of T-1. These less sophisticated users are also less likely to be aware of the security risk or to have the technical expertise or budget to implement the proper level of security.

Most small offices and a growing number of home users run Network Address Translation (NAT) software of some type to share Internet access with multiple PCs on a small LAN. This provides a small measure of security to the systems on the local network because NAT assigns private IP addresses to the NAT client computers. These addresses are not visible on the Internet. However, the NAT host computer that is directly connected to the Internet is exposed.

How to Protect Your Broadband Connection

If you have a computer that uses a broadband Internet connection and the computer is *not* connected to a LAN and is not functioning as an Internet server, one step you can take is to be sure file and print sharing is not enabled on that computer.

Another common security hole on Windows systems is called an *IRDP vulnerability*. This is caused by the ICMP Router Discovery Protocol (IRDP) that is enabled by default on Windows machines that are configured as DHCP clients. IRDP isn't needed when the DHCP server specifies router information, but hackers can use it to add default route entries that will then override the default route that the DHCP server provides. You can disable IRDP by editing the Windows Registry.

Some cable users have found that when the NIC used to connect to the cable modem was installed by the cable company (or by the user), Windows automatically binds the card to both TCP/IP and the Microsoft Networking service. Having this interface bound to Microsoft networking opens their systems to others on the cable segment.

NOTE

Chapter 8, "Implementing System Security," provides details on how to disable file and print sharing on Windows, UNIX/Linux, and Macintosh computers; how to edit the Registry to protect against IRDP vulnerability; and how to check and change NIC bindings.

Which is more secure: DSL or cable? Cable is a shared connection (that is, everyone in your neighborhood is part of the same network segment). In essence, this creates a local area network. That means that your neighbors have access to your system, much as neighboring computers on any LAN have access to one another.

As on a regular LAN, there are ways to protect yourself from your LAN-mates. The Data Over Cable Service Interface Specification (DOCSIS) standard for cable modems provides some measure of security because modems that comply with this specification support data encryption between the provider's hub and the user's computer. Data is *not* encrypted between the provider and the end destination (that is, when traveling over the Internet), but this standard does help to address the "neighborhood segment sharing" problem, since others on your cable segment will not be able to read your data if they intercept it. Cable networks that use DOCSIS standards also prevent your computer from announcing its shares to the network using NetBIOS protocols (which cause other computers on the network to show up in the Network Neighborhood or Network Places window on computers running Windows). Be aware, though, that a hacker could still connect to your computer if he or she knows your computer name or IP address.

DSL users are connected directly via their phone lines to the telephone company central office (CO). Thus DSL provides fewer vulnerabilities to hackers—but this does not mean a DSL connection is a secure one.

No one should use a broadband Internet connection without also using a firewall to protect from outside intruders. Firewalls can filter both incoming and outgoing data and block open ports to cut hackers off from their usual entry points. A firewall can be either a hardware device or a software program that runs on the Internet-connected computer. Microsoft's newest desktop operating system, Windows XP, even comes with built-in firewall software.

We discuss how firewalls work and the various types of firewalls that are available in Chapter 7, "Understanding Cybercrime Prevention."

Why Cybercriminals Love Wireless

Wireless technologies are emerging as the Next Big Thing in computer networking for the twenty-first century. The IEEE's 802.11b specifications provide standards for wireless networking at 11Mbps using spread-spectrum radio transmission. A newer specification, 802.11g, allows for wireless communications at about twice that rate: 22Mbps. This specification gives mobile computers the ability to boldly go where no Ethernet cable has gone before—and still stay connected to the local network and/or the Internet.

Microsoft's latest operating system, Windows XP, includes built-in support for 802.11b wireless networking. Setup of a wireless network is easy using the XP interface, as shown in Figure 2.1.

Figure 2.1 You can set up wireless networking quickly and easily with Windows XP.

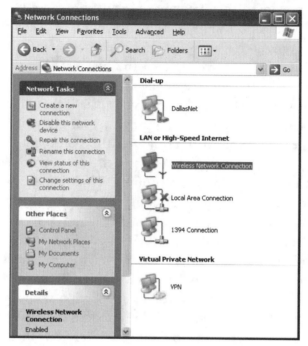

Bluetooth is a wireless technology designed to enable a wide variety of portable devices, such as personal digital assistants (PDAs) and mobile phones—as well as more traditional laptop and notebook computers—to connect to the Internet.

Unfortunately, the ability to access a network without any physical connection makes it that much easier for hackers to do the same, because they don't have to worry about "plugging in" to the cable. If a network includes a wireless access point, it is vulnerable to outside intruders even if there is no remote access server or Internet connection on the network.

The Problem with Wireless Technologies

How secure are today's wireless technologies? It's important to understand that most are based on radio transmissions that go out over the airwaves. For example, Bluetooth devices transmit in the 2.4GHz spectrum. This is an unlicensed range, so anyone can transmit and receive on it.

Transmissions over the airwaves can be intercepted, and 2.4GHz antennas, amplifiers, and transceivers are readily available. The signals can be picked up hundreds of feet from the access point; high-gain antennas increase this distance. All this is fodder for the cybercriminal.

It's not quite as bad as it sounds, though. Two types of spread-spectrum radio transmission are supported by IEEE 802.11:

- Frequency Hopping Spread Spectrum (FHSS)
- Direct Sequence Spread Spectrum (DSSS)

The first type, FHSS, uses *frequency hopping*, which means the signal "hops" or changes from one frequency to another. (For Bluetooth, the hops span 79 frequencies at 1MHz intervals and can make up to 1600 hops per second.) This means a hacker can't just tune into a set frequency and listen in, as you can do with narrowband radio broadcasts that use a fixed frequency. This provision gives only a small measure of security, however.

DSSS uses a redundant bit pattern for each bit of data that is transmitted (called a *chipping code*). The purpose is to make the signal more resistant to interference and provide some fault tolerance; if some of the bits get damaged during transmission, the redundancy allows for the original data to be recovered.

CyberStats...

A World Without Wires?

Bank of America projections anticipate that there will be 400 million wireless users by 2003, according to Eric W. Pfeiffer, writing on Forbes.com. International Data Corporation (IDC) reports that over 15 million subscribers already have wireless access to the Internet through PDAs and smart phones.

The 802.11 wireless standards actually do provide for security measures, such as authentication and encryption. Unfortunately, the encryption used by these technologies is weak and can be broken relatively easily. Small handheld devices, such as mobile phones, have limited memory and processing power. This means larger encryption algorithms that require heavy processing can't be used.

A program named AirSnort that runs on Linux exploits the weaknesses of wireless encryption to discover the WEP encryption key simply by passively monitoring the wireless network. The fact that WEP uses static keys (rather than more secure dynamic keys that change at regular intervals) makes this technology especially dangerous.

NOTE

The IEEE 802.11b standards governing wireless technology defines WEP as Wireless Equivalent Privacy. This protocol is also referred to as the WEP Encryption Protocol (the acronym for which is also WEP) or in much technical literature, simply as the Wireless Encryption Protocol (you guessed it—WEP).

On the Scene...

Real Life Experiences

In 2001, Sun Microsystems' network was hacked by two intruders who were in the company's parking lot, using standard wireless networking cards.

In 2002, a security firm named i-sec showed how hackers could use a Pringles potato chip can to make a directional antenna that was able to locate wireless networks in the London financial district. Coffee cans or similar metal containers can also be used. These homemade antennas can increase the signal by up to 15 decibels.

The weakness of the encryption algorithms aside, wireless encryption covers only the transmission between a user's computer and the wireless gateway that connects the wireless network to the Internet. When the data reaches the Wireless Application Protocol (WAP) gateway, it must be transferred from the wireless network to the wired network. In order to do this, the wireless communication, which is in the form of encrypted Wireless Markup Language (WML), must be decrypted and then re-encrypted in order to be transmitted on the cabled network. The data is vulnerable during this "encryption gap."

Another problem is that even though the data is encrypted, the source and destination addressing information is not. Finally, encryption is not necessarily enabled by default when wireless networking components are installed. According to a BBC News broadcast of March 8, 2002, an informal survey conducted by i-sec discovered that 67 percent of networks in the survey had encryption disabled.

According to an article, *Exploiting and Protecting 802.11b Wireless Networks*, published on the ExtremeTech Web site in April 2002, security tests were conducted using a Yagi antenna on the deck of the Ziff Davis office building in Manhattan. Testers were able to find over 60 wireless access points, and an astonishing 79 percent of them did not have encryption enabled. Similar vulnerabilities were found in Jersey City and Silicon Valley.

The practice of driving around with a portable computer that's equipped with a wireless NIC, searching for wireless network signals, is called *war driving* (a term coined by security expert Peter Shipley) or *drive-by hacking.*

How to Protect Your Wireless Connection

Organizations and individuals who use wireless technologies don't want to give up the convenience, but they are recognizing that extra security precautions are necessary. One way to add security to wireless networks is the use of hardware-based security devices such as smart cards; users are not able to access resources without swiping the issued card through a card reader.

NOTE

We discuss smart card authentication and access control in more detail in Chapter 7, "Understanding Cybercrime Prevention."

Other wireless security measures that can be implemented either by wireless device manufacturers or by wireless LAN (WLAN) administrators include:

- Moving wireless hubs away from windows and toward the center of buildings

- Ensuring that wireless encryption is enabled

- Disabling broadcasts on the network's hubs

- Changing the default settings such as the Service Set Identifier (SSID) and the default password on the wireless access point or router

- Limiting the number of wireless access points can also make the WLAN less vulnerable to unauthorized access

- Assigning static IP addresses to wireless NICs and disabling DHCP on the wireless router

- Security auditing, in the form of a media access control (MAC) address-tracking system that can be used to track the devices that access the wireless network

- Installing a firewall between the WLAN and the wired LAN

- Putting the wireless access points in what is known as a *demilitarized zone (DMZ),* also referred to as a *perimeter network* or *screened subnet,* and configuring wireless users to use a virtual private network (VPN) to create a secure tunnel into the network

- Treating the wireless network as though it were a public network and not sending sensitive data over it without taking precautions (such as using another encryption method along with WEP)

Why Cybercriminals Love Mobile Computing

Over the past decade, the high price of portable computers—laptops, notebooks, and handhelds—has steadily dropped while the processing power has come to equal that of desktop machines. This trend has been great for on-the-go business-people, who can now continue to work when they're on the road, with little loss in productivity.

Often, getting the work done requires access to the corporate network, and accordingly, most of today's laptops come with built-in modems and Ethernet ports. Travelers can dial directly back to the remote access server on the company LAN or dial up a local ISP and "tunnel" back to the corporate network through the Internet. More hotels are now providing high-speed Internet services, to which you connect via your portable computer's Ethernet port or PCMCIA (PC Card) NIC.

Once you connect to the company's LAN via one of these remote access methods, your computer becomes another (temporary) node on that local network, and remote access technology allows you to perform any task you could do from a wired workstation on site. This is great for employees who must be away from the office—but it's also great for hackers looking to come in uninvited.

The Problem with Mobile Computing

Remember that every point of access on the network creates one more vulnerability. A remote access server provides a point of access, as does a VPN server.

Of course, mobile computing also provides an additional security consideration: the possibility that the entire computer will be stolen. You might think this isn't a security problem if you don't store sensitive information on the portable's hard disk—but what about your VPN or remote access software configuration, which would allow anyone in possession of the computer to connect to the company network? Although a password may be required for network logon, many users set up their systems to "remember" their passwords so they won't have to take the time to type them in each time they connect, thus defeating the purpose of password security if someone else takes possession of the computer.

CyberStats...

Telecommuting Numbers Continue to Grow

According to ebizChronicle.com, in 2001 the number of employees telecommuting—working away from the office and connecting to the company network via remote access—grew to 32 million in the United States alone. Projections estimate that by 2004, almost 40 million workers will telecommute.

Mobile computing presents some special security concerns. User authentication is one of the biggest. Unlike the corporate environment, where there are security guards, surveillance cameras, and fellow employees to physically recognize the presence of suspicious strangers around the computer systems, a user connecting remotely to the network offers no assurance that he or she really is the person whose credentials are being used.

Oh, and there's one more reason cybercriminals love today's powerful, low-cost mobile computers: Now they *can* take it with them. Lightweight, compact computers are much easier to transport to a "secure" location such as a pay phone, from which a hacker can initiate a hard-to-trace online session, or to take on "drive-by hacking" expeditions to find wireless LANs to which they can connect surreptitiously.

How to Protect Your Mobile Computers and Remote Access Connections

The first line of defense in mobile security is physical security of the portable computer. There are many laptop locking devices on the market. Mobile users should be instructed to keep a close watch on their computers, especially in airports and other crowded public places. You can buy hardware devices that will emit a "homing" signal and software programs that can be set to automatically dial in or contact "home base" through the Internet the first time the computer goes online after someone uses an incorrect password.

Various means are available to address the mobile user authentication problem. For example, Windows-based remote access servers offer the ability to configure user accounts so that *callback security* is required. This means that a specific telephone number is associated with that user's account. When the user dials into the network and enters the username and password, the server doesn't provide immediate access. Instead, it disconnects and calls the user back at the specified telephone number and only then allows access to network resources.

This means that someone who has stolen a user's laptop with "remembered" passwords (or who has somehow discovered the user's password and is dialing in from another location) will not be able to access the network unless the hacker is also calling from the user's home or other previously specified location. This system works well for telecommuters, who usually dial into the network from their homes. It is less useful for traveling employees, who might be calling from a different hotel each day. Similar systems are available that, instead of hanging up and calling the user back, identify the caller's number through caller ID and check it against a list of approved remote user numbers. If the number is on the list, the user can access the network. This would work better than callback for users who dial in from several different fixed locations.

Windows remote access servers allow you to set remote access policies that control whether remote connection attempts are authorized. Another method of authenticating remote users is the Remote Access Dial In User Service (RADIUS) server. RADIUS is a security protocol that supports multiple authentication methods and allows encrypted transmissions between client and server. RADIUS allows administrators to place limitations and restrictions on the tasks that a remote user can perform once that user is logged onto the network, based on settings for that user account. RADIUS can be used to centrally manage multiple remote access servers or VPN servers using the same set of policies.

NOTE

Companies should also have written policies that specify rules governing remote access to the network. These rules should be distributed to all employees whose accounts allow remote logon. A sample dial-in access policy is available through the SANS Institute Web site at www.sans.org/newlook/resources/policies/Dial-in_Access_Policy.pdf. The document is in .PDF format; you'll need Adobe Acrobat or Acrobat Reader (the latter is free from the www.adobe.com Web site) to open it.

Other measures that can improve the security of remote access connections include:

- Use of dedicated application access so that the remote user connects to a specific application on the network server using proprietary protocols. This means the connected user will not have access to any other network resources. This system works well in cases in which remote users need to perform only a specific task, such as checking e-mail.

- Use of two-factor authentication. In this system, two separate components are required to successfully access the network: the first is *something you know*, and the second is *something you have* or *something you are*. In addition to providing a password (something you know), you must also provide a hardware token, smart card, or a biometric identifier such as a fingerprint (something you have).

- Deployment of callback security for telecommuters and other remote access users who connect from the same location all the time.

- Use of encryption for sensitive communications over public phone lines or through the Internet.

- Use of remote access policies to restrict what dial-in users can do on the network as well as the days and times of day they can connect and other parameters.

Remote access opens company networks to employees, partners, and customers—and to unwanted intruders. It is important to take extra security precautions at every point at which your network can be accessed from the outside.

Why Cybercriminals Love Sophisticated Web and E-Mail Technologies

Today's World Wide Web is a different "place" from that of 10 years ago. In the early 1990s, most Web pages consisted of plain text and graphics. The limitations of HTML and the slow bandwidth of most Internet connections dictated that Web designers follow the "keep it simple, stupid" caveat.

Today it's a whole different ballgame. Web sites flash and dance. Increasingly sophisticated presentations and interaction are possible with technologies such as Java and Visual Basic scripting and ActiveX controls. New markup languages such as Dynamic HTML (DHTML) and XML provide opportunities for Web designers to push the envelope. The prevalence of high-speed connections makes bandwidth-intensive Web applications feasible.

But once again, one man's (or woman's) feature enhancement is another's security hole. *Scripts* are programs that run when you access Web sites in which they are embedded. What the program does is up to the programmer. Most Web scripts serve useful, harmless purposes; for example, a Java script can produce visual effects such as falling snow or animated text. Applets and scripts can also create calculator tools, chat interfaces, games, or clocks.

Malicious programmers, however, can use these technologies for their own nefarious purposes. Although there are many kinds of attachments, Web page components, and other aspects of Web and e-mail technologies that can present security risks, the most worrisome are those that can actually run code and do things on (or to) your computer. In most cases, this kind of material—sometimes known as *active content* because it can run itself on your machine—is benign and is designed to perform specific tasks to manage or update a page display, run an animation, perform a calculation, and so forth. But active content can also include malicious code that can do all kinds of nasty things to your PC if allowed to run unchecked. That's why most security experts recommend that users (and network administrators) screen active content. By far, the safest security policy is to refuse to accept active content. However, this alternative could also prevent you from being able to use features that you need that depend on active content. Other strategies include requiring the active content to show valid credentials before being allowed to run or accepting active content only from specified (known safe) Internet locations or addresses. If written by a malicious programmer, active content can introduce viruses, worms, back doors, and all kinds of other questionable code and access points to your systems and networks.

This same problem (along with a few others) that applies to Web browsers also applies to today's sophisticated e-mail client programs that allow the display of HTML mail, running of scripts embedded in mail messages, and sending of attachments. Here again, active content—which makes sophisticated presentations and interaction work—opens the door to potential security breaches.

The Problem with Web Scripts and Controls

Scripts and controls can be used to perform tasks on your computer without your knowledge—including monitoring your communications with others or deleting key files on your hard disk. Java and ActiveX give programmers a way to run any program they like on your computer. Malicious code can emulate a login box request and send the password credentials you enter to the hacker, all without your knowledge.

There are many ways that your Web browser can be exposed to malicious code. Following links from other Web sites or clicking on links in e-mail messages or newsgroup posts can take you to a page that runs a malicious script.

How to Protect Your Web Browser from Malicious Code

Because of these very security concerns, a number of mechanisms have been developed to protect unwary Web users from potentially dangerous content. Code can be digitally signed to verify that it is from a legitimate vendor and thus safe to download. Most modern Web browsers allow you to select the level of security you desire. You can disable Java and/or ActiveX, or you can set the browser to prompt you when a script is encountered so that you can make the decision about whether to run it based on your trust (or lack thereof) in the site.

For example, the Microsoft Internet Explorer Web browser allows you to either select a predefined security level (Low, Medium Low, Medium, or High), as shown in Figure 2.2. The level selected determines whether unsigned ActiveX controls will be downloaded and whether you will be prompted before downloading any content that is considered potentially unsafe.

If none of the preset security levels works for you, you can also create your own customized security settings, as shown in Figure 2.3.

Figure 2.2 Modern browsers allow you to set security levels.

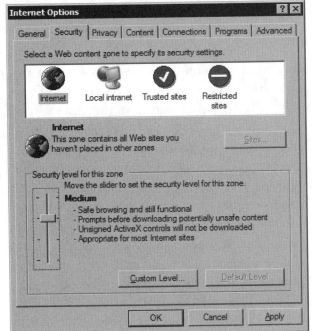

Figure 2.3 You can create custom security settings instead of using predefined levels.

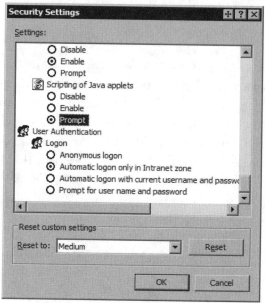

Because the Web is one of the most-used Internet applications, it is important to ensure that you don't expose your system and your network to a hack attack through the code that is run by your browser.

The Problem with Fancy E-Mail Clients

All of the same risks that are inherent in Web browsers that run scripts and controls surface again when you use an e-mail client that allows you to receive messages formatted in HTML, which can have the same sorts of malicious code embedded.

In the early days of e-mail, programs were simple and messages were basically text only. This system provided much less opportunity for security breaches, but it also limited the usefulness of e-mail communications. When it became possible to send files as attachments to messages, the doors opened to a new risk. Initially, attachments were usually photos (.jpg, .gif, etc.) or text files that were too large to include in the message itself. The problem arises when an attachment is or contains an executable program. Files with .exe, .com, or .bat extensions are obvious examples, but there are many other files that can run code, infect your system with viruses, and otherwise do great damage. These files include screen-saver files (.scr) and link files (.lnk). Registry (.reg) files can edit the Windows

On the Scene...

Real Life Experiences

In 1999, a Word macro virus called Melissa began propagating throughout the Internet and caused performance problems and denial of service due to overload on mail servers throughout the world. According to the Computer Emergency Response Team (CERT) Coordination Center at Carnegie-Mellon University, Melissa affected at least 100,000 computers within the first week after it appeared.

The original Melissa was relatively benign (it shut down servers due to the overload but didn't damage anything on users' computers). Soon after the major virus makers (such as Symantec and McAfee) updated their definition files to protect their products' users from Melissa, virus writers began to create modifications to the original code. Some of these modifications were more destructive, carrying payloads that destroyed files or sent personal information back to the virus writer.

A New Jersey computer programmer named David Smith was arrested by federal prosecutors and pled guilty to creating the virus. Estimates of the damage done by Melissa in North America alone range from US$80 million to US$385 million. Much of the evidence linking Smith to Melissa was gathered by ICSA.net, which operates a team of undercover security experts called IS Recon. This group gathers intelligence about underground hackers and potential computer and network security threats.

Registry, and .url files can open Web pages that run malicious code. Document files (such as Word .doc files) can include macros, which are simply small programs; virus writers have taken advantage of the powerful Visual Basic for Applications (VBA) support in Microsoft's Office applications to create macro viruses that can infect your system if you open the macro-containing document.

How to Protect Your E-Mail

To avoid the problems associated with modern e-mail programs, you might want to configure your e-mail client not to display a "preview pane" (which displays messages, including HTML messages, without you having to click on them to open them), install an antivirus package that checks both incoming and outgoing mail for viruses, and take care not to open e-mail attachments with suspicious extensions unless you are absolutely certain of their origin.

In the case of most e-mail–distributed viruses, once a virus has infected a machine, it automatically sends itself to everyone in the victim's address book, appearing to be a message from the victim. This means that you can't assume an attachment is safe just because you recognize the name in the "From" field of the message.

In recognition of these problems, e-mail programs are building in more security—sometimes so much that the functionality of the mail client is severely crippled. For example, Microsoft Outlook 2002 by default will not allow you to open executable file attachments, even if you are absolutely certain of the file's validity and safety. This restriction might be fine for the "average" user, but not for people like software developers who need to send programs back and forth on a regular basis. Luckily, you can get add-on software that will allow you to change this overprotective behavior if it's a problem for you.

In many cases, the correct application configuration can save you a good deal of grief. For example, Microsoft Word now allows you to set security so that the system will prompt you before running any macros. If you open a document that shouldn't have macros and get the dialog box asking you whether to disable macros, elect to do so and you can read the document itself without running the potentially dangerous code.

Why Cybercriminals Love E-Commerce and Online Banking

Most of us have heard the quote erroneously attributed to famous bank robber Willie Sutton in response to the question, "Why do you rob banks?" The answer: "That's where the money is." Regardless of who really said it, it makes sense.

It also makes sense that criminals are showing up in greater numbers online, because increasingly, that's where the money is. E-commerce, online banking, and related technologies have resulted in millions of dollars of financial transactions taking place across network connections.

CyberStats…

E-Commerce Predictions

Forrester Research (www.forrester.com) predicts that by 2004, total e-commerce transaction figures will reach US$3.5 *trillion* in North America alone, with another US$1.6 trillion in Asia and US$1.5 trillion in Western Europe.

Perhaps the growing popularity of online shopping, banking, stock trading, and other financial activities is best summed up by the title of an article published by Nua about a Penn State study of Internet activities: *Sex out, E-commerce in*. The study indicated that Internet users as a whole are spending proportionately less time each year (based on 1997–2001 data) searching for sexually oriented material online and more time on business and financial transactions.

The Problem with E-Commerce and Online Banking

The open nature and wide scope of the Internet make it a perfect forum for conducting business; transactions can be conducted between a business and a customer across the street or across the globe. Those wide-open cyberspaces also expose both seller and buyer to risks that aren't present, or at least not to the same extent, in face-to-face transactions.

CyberStats...

Fraudulent Online Transactions

According to Nua's Internet trends and statistics resource site (www.nua.com), online fraud reached US$700 million in 2001.

Epaynews.com reported that Meridien Research estimated that the cost of Internet fraud would reach between US$5 billion and US$15 billion by 2005. The lower number is based on companies investing in antifraud software; the higher figure predicts what will happen without such an investment. (See www.epaynews.com/statistics/fraud.html#1.)

When buyers must enter their credit card information to make a purchase, they are rightfully concerned that the information could fall into the wrong hands. Some would say that providing this information to a Web-based vendor is no different than giving it out over the telephone—but that philosophy doesn't take into account the difference between a telephone connection and an Internet transaction.

A phone call establishes a temporary dedicated private circuit directly between the caller and recipient; although it is possible to tap into a telephone line, it is relatively difficult and expensive. Information sent via e-mail or a Web form travels over the very public Internet and goes through a number of nodes (servers and routers) along the way. It is vulnerable to interception and, unless the information is encrypted, could then be used to make unauthorized purchases.

On the Scene...

Real Life Experiences

As more companies have taken their sales online, security breaches that expose consumers' credit card information have occurred many times. Bibliofind.com, a book vendor, revealed in March 2001 that its servers, holding customers' credit card data, had been subjected to a security breach that lasted for four months. In December of the same year, CreditCards.com, a credit card processing firm, had more than 50,000 credit card numbers stolen from its Web site.

Charles Schwab Corporation and the E*TRADE online brokerage company both discovered security holes in their networks that exposed clients' stock-trading accounts.

The Internet also makes it easy for criminals to exchange this illegally obtained information. Lists of stolen credit card numbers are posted in newsgroups that are frequented by criminally minded individuals.

In fact, the incidence of credit card fraud in online transactions is significantly greater than that for more traditional purchase methods. According to a paper on credit card fraud published by the National White Collar Crime Center (NW3C) Research Section, estimates put the overall percentage of credit card fraud at about .08 percent of all credit card transactions, but the same source estimates fraud accounts for 3 percent to 5 percent of all those transactions conducted online.

Credit card purchases are not the only online financial transactions that expose consumers to risk. An increasing number of busy professionals are turning to the convenience of online banking for depositing and transferring money and paying bills. Although one might assume that banks, of all businesses, would be certain to have adequate security measures in place, a number of serious security holes have been discovered in some online banking systems.

In 2000, a flaw in the software used by an online bank based in Palo Alto, California, allowed anyone to open an account and then use that account to transfer funds from other customers' accounts without their permission using the account and routing numbers for the victim's account. (These numbers are printed on account holders' checks, so all the thief would need is a look at a victim's checks.) Barclays Bank in the United Kingdom has reported security breaches in its online services that allowed customers' account information to be displayed to others. Similar problems have haunted other online banks around the world.

Today it seems that almost any financial transaction—from buying Girl Scout cookies to financing a home loan—can be conducted online. Any time you send sensitive information across the Net, you need to be aware of the risks. Last November, a computer security firm discovered a security flaw in the software that many mortgage brokers use to process loan applications. The flaw resulted in the display on the Internet of applications filed by hundreds of consumers, exposing such information as their Social Security numbers that could be used to steal their identities.

On the Scene...

Real Life Experiences

In May 2001, FBI investigators filed charges for credit card fraud, bank fraud, and other online fraud totaling an estimated US$117 million against almost 100 individuals and businesses as part of Operation CyberLoss.

How to Protect Your E-Commerce and Online Banking Transactions

Protecting e-commerce and online banking transactions must be a joint effort involving everyone who participates. The "protection triad" includes:

- The IT professionals who run the e-commerce or bank servers

- The consumer who uses e-commerce or online banking services

- The law enforcement community

The role of the IT professional is to secure the servers that are used for financial transactions, using technologies such as firewalls to keep outsiders from breaking in and stealing confidential information and strong encryption to protect the data when it travels from customers through ISPs to the server. Chapters 7 and 8 discuss Web server security and protocols such as Secure Sockets Layer (SSL), Transport Layer Security (TLS), and Secure HTTP (S-HTTP) that can be used to transmit data securely through Web browsers.

Consumers must also be made aware of the dangers of online transactions so that they can take precautions, such as never giving credit card numbers and similar information online unless the Web site or form is a secure site. Consumers need to understand how to secure the home or office computers that they use to conduct online transactions, because their passwords and other personal information can be stored on their own local hard disks, and how to properly configure security options on their Web browsers.

On the Scene...

Real Life Experiences

A popular online bank called Egg, based in the United Kingdom, detected attempts to set up fraudulent online bank accounts in 2000 and contacted the National Crime Squad, which was able to track down and arrest the would-be crooks.

Law enforcement agents must understand the scope and nature of the online fraud problem and should be educated in what information to gather, how to track down and preserve the evidence, and federal and private resources that can provide guidance and information in handling these types of cases.

Jurisdiction, as always, is an issue. The U.S. government established the Internet Fraud Complaint Center (IFCC) in May 2000 to provide an avenue for victims of online crime to file complaints and submit information to a centralized source rather than having to figure out what law enforcement agency has jurisdiction in their particular situations. The IFCC is operated by the FBI in partnership with the NW3C.

Why Cybercriminals Love Instant Messaging

Instant messaging (IM) gives Internet users the ability to communicate in near real time with others anywhere in the world. It's an application that inspires a lot of passion: You either love it or hate it. Some people consider "IM'ing" a time waster and an intrusion, but others happily spend hours at home and work communicating this way. It does have advantages even in a business environment; you can get immediate questions answered without waiting for e-mail to go through or paying for long distance telephone calls.

Convenient as it might be, instant messaging software (AOL's AIM and ICQ, Microsoft's MSN Messenger, Yahoo Instant Messenger, and others) poses serious security risks, along with providing criminals an easy way to communicate with one another to plan or discuss their crimes.

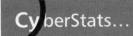

CyberStats...

The Popularity of Instant Messaging

According to an article from Reuters printed in *USA Today* in January 2002, at that time approximately 100 million users were registered with AOL's AIM service.

The Problem with Instant Messaging

By default, most of the IM products are configured to stay active all the time, running in the background, and broadcast that the user is online even when the program interface is closed. This wouldn't be so bad except that the IM software also allows for sending of files between users, which means it's not that difficult for a knowledgeable hacker to use this open channel to transfer viruses hidden in Trojans or other unwanted "gifts."

Other IM programming flaws can be exploited to execute malicious code as well. For example, some versions of AOL's ICQ and AIM programs were subject to a "buffer overflow" error if the application was sent more code than it could handle; this error allowed hackers to download malicious code to the targeted computer. Although this particular problem was fixed in subsequent software versions, it is impossible to know how many people unknowingly continued to use the flawed version of the software after the problem was revealed.

In February 2002, two bugs were reported in Microsoft's MSN Messenger software: one that exposes names and e-mail addresses on the victim's contact list and another potentially more dangerous bug that can allow a hacker to take control of the program and perform tasks on the user's computer by exploiting a security hole in Internet Explorer known as the *Document.Open()* bug.

Although IM vendors are pretty good about releasing fixes for these security flaws when they become known, new exploits are continuously being found, and many users don't update their software often. They could remain unaware of the problem until they are victimized. Network administrators and other IT professionals should stay current on these issues by subscribing to security newsletters and regularly visiting security bulletin Web sites. They should then work to educate the users in their organizations about security vulnerabilities and see that updates and fixes are installed when they become available.

Another possible security problem is the IM log that records the content of online discussions. These could be accessed by a hacker, exposing private conversations.

In fact, IM vendors generally admit that their products are not secure and, in their end-user agreements, they recommend that you not use them for sensitive communication. Nevertheless, many business users discuss personnel matters, financial and budgeting decisions, marketing strategies, and other confidential information via instant messages.

Another problem with IM software is that there is no reliable authentication mechanism to verify that a person sending you a message across the Internet really is who he or she claims to be. Anyone can set up an IM account using a false name and information. For this reason, instant messages are also a popular way for pedophiles, scam artists, and other criminals to make contact with their victims and get to know those they target for their crimes.

How to Protect Your System from Instant-Messaging Security Flaws

The best way to avoid the security problems inherent in instant messaging is not to use the programs or to use them only when necessary and never for sensitive or mission-critical communications. Many businesses block the ports used by IM software in their firewalls to prevent employees from using the programs.

If you must use IM, here are a few things you can do to reduce the risk:

- Block file transfers and game-playing capability at the firewall.

- If users only need to communicate with others within the company, administrators can install IM programs that run on the intranet, reducing exposure to the Internet.

- Users should close the program completely when not using it (just closing the interface can result in the program still running in the background— check the system tray or the list of running processes to be sure).

- Users should not accept messages from people they don't know.

- Some IM programs allow you to block the display of your IP address to recipients. If you don't completely trust the person with whom you're conversing, you might want to enable this feature.

- Turn off message logging or, if you need to keep logs, move the files to a location other than the default and encrypt them.

Like the other technologies we've discussed, IM software can be used for either good or evil. Because the programs were originally designed for recreational chatting, security hasn't been a high priority, but if you use instant messaging in a business environment or on a home machine that has sensitive data stored on it, it's important to consider the security ramifications.

Why Cybercriminals Love New Operating Systems and Applications

User demands and rapidly increasing hardware capabilities result in new operating systems (or at least new versions) being released every few years. Each new incarnation includes nifty new features, and in many cases, the new versions are more stable and faster performers than their predecessors. It seems as though users hardly have time to learn one operating system before it's time to upgrade. The same goes for productivity applications; once you upgrade the operating system, you often need a new version of your word processing or graphics software to go with it.

This system is great for the software companies, which get to make a lot of new sales, of course—but it's also great for hackers, for a couple of reasons:

- New software, especially operating systems that include dramatic changes such as Microsoft's Windows 2000 or Apple's Mac OS X, never comes out of the box perfect, regardless of how many tireless hours of beta testing went into it. Version 1.0 (and sometimes several more versions following it) is almost always at least a little buggy, and hackers can often exploit those bugs.

- Even if the software *is* perfect, users are not yet well acquainted with it and could misconfigure it in ways that open up security vulnerabilities.

Thus cybercriminals are happy when you upgrade to the latest and greatest. It opens up a window of opportunity for them before bugs are reported and security patches released—and before users learn to configure the new systems for best security.

There's not a lot you can do about this, other than perhaps foregoing the temptation to be an "early adopter" of every new software program that comes along. Even if you wait for version 2.0 or later, you'll still have to deal with users' learning curve. Network administrators should be especially wary and monitor closely for security breaches during the period immediately following major upgrades or the rollout of completely new software.

Why Cybercriminals Love Standardization

It might sound like a contradiction to say that cybercriminals love the new and different and then turn around and say that they love standardization, but it's really not. What we mean by standardization is everyone (or a vast majority) using the same operating systems, applications, protocols, and hardware.

Standardization makes things easier for hackers because they don't have to learn how to manipulate dozens of different types of systems. When a product becomes a standard, it also becomes a favorite target of hackers, crackers and virus writers. Users of Windows operating systems are more vulnerable to attack than users of other systems in large part because the vast majority of computer users run Windows. It's common sense: If you want to do the largest amount of damage with a virus, you write one that targets the most popular operating system.

You don't see many hackers out there working on how to crack OS/2 Warp (IBM's client operating system that has a very small percentage of the desktop market). It might not be a coincidence that many of the existing OS/2 client deployments are in the banking industry, a business that needs all the security it can get.

Standardization makes possible networking and computer communications on a large scale, but it also makes it possible for hackers to do their damage on a large scale. Standards are good in that they make computer hardware and software work more smoothly, but if your business deals with particularly sensitive information, one way to make your systems less vulnerable is to go with a proprietary rather than an industry-standard solution.

Planning for the Future: How to Thwart Tomorrow's Cybercriminal

What does all of this information mean as we make plans for a future in which we will all be less likely to be victimized by cybercrime? Must we give up our fast, always-on connections and go back to dialup modems? Must we forego the conveniences of wireless and mobile computing, and go back to the Lynx text-based Web browser and the PINE e-mail program? Must we stop chatting online and start waiting in line at the drive-through bank again? Should we hang on to our ancient software once we've learned to use it, or should we switch to some exotic proprietary software that no one else has ever heard of?

Of course, we won't—probably can't—do any of this. What we *can* do is be aware of the dangers that each brave new technological miracle poses and take steps that will protect us from criminal exploitation of these technologies while still allowing us to enjoy their benefits. Chapters 4 through 8 of this book provide very specific details of how this goal can be achieved.

Summary

Those who cannot remember the past are condemned to repeat it. —George Santayana

Computers and networking have only been around for a few decades. Cybercrime thus far has a short but colorful history. What can we learn from that history that will help us build a more secure online future?

As we read through some of the events that brought us to where we are today, we can see that cyberspace is still much like the American West was in the 1800s: chaotic and unsettled, a new frontier that hasn't yet been tamed. The ARPA had its own agenda, the research universities that were involved in the Net's beginnings had their big dreams, the companies that flocked online in the 1990s had their marketing plans, the individuals who "live online" have their reasons, and the criminals who take advantage of the technology have their motives. However, there was no grand master plan by which the Internet evolved into the integral part of our lives that it occupies today. Rather, it "just grew that way," and the result was a hodgepodge of systems and technologies that work amazingly well in spite of its haphazard nature.

As we enter the twenty-first century, the Internet enters a new phase in its existence. Law and order are coming to the new frontier, making it a safer—and perhaps a less creative and less fun—"place" to work and play. Those who long for the "good old days" when the Net was the province of only an elite few and online crime wasn't—or didn't seem to be—a problem are missing the point: The genie won't go back into the bottle.

Law enforcement specialists know that the policing methods that work in rural areas are not necessarily appropriate in the inner city, and vice versa. Today's Internet is not the virtual small town that it used to be; it's now a bustling international urban environment. If we are to make it an environment that's safe for us

Frequently Asked Questions

The following Frequently Asked Questions, answered by the authors of this book, are designed to both measure your understanding of the concepts presented in this chapter and to assist you with real-life implementation of these concepts. To have your questions about this chapter answered by the author, browse to **www.syngress.com/solutions** and click on the **"Ask the Author"** form.

and for our children, our cybercrime-fighting tactics will have to reflect that— much as we might wish it weren't so.

Q: What about satellite Internet service? Does it suffer the same security vulnerabilities as DSL and cable?

A: Satellite Internet services such as DirecPC and Starband use a dish-type antenna to transmit signals to and from a geostationary (fixed-position) satellite that is 22,300 miles above the earth. Radio waves (which travel at the speed of light, or approximately 186,000 miles per second) must make this trip twice when you send a communication via satellite to a computer elsewhere in the world. During this journey, the radio waves are vulnerable to interception, just as other wireless technologies. Unlike a land-based wireless transmission, satellite transmission allows an attacker to eavesdrop from anywhere within a huge area (the satellite's reception range). Satellite systems use frequency hopping and multiple-access technologies that divide the signal, making it somewhat more difficult to intercept. In addition, some systems such as DirecPC use a VPN for the connection, which prevents users from setting up their own VPNs to address security concerns. On the other hand, because satellite offers greater bandwidth than most wireless technologies, it is easier to deploy strong encryption and authentication methods.

Q: Does it matter whether I have a static or dynamic IP address?

A: Yes. Although there are advantages to having a static IP address (such as the ability to run a Web server, FTP site, or VPN), security isn't one of them. Many broadband providers issue a static IP, but others use technology that automatically changes your IP address on a regular basis (every day or even every hour), and some issue you several IP addresses so that you can manually change the address yourself when you want. This makes it more difficult for a hacker to continue attacking your site once it's been found.

Q: Does it matter which remote access authentication protocols are used? Are some more secure than others?

A: The answer is another, resounding "yes." The two most common authentication protocols used for dialup Point-to-Point Protocol (PPP) connections are Password Authentication Protocol (PAP) and Challenge Handshake Authentication Protocol (CHAP). PAP merely sends the user's name and password across the network to the server, in plain-text form. If the packets are intercepted in transit, the password can be read and stolen. CHAP uses symmetric encryption to protect the passwords that are sent over the network. However, the way CHAP works creates a new problem. The server generates a random key called the *challenge* and sends it to the client; the client uses the key to encrypt the password and sends the encrypted password back to the server. The server looks up the user's password in its database, uses the same key to encrypt it, and compares the result with the encrypted password sent by the client. Although the plain-text password doesn't ever pass across the network with this method, the server must store a plain-text version of the user's password in its database in order to make the encryption for comparison. If an intruder accesses the server's database, the intruder will have the passwords for all the users. RADIUS is a more secure alternative.

References

- John Draper: *Life as a Hacker*
  www.rit.edu/~gpm8967/imm/Draper/index.html

- Hobbes' Internet Timeline v5.6
  www.zakon.org/robert/internet/timeline

- The Internet Worm of 1988
  http://world.std.com/~franl/worm.html#p3

- Internet Fraud Complaint Center
  www1.ifccfbi.gov/index.asp

- ComputerUser.com: *Serious Online Banking Breach*
  www.computeruser.com/newstoday/00/01/31/news4.html

- Cable Datacom News, Cable Modem Info Center
  www.cabledatacomnews.com/cmic

- DSL/Cable Security: Links to Guide Picks
  http://compnetworking.about.com/cs/dslcablesecurity

- *Remote Access Network Security*
  http://home.indy.net/~sabronet/secure/remote.html

- ExtremeTech: *Exploiting and Protecting 802.11b Wireless Networks*
  www.extremetech.com

- SANS Institute: *Security on Internet Satellite*
  http://rr.sans.org/wireless/satellite.php

Chapter 3

Understanding the People on the Scene

Topics we'll investigate in this chapter:

- **Understanding Cybercriminals**
- **Understanding Cybervictims**
- **Understanding Cyberinvestigators**

☑ **Summary**

☑ **Frequently Asked Questions**

☑ **Resources**

Introduction

Cybercrime, by definition, involves computers and networks. However, as sophisticated as technology has become and as fascinating as the science of artificial intelligence (AI) might be, we are not yet at the point where computers can—by themselves—engage in criminal activity. The machines are wonderfully compliant (difficult as that sometimes might be to believe when we're struggling to make them work) and totally amoral. They do whatever we tell them to do, with no protests, no regrets, and no ulterior motives. A cybercrime always involves at least one human being who originates, plans, prepares, and initiates the criminal act.

The cybercriminal is usually not the only person on the scene of the cybercrime, however. Some cybercrimes appear to be victimless, such as a network intrusion that occurs without anyone knowing about it, in which no files are harmed and no information is "stolen" or misused. In most cases, though, some person(s) are ultimately harmed by the cybercriminal's actions. These victims might be workers who lose productive time due to a DoS attack or have to redo their work because of cybervandalism. They might be company shareholders who lose money due to extra charges for the bandwidth that a hacker uses. They might be managers who lose "brownie points" in their bosses' eyes because of the impact on their budgets. They might be IT administrators who lose their jobs for "allowing" the attack to happen. In most cases of cybercrime, if you look hard enough, you'll find a victim.

When cybercrimes are reported to the police or other enforcement agencies, more people get involved. The investigators who collect clues to discover the identity of the cybercriminal and build up the evidence can spend days, weeks, or months on a single case. The skills, knowledge, perseverance, and determination of the investigator might have a profound impact on the outcome of the case.

When cybercrime occurs in the business environment, management personnel inevitably become involved as well. As we've mentioned in earlier chapters, the law enforcement personnel and the IT professionals who need to cooperate in the investigative process often find themselves at odds. Managers, who know that cybercrime is hurting the company's bottom line and have a vested interest in minimizing the damage and seeing the cybercriminals brought to justice, are often in a unique position to facilitate cooperation among the other players.

In this chapter, we take a look—up close and personal—at all these people on the scene of the cybercrime. We examine the roles of both cybercriminals and cybervictims and how they interact—sometimes in ways that mirror the "real-world" criminal-victim relationship and sometimes in ways that are quite different.

We try to get inside the heads of the cybercriminals and understand what motivates them. We show how cybercriminals can be divided into a number of different categories and how determining which category a cybercrook fits into can help you protect yourself from his or her actions. We also look for patterns that can help us predict who will be victimized by cybercrime, and we discuss ways of making potential victims less vulnerable.

Then we turn to the professionals on the scene: the law enforcement officers and private or corporate investigators and the IT professionals who are employed by the victimized companies or who are brought in as consultants. We discuss the characteristics of a good cybercrime investigator and the type of background and training that can give the aspiring cyberdetective a head start on the job. We also focus on the specific problems of IT and law enforcement pros when they try to work together and how they can overcome these problems.

Finally, we take a special look at the role of the chief executive officer (CEO) or manager in business-related cybercrimes. We examine what the IT team and the police need—and don't need—from upper management and how managers can become facilitators in the sometimes adversarial investigative process.

At this point, you could be wondering why this book seems to be suddenly stepping away from the technical topics of computer science and law to delve into a "soft science" like psychology. Why do you—an IT professional or law enforcement officer—need to "understand" the cybercriminal? Why should you care what motivates such a person to break the law? What difference does it make to you if some personality types (and remember that companies have "personalities," too) are more likely than others to find themselves victims of cybercrimes? Isn't an investigator still an investigator, regardless of the type of crime that's been committed? Why are special skills or personal characteristics necessary for a cybercrime investigator? We provide answers to these questions as you progress through this chapter. Specifically:

- We show you how an understanding of the basics of *criminal psychology* can put you one step ahead of the cybercriminal. You'll see how knowing what motivates a criminal can help you catch that criminal— or even help you take steps to prevent the next crime from occurring.

- You'll learn about *criminal profiling*, a subject that has been frequently discussed, and frequently misrepresented, in the popular media.

- We talk about the science of *victimology*—the study of crime victim characteristics, with the goal of determining why criminals target certain people as their victims.

- We discuss *career aptitude* as it applies to the criminal investigator. You'll find out why some people are better suited for this role than others. You'll learn why, in many cases, investigation is as much an art as a science.

The human element is not only an important component of every crime case, including cybercrimes—it is often the most fascinating. We get down to the nitty-gritty technical details (and there will be plenty of those!) in upcoming chapters. But first, let's delve into the complex and often confusing issues surrounding the people who engage in, are victimized by, or devote their workdays to preventing, solving, and prosecuting cybercrime.

Understanding Cybercriminals

A number of scientific disciplines are devoted to gaining a better understanding of criminals and criminal behavior. *Criminal psychology* is the study of the criminal mind and what leads a person to engage in illegal or socially deviant behavior. You can think of criminal psychology as a subcategory of *forensic psychology*, which concerns itself with emotional and behavioral issues that pertain to the law and legal systems and includes police psychologists (who address emotional and behavioral issues with police officers), social psychologists (who study group behavior and broader societal implications of psychological issues), and others. The job of the criminal psychologist may also overlap with that of the *criminologist*, who studies criminals, crime, and the effect of the criminal justice system and societal factors on criminal behavior and crime rates.

NOTE

Forensic psychology is a different discipline from *forensic psychiatry*, which the American Academy of Psychiatry and the Law (AAPL) defines as "a medical subspecialty that includes research and clinical practice in the many areas in which psychiatry is applied to legal issues." (See http://flash.lakeheadu.ca/~pals/forensics/forensic.htm.) Forensic psychiatrists are medical doctors and can treat patients, prescribe controlled drugs, and otherwise practice medicine. Forensic psychologists may also work directly with patients, but criminal psychologists often focus on studying the cases of criminals to detect patterns, analyze behaviors, and make predictions and profiles based on their analyses.

On the Scene...

At the FBI

Behavioral science is a broad term that refers to use of scientific methods to study the behavior of living creatures (including humans). *The behavioral sciences* is often used as a collective term referring to psychology, sociology, anthropology, and other sciences that study behavior of people or animals. The FBI uses the term much more specifically, as in the name of its Behavioral Science Unit (BSU) at its Quantico, Virginia, training academy.

The BSU focuses on the study of human behavior as it applies to criminals and crime. FBI personnel who work in the BSU are trained special agents who also have advanced degrees in psychology, sociology, criminology, and the like. The BSU is famous for its success in criminal profiling of serial killers and other violent criminals. The BSU uses a number of methodologies, such as computerized crime analysis, clinical forensic psychology, and applied criminal psychology, to provide assistance to other law enforcement agencies in solving crimes and capturing criminals.

Many of the FBI's behavioral science specialists have made names for themselves outside the agency. Robert Ressler, John E. Douglas, James T. Reese, and Roy Hazelwood all became famous for their work, as part of the BSU, on various high-profile cases.

A new psychological specialty has evolved over the last few decades: that of the *investigative psychologist*. Investigative psychology involves applying knowledge of psychological principles to police work and criminal investigation.

Despite the FBI's and many large law enforcement agencies' focus on bringing scientific methods such as criminal psychology into police investigations, many police officers at the local level are still skeptical. "Why should I care about *understanding* criminals?" they ask. "All I want to do is catch them and put them behind bars."

This attitude is usually due to a misunderstanding about the meaning of the word *understanding*. One of its meanings is indeed "sympathetic, empathetic, or tolerant." Police (understandably!) see no reason to show this sort of feeling toward lawbreakers, especially people who cause harm to others in doing so. We're not asking them to exhibit this meaning of the word *understanding*.

The other meaning of the word is "to perceive and explain the meaning or nature of somebody or something." This is the kind of understanding you need as a law enforcement officer or IT professional involved in investigating cybercrimes as it relates to the cybercriminal's mindset and motivations. You need that kind of understanding because it will help you catch the criminal and put him or her behind bars.

Profiling Cybercriminals

Criminal profiling is the art and science of developing a description of a criminal's characteristics (physical, intellectual, and emotional) based on information collected at the scene(s) of the crime(s). A *criminal profile* is a psychological assessment made before the fact—that is, without knowing the identity of the criminal. The profile consists of a set of defined characteristics that are likely to be shared by criminals who commit a particular type of crime. The profile can be used to narrow the field of suspects or evaluate the likelihood that a particular suspect committed the crime.

Profiling by police has taken on a number of unfortunate connotations due to media focus on the term when describing discriminatory police practices. In the mind of some members of the public, all police profiling has become associated with *racial* profiling, which in turn has come to mean treating people as criminal suspects based solely on their ethnicity or the appearance of ethnicity.

On the other hand, in some circles the perceived effectiveness of profiling has been elevated to almost mythical proportions. Movies such as Jonathan Demme's *Silence of the Lambs* and Michael Mann's *Manhunter* have glorified and glamorized the role of the criminal profiler, making it seem that profiling is almost akin to magic. Profilers in movies are able to take a look at the crime scene and unerringly describe the criminal's physical characteristics and background.

It's not quite that easy or certain in real life, but criminal profiling is a valuable tool that can give investigators many clues about the person who commits a specific crime or series of crimes. Nonetheless, it's important to understand that a profile—even one constructed by the top profilers in the field—will provide only an idea of the general *type* of person who committed a crime; a profile will *not* point to a specific person as the suspect. Although good profiles can be amazingly accurate as to the offender's occupation, educational background, childhood experiences, marital status, and even general physical appearance, there will always be many individuals who fit a given profile.

Profiling is just one tool among many for conducting an investigation and building a criminal case. A profile is *not* evidence; rather, it is a starting point that can help investigators focus on the right suspect(s) and begin to gather evidence.

NOTE

Profiling has been in use in law enforcement for quite some time. Although the FBI is often credited with its "invention," a less sophisticated form of profiling and crime reconstruction was used in the Jack the Ripper case in London in the 1880s. See the article *Criminal Profiling: How It Got Started and How It Is Used* by Wayne Petherick, located on the Crime Library Web site at www.crimelibrary.com/criminology/criminalprofiling2, for a historical examination of criminal profiling.

Understanding How Profiling Works

Criminal profiling is considered by some people—including, still, some law enforcement officers—to be an exotic "last resort" investigative tactic. Those skeptics equate the profiler's work with that of "forensic psychics" who offer their clairvoyant powers to assist in solving crimes. Profiling, however, is a process that is based on collecting information and then analyzing that information by applying logic.

Profilers draw inferences about the criminal's personality and other characteristics based on the following indicators:

- Their observations of the crime and crime scene

- The testimony of witnesses and victims

- Their knowledge of human psychology and criminal psychology

- The existence of patterns and correlations between different crimes

John E. Douglas, former FBI profiler, says in his book *MindHunter,* "Behavior reflects personality." Profilers examine the criminal's behavior and develop a description of his personality.

Often, an important part of a criminal profiler's work involves comparing the facts and impressions from a group of crimes and determining whether it is likely that the crimes were committed by the same person. Repeat criminals are, not surprisingly, creatures of habit in ways other than the fact that they continue to commit crimes. They tend to do things in the same way each time; this is known in popular parlance as the criminal's *modus operandi* (method of operation, or MO). Behaviors that a criminal repeats at each crime scene, especially if the behavior seems to fulfill a psychological need (as opposed to being a matter of practicality), are also known as the criminal's *signature.* Cybercriminals, like other criminals, often give themselves away by their MOs or signatures.

There are two basic profiling methods: inductive and deductive. Each is based on a particular method of reasoning or logic. Generally, *inductive reasoning* works from the specific to the general, whereas *deductive reasoning* works from the more general to the more specific.

With inductive reasoning, you begin with observations or information, then come up with a theory that you apply to new circumstances. With deductive reasoning, you begin with a premise and then come up with specific conclusions based on the premise. For better understanding, see San Jose State University's exercises in inductive and deductive reasoning at www.sjsu.edu/depts/itl/graphics/induc/ind-ded.html.

Inductive Profiling

The *inductive profiling* method relies on statistics and comparative analysis to create a profile. Information is collected about criminals who have committed a specific type of crime. The information can take the form of formal studies of convicted criminals, informal observation of known criminals, clinical or other interviews with criminals known to have committed certain crimes, and data already available in databases.

By analyzing the data and establishing correlations, the profiler infers that characteristics common to a statistically significant number of offenders who commit a particular type of crime are applicable to other criminals who commit the same type of crime. The inductive-profiling model tends to produce results that are nonspecific and generalized.

Deductive Profiling

A deduction *is an argument in which, certain things being laid down, something other than these necessarily comes about through them.*—Aristotle

The *deductive profiling* method relies on the application of deductive reasoning to the observable evidence. Investigators collect general information about the crime, and the profiler draws specific conclusions about the criminal's characteristics, based on the profiler's experience, knowledge, and critical thinking. Victimology, the crime scene, forensic evidence, and behavioral analysis are all components of the deductive process.

The deductive method involves several distinct steps:

1. A problem is stated.
2. Information is collected.
3. A working hypothesis is formulated.

4. The hypothesis is tested.

5. Results of the test are examined.

6. One or more conclusions are reached.

Hypotheses can be tested using *if/then thinking*. We might start with a hypothesis such as, "Hackers are mostly harmless." If our hypothesis is correct, the data should show that the vast majority of hacking incidents cause no monetary loss or other harm to the companies or individuals whose systems are hacked. Finding one or two incidences of loss or harm would not disprove the hypothesis—but if we find large numbers of cases that are inconsistent with our hypothesis, we can consider it to be invalid. Our conclusion, then, could be the opposite of the hypothesis we started with: Hackers are *not* "mostly harmless."

Profilers using the deductive method often mention that success depends on being able to "get inside the mind" of the criminal, to think like the criminal thinks, in order to understand the criminal's motives and predict his future actions. The best deductive profilers might state that they rely on intuition or that they use common sense to develop profiles. However, close examination usually reveals that the "common sense" to which they refer is a process of logical thinking, applied to the hard evidence they've gathered and observed. This thinking process can take place subconsciously, leading to the "intuitive feelings" that don't really come out of nowhere but are instead the result of long hours or days of subconsciously processing masses of information.

Unlike the inductive process, which is based on statistical data (and which can be processed by a computer as well as or better than by a human being), deductive reasoning requires intelligence of a kind of which machines are not yet capable. Deductive thinking is not only a skill, it is a talent that some people seem to be born with and that other people can never learn. The most talented detectives tend to be masters of deductive reasoning. We discuss the qualifications and characteristics of a good investigator later in this chapter, in the "Understanding Cyberinvestigators" section.

NOTE

Perhaps one of the most famous proponents of deductive reasoning was Sir Arthur Conan Doyle, the Scottish writer and physician who created the Sherlock Holmes character in the 1880s. Doyle summed up the deductive method rather succinctly: "It is an old maxim of mine that when you have excluded the impossible, whatever remains, however improbable, must be the truth."

Uses of the Criminal Profile

A profile cannot, by itself, solve a criminal case. However, the profile can be used for several purposes:

- To narrow the field of suspects

- To link related crimes

- To give investigators valuable leads to follow

Although the profile is not itself evidence of a particular suspect's guilt, it can be used in court in conjunction with expert witness testimony. *Expert witnesses*, unlike other witnesses in a criminal case, are allowed to state opinions. An expert witness can reference a criminal profile as the basis of an opinion that there is a high probability of a link between a particular suspect and a particular crime scene. We discuss expert witnesses and expert testimony in more detail in Chapter 11, "Building the Cybercrime Case."

Profiling that is based on collecting large amounts of data about cybercrime and those who commit it can serve another purpose. As a picture of the typical cybercriminal begins to come into focus, we could be forced to reexamine our own misconceptions about cybercriminals based on media myths and a few anecdotal cases.

Reexamining Myths and Misconceptions About Cybercriminals

Movies such as *WarGames* and *Hackers* have given us Hollywood's image of the cybercriminal, one that tends to be simplified and romanticized. In those movies, hackers are all misunderstood geniuses with hearts of gold who are just trying to save the world, despite the interference of the big, bad government. News stories, on the other hand, often go overboard in the opposite direction. They paint anyone who believes in the distribution of open-source software as a dangerous pirate who is determined to undermine the very foundations of our capitalistic society. The truth, as usual, lies somewhere in between these two extremes.

Now that Internet access is a mainstream activity, most members of the general public have heard of cybercrime, and many hold opinions at the extreme ends of the spectrum. Some of the most common misconceptions regarding cybercriminals include:

- All cybercriminals are "nerds"—bright but socially inept.

- All cybercriminals have very high IQs and a great deal of technical knowledge.

- All cybercriminals are male, usually teenage boys.

- All teenage boys with computers are dangerous cybercriminals.

- Cybercriminals aren't "real" criminals because they don't operate in the "real world."

- Cybercriminals are never violent.

- All cybercriminals neatly fit one profile.

Most of these misconceptions are based on stereotypes. We could argue that stereotyping is what profiling is all about. What is a stereotype, anyway? The dictionary defines the term as "an oversimplified standardized image or idea held by one person or group of another." The key here (and the difference between a stereotype and a profile) is *oversimplification*. A criminal profile is complex and based on hard data. A stereotype is a device that allows you to bypass collecting hard data and apply a "known" fact (or a statement widely accepted as such) to individual situations.

Are stereotypes always wrong? Of course they're not. If there were not some truth in a belief, at least some of the time, it would never become a stereotype. The danger of relying on stereotypes—especially in the context of investigating crime and enforcing the law—is that it puts blinders on the investigator and closes his or her mind to all the possibilities. Savvy criminals can take advantage of these stereotypes and literally "get away with murder" (and lesser crimes) simply by not fitting the known stereotype.

On the Scene...

How and Why We Stereotype

The word *stereotype* is derived from the process of creating metal-engraved plates for printing. Once the plate is created, the image is "set" and cannot be easily changed. Thus the word evolved into a description of the "set image" or opinion that people apply to an entire category of people.

Continued

www.syngress.com

> Stereotypes often contain a grain of truth; women *do* tend to be more emotional than men, more Asians than Westerners *do* practice and master the martial arts, the rich *are* different from you and me and Ernest Hemingway (they have more money). The danger of stereotypes is that they provide a "quick and dirty"—and often misleading and inaccurate—way of judging people we don't know.
>
> Stereotyping is a handy "shortcut," and the human brain is attracted to that. We all base some of our beliefs on stereotypes; when we simply don't have enough information to form an opinion, we tend to default to what we've heard from others, read in books, or seen on television. The media is one of the biggest perpetuators of stereotypes. Much comedy is based on common stereotypes. This is not necessarily out of any evil intent; when you have to tell a story in the space of a half-hour sitcom or a two-hour movie, shortcuts become a necessity. The more a particular stereotype is repeated, however, the more likely we are to believe it.
>
> An excellent, detailed discussion of stereotyping and how it is used in social interaction is available at www.psc-cfp.gc.ca/publications/monogra/mono3_e.htm.

Let's take an up-close look at each of the misconceptions on our list and discuss how each came about and why each is generally an inaccurate assumption.

All Cybercriminals Are "Nerds"—Bright But Socially Inept

As with many misconceptions, this one grew out of a past when it was more often true than it is today. Recall from the history discussion in Chapter 2 that in the early days of computers and networking, few common folks had access to the huge, expensive, user-unfriendly mainframe systems that defined the word *computer*.

Who *did* have access? "Scientific types" at places like MIT. These were the guys with crew cuts and slide rules in their pockets. Working with the first computers required extensive math skills. There were no computer "users" back then; if you wanted to interact with the machine, you needed to be a programmer. Programming was a painstaking process that required patience and the willingness to devote huge chunks of your time to coding. It was hardly conducive to cultivating opportunities to appear on the newspaper's society pages. When (if) you *did* get out into the world at night, what did you have to talk about after spending your days locked up with a bunch of vacuum tubes, poring over printouts of 1s and 0s? Not much that anyone else could understand or care about.

The word *nerd* has a couple of different meanings and even more connotations. Microsoft's *Encarta World Dictionary 2001* defines it as "a single-minded enthusiast, whose interest is regarded as too technical or scientific and who seems obsessively wrapped up in it." That's an apt description of a large proportion of the computer hobbyists of the 1950s, 1960s, and 1970s. Today, though, computers are almost ubiquitous. The skills needed to use the Net for mischievous or malicious purposes are far less complex than they used to be. The "nerd" stereotype still fits some people, but many of today's cybercriminals—especially computer scam artists and sexually motivated criminals who use the Internet to find victims—are smooth and charming and have highly developed social skills.

On the Scene...

Cyber Serial Killer

In 2000, a Kansas man named John Robinson was arrested for sexual assault and became a suspect in the killings of several women over a span of 15 years. What made this case unique was the method of procuring victims: through Internet chat rooms, most of them dedicated to sadomasochism. Although he had a criminal record (he had previously been arrested for theft and fraud), he represented himself to his victims as a rich, professional businessman. Robinson's trial for three of the murders, which has been postponed several times, is scheduled for September 2002. See www.mayhem.net/Crime/robinson.html for more information.

All Cybercriminals Have Very High IQs and a Great Deal of Technical Knowledge

Again, this is a stereotype based on outdated facts. Those early MIT math majors tended to fit it, but it bears little relevance to today's cybercriminal. Getting online now is as easy as pointing and clicking. Although some cybercrimes—such as writing and distributing new viruses or mounting intrusion attacks against highly protected networks—require technical expertise, many other cybercrimes can be (and are) committed by people of average or below-average intelligence with little or no technical training or skill.

Cyber con games can be played by anyone who is capable of sending e-mail or using Internet chat programs. Data theft is often a simple matter of dragging and dropping. Even crimes that depend on complex technical exploits can be performed by unskilled hackers called *script kiddies,* who merely use the code written by others to do their mischief. Hundreds of Web sites and newsgroups provide technologically clueless "wannabe" hackers with these preconfigured or automated tools that can be used to crack systems.

For more information, see the article *Don't Fear the Reaper, Fear the Script Kiddie* on the About.com Web site at http://netsecurity.about.com/library/weekly/aa111600a.htm.

All Cybercriminals Are Male, Usually Teenage Boys

This is a double stereotype. It makes assumptions about two groups: cybercriminals and women. Science and math in general, and computer technology in particular, have traditionally been predominantly male domains. Furthermore, law enforcement statistics show that males are more likely to commit crimes of all types than are females.

On the Scene...

From Script Kiddies to Click Kiddies

Script kiddies, who use scripts written by others to break into networks, crack passwords, and wreak other mischief, must have at least enough technical ability to enter the proper commands to execute the script. The newest phenomenon in the "devolution of hacking," according to security expert David Rhoades, is the *click kiddie,* who hacks simply by pointing and clicking, cutting and pasting. This is made possible by Web sites that do all the work for them. Rhoades's excellent presentation on this topic, called *Hacking for the Masses,* is available online at www.clickkiddie.net.

However, statistics also show that the gender gap is closing. Near the end of the 1990s, arrests of women comprised about 22 percent of all arrests (with women accounting for about 14 percent of violent offenders and about 29 percent of property-related crime offenders), according to the U.S. Department of Justice's Bureau of Justice Statistics (www.ojp.usdoj.gov/bjs/crimoff.htm#women). That same source states that during the 1990s, the number of female defendants convicted of felonies in the state courts increased at more than twice the rate of the increase of male convictions.

White-collar criminals have traditionally been male—but some experts theorize that this was because, until recent years, high-level corporate positions (which pose the greater opportunities and temptations) were almost exclusively held by men. Now that women are making it into the executive suite, more and more female offenders are being arrested on embezzlement, fraud, and other white-collar crime charges. See the paper *Integrity in the Corporate Suite: Predictors of Female Frauds* by Collins, Muchinsky, Mundfrom, and Collins, at www.cj.msu.edu/~faculty/collinsintegrity.html for theoretical and statistical information.

Computer science is no longer an all-male occupation. The U.S. Department of Commerce statistics show that 28.5 percent of programmers are now female. Although only a small percentage of programmers (of either gender) use their skills for illegal purposes, women are definitely acquiring the means to commit computer crimes in greater numbers than ever before.

Randy Nichols, president of Comsec Security and lecturer on cryptography and security at George Washington University in Washington, D.C., was quoted in the *Irish Times* in January 2000 as saying, "Worldwide, not one single female has been charged with a felony committed with a computer." However, there have been a few noted female hackers. See the ABC News Web site at http://abcnews.go.com/sections/tech/dailynews/hackerwomen000602.html for an article that contains interviews with female hackers discussing sexism in the hacker community.

On the Scene...

The World's Oldest Profession and the World's First Famous Female Hacker

A woman who used the pseudonym Susan Thunder evolved from a rock-star groupie and prostitute into a phone phreaker and computer hacker. She specialized in breaking into military computers and eventually become associated with infamous hackers Ron and Kevin Mitnick. She was, in fact, granted immunity from prosecution for testifying against them when they were arrested for their own hacking exploits.

Given her background, it was only logical that Susan became adept at what is known in the hacking world as *social engineering*—that is, persuading authorized users to reveal their passwords. Legend has it that she often accomplished this goal by engaging in sexual relationships with the military personnel who had the information she sought.

The "typical cybercriminal" profile offered by Nichols—male, white, and 19 to 30 years of age—is still valid for speaking in generalities, but it is becoming less so every year. Increasingly, those who commit cybercrimes come from both genders, all races, and every age group.

All Teenage Boys with Computers Are Dangerous Cybercriminals

Once again, the media is mostly responsible for this stereotype. It is a common belief in some quarters that every teenage boy with a computer spends his nights breaking into the defense department computers in search of the codes to fire nuclear missiles. This image is reinforced by stories such as the report in the summer of 2001 that a "secret society of teenage cyberanarchists" had brought down the corporate Web site of Steve Gibson, a well-known security expert. Even the FBI was unable to help Gibson track down the hackers. (For the full story, see http://grc.com/dos/grcdos.htm.) The TV networks run documentaries such as the *20/20 Monday* episode that featured an online "gang" of teenage hackers called Global Hell. Books such as *The Hacker Diaries: Confessions of Teenage Hackers,* published by McGraw-Hill/Osborne Media, further perpetuate many people's fear and suspicion of teenagers with computers.

No one can dispute that teenagers who get their kicks by vandalizing corporate Web sites or trying to penetrate government computer systems are criminals, and that such behavior constitutes a problem. Neither can anyone dispute that teenagers full of rage who open fire on their classmates and teachers are dangerous criminals. However, most of us realize that the vast majority of teens—even sullen, angry, rebellious teens—will never engage in such extreme behavior.

The same is true of the vast majority of teenage boys who have computer skills. The farthest most will go in using their computers for illegal activities is to download music or software for their own personal use through services like Napster or "warez" newsgroups. Although this activity might be "dangerous" to the record companies' and software vendors' bottom lines, it's a crime on the same level as copying songs from a CD to cassette tape to share with a friend. It's hardly in the same category as bringing down the systems that run Wall Street or infiltrating the international banking system's computers.

Cybercriminals Aren't "Real" Criminals Because They Don't Operate in the "Real World"

Many cybercriminals buy into this myth themselves—or at least they use it to justify and rationalize their behavior. Even people who stop short of illegal activity often behave online in ways they would not think of behaving in their "real lives"—lying, cheating on their spouses via "virtual" relationships, or merely acting rude and obnoxious.

This phenomenon is so commonplace that an entire field of study, *cyberpsychology,* has grown up around it. Publications such as *CyberPsychology & Behavior* (www.liebertpub.com/CPB/default1.asp), professional mailing lists, and Web sites such as the Computer-Mediated Communication (CMC) Studies Center (www.december.com/cmc/study/center.html) have examined the double illusion of unreality and anonymity that leads people to behave differently (and often badly) in cyberspace.

Technology such as online chat, multiple-user dungeons (MUDs), and virtual reality programs have distorted some users' ability to distinguish between what is real and what is unreal. Many Internet users, especially those who are new to the online world, seem to see the people on the other end of their modem line as akin to characters in an interactive program, and they see the interactions and relationships they engage in with those people as nothing more than a game.

Because these people are not being their "real selves" in online interactions, they perhaps believe that no one else is, either. Hence, it becomes okay in their minds to concoct elaborate stories and deceptions, which might cross the line into illegal fraud. Furthermore, because they can sign on using pseudonyms (online services like AOL let you easily and quickly create new screen names, making it even more tempting to do so), they think nobody knows who they are or what they do online. For those people who have no real internal controls in the form of personal ethics and morals and who behave "properly" only out of fear of external consequences (societal disapproval or jail), this forum provides an excuse to throw off all inhibitions. Add to this the anecdotal evidence that many of those who frequent chat rooms lower their inhibitions even further by indulging in alcohol while they surf the Net, and you have a recipe for antisocial behavior.

Of course, this idea that nothing online is real and therefore nothing you do there "counts" is a fallacy. But it's an old trick of the criminal to depersonalize his or her victims; seeing them as something less than true human beings makes it easier to hurt them. This self-deception is made much easier in cyberspace because they never have to see the faces or hear the voices of the people they're victimizing; the people with whom the criminal deals can conveniently remain nothing more than words on a computer screen.

Cybercriminals Are Never Violent

Because the Internet is more a virtual than a physical medium, it seems logical to assume that even if cybercrime is real crime, it isn't *violent* crime. After all, it's the ability to commit their crimes from a distance that attracts many criminals to the Net in the first place.

It's true that a large percentage of reported cybercrimes are frauds, thefts, and cases of unauthorized access. However, it is interesting to note that the most frequently reported cybercrime in the Cybersnitch database (www.cybersnitch.net) is child pornography, which is generally classified as a violent or potentially violent crime for two reasons: the harm done to the children who are used to make the photographs, and the potential of the material to incite pedophiles to act out their fantasies with real children. Hacker intrusions are the second most frequently reported crime type; the third is electronic stalking, which can also be considered a violent crime because it terrorizes the victim, and cyberstalkers have often been known to progress to actually stalking their victims in real life.

Some people might argue that child porn and cyberstalking aren't in themselves physically violent crimes, but it would be difficult to make such a claim of the predators who use the Internet to find vulnerable people they can lure into a meeting in order to rape, assault, or kill them. In addition to these violent offenders who usually act alone, the terrorists who use the Internet to raise money, plan their activities, recruit new members, and communicate with one another are violent criminals of the most dangerous sort.

Cybercriminals, like criminals in general, span a continuum that reaches from the kid whose curiosity causes him or her to try hacking into someone's network just to see if it can be done, with no intent to do damage, all the way up to the men who carried out the attack on the World Trade Center in New York City. This realization leads us to our last misconception.

All Cybercriminals Neatly Fit One Profile

We might be able to construct a profile of the type of person who commits a particular cybercrime, but it is impossible to create one profile that fits all cybercriminals, just as it is impossible to make an accurate profile of all traffic law violators. The casual speeder is likely to have a different personality and different motivations from the habitual drunk driver or the outraged motorist who uses his vehicle as a weapon to mow down pedestrians. Likewise, the computer scam artist is an entirely different creature from the cyberstalker, who is, in turn, nothing like the typical hacker.

Even within a particular category of cybercrime, the physiology, psychology, and motivations of each cybercriminal is different from every other. Nonetheless, some commonalities allow us to paint a very broad picture of the "typical" cybercriminal. We must keep in mind, however, that in order for a profile to be useful in our investigations, it must be based on the facts of an individual case.

Constructing a Profile of the Typical Cybercriminal

As a first step in building a profile (and remembering that it is *only* the first step), we can look at some generalities that, more often than not, apply to cybercriminals in all categories. It is important to see these characteristics as *probabilities*, not as absolute rules. There are exceptions to each case. That said, a majority of cybercriminals exhibit at least some of these characteristics:

- **At least a minimal amount of technical savvy** This assumption is based on common sense. Although, as we've mentioned before, it is easier than ever to get online without being a computer whiz, most people who use the Internet for illegal purposes are able to find their way around in cyberspace without a lot of assistance. People generally use the tools with which they feel comfortable, especially when engaging in high-risk activities such as committing crime. In order to use the Internet to carry out a planned act such as a crime, you must be capable of basic tasks such as sending e-mail, surfing the Web, or logging onto a chat line. Some crimes require a good deal more expertise. The typical cybercriminal isn't a computerphobe or someone who's just signed onto the Net for the first time.

- **Disregard for the law or a feeling of being above or beyond the law** Few people, including criminals, think of themselves as "bad." Most—though not all—lawbreakers justify their actions by instead seeing the laws themselves (at least the ones they break) as bad laws. Cybercriminals, like other habitual criminals, often exhibit disregard or disdain for the law. They are not the types of people who believe you should comply with the law just *because* it's the law. Rather, they tend to believe that laws they consider unreasonable are fair game to be broken. In some cases, they feel that they themselves, because of their special skills, intelligence, positions, or circumstances, are above the law. For example, an employee who regards the common thief as a crook might believe that embezzling money from his or her employer is okay because the company underpays and overworks its employees. Other cybercriminals believe that the law simply doesn't apply in cyberspace, hearkening back to the "unreality" aspect we mentioned earlier.

- **An active fantasy life** Many cybercriminals use the Internet as an outlet for their fantasies. They often construct entirely new personas that they use online—both to hide their true identities and avoid detection and because they enjoy "playing the part" of someone different from themselves. Con artists can concoct elaborate schemes based on their fantasies. Cyberstalkers build fantasies around their victims. Child pornographers deal in sexual fantasies. Hackers fantasize about "hacking the world," gaining control over other people by controlling their computer systems. This ties into the next common characteristic of cyber-criminals.

- **A "control freak" and/or risk-taking nature** Criminals often expend more energy, for less practical return, in committing crimes than they would if they turned their efforts to more socially acceptable work. Why then do they engage in such high-risk behavior? For some, it is the risk of getting caught, the thrill of doing something that's forbidden, that makes a life of crime attractive. For others, it is the sense of control they get from manipulating or outwitting others. Although these two character-istics seem to conflict, they can exist simultaneously in the same person. The risk-taking element provides the "rush," while escaping detection one more time makes the cybercriminal feel safe and in control.

- **Strong motivations—but the motivations might be wildly different** As noted, it takes time and energy to commit most crimes. It takes extra effort, and a certain amount of skill, to commit cybercrimes. Most cybercriminals are strongly motivated, but the motivations range from just wanting to have fun to the need or desire for money, emo-tional or sexual impulses, political motives, or dark compulsions caused by mental illness or psychiatric conditions. Discerning the motivation for a particular crime is an important aspect of building a useful profile of the criminal who committed it.

Recognizing Criminal Motivations

In the words of one police academy instructor, "Why do criminals commit crimes? Because they're criminals." If only it were that simple. People break the law for many different reasons. Some of those reasons might even seem reason-able, such as the out-of-work mother with no money left who steals baby food to feed her child. On the other hand, many people in dire straits find solutions to their problems that don't involve breaking the law. Some cybercriminals—for example, the longtime loyal employee who suddenly embezzles company funds to pay unexpected medical bills or get a relative out of trouble—might do so out of desperation, too. Most, though, are driven by far less noble motives: greed, anger, lust, or just plain boredom.

Why does motive matter? In many jurisdictions, an important element of proving guilt is showing that the accused possesses each component of the so-called *crime triangle:* means (a way to commit the crime), motive (a reason for committing the crime), and opportunity (being in the right place at the right time to commit the crime). Thus understanding the criminal's motive is useful at two points in the investigation: when we are creating a profile to help us identify the correct suspect(s) and later when we present the case against our suspect.

Common motives for committing cybercrimes include:

- Just for fun
- Monetary profit
- Anger, revenge, and other emotional needs
- Political motives
- Sexual impulses
- Serious psychiatric illness

Let's examine each of these motives individually and look at how each can apply to the cybercriminal.

Just for Fun

Young hackers are the cybercriminals most likely to fall into this category. According to J. Maxwell in the *Electronic Data Processing Audit, Control, and Security Newsletter* (cited at http://faculty.ncwc.edu/toconnor/315/315lec12.htm), the hackers who do it for fun can be further broken down into several categories:

- *Pioneer types*, who are fascinated by the technology. They enjoy learning how the systems work via a trial-and-error process and hack as a learning experience.
- *"Scamps,"* playful hackers who don't intend to do any harm. This is the type who might hack into a Web site and leave an innocuous message such as "J.B. was here."
- *Explorers*, who get their kicks out of "going where no hacker has gone before"—or at least, where they themselves have never been. Their curiosity leads them to break into networks just to look around and see what's there.
- *Game players*, who look at hacking into systems as a game, pitting themselves against the network's security measures and motivated by the desire to "win" by breaking in.

Another of Maxwell's hacker personality types, the *addict,* might start as any of these character types but becomes psychologically dependent on the activity. At that point, the pioneer, scamp, explorer, or gamester is no longer really hacking just for fun, but because he or she *needs* to hack in order to feel okay or normal.

The distinguishing characteristic of the "for fun" hacker is enjoyment. Unlike other cybercriminals who use the computer and Internet as the means to an end, for these hackers, hacking is an end in itself. They might view the computer as a toy and the entire Internet as their playground.

These "for fun" hackers realize no practical or financial gain from their hacking; in fact, hacking could be an expensive hobby for those who are continually upgrading their own computer systems to make the hacking experience faster and more satisfying.

Monetary Profit

If love of money is the root of all evil, it's no surprise that many cybercrimes—like many offline crimes—are motivated by the desire for financial gain. "Hacking for dollars" can cover many different offenses, including embezzlement, corporate espionage, and selling one's hacking services to others who have monetary or nonmonetary motives (the "hacker for hire").

Most cyberscam artists are in it for the money. Their motive could be to get money into their own hands or obtain properties or services without paying.

Money-motivated cybercriminals come in all "flavors"—male, female, young, old, wealthy, poor, or middle class. Some never made it through high school; others have advanced degrees. *White-collar criminals* (embezzlers, trade-secret thieves, and the like) tend to be educated professionals, often in the midst of career stagnation or burnout. *Scam artists* are usually sociable and charming, able to persuade others to do what they want. *Hired hacks* are generally highly skilled technicians who, in their own eyes, are "just doing a job."

Anger, Revenge, and Other Emotional Motivators

Money is not the only motive, or even the strongest one, for committing crimes. Many criminal offenses, especially those that involve violence (and threat of violence) or property destruction, are committed out of emotional motivations: anger, rage, or revenge for real or imagined wrongs.

Anger can drive people to do things they otherwise might not. Psychologists note that dealing with a person who is very angry, hurt, or emotionally distraught is like dealing with someone who is mentally disturbed or under the influence of alcohol or drugs. Indeed, strong emotions cause a release of adrenaline, which does act on the body and brain like a drug, resulting in both physiological and psychological changes (enhanced physical strength, heightened alertness, "tunnel vision," or obsession with the problem immediately at hand). A very angry person *is*—temporarily, at least—an emotionally disturbed person.

Cybercriminals who act out of anger might be spurned lovers or spouses, fired employees, business associates who feel they've been cheated or ripped off, or others who believe some great wrong has been done to them or someone they care about. Their crimes range from terrorist threats (for example, e-mail threatening to assault or kill someone) to defacing a company's Web site with profanities or bringing down an organization's network with DoS attacks or computer viruses.

Revenge differs from anger in that it is usually better planned and not an immediate response. This makes it a less emotional act; consequently, it could be more dangerous because the vengeance-motivated cybercriminal has more time to think through the plan, cover his or her tracks, and reduce the probability of being caught.

Almost anyone, pushed hard enough and far enough, is capable of lashing out in anger. Thus the anger-motivated cybercriminal can be someone who doesn't ordinarily engage in criminal activity. The crime could seem completely out of character. Just as an investigator asks, in the case of a money-motivated crime, "Who was in a position to benefit financially?" the investigator should approach a crime that appears to be motivated by anger with the question, "Who has been harmed or is close to someone who has been harmed by the victim?"

Anger and revenge are not the only motives that involve emotions. Cybercriminals commit crimes out of other emotional and psychological needs. For example, hackers could break into protected systems in order to prove themselves to their friends, to obtain a sense of belonging to the group. In fact, hackers sometimes commit acts in groups that they would not commit individually. The "crowd mentality" (or *mob* mentality, in extreme cases) is a phenomenon with which psychologists are familiar and is something most law enforcement officers are aware of. Large groups can take on personalities of their own, becoming more or other than the sum of their parts. Hackers might egg one another on, daring each other to go farther, with no one willing to be the first to say "no" and lose status in the eyes of his or her peers.

Hackers also commit crimes to gain attention. This is especially true of teenage hackers who want to embarrass their families or simply make family members or authority figures notice them.

Another emotional motivation for hacking is loyalty to a friend or the desire to "help" someone—for example, the high school hacker who doesn't want his girlfriend to flunk calculus and have to go to summer school, so he breaks into the school's computer system and changes her grade from an F to a C.

Political Motives

Politically motivated cybercriminals include members of extremist and radical groups at both ends of the political spectrum who use the Internet to spread propaganda, attack the Web sites and networks of their political enemies, steal money to fund their militant activities, or plan and coordinate their "real-world" crimes. Examples include:

- The 1996 case in which "hacktivists" infiltrated the U.S. DoJ through its Web site, deleted the DoJ's Web files and replaced them with their own pages protesting the recently passed Communications Decency Act

- The rash of Web site defacements that included the message "Free Kevin" (in reference to Kevin Mitnick, who was arrested for computer crimes) in 1998

- The "cyberwars" between U.S. and Chinese hackers in the summer of 2000, following international disputes over the landing of a U.S. spy plane in China

Cybercriminals with political motivations range from relatively benign hackers who just want to make a political statement to organized terrorist groups such as Hezbollah, Hamas, and al Qa'ida. *Cyberterrorism* refers to using the Internet and computer skills to disrupt or shut down the critical infrastructure and government services of a country. Although no such large-scale attacks have thus far been implemented at this writing, security experts warn that such attacks are or will be within the capabilities of some terrorist organizations and could pose a huge threat to government and business operations.

The politically motivated cybercriminal usually devotes a good deal of time to his or her cause and often (though by no means always) has a prior criminal record for offenses such as criminal trespass, rioting, and similar activities. True terrorists are especially dangerous because they are willing to die for their cause. They also often have large networks of like-minded people they can call on to help them carry out their missions and to hide them from law enforcement.

Sexual Impulses

Sex is one of the strongest instincts in any animal, including humans. Psychologists and psychiatrists argue over what causes normal sexual feelings to become perverted, but there is no question that sexual deviance (defined as sexual behavior that is out of the norm or breaks societal rules) is common among certain types of criminals.

Not all sexually deviant behavior is illegal or considered harmful. However, when sexual arousal becomes associated with violence or with inappropriate objects of desire, such as children, serious harm and criminal activity can result.

Sexually motivated cybercriminals include these types:

- *Passive pedophiles*, who use the Internet to access and download kiddie porn and use photos and stories of children engaging in sex (usually with adults) to feed their own fantasies. Even if they never act out those fantasies in real life, in the United States and many other countries, it is illegal to even possess child pornography in photographic form. This law is based on the assumption that children were harmed in the making of the pictures. The pornography laws generally apply to visual depictions only; the written word (stories about child sex) is protected by the First Amendment. The issue of "virtual child pornography" that uses high-quality, computer-generated images instead of real photographs is a matter of intense debate. In April 2002, the Supreme Court struck down the federal laws making this form of kiddie porn illegal. At the time of this writing, the Justice Department and members of Congress were intent on rewriting those laws more narrowly, in a way that would outlaw virtual child pornography that is indistinguishable from the real thing while still allowing the law to pass Constitutional muster.

- *Active pedophiles*, who use the Internet to find their victims. These criminals usually also collect child pornography, but they don't stop at fantasies. They often hang out in chat rooms that are frequented by children and engage them in virtual conversations, attempting to gain their trust and lure them into an in-person meeting. They might then rape the children, or they could simply "court" them, preferring to gradually seduce them into sexual relationships. Because children under a certain age (which varies from one state to another) are not considered capable of consenting to sex, sexual conduct with a minor is still a crime, even if the child agrees to it. Usually the offense is defined as *statutory rape* or some category of *sexual assault*.

- *Fans of S&M*, or sadomasochistic sex, who are aroused either by inflicting pain on others (sadists) or by having pain inflicted on them (masochists). Although S&M behavior between consenting adults is generally not considered a crime, some sadistic individuals hunt for partners on the Internet and then take the activities beyond the level that the partner bargained for or consented to, seriously injuring or sometimes even killing their victims.

- *Serial rapists*, who develop relationships (hetero- or homosexual) online and then invite their victims to meet in real life, only to rape them. Serial rapists often have problems performing sexually in a normal, loving situation. They are able to become aroused only when the sex is violent and forced. Psychologists call rape an anger-motivated or power-motivated crime rather than a sexually motivated one, but sex is certainly an important element, if only as the "tool of the crime."

- *Sexual serial killers*, who—like serial rapists—cruise Internet chat rooms and forums looking for victims. Psychiatric literature recognizes two types of serial killers: organized and disorganized. The *organized killer* is often of above-average intelligence, socially gregarious and charming, and is usually married or living with a partner. *Disorganized killers* are almost exactly the opposite; their IQ is usually below average, and they are socially inadequate loners and are anxious during the commission of the crime. Organized killers tend to be very controlled and unemotional and are often diagnosed (as was Ted Bundy, one of the country's most famous sexual serial killers) as sociopathic. In fact, sexual serial killers, despite the sexual motivation for their crimes, belong in the next category of motivation: serious psychiatric illness.

Serious Psychiatric Illness

Criminal behavior is not, itself, indicative of mental illness. If it were, perhaps it could be treated medically. However, some criminals are motivated to engage in illegal and antisocial behavior by underlying psychiatric conditions, especially those conditions that manifest themselves in symptoms such as lack of impulse control and lack of inhibition, hallucinations and delusions, paranoia, hyperactivity, and inability to concentrate or possession of impaired communications skills.

Persons suffering from personality disorders, schizophrenia, bipolar affective disorder, aggression, depression, adjustment disorders, and sexual disorders such as paraphilias are prone to criminal behavior, according to *Psychiatric Illness Associated with Criminality*, by William H. Wilson, MD, and Kathleen A. Trott, MD (www.emedicine.com/med/topic3485.htm). Illegal conduct can also stem from drug- or alcohol-induced psychosis or conditions caused by traumatic brain injury.

It might be easier for such persons to hide their mental illness in the online community, where they don't have to come into physical contact with others, than in the offline world. Cybercrime that is motivated by psychiatric illness can be difficult to investigate and solve, precisely because the criminal's motivations don't seem logical or rational. We can understand why a money-motivated offender commits crimes, even though we don't approve of the behavior. However, we might not be able to easily understand the actions of a mentally ill person.

Recognizing the Limitations of Statistical Analysis

According to author Samuel Clemens, writing under the famous pseudonym Mark Twain, "There are three kinds of lies: lies, damn lies, and statistics." Many members of the public are suspicious of statistical analysis and statistics-based arguments, and rightly so. Everyone who has worked with statistical data or has followed both sides in a political campaign knows that the same set of facts can be manipulated during presentation to support divergent conclusions.

Criminal profiles are based on probabilities. The probabilities are based on statistical patterns that have been discerned by studying similar past cases. As we've seen, profiling can be a useful tool, and cybercrime investigators—who face special challenges due to the complexity and global nature of the Internet—need all the tools they can get. However, it is important to remember that a carefully constructed profile can be completely wrong. The investigation should shape the profile; the profile should never shape the investigation.

Categorizing Cybercriminals

In Chapter 1, we discussed the importance of categorizing cybercrimes. In the previous section, we touched on one way that cybercriminals could be categorized, based on their motivations for committing crimes. There is another way to categorize Internet-using offenders: by the role that the Internet plays in their criminal activity. This role generally breaks down into two broad categories:

- Criminals who use the Net as a tool of the crime
- Criminals who use the Net incidentally to the crime

In the following sections, we examine the differences between these two categories. We also take a look at a special category of cybercriminal: the one who would never engage in illegal activity in "real life" but who becomes a criminal via an online persona.

Criminals Who Use the Net as a Tool of the Crime

Many types of cybercrime depend on the use of a computer network to accomplish the criminal act. This doesn't mean that the same offense couldn't be committed without computers and networks; it means that in this instance, the network was directly used to commit the crime.

Here's an analogy to make it easier to understand this concept: A murder can be committed using any of a number of methods—a gun, a knife, poison, even a motor vehicle. Although the end result (death of the victim) is the same in all cases, the killing cannot be done in the same way if the tool is different. Likewise, an embezzler could steal company money without using a network, but it would be done in a different way. If the embezzler does use a network to divert funds, the network is a tool of that crime.

A network can be used as a crime tool by different types of cybercriminals. Most frequently, a network is used as a tool by:

- White-collar criminals
- Computer con artists
- Hackers, crackers, and network attackers

White-Collar Criminals

The term *white-collar criminal* is derived, of course, from the image of the office worker or professional who traditionally wears business attire (white shirt and tie) to work. White-collar cybercrimes can include many different offenses, such as:

- Changing company computer records to provide the criminal with an unauthorized pay raise or to eliminate or change bad employee evaluations or pad expense accounts

- Accessing and using insider information for purchasing stocks or securities, which are U.S. Securities and Exchange Commission (SEC) violations

- Selling company information to outsiders; using insider information to obtain kickbacks from clients, business partners, or competitors; or using confidential information for blackmail purposes

- Manipulating electronic accounts to appropriate the company's or clients' money or property for oneself

- "Cooking" the company books or financial statements to provide false information to creditors, investors, the Internal Revenue Service, internal auditors, and so on—often to cover other crimes

Studies of white-collar crime have shown that these offenders can fall into several subcategories, based on their underlying motivations:

- The *resentful* white-collar criminal cheats the company because he or she feels cheated *by* the company. This is often a long-time employee who has been passed over several times for a raise or promotion or has received a negative employee evaluation that, in the employee's eyes, is undeserved. These cybercriminals adopt something of a Robin Hood mentality, convinced that they are merely taking from the rich company—which can afford the loss and even deserves it—and giving to the poor (usually themselves).

- The *deliberate* white-collar criminal has no personal ethics that would prohibit stealing. Unlike the previously described offender, there is no period of building anger or resentment; this type begins criminal activity as soon as the opportunity arises. These cybercriminals can be quite bright and plan their crimes meticulously. They often have a timeline or monetary goal in mind; the master plan is to put the stolen money away in a safe place (such as an offshore bank account). After a certain number of years or after a specific amount of cash is built up, they plan to retire and live in luxury someplace beyond the jurisdiction of the law. They are often very disciplined and careful, taking only small amounts of money at a time so as not to be noticed.

- The *desperate* white-collar criminal steals in response to serious personal financial problems. These problems can be unpredictable, such as a medical or legal crisis in the family. More often, though, they are the result of bad judgment: gambling, alcohol, or drug problems, losing money in bad business investments, or living beyond their means to impress others. These cybercriminals are often careless, becoming more blatant as their situations worsen. Thus they are the most likely type of white-collar cybercriminal to be caught.

White-collar criminals often give themselves away by leaving clues that arouse investigators' suspicions, such as:

- Unexplained income, property, or lifestyle that is far greater than the person's job makes feasible

- Many large cash transactions

- Multiple bank accounts in different banks, especially banks in different cities or countries

www.syngress.com

- Multiple businesses listed at the same address
- "Paper" corporations that have no physical assets and seem to make no product and provide no services

A detailed list of types of white-collar crimes and scams is available at the National Check Fraud Center Web site at www.ckfraud.org/whitecollar.html. Some of the crimes described on this list more appropriately belong in our next section, about computer con artists.

Crimestoppers...

The White-Collar Crime Fighter

White-Collar Crime Fighter magazine is a good source of information about white-collar crime, with tips and tricks on how to avoid being victimized and information for law enforcement officers and prosecutors who deal with white-collar offenses. A sample copy and subscription information are available on the magazine's Web site at www.wccfighter.com.

Computer Con Artists

Con artists use the Internet as a tool, to reach "marks" (their terminology for victims) that they could never reach otherwise. E-mail, Web sites and chat rooms can all become tools for scammers to propagate their fraudulent schemes.

According to the Online Buyer's Guide (at www.netaction.org/shoppers/fraud.html), the FTC lists the most frequently reported "dot-cons" as:

- **Internet auctions** Bidders send their money but do not receive the promised product, or they receive property that is not what it was represented to be.

- **Internet service scams** Customers prepay for access services and then companies fold and disappear, or customers are enticed into paying for services they don't want (for example, by official-looking notices that imply that you will lose your domain name registration if you don't send money to the scam artist). In another variation, an ISP mailed checks for $3.50 to people on a mailing list; unless the recipients read the fine print, they didn't realize that by cashing the check, they were agreeing to purchase Internet services that would be billed through their phone companies.

- **Credit card fraud** This type of fraud involves individuals and shady companies that pretend to (or actually do) sell a service or product via credit card, for the purpose of collecting the victim's credit card information and using it to make fraudulent purchases. Transferring the information from a card to another counterfeit card is a practice called *skimming*.

- **International modem dialing** Internet users are persuaded to download a free dialer or viewer program (often for the purpose of downloading "free" pornography) that disconnects their modems and redials an international long distance number or pay-per-minute 900 number that results in huge, unexpected charges on the user's phone bill.

- **Web "cramming"** This crime involves offers for free services such as Web hosting for a trial period with no obligation, after which users are charged on their phone bills or credit cards, even though they never agreed to continue the service after the trial period. (See www.ftc.gov/bcp/conline/pubs/alerts/webalrt.htm for more information.)

- **Multilevel marketing (MLM) and pyramid schemes** Con artists play on users' greed and desire to get rich quick by signing recruits—for a hefty fee—and promising them huge profits if they recruit others. The *chain letter* is a variation on the pyramid scheme, as is the *Ponzi scheme* (named after Charles Ponzi, who successfully defrauded hundreds of people using this method in the 1920s). All these con games were around long before the Internet, but today's ability to communicate quickly and easily with a huge number of people all over the world has given them new life. (See http://skepdic.com/pyramid.html for detailed explanations of how the pyramid, chain letter, Ponzi, and other MLM schemes work—and why they *don't* work for the naïve recruits who are their victims.)

- **Travel and vacation scams** These are the Internet-age variant on a time-honored telemarketing con. Travel "bargains" and "free" vacation scams (that include all manner of hidden costs) abound. These include selling frequent-flyer miles that are on the verge of expiration, selling travel vouchers in conjunction with pyramid schemes, bait-and-switch offers, and other too-good-to-be-true travel deals.

- **Business and investment "opportunities"** These range from work-at-home scams that require you to purchase an expensive starter kit and don't provide actual jobs to day-trading programs and solicitations for investment in worthless real estate. According to the Better Business Bureau (www.bbb.org/library/faithscams.asp), the number of investment con artists who attempt to take advantage of their victims' religious beliefs has been rising dramatically. The SEC maintains a Web site on how to prevent Internet investment scams at www.sec.gov/investor/pubs/cyberfraud.htm.

- **Scams involving health-care products and services** These include weight loss, antiaging, and alternative health products that are marketed under false or unproven claims; online prescription drug sales that don't require the patient to be seen by a physician; multilevel marketing of health products; and other con games that seek to take advantage of people who are ill or frightened about their health. A number of organizations and agencies exist to combat health-care fraud, such as the National Council Against Health Fraud (www.ncahf.org).

Crimestoppers...

The FTC Scam Line

The Federal Trade Commission provides consumer information, takes complaints, and maintains a database of companies reported to engage in online fraud. Consumers who have been victims of fraud or deceptive or unfair business practices (online or off) can contact the agency via their toll-free telephone help line at 1-877-FTC-HELP, or they can fill out the online complaint form at https://rn.ftc.gov/dod/wsolcq$.startup?Z_ORG_CODE=PU01. Internet fraud cases, telemarketing frauds, and identity theft cases are entered into a secure database called the Consumer Sentinel (www.consumer.gov/sentinel). The database is made available to law enforcement agencies all over the world. The state attorney general's office in most states also handles these types of fraud cases.

A good source of news, information, and links pertaining to all types of con games and fraud cases (including a Scam Alerts section) is the Scams & Swindles site at www.swindles.com. This site is updated daily. Scamwatch, part of InterGOV International (www.scamwatch.com), is another good resource for reporting scams and other crimes. A huge number of scams are listed in the InterGOV database; as well as the FTC's most frequently reported types, these include gambling scams, credit-repair scams, college degree scams, prize offer scams, and many more.

Hackers, Crackers, and Network Attackers

The network is an important tool that makes white-collar criminals' and scam artists' "jobs" easier, but it is an absolutely essential tool for hackers. It would be impossible for hackers to commit their crimes without the Net.

In Chapter 1 we discussed the types of crimes hackers commit: unauthorized access, theft of data or services, and destructive cybercrimes such as Web site defacement, release of viruses, DoS and other attacks that bring down the server or network. In Chapter 6, you will learn the technical details of how most of these attacks work.

Hackers learn their "craft" in a number of ways: by trial and error, by studying network operating systems and protocols with an eye to learning their vulnerabilities, and perhaps most significantly, from other hackers. There is an enormous underground network (in the traditional, rather than technical, sense of the word) where those new to hacking can get information and learn from more experienced hackers.

Web sites such as www.2600.com (originally a phone phreakers' magazine), www.hackers.com (which advertises itself as "for hacker to housewife, student to scientist"), and www.atomicvoid.net (a source of hack/attack tools) provide opportunities to meet other hackers online. So do newsgroups such as alt.hackers and alt.2600.hackerz and mailing lists such as the FreeBSD Hackers Digest at FreeBSD.org. Online papers such as *How to Become a Hacker* (www.tuxedo.org/~esr/faqs/hacker-howto.html) provide guidance to people who are attracted to the hacker lifestyle. Hacker conferences such as DEF CON and the Black Hat Briefings provide real-world opportunities for hackers to meet. Interestingly, the organizations that sponsor these meetings have become more and more mainstream over the past few years, now attracting security professionals and government officials as well as hackers.

There is a definite hierarchy in the hacker community. "Real" hackers— expert programmers and networking wizards who write the code and discover the exploits—have disdain for the script kiddies who merely use software written by others to break into systems or launch attacks, without really understanding how it works. The hacker culture also divides itself into two groups:

- **Black hats** break into systems illegally, for personal gain, notoriety, or other less-than-legitimate purposes.

- **White hats** write and test open-source software, work for corporations to help them beef up their security, work for the government to help catch and prosecute black-hat hackers, and otherwise use their hacking skills for noble and legal purposes.

There are also hackers who refer to themselves as *gray hats*, operating somewhere between the two primary groups. Gray-hat hackers might break the law, but they consider themselves to have a noble purpose in doing so. For example, they might crack systems without authorization and then notify the system owners of the systems' fallibility as a "public service," or find security holes in software and then publish them in order to force the software vendors to create patches or fixes for the problem.

NOTE

The white-hat/black-hat distinction has become more muddled as former criminal hackers have gone on the lecture circuit or gotten corporate jobs as security experts and as organizations like Black Hat, Inc., have added a "white-hat track" to their conference training programs. Only in old Western movies can you rely on a person's hat color as a dependable indication of his character. In today's cyberworld, most people— including hackers—are neither all good nor all bad. A hacker who identifies him- or herself as a white-hat hacker might succumb to the temptation to engage in an illegal act, and a self-professed black hat can reform and become one of the "good guys."

So-called "ethical hacking" can be a lucrative business, if a hacker has the requisite skills, including the social skills necessary to function in the corporate world. Consultants charge companies $10,000 or more to test their security by attempting to hack into their systems and providing reports and recommendations on plugging the security holes that they find. (See www.research.ibm.com/journal/sj/403/palmer.html for more information about ethical hacking.)

Criminals Who Use the Net Incidentially to the Crime

Some criminals use the network in relation to their crimes, but the Net is not an actual tool of the crimes. That is, the network is not used to commit the *criminal* activity, although it can be used to prepare for or keep records of that criminal activity. Examples of this type of criminality include:

- Criminals who use the Net to find victims
- Criminals who use computers or networks for record keeping
- Criminals who use e-mail or chat services to correspond with accomplices

Even in cases in which the network is not a tool of the crime, it can still provide evidence of criminal intent and clues that help investigators track down the criminals. We discuss each of these situations in the following sections.

Criminals Who Use the Net to Find Victims

It might seem that using the Net to find victims would make it a tool of the crime. In some cases, the criminal goes on to use the Internet to actually commit the crime—for example, sending electronic chain letters, e-mailing fictitious notices purporting to be from the victims' ISPs that request their credit card information, or directing victims to a Web site that tries to sell them products under false pretenses). In those cases, the Internet *is* a tool of the crime, but the initial act of searching out potential victims is not, by itself, criminal. Thus a pedophile or rapist or other criminal who uses the Net to find victims but then commits the criminal activity in the real world is using the Internet incidentally to the crime. However, the Internet can be used to set up a sting operation that will turn the tables and lure the criminal into revealing his identity to law enforcement.

Criminals Who Use Computers or Networks for Record Keeping

People who engage in noncomputer-related criminal activity such as drug dealing, illegal gambling, or other illicit "businesses" can use computers to keep financial records, customer lists, and other information related to the criminal activity and use the Internet to transfer these files to an offsite location where they will be safer from law enforcement.

Transferring business records to a friend's computer or an Internet data storage service is not against the law, so Net use is incidental to this criminal activity, even though those files might be important evidence of the actual crime.

Criminals Who Use E-mail or Chat Services to Correspond with Accomplices

Criminals who work in groups—terrorist groups, theft rings, black-hat hackers—often use e-mail and chat in the same way that legitimate users do: to correspond with people they work with. The correspondence itself is not a crime; it is the illegal activity being planned or discussed that is criminal. However, the correspondence can be used not only to show the criminal's intent and help track him down but also, in some cases, to prove the existence of a criminal conspiracy. This is important because if the elements of conspiracy exist, charges can be brought against all members of the conspiracy, not just the person(s) who physically committed the crime.

CyberLaw Review...

Criminal Conspiracy

The wording of conspiracy statutes varies in different jurisdictions, but most states address conspiracy as an inchoate or preparatory offense. The conspiracy charge is a separate offense, but it must be charged in conjunction with another criminal offense. Generally, a criminal conspiracy exists when two or more persons agree that one or more of them will commit a felony offense *and* one or more of the conspirators performs some overt act in furtherance of the agreement. In other words, if in court the prosecution can show (for example, via e-mail collected pursuant to a search warrant or intercepted legally under court order) that such agreement was made and can further prove that at least one of the parties took some step toward committing the crime, *all* parties can be charged with criminal conspiracy, whether or not the crime was completed successfully.

Real-Life Noncriminals Who Commit Crimes Online

In some situations, people who are not criminals in real life engage in criminal conduct online. These include accidental cybercriminals and situational cybercriminals. *Accidental cybercriminals* have no criminal intent. They commit illegal acts online because of ignorance of the law or lack of familiarity with the technology.

An example is someone who has a cable modem connection or is using the broadband Internet access available in some hotels and opens up the Network Neighborhood folder on his computer (the network browse list) and sees other computers listed there. Curious, he might click one of the icons just to see what happens. If he has stumbled upon a computer on the network that is running a low-security operating system or doesn't require a username and password to log on, and it has network file sharing enabled, he might be able to access the shared files on that computer.

If our hypothetical user is not very technically or legally savvy, he might not even realize that those files are on someone else's private (or so the owner thought!) computer. Or he might think that because they're accessible, it is legal to look at them. However, depending on how the state's unauthorized access statutes are written, it might be a crime to access any other computer across a network without permission, even if that computer's users have, perhaps unwittingly, made it technologically easy to do so.

The behavior of *situational cybercriminals* reflects an interesting phenomenon that we discussed earlier—the psychological dissociation experienced by some people when they go online. This dissociation can cause some people who, in real life, consider themselves upstanding, law-abiding citizens and would never deliberately commit a crime to engage in illegal activity when they don their "alternate persona" while online.

These people might have repressed desires to indulge in illicit conduct that they control through self-discipline but which they feel free to unleash when they log onto the Internet because there they can be (in their own minds) "someone else." They literally lead double lives, like a modern-day drjekyllandmrhyde@aol.com.

Understanding Cybervictims

The term *victim* is derived from the Latin word *victima,* which means "an animal offered as a sacrifice." Today the word is used to refer to someone or something that is harmed by some act or circumstance. The crime victim is the person *to whom* the crime happens, the one who is harmed by a criminal's illegal act.

The field of *victimology* involves collecting data about, and in effect profiling, the victims of crime. This information is useful for several reasons:

- It allows law enforcement officers to predict what people or personality types are likely to become victims of certain crimes and warn them. This in turn gives the potential victims the opportunity to take steps to protect themselves.

- It allows law enforcement officers to better profile the criminal, because patterns in victim choice are an important part of the criminal profile.

- It allows law enforcement officers to use the victim profile to bait criminals, to draw them out into the open.

The victim of a crime is often the key witness against the offender. Using victimology techniques, even a deceased victim can provide important clues for investigators. According to Amy Goldman, author of *The Importance of Victimology in Criminal Profiling,* "Each question answered regarding the victim is actually a window to the offender's psyche and, in turn, answers questions about the offender."

On the Scene...

Using Victimology to Develop a Sting

Officers had been investigating an online pedophile who was suspected of luring children into in-person meetings and raping them. An undercover office created an online persona—that of a 12-year-old girl—based on the characteristics of a pedophile's past victims. The officer then frequented the chat rooms where the offender was known to hang out, in hopes that the pedophile would try to set up a real-life meeting with the officer in her guise as a child. In this way, police could monitor the meeting place and positively identify the criminal.

It is very important, in any sting operation, to avoid committing entrapment, which will cause evidence against the offender to be thrown out of court. Generally, courts have held that officers can "provide a mere opportunity" for someone to commit a crime—as the officer in our example did by pretending to be a child who fit the profile of the pedophile's victims and waiting for the pedophile to initiate contact and pursue her. Entrapment occurs when officers go beyond providing the opportunity, overtly attempting to induce, entice, or persuade the suspect to commit the criminal act. For example, if our officer (playing the role of the child) had contacted the pedophile, had "come on" to him and asked him to meet her for sex, that could be held to constitute entrapment.

Categorizing Victims of Cybercrime

We can create categories of cybercrime victims, just as we were able to do with cybercriminals. Again, it is important to note that not all victims fit neatly into these categories, and some of the categories overlap at times. Some common victim characteristics include:

- People who are new to the Net
- People who are naturally naïve
- People who are disabled or disadvantaged
- "Desperados" who are greedy, lonely, or have other emotional needs
- Pseudo-victims who report having been victimized but actually were not
- People who are simply unlucky enough to be in the wrong (virtual) place at the wrong time

Let's take a moment to review each of these characteristics and understand why people in these groups are especially vulnerable to cybercrime.

New to the Net

Internet "newbies" might not yet be familiar with the common scams that would cause a Net veteran to sigh and say "Ho, hum, not *that* sob story again." In addition, newbies are often unaware of common security practices and known software security holes. Newcomers might not realize that their systems can be infected with viruses simply by opening an e-mail attachment or visiting the wrong Web site, nor might they be aware that viruses can be sent from their own machines without their knowledge.

Computer users who have not had a lot of experience interacting online could be more trusting of those they "meet" via chat. They could believe that because *they* are honest in their online communications, everyone else is, too.

With huge numbers of people connecting to the Internet for the first time every year, cybercriminals always have a fresh crop of Net newbies on which to prey. In their efforts to educate the public about cybercrime, law enforcement and IT professionals should pay special attention to new Internet users, let them know that they can be the targets of scam artists and other offenders, and provide them with information on how to recognize and avoid questionable schemes.

Naturally Naïve

Some groups are naturally more naïve, as a whole, than others—although individual members of those groups might not be naïve at all. The very young and the elderly have long been the favorite marks of con artists, and that preference carries over to the online world.

Youngsters often have distorted world views, especially if they've led sheltered lives. They might not yet have internalized the idea—even if they've been told—that there are bad people who want to hurt others. They might think that if they are nice to others, everyone will be nice to them. Furthermore, kids are naturally curious and eager to please, which can be a dangerous combination of qualities when they come into contact with a cybercriminal. Children are, of course, the targets of some of the Internet's worst of the worst: pedophiles.

Many elderly people feel uncomfortable with new technology because they didn't grow up with it. They might enjoy helping people, a trait that scam artists can exploit. When elderly people do fall victim to criminal behavior, they might be hesitant to report it—even when they've been cheated out of thousands of dollars—because they feel that they were themselves somehow to blame for being "dumb." Traditional mail-fraud schemes that targeted the elderly are being reborn in a new incarnation: e-mail fraud.

Enforcement agencies are recognizing the growing problem faced by young and old victims and are developing programs designed to help these "student drivers" and folks who have slowed down a little ease onto the information superhighway without getting run down. Law enforcement and IT professionals can join together with schools and senior citizens' centers to increase awareness and educate these vulnerable groups.

Disabled and Disadvantaged

The mentally and physically disabled and the disadvantaged can also be targeted by particularly reprehensible cybercriminals who—with the goal of identifying potential victims—search online databases and join mailing lists that are intended as support groups for people with disabilities.

Online forums can be especially important as a means of social interaction and a source of friendship for people with certain disabilities that limit their mobility, such as paraplegia, or that make it inadvisable for them to be around groups of people, such as immune system disorders, or that have altered their appearance, such as traumatic injuries. Law enforcement agencies can partner with IT firms to provide a valuable service by helping these people develop a greater awareness of cybercrime while assisting them in learning to take full advantage of computer technology's ability to enhance their lives.

Desperados

Desperate people make excellent targets for cybercriminals. They could be looking for love in all the wrong online places, desperately seeking salvation through Internet religious groups, direly in need of money, or have some other immediate emotional or physical need. In any event, their desperation makes them vulnerable—to Lothario-style scam artists who enter romantic relationships with the intent to defraud the partner, or unethical online evangelists who are out to make money off others' spiritual longings, to get-rich-quick schemers, Internet loan sharks, or fraudulent job brokers.

Because desperation is usually a temporary or intermittent condition, and because, to paraphrase Henry David Thoreau, those suffering from it usually lead lives of *quiet* desperation, it might be more difficult to identify and warn these potential victims of their vulnerability. Investigators who detect this victimization pattern for a particular cybercriminal can, however, use the information in constructing stings, by posing as "marks" who fit the victim profile.

Pseudo-Victims

Sigmund Freud might have been right when he said that sometimes a cigar is just a cigar, but sometimes a victim is *not* just a victim. There are people who, for various reasons, report crimes that never occurred or represent themselves as victims when they are not (and could, in fact, actually be the perpetrator).

The motivations of these *pseudo-victims* run the gamut:

- People who take revenge or express their anger at another person by falsely accusing that person of a crime

- People who want attention; pretending to be a crime victim makes them feel "special"

- People who claim to be crime victims to cover up the fact that they themselves committed the crime

- People who pretend to be victims in order to claim money from victim relief funds, charitable organizations, or insurance companies

- People who honestly believe that a crime has been committed against them when they have been the victims of unethical or immoral—but not illegal—behavior

Although the vast majority of victim reports are genuine, when investigators interview crime victims they should always be cognizant of the possibility of pseudo-victimhood. In most states, statutes make it a criminal offense to file a false crime report; such charges might be appropriate in all except the last example.

In the Wrong (Virtual) Place at the Wrong Time

It is true that human predators, like their animal counterparts, often seek as prey the weakest members of the herd, or those they perceive to be weakest. However, not all crime victims are selected because they exhibit some vulnerability. Some criminals are indiscriminate and choose their victims at random—first come, first served. Sometimes ending up a cybercrime victim is just a matter of being in the wrong (virtual) place at the wrong time.

In building profiles, whether of criminals or of victims, just as profilers must be on the lookout for patterns, they must also take care not to imagine patterns where none exist. The fact that a criminal's victims *don't* fit a profile can also be valuable information for the investigator.

Making the Victim Part of the Crime-Fighting Team

When the field of victimology first emerged in the 1940s, those who studied victimization tended to see victims as objects of pity, weak people who were often viewed as contributing to their own bad fortune. This later became known as the "blame the victim" mentality and gave way to the more prevalent attitude today—that victims should be "empowered" through education and access to resources. In large part, the shift was in response to feminists who protested the denigrating and humiliating treatment that female crime victims—especially the victims of rape or sexual assault—sometimes suffered at the hands of law enforcement and the courts.

Many victims today prefer not to define themselves as victims because of the image of weakness and helplessness that implies. According to *Victimology Theory,* by T.O. Connor (http://faculty.ncwc.edu/toconnor/300/300lect01.htm), the preferred term now is *survivor,* a word that implies strength.

Many states have enacted a Crime Victims' Bill of Rights and other legislation that imposes requirements on law enforcement agencies to follow certain guidelines in dealing with crime victims. Many agencies now appoint crime victims' liaisons, professionals who are trained to offer counseling and guidance to victims and in some cases to "protect" the victims from hostile or overeager law enforcement personnel.

Victims' rights granted by these laws often include:

- The right to be notified when the offender will come to trial
- The right to be present at the trial, either personally or through representation of an attorney
- The right to be informed of the disposition of the case

- If the suspect is convicted, the right to be informed and to give input when the suspect comes up for parole

- The right to be informed if and when the suspect is released from prison

- The right to be treated with dignity by the criminal justice system

- The right to be informed of victim social services and financial assistance that are available

- The right to be compensated for their loss, when possible

Victim compensation programs are usually state-funded programs designed to help pay medical and other expenses associated with being the victim of crime. In some cases, the courts require offenders to pay restitution directly to victims or to pay restitution into a compensation fund. These programs are usually administered by the state attorney general's office.

CyberLaw Review…

Victim Services Programs

The U.S. Department of Justice operates the Office for Victims of Crime (OVC), which organizes events for National Crime Victims' Rights Week in April and provides news, research, and statistics and other resources at www.ojp.usdoj.gov/ovc. You can find examples of state victim services programs at these sites:

www.oag.state.tx.us/victims/victims.htm (Texas)

http://legal.firn.edu/victims (Florida)

www.scattorneygeneral.org/public/victimassist.html (South Carolina)

www.ago.state.nm.us/Advocate/victim_services_advocate.html (New Mexico)

www.ag.state.il.us/crimevictims/crime.htm (Illinois)

www.ago.state.ma.us/videfault.asp (Massachusetts)

www.doj.state.wi.us/cvs (Wisconsin)

www.caag.state.ca.us/cvpc/fa_victims_services.html (California)

www.oag.state.ny.us/crime/crime.html (New York)

Other states run similar programs.

Understanding Cyberinvestigators

Are cybercrime investigations just the "same old stuff" for police detectives? Are the same personality characteristics, skills, and knowledge required for cyberinvestigations as for general criminal investigations? Do investigators who deal with cybercrime need special training? In the following sections, we address these questions and build a profile of an effective cyberinvestigator.

> ## NOTE
>
> There is generally no official job title or position called *cyberinvestigator*, although local agencies are usually free to create their own titles, so we can't say with certainty that such a title doesn't exist. We use the term here to refer to people whose investigative duties include cybercrimes. In most agencies, not enough computer-related offenses are reported and investigated to justify dedicating personnel to investigating only those types of crimes. Even in large agencies such as the Los Angeles Police Department (LAPD), only a few of the 9000 employees are part of the department's computer crimes unit.

Recognizing the Characteristics of a Good Cyberinvestigator

A good cyberinvestigator must possess the qualities that are necessary for any good criminal investigator, including:

- **Excellent observation skills** An investigator must notice things, including the "little things."

- **Good memory** In order to put together the many clues that pop up over the course of an investigation, a detective must be able to remember facts, names, places, and dates, or the investigator could miss a vital connection.

- **Organization skills** A good investigator not only remembers information but is able to organize it in a logical way so that patterns and correlations become apparent.

- **Documentation skills** A good investigator doesn't keep all this information in his head; instead, he is able and willing to meticulously put it into writing so that it can be shared with others and used as a foundation for building the case.

- **Objectivity** The investigator must not allow personal prejudices, relationships, or feelings to affect his or her ability to evaluate the evidence objectively.

- **Knowledge** An effective investigator knows the criminal laws, the rules of evidence, victimology theory, criminal psychology, and investigative concepts and procedures and knows about scientific aids, lab services, and resources inside and outside the agency.

- **Ability to think like a criminal** The best investigators have a "native" awareness of criminal mental processes and can put themselves in the place of an offender and predict the offender's actions.

- **Intellectually controlled constructive imagination** The investigator must be creative enough to consider all possibilities, to examine facts and then extrapolate conclusions.

- **Curiosity** The best investigators are innately curious. They aren't satisfied with simply clearing the case. It's not enough for them to determine that the suspect committed the crime; they want to know why and exactly how the crime was committed.

- **Stamina** Investigation is hard work, often involving long hours. A good investigator must be physically up to the challenge.

- **Patience** Investigation is often a drawn-out process. Progress is frequently made one tiny step at a time. Leads often lead to nowhere, prime suspects turn out to have airtight alibis, and the investigator must back up and start over from scratch.

- **Love of learning** Learning is really what investigation is all about— learning the facts of a case, learning about the people involved, sometimes even becoming an "instant expert" in another field, such as computer networking, in order to understand the technical aspects of the crime.

In addition to these generic qualities, an investigator who specializes in cybercrime needs a few additional characteristics:

- **A basic understanding of computer science** The more the investigator knows about how computers work (including both hardware and software), the better.

- **An understanding of computer networking protocols** Cybercrime, by definition, involves a network. Even if the investigator has a good grasp of computer technology in a standalone context, it doesn't mean he or she will understand how network intrusions and attacks work, what happens to e-mail when it leaves the sender's system, or how a Web browser requests and downloads pages, graphics, or scripts.

- **Knowledge of computer jargon** All vocations and most avocations have a unique *jargon,* terminology that has little meaning outside the field that members use as "shorthand" to communicate with one another. A good investigator must be able to "speak the language."

- **An understanding of hacker culture** It's been said that it takes a hacker to catch a hacker (usually by reformed hackers selling their services as security experts). There is a grain of truth in this axiom; it's much easier to track down hackers if you understand their mentality and the protocols (in the nontechnical sense this time) of interacting in the hacker community. Just as narcotics officers need to be intimately familiar with how drug dealers interact with each other, cybercrime investigators likewise should be experts in hacker culture.

- **Knowledge of computer and networking security issues** In order to investigate hacking or intrusion and network-attack crimes, the investigator should be familiar with common security "holes," security products (such as firewalls), and security policies and practices.

It should be apparent from the preceding list that cybercrime investigators usually need extensive training in order to operate effectively in this specialty area. This need is usually recognized in large law enforcement agencies, where IT professionals and computer science graduates might be recruited to handle cybercrime investigations or outside consultants might be called in to assist detectives with those investigations. In small agencies, however, too often the detective on duty is assigned to the cybercrime case, whether or not he or she knows anything about computers. Almost as bad is the common situation in which the officer in the department who is considered the computer whiz (which can mean anything from "expert programmer" to "the only one in the department who knows how to format a diskette") is assigned to all cybercrime cases. Because this officer is perceived as a computer expert by the agency administrators—even though he or she might be far from that—the newly anointed cybercrime investigator is expected to handle matters that are far beyond his or her capabilities.

Categorizing Cyberinvestigators by Skill Set

While the skill *level* of those doing cybercrimes investigations varies tremendously, we can categorize most cyberinvestigators according to skill set:

- **Investigators who specialize in computer/network crime** They are investigators first, with a secondary interest in technology. They are usually law enforcement officers or corporate security personnel.

- **Computer specialists who conduct investigations** They are IT professionals first, with a secondary interest in law enforcement/investigation. They often work as consultants to law enforcement agencies.

- **Those who are equally skilled, trained, or interested in investigation and IT** They are involved in computer/cybercrime from the beginnings of their careers; they may have parallel training in both fields, such as a double major in criminal justice and network engineering or programming. They may work for law enforcement agencies or as independent consultants and are generally in great demand and command high salaries.

- **Those who have no real skills or interest in either investigation or IT** These could be police officers who were "kicked upstairs" to the detective division and drew a cybercrime case randomly. They aren't really interested in investigative work and would prefer to be working patrol, and they have no training in or love of computers and networking. Fortunately, there aren't many cyberinvestigators who fit in this category.

Recruiting and Training Cyberinvestigators

The question has been asked before: Is investigation a skill or a talent? You might wonder what the difference is, and what difference the answer to that question makes.

A *skill* can be learned; a *talent* is inborn. Most creative activities involve both. Almost anyone can take piano lessons, learn to read music, and be able to play simple songs. That's a skill that can be developed through practice. Some people, however, are born with the ability to "play by ear," to sit down at a piano and perform any song they've ever heard, without sheet music, or to compose original pieces of their own. That's talent, and the best teacher can't teach you to do it if you don't have it.

Investigation is, as we've mentioned, a creative process. It requires certain skills that can be learned and developed, but the best investigators are also talented; they can be said to have "a nose for it" or thought to possess some quasi-magical sense of intuition. There are also people who seem to have a natural way with computers. The rare individual who is talented in both of these areas should be recruited vigorously by law enforcement agencies.

But raw talent is not enough to become a master cyberinvestigator, any more than it's enough to make you a concert pianist. Training is required to develop and perfect the skills to go along with the talent.

State police training oversight commissions (often called POST, for *Peace Officers Standards and Training,* although in Texas it's the Texas Commission on Law Enforcement Officer Standards and Education, or TCLEOSE) should incorporate basic cybercrime training into their academy programs. Almost all officers working in today's world eventually encounter cybercrimes. As first responders, patrol officers need to know how to handle computer evidence, even if they won't be conducting the investigation.

Advanced training in cybercrimes should be available—and mandatory—for those who actually handle the investigation. New technologies (and new ways to use them to commit crimes) are emerging constantly, so cybercrime investigators must stay up to date on the latest information.

Organizations such as the International Association of Chiefs of Police (www.theiacp.org), the High Technology Crime Investigators Association (www.htcia.org), and the International Association of Computer Investigative Specialists (www.iacis.com) can provide training guidelines and resources.

Facilitating Cooperation: CEOs on the Scene

There is one more important person involved in cybercrimes that victimize businesses and large organizations: the corporate chief executive officer (CEO) or manager. Corporate executives are finding their organizations increasingly exposed to the threat of criminal activity—and in some cases, criminal liability—from people both inside and within the organization who use computers and networks to commit illegal acts.

The first step company executives must take on discovering criminal activity is to report it to law enforcement. The choice to report the crime is not always as simple as it sounds. If every violation of the law were reported, investigated, and prosecuted, our criminal justice system would soon break down from the overload. For example, in many states it's a criminal offense to call someone a profane name in a public place. However, if this happens to you, unless the situation escalates, you probably won't call in the police. Why? Because consciously or subconsciously, you do a cost/benefits analysis and determine that the time and effort you would have to spend to give an official sworn statement and perhaps return to testify in court, along with the risk of making the offender *really* mad at you, isn't worth the benefits of pressing charges.

Similarly, if company officials discover that a hacker has broken into their network, but there has been little or no loss or damage, they might decide that the downtime of key personnel, the risk of bad publicity to the company if others find out they were hacked, and other factors make the cost of reporting outweigh the benefits.

Another reason victimized companies hesitate to report cybercrime is the issue of their own liability. Even though the crime was committed against them, it is conceivable that their customers might sue them for negligence for allowing the crime to happen (as some of the victims of the terrorist attacks on New York City's World Trade Center sued the airlines that were also victimized). The perception today is that a company is legally responsible for preparing for every possible contingency to protect itself and its clients; this view has been upheld by juries, which have awarded big bucks to plaintiffs in many negligence cases. Even if clients don't sue, shareholders could be upset and investors might withhold funding if the company's network is seen as less than secure.

Managers could also be reluctant to open up the information stored on their network to government investigators. This is especially true if any less-than-legal activities are going on—"creative" tax strategies, for example. It's easier simply to absorb the costs accrued by the crime, if there are any, and spend the time and money to secure the network rather than pursue justice against those who breached it. In fact, in some cases, the discovery of unauthorized access might never make it up the management ladder at all; the network administrator or security specialist whose job it is to prevent such incidents will not be eager to tell the bosses that hackers found their way around his or her security measures.

It is important for managers to realize that they have a vested interest in working with law enforcement to track down and bring charges against the cybercriminals who cost the company time and money and, in some cases, do irreparable damage to the business's reputation. Managers are more likely to cooperate with law enforcement if the investigative process isn't shrouded in mystery. Education, as always, is the key.

It is essential that managers, as well as their IT teams, understand how a criminal investigation works, their own roles in the investigation, and special issues that pertain to the collection, preservation, and presentation of digital evidence. We mentioned before that IT professionals and law enforcement officers often find themselves at odds in their efforts to reach a common goal: bringing the cybercriminal to justice. Managers, who see cybercrime hurting their bottom lines, can be in a unique position to facilitate cooperation between the two if they are made a part of the cybercrime-fighting team from the beginning.

Summary

Cybercrime is not just about computers. It is also about people. Understanding cybercrime is the first step in combating it. Understanding the people on the scene of the cybercrime—those who commit it, those who are injured by it, and those who work to stop it—is the first step toward understanding cybercrime.

Cybercriminals cannot be easily understood as a group because they engage in a wide range of very different criminal activities for very different reasons. However, we can gain more understanding if we categorize them and analyze each group separately. Understanding the motives, characteristics, and typical behaviors of criminals in each group, along with analyzing the evidence in each particular case, can help us develop a criminal profile that will assist in identifying and capturing offenders.

Part of the criminal profile involves studying the type of people that criminals choose as victims. Victimology also serves other purposes; it allows us to predict where the cybercriminal might strike next and warn potential future victims. Victim profiles can also be used in concocting sting operations that lure the cybercriminal out of the virtual world and into the real one.

Investigators of cybercrime need all the characteristics that are required of any criminal investigator, plus a few extra ones to boot. Not only must cyberspace detectives be smart, logical, objective, patient, curious, and physically fit, but they must also have some knowledge and understanding of computers, networking, technical jargon, the hacker underground, and IT security issues. That's a tall order, and talented, skilled, well-trained cybercrime investigators are highly in demand. Law enforcement agencies might have to pay premium salaries to get them—especially considering the discrepancy between compensation in the public sector and the corporate world for IT professionals. However, a professional cyberinvestigator can be invaluable to law enforcement agencies, which can expect to see the incidence of cybercrime continue to rise at an exponential rate for the foreseeable future.

Understanding the technology of cybercrime is easy compared with understanding the people who carry out the crimes. The human factor is often the most inexplicable component in an investigation.

Frequently Asked Questions

The following Frequently Asked Questions, answered by the authors of this book, are designed to both measure your understanding of the concepts presented in this chapter and to assist you with real-life implementation of these concepts. To have your questions about this chapter answered by the author, browse to **www.syngress.com/solutions** and click on the **"Ask the Author"** form.

Q: Internet auctions are mentioned as one of the most frequently reported online crimes. Does this mean that all online auctions are con games?

A: No. Most online auctions are legitimate. Recognized auction sites such as eBay attempt to provide protections by publishing ratings of their sellers that are provided by people who have done business with them. The auction sites usually post security recommendations and guidelines that will help users protect themselves against fraud. However, the auctions do provide an opportunity for unscrupulous dealers to cheat their customers. It is important to be very careful when buying merchandise through an auction site.

Q: Why do con artists continue to engage in scams, even when they can make more money doing legitimate work, or even when the scam doesn't benefit them financially—or benefits them only minimally?

A: According to the study *Deceivers and Deceived: Observations on Confidence Men and Their Victims, Informants and Their Quarry, Political and Industrial Spies and Ordinary Citizens,* by Richard Blum (see www.fraudaid.com/ Why-Con-artists-Scam.htm), the typical con artist is both impulsive and compulsive and is addicted to the con games he plays because they give him the "high" of having put something over on someone. Blum concludes that most con artists exhibit the symptoms of antisocial personality disorder. According to the *Diagnostic and Statistical Manual of Mental Disorders,* fourth edition (DSM-IV), which is the primary diagnostic reference used by U.S. mental health professionals, characteristics of people with antisocial personality disorder include:

1. Failure to conform to social norms with respect to lawful behaviors, as indicated by repeatedly performing acts that are grounds for arrest

2. Deceitfulness, as indicated by repeated lying, use of aliases, or conning others for personal profit or pleasure

3. Impulsivity or failure to plan ahead

4. Irritability and aggressiveness, as indicated by repeated physical fights or assaults

5. Reckless disregard for safety of self or others

6. Consistent irresponsibility, as indicated by repeated failure to sustain consistent work behavior or honor financial obligations

7. Lack of remorse, as indicated by being indifferent to or rationalizing having hurt, mistreated, or stolen from another

Q: What factors should a company consider before recruiting hackers to work as corporate security specialists or computer crimes specialists for law enforcement agencies?

A: This is a trend based on the notion that "it takes a hacker to catch a hacker" (or to protect a network from another hacker). It is certainly true that those who have committed the crimes are intimately familiar with how they are committed and with how they might be thwarted. Police have traditionally utilized the expertise of criminals, using studies made of people convicted of crimes. However, police agencies would not consider hiring former burglars as property-crime detectives or convicted murderers as homicide investigators. Hiring hackers who have broken the law in the past presents a number of problems that both private and public sector employers should keep in mind.

For one, many hacker types are philosophically opposed to big business. Although they could be persuaded to work for a corporation if tempted by enormous salaries to do what they do anyway—play with computers—they might not fit in well in the structured corporate environment. Hackers are often loners who do not conform to the corporate model, which stresses teamwork. Perhaps more important, a hacker who has been guilty of criminal activity in the past can expose your company to substantial risks if he or she hasn't truly reformed. Your organization's network could be used to launch hack attacks when your "professional hacker" gets bored with assigned duties. This can leave the company open to serious liability issues. Your hacker could also build "back doors" into your system so that if you fire him or if he gets tired of playing the corporate game and leaves, he can get back in and have full access to your network.

There are computer security specialists who are as skilled as the hackers but have never chosen to use their skills to go outside the law. Company officials should think long and hard and consider all the advantages and disadvantages before hiring a hacker just because it's currently the "thing to do." Law enforcement agencies, in most cases, are constrained by their own policies and their state commission rules from hiring people who have been convicted of serious criminal offenses. Many criminal hackers, however, have never been arrested or convicted. Agencies are finally realizing that it's in their interest to recruit people with computer skills. Most of them conduct thorough background investigations that reveal how those people acquired their skills and how they've used them in the past.

References

- *Forensic Psychology and Forensic Psychiatry: An Overview*
  http://flash.lakeheadu.ca/~pals/forensics/forensic.htm

- *Criminal Profiling: How It Got Started and How It Is Used*
  www.crimelibrary.com/criminology/criminalprofiling2

- Cornell University Research Methods Knowledge Base:
  Deductive and Inductive Thinking
  http://trochim.human.cornell.edu/kb/dedind.htm

- Public Service Commission of Canada monograph: *Stereotyping*
  www.psc-cfp.gc.ca/publications/monogra/mono3_e.htm

- About.com: *Don't Fear the Reaper, Fear the Script Kiddie*
  http://netsecurity.about.com/library/weekly/aa111600a.htm

- U.S. Department of Justice's Bureau of Justice Statistics: *Women Offenders*
  www.ojp.usdoj.gov/bjs/crimoff.htm#women

- *Integrity in the Corporate Suite: Predictors of Female Frauds*
  www.cj.msu.edu/~faculty/collinsintegrity.html

- *The Irish Times: WAP Challenges Security Experts*
  www.ireland.com/newspaper/finance/2000/0121/fin41.htm

- Netaction Online Buyers Guide
  www.netaction.org/shoppers/fraud.html

- Federal Trade Commission
  www.ftc.gov

- National Check Fraud Center: *Types of White-Collar Crime*
  www.ckfraud.org/whitecollar.html

- *Psychiatric Illness Associated with Criminality*
  www.emedicine.com/med/topic3485.htm

- *IBM Systems Journal: Ethical Hacking*, by C.C. Palmer
  www.research.ibm.com/journal/sj/403/palmer.html

- *The Importance of Victimology in Criminal Profiling*, by Amy Goldman
  http://isuisse.ifrance.com/emmaf/base/impvic.html

- *Victimology Theory*, by T.O. Connor
  http://faculty.ncwc.edu/toconnor/300/300lect01.htm

Chapter 4

Understanding Computer Basics

Topics we'll investigate in this chapter:

- **Understanding Computer Hardware**

- **Understanding the Language of the Machine**

- **Understanding Computer Operating Systems**

☑ **Summary**

☑ **Frequently Asked Questions**

☑ **Resources**

Introduction

In Chapter 3, we mentioned that, in addition to traditional investigative skills, a good cybercrimes investigator needs a thorough understanding of the technology that is used to commit these crimes. Just as a homicide investigator must know something about basic human pathology to understand the significance of evidence provided by dead bodies—rigor mortis, lividity, blood-spatter patterns, and so forth—a cybercrimes investigator needs to know how computers operate so as to recognize and preserve the evidence they offer.

A basic tenet of criminal investigation is that there is no "perfect crime." No matter how careful, a criminal always leaves something of him- or herself at the crime scene and/or takes something away from the scene. These clues can be obvious, or they can be well hidden or very subtle. Even though a cybercriminal usually never physically visits the location where the crime occurs (the destination computer or network), the same rule of thumb as for traditional crimes applies: Everyone who accesses a network, a system, or a file leaves a track behind. Technically sophisticated criminals might be able to cover those tracks, just as sophisticated and careful criminals are able to do in the physical world— but in many cases, they don't completely destroy the evidence; they only make the evidence more difficult to find.

For example, a burglar might take care to wipe all fingerprints off everything he's touched while inside a residence, removing the most obvious and often the most helpful evidence that proves he was there. But if as he does so, tiny bits of fabric from the rag that he uses adhere to some of the surfaces, and if he takes that rag with him and it is later found in his possession, police could still have a way to link him to the crime scene. Likewise, the cybercriminal may take care to delete incriminating files from his hard disk, even going so far as to reformat the disk. It will appear to those who aren't technically savvy that the data is gone, but an investigator who understands how information is stored on disk will realize that evidence could still be on the disk, even though it's not immediately visible (much like latent fingerprints), and will take the proper steps to recover and preserve that evidence.

IT professionals who are reading this book and who already have a good understanding of technology might wonder if they can skip this chapter. We recommend they read the chapter. It might be useful for those who anticipate working with law enforcement officers and crime scene technicians to see computer technology from a new perspective: how it can serve as evidence and which technological details are most important to understand from the *investigative* point of view. Most IT professionals are used to looking at computer and networking hardware, software, and protocols in terms of *making things work.* Investigators see these items in terms of what they can reveal that is competent, relevant, and material to the case. A network administrator familiar with the Windows operating system, for example, knows that it can be made to display file modification dates, but he or she might not have considered how crucial this information could be in an investigation. Similarly, a police investigator who is not trained in the technology might realize the importance of the information but not realize that such information is available, because it isn't obvious when the operating system is using default settings. Once again, each side has only half the pieces to the puzzle. If the two sides work together, the puzzle falls into place that much more quickly.

In this chapter, we provide an overview of how computers process and store information. First we look at the hardware, then we discuss the software (particularly the operating system) on which personal computers run. At the end of each section, we summarize how the information in that section can be useful to cybercrimes investigators.

Understanding Computer Hardware

Today, most people who operate in the business world or in any administrative or clerical capacity in the public sector gain some exposure to computers. The fact that they use computers every day doesn't mean that they understand them, however. This makes sense. Most of us drive cars every day without necessarily knowing anything about mechanics. Even people with enough mechanical aptitude to change their own car's oil and spark plugs might not really understand how an internal combustion engine works. Similarly, we can turn on our televisions and change the channels (some of us can even set the clocks on our VCRs!) without really knowing how programs are broadcast over the airwaves or via cable.

Most casual users take it for granted that if they put gas in a car, it takes them where they want to go, and if they pay the cable bill, the show goes on. Even though we don't understand these technologies, they've been around long enough that we're comfortable with them. To "first-generation" users, though, the old Model T Ford must have seemed like quite a mysterious and scary machine, and pictures that somehow invisibly flew through the air and landed inside a little box in people's living rooms seemed nothing short of magic to early TV owners.

We must remember that many of the people using computers today are members of the "first generation" of computer users—people who didn't grow up with computers in every office, much less in almost every home. To them, computers still retain the flavor of something magical, something unexplainable.

Some skilled criminal investigators fit into this category. Just as effective cyber-crime fighting requires that we acquaint IT professionals with the legal process, it also requires that we acquaint law enforcement personnel with computer processing—how the machines work "under the hood."

The first step is to open up the case and look inside at all the computer's parts and pieces and what they do so that we can understand the role that each plays in creating and retaining electronic evidence.

Looking Inside the Machine

Machines have been making our lives easier for many centuries. Scientists agree that one of the features distinguishing man from most other species is the ability to make and use tools. In many ways, historical eras are defined by their tools. The agrarian age, when most humans were farmers, gave way to the industrial age of the nineteenth century, when the manufacturing companies reigned and the steam engine and railroad provided a way to get manufactured products to market. By the early twentieth century, commercial electrical-generating stations were becoming widespread, which led us into the electronic age, giving our machines the "power of lightning." As we venture into the twenty-first century, we find ourselves smack in the middle of the digital age, a.k.a. the information age, in which we have become (frighteningly so, many feel) dependent on computers to run our national infrastructures.

Regardless of how you feel about these machines, they seem to be here to stay—at least, unless and until some global catastrophe such as a solar-generated worldwide electromagnetic pulse of huge proportions renders them all useless and plunges us all back into chaos. As they become more powerful, computers are capable of performing more complex tasks, and performing these tasks with increasing speed.

Nonetheless, at its most basic level, all a computer really does is crunch numbers. As explained later in this chapter, all data—text, pictures, sounds, programs—must be reduced to numbers for the computer to "understand" it. According to Microsoft's *Encarta World English Dictionary 2001,* the definition of a computer is an electronic device that accepts, processes, stores, and outputs data at high speeds according to preprogrammed instructions.

Components of a Digital Computer

Regardless of whether it is a tiny handheld model or a big mainframe system, a digital computer consists of the same basic components:

On the Scene...

Analog vs Digital Computers

The machines we usually think of today when we hear the word *computer* are *digital computers.* There is another type of computer, the *analog computer.* Both types of machines perform mathematical calculations, but analog computers represent numbers using voltages. The most important difference between analog and digital computers is that analog systems operate on continuous variables rather than adding and subtracting digits. Analog computers are considered obsolete by many today, but in fact there are still analog computers in use. Some computer theorists believe that analog computers are actually more powerful than digital computers. For a description of analog computers, visit www.science.uva.nl/faculteit/museum/AnalogComputers.html. (Additional resources on this topic appear in the "References" section at the end of the chapter.)

- A control unit
- A processing unit
- A memory unit
- Input/output units

Of course, there must be a way for all these components to communicate with one another. PC architecture is fairly standardized, which makes it easy to interchange parts between different computers. The foundation of the system is a main circuit board, fondly referred to as the *motherboard.*

The Role of the Motherboard

Most other components plug into the main board, and they all communicate via the electronic paths (circuits) that are imprinted into the board. Additional circuit boards can be added via *expansion slots.* The electronic interface between the motherboard and these additional boards, cards, and connectors is called the *bus.* The bus is the pathway on the motherboard that connects the components and allows them to interact with the processor.

The motherboard is the PC's control unit. The motherboard is actually made up of many subcomponents:

- The printed circuit board (PCB) itself, which may be made of several thin layers or a single planar surface onto which the circuitry is affixed

- Voltage regulators, which reduce the 5V signal from the power supply to the voltage needed by the processor (typically 3.3V or less)

- Capacitors that filter the signals

- The integrated chipset that controls the interface between the processor and all the other components

- Controllers for the keyboard and I/O devices (integrated SCSI, onboard sound and video, etc.)

- An erasable programmable read–only memory (EPROM) chip that contains the core software that directly drives the system hardware

- A battery-operated CMOS chip that contains the BIOS settings and the real-time clock that maintains the time and date

- Sockets and slots for attaching other components (processor, main memory, cache memory, expansion cards, power supply)

- Ports and/or pins (headers) for connecting cables and devices (serial, parallel, USB, IDE, SCSI, IR, IEEE 1394/FireWire) and pin connectors for the case power switch, LED indicators, case speaker, and processor fan

The layout and organization of the components on the motherboard is called its *form factor.* The form factor determines the size and shape of the board and where its integrated ports are located, as well as the type of power supply it is designed to use. The computer case type must match the motherboard form factor or the openings in the back of the case won't line up correctly with the slots and ports on the motherboard. Typical motherboard form factors include:

- ***ATX/mini ATX***, currently the most popular form factor; all current Intel motherboards are ATX. Port connectors and PS/2 mouse connectors are built in; access to components is generally more convenient, and the ATX power supply provides better air flow to reduce overheating problems.

- ***AT/Baby AT***, the most common PC motherboard form factor prior to 1997, still in wide use. The power supply connects to the board with two connectors labeled P8 and P9; reversing them can destroy the motherboard.

- **LPX/Mini LPX**, generally used by big brand-name computer manufacturers to save space in small cases. Uses a "daughterboard" or riser card that plugs into the main board. Expansion cards then plug into the riser card.

- **NLX**, a modernized and improved version of LPX. This form factor is also used by name-brand vendors.

NOTE

For a more detailed discussion of motherboard components and form factors, see www.pcguide.com/ref/mbsys/index.htm.

The Roles of the Processor and Memory

Two of the most important components in a computer are the processor and memory. Let's take a brief look at what these components do.

The Processor

The *processor* (short for *microprocessor)* is an integrated circuit on a single chip that performs the basic computations in a computer. The processor is sometimes called the *CPU* (for *central processing unit*), although many computer users use that term to refer to the PC "box"—the case and its contents—without monitor, keyboard, and other external peripherals.

The processor is the part of the computer that does all the work of processing data. Processors receive input in the form of strings of ones and zeros (called *binary communication*, which we discuss later in this chapter) and uses logic circuits, or formulas, to create output (also in the form of ones and zeros). This system is implemented via digital switches. In early computers, vacuum tubes were used as switches; they were later replaced by *transistors,* which were much smaller and faster and had no moving parts (making them *solid-state* switches). Transistors were then grouped together to form *integrated circuit* chips, made of materials (particularly silicon) that conduct electricity only under specific conditions (in other words, a *semiconductor)*. As more and more transistors were included on a single chip, the chips became smaller and smaller and less expensive to make. In 1971, Intel was the first to use this technology to incorporate several separate logic components into one chip and call it a *microprocessor.*

Processors are able to perform different tasks using programmed instructions. Modern operating systems allow multiple applications to share the processor using a method known as *time slicing,* in which the processor works on data from one application, then switches to the next (and the next and the next) so quickly that it appears to the user as if all the applications are being processed simultaneously. This method is called *multitasking,* and there are a couple of different ways it can be accomplished. Some computers have more than one processor. In order to take advantage of multiple processors, the computer must run an operating system that supports multiprocessing. We discuss multitasking and multiprocessing in more depth in the section "Understanding Computer Operating Systems" later in this chapter.

The processor chip itself is an ultra-thin piece of silicon crystal, less than a single millimeter in thickness, that has millions of tiny electronic switches (transistors) embedded in it. This embedding is done via *photolithography,* which involves photographing the circuit pattern and chemically etching away the background. The chip is part of a *wafer,* which is a round piece of silicon substrate, on which 16 to 256 individual chips are etched (depending on wafer size). The chips are then *packaged,* which is the process of matching up the tiny connection points on the chip with the pins that will connect the processor to the motherboard socket and encasing the fragile chip in an outer cover.

NOTE

The processor package determines the type of slot or socket it will fit into. Package styles include Dual Inline Package (DIP), Pin Grid Array (PGA) and its variations (a square flat package that connects to a socket on the motherboard with rows of pins, as in the Intel 80286 through 80486 and early Pentiums), and Single Edge Contact (SEC) that mounts the chip on a small circuit board (sometimes called a *daughtercard*), the edge of which plugs into a slot on the motherboard. Notebook PCs sometimes have the processor chip soldered directly onto the motherboard to save space, or they use a special mobile module that includes processor, secondary cache, and chipset.

Before they're packaged, the chips are tested to ensure that they perform their tasks properly and to determine their rated speed. Processor speed is dependent on the production quality, processor design, process technology, and the size of the circuit and die. Smaller chips generally can run faster because they generate less heat and use less power. As processor chips have shrunk in size, they've gotten faster. The circuit size of the original 8088 processor chip was 3 microns; modern Pentium chips are 0.25 microns or less. Overheating decreases performance, and the more power is used, the hotter the chip gets. For this reason, new processors run at lower voltages than older ones. They also are designed as dual voltage chips, in which the *core voltage* (the internal voltage) is lower than the *I/O voltage* (the external voltage). The same motherboard can support processors that use different voltages, because they have voltage regulators that convert the power supply voltage to the voltage needed by the processor that is installed.

Even running at lower voltages, modern high-speed processors get very hot. Heat sinks and processor fans help keep the temperature down. A practice popular with hackers and hardware aficionados, called *overclocking* (setting the processor to run faster than its rating), causes processors to overheat easily. Elaborate—and expensive—water-cooling systems and Peltier coolers that work like tiny solid-state air conditioners are available to address this problem.

Note

For more information about how overclocking of processors works, see www.hiphardware.com/editorials/overclocking/index.shtml. Numerous Web sites, such as www.overclockers.com and www.overclockershideout.com, provide advice on overclocking and sell cooling products and other related accessories.

System Memory

The term *memory* refers to a chip on which data is stored. Some novice computer users might confuse the terms *disk space* and *memory;* thus you hear the question, "How much memory do I have left on my hard drive?" In one sense, the disk does indeed "remember" data. However, the term *memory* is more accurately used to describe a chip that stores data temporarily and is most commonly used to refer to the *system memory* or *random access memory (RAM)* that stores the instructions with which the processor is currently working and the data currently being processed. Memory chips of various types are used in other parts of the computer; there's cache memory, video memory, and so on. RAM is called *random access* memory because data can be read from any location in memory, in any order.

The amount of RAM installed in your computer affects how many programs can run simultaneously and the speed of the computer's performance. Memory is a common system *bottleneck* (that is, the slowest component in the system that causes other components to work at less than their potential performance speed). The data that is stored in RAM, unlike data stored on disks or in some other types of memory, is *volatile.* That means the data is lost when the system is shut down or the power is lost.

Each RAM chip has a large number of memory *addresses* or *cells,* organized in rows and columns. A single chip can have millions of cells. Each address holds a specified number of bits of data. Multiple chips are combined on a *memory module,* which is a small circuit board that you insert in a memory slot on the computer's motherboard. These modules are called *single inline memory modules (SIMMs)* or *dual inline memory modules (DIMMs).* The memory controller, which is part of the motherboard chipset, is the "traffic cop" that controls which memory chip is written to or read at a given time. How does the data get from the memory to the processor? It takes the bus—the memory bus (or data bus), that is. As mentioned earlier, a *bus* is a channel that carries the electronic signals representing the data within the PC from one component to another.

RAM can be both read and written. Computers use another type of memory, *read-only memory (ROM),* for storing important programs that need to be permanently available. A special type of ROM mentioned earlier, erasable programmable ROM (EPROM), is used in situations in which you might need to occasionally, but not often, change the data. A common function of EPROM (or EEPROM, which is *electrically erasable PROM)* is to store "flashable" BIOS programs, which generally stay the same but might need to be updated occasionally. Technically, EPROM is not "read only" 100 percent of the time, since it can be erased and rewritten, but most of the time it is only read, not written. The data stored in ROM (including EPROM) is *not* lost when the system is shut down.

Yet another type of memory used in PCs is *cache memory.* Cache memory is much faster than RAM but also much more expensive, so there is less of it. Cache memory holds recently accessed data. The cache is arranged in layers between the RAM and the processor. Primary, or Level 1 (L1), cache is fastest; when the processor needs a particular piece of data, the cache controller looks for it first in L1 cache. If it's not there, the controller moves on to the secondary, or L2, cache. If the controller still doesn't find the data, the controller looks to RAM for it. At this writing, L1 cache memory costs approximately 100 times as much as normal RAM or SDRAM, whereas L2 cache memory costs 4 to 8 times the price of the most expensive available RAM. Cache speeds processing considerably because statistically, the data that is most recently used is likely to be needed again. Getting it from the faster cache memory instead of the slower RAM increases overall performance.

NOTE

> **NOTE**
>
> There are other types of cache in addition to the processor's cache memory. For example, Web browsers create a cache on the hard disk where they store recently accessed Web pages, so if those same pages are requested again, the browser can access them from the local hard disk. This system is faster than going out over the Internet to download the same pages again. The word *cache* (pronounced "cash") originally meant "a secret place where things are stored," and appropriately, the Web cache can provide a treasure trove of information that might be useful to investigators, as we discuss in Chapter 10, "Collecting and Preserving Digital Evidence."

Cache memory uses static RAM (SRAM) instead of the dynamic RAM (DRAM) that is used for system memory. The difference is that SRAM doesn't require a periodic refresh to hold the data that is stored there, as DRAM does. This makes SRAM faster. Like DRAM, though, SRAM loses its data when the computer's power is turned off.

The Role of Storage Media

The term *storage media* is usually used to refer to means of storing data permanently (that is, nonvolatile storage that retains the data without electrical power). Data can be stored more or less permanently on several different media types, including:

- Hard disks
- Floppy disks
- Compact discs (CDs) and digital versatile/video discs (DVDs)
- Tape
- Flash memory (CompactFlash, SmartMedia, Memory Stick)
- Other removable media (Zip and Jaz disks, microdrives, magnet-optical)

Let's look briefly at how each of these media works.

Hard Disks

Today, the hard disk is usually the primary permanent storage media in a PC. However, the earliest PCs didn't have hard disks. In fact, early computers (prior to the PC) didn't have any sort of data storage medium. You had to type in every program that you wanted to run, each time you ran it. Later, punched cards or tape were used to store programs and data. The next advancement in technology brought us magnetic tape storage; large mainframes used big reels of tape, whereas early microcomputers used audiocassette tapes to store programs and data. By the time the IBM PC and its clones appeared, computers were using floppy disks (the 5.25-inch type that really *was* floppy). More expensive models had two floppy drives, one for loading programs and a second for saving data—but still no hard disk.

CyberStats...

Hard Disk Sizes

IBM introduced its first hard disk in 1956, but the real "grandfather" of today's hard disks was the Winchester drive, which wasn't introduced until the 1970s. The standard physical size of disks at that time was 14 inches (the size of the platters that are stacked to make up the disk). In 1979, IBM made an 8-inch disk, and Seagate followed that in 1980 with the first 5.25-inch hard disk, which was used in early PCs. Three years later, disks got even smaller; the 3.5-inch disk was introduced. This became a standard for PCs. Much smaller disks (less than 2 inches) were later developed for use in laptop and notebook computers. The IBM "microdrive" shrunk the diameter of the platter to 1 inch.

The platter size of a hard disk is called its *form factor.* Smaller platter sizes do more than save space inside the computer; they also improve disk performance (seek time) because the heads don't have to move as far.

The first hard disks that came with PCs provided 5MB of storage space—a huge amount, compared to floppies. The IBM PC XT came with a gigantic 10MB hard disk. Today's hard disks are approaching 200GB capacities at prices far lower than those first comparatively tiny disks. Despite the fact that they're much bigger, much faster, less fragile, and more reliable, the hard disks of today are designed basically the same way as those of years ago.

Hard disks comprise from one to several *platters* (flat, round disks). The platters are stacked one on top of another on a spindle that runs through a hole in the middle of each platter, like LPs on an old-time record player. There is a motor attached to the spindle that rotates the platters, which are made of some rigid material (often aluminum alloy, glass, or a glass composite) and are coated with a magnetic substance. Electromagnetic *heads* write information onto the disks in the form of magnetic impulses and read the recorded information from them.

Data can be written to both sides of each platter. The information is recorded in *tracks,* which are concentric circles in which the data is written. The tracks are divided into *sectors* (smaller units). Thus a particular bit of data resides in a specific sector of a specific track on a specific platter. Later in this chapter, when we discuss computer operating systems and file systems, you will see how the data is organized so that users can locate it on the disk.

Hard disks generally connect to the computer's motherboard via one of the following interfaces:

- Integrated Drive Electronics/Enhanced IDE (IDE/EIDE), so named because the disk controller is built into, or integrated with, the disk drive's logic board. It is also referred to as Advanced Technology Attachment (ATA), a standard of the American National Standards Institute (ANSI). Almost all modern PC motherboards include two EIDE connectors. Up to two ATA devices (hard disks or CD-ROM drives) can be connected to each connector, in a *master/slave configuration.* One drive functions as the "master," which responds first to probes or signals on the *interrupt* (a signal from a device or program to the operating system that causes the OS to stop briefly to determine what task to do next) that is shared with the other, "slave" drive that shares the same cable. User-configurable settings on the drives determine which will act as master and which as slave. Most drives have three settings: master, slave, or cable-controlled. If the latter is selected for both drives, the first drive in the chain will be the master drive.

- Small Computer System Interface (SCSI, pronounced "scuzzy"), another ANSI standard that provides faster data transfer than IDE/EIDE. Some motherboards have SCSI connectors and controllers built in; for those that don't, you can add SCSI disks by installing a SCSI controller card in one of the expansion slots. There are a number of different versions of SCSI; later forms provide faster transfer rates and other improvements. Devices can be "chained" on a SCSI bus, each with a different SCSI ID number. Depending on the SCSI version, either 8 or 16 SCSI IDs can be attached to one controller (with the controller using one ID, thus allowing 7 or 15 SCSI peripherals).

NOTE

For more information about SCSI, including comparisons between SCSI and other disk interfaces, see the articles at www.scsi-planet.com/vs.

Although most hard disks use the IDE/EIDE or SCSI interface, there are other ways to connect disks to your computer. The microdrive, mentioned earlier, connects via a PC Card (also called *PCMCIA,* for the Personal Computer Memory Card International Association that created the standard). FireWire (IEEE 1394) and USB hard drives are also available.

Data written on a hard disk generally stays there unless or until it is either overwritten by more data or physically erased by a magnet. Simply deleting the data using operating system file management utilities does *not* get rid of the data. It only removes the pointer used by the file system to locate that data physically on the disk. The data itself (in the form of the physical changes to the disk's magnetic surface) is still there and can be recovered using special recovery software.

Many users think that formatting a hard disk erases all its data, but this isn't necessarily so. Formatting defines the structure of the disk. *Low-level formatting (LLF),* which physically defines where the tracks and sectors are on the disk, does erase data. However, modern disks are formatted at the low level at the factory; users do not perform LLF on today's IDE and SCSI disks. So, when we discuss formatting, we are generally talking about *high-level formatting (HLF).* This term refers to the process of defining the file system structure. Thus, we say a disk is formatted in FAT or formatted in NTFS (file systems that we discuss later in this chapter).

Before we can format a hard disk, we must *partition* it. This involves dividing the disk into *volumes,* which generally appear to the operating system as *logical drives,* identified by different drive letters. The disk is divided into logical drives for the purposes of performance and organization of the data. Each logical drive can be formatted separately. Of course, you can partition the disk as a single partition. Partitioning schemes and tools differ depending on the operating system and file system. Contrary to popular belief, FDISK and other partitioning utilities do not erase the data on a disk; they only delete and manipulate the partition tables. Even though tools such as Partition Magic warn that their use will erase the data on a disk, this is not true; the warning is intended for the average user who will not be able to recover the data after using the utility. However, professional data recovery techniques *can* still recover the data (although the data might be *fragmented*—that is, the contents of a file could be spread out in different areas of the disk and recoverable in bits and pieces).

On the Scene...

Wiping a Hard Disk Clean

There *are* ways to completely erase the data on a disk, but the average user (and the average cybercriminal) will not usually take these measures. Software programs that "zero out" the disk do so by overwriting all the ones and zeros that make up the data on the disk, replacing them with zeros. These programs are often called "wiping" programs. Some of these programs make several passes, overwriting what was already overwritten in the previous pass, for added security. However, in some cases, the data tracks on the disk are wider than the data stream that is written on them. This means that some of the original data might still be visible and recoverable with sophisticated techniques.

A strong magnet can also erase or scramble the data on magnetic media. This process is called *degaussing*. It generally makes the disk unusable without restoring the factory-installed timing tracks. The platters might have to be disassembled to completely erase all the data on all of them, but there is equipment available that will degauss all the platters while they remain intact.

In very high-security environments such as sensitive government operations, disks that have contained classified information are usually physically destroyed (pulverized, incinerated, or exposed to an abrasive or acid) to prevent recovery of the data.

Removable Storage

There are several popular types of *removable media,* so called because the disk itself is separate from the *drive,* the device that reads and writes to it. Of course, some hard disks can be removed from the computer. Removable disk racks and bays allow you to easily slide an IDE or SCSI hard disk drive (mounted in a carrier rack) in and out of a docking bay that remains attached to the computer's ATA or SCSI interface. Hard disk drives can also be inserted into external bays that are easily plugged into and removed from the computer's USB port. The distinction is that in these cases you are removing the *entire drive,* not just the disk itself, whereas with true removable storage media, the drive stays attached to the computer and only the media—disk, tape or card—is removed. Removable media includes the following:

- **Floppy disks or diskettes** In the early days of personal computing, floppy disks were large (first 8 inches, then later 5.25 inches in diameter), thin, and flexible. Today's "floppies," often and more accurately called *diskettes*, are smaller (3.5 inches), rigid, and less fragile. The disk inside the diskette housing is plastic, coated with magnetic material. The drive into which you insert the diskette contains a motor to rotate the diskette so that the drive *heads,* made of tiny electromagnets, can read and write to different locations on the diskette. Standard diskettes today hold 1.44MB of data; SuperDisk technology (developed by Imation Corporation) provides for storing either 120MB or 240MB on diskettes of the same size.

- **CDs and DVDs** CDs and DVDs are rigid disks a little less than 5 inches in diameter, made of hard plastic with a thin layer of coating. CDs and DVDs are called *optical media* because CD and DVD drives use a laser beam, along with an optoelectronic sensor, to write to and read the data that is "burned" into the coating material (a compound that changes from reflective to nonreflective when heated by the laser). The data is encoded in the form of incredibly tiny pits or bumps on the surface of the disk. CDs and DVDs work similarly, but the latter can store more data because the pits and tracks are smaller, because DVDs use a more efficient error correction method (that uses less space), and because DVDs can have two layers of storage on each side instead of just one.

- **Tape** Magnetic tape is a relatively inexpensive form of removable storage, especially for backing up data. It is less useful for data that needs to be accessed frequently because it is a *sequential access* media. You have to move back and forth through the tape to locate the particular data you want. In other words, to get from file 1 to file 20, you have to go through files 2 through 19. This is in contrast to *direct access* media like disks, in which the heads can be moved directly to the location of the data you want to access without progressing in sequence through all the other files.

- **Flash memory** Flash memory cards and sticks are popular for storing and transferring small amounts of data (typically from 8MB to 512MB). For example, they are commonly used for storing photos in digital cameras (and transferring them to PCs) and for storing and transferring programs and data between handheld computers (pocket PCs and Palm OS devices). Although called "memory," unlike RAM, flash media is nonvolatile storage; that means that the data is retained until it is deliberately erased or overwritten. Flash cards and sticks include Compact Flash and SmartMedia cards and Sony's Memory stick. PCMCIA flash memory cards are also available. Flash memory reader/writers come in many handheld and some laptop/notebook computers, and external readers can be attached to PCs via USB or serial port.

- **Other removable media** There are a number of other types of removable media, such as the venerable Zip and Jaz disks made by Iomega that contain one or more hard disk platters in a removable cartridge that is inserted into a drive (which contains the motor and heads). Iomega recently introduced high-capacity Peerless cartridges and drives for backing up large hard disks (up to 20GB). Magneto-optical (MO) technology uses a combination of magnetic and laser (optical) technology.

New removable storage options are appearing all the time. Removable storage provides convenience in an increasingly mobile computing world. Technologies such as holographic storage are in development and expected to greatly increase data storage capacities in the future.

NOTE

For more information about the theoretical possibilities of holographic storage techniques, see the *Scientific American* article "On the Horizon: Holographic Storage" on the magazine's Web site at www.sciam.com/ 2000/0500issue/0500toigbox5.html.

Why This Matters to the Investigator

Why does the cybercrime investigator need to know the difference between RAM and disk space, what a microprocessor does, or the function of cache memory? Understanding what each part of a computer does will ensure that you also understand where in the machine the evidence (data) you need might be— and where *not* to waste your time looking for it.

For example, if you know that information in RAM is lost when the machine is shut down, you'll be more careful about immediately turning off a computer being seized pursuant to warrant. You'll want to evaluate the situation; was the suspect "caught in the act" while at the computer? The information that the suspect is currently working on will *not* necessarily be saved if you shut down the system. The contents of open chat sessions, for example, could be lost forever if they're not automatically being logged. You will want to consider the best way to preserve this volatile data without compromising the integrity of the evidence. You might be able to save the current data, print current screens, or even have your crime scene photographer take photos of the screens to prevent information in RAM from being lost.

Understanding how data is stored on and accessed from hard disks and removable media will help you recognize why data can often be recovered even though the cybercriminal thinks he or she has "erased" it, either by merely deleting the files or by formatting the disk.

Investigators should also be aware of the many existing removable media options that allow cybercriminals to store evidentiary data in a location separate from the computer, easily transfer that data to another computer, or make copies of the data that can be used in case the original data on the computer's hard disk is destroyed. The presence of any removable media drive (diskette drive, CD-R, tape drive, or the like) means that there is definitely a possibility that data has been saved and taken away. Unfortunately, the absence of such a drive does not negate that possibility, because many removable media drives are external and portable; they can be quickly and easily moved from one computer to another, attaching to the machine by way of a serial, parallel, USB, or other port.

The Language of the Machine

Computer hardware and accessories, such as hard disks and removable media, might provide the physical evidence of cybercrime. However, in most cases the hardware itself is not really the evidence; it merely *contains* the evidence. Similarly, a letter written by a criminal might be entered into evidence, but it is not the physical page and ink that provide proof of guilt, it is the words written on the page that indicate the criminal's culpable mental state or that provide a written confession of the criminal's actions. If those words are in a language that the police, prosecutors, and jury can understand, using them as evidence is easy. On the other hand, if the words are written in a foreign language, using them as evidence might be more difficult because they will have to be interpreted by someone who understands both languages.

In a sense, most computer data is written in a foreign language. The data stored in computers is written in the "language" of ones and zeros, or *binary language* (also called *machine language* or *machine code*). Although relatively few humans can program in pure machine language and few cybercrime investigators learn to translate the magnetic encoding representing ones and zeros on a disk into "real" (understandable) data, it is helpful for investigators to understand how binary language works in order to anticipate questions that can be raised by the defense in a case that relies on computer data as evidence.

On the Scene...

Getting Down to the Lowest Level

Machine language is the lowest level of programming language. The next step up is *assembly language*, which allows programmers to use names (or *mneumonics*) represented by ASCII characters, rather than just numbers. Code written in assembly language is translated into machine language by a program called an *assembler.*

Most programmers, however, write their code in *high-level languages* (for example, BASIC, COBOL, FORTRAN, or C++). High-level languages are "friendlier" than other languages in that they are more like the languages that humans write and speak to communicate with one another and less like the machine language that computers "understand." Although easier for people to work with, high-level languages must be converted into machine language for the computer to use the program. This is done by a program called a *compiler*, which reorganizes the instructions in the source code, or an *interpreter*, which immediately executes the source code. Because different computing platforms use different machine languages, there are different compilers for a single high-level language to enable the code to run on different platforms.

Wandering Through a World of Numbers

Working with numbers, beyond the primitive method of simply representing each item counted as a one (for example, carving one notch on the investigator's wooden desktop for each case solved), requires that we use a *base system* to group items in an ordered fashion, making it easier for us to keep count.

Who's on Which Base?

Most of us are most familiar with the base–10 numbering system, also called the *decimal numbering system*. Many sources credit early Indian cultures with creating this numbering system approximately 5000 years ago; it was later refined in the Arab world. This system uses 10 digits (0 through 9) to represent all possible numbers. Each digit's value depends on its *place;* as you move left in reading a number, each place represents 10 times the value to its right. Thus the digit *1* can represent 1, 10, 100, 1000, and so on, depending on its place as defined by the number of digits to its right. A *decimal point* is used to allow numbers less than 1 to be represented.

We use base 10 all the time; it is our day-to-day numbering system. When we see a decimal number such as *168*, we understand that the 1 represents one *hundred,* the 6 represents six *tens,* and the 8 represents eight *ones,* based on the place occupied by each digit in relation to the others.

Base 10 works great for human counting because we have 10 fingers (also called *digits*) that we can use to count on. Historians believe this explains the development and popularity of decimal numbering; primitive people found it easy to count to 10 on their fingers and then make a mark in the sand or on stone to represent each group of 10.

Computers, however, work with electrical impulses that have two discrete states. You can visualize this system by thinking of a standard light switch. The bulb can be in one of two possible states at a given time; it is either on or off. This is a *digital* signal. We don't have 10 different states to represent the 10 digits of the decimal system to the computer, but we can still represent all possible numbers using the base-2 numbering system, also called the *binary numbering system.*

Understanding the Binary Numbering System

Binary numbering uses only two digits, 0 and 1. Each binary digit (each 0 or 1) is called a *bit.* In binary numbering, as in decimal, the value of a digit is determined by its place. However, in binary, each place represents 2 times the value of the place to its right (instead of 10 times, as in base 10).

NOTE

A *byte* generally equals 8 bits. Bytes are the units that computers usually use to represent a character (a letter of the alphabet, a numeral, or a symbol). Eight bits is also called an *octet,* especially in the context of IP addressing.

This means the binary number *1000* does not represent one thousand; instead, it represents eight (its decimal equivalent) because that's the value of the fourth place to the left. A zero is a placeholder that indicates that place has no value, and a one indicates that a place has the value assigned to it. Thus *1111* represents 15 in decimal, because each place (starting from the right) has a value of 1, 2, 4, and 8. Adding these values together gives us 15.

Converting Between Binary and Decimal

Although computer processors must work with binary numbering, humans prefer to work with numbering systems that use more digits, because it is less confusing for us to deal with a number that looks like 139 than its binary equivalent of 10001011.

Table 4.1 shows the place values of the first 12 places of a binary number, starting from the right. If the binary digit is a 1, the value shown is assigned to it; if it's a 0, no value is assigned. The second line of the table shows the digits of a typical binary number.

Table 4.1 Place values of binary digits

Value	2048	1024	512	256	128	64	32	16	8	4	2	1
Binary Digit	1	1	0	1	0	0	0	1	1	0	0	1

Looking at this binary number, 110100011001, we see that the bits that are "on" (represented by 1s) have values of 1, 8, 16, 256, 1024, and 2048. If we add those values together, we get 3353. This is the decimal equivalent of the binary number.

Converting Between Binary and Hexadecimal

Another numbering system that is sometimes used to make binary more palatable for humans is the *hexadecimal,* or *hex, system,* or base 16. Why not just use our familiar decimal system and convert it to binary instead of learning yet another numbering system? Hex is useful because it is easier to convert hex to binary. Since hex uses 16 digits, each byte (8 binary digits) can be represented by 2 hex digits. Hex also produces shorter numbers to work with than decimal.

Hex needs six more symbols than decimal to represent all its digits, so it uses the standard decimal digits 0 to 9 to represent the first 10 digits and then uses the first six letters of the alphabet, A to F, to represent the remaining six digits. Table 4.2 shows the hexadecimal digits and their decimal equivalents.

Table 4.2 Hexadecimal digits and their decimal equivalents

Hexadecimal	0	1	2	3	4	5	6	7	8	9	A	B	C	D	E	F
Decimal		0	1	2	3	4	5	6	7	8	9	10	11	12	13	14	15

Using this system, for example, the decimal number 11,085 is equivalent to the hex number 2B4D, and the decimal number 1409 is equivalent to the hex number 581. In the first case, it's obvious that we're dealing with a hexadecimal number, but if we see the number 581, how do we know whether it's a decimal or hexadecimal number? To solve this problem, hex numbers are indicated by either a prefix of *0x* or a suffix of *H*. Thus, our hex equivalent of 1409 would be written either *0x581* or *581H*.

In the computer world, you'll find that some numbers (such as IP addresses) are traditionally represented by their decimal equivalents, whereas others (such as memory addresses and MAC addresses) are traditionally represented by their hexadecimal equivalents.

Converting Text to Binary

Computers "think" in binary, but people (aside from the rare mathematical genius) don't. We tend to work with words, and much of the data that we input to our computers is in the form of text. How does the computer process this data? Ultimately, it must be converted to the binary "language" that the computer understands.

Text files are commonly encoded in either ASCII (in UNIX and MS-DOS-based operating systems) or Unicode (in Windows NT/2000). *ASCII* stands for *American Standard Code for Information Interchange,* which represents binary numbers as text. Assembly language uses ASCII characters for programming. Each character of the alphabet, numeric digit, or symbol is represented by a specific 1–byte string of binary digits. (In a binary file, there is no one-to-one correlation between characters and bytes.)

ASCII characters are used by text-based operating systems and programs such as MS-DOS and WordPerfect versions prior to 5.0. By contrast, graphical programs use bitmaps or geometrical shapes instead of characters to create display objects.

NOTE

The *extended ASCII* character set includes additional characters, such as shapes for drawing pictures so that graphics objects can be simulated. MS-DOS uses extended ASCII to display menus, bar charts, and other shapes that are based on straight lines.

Encoding Nontext Files

The original ASCII encoding scheme used 7-bit characters and is designed to handle plain text only. Then along came the Internet, and people wanted to send files to one another via e-mail. E-mail server software was designed to handle the ASCII character set and another 7-bit encoding scheme, Extended Binary Coded Decimal Interchange Code (EBCDIC) that was developed by IBM for their minicomputers and mainframes. This worked fine as long as everyone was sending plain text files. However, it was a problem if you wanted to send pictures, audio, programs, or files created in applications that did not produce plain text, because most nontext files use 8-bit characters. Even the documents created by word processors are usually not saved as ASCII files but as binary files (in order to preserve formatting information).

The answer to this problem was to use an encoding scheme that could represent nontext files as text. Programmers came up with solutions such as uuencode and Multipurpose Internet Mail Extensions (MIME) to convert nontext files into ASCII text. Thus a photo or other nontext file could be sent across the Internet without a problem. An encoded file looks like a mass of meaningless ASCII characters to the human eye, but when it is decoded by software at the recipient's end, it is converted back into its original form. MIME provided a number of advantages over uuencode in that it supported sending multiple attachments and interactive multimedia content. Perhaps most important, it supports languages such as Japanese, Chinese, and Hebrew that don't use the Roman alphabet.

Another encoding scheme, called BinHex, is often used by Apple Macintosh software. Mac files differ from those created by Windows and some other operating systems in that the Mac files consist of two parts, called *forks*—one that contains the actual data and one that contains attribute information and parametric values. There are programs available to convert the files into a single byte stream for sending over a network. Macintosh files can be sent via MIME, using the MIME encapsulation specifications outlined in RFC1740.

Web browsers also support MIME so they can display files that are not in HTML format. There is also a version of MIME called *S/MIME* that supports encryption of messages.

Why This Matters to the Investigator

Investigators might not be capable of interpreting machine language, but they should understand what it is when they see it. The 1s and 0s of binary computation, the odd-looking hexadecimal numbers used in some types of addressing, and the indecipherable "gibberish" of MIME-encoded files might look meaningless, but when properly translated they can contain valuable evidence.

Just as an investigator should not throw away a letter found at the scene of a crime just because it happens to be written in Chinese, neither should computer data be dismissed as useless just because the investigators can't understand it. Pure binary data, or data that has been encoded for sending across a network, might be less convenient to work with than text or unencoded pictures, but often it can be converted to a readable form by the proper software.

It is also important for investigators to understand the difference between the type of encoding we are discussing here, which is done to make data recognizable and usable by a computer, and *encryption,* the purpose of which is to make data unrecognizable and unusable by unauthorized humans. Encoded data is intended to be easily decoded, and the software for doing so is widely available; encrypted data is intended to be difficult or impossible to decrypt without the proper key.

The very fact that a file has been encrypted can in some cases be a red flag that arouses suspicion or a building block of the probable cause needed to get a warrant or effect an arrest. Thus knowing the difference between an encoded file and an encrypted file will save investigators time and strengthen their credibility before a judge.

On the Scene...

Does File Encryption Create Probable Cause?

Investigators know that probable cause is usually not based on one fact or piece of evidence but rather comprises multiple building blocks that, when taken together, would cause a reasonable and prudent person to believe that a crime has been committed by the suspect. Law enforcement professionals sometimes refer to these building blocks collectively as the *totality of the circumstances.* The fourth amendment to the U.S. Constitution requires that probable cause, based on the totality of the circumstances, be shown before a search warrant can be issued.

Does the existence of an encrypted file (or files) on a computer establish probable cause to seize that computer and examine the files, going on the theory that "only guilty people have something to hide"? In other words, if the girlfriend of a child-pornography suspect tells you that there are files on the family computer that are encrypted so that she

Continued

can't open them, is that enough cause for a search warrant? Given the nature of probable cause, the answer is no—at least, not by itself. Encryption alone generally would not be enough to satisfy the definition of probable cause. Use of encryption is not illegal in the United States (it is in some countries), and many people concerned with privacy use encryption to protect data that has nothing to do with criminal activity.

However, the fact that data is encrypted can be used as one of your building blocks of probable cause. If you have other evidence that indicates, for example, that a suspect regularly downloads pornographic photos of children (such as testimony of a known child pornographer that the suspect requested such photos from him, intercepted e-mail messages, or the like), the existence of encrypted files on the suspect's hard disk would add to the suspicion that illicit photos were stored there.

Other considerations include whether all the files on the disk are encrypted or only some select ones. The former situation is more indicative of someone who is just generally concerned about privacy, whereas the latter situation serves as a red flag that those particular files could contain something of interest to law enforcement. We discuss encryption in more detail in Chapter 7, "Understanding Cybercrime Prevention," in the section on cryptography.

Understanding Computer Operating Systems

As a computer starts, the operating system is loaded into its memory and provides the foundation or *platform* on which application programs run. Although the vast majority of today's personal computers run some version of one of the three most popular PC operating systems (Windows, UNIX/Linux, or Macintosh OS), thousands of different computer operating systems exist. Some of these are network operating systems such as NetWare that run servers but don't function as desktop/client operating systems. Some run on mainframe or mini-mainframe computers, such as IBM's z/OS and OS/400, and some are designed for high-end workstations, such as Sun's Solaris and IBM's AIX (both based on UNIX). Others are proprietary operating systems used for specific devices, such as Cisco's Internetworking Operating System (IOS) that runs on Cisco routers or SCOUT, which runs network appliances. Some are used as embedded operating systems in a variety of devices, such as Windows CE Embedded, QNX, and Symbian. Some are experimental operating systems such as GNU HURD and SkyOS.

> **NOTE**
>
> For a list of many operating systems that are in development, see the Current Operating Systems Projects page at www.cs.arizona.edu/people/ bridges/oses.html.

Understanding the Role of the Operating System Software

The operating system acts as a sort of liaison between the computer hardware and the application programs that are used to perform specific tasks (such as word processing or downloading and sending e-mail). It also provides file management, security, and coordination of application and utility programs that are running simultaneously. Operating systems can be classified in a number of different ways:

- *Text-based (or character-based) operating systems* such as MS-DOS and UNIX/Linux are faster performers because they don't have the overhead required to display complex graphics, but many people find them to be less user-friendly than GUI operating systems because you must learn and type commands to perform tasks. Most text-based operating systems can run shell programs to give them a graphical interface. Examples include Windows 3.*x* for MS-DOS and KDE for Linux.

- *Multiuser operating systems* generally run on mainframe systems and allow more than one user to log on, through terminals, and run programs simultaneously. The term is sometimes also used to refer to operating systems (such as Windows NT/2000/XP) that allow only one user at a time to log on but identify different users by a user account that is assigned a *profile* that defines settings, preferences, and documents that are specific to that user. Server operating systems (such as Windows NT/2000/.NET Server, Novell NetWare, and UNIX) allow multiple users to log onto the server over the network and access its resources, although only one user is logged on interactively (at the local machine).

- *Multitasking operating systems* are those that allow you to run more than one program at a time. MS-DOS is a *single-tasking* operating system; in other words, you have to close one application before you can start another. The Windows shell, running on top of DOS, allows it to multi-task. UNIX, IBM's OS/2, and Windows 9*x*/ME and NT/2000 and later are all true multitasking operating systems.

■ *Multiprocessing operating systems* are able to use the capabilities of more than one microprocessor installed in the system, either by assigning different programs to run on different processors or by allowing different parts of a single program to run on different processors. For example, Windows 9*x*/ME operating systems do not recognize or use multiple processors, but Windows NT/2000/XP/.NET do. (The number of processors depends on the OS version.) UNIX and Macintosh also support multiple processors.

Differentiating Between Multitasking and Multiprocessing Types

Different operating systems support such features as multitasking and multiprocessing in different ways. The type of multitasking or multiprocessing that is used by a particular operating system depends on its *architecture*—that is, its design and structure.

Multitasking

Multitasking works by *time slicing*—that is, allowing multiple programs to use tiny slices of the processor's time, one after the other. Two basic types of multitasking are used by PC operating systems: cooperative and preemptive. *Cooperative multitasking* was used by Windows 3.*x* and prior, running on top of MS-DOS, as well as Macintosh operating systems prior to OS X. In this type of multitasking environment, each program must be written so that its *processes* (tasks or executing programs) use the processor for a short amount of time and then give up control of the processor to other processes. As long as the programs are written to cooperate, this system works. However, poorly written programs can take over the processor and refuse to relinquish control. When this happens, the system can freeze or crash.

Preemptive multitasking is more efficient. This method puts the operating system itself in charge of the processor. This way, a badly written program can't hog control of the processor; if it tries to do so, the operating system preempts its use of the processor and gives it to another process. A component in the operating system's kernel called the *scheduler* is responsible for allotting use of the processor to each process in turn. Some operating systems allow you to assign priorities to certain processes so that they come first when they need to use the processor. Preemptive processing is used by Windows 9*x* and later, UNIX, OS/2, and Macintosh OS X.

Multiprocessing

Even if a computer has more than one processor physically installed, it might not be able to perform multiprocessing. In order to perform multiprocessing, the operating system must be capable of recognizing the presence of multiple processors and be able to use them. Some operating systems, such as Windows 9x, do not support multiprocessing. Even among those that do, not all multiprocessing operating systems are created equal.

There are three methods of supporting multiple processing:

- Asymmetric multiprocessing (AMP or ASMP)
- Symmetric multiprocessing (SMP)
- Massively parallel processing (MPP)

With *asymmetric multiprocessing,* each processor is assigned specific tasks. One primary processor acts as the "master" and controls the actions of the other, secondary processors.

Symmetric multiprocessing makes all the processors available to all individual processes. The processors share the workload, distributed more or less equally, thus increasing performance. Symmetric multiprocessing is also called *tightly coupled multiprocessing* because the multiple processors still use just one instance of the operating system and share the computer's memory and I/O resources.

Massively parallel processing is a means of crunching huge amounts of data by distributing the processing over hundreds or thousands of processors, which might be running in the same box or in separate, distantly located computers. Each processor in an MPP system has its own memory, disks, applications, and instances of the operating system. The problem being worked on is divided into many pieces, which are processed simultaneously by the multiple systems.

NOTE

MMP is generally used in research, academic, and government environments running large, complex computer systems. It is seldom used on desktop machines or typical business servers, although there is a type of parallel processing called *distributed computing* that uses large numbers of ordinary PCs on a network to work together on a problem, dividing the task among multiple machines. One of the best-known examples of this type of processing is done on the Search for Extraterrestrial Intelligence (SETI) project. SETI@Home recruits volunteers across the

---

Continued

Internet who install software on their home computers that allows their systems, during idle time, to process a portion of the massive amount of data collected from radio telescopes and analyze it for signals that might have originated from intelligent beings in space.

A paper that outlines the advantages of the distributed computing model of parallel processing used in SETI and other projects is available at http://roland.grc.nasa.gov/~mallman/papers/prime-delay.pdf (PDF format).

Symmetric multiprocessing is the type supported by mainstream operating systems, including Windows NT/2000/XP/.NET, Linux, BSD and other UNIX versions, BeOS, and OS/2 Warp. To take advantage of the multiprocessing capabilities, the programs running on multiprocessor machines and operating systems must be *multithreaded*—that is, they must be written in a way that allows them to execute tasks in small executable parts called *threads*. Windows 2000, XP, and .NET also support a feature called *processor affinity* that provides AMP-like functionality.

Differentiating Between Proprietary and Open Source Operating Systems

Most commercial operating systems are *proprietary*—that is, the vendors keep the source code (the programming instructions) secret, and the licensing agreements prohibit "reverse engineering" (that is, dismantling the software's components and replicating them). Vendors don't depend on the licensing agreement alone to prevent you from performing reverse engineering. When you buy the software, it has been *compiled;* in other words, a compiler program has translated the source code (written in a higher-level language understandable to the programmer) into machine language that is understandable by the computer. This compilation process makes it difficult or impossible for programmers to replicate the original source code, which is needed in order to make changes to the software.

However, some operating systems are distributed as *open source products*, meaning that the source code is made available to the public and developers at no cost. Anyone is free to modify the code to improve it. The only "catch" is that the license, although free, usually obligates programmers to disclose their improvements or even to make them available to the public at no cost.

The most notable (though not the only) open source operating system is Linux, which is based on the UNIX operating system. (Some versions of UNIX, such as FreeBSD, are open source; others, such as AIX, HP-UX, and Solaris, are not.) To confuse matters more, although the source code for Linux is free, vendors such as Red Hat, Caldera, and Corel market their own "distros" (Linux-speak for *distributions*) commercially. The term *open source* doesn't necessarily mean that the compiled version is free—only the source code is.

Linux was developed by and is named after Linus Torvalds, under the GNU General Public License (GPL). The licensing agreement makes it clear that developers who modify or distribute the software can charge for the service if they like; what they *can't* do is keep the source code secret or patent the products (unless the patent is licensed for everyone's free use).

NOTE

You can read all the terms of the entire GNU GPL on the GNU Web site at www.gnu.org/licenses/gpl.html#SEC1. For information about the Open Source Initiative (OSI), visit www.opensource.org.

If open source software is free—or at least the source code is—why doesn't everyone use it instead of proprietary commercial software that costs big bucks? There are several reasons:

- There are dozens of different versions or "distros" of each open source operating system or application. This can be confusing to users, who don't know which one to select.

- Because anyone and everyone can make modifications to the operating system, you don't have the standardization that you have with proprietary software. In other words, one version of Linux might work fine with your hardware configuration, but another distro might not.

- Often, device drivers are not readily available for open source operating systems, so you must write your own. This is beyond the capabilities of many consumers and business users (in other words, people who aren't "geeks").

- Generally, no warranty is included with open source software, and no technical support is available (although some companies, such as Red Hat, package their distros of Linux and in essence sell the warranty/tech support services accompanied by the "free" software). This is especially important to business users, who generally will not use software that doesn't include tech support from the vendor.

The open source community has criticized vendors of proprietary software, such as Microsoft and Apple, for keeping their source code secret. As a result, Apple Computer has, for the first time, opened its source code for Darwin, the Mac OS X kernel, which is based on UNIX. For more information about the OpenDarwin project, see Apple's Web site for developers at http://developer .apple.com/darwin/projects.

An Overview of Commonly Used Operating Systems

The most commonly used operating systems for microcomputers today include those made by Microsoft, Apple's Macintosh operating systems, and the various "distros" of Linux and other UNIX-based operating systems. In this section, we look briefly at the following operating systems:

- DOS
- Windows 3.*x*
- Windows 9*x* (95, 95b, 95c, 98, 98SE, ME)
- Windows NT 3.51 and 4.0 (Workstation and Server versions)
- Windows 2000 (Professional and Server versions)
- Windows XP (Home and Professional versions)
- Linux/UNIX
- OS/2 and BeOS
- Macintosh

At the time of this writing, Microsoft's .NET Server operating system was still in beta testing, but it can be expected to be deployed widely in the corporate environment when it is released. Figure 4.1 shows the Microsoft "family tree," diagramming the chronological evolution of the current Windows operating systems.

Understanding DOS

DOS is the Disk Operating System, which was the operating system first used on the original IBM PCs. Today many computers still run some form of DOS. The most popular "flavor" of DOS is Microsoft's version, MS-DOS. IBM licensed DOS from Microsoft and marketed a version called PC-DOS that was bundled with its early PCs. Digital Research sold a version called DR–DOS that was later marketed by Caldera as DR-OpenDOS. There is an open source version of DOS called FreeDOS; for more information on this product, see the FreeDOS Web site at www.freedos.org.

The earliest versions of DOS used a file system called FAT12 (we'll discuss file systems in more detail in the next section). MS-DOS versions 3.*x* through 6.*x* supported FAT16 along with FAT12 and were used both as standalone operating systems and as the operating system on which Windows (through version 3.11) was loaded, because early versions of Windows were not full-fledged operating systems, only graphical shells that required DOS underneath. MS-DOS version 7.0, which also supported FAT12 and FAT16, was part of the Windows 95 operating system. At that point in the evolution of Microsoft operating systems, the shell was integrated with the operating system, and users no longer installed MS-DOS and Windows as two separate products. Windows 95b (also called OEM Service Release 2 or OSR 2) was integrated with a new version of MS-DOS, version 7.1, which supported the FAT32 file system.

Figure 4.1 The Microsoft family tree

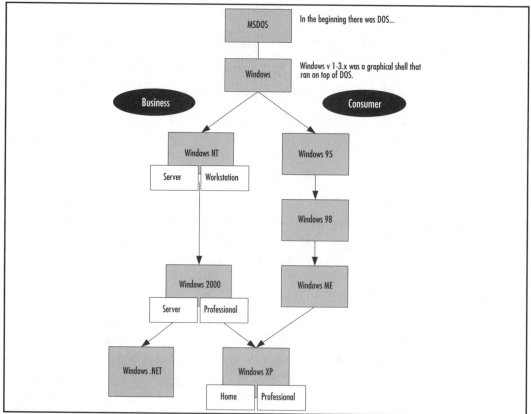

MS-DOS as a standalone operating system is text-based and is not capable of multitasking. It has several limitations, such as the inability to work with disk partitions larger than 2GB or memory greater than 1MB (unless you use the Expanded Memory Scheme, or EMS, software). Windows 3.*x* uses EMS to provide multitasking. DOS was built on the BASIC programming language, and most versions include a version of BASIC. The MS-DOS interface is shown in Figure 4.2.

Figure 4.2 MS-DOS has a text-based interface.

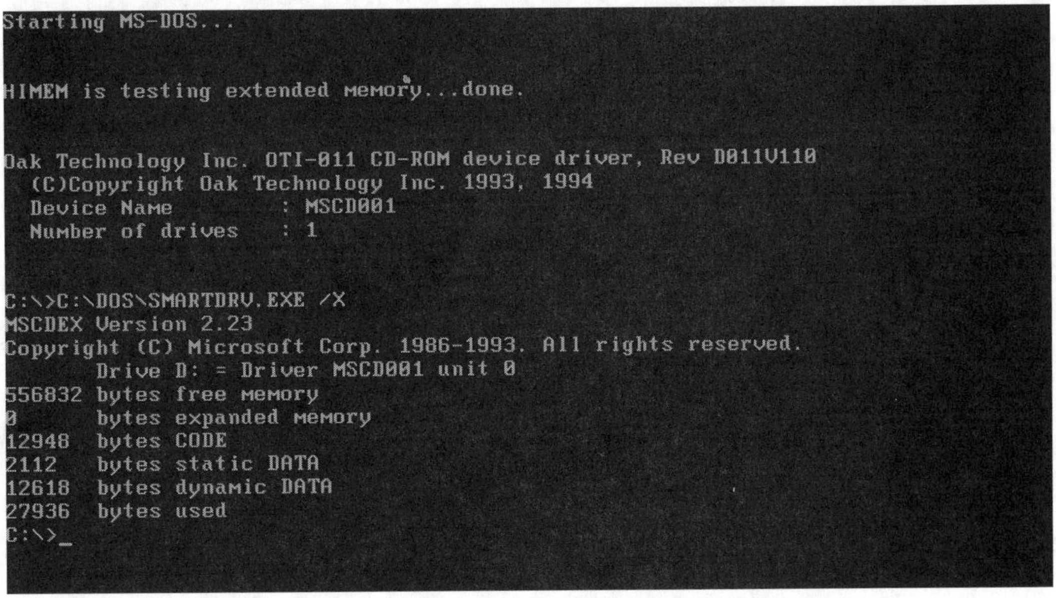

Advantages of MS-DOS include size (version 6.22 fits on three diskettes), relative simplicity, low cost, and the fact that it will run on older, low powered hardware that doesn't have enough memory or disk space to support more modern operating systems.

Windows 1.*x* Through 3.*x*

Not really operating systems in their own right but rather add-ons to MS-DOS, Windows versions 1.*x* through 3.*x* were designed to bring a graphical interface to the Microsoft computing environment. Versions 1 and 2 were not very popular, but as the old adage says, the third time is a charm, and Windows 3.0, released in 1990, was the beginning of Microsoft's dominance in the operating system market.

On the Scene...

Who "Stole" What from Whom?

It is a popular truism in the personal computing community that Microsoft "stole" (or at least derived) the idea of a graphical interface for Windows from its chief competitor at the time, Apple. Like most truisms, it is only partially true. It is true that Apple did develop a graphical operating system for its Local Integrated Software Architecture (LISA) computer, which it officially released in 1983, just prior to Microsoft's announcement of Windows and almost two years before Windows 1.0 actually became available to the public. However, Apple didn't "invent" the idea of the mouse-driven GUI, as many people believe. The Xerox Alto (named after the Palo Alto Research Center, where it was developed) and Star computers were actually the first personal computers to use these features, way back in the 1970s. Both Steve Jobs (of Apple) and Bill Gates (of Microsoft) visited Palo Alto and "borrowed" the ideas from Xerox, which later showed up in the Lisa (and later the Macintosh) and in Windows.

For more information about the Alto, see www.fortunecity .com/marina/reach/435. To view the Lisa interface, see http://members .fortunecity.com/pcmuseum/lisadsk.htm. For a look at the interface on Windows 1.0 and subsequent versions of Windows (up through XP), visit www.infosatellite.com/news/2001/10/a251001windowshistory_ screenshots.html#win101.

Windows 3.x is still in use on many computers in the world today. Like MS-DOS alone, it will run on older hardware, and many applications were made for it. Windows 3.x over MS-DOS is known as a *16-bit operating system*, meaning that it can process 2 bytes (which equals 16 bits) at a time. One of its limitations is the inability to handle filenames that have more than eight characters (with a three-character extension).

NOTE

The first microcomputer operating systems, used by the Commodore PET, Tandy TRS-80, Texas Instruments TI/99, and Apple II, were 8-bit operating systems.

Windows 3.11 added 32-bit file access (a new way of accessing the disk), updated device drivers, and bug fixes. Another popular version of Windows 3.1 and 3.11 was called Windows for Workgroups, which included integrated networking components for the first time. It included Microsoft Mail support and remote access services, and it claimed 50- to 150-percent faster disk I/O performance. Windows for Workgroups made peer-to-peer networking much easier and more convenient than earlier Microsoft operating systems and became very popular in small business environments. The Windows 3.11 interface is shown in Figure 4.3.

Figure 4.3 Windows 3.*x* ran on top of MS-DOS, providing a graphical interface.

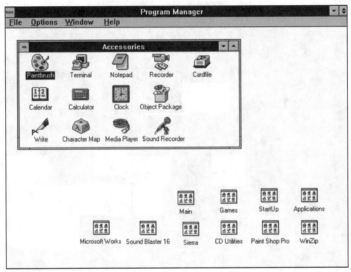

Windows 9*x* (95, 95b, 95c, 98, 98SE, and ME)

Windows 95 was a major new operating system release that was accompanied by heavy fanfare from Microsoft and the computing community. Released in August 1995, Windows 95 was Microsoft's first 32-bit consumer operating system; however, it is a *hybrid* operating system rather than a true 32-bit OS. For backward compatibility with older programs written for Windows 3.*x*, there is still a good deal of 16-bit code in Windows 95.

Windows 95 was designed to provide users with an entirely new interface (doing away with the old Program Manager and incorporating the now-familiar Start button and taskbar) and many enhanced features, such as:

- Preemptive multitasking (for 32-bit programs only)
- Support for long filenames (up to 256 characters) through the VFAT file system

- Plug and Play (which makes hardware installation easier)

- Power Management (a boon for laptop users)

- The Recycle Bin (which makes it easier to recover deleted files)

- Dialup networking support built into the operating system

Windows 95 became tremendously popular and was the beginning of the Windows 9*x* family tree, which includes Windows 98 and ME. The Windows 95 interface is shown in Figure 4.4.

Figure 4.4 Windows 95 provided a whole new look and many new features.

The second release of Windows 95, popularly called 95b and officially referred to as OSR 2, was not available to consumers on the shelves. It was released to original equipment manufacturers (OEMs, or PC hardware vendors) to install on the machines they sold. Version 95b added support for the FAT32 file system. A variant of 95b, called OSR 2.1, added rudimentary USB support. Another variant, OSR 2.5, which is often called Windows 95c, added the Internet Explorer 4.0 Web browser as an integrated component.

The next upgrade to Microsoft's 9*x* line of consumer operating systems was Windows 98, released, appropriately enough, in June 1998. This was the first version available as packaged software to consumers that supported FAT32 (in addition to the "old" file systems FAT12 and FAT16). Windows 98 also added networking and dialup enhancements, better hardware support, infrared (IrDA) support, and Advanced Configuration and Power Interface (ACPI). It also included the Active Desktop (which could be added to Windows 95 by installing the Internet Explorer 4.0 browser) and provided for multiple monitor support. Windows 98 replaced the old Help files with an indexed, searchable HTML system that is far more functional and added a number of interactive Trouble-shooting Wizards, along with the Windows Update online driver/component update feature. Windows 98SE (second edition) added a few new features such as Internet Connection Sharing (ICS) and DVD-ROM support.

Next (and presumably last) in the Windows 9x line is Windows ME, short for Millennium Edition, released in September 2000. ME added several multimedia features such as a video-editing program and included better home networking support, but it was not a major upgrade. ME is presumably the last in the 9x line because the Windows 9x line of operating systems, geared to home users, and the Windows NT/2000 line, geared toward businesses, have been merged into one with the advent of Windows XP.

Windows NT

Microsoft designed Windows NT for the corporate desktop and server market. NT comes in two versions: Workstation for desktops and Server for servers. NT was released in 1993 and was based in part on the work done jointly by Microsoft and IBM, before they parted ways, on OS/2. Thus many of NT's features, such as its pure 32-bit code and its high-performance, secure file system, are similar to features in OS/2. NT is Microsoft's first operating system that is *not* based on MS-DOS. However, it can run MS-DOS programs by creating a virtual machine that emulates the DOS environment on which DOS applications can run.

NOTE

What does *NT* stand for? In its early days, Microsoft said the letters stood for *New Technology*. Later (when the technology could no longer be called "new"), Microsoft changed its story and said it doesn't stand for anything. David Cutler was the driving force behind the development of Windows NT.

Primary differences between Windows 9x and Windows NT are stability and security. The business environment requires an operating system that does not crash frequently, one that is secure enough to protect the sensitive data stored often stored on corporate computers. Windows NT's architecture incorporates a hardware abstraction layer (referred to fondly as *HAL*) that prevents software applications from making direct calls to the hardware. This makes NT more stable and less crash-prone, but it also means that some applications written for Windows 9*x* won't run on Windows NT.

NT 3.1 was released in 1993, a year prior to the release of Windows 95. The interface resembled Windows 3.*x*, but the kernel was completely different. A significant factor was the way NT handled memory. Unlike with Windows 3.*x* before it, each program ran in its own separate memory address. This meant that if one program crashed, it would not bring down all the rest of the currently running programs with it. Security features included mandatory logon (a user must have an account name and password to log onto the computer). NT also introduced support for a new file system, NT File System (NTFS), that offers better performance as well as the ability to set permissions (called *NTFS permissions* or *file-level permissions*) on individual files and folders. NT 3.51 and prior versions also included support for the native file system of IBM's OS/2, High Performance File System (HPFS).

NT 4.0 was a major upgrade released in 1996. The interface resembled that of Windows 95, and it included advanced user administration tools, wizards, a network monitor (a built-in protocol analyzer or "sniffer" software), a task manager (a tool that provides information on running applications and processes), and support for system policies and user profiles to allow administrators to more easily control the users' desktop environment. Remote access services and built-in virtual private networking (VPN) support via the Point-to-Point Tunneling Protocol (PPTP) were other improvements. NT 4.0 dropped support for HPFS. The Windows NT 4.0 interface is shown in Figure 4.5.

Although Windows NT Workstation has many advantages over the Windows 9*x* operating systems, it never became popular for home computing, for several reasons:

- NT does not support Plug and Play, so hardware installation is more difficult and NT is "pickier" about the hardware it supports.

- NT is not optimized for gaming; many popular Windows 9*x* and DOS games won't run on NT, because the game software needs direct access to the hardware, which NT doesn't allow.

- NT Workstation costs about twice as much as Windows 9*x*.

- NT is more complex and less "user friendly," and its extra security measures are considered unnecessary and inconvenient by many home users.

Figure 4.5 Windows NT 4.0 provided an interface similar to that of Windows 95.

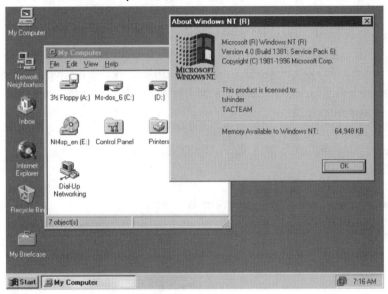

Despite its lack of popularity in the consumer market, Windows NT—both Workstation and Server versions—became immensely popular in the business environment, with Microsoft's server product eventually overtaking and surpassing Novell's NetWare as a network authentication server. Windows NT made huge inroads into the Internet mail and Web server markets, which were previously dominated by UNIX.

Windows 2000

Although Windows NT provided significantly more stability and security than the 9x operating systems, in order to continue to grow in market share among business customers, especially when competing with UNIX, Microsoft needed something better. Windows 2000 was released in February 2000, representing at least as many changes as the upgrade from Windows 3.x to 95. Like NT, Windows 2000 is really a family of products: Professional (the desktop/client operating system that replaces NT Workstation) and three versions of the server software (Server, Advanced Server, and Datacenter Server). The startup screen for Windows 2000 Pro is shown in Figure 4.6.

The Windows 2000 operating systems are built on the NT kernel but with the Windows 98 interface and literally hundreds of enhancements and improvements. Many features that were missing in NT (although some of them could be added via third-party add-on software) such as file encryption, disk quotas, and—

finally!—Plug and Play are included in Windows 2000. New security features include support for the Internet-standard Kerberos authentication protocol, IP Security (IPSec) for encrypting data that travels over the network, Group Policy (a much more robust and powerful replacement for system policies), and the Layer 2 Tunneling Protocol (L2TP) for more secure VPNs. The biggest difference between NT and Windows 2000 networking is the addition of the Active Directory, a directory service similar in some ways to Novell's NDS, which provides a central-ized database for managing security, user data, and distributed resources.

For more information about Windows 2000 and Active Directory, a good starting point is Microsoft's Windows 2000 Web site at www.microsoft.com/ windows2000.

Figure 4.6 Windows 2000 is built on NT technology.

Windows XP

In October 2001, Microsoft released another semi-major desktop upgrade, this one called Windows XP. One thing that makes XP special is the fact that it is an upgrade to both the Windows 9*x* line and the Windows NT/2000 line of desktop operating systems, which have been merged back together into one product line—sort of. Although both are based on the more stable NT kernel, XP comes in two different versions: XP Home Edition for consumers and XP Professional for business users.

The Home Edition of XP focuses on entertainment (digital photography, music, and video), gaming, and other consumer-oriented activities, along with features that make Internet connectivity and home networking easier than ever. The Professional Edition includes all the features of XP Home plus additional features that are geared toward the corporate user, such as Remote Desktop (a "lite" terminal server application that allows you to access your XP desktop from anywhere across the network), file encryption, support for multiple-processor systems, and advanced networking features. The Windows XP Professional interface is shown in Figure 4.7. Note that this is not the default XP desktop; it has been highly customized to show the great flexibility provided by the operating system to allow users to "have it their way."

Figure 4.7 Windows XP combines the best of the 9*x* and NT/2000 worlds.

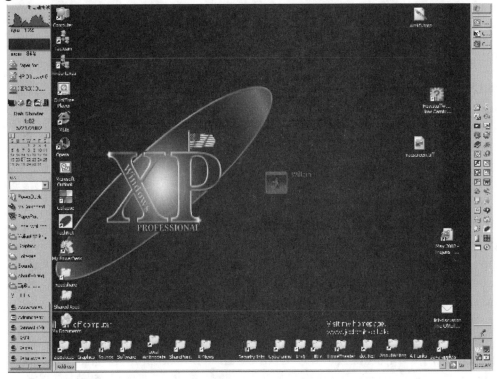

A Windows XP Pro computer, like NT Workstation and Windows 2000 Pro, can be a member of a Windows domain (a server-based network), whereas XP Home computers, like Windows 9*x* systems, can be used to access domain resources but cannot belong to the domain. Useful features included in both versions of XP are:

- Built-in Internet firewall for better security

- Windows file protection feature that prevents accidentally changing the core operating system files

- Fast user switching that allows users to change the currently logged-on user account without closing applications (on nondomain computers)

- A number of new wizards that walk you through commonly performed tasks such as transferring files and settings from one computer to another, setting up a network, publishing to the Web, and so on

Windows XP is a desktop/client operating system only. Although it had not been released at the time of this writing, its corresponding server operating system is Windows .NET Server (currently in beta testing). For more information about Windows XP, a good starting point is Microsoft's XP home page at www.microsoft.com/windowsxp/home/default.asp. You can find more information about .NET Server at www.microsoft.com/windows.netserver.

Linux/UNIX

UNIX has been around since the 1960s, when it was developed at Bell Labs in conjunction with MIT computer scientists and thus has a "head start" on most of the competition in the PC operating system market. Generally used for servers rather than desktop machines, UNIX is a very powerful but complex (and somewhat user-hostile) text-based operating system that runs many of the mail, Web, and other servers on the Internet.

UNIX grew out of the Multiplexed Information and Computing Service (Multics) mainframe system developed at MIT but was a completely new operating system designed to create a multiuser computing environment that would support a large number of users. It originally ran on the huge PDP timesharing machines in use at universities and government facilities in the 1960s and 1970s. The first versions of UNIX were written in assembler language, but later versions were written in the high-level C programming language. In the late 1970s, the popularity of UNIX began to spread beyond the academic world, and in the early days of the Internet, it ran on most of the VAX computers that were connected to the internetwork. In the 1980s, more versions of UNIX were developed, and its use spread throughout the business world.

Today there are still a large number of different versions of UNIX, including IBM's AIX, Sun Microsystems' Solaris, Hewlett-Packard's HP-UX, Berkeley's BSD, Santa Cruz Operations' SCO UNIX (which that company bought from Novell in 1995), and others. The X Window system was developed to add a graphical shell to UNIX and make it more user-friendly. It's not really a GUI but is instead a protocol that can be used to build a GUI, such as Common Desktop Environment (CDE). However, UNIX graphical interfaces tend to be somewhat clunky and ugly compared to Windows interfaces, and UNIX purists shun the GUI, preferring the higher-performance command-line environment.

In 1991, Finnish student Linus Torvalds wrote a UNIX-based operating system that he called Linux (mentioned briefly earlier in this chapter) and distributed free through Internet newsgroups. Linux caught on with programmers and then with users who were looking for an alternative to Microsoft Windows. Although Linux is often used to run servers (especially Web servers running the open source Apache Web server software), it is more suitable for the desktop than UNIX. Linux is a text-based operating system like UNIX, but when it became popular as a desktop operating system, developers soon created a variety of graphical shells that ran on top of it, much as Windows 3.*x* ran on MS-DOS. These shells included Kool Desktop Environment (KDE) and GNOME, which is part of the GNU project and is available as a free download from the GNOME Web site at www.gnome.org. You can see the KDE interface in Figure 4.8.

Figure 4.8 The KDE graphical interface makes Linux more user-friendly.

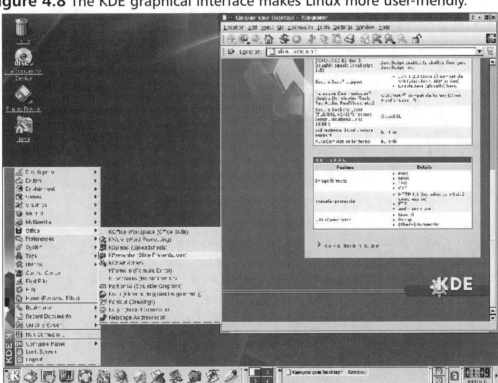

In 1994, Red Hat released a commercial version of Linux, which was followed by a release from Caldera in 1997 called OpenLinux. A large number of versions of Linux are available today. Some of the most popular are:

- Red Hat (www.redhat.com)

- Caldera (www.caldera.com)

- Debian (www.debian.org)

- SuSE (www.suse.com)

- Mandrake (www.linux-mandrake.com)

- Slackware (www.slackware.com)

- TurboLinux (www.turbolinux.com)

At least 70 distributions are available; you can find information and comparisons at the Linux Distrowatch Web site at www.distrowatch.com.

Other Operating Systems

Other operating systems in use on personal computer systems include:

- OS/2

- BeOS

- Macintosh operating systems

Operating System 2 (OS/2) began as a joint effort between IBM and Microsoft in the 1980s to replace DOS. The original OS/2 (version 1) was text-based but was a 16-bit operating system, unlike the then-current version of DOS (version 3.0), which was 8-bit. Version 2.0 included a graphical interface and was a true 32-bit operating system. OS/2 was designed to feature stability and multitasking capabilities that DOS didn't have. The OS/2 desktop is shown in Figure 4.9.

After Microsoft's Windows 3.0 started to become popular, Microsoft dropped its support for OS/2, although it based the Windows NT kernel on the OS/2 kernel. IBM was really a hardware company rather than a software company, so when Microsoft left the project, IBM contracted with Commodore and borrowed from the Amiga for OS/2's object-oriented GUI. Version 2.11 added support for symmetric multiprocessing and was able to run Windows 3.x programs as well as applications written for OS/2. In 1994, IBM released OS/2 Warp 3.0. It included built-in Internet support (the first consumer OS to do so), and its successor, OS/2 Warp Connect, supported all the major networking protocols: TCP/IP, IPX, and NetBIOS.

In 1996, "Merlin" (OS/2 4.0) was released, with a more attractive interface and support for OpenGL and the Java virtual machine. Unfortunately for IBM, by this time Windows had gained momentum and most applications were written for it. OS/2 was unable to run 32-bit Windows applications, a limitation that severely hurt its popularity. IBM stopped development on OS/2 and it is still stuck at version 4 as of this writing, although it has continued to be popular in certain industries such as banking and IBM continues to support it while also marketing OS/2 Warp Server for e-business.

Figure 4.9 OS/2 featured the Workplace Shell interface.

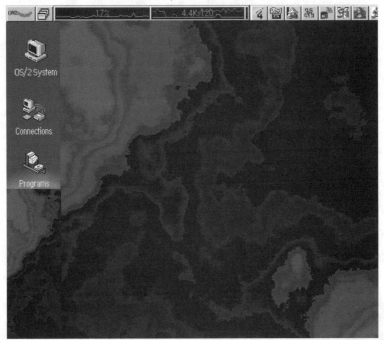

BeOS is a single-user operating system that has some similarities to UNIX, but it is not a UNIX clone (UNIX is a multiuser operating system). BeOS was designed for a specialized purpose: to serve as a platform for audio, video, and other "near real-time" applications. BeOS supports multithreading and multiprocessing. It was developed by two former Apple employees, and the first public version was released in 1995 for the PowerPC, then was ported to the Intel x86 platform in 1998. The current version supports TCP/IP networking and PPP dialup connections. The OS has also been used for Internet appliances (dedicated e-mail/Web machines that don't have the functionality of full fledged computers) and digital VCRs.

The Apple Macintosh computers differ from Intel-compatible PCs in many ways, one of which is the fact that they are proprietary; Apple makes both the hardware and the operating system software. Mac operating systems don't run on PCs, and PC operating systems don't run on Macs (although it is possible to use special *virtual machine* software to allow you to run a PC operating system in a window on top of your Mac OS).

The latest version of the Mac OS, called OS X, is a big departure from prior versions because it is based on a version of UNIX called Darwin. Macintosh OS X combines the power of underlying UNIX code with a beautiful, user-friendly GUI called Aqua. The Mac has always been popular with educational institutions and graphic designers, but OS X is gaining popularity among both traditional UNIX users and die-hard Windows fans. The Mac OS X interface is shown in Figure 4.10.

OS X features built-in support for writing CDs and DVDs and is easy to connect to a local area network and/or the Internet. Built-in support is included for accessing files on Windows PCs across the network, and software such as SAMBA is available to allow you to share your Mac files with networked Windows machines. With OS X, the Mac finally adds such advanced features as preemptive multitasking and protected memory and includes support for symmetric multiprocessing, USB, and FireWire (IEEE 1394). Apple is also marketing a server version, OS X Server, that supports clients running Mac, Windows, UNIX, and Linux. For more information about OS X, see the Apple Web site at www.apple.com/macosx.

Figure 4.10 Macintosh OS X features an attractive, usable interface on a UNIX OS.

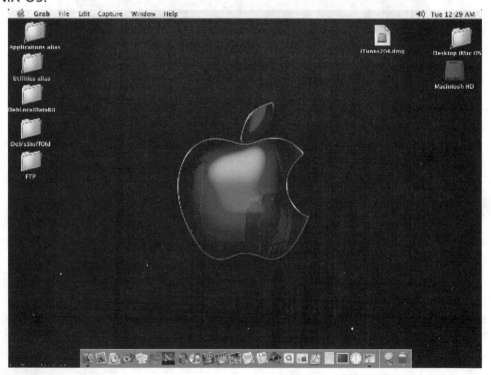

Understanding File Systems

An important factor related to the operating system used by the computer is the *file system,* which defines the structure for organizing and locating data on the disk. Data is stored in *clusters,* which are units measuring a specified size in bytes. A file can be stored across many clusters, but data from different files is not stored in the same cluster. This means that if, for example, a cluster is 12KB in size and a file is only 2KB, there will be 10KB of wasted space in that cluster. Handling of clusters and cluster sizes comprise a major difference between different file systems. Other differences include the maximum partition size supported, reliability, and security.

Most file systems store data in a hierarchical tree structure. Containers called *directories* or *folders* hold files (and can also hold subdirectories or subfolders), organized into groups for better management. The top level of the hierarchy is called the *root* or *root directory.* The file system is the entire directory structure, consisting of the root directory and all the subdirectories and files underneath it in the hierarchy.

Different operating systems use different file systems, and some operating systems support more than one file system. The most familiar are those used by the Microsoft operating systems:

- FAT12
- FAT16
- VFAT
- FAT32
- NTFS

In the following sections, we look at some of the characteristics of each file system, along with some less commonly encountered file systems used by non-Microsoft operating systems.

FAT12

FAT stands for *file allocation table;* the FAT file system was developed for use by the DOS operating systems. The first version of FAT was called FAT12 because its allocation tables used a 12-digit binary number (12 bits) for cluster information. FAT12 was useful for the very small hard disks that came with the original IBM PC (under 16MB in size). It is also used to format floppy diskettes.

FAT16

FAT16 was developed for disks larger than 16MB, and for a long time it was the standard file system for formatting hard disks. As you can probably guess, it uses 16-bit allocation table entries. FAT16 (often referred to as just *FAT*) is supported by all Microsoft operating systems, from MS-DOS to Windows XP. It is also supported by some non-Microsoft operating systems, including OS/2 and Linux. This support makes it the most universally compatible file system. However, it has many drawbacks, including:

- FAT16 doesn't scale well to large disks; because the cluster size increases as the disk partition size increases, a large disk (over about 2GB) formatted with FAT16 will have a lot of wasted space.

- FAT16 doesn't support file-level compression; the compression scheme used with FAT16, such as that implemented by DriveSpace, requires that the entire logical drive be compressed.

- FAT16 doesn't support file-level security (assignment of permissions to individual files and folders).

> **NOTE**
>
> You may read in some sources that FAT16 is limited to 2GB in size, but that's not really the case (although it does become inefficient at larger disk sizes). MS-DOS will not allow you to create a FAT16 partition larger than 2GB, but you *can* create larger FAT16 partitions (up to 4GB) in Windows NT/2000. These larger FAT16 partitions are not supported and recognized by MS-DOS or Windows 9x.

VFAT

Virtual FAT, or *VFAT*, is a file system driver that was introduced in Windows for Workgroups 3.11 and supported by Windows 95. Its advantages are that it operates in protected mode and provides the capability for using long file names with FAT16. VFAT is not a file system; rather, it is a program extension that handles filenames over the 8.3 limitation imposed by the original FAT16.

FAT32

FAT32 uses a 32-bit allocation table. It was first supported by the OSR 2 version of Windows 95 (95b) and was designed to improve on the functionality of FAT16 by adding such features as:

- More efficient use of space with large hard disks by using smaller cluster sizes.

- Support for larger partitions, up to 2 terabytes in size, in theory (Windows supports FAT32 partitions of up to 32GB)

- Greater reliability, due to the inclusion of a backup copy of important data structure information in the boot record

FAT32 also has its disadvantages, including the fact that it is incompatible with MS-DOS, Windows 3.*x*, Windows 95a, Windows NT, and some non–Microsoft operating systems (although FAT32 drivers are available from third-party vendors for Windows 95, NT, and even non–Microsoft operating systems such as Linux). Additionally, the overhead used by FAT32 can slow performance slightly.

NTFS

NTFS, Windows NT's native file system, was designed to be more robust and secure than other Microsoft file systems. It supports very large partition sizes (up to 16 exabytes, in theory) and allows you to create volumes that span two or more partitions. You can set access permissions at the file level to control who can read, change, or otherwise access a file. This applies to users accessing the file from the local machine as well as over the network and is in addition to network share permissions that are set at the folder/directory level. NTFS is more reliable because it supports a feature called *hot fixing,* a process by which the operating system detects a bad sector on the disk and automatically relocates the data stored on that sector to a good sector, then marks the bad sector so that it won't be used by the system. This process is done on the fly, without the awareness or intervention of the user or applications.

The compression scheme used by NTFS allows you to compress data on a file-by-file basis to save disk space and archive older files. This is much safer than the drive-level compression used by Windows 9x, in which the loss of the single compressed file that held the contents of the entire drive meant all data on that drive was lost.

The version of NTFS included in Windows 2000 and above (NTFS 5.0) supports file encryption. This feature is called Encrypting File System (EFS) and relies on public key cryptography and digital certificates. For more information about EFS, see the *Windows & .NET Magazine* at www.winntmag.com/Articles/Index.cfm?ArticleID=5387&Key=Internals. Note that NTFS 5.0 also supports *disk quotas,* which involve the administrator's capability to set limits on how much disk space can be used on a per-user, per-disk basis.

NOTE

Service Packs 4 and later for Windows NT 4.0 add support for NTFS 5.0 so that NT can access local drives formatted in NTFS 5.0. However, NT is not able to use all the functionality of NTFS 5.0 (for example, EFS encryption is not supported in NT).

Other File Systems

Other file systems you might encounter include:

- CDFS, the file system used to write data to CDs
- HPFS, the high-performance native file system of OS/2
- Ext2fs, VFS, and Journaling file systems, used by Linux
- Macintosh Hierarchical File System (HFS)
- Network file systems

Because the file system determines how data is stored on the disk, it is important to be familiar with the file system when you're performing data recovery. Table 4.3 shows at a glance which file systems are supported by various Microsoft operating systems (without adding third-party drivers).

Table 4.3 Microsoft operating system and file system correlation

Operating System	FAT12	FAT16	FAT32	NTFS
MS-DOS	X	X		
Windows 3.x	X	X		
Windows 95a	X	X		
Windows 95b	X	X	X	
Windows 98	X	X	X	
Windows ME	X	X	X	
Windows NT	X	X		X
Windows 2000	X	X	X	X
Windows XP/.NET	X	X	X	X

Summary

Cybercrime investigators need to be as intimately familiar with the internal workings of computers and the software that runs on them as homicide investigators must be with basic human pathology. That includes understanding the function of all the hardware components that go together to make up a computer and how these components interact with one another.

It would be difficult for an investigator to conduct a proper investigation in a foreign country where he or she does not speak the local language, because many clues might go unnoticed if the investigator cannot understand the information being collected. Likewise, a cybercrime investigator must have a basic understanding of the "language" used by the machines to process data and communicate with one another. Even though an investigator in the field might not be able to speak all human languages, it is helpful to at least be able to recognize what language written evidence is in, because this evidence might be significant and will certainly help the investigator find someone who can translate it. Similarly, even though a cybercrime investigator is not expected to be able to program in binary, it helps to recognize the significance of data that is in binary or hexadecimal format and when it can or can't be valuable as evidence.

Computers today run a variety of operating systems and file systems, and the investigator's job of locating evidence will be done differently depending on the system being used. A good cybercrime investigator is familiar with the most common operating systems and how their file systems organize the data on disk.

Although all this information might seem far too technical to the "non-geek" police professional—and could perhaps seem too obvious to the computer or networking professional—it is important that investigators who aspire to specialize in computer crimes and cybercrimes have a good grasp of how technical understanding can lead to understanding of cybercrime and cybercriminals. Now that you understand how computers work, in the next chapter we delve into how they communicate on a network.

Frequently Asked Questions

The following Frequently Asked Questions, answered by the authors of this book, are designed to both measure your understanding of the concepts presented in this chapter and to assist you with real-life implementation of these concepts. To have your questions about this chapter answered by the author, browse to **www.syngress.com/solutions** and click on the **"Ask the Author"** form.

Q: What is meant by terms such as *data transfer rate* and *seek time* in relation to hard disks?

A: These are ways to measure the performance of a hard disk. The *data transfer rate* refers to the number of bytes per second (bps) that the disk drive is able to transfer to the processor. This is usually measured for today's disks in megabytes per second, and rates between 5 and 40 are common. The higher this number, the better the disk performance. *Seek time* refers to the time interval between the time that the processor makes a request for a file from disk and the time at which the first byte of that file is received by the pro-cessor. This time is measured in milliseconds (typically between 7 and 20), and the lower this number, the better the performance.

Q: How does a CD-R drive write data on a CD?

A: CD-Recordable, or CD-R, discs, unlike regular read-only CDs, have a layer of dye (usually a greenish color) on the disk that is then covered with a reflective gold layer. Both of these thin layers sit on top of a rigid piece of plastic called the *substrate*. The CD-R drive has a *writing laser* that is more powerful than the reading laser in a regular CD-ROM drive. This more pow-erful laser heats the layer of dye from the bottom, going through the sub-strate. The heating process changes the transparency of the dye at that spot, creating a "bump" that is not reflective. This bump forms a readable mark that is then read by the CD drive as data. The same encoding scheme is used as for regular CDs; that's why a regular CD-ROM drive can read CD-R discs.

Q: How does virtual memory work?

A: When an operating system supports the use of virtual memory, it creates a file on the hard disk (called a *swap file* or a *page file*) in which it can "swap out" data between the RAM and the disk. The system detects which areas of the physical memory (RAM) haven't been used recently. Then it copies the data from that location in memory to the file on the hard disk. This means there will be more free space in RAM, which allows you to run additional applications or speeds the performance of applications that are currently running. When the data stored in the swap/page file is needed by the processor, it can be loaded from the hard disk back to RAM. The data is stored in units called *pages*. Using virtual memory can degrade performance if the system has to frequently swap the data in and out of RAM. This is because the hard disk is much slower than the RAM. Frequent swapping results in *disk thrashing*, which is usually a sign that you need to add more physical memory to the computer.

Resources

- Analog computers
  www.science.uva.nl/faculteit/museum/AnalogComputers.html

- Analog Computer Museum
  http://dcoward.best.vwh.net/analog/analog1.htm

- EETimes: *Analog Computer Trumps Turing Model*
  www.eetimes.com/story/OEG19981103S0017

- Overclocking information
  www.overclockers.com and www.overclockershideout.com

- PC Guide: *Hard Disk Drives*
  www.pcguide.com/ref/hdd/index.htm

- *How Hard Disks Work*
  www.howstuffworks.com/hard-disk.htm

- *How Floppy Disk Drives Work*
  http://howstuffworks.lycoszone.com/floppy-disk-drive.htm

- *How Flash Memory Works*
  http://howstuffworks.lycoszone.com/flash-memory.htm

- *How Removable Storage Works*
  http://howstuffworks.lycoszone.com/removable-storage.htm

- *How Operating Systems Work*
  http://howstuffworks.lycoszone.com/operating-system.htm

- GNU General Public License
  www.gnu.org/licenses/gpl.html#SEC1

- Open Source Initiative
  www.opensource.org

- Apple's Open Source Projects
  http://developer.apple.com/darwin/projects

- The FreeDOS Project
  www.freedos.org

- Windows 2000
  www.microsoft.com/windows2000

- Windows XP
  www.microsoft.com/windowsxp/home/default.asp

- Windows .NET Server
  www.microsoft.com/windows.netserver

- Linux DistroWatch
  www.distrowatch.com

Chapter 5

Understanding Networking Basics

Topics we'll investigate in this chapter:

- **Understanding How Computers Communicate on a Network**

- **Understanding the TCP/IP Protocols Used on the Internet**

- ☑ **Summary**

- ☑ **Frequently Asked Questions**

- ☑ **Resources**

201

Introduction

In Chapter 4, we discussed how computers—both the hardware and the software—accept, process, and store data. A decade ago, that might have been as far as we needed to go in our discussion. Many PCs, especially home computers, functioned as standalone systems. Today, however, the local machine is only the starting point for computer crime investigators. Now most computers—and by the very nature of cybercrime, all computers that are involved in this special type of offense—are connected to a network. That network might be a local area network, the global Internet, or both.

Network connectivity opens up new opportunities for criminals as well as for legitimate computer users. Understanding the more technically oriented cybercrimes, such as unauthorized access across the network (hacking)—and indeed, even determining whether or not a crime has occurred—can depend on an understanding of how networked computers communicate with one another.

Many hack attacks, which are designed to bring down a computer or network or to congest the system so that legitimate users are unable to get through, are based on exploiting the characteristics of the network protocols, typically the Transmission Control Protocol/Internet Protocol (TCP/IP) suite. To launch these attacks, a criminal must understand how TCP/IP works. Likewise, in order for an investigator to document how the attack was made and determine from where it might have been launched, the investigator must understand the workings of the TCP/IP protocols.

A burglary investigator who doesn't understand how door locks (both mechanical and electronic) work and how they can be picked might miss clues and overlook ways that a real-world intruder could have gained entry to a residence or business. Knowing this type of information could help to narrow down the burglar's identity. It is an important part of proving the case, because if you can show that the criminal used special skills or tools to get in (as opposed to finding the door unlocked and walking in), you usually create a stronger case in the minds of jury members. Forced entry indicates premeditation rather than a "spur of the moment" offense. Similarly, a cybercrime investigator who doesn't understand the process of gaining entry to a networked computer is likely to have a harder time interpreting the digital clues, tracking down the criminal, and building the case.

Even for crimes that are less technical in nature, the network gives criminals an infinite number of additional locations for storing files that provide evidence of the crime. Investigators must be aware of this fact or they could overlook crucial pieces of evidence. For example, a child pornographer might be careful to upload all his illegal graphics files to a location someplace geographically far away from his home computer, deleting the originals from his hard disk. Examination of the suspect's own computer might reveal nothing incriminating. However, network logs could show when and to where the transmissions were made, and sniffer software can capture the actual packets during transmission. The logs of FTP clients or other programs used to transfer the data could reveal the site to which uploads were made. An investigator who doesn't understand how data is sent across networks or who is not aware of the existence of log files or the significance of program settings would not even know how to begin looking for this evidence.

In this chapter, we pick up where Chapter 4 left off, continuing to discuss how computers work but now focusing on how they work on the network: sending and receiving data (at the physical level), implementing standardized networking models, and using industry-standard protocols. Once again, each section is summarized with an explanation of why the information matters to cybercrime investigators and how it can be used in the detection and prosecution of criminal offenses.

Understanding How Computers Communicate on a Network

The purpose of a network is to allow computers to share; that means sharing data, sharing application programs, sharing hardware peripherals such as printers, and even sharing a common authentication mechanism so that all the other sharing will occur more easily and more transparently to the user.

The earliest form of "networking" (when most computers were standalones) was called *sneakernet* because it involved physically transporting the data, software, or hardware being shared to the remote computer. In other words, if you wanted to share a data file or software program with someone using a different machine, you copied it to a floppy disk and trekked across the room or building (or, in some cases, used the postal service or private courier to deliver it across town or across the country). Sharing a printer could be even more inconvenient; you copied the file you wanted to print onto a floppy and take it to the lucky (or unlucky) user who had a printer attached to his or her computer. That user got to stop what he or she was doing and insert the floppy, bring up the document, and send it to the printer for you. Alternatively, you could transport the printer itself from one computer to another. Printers often resided on wheeled carts for that very purpose. No matter how you did it, sharing printers was awkward and time-consuming prior to the advent of local area networking. The alternative—providing a separate printer for each user—was often too expensive to be feasible.

It soon became obvious that there was a better way: connect the computers via cable so that data (including documents to be printed) could be sent from one computer to another without anyone having to make the physical journey. In fact, this was one of the most popular reasons for companies to implement local networks in the early days of networking. Networking hardware and software have grown more sophisticated over the years, and now we can do much more than send files. Network applications allow us to communicate quickly and easily via e-mail, chat, or instant messaging, make information available to other network users on Web sites, run applications on remote servers from our own desktops via terminal services, and much more.

Sending Bits and Bytes Across a Network

Because all data processed by computers is ultimately reduced to strings of 0s and 1s, all network communication involves transmitting and receiving this binary data (bits and bytes). This binary information can be sent across copper-based cabling as electrical impulses, across optical cabling as pulses of light, or through the air as radio or microwave signals, infrared, or laser pulses. Regardless of the medium, the signals represent the 0s and 1s that comprise all computer data. The process of turning the 0s and 1s into these energy pulses is called *signal encoding* or *signal modulation*.

There are a number of different encoding methods that specify exactly how the binary 0s and 1s are to be represented electrically. For example, the Manchester encoding scheme dictates that a binary 1 is represented by low voltage for the first half of the bit and high voltage for the second half. A 0 is represented by the opposite signal; the first half is high voltage and the second is low voltage. This system is represented graphically in Figure 5.1.

As you can see, each bit consists of a voltage change, either from low to high (representing a 1) or from high to low (representing a 0). The transition, called the *clock transition,* is used by the network adapter receiving the signal to determine the beginning and end of each bit. This encoding method is used for 10BaseT Ethernet networks—networks that send signals over unshielded twisted pair (UTP) cabling at the rate of 10Mbps. The encoding schemes used for other network architectures (such as Fast Ethernet, also called 100BaseX) are different. This is because Manchester encoding increases the frequency at which the signal is transmitted and is difficult or impossible to implement at the 100Mbps transmission rate of Fast Ethernet.

Figure 5.1 The Manchester encoding scheme is one method of representing binary data electrically.

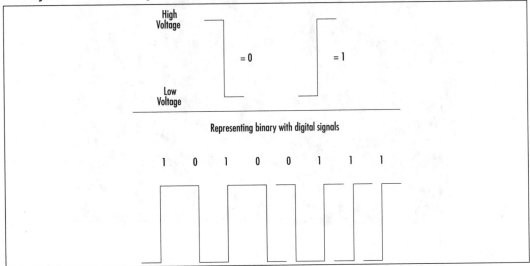

NOTE

If there is interference from an outside source (a motor, radio transmission, or other source that creates a strong electromagnetic field), the signal can be disrupted. This could destroy some of the bits, resulting in a loss of data.

Digital and Analog Signaling Methods

The type of signaling that best represents binary information, in which there are two possible states (off or on) that represent two specific values (0 or 1), is called *discrete state signaling*. *Digital signals* are discrete state, whereas *analog signals* are not. Analog signals change state gradually, on a continuum, rather than going directly and instantaneously from one discrete state to another. Analog signals can be drawn as waveforms, as shown in Figure 5.2.

If an ordinary light switch that has two positions—on and off—represents digital signaling, then a "dimmer" switch, which allows you to use a knob or slider to move through stages of "on" before you reach "off," represents how analog signals work. Hundreds of devices in our everyday world illustrate the difference between digital and analog signals—for example:

Figure 5.2 Analog signals are continually changing waves of energy.

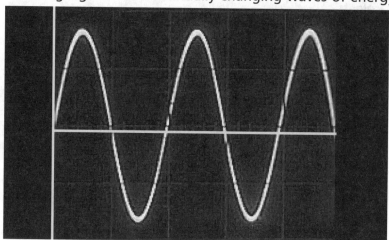

- Analog clocks with a hand that sweeps continuously through the time markings and digital clocks that instantly change from one minute to the next

- Analog radio tuners with a dial that lets you tune gradually through the frequencies and digital tuners that allow you to punch in the exact frequency you want

- Analog thermometers in which mercury rises gradually and digital thermometers that display a specific temperature

Analog signals are obviously more complex than digital signals. Measurement of analog signals involves measuring the following three characteristics: amplitude, frequency, and phase. *Amplitude* is the signal strength; in the illustration, the height of the wave represents its amplitude. *Frequency* refers to the amount of time it takes for a wave to complete a cycle. Frequency is denoted by the number of cycles per second, called *hertz*. *Phase* measures the state of one wave relative to another; this is measured in *degrees*.

We live in a world that can be thought of as mostly analog in nature. Even though time, radio frequencies, and temperature can be represented digitally, we know that in reality there are "in between" states that aren't being represented by digital devices. However, for most purposes, digital representation is good enough or even preferable. It is simpler than analog, and it's usually less vulnerable to interference. A continuous waveform can be disrupted by small distortions that won't affect the discrete states of digital signals.

NOTE

Although digital signals are less vulnerable to interference than analog signals, the opposite is true when it comes to *attenuation,* which is the loss of signal strength over distance. Analog signals are generally able to go further than digital ones without becoming so weak that the transmission is unreliable.

Other advantages of digital transmissions over analog include:

- **Performance** Digital connections usually offer faster performance.

- **Cost effectiveness** It is generally less expensive to manufacture digital devices than their analog counterparts.

- **Reliability** Due to its simplicity, digital signals are generally more reliable.

- **Security** It is generally easier to secure digital transmissions.

On the other hand, analog signals are generally easier to multiplex. *Multiplexing* refers to using a single link to send multiple streams, or *channels,* of information. Multiplexing is how cable TV works, transmitting dozens or even hundreds of different channels of programming over one cable.

How Multiplexing Works

Signals can be multiplexed in several different ways. For example, different streams of information can be sent on separate frequencies. This is called *frequency division multiplexing* (FDM) and is the typical method for multiplexing analog signals. Each channel is transmitted at a different frequency but on the same line. Special equipment called a *multiplexer/demultiplexer* is required at both the sending and receiving end of the transmission so that the frequency channels can be separated for use when they reach the destination.

Another multiplexing method is called *time division multiplexing,* or TDM. This method can be used for multiplexing digital signals. Instead of using different frequencies, TDM breaks each of the signals into small pieces called *segments,* and these are transmitted over the link one after the other. At the other end, the segments that make up each individual signal stream are put back together. This system is similar in some ways to the *time slicing* used by computer processors to give the appearance of working on multiple tasks simultaneously.

If the transmission medium is optical cable, another method of multiplexing, called *dense wavelength division multiplexing (DWDM),* can be used. Because light can be separated into different wavelengths, separate signals can be transmitted using separate wavelengths.

NOTE

This discussion of multiplexing is a highly simplified overview of a complex subject. If you are interested in more technical details, refer to the following resources:

- Bell Labs: *What Does Multiplexing Do for Communications?* www.bell-labs.com/technology/multiplex
- Explanation of FDM: www.cs.williams.edu/~cs105/f01/text/ch3/DigitalTrans_13.html
- Explanation of TDM: www.cs.williams.edu/~cs105/f01/text/ch3/DigitalTrans_9.html
- Tutorial on DWDM by the International Engineering Consortium: www.iec.org/online/tutorials/dwdm

---

Directional Factors

Depending on the signaling method, signals can travel in one direction only (unidirectional) or in both directions (bidirectional). Bidirectional signals can either travel in both directions sequentially or in both directions simultaneously. These three different methods of signal travel are identified as follows:

- **Simplex transmissions** These are unidirectional transmissions that work like a one-way street; travel is permitted in only one direction. Early cable TV systems used this type of transmission because the information (TV programming) was being delivered to the customer; there was no need for the customer to send return transmissions. Most cable companies have upgraded their infrastructures to support two-way signaling, which is necessary for cable Internet services and for entertainment services that require the customer to communicate back to the cable company (such as Pay-Per-View). Other cable companies have retained their one-way signaling schemes and use the phone lines for customers' upstream transmissions. Another example of one-way transmission is a public address system. Amplified voice messages are broadcast, but there is no mechanism for receiving return messages.

- **Half-duplex transmissions** In these transmissions, signal transmission is bidirectional, but the signal can travel only one way at a time. This is similar to a two-way road over a bridge that is so narrow that only one vehicle can fit on it at a time. A car coming in the opposite direction must wait to enter the bridge until the oncoming vehicle has exited it. Half-duplex signals are often used for two-way radio communications; law enforcement officers are familiar with this type of transmission because this is the way most police radios operate. When you hold the Transmit button down, you can talk, but you can't hear anything being said on the other end of the transmission. The other party must wait until you're finished transmitting before he or she can reply. If you both try to transmit at once, you'll "step on" each others' signals and no transmission will get through.

- **Full-duplex transmissions** Signals are transmitted both ways and can travel across the air or cable simultaneously. This is akin to a two-lane, two-way road over a bridge, where vehicles can pass one another going in opposite directions. Regular phone lines work this way; when you're having a telephone conversation with someone else, you can both talk at the same time, and while you're talking you're able to hear (although you might not be able to understand) what the other person is saying.

If we apply these transmission methods to computer networking, it should be obvious that full duplex provides faster performance than the other methods. Data can be sent and received simultaneously. Network cards and modems are capable of transmitting in either half-duplex or full-duplex modes. The line must also support full-duplex transmission. Digital connections require two separate wire pairs: one for sending and one for receiving. Analog transmissions can divide the sending and receiving signals into two separate frequencies.

Timing Factors

When a network adapter or other network device receives an incoming signal, it needs *timing information* in order to interpret the signals correctly. This is referred to as *synchronizing the bits*. There are two basic ways to accomplish this goal, and the transmission method is said to be either *synchronous* or *asynchronous,* depending on which method is used. The difference is as follows:

- **Asynchronous** A *start bit* is included at the beginning of each message; this bit is used as a signal for the receiving device to synchronize its clock with that of the sending device.

- **Synchronous** A timing mechanism built into the transmission synchronizes the clocks of the sending and receiving devices.

Signal Interference

Network signals can be disrupted by outside interference, which can cause loss or garbling of data. We mentioned earlier that digital signals are less vulnerable to interference; the type of media used to transmit the signals (copper cable, optical cable, or airwaves) also affects vulnerability to interference. Two common types of interference you'll hear about are:

- **Electromagnetic interference (EMI)** Electromagnetic energy (EM) is made up of alternating waves of electric and magnetic fields. The electromagnetic spectrum ranges from X-rays and gamma rays at the short end through light waves near the middle to radio waves at the long end. The U.S. Navy uses signals with very long wavelengths, called *extra-long frequency (ELF),* for communicating with submarines. Microwaves have short wavelengths of approximately a millimeter. All types of electronic equipment can generate EMI, or unwanted electromagnetic signals. When EMI interferes with audio transmissions (such as telephone conversations), it is often called *noise.* When it interferes with data transmissions, it can cause loss of or changes to the data.

- **Radio frequency interference (RFI)** Radio frequencies are the wavelengths between about 10kHz and 100GHz. RFI refers to the reception of unwanted radio signals and is really a subset of EMI. Wireless networking uses radio frequencies to send and receive network signals. If nearby radio transmitters use the same (or close) frequencies to broadcast, this can interfere with the network's data transmissions. Computer monitors, processors, and other devices also generate signals on radio frequencies and can be sources of interference. RFI can originate from many sources.

Electromagnetic energy is capable of different effects, depending on the frequency. EM at the lowest end (X-rays) can ionize atoms because their wavelengths are so tiny. Microwaves, a bit further up the spectrum, are capable of making water molecules vibrate, which heats them (this is how a microwave oven works). Metal objects (for example, antennae) generate currents when struck by EM; this signal can then be passed to circuits that are able to decode the signal, such as a radio or television receiver. EM waves are generated constantly, so EMI can be a major source of transmission disruption.

On the Scene...

Preparing for the EMP

A sudden huge burst of EM is called an *electromagnetic pulse,* or EMP. An EMP can be produced by a nuclear explosion; gamma rays are produced that interact with the air molecules to produce a very strong electric field followed by a conduction current that flows in the opposite direction. An EMP can destroy or damage electronic equipment, power generators, metal pipes and wiring, and anything else that is vulnerable to electric voltage surges. Semiconductor chips—which are embedded in everything from elevators to airplanes and control many of the machines on which our modern society, including our military system, depends—are especially susceptible to EMP. The EM energy heats up the chip and can melt it completely.

Metallic shielding can be used to "harden" vulnerable devices against the possibility of EMP. However, the process is very expensive, and in some cases it decreases the functionality of the equipment. Most discussions of nuclear detonation have centered on the effect of radiation on organic life, but the effects of an accompanying EMP on electronic devices could create a different type of devastation, for which we might not be prepared.

For more information about the threat of EMP, see the transcript of testimony before the House of Representatives' Committee on National Security in 1997, *Threat Posed by Electromagnetic Pulse to U.S. Military Systems and Civilian Infrastructure,* on the Web at http://commdocs .house.gov/committees/security/has197010.000/has197010_1.HTM.

Packets, Segments, Datagrams, and Frames

Signals represent individual bits, and those bits are often grouped together in bytes for convenience, but computers send data across the network in larger units: packets, segments, datagrams, or frames. A *packet* is a generic term, generally defined as a "chunk" of data of a size that is convenient for transmitting. Rather than send an entire, large file as one long stream of bits, the file is divided into blocks, and each of these blocks is transmitted individually. This system allows for more efficient network communications because one computer doesn't "hog" the network bandwidth while sending a large amount of data. On an internetwork, where there are multiple routes from a particular sender to a particular destination, this system also allows the separate blocks of data to take different routes.

Most networks, including the Internet, run on the TCP/IP protocols. At the transport level, a unit of data is called a *segment* when TCP is the transport layer protocol. To further confuse an already confusing issue, it's called a *user datagram* when User Datagram Protocol (UDP) is used. One step down, at the network (IP) level, the chunks of data that are routed across the network are called *datagrams*. When we move down to the data link level (at which Ethernet and other link layer protocols operate), the unit of data we work with is called a *frame*.

The Internet uses *packet-switching technology* to most effectively move large amounts of data being transmitted by multiple computers along the best pathways toward their destinations. Each packet travels independently; when all the packets that make up a communication arrive at the destination computer, they are reassembled in proper order using information contained in their *headers*. A packet can be thought of as an electronic envelope that contains the data as well as addressing and other relevant information (such as sequencing and checksum information).

Access Control Methods

When signals are transmitted on a network, there must be some mechanism for "directing traffic"—that is, a way to ensure that when multiple computers are sending signals, all the data packets make it safely to their destinations. This is called the *access control method*.

The popular access control methods are grouped in three categories: contention methods, token passing, and polling methods. Let's take a brief look at each:

- **Contention methods** These include Carrier Sense Multiple Access Collision Detection (CSMA/CD), used in Ethernet networks, and Carrier Sense Multiple Access Collision Avoidance (CSMA/CA), used in Appletalk networks. In both cases, computers that want to transmit data on the network must compete, or *contend*, for the use of the wire or other media. If two stations attempt to send at the same time, a collision occurs. CSMA/CD and CSMA/CA differ in their ways of addressing this collision problem; with the former, data collisions are detected and the data is sent again after a random amount of time. With the latter, an "intent to transmit" message is put out as a "feeler" before the computer transmits the actual data.

- **Token-passing methods** These eliminate the possibility of collision by using a circulating signal called a *token* to determine which computer can transmit. A computer on a token-passing network is more "polite";

rather than blurting out its transmission whenever it has something to say, it waits patiently for its turn (when the token gets around to it) and sends data only when it "has the floor."

- **Polling methods** These are similar in some ways to token passing, except that instead of the group of computers policing itself by passing around a token, a central unit acts as a "chairperson," asking members of the "committee" in turn whether they have something to say. Since the computers follow these "rules of parliamentary procedure," data transmission proceeds in an orderly fashion, and again, there is no danger of data collision.

Network Types and Topologies

Networks can be categorized in many ways. For example, networks are classified according to their physical *scope* (the size of the area that a network spans geographically) as follows:

- **Local area network (LAN)** Confined to one geographic area, such as a single building or several buildings in close proximity.

- **Wide area network (WAN)** Connects locations in widely dispersed areas, using technology such as regular telephone lines, dedicated leased lines, or satellite.

- **Metropolitan area network (MAN)** Covers an area about the size of a typical city.

Different media, protocols, and technologies are used in these networks, depending on which of these three categories a network fits into.

Another important issue is the layout, or topology, of the network. The term *topology* refers to whether the cables are arranged in a line going directly from computer to computer (a bus), in a circle going from computer to computer with the last connecting back to the first (a ring), or in a spoke-like fashion with each connecting directly to a central hub (a star). A fourth topology, the *mesh*, is created when every computer is connected to every other computer, creating redundant data pathways and high fault tolerance, at the cost of increasing complexity as the network grows.

Wireless communications can use a *cellular topology*, such as is widely used for wireless telephone networks. In this case, an area is divided into slightly overlapping cells, representing connection points.

The physical layout of a network influences other factors, such as the media access method (and thus the cable type) that is used. All the physical layer factors (cable type, access method, topology, and so on), considered together, define the *architecture* of the network. Popular network architectures include Ethernet, ARCnet, Token Ring, and AppleTalk.

You can classify networks based on their architecture—the standards and specifications for media type, physical and logical topology, access method, distance limitations, packet sizes, and headers and other criteria. The most popular architectures are:

- **Ethernet** Developed in the 1960s and based on the CSMA/CD access method, with specifications created by Digital, Intel, and Xerox (governed by the IEEE 802.3 standards).

- **Token Ring** Developed by IBM and based on the token-passing access method (governed by the IEEE 802.5 standards).

Ethernet networks can be divided into subcategories, depending on the type of cabling used, the topology, and the transfer speed supported, as follows:

- **10Base5 Ethernet** Uses thick coax cable and a bus topology and transfers data at 10Mbps. Sometimes called "standard" Ethernet, although it is less common than other types today.

- **10Base2 Ethernet** Uses thin coax cable and a bus topology and transfers data at 10Mbps.

- **10BaseT Ethernet** Uses UTP cable and a star topology and transfers data at 10Mbps.

- **100BaseT** Similar to 10BaseT but transfers data at 100Mbps. Sometimes called *Fast Ethernet*.

- **1000BaseT** Similar to 10BaseT but transfers data at 1000Mbps (1Gbps). Sometimes called *Gigabit Ethernet*.

NOTE

There are other Ethernet subarchitectures that use different media or have slightly different specifications. For example, 100BaseFL uses fiber optic cabling.

Why This Matters to the Investigator

Understanding how binary data is translated into electrical or optical signals helps investigators understand how those signals can be captured off the cable or airwaves and, in some cases, translated back to their data form. This is a most insidious form of "breaking and entering" the network, because it doesn't leave behind the same number or type of clues that might be present when a criminal uses higher-level methods to steal data. Being able to identify the type of network with which you're working gives you a head start on understanding how the data is packaged and transmitted and what the particular vulnerabilities are at the physical level.

In the next sections, you will learn about specific media types and how some are more susceptible to unauthorized interception than others. Putting that information together with a good grasp of signaling theory will help you recognize what is and isn't possible for technically savvy cybercriminals to accomplish when they're determined to break into a network.

Understanding Networking Models and Standards

A *network protocol* is a set of rules computers use to communicate. Protocols had to be developed so that two computers attempting to transfer data back and forth would be able to "understand" one another.

The first networking protocols were *proprietary*—that is, each vendor of networking products developed its own set of rules. Computers using one particular product would be able to communicate with each other, but they could not communicate with computers that were using a networking product from a different vendor. This situation had the effect of locking a business into a particular set of equipment from a particular vendor—in other words, a company was limited to buying the products of a specific vendor if its systems were all to be able to communicate with one another.

The solution to this problem was the development of protocols based on *open standards*. The U.S. Department of Defense (DoD) developed the original networking model on which TCP/IP is based. Later, the International Organization for Standardization (ISO) refined and expanded on this model, creating the *Open System Interconnection,* or *OSI, model*. These standards were published so that they would be available to any vendor that wanted to create products that adhered to them. As a result, consumers are no longer forced to buy all products from one vendor, and the advantage to the vendor is that its products are more widely compatible and thus can be used in networks that also use a different vendor's products.

A model provides an easy-to-understand description of a networking architecture and serves as the framework for standards. As we look at each of the popular networking models, you'll see that all use layers to represent areas of functionality. In OSI's terms, each layered specification uses the services of the layer below it to build an enriched service. The layered approach provides a logical division of responsibility, where each layer handles prescribed functions.

The OSI Networking Model

Although the DoD model was developed first, we start by looking at the OSI model, because it has become the common reference point for discussion of network protocols and connection devices. The OSI model is used as a broad guideline for describing the network communications process. Not all protocol implementations map directly to the OSI model, but it serves as a good starting point for gaining an understanding of how data is transferred across a network.

The Seven Layers of OSI

The OSI model consists of seven layers. The number 7 carries many historical connotations; it is thought by some to signify perfect balance or even divinity. Whether or not this was a factor when the OSI model's designers decided how to break down the functional layers, it's safe to say that within the technical community, the Seven Layers of the OSI model are at least as legendary as the Seven Deadly Sins and the Seven Wonders of the World.

The data is passed from one layer to the next layer below it at the sending computer, until the physical layer finally puts the data out onto the network cable. At the receiving end, the data travels back up the stack in reverse order. Although the data travels down the layers on one side of the transmission and up the layers on the other, the logical communication link is between each layer and its matching counterpart, as shown in Figure 5.3.

Here's how the system works: as the data goes down through the layers, it is *encapsulated*, or enclosed within a larger unit, as each layer adds its own header information. When the encapsulated data reaches the receiving computer, the process occurs in reverse; the information is passed upward through each layer, and as it travels, the encapsulation information is stripped off, one layer at a time. The information added by the network layer, for example, is read and processed by the network layer on the receiving side. After processing, each layer removes the header information that was added by its corresponding layer on the sending side.

When the application layer finally presents the incoming data to the user application at the receiving computer, the data is once again in approximately the same form it was in when sent by the user application at the originating machine. (The form is identical only if the computers, operating systems, applications, and configuration settings used by sender and recipient are identical.) Figure 5.4 illustrates how the header information is added to the data as it progresses down through the layers.

Figure 5.3 The OSI networking model uses seven layers to represent the communication process.

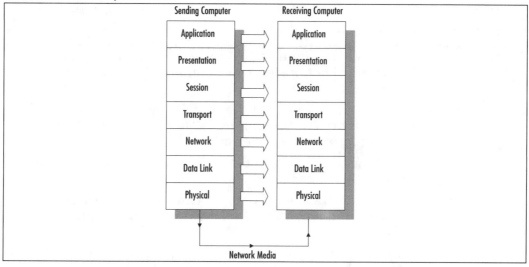

Figure 5.4 Protocols at each layer (except the physical layer) add header information to the data.

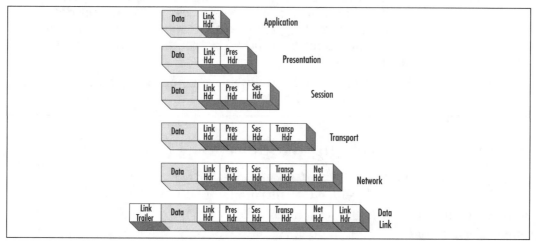

Many books teach the OSI layers "upside down"—that is, starting with the bottom layer. In fact, the physical layer is often referred to as Layer 1, the data link layer as Layer 2, and so on. Other descriptions start (seemingly logically) at the topmost layer. The way you look at it depends not on which hemisphere you live in but on whether you're addressing the communication process from the viewpoint of the sending or the receiving computer.

Table 5.1 shows the function of each of the seven layers, from the "top down," but retaining the traditional numbering scheme.

Table 5.1 Each layer of the OSI model prescribes a specific set of functions.

Layer Number/ Layer Name	Function
7 Application	Supports application and end-user processes; provides services for file transfer, e-mail, and other network software services.
6 Presentation	Deals with differences in the way data is represented (compression, encryption), translating from application to network format or vice versa.
5 Session	Establishes, manages, and terminates connections between applications at each end.
4 Transport	Provides for transfer of data between hosts; handles acknowledgment, error checking, and recovery and flow control.
3 Network	Handles routing and switching using logical addresses (IP addresses) by creating virtual circuits. Responsible for congestion control and packet sequencing.
2 Data link	Divided into two sublayers: media access control (MAC), which handles how computers access and transmit data on the network, and logical link control (LLC), which handles frame synchronization, flow control, and error checking at the link level.
1 Physical	Interacts with the hardware to provide the actual stream of bits as signals at the electrical and mechanical levels.

The DoD Networking Model

When the DoD developed the TCP/IP protocol stack for ARPANet, the OSI model had not yet been developed, so the model used was a slightly different, somewhat simpler model. It is sometimes called the TCP/IP model, but it's more often referred to as the DOD model. It consists of only four layers, compared with the OSI model's seven layers. The DoD model layers can be roughly mapped to those of the OSI model, as shown in Figure 5.5.

The various protocols in the TCP/IP suite fit nicely into the layers of the DOD model. Remember that the DOD model was designed in the 1970s; the OSI model came along a decade later, with the goal of more specifically defining the layers of functionality for the network components.

Figure 5.5 The four layers of the DoD model map roughly to the seven OSI layers.

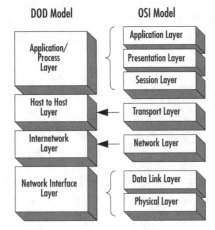

The Application/Process Layer

The top layer of the DOD model encompasses all three OSI upper layers: application, presentation, and session. Thus when an article or book refers to TCP/IP, you may read that encryption of data or checkpointing and dialog control take place at the application layer. Remember that this does *not* mean the OSI application layer and you'll avoid confusion.

The Host-to-Host (Transport) Layer

The host-to-host layer is sometimes labeled the transport layer, even on four-layer DoD diagrams, and it maps to the transport layer on the OSI model. TCP, UDP, and DNS operate here.

The Internetworking Layer

The internetworking layer corresponds closely to the OSI network layer. IP, Internet Control Message Protocol (ICMP), and Address Resolution Protocol (ARP) function at this layer. As we discussed earlier, IP deals with routing based on logical IP addresses. ARP translates logical addresses to MAC addresses. This translation is necessary because the lower layers can process only the MAC addresses.

The Network Interface Layer

The network interface layer maps to OSI's data link and physical layers. The TCP/IP suite itself has no protocols that operate at these lower layers but uses the standard Ethernet and Token Ring data link and physical layer protocols.

The Physical/Data Link Layer Standards

The Institute of Electrical and Electronics Engineers (IEEE), like the ISO, develops standards. The 802 Project was named after the year and month that the original committee met, February 1980. The IEEE 802 specifications address various physical and data link layer issues. Those most pertinent for the average network administrator are:

- **802.2** Establishes standards for the implementation of the LLC sublayer of the data link layer.

- **802.3** Sets specifications for an Ethernet network using CSMA/CD, a linear or star bus topology, and baseband transmission.

- **802.5** This specification sets standards for a token-passing network using a physical star/logical ring topology such as Token Ring.

- **802.7** Establishes criteria for networks using broadband transmission.

- **802.8** Sets specifications for using fiber optic as a network medium.

- **802.11** Establishes standards for wireless networking.

Why This Matters to the Investigator

The OSI and DoD networking models form the basis of understanding how network communications are prepared for transmission and how the signals that go across the media are processed when they reach the destination.

Networking professionals are taught to troubleshoot communications problems "from the ground up," starting with the physical layer and moving up through the models. Investigators are also troubleshooters of a sort, and the same problem-solving methods are appropriate when investigating cybercrimes that rely on technical implementation, such as unauthorized access or network attacks. Understanding header information can be crucial in tracking down the source of an attack, and the first step in that understanding is awareness of how, when, and where that information is added to the data packet.

Understanding Network Hardware

Just as you need a working knowledge of the hardware that makes up a PC to understand how a computer works, you need to be familiar with the hardware that enables network communication in order to understand how that communication process works. Networks range from very small (two directly linked computers) to very large (wide area internetworks that rely on complex hardware devices to link entire local networks in distant locations). Thus, the number and type of network hardware devices on a network will vary. However, all computer networking begins with an *interface* connecting each networked computer to the network.

The Role of the NIC

The *network interface card (NIC)* is the hardware device most essential to establishing communication between computers. Although there are ways to connect computers without a NIC (by modem over phone lines or via a serial "null modem" cable, for instance), in most cases where there is a network, there is a NIC (or, more accurately, at least one NIC for each participating computer).

The NIC is responsible for preparing the data to be sent over the network media. Exactly how that preparation is done depends on the medium being used. A Token Ring NIC is different from an Ethernet NIC, for example; it logically would have to be, since they use different access methods. And even though 10Base2, 10Base5 and 10BaseT Ethernet networks all use CSMA/CD as their access method, they use different cable and connector types, although it is possible to get a "combo" card that has connectors for all three.

The NIC must match the bus type for which you have an open slot in the computer, it must be of the correct media access type, it must have the correct connector for the cable your network uses, and it must be rated to transfer data at the proper speed. (Ethernet normally transmits at either 10Mbps or 100Mbps, and Token Ring runs at 4Mbps or 16Mbps.)

The Role of the Network Media

The *network media* are the cable or wireless technologies on which the signal is sent. Cable types include thin and thick coaxial cable (similar to but not the same as cable TV media), twisted-pair cable (such as is used for modern telephone lines, available in both shielded and unshielded types), or fiber optic cable, which sends pulses of light through thin strands of glass or plastic for fast, reliable communication but is expensive and difficult to work with. Wireless media include radio waves, laser, infrared, and microwave.

Data can be captured by unauthorized people directly from the media, by "tapping into" the cable and using a protocol analyzer to open packets and view the data inside. Copper cables are especially easy to compromise in this way, but data can also be intercepted on fiber optic cabling using a device called an *optical splitter*. Wireless transmissions are also easy to intercept; the practice of "war driving" is popular with hackers, who set up laptop systems with wireless network cards and then drive around looking for open wireless networks to connect to. Because many businesses leave the default settings on their wireless access points and don't elect to use wireless encryption protocols, their networks are wide open to anyone with a portable computer, a wireless NIC, and a small amount of technical knowledge. (Wireless security is addressed in detail in Chapter 8, "Implementing System Security.")

On the Scene…

When the Medium Is the Phone Line

Remote access networking uses the phone lines as the network medium and a *modem* (a device that modulates and demodulates signals to convert them from the computer's digital format to the public telephone system's analog format and back again) in place of a NIC. To establish a dialup connection to a remote computer, *link protocols* such as Point-to-Point Protocol (PPP) or Serial Line Internet Protocol (SLIP) are used. Then a regular network/transport protocol stack such as TCP/IP is used to communicate with the remote computer and other computers on its local network. This is the way you connect to your ISP's remote server and, through it, to the ISP's connection to the Internet. Once connected to the remote network, you can log on using the same user account and password that you use when logging on at the site, and you can do everything (if given the proper access permissions) that you could do from a machine physically cabled to the remote network. The only difference is speed; the phone lines are much slower than even the slowest LAN connections.

Another type of remote access involves creation of a *virtual private network (VPN)*, which allows you to "tunnel" through the Internet using special tunneling protocols, such as:

Continued

Point-to-Point Tunneling Protocol (PPTP)

The Layer 2 Tunneling Protocol (L2TP)

Layer 2 Forwarding (L2F)

IP Security Protocol (IPSec)

These protocols allow for a private (encrypted) connection to a remote computer when both are connected to the Internet, thus allowing for private communications through a public infrastructure (and saving the cost of long distance if the remote server is geographically distant). For more information about VPN, see the tutorial at www.wkmn.com/newsite/vpn.html or the VPN overview at www.intranetjournal.com/foundation/vpn-1.shtml.

The Roles of Network Connectivity Devices

Network connectivity devices do exactly what the name implies: They connect two or more segments of cable. Complex connectivity devices can serve two seemingly opposite purposes: They are used to divide large networks into smaller parts (called *subnets* or *segments*, depending on the device type), and they are used to combine small networks into a larger network called an *internetwork* or *internet*. Less complex connectivity devices do neither; they are used merely as connection points for the computers on a network (or network segment) or to amplify the signals of networked computers, which extends the distance over which transmissions can be sent. They can also:

- Connect network segments that use different media types (for instance, thin coax and UTP)
- Segment the network to reduce traffic without dividing the network into separate IP subnets

We look briefly at some of these devices in the following subsections.

Repeaters and Hubs

Hubs and *repeaters* are connection devices. We discuss them together because, in many cases, they are the same thing. In fact, you will hear hubs referred to as *multiport repeaters*. Repeaters connect two network segments (usually thin or thick coax) and boost the signal so the distance of the cabling can be extended past the normal limits at which attenuation, or weakening, interferes with the reliable transmission of the data.

A repeater is used to extend the usable length of a given type of cable. For instance, a 10Base5 Ethernet network, using thick coax cable, has a maximum cable segment length of 500 meters, or 1640 feet. At that distance, *attenuation* (signal loss due to distance) begins to take place. But when you place a repeater at the end of the cable and attach another length to the repeater's second port, the signal is boosted and the data can travel further without damage or loss, as shown in Figure 5.6.

Figure 5.6 Repeaters address the problem of attenuation (signal loss due to distance).

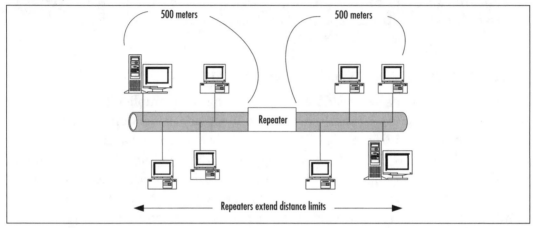

NOTE

Repeaters are not very "smart" devices. They simply boost whatever signal they receive, without distinguishing between data and noise, and pass the signal on. They also aren't very "polite." They don't follow the usual CSMA/CD process that NICs use, listening for traffic on the network before transmitting. A repeater just goes ahead and transmits, even if another node is in the middle of a transmission. This situation, of course, results in a data collision, which means data must be resent and network performance is negatively impacted. Also note that repeaters do not logically segment or subnet the network and do no filtering of traffic. You cannot reduce the traffic load or increase available network bandwidth by using repeaters; you can only amplify the signal and extend the maximum length of the cable.

On the Scene...

The Difference Between Repeaters and Amplifiers

A repeater boosts the signal traveling across an Ethernet cable in much the same way that an amplifier boosts the signal input from an old radio tuner. The difference between a repeater and an amplifier lies not in what they do but in the kind of signals they do it to.

Amplifiers boost analog signals (such as those used in the public telephone network or in older home stereo systems); repeaters boost the digital signals used in most computer communications.

Hubs are different from basic repeaters in that the repeater generally has only two ports, whereas the hub can have many more (typically from 5 to 64 or more). Hubs can also be connected to one another and stacked, providing even more ports. Hubs are generally used with Ethernet twisted-pair cable, and most modern hubs are repeaters with multiple ports; they also strengthen the signal before passing it back to the computers attached to it. Hubs can be categorized as follows:

- **Passive hubs** These hubs serve as connection points only; they do not boost the signal. Passive hubs do not require electricity and thus don't use a power cord as active hubs do.

- **Active hubs** These hubs serve as both a connection point and a signal booster. Data that comes in is passed back out on all ports. Active hubs require electrical power.

- **Intelligent or "smart" hubs** These are active hubs that include a microprocessor chip with diagnostic capabilities so that you can monitor the transmission on individual ports.

Another type of hub, called a *switching hub*, operates at the data link rather than the physical layer and is more commonly called simply a *switch*.

NOTE

Hubs present a security risk because all messages, to all computers, go out over every port. This makes it easy for an unauthorized person who can gain access to the server rooms or offices where the hubs are located to simply plug in a laptop and intercept data.

Bridges

Bridges operate at the data link layer of the OSI model. Bridges can separate a network into segments, but they don't *subnet* the network as routers do. In other words, if you use a bridge to physically separate two areas of the network, it still appears to be all one network to higher-level protocols.

A bridge monitors the data frames it receives to construct a MAC address table, using the source addresses on the frames. This is a simple table that tells the bridge on which side a particular address resides. Then the bridge can look at the destination address on a frame and, if it is in the table, determine whether to let it cross the bridge (if the address is on the other side) or not (if the address is on the side from which it was received).

In this way, less unnecessary traffic is generated, because when a computer on Side A sends a message to another computer that is also on Side A, the signal goes only to those computers on Side A. The computers on Side B, on the other side of the bridge, go blithely on with their business and never have to deal with the message.

Bridges can decrease network congestion because they can do some basic filtering of data traffic based on the destination computer's MAC address. When a transmission reaches the bridge, the bridge will not pass it to the other side of the network if the destination computer's MAC address is known to be on the same side of the network as the sending computer, as shown in Figure 5.7.

Figure 5.7 Bridges segment networks to reduce traffic.

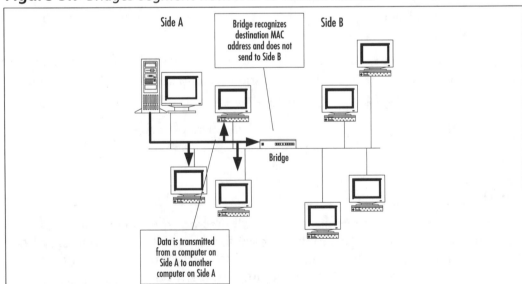

On the Scene...

Types of Bridges

There are different types of bridges. Although all types work at the data link layer, some operate at the lower MAC sublayer and others at the higher LLC sublayer. There are some important differences between bridge types. One practical question is whether you can use a bridge to connect network segments that use different media access methods (for instance, an Ethernet segment and a Token Ring segment). The answer is yes—or no, depending on which type of bridge you're referring to.

A bridge that operates at the LLC sublayer, sometimes called a *translation bridge,* can connect segments using different access methods. However, a lower-level bridge (one that operates at the MAC sublayer) cannot. Either type, however, can connect segments using different physical media—that is, a segment cabled with thin coax and a segment running on UTP cable.

Translation bridges do *not* translate between protocols. Bridges are unaware of and not dependent on the network/transport protocols used for communication. Bridges can use only the MAC addresses. Because bridges do not look at the upper-layer protocols such as IP, they cannot make decisions about where to send data frames based on IP address.

Switches

Layer 2 switches, or switching hubs, work at the data link layer, and they are installed in place of the active hubs that have been more typically used to connect computers on a UTP-cabled network. Replacing hubs with switches costs a bit more than using only hubs but offers several important advantages.

A switch combines the characteristics of hubs and bridges. Like a bridge, a switch constructs a table of MAC addresses. The switch knows which computer network interface (identified by its physical address) is attached to which of its ports. It can then determine the destination address for a particular packet and route it only to the port to which that NIC is attached. Obviously, this system cuts down a great deal on unnecessary bandwidth usage since the packet is not sent out to all the rest of the ports, where it will be disregarded when those computers determine that it is not intended for them. This process is illustrated in Figure 5.8.

Figure 5.8 Switches reduce traffic by sending data only out the port with which the destination MAC address is associated.

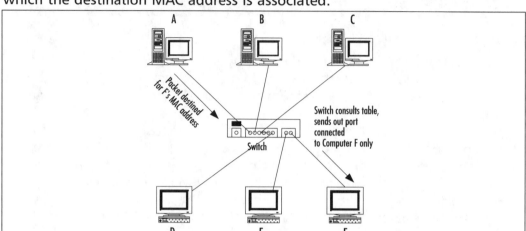

Using switches instead of hubs creates individual "collision domains" for each segment (the cable length between the switch and each node). This means a particular computer receives only the packets addressed to it, to a multicast address to which it belongs, or to the broadcast address. You increase potential bandwidth in this way by the number of devices connected to the switch, because each computer can send and receive at the same time that one or more other nodes are doing so.

Switches can forward data frames more quickly than bridges because instead of reading the entire incoming Ethernet frame before forwarding it to the destination segment, the switch typically only reads the destination address in the frame, then retransmits it to the correct segment. This is why switches can offer fewer and shorter delays throughout the network, resulting in better performance.

Recently a type of switch that operates at the network layer, or Layer 3 of the OSI model, has become a popular connectivity option. A Layer 3 switch, sometimes referred to as a *switch router*, is in fact a type of router. Although a Layer 2 switch (switching hub) is unable to distinguish between protocols, a Layer 3 switch actually performs the functions of a router. A Layer 3 switch can filter the packets of a particular protocol to allow you to further reduce network traffic.

Layer 3 switches perform the same tasks as routers and can be deployed in the same locations in which a router is traditionally used. Yet the Layer 3 switch overcomes the performance disadvantage of routers, layering routing on top of switching technology. Layer 3 switches, manufactured by such companies as Cisco (one of the most well-known makers of traditional routers), is quickly becoming the solution of choice for enterprise network connectivity.

Routers

Like hubs and switches, routers are multiport connectivity devices. Unlike hubs and Layer 2 switches, routers are appropriate for use on large, complex networks because they are able to use the logical IP address to determine where packets need to go.

How does using the IP address help simplify the routing process? Recall that an IP address is divided into two parts: the network ID and the host ID. The network ID is the key here because it "narrows down" the location of the particular destination computer by acting somewhat the way a ZIP code does for the post office.

Routers are used to handle complex routing tasks. Routers also reduce network congestion by confining broadcast messages to a single subnet. A router can either be a dedicated device (such as those made by Cisco) or a computer running an operating system that is capable of acting as a router. Windows 2000, like Windows NT, can function as a router when two network cards are installed and IP forwarding is enabled.

Routers are capable of filtering so that you can, for instance, block inbound traffic. This capability allows the router to act as a *firewall*, creating a barrier that prevents undesirable packets from either entering or leaving a particular designated area of the network. However, in general, the more filtering a router is configured to do, the slower its performance. We look at how IP routing works in detail later in this chapter, in the section on IP addressing.

On the Scene...

The Marriage of the Bridge and the Router

Although its name might sound like the weird result of some recombinant DNA experiment, the *brouter* is a device that attempts to combine the features of bridges and routers into a "best of both worlds" solution. This can be useful when some nodes on the network are running unroutable protocols, such as NetBEUI, while others use protocols that can benefit from routing. A brouter functions like a router, using IP addresses to make routing decisions when packets are sent using a routable protocol such as TCP/IP, but if a nonroutable protocol is used, it the brouter uses the MAC address to function as a bridge. Because it performs the functions of both a router and a bridge, brouters operate at both the data link and network layers of the OSI model. Brouters are not often seen on networks today.

On the Scene...

Using the Network ID to "Narrow the Search"

In a small town, all streets might share the same ZIP code, so a letter addressed to 100 Hall Street, Somecity, Texas, doesn't really need a ZIP code. It will reach its destination because there is only one Somecity post office, and it can easily keep track of the location of all the streets in town. In a big city with several ZIP codes, however, a letter addressed to 100 Hall Street, Bigcity, Texas, will have more difficulty reaching its destination. That's because there are several post offices in Bigcity, each designed to serve only a designated part of the city. It's the ZIP code that identifies which of these post office stations will handle the delivery of the letter, much as the network ID identifies which subnet, or part of the network, a destination computer is on.

In order to use this information, though, the post office must be "ZIP code aware." That is, the employees who sort the mail in the post office must understand what the ZIP codes mean. If employees performing this task came from the era before the advent of ZIP codes, they would see the series of numbers at the end of the address and, not understanding its significance, disregard it. Like those postal employees from a former time, bridges and other lower-layer devices don't recognize IP addresses or utilize them in making decisions about where to send the data.

Routers, however, working at the network layer where IP operates, can understand and use IP addresses. A router keeps a table, too, but unlike a bridge or switch, which deals in only MAC addresses, the routing table tells the router how to get to other known networks (or subnets) based on the network ID. Then when a packet reaches the appropriate network, the host ID is used to get it to the particular computer for which it is destined.

Gateways

Gateways are usually not implemented as "devices" (although they can be). Rather, they are implemented as software programs running on servers. However, because they are also used to connect disparate networks, we touch briefly on what they are and why they are implemented in many networks.

Gateways normally operate at higher levels of the OSI model—typically at the application layer—and can be used to connect two networks that use entirely different protocols. For instance, an SNA gateway (Microsoft's latest version is called Host Integration Server) allows personal computers running Windows operating systems to communicate with an IBM mainframe computer, even though the two systems are "alien" to one another. Another type of gateway is used to allow Windows machines, which use the SMB file-sharing protocol, to "talk" to a file server that runs the NetWare NOS and uses NetWare Core Protocol (NCP). There are many other different types of gateways, such as e-mail gateways, which translate between e-mail protocols.

Why This Matters to the Investigator

The network hardware controls how data is handled once it leaves the computer and begins its journey across the network. Understanding how network devices work helps investigators understand how data signals can be captured while in transit over the network and how an unauthorized person who is able to gain access to the premises can plug a laptop into a hub and capture data traffic or tap into the cable using a splitter and intercept the data flowing through it.

Understanding Network Software

Modern operating systems have networking capabilities built in. Early PC operating systems such as DOS (and the Windows shell that ran on it) did not; it wasn't until version 3.11, with Windows for Workgroups, that Microsoft included networking components. As the name implied, that version of Windows was designed to function in a small peer-to-peer local network. Windows NT added authentication server functionality (Microsoft called the authentication server a *domain controller*), but with the early versions of NT, the focus was still on the LAN, not the WAN. At that time, Microsoft operating systems were not considered scalable enough for enterprise networking, and most Web servers on the Internet were UNIX machines. With Windows 95, it became easier for users to connect to the Internet, and NT 4.0 supported Web services (Internet Information Server) that made it easy to host Web sites on the Internet or intranets. Windows 2000 built more heavily on Internet connectivity and added features to the server products that made it more suitable for enterprise-level computing, including a robust directory service (Active Directory), industry-standard security protocols such as Kerberos and IPSec, and load-balancing and clustering support. The next generation of Windows servers, .NET, continues this trend and embraces the idea that "the network *is* the computer" to a larger extent than ever.

The term *network operating system (NOS)* is used in three different ways:

- It is sometimes used to refer to any computer operating system that has built-in networking components, as do all of today's popular PC operating systems. Thus Windows 9x, NT, 2000, XP, and .NET (along with most distros of Linux, UNIX, Macintosh, and OS/2 Warp) are considered NOSs, whereas MS-DOS and Windows 3.1 and earlier are not.

- It is sometimes used to refer to the components of the operating system that make networking possible. For example, today's Windows operating systems include file and print sharing services (known as the Server service in NT), which allow the computer to act as a server and share its resources with other systems, and the Client for Microsoft Networks (known as the Workstation service in NT) which allows the computer to connect to and access the shared resources of other systems. These components, along with the protocol stacks on which the network operates, are sometimes referred to as the NOS.

- It is sometimes used to refer to the server operating system software—such as Windows NT Server, Windows 2000 Server, UNIX, or NetWare—especially when functioning as an authentication server that maintains a security accounts database for the network.

In the following sections, we look at how client/server computing works and discuss both the server software and client software that work together to enable network communications. We also take a look at network file systems and how they differ from local file systems as well as the protocols that govern the network communication process.

Understanding Client/Server Computing

The term *client/server computing* has different meanings, depending on the context in which it is used. Some documentation uses the term narrowly, to refer to applications in which the bulk of the processing is performed on a server. For example, SQL Server is a database application that uses the server's power to sort the data in response to a query and then returns only the results back to the client. Contrast this system with Microsoft's Access, in which database files are stored on a server, but a client query results in the entire file being transferred to the client machine, where the sorting takes place.

Using this meaning of the term, *thin client computing* is the ultimate form of client/server computing. With thin client software such as Microsoft's terminal services, the operating system runs on the server, and all applications run there; only the graphical representation of the desktop screen runs on the client machine. This means that client machines can be low-power systems with modest processors and small amounts of RAM—machines that are not capable of running the operating system themselves. Thus a user can work in Windows 2000 using an old 80486 system that only has 16MB of RAM, because the operating system isn't really running on that old system—it's only being used as a terminal to access the OS on the server.

Authentication Server-Based Networks

A second, broader meaning of the term *client/server computing* refers to a network that is based on an authentication server. This is a server that controls access to the network, storing a security accounts database that holds users' networkwide account information. When a user wants to log onto the network, the client computer contacts this authentication server. The server checks its database to ensure that the user is authorized and to determine the level of access allowed that user (usually based on security groups to which the user belongs). The authentication server is a centralized point of security and network resource management and must run special (and usually expensive) server software. In Microsoft networking, this type of network is called a *domain* and the authentication server is called a *domain controller*. UNIX and NetWare servers also provide network authentication services.

NOTE

We discuss *authentication*, which refers to the verification of a user's or computer's identity, in much more detail in Chapter 7, when we discuss security concepts.

Authentication server operating systems such as NT Server used a flat accounts database, but the trend is toward the use of hierarchical databases called *directory services,* such as Novell's NDS and Microsoft's Active Directory. The new Macintosh OS X Server uses a somewhat less robust directory service called NetInfo. All these services have something in common: They are compatible with the *Lightweight Directory Access Protocol (LDAP)* standards. This is an industry-standard based on the ISO's X.500 specifications, and adherence to the standards allows directory services from different vendors to interoperate on a network.

These client/server (or server-based) networks provide many advantages, especially for large networks. Because security and management are centralized, this type of network can be more easily secured and managed than the alternative network model.

Peer-to-Peer Networks

Networks without an authentication server are called *workgroups* or *peer-to-peer networks*. This model is appropriate for small networks with only a few computers, in environments where high security is not required. In a workgroup, all computers can provide both client and server services.

NOTE

In this context, the term *server services* means only that the computers make their resources accessible to (share them with) other computers on the network. The computers in a workgroup do not have to run expensive server software, although a workgroup can have machines running such software as Windows 2000 Server, operating as *member servers* instead of domain controllers. The key differentiating factor is that in a workgroup, there is no *authentication* server, although there can be other types of servers (file and print servers, remote access servers, fax servers, and the like).

Workgroups are less expensive to implement than server-based networks, for several reasons:

- Server operating system software, which costs from several hundred to several thousand dollars, must be purchased to implement a server-based network.

- Server software generally requires more powerful hardware than do desktop operating systems, so you might need to purchase more expensive machinery to run it.

- Server-based networks generally require a dedicated network administrator to perform the many tasks involved in network administration and maintenance, necessitating hiring additional personnel or extra work on the part of an existing employee.

Despite workgroups' cost advantage, they are less secure, because the user of each computer must manage its resources. In order to access resources on any other computer in the workgroup, a user must have a local account created on that machine, or alternatively, each individual shared resource can be protected by a password. Either of these methods gets very cumbersome when there are more than a handful of users and/or more than a few shared resources.

With the first method, a user might need accounts on a dozen or more computers; with the second method, that user would have to remember dozens or even hundreds of different passwords in order to access different shared folders or printers. Contrast this scenario with the authentication server-based network, where each user has a single username and password for logging onto the entire network. The user can then access any resource on any machine in the network for which the appropriate permissions have been assigned. Although administrators do have to assign permissions to each shared resource, from the user's point of view this is a much simpler system. When workgroups grow beyond 20 or 25 computers, it is usually advantageous to convert to a centralized (server-based) model.

Server Software

Remember that all modern operating systems, even consumer/home editions, have a *server component* (such as file and print sharing for Microsoft Networks) that allows them to share their resources. When we refer to server software here, we're talking about operating systems capable of providing network authentication services (as well as other server services such as DNS, Web services, or remote access services). There are also many server *applications* (such as the SQL database server, the ISA proxy/firewall server, the Exchange mail server, and the like) that can be installed only on a system running a server operating system.

The major server operating systems in use today include:

- **Microsoft Windows NT and 2000 Server** There are several versions of each; the NT 4.0 family includes Standard Server, the Enterprise Edition, and the Terminal Server Edition. The Windows 2000 family includes Standard Server, Advanced Server, and Datacenter Server. The higher-level products include additional features and/or support more memory and a greater number of processors. As of this writing, the next generation of Microsoft's server product, .NET Server, has not yet been released.

- **Novell NetWare** Only a decade ago, NetWare had the majority of the installed base for network authentication server software in the United States. It lost ground to Microsoft with the introduction of Windows NT 4.0 and then Windows 2000 (which included a directory service similar to NetWare's NDS). Prior to NetWare 5, the IPX/SPX protocol stack was required for connecting to NetWare servers. Now NetWare can run on pure IP. As of this writing, the current version of NetWare is version 6.

- **UNIX/Linux in many, many different "flavors"** UNIX has been around since the beginning of networking and the Internet. Linux is a UNIX-based OS that can also be run on the desktop. UNIX is a very powerful server operating system, but it is considered to have a steep learning curve. It is a character-based OS, but GUI interfaces are available. There are dozens of different popular commercial and free distributions of UNIX and Linux.

Apple makes its OS X in a server version, which supports Macintosh, Windows, UNIX, and Linux clients and includes Apache Web server, POP and IMAP mail, and DNS and DHCP services. OS X Server runs only on Macintosh systems (G3, G4, and iMac). Although not widely implemented at this time, the server version of OS X is less costly than Microsoft's and Novell's products and much more user-friendly than other versions of UNIX. For more information about OS X Server, see the FAQ at www.apple.com/macosx/server/faq/index.html.

Client Software

Most modern operating systems can also function as network clients. These include the server operating systems discussed earlier, with the possible exception of NetWare. However, it would be inefficient and costly to run NT Server or Windows 2000 Server, for example, as a desktop client—the OS itself costs 10 times more than Windows operating systems designed for the desktop (9x/ME, NT Workstation, 2000/XP Professional, and the like). UNIX is most often used as a server, but Linux is growing in popularity as a desktop/client OS. Mac OS X comes in both client and server forms. Novell doesn't make a client OS of its own; NetWare clients generally run Windows or UNIX operating systems with NetWare client software (and the IPX/SPX protocols, if necessary) installed.

This brings up an important point: Client machines don't necessarily have to run an operating system made by the vendor of the network's server software. With the proper add-on software installed, Macintosh and UNIX-based clients can access Windows servers, Windows and Macintosh clients can access UNIX servers, and so forth.

The most popular client operating systems are:

- **NT Workstation, and 2000/XP Professional** Windows-based clients are by far the most popular client operating systems, regardless of the server type running on the network. Novell makes client software for all versions of Windows, and Microsoft includes its own NetWare client software with Windows operating systems as well. SAMBA is software that runs on a UNIX machine and allows Windows computers to access its resources. (MS-DOS and Windows 3.*x* clients are also still in use in some businesses, and Windows 9*x*/ME or XP Home Edition can be used to access a Windows domain, although those computers cannot actually join the domain. This means that a user with a valid domain account can log on from the system, but the computer has no computer account and thus is less secure and cannot be managed as an NT/2000 or XP Pro machine can.)

■ **Linux** Novell, Microsoft, and Apple all provide add-on client software to allow Linux and UNIX machines to access some or all of their resources. For example, Microsoft's Services for UNIX is added to an NT or Windows 2000 server to allow NFS authentication for Linux and UNIX clients. (Note that not all distros are supported.) The SAMBA project has also developed a program called Winbind to allow UNIX-based workstations in networks with multiple operating systems (sometimes called *hybrid* or *heterogeneous networks*) to log onto Windows domains with full functionality. NetWare v6 allows Linux clients to access resources without installing NetWare client software, either using a Web browser or through the native file access feature for Linux clients using the Network File System (NFS).

■ **Macintosh OS 8/9 and OS X** Microsoft's Services for Macintosh allow Mac clients to access Windows servers. The Microsoft User Authentication Module (UAM) provides a mechanism for encrypting passwords used by Mac users to log onto Windows' Apple File Protocol (AFP) services. Novell provides the NetWare Client for Mac OS, which can be installed on Macintosh machines to access NetWare 5 servers, or alternatively, NetWare's Services for AppleShare can be installed on the NetWare server (in which case no client software is required). NetWare 6 allows access through the browser or native file sharing without installing client software. The latest Mac OS, OS X, is UNIX-based and connects easily to UNIX servers. Older versions of Mac OS can use terminal emulation software to connect to UNIX servers.

Network File Systems and File Sharing Protocols

Network file systems and *file sharing protocols* allow users to access and update files on remote computers as though they were on the local computer. They can make different file systems on the remote machine irrelevant when accessing that machine's resources across the network. This is the reason that a Windows 9*x* computer, which does not support NTFS and can't access NTFS files locally, is able to read and write to NTFS files that are stored on a remote Windows NT/ 2000 computer. Popular mechanisms for file sharing across a network include:

- **Server Message Block (SMB) Protocol** Microsoft uses this protocol to allow client applications to access and write to remote files and request services from server applications on remote systems. SMB is included with Windows operating systems. SAMBA is an implementation of SMB and the Common Internet File System (CIFS) that can be installed on UNIX computers to allow Windows clients to access their files as though they were SMB servers.

- **Common Internet File System (CIFS)** CIFS is a protocol proposed as an Internet standard for allowing access to remote files across the Internet. CIFS is considered an open (nonproprietary) version of SMB. Both SMB and CIFS run on top of the TCP/IP protocol stack.

- **NetWare Core Protocol (NCP)** NCP is actually a set of protocols that provide file and printer access, among other services, between clients and remote servers on NetWare networks. NCP runs over IPX or IP.

- **Network File System (NFS)** NFS is a client/server application developed by Sun Microsystems that runs on TCP/IP to allow remote file access. NFS uses the Remote Procedure Call (RPC) communication method. NFS is used for remote file access by UNIX/Linux machines and can be installed on Windows and Macintosh computers.

A Matter of (Networking) Protocol

In order for any network communication to take place between computers, the computers must be running a common *network protocol*. Protocols are simply sets of rules that define the communication process. Some texts compare protocols to languages, but a better comparison is to the grammar and syntax of a language— the rules that govern the language's use. Think of it this way: Even if you learn all the words or vocabulary of a foreign language, you will not be able to effectively communicate with a speaker of that language if you don't understand the rules for putting those words together in sentences.

Networking protocols generally work together in protocol stacks or suites. A *stack* is two or more protocols working at different layers of the OSI or DoD model. For example, TCP and IP form a protocol stack, with TCP working at the transport layer and IP working at the network layer. Similarly, Sequenced Packet Exchange (SPX) and IPX work together, with SPX performing transport layer duties and IPX performing network layer tasks. A suite includes additional protocols such as the application-layer FTP and Telnet protocols included in the TCP/IP suite.

In the early days of Microsoft networking, most networks were small LANs, so simple protocols sufficed to enable communication. The NetBIOS Extended User Interface (NetBEUI), an outgrowth of the Network Basic Input/Output System (NetBIOS) protocol developed by IBM, was used for network communications. NetBIOS and NetBEUI rely on assigned computer names, called *NetBIOS names*, to identify computers on a network. There is no mechanism for identifying the network itself, which means that transmissions using this protocol cannot travel between two different networks.

On the Scene...

How Protocols Work

Networking protocols set rules for such things as how computers are identified and located on the network. For example, both the Internet Protocol (IP) and the Internet Packet Exchange (IPX) protocol handle addressing and routing of packets at the network layer of the OSI model. However, they use completely different addressing schemes. It's like the difference between the postal service, which uses your street number and name to locate your house, and a satellite system that uses the geographic coordinates to find the same structure. Geographic coordinates would be of little help to a postal worker in delivering a letter, and your street address would mean nothing to the satellite system.

As networks grew and became interconnected, more complex protocols were required so that messages could be *routed* between different networks. NetWare networks depended, until recently, on the IPX/SPX protocols. IPX/SPX is a routable protocol stack that uses a system of network addresses and internal network addresses to identify both network and computer.

The most popular protocol stack today is TCP/IP, primarily because it is the protocol of the Internet and any computer that connects to the Internet must have TCP/IP installed. TCP/IP uses an addressing scheme that makes it extremely routable, so it is suitable for the largest networks. It can also be run on the smallest networks, although its slower performance and complexity of administration may make it less desirable than NetBEUI for small, nonrouted networks. Nonetheless, TCP/IP is the networking protocol stack of choice for most of today's networks. In the following section, we examine the TCP/IP protocol suite in detail.

NOTE

IPX/SPX can also be used on networks that don't have NetWare servers. Some Microsoft networks run IPX/SPX—or Microsoft's version of it, called NWLink—to provide greater security when the local network is connected to the Internet. Because most computers on the Internet don't have IPX/SPX installed, they aren't able to access machines running only that protocol stack.

Understanding the TCP/IP Protocols Used on the Internet

The Transmission Control Protocol/Internet Protocol (also referred to as the *TCP/IP protocol stack*, or just plain *TCP/IP*) is a familiar, if poorly understood, networking component to most modern network administrators and information technology professionals.

If you work in any but the smallest networked environment, chances are you've encountered TCP/IP. However, only a few short years ago, TCP/IP was regarded as a somewhat sluggish, difficult-to-configure protocol used primarily by university or government networks that participated in an exotic wide area networking project called the ARPANet. TCP/IP was considered too slow and complex to be an appropriate choice for most private organizations' LANs.

Microsoft and IBM workgroups ran fine on NetBEUI, a fast and simple transport protocol that could be set up easily and quickly by someone without a great deal of expertise. Novell NetWare LANs used the IPX/SPX stack, which was routable and thus could be used with larger server-based networks. Few business networks had any need for a powerful but high-overhead set of protocols like TCP/IP. Then something happened: the Internet.

The Need for Standardized Protocols

The ARPANet's reach expanded and grew into the commercial Internet that we know today. Although changed in many ways from its early days, the global network still runs on the TCP/IP protocol suite developed for the ARPANet. In order for computers all over the world to communicate with one another, there must be a common, standardized set of protocols—and TCP/IP fills that role.

Although TCP/IP is a "universal" protocol stack that allows communication between machines running different operating systems or even running on different platforms, different vendors' implementations of the protocols might differ slightly. You'll see this in the different commands used to perform the same utilitarian tasks. For example, on Microsoft networks, the **ipconfig** command is used to view TCP/IP configuration information. On UNIX-based networks, the same task is performed using the **ifconfig** command. Likewise, Microsoft's **tracert** is UNIX's **traceroute,** and so forth.

On the Scene...

The Effort to Dethrone TCP/IP as King of the Internet

There have been occasional attempts to usurp TCP/IP's position as the protocol of choice for internetworking. The Open Systems Interconnection protocol suite, based on the famous (or infamous) seven-layer OSI networking model, was conceived with the idea of unseating the incumbent and replacing TCP/IP as a universal standard for internetworking communications. In fact, in the late 1980s, the U.S. government, which had played an important part in creating and developing TCP/IP, made plans to phase it out in favor of the OSI suite. It didn't quite work out that way. TCP/IP turned out to be the protocol stack that refused to go quietly into that good night.

It was as though someone announced that they had discovered a replacement for dirt and suggested that we uproot all the trees and plants and then "reinstall" them in the new, superior substance. Restructuring the huge, sprawling global Internet to "plant" it in a different protocol environment—regardless of any advantages that new environment might offer—is just too overwhelming an undertaking.

A Brief History of TCP/IP

As German philosopher Friedrich Schlegel said, "The subject of history is the gradual realization of all that is practically necessary."

Practical necessity is the driving force behind most important inventions and developments, and the necessity for a reliable set of communications protocols suitable for connecting large networks led to the creation of the TCP/IP stack.

In the 1960s, computer networking was in its infancy. The many benefits of connecting computers so that they could share resources were only beginning to become apparent. The equipment was expensive, and products from different manufacturers were largely incompatible. Few business entities had the money or inclination to bother with creating local networks, much less attempt to get their computers to "talk" to distant systems.

The U.S. Department of Defense recognized the value of establishing electronic communications links between major military installations. (Grim as it might seem, a primary motivation was the desire to maintain communication capabilities in the event of the mass destruction that would come with nuclear war.) Major universities were involved in networking projects as well. The DoD funded research sites throughout the United States, and in 1968, the Advanced Research Projects Agency (ARPA) contracted with a company called Bolt, Beranek and Newman (later called simply BBN) to build a network based on packet-switching technology.

The next year, ARPANet was born when its first *node*, or connection point, was installed at the University of California at Los Angeles. Within three years, the network had spread across the United States and two years after that, to the European continent.

It was important that the networking protocols, the set of rules governing the communications process, be reliable and scalable to accommodate multiple redundant sites and anticipated growth (although no one at that time expected the rate of growth that was to come). Perhaps following the timeworn advice that "if you want it done right, you have to do it yourself," the ARPANet's developers designed a new group of protocols that fit the bill. Their first attempt was the Network Control Protocol (NCP), but it proved to be unsuitable as traffic increased. By the mid-1970s, necessity had mothered invention again, and the TCP/IP protocol suite was implemented.

The Internet Protocol and IP Addressing

One of TCP/IP's great strengths—and a primary reason that it has become the standard for large networks, including the Internet—is its scalable addressing scheme, which can accommodate networks of all sizes. In order to communicate over a network using the TCP/IP protocols, a computer must have an IP address that is unique on that network. The IP address can be manually assigned by a network administrator or it can be automatically assigned by an automatic addressing service (see the following section on automatic addressing). In any event, there will be no IP communication without an address.

Under the current IP addressing system, IPv4, there are "only" a little over 4 billion possible IP addresses (4,294,967,296, or 2^{32}, for those who like to be precise). In the beginning (the early 1980s), this seemed to be more than enough for the foreseeable future. At that time, when IP specifications became standardized, a two-level hierarchical addressing structure was imposed, consisting of the network ID (sometimes called the *network prefix*) and the host ID. Networks were divided into "classes" A, B, and C (as well as D and E, but the latter two were not allocated to networks; rather, they were reserved for special purposes). This is referred to as *classful addressing*. A newer method of identifying networks via an "IP prefix" is called *classless interdomain routing (CIDR)*, which we discussed briefly in Chapter 4. Instead of designating networks as Class A, B, or C, a network is referred to as a */16*, a */24*, and so on, depending on the number of bits used for the network ID portion of the address.

Logical IP Addresses vs. Physical MAC Addresses

The IP address is a "logical" address assigned by the network administrator. It bears no direct relation to the network interface card's "physical" address (often referred to as the *MAC address* because it is used at the media access control sublayer of the OSI data link layer).

Changing a computer's (or more precisely, an individual NIC's) IP address is a software function. If you have administrative privileges, it's as simple as clicking the mouse a few times to open the proper dialog box and typing in a new number. (The hardest part is knowing what number to type in.)

The MAC address, on the other hand, is hardcoded into the chip on the network card in the typical Ethernet network. Some network cards provide for a way to change the MAC address via jumper settings or by "flashing" the chip with special software, but this is not usual; in most cases, the MAC address stays the same.

NOTE

You could think of the IP address as analogous to your street address, with two parts representing the street on which you live and the particular house on that street (as the two parts of an IP address represent the network on which the computer "lives" and the specific host on that network). The street address is a "logical" address, in that it was assigned (probably by the city). A vote of the municipal government can change the name of the street or even the numbering scheme, just as the network administrator can easily change the IP address of a computer. The MAC address is more like the geographic coordinates (latitude and longitude) that identify the location of your house. These are permanent and can't be changed at the whim of the city government.

An Ethernet MAC address is a 48–bit number represented in hexadecimal, so it looks something like this: 00–80–C8–6A–FA–00. If you're using a Windows computer, you can find out the physical address of your Ethernet card by typing **ipconfig /all** at the command line, which will give you the information shown in Figure 5.9.

Figure 5.9 You can find out a computer's IP address using the **ipconfig** command in Windows.

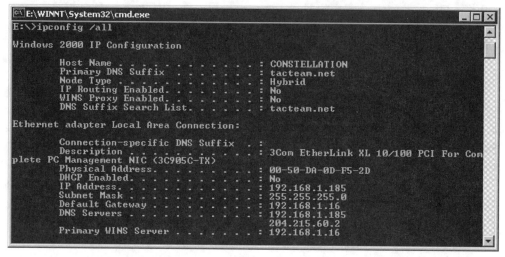

Figure 5.10 You can use the GUI to find out your Ethernet address with an OS X system.

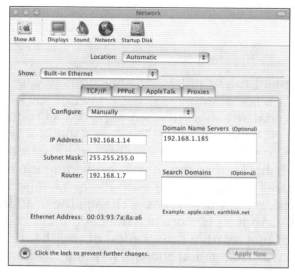

On Linux systems, the command for finding out your MAC address is **ifconfig –a**. The method differs on different "flavors" of UNIX; for example, in HP-UX, you use the **lanscan** command. With Macintosh OS X, you select **System Preferences** from the **Apple** menu, then select **Network**, select your Ethernet adapter from the drop-down box in the **Show** field, and the hardware address will be displayed (along with TCP/IP configuration information), as shown in Figure 5.10.

As you can see in these screenshots, the IP and MAC addresses are in two very different formats and have no logical relationship to one another. The Address Resolution Protocol (ARP) is responsible for "keeping tabs" on which IP addresses match up with which physical addresses and relaying that information so computers can communicate at the physical (network interface) level.

Static Addressing

Administrators can manually assign IP addresses to each computer on a network, using the TCP/IP configuration utilities (which vary depending on the operating system). This works fine when the network is small and is necessary when you have computers (typically servers) that need to always have the same IP address. Figure 5.11 shows the TCP/IP properties sheet that is used to assign a static IP address to a Windows 2000 computer.

Figure 5.11 Network administrators can manually assign IP addresses (called "static addresses") to computers.

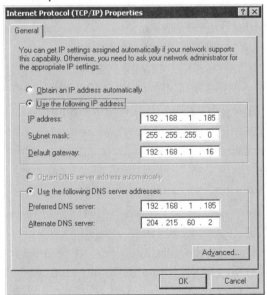

When you manually assign an address, you must also enter the correct subnet mask and, if the network is routed, the IP address of the default gateway (the router or computer performing routing functions). Although manual addressing is more time consuming if you have more than a few computers, and it is easy to make errors entering the data, which could result in loss of connectivity or odd network behavior, there are sometimes good reasons to manually assign addresses. If there is no mechanism for automatic addressing on the network, obviously the addresses need to be assigned manually. There are also certain systems, such as domain controllers and DNS and WINS servers, that need to have static addresses.

Automatic Addressing

With very large networks, manual addressing is time-consuming and prone to error (duplication of addresses). Automatic address assignment can be done by a server running the Dynamic Host Configuration Protocol (DHCP) service. DHCP can be a network administrator's best friend—unless that administrator fails to configure it properly, in which case it can be a source of nightmares. DHCP's purpose is to assign IP addresses dynamically as computers come onto the network. Each computer only has to be set up in TCP/IP properties to get an IP address (and other TCP/IP configuration information) from a DHCP server, and the service does the rest. This system has several advantages:

- **Time savings** Network administrators don't have to tediously enter the IP address, subnet mask, DNS and WINS server addresses, and other information over and over, for every machine on the network. Likewise, if the IP address for the network's DNS server changes, the change does not have to be made on every machine; the change is made in the DHCP server's configuration and the new address is automatically disseminated to client computers when they obtain an address.

- **Better accuracy** The possibility of mistyping an address in one of the machines is eliminated. A scope of addresses is defined only once, on the DHCP server, and the addresses are managed by the server. There is no possibility of the server "forgetting" that a particular address was already assigned to another machine and duplicating the address.

- **More efficient use of addresses** If the number of available addresses is limited, DHCP optimizes their use, since it only "leases" the addresses to computers for a predetermined period of time instead of assigning them permanently, as with manual assignment. When a computer goes offline, its address can be released so that it can then be assigned to a different system.

You must set up the client computers to seek an address from the DHCP server. In Windows, configuring a computer to obtain an address from a DHCP server is simple. In the TCP/IP properties box, simply check the radio button option **Obtain an IP address automatically**.

NOTE

DHCP works with most operating systems. It grew out of BootP, the bootstrap protocol that was originally designed to allow diskless work-stations to boot an operating system from the network. DHCP adds much more functionality, allowing administrators to configure many dif-ferent options. The DHCP server can assign other TCP/IP information, such as the default gateway and DNS and WINS server addresses, as well as assigning an IP address.

Other services can assign IP addresses under some circumstances. For example, in Windows 98/2000 and later, the Automatic Private IP Addressing (APIPA) service and Internet Connection Sharing (ICS) can assign IP addresses. APIPA was included in Windows 2000 to make TCP/IP configuration easier and to help ensure that a computer would be able to communicate on a small (unsubnetted) TCP/IP network that does not have a DHCP server. In past ver-sions of Microsoft's operating systems, prior to the release of Windows 98 and then Windows 2000, if a computer did not have a manually entered address and was not able to contact a DHCP server when it came online, it would not be able to join the TCP/IP network. With APIPA, the computer first attempts to reach a DHCP server and negotiate a lease for an IP address. However, if this fails, the computer then takes the initiative and assigns itself an address from the reserved APIPA range of 169.254.0.1 through 169.254.255.254 with a subnet mask of 255.255.0.0. This allows the computer to communicate on the network, using the APIPA address temporarily until a DHCP server can be reached.

ICS is another new feature introduced in Windows 98/2000. ICS is used to allow multiple computers to access the Internet or another outside connection via a single public IP address. ICS is a part of Windows 2000 Network and Dialup Connections and can be enabled on a Windows 2000 Professional or Server computer that has a dialup connection to the Internet, thereby allowing other computers on the LAN to share that connection using Network Address Translation (NAT).

When you enable ICS, the host machine that is sharing its connection will be configured with an IP address of 192.168.0.1 with a subnet mask of 255.255.255.0. The ICS computer also becomes a *DHCP allocator*. This role differs from that of a full-fledged DHCP server in that the computer does not have to be running a server operating system. The DHCP allocator has a predefined scope of IP addresses that it can hand out to the client computers sharing its Internet connection. These addresses fall into a private Class C address range, the 192.168.0.0 network.

The Future of IP

The current version of IP (IPv4) uses 32-bit addresses. This provides for a total of approximately 4 billion individual unique addresses, in theory. Unfortunately, in practice, there are far fewer usable addresses. This situation is unfortunate because every computer that connects to the Internet—with the exception of those connecting through proxies and NAT—must have a unique address. The Internet's popularity has exceeded the wildest dreams of those who developed the Internet Protocol. Additionally, address assignments in the early days were not made with efficiency in mind. Many addresses were "wasted"—for example, the entire 127.x.y.z address range is not used because it is assigned as a "loopback" address for testing the local TCP/IP stack, wasting over 16 *million* addresses. In the early days of the Internet, Class A and B address blocks, with approximately 16 million and 65,000 host addresses, respectively, were assigned to organizations that didn't need nearly that many addresses.

NOTE

In 1991, there were a little over 1 million hosts on the global Internet. By 1997, there were over 16 million. By 2000, according to the Internet Society, there were an estimated 50 million. If growth continues at this rate, the prospect of using up all the available addresses will become very real.

As a consequence, the world is running short on available IP addresses. As the number of Internet devices increases, with PDAs, cell phones, and household appliances expected to be connected to the Net in the future, the need for more addresses will become critical. A new version of IP is needed—one that provides for a larger number of addresses. That's where IPv6 comes in.

IPv6, or IPng (the *ng* stands for *next generation*), is the new version of IP. It was designed by the Internet Engineering Task Force (IETF) as the next step up from IPv4. It builds on IPv4 and is a natural progression. IPv6 uses 128-bit addresses. This provides for a total number of IP addresses that, represented exponentially, is 2 to the 128th power. The actual number would take up an entire line of space in this paragraph; it's safe to say it definitely adds up to "a lot." You can install it as a software implementation, and it is compatible with IPv4, which is currently used on the Internet and other TCP/IP networks. The specific intent of IPv6 was to work efficiently in high-performance networks such as asynchronous transfer mode (ATM), while still working efficiently over low-bandwidth networks (which include many wireless technologies).

It's not likely you'll wake up one day and suddenly see an announcement that on a particular date, at a particular time, the Internet is switching to IPv6. The new version is expected to replace IPv4 gradually, and the two will coexist for a number of years as the transition occurs. Because IPv6 provides for so many possible addresses, the entire original IPv4 address space will remain as is to ensure maximum compatibility with IPv6 addresses, making the transition easier to implement.

How Routing Works

Computers on an internetwork send packets to one another in one of two ways:

- Directly (if the source and destination computers are on the same subnet)

- Indirectly (if the source and destination computers are on different subnets) by forwarding the packets to a router

IP routing involves discovering a pathway from the sending computer (or forwarding router) to the destination computer whose address is designated in the IP header. In concept, this process is not unlike what you do when planning a trip from your home to a distant location. To navigate a course, you sit down with a map and plot out the best route based on several factors. Distance, simplicity, and congestion might be some things you consider when deciding which roads to take.

IP routing refers to forwarding of packets from a source computer to a destination computer by going through routers that support IP routing. Every computer has a table of network numbers, known as a *routing table*. A gateway address is listed there for each network number, and the gateway is used to reach that network. The gateway doesn'' have to connect directly to the destination network; it is just the starting point. Each gateway, or router, that the message must go through is called a *hop*. At each router, the destination IP address on the packet is compared to the routing table, and the best route is used to decide the endpoint of the next hop. You might say a journey of 1000 hops begins with a single step: the gateway address listed in the routing table for a particular network number.

Typically, a router is connected to two or more networks or subnets. The router, a dedicated device or a computer acting as a router, is said to have an *interface* to each network to which it is connected.

The router's interface can connect to a LAN or to a WAN. The wide area networking interface can be a modem or ISDN terminal adapter or other WAN media connection device; the LAN interface is a network adapter card.

Each interface must have an IP address with a network ID appropriate for the network to which it is connected. The router functions at the internetwork layer of the DoD networking model (the network layer of the OSI model).

Static Routing

Routing comes in two basic "flavors," static and dynamic. With static IP routing, the routing table must be constructed manually; an administrator must enter the IP addresses defining the routes to remote networks one by one. Static routing not only requires that you painstakingly set up the routing table; you also must manually enter every change, addition, and deletion that occurs. This reprogramming of the routers each time a change is made can be time-consuming and tedious. Why would anyone ever use static routing? Actually, most networks today don't, but static routing does have a couple of advantages:

- Static routing can be implemented with a minimum of equipment. No dedicated routing device is needed; you can set up a *multihomed* Windows NT or Windows 2000 computer to be a static router. A multihomed computer is one that has two (or more) network interfaces.

- The initial cost of implementing static routing is less than dynamic routing because of the cost of routing devices. However, these initial savings can be offset by the simplification of administration and reduction in person-hours needed to maintain the dynamic routers.

- You have more specific control over routes used in a static routing situation, since you enter the routes into the table manually. You can delete or change routes and ensure that packets use the desired route.

These benefits are usually not enough, however, to make static routing an attractive solution to network administrators, due to the method's many disadvantages:

- There is no real fault tolerance in a static routing environment. If one of the routers becomes unavailable, others cannot detect its absence. Since a static routed internetwork is generally a single-path environment (only one path available between any two endpoints), this can result in some hosts' inability to communicate with others on the network.

- A great deal of administrative maintenance is required to keep routing tables updated on a static network if new routes need to be added or removed.

- Static routing is appropriate only for small internetworks (those having from two to 10 networks). Beyond this, administration becomes unmanageable.

Using a dynamic routing protocol, the table is configured and maintained automatically because the dynamic router can communicate with and "learn" from other routers on the network. This system saves the administrator a great deal of time.

Dynamic Routing Protocols

Routers running dynamic routing protocols can automatically build their routing tables and make modifications when the network changes. These changes are propagated throughout the network as the dynamic routers communicate with one another. Two popular dynamic routing protocols are the Routing Information Protocol (RIP) and Open Shortest Path First (OSPF).

RIP has been in use for many years and works well with small and medium-sized networks, although it does not scale well to large internetworks. RIP is a distance vector protocol (for more information, see the On the Scene sidebar) with a maximum hop count of 15. For practical purposes, this means that if it takes more than 15 hops to reach another network (subnet), RIP will not work.

RIP for IP works by sending at regular intervals an announcement message that contains the information in its routing table. Other RIP routers receive this message and add the information to their own tables. In this way, route information spreads throughout the network. Version 1 of RIP sends its announcements via broadcast packets. Version 2 can also send announcements via broadcast packets but can use multicast packets, too. RIP routers also use *triggered updates* to spread their information. An update is triggered by a change in the network, such as the failure of a gateway. When a router detects the failure, it updates its own table and then sends out the new information immediately instead of waiting for the next scheduled update period.

OSPF overcomes some of the limitations imposed by RIP. OSPF was designed to handle the types of networks that RIP doesn't handle well: large, complex internetworks. OSPF is efficient; it does not require much overhead. This is especially important in the large internetwork environments for which it is designed. Furthermore, OSPF's Shortest Path First (SPF) algorithm is not vulnerable to routing loops that can plague RIP routes. SPF calculates the shortest path between the router and remote networks by creating and maintaining a map of the internetwork. The map is called a *link state database*, and OSPF is referred to as a *link state protocol*.

On the Scene...

Distance Vector vs. Link State Routing Protocols

One of the significant ways in which RIP and OSPF differ is in the algorithms used to calculate routing decisions. RIP is what is called a *distance vector protocol;* OSPF is referred to as a *link state protocol*.

Distance Vector Algorithms

Distance vector algorithms are also called Bellman-Ford or Ford-Fulkerson algorithms. The latter authors were the first to document the distance vector algorithm class, which is based on Bellman's equation that forms the foundation of dynamic programming.

The distance vector algorithms are a long-standing standard that was in use for network routing calculations in global networking's infancy in the 1960s, in the ARPANet that was the predecessor of today's Internet.

The distance vector algorithms allow gateways (routers) to share and exchange routing table information. This provides a huge benefit over static routing protocols, which require tables to be constructed and maintained manually. RIP descended from the Xerox networking protocols and the name *Routing Information Protocol* was first used in conjunction with XNS. Another variation is called Berkeley's Routed.

Distance vector algorithms, although a vast improvement over static routing, suffer from several limitations. The maximum path length

Continued

is 15 hops, and they are vulnerable to routing loops, caused by a behavior called *count to infinity*. RIP and the other distance vector protocols were designed for use in moderately sized networks, not for an internetwork as vast as the Internet. That's why they are implemented as IGPs.

This brings us to the need for another type of routing protocol that can better handle routing over enormous, disparate networks. That's where link state algorithms come in.

Link State Algorithms

The link state protocol used by OSPF maps the network and updates the mapping database (called the *link state database*) whenever any changes are made to the network. Link state protocols are also referred to as *Shortest Path First (SPF)* or *distributed database protocols*. The first link state protocol was designed for use in the ARPANet. Later modifications were made to reduce traffic overhead and add fault tolerance.

A link state routing protocol builds a consistent view of a network by mapping the network topology. Each router broadcasts (or multicasts) data about the cost of the path to each of its neighboring routers. This information is disseminated to all nodes on the network. Link state protocols are more efficient but more complex than distance vector protocols.

As the link state database grows, memory and processor requirements and the time required to calculate routes increase. In order to address this problem with link state protocols, OSPF divides the internetwork into areas (groups of contiguous networks) that are connected to each other through a backbone area. Each router then keeps a link state database only for those areas that are connected to the router. Link state protocols use TCP-directed packets to communicate with other routers directly in an area, thus reducing broadcast traffic on the network.

With link state protocols, convergence occurs as soon as the databases are updated, avoiding the slow convergence problems of distance vector algorithms. Link state routing protocols also allow for security of the record update messages. The database description packets are transmitted in a secure manner and protected by a checksum. Link state records are also protected by timers that remove them from the database if a refresh packet doesn't arrive within the timeout specified. For even more security, the messages can be authenticated via password.

In an OSPF network, the database is synchronized between the OSPF routers, which use it to calculate routes in the routing table. OSPF uses the Dijkstra algorithm, which comes from the branch of mathematics called *graph theory*, to calculate the lowest-cost path to a destination from a given source. OSPF supports load balancing and multipath routing and can be used with both broadcast networks (such as Ethernet) or nonbroadcast networks (such as ATM or X.25). OSPF has different protocols for broadcast and multicast network types.

The routing tables used by a distance vector protocol like RIP have a flat structure; every RIP router on the internetwork must contain an entry for every network. The networks are not divided into areas or groups; all are seen as individual entities—thus the "flat" description. Link state protocols like OSPF create a hierarchical structure by dividing the internetwork into areas. Every OSPF router belongs to an area, identified by a 32-bit number called the *area number*. This area greatly reduces the size of the routing table for each router, since it has to keep entries only for its area.

The Transport Layer Protocols

The TCP/IP protocols that operate at the transport layer of the OSI model (the host-to-host layer of the DoD model) are the Transmission Control Protocol (TCP) and the User Datagram Protocol (UDP). These two protocols provide two different types of connection services:

- TCP is a connection-oriented protocol.
- UDP is a *connectionless* protocol.

The protocol most appropriate for sending a given message depends on whether reliability or speed is of highest priority. A connection-oriented protocol such as TCP offers better error control, but its higher overhead means a loss of performance. A connectionless protocol like UDP, on the other hand, suffers in the reliability department but, unhampered by error-checking duties, is faster. Here is more information about the two types of service:

- **Connection-oriented services** As a provider of connection-oriented services, TCP first establishes a virtual connection between the sending and receiving computers. This is done through the use of acknowledgments and response messages.

- **Connectionless services** A connectionless transport protocol like UDP doesn't provide the service of dividing a message into packets (also called *datagrams*) and reassembling it at the other end, as the connection-oriented TCP does. Since UDP doesn't sequence the packets that the data arrives in, an application program that uses UDP has to be able to make sure that the entire message has arrived and is in the right order. To save processing time, network applications that have very small data units to exchange, and thus very little message reassembling to do, may use UDP instead of TCP.

On the Scene...

The Difference Between Connection-Oriented and Connectionless Services

The most common analogy for differentiating between connection-oriented and connectionless communications compares different services available from the post office. If you're in Boston and you need to send an important report to the manager of your company's branch office in El Paso, you could put it in an envelope, affix the required amount of postage, and drop it in the corner mailbox. This would be the easiest, quickest way to take care of the task, but you would have no idea whether or when the report reached its destination.

On the other hand, you could go to the post office and fill out a card to send the report via registered, certified mail, with a return receipt requested. It would cost more and it would take more time and effort on your part, but it would be a more reliable form of communication. You would get back an acknowledgment when the package was delivered, showing that it was indeed received by the person to whom it was addressed.

Connection-oriented services resemble the second example, although they actually go one step further: They establish the connection before sending the data. This would be as though, before you sent your certified mail, you first got on the phone with the El Paso manager and let him know the report was coming so he could be on the lookout for its arrival. If you're really detail-minded (or paranoid) you could even ask that he call you back when it gets there, and let you know that all the pages are there in sequence and it wasn't damaged along the way. That is essentially what a connection-oriented service does. You've taken pains to make sure your communication is as reliable as possible, but at a cost in time (and long distance phone charges) to both you and the intended recipient.

Which Port in a (Broadcast) Storm?

Thanks to the multitasking capabilities of Windows 2000 and other modern operating systems, you can use more than one network application simultaneously. For example, you can use your Web browser to access your company's homepage at the same time your e-mail software is downloading your e-mail. You know that TCP/IP uses an IP address to identify your computer on the network and get the messages to the correct system, but how does it separate the response to your browser's request from your incoming mail when both arrive at the same IP address?

That's where ports come in. If the two parts of an IP address that represent the network identification and the host (individual computer) identification are somewhat like a street name and an individual street number, you might think of the port number as the identifier of the specific apartment or suite within the building.

TCP and UDP, the transport layer protocols, assign port numbers to each application, so the data intended for the Web browser in Apartment A doesn't get sent to the e-mail program in Apartment B.

Table 5.2 shows some of the commonly used ports (the designated ports used by certain services or applications by default).

Table 5.2 Specific ports are designated for the use of certain services and applications.

Port Number	Service/Application
7	Echo
20, 21	File Transfer Protocol (FTP)
23	Telnet
25	Simple Mail Transfer Protocol (SMTP)
53	Domain Name System (DNS)
68	Dynamic Host Configuration Protocol (DHCP)
69	Trivial File Transfer Protocol (TFTP)
80	Hypertext Transfer Protocol (HTTP)
88	Kerberos
110	Post Office Protocol, version 3 (POP3)
119	Network News Transfer Protocol (NNTP)
143	Internet Message Access Protocol (IMAP)
161	Simple Network Management Protocol (SNMP)
220	IMAP 3

The MAC Address

When we discuss a computer's "address," in the context of TCP/IP, we are usually referring to its IP address. The IP address is a *logical* address; it can be assigned by the administrator (or by a DHCP server) and can be changed easily. However, each network card or interface also has a *physical* address, called the *Media Access Control (MAC) address*. This address is usually permanently burned into a chip on the NIC and is not as easily changed (although some NIC manufacturers allow you to change the MAC address by "flashing" the card with special software).

How does the MAC address correlate to the IP address? Think of it this way: A city or county can assign a street name and house number to a physical structure, but this is really only a "logical" address. This address can be changed; sometimes a neighborhood group will petition to have a street renamed, or the city council will change the numbering scheme to facilitate emergency response or to accommodate new construction. But the location where the building stands also has a "physical" address—its geographic coordinates. When the land is surveyed, the location is identified by degrees of longitude and latitude, and these points will remain constant regardless of changes to the street name and number. That physical address is like the NIC's MAC address; it will (almost always) remain the same.

MAC addresses on Ethernet cards are generally 12-digit hexadecimal numbers, with one part of the address identifying the NIC vendor. The IEEE assigns this part to the vendor. The rest of the address is a unique identification for that card, assigned by the vendor. No two NICs should have the same MAC address (although this doesn't really become a problem unless the two identical addresses are on the same network). ARP maps IP addresses to MAC addresses.

Name Resolution

What's in a name? When it comes to computer networking, the answer is, a lot. On TCP/IP-based networks, the endpoints of communication are the IP address of the hosts and destination computers. But IP addresses are difficult for humans to remember. Just imagine a world in which people were identified solely by numbers—how much more difficult would it be to keep those identifications straight if you had to remember that the colleague you just met is called 1000101000110111 instead of Bob? Most software programs are not written to be "aware" of IP addresses, either. Network access would be fraught with error if everyone had to remember the IP address of every host with which they wanted to communicate.

There must be a mechanism, then, that allows users and programs to access network resources via computer or host name, rather than just IP addresses. This is the role of the *name resolution service*. Name resolution services in use on today's networks fall into two broad categories:

- NetBIOS name resolution
- Hostname resolution

In the following sections, we look at the "how's and why's" of NetBIOS name resolution, and we define and analyze the major methods of resolving NetBIOS names, including the Windows Internet Naming Service. Then we move to hostname resolution and examine how the hierarchical names used on the Internet (such as www.shinder.net) are resolved to IP addresses, with a focus on the Domain Name System and its latest incarnation, Dynamic DNS.

NetBIOS Name Resolution

A company called Sytek, Inc., developed NetBIOS in 1983 for IBM. The NetBIOS transport protocol was designed to accommodate small LANs located on a single segment, and the NetBEUI transport protocol is an outgrowth of the NetBIOS transport protocol. NetBEUI uses the instruction set provided with the NetBIOS standard and has "extended" it—hence the name NetBIOS Extended User Interface (NetBEUI).

Programs written to the NetBIOS interface use NetBIOS names as the "end-point" of communications. Each computer on a NetBIOS network must have a NetBIOS name, which consists of 16 bytes. Only the first 15 bytes of the NetBIOS name are configurable by the user. The sixteenth byte is used by the operating system to denote the availability of network services. NetBIOS programs *must* know the name of the destination computer in order to establish a session.

In order to access the destination computer, a broadcast is used. Broadcast messages are sent to all computers on the network segment, rather than to a specific destination. This means that all computers must be on the same physical subnet, since normally broadcast messages don't cross routers. In larger network installations (more than about 40 or 50 computers), the volume of broadcast traffic will become so "loud" from network congestion that no useful information will be able to get through.

So NetBIOS is broadcast-based, limited to a single segment, and uses NetBIOS names as the endpoint of communications. This presents a significant challenge to NetBIOS programs that need to function on a TCP/IP-based network. The TCP/IP protocol stack was designed to work on large internetworks, with the segments separated by routers. Routers do not forward broadcasts by default. Therefore, NetBIOS applications would not be able to access resources on computers located on another segment. Even if we open up the NetBIOS ports on the routers, we still have the problem of NetBIOS applications using only NetBIOS names. Before the request can be passed down the TCP/IP protocol stack, the NetBIOS name must be converted, or *resolved,* to an IP address.

The entire process of matching a NetBIOS name with an IP address is called *NetBIOS name resolution.* In order to get TCP/IP to "care" about NetBIOS names and deal with them in an orderly fashion, we need to add something to the TCP/IP protocol stack. This "add-on" is called *NetBIOS over TCP/IP,* shortened to NETBT or NBT. NetBT is implemented in the NetBIOS session layer interface.

When a request for network services is passed from the user application to the application layer of the TCP/IP stack, NetBT intercepts the request and the NetBIOS name is resolved to an IP address. After the IP address is discovered, the request is passed on, now including the destination computer's IP address. It moves down the stack to the transport layer, then to the network layer, through the data link and physical layers and onto the wire (or wireless media).

On the Scene...

Understanding The Need for NetBIOS Name Resolution

Here's an analogy to help you understand the need for NetBIOS name resolution. A young child writes a letter to his mother and addresses it to "Mom," the *friendly name* by which he identifies her. If the child were to leave this letter on the kitchen table, there would be no problem getting it to its destination host (Mom). This is because the kitchen table is on the local segment (the kitchen of Mom's home). But if the child put the letter in the mailbox, the post office would encounter quite a challenge in trying to get the letter to the correct destination. "Mom" is like a NetBIOS name in that it is not a routable address. However, if the child's father took that letter and put it into another envelope that had both "Mom" and the house address on the front, the post office would be able to deliver the message. The house address is a routable address, so the letter will now find its way to the right mom. What Dad did is similar to what NetBT does for NetBIOS names. It converts NetBIOS name requests to IP address requests so that the message or communication will get to the intended host.

NetBIOS and NetBEUI, which use a flat namespace for computer identification and don't include any method of identifying the network on which a computer resides, are consequently *nonroutable* protocols. But when the NetBIOS name is converted to an IP address, which *does* provide for network identification, our message becomes a routable request.

Microsoft operating systems use several different ways to resolve NetBIOS names to an IP address. This is because it is vitally important for NetBIOS applications to be able to access the IP address of a destination host on a TCP/IP-based network. If the NetBIOS name cannot be resolved, the NetBIOS application will not be able to establish a session with the destination host. NetBIOS names can be resolved by the following mechanisms:

- NetBIOS name cache
- NetBIOS name servers
- Broadcasts
- LMHOSTS file

The NetBIOS remote name cache contains the name and IP address mappings of recently accessed machines. This cache is searched first before any other method of NetBIOS name resolution takes place.

A NetBIOS name server keeps track of NetBIOS names and their associated IP addresses. In the real world, NetBIOS is in widespread use only on Microsoft networks, and almost all NetBIOS name servers run Microsoft's WINS. It's unlikely that you'll ever run into any other implementation of NetBIOS names servers, so from this point forward we refer to NetBIOS name servers as WINS servers. WINS servers provide two basic functions. First is NetBIOS name registration, where the WINS server registers computers' NetBIOS names and IP addresses. A WINS server dynamically and automatically updates WINS clients' NetBIOS names when WINS clients start. The second major function of a WINS server is to resolve NetBIOS name queries when NetBIOS clients query the WINS server for the IP address of a destination NetBIOS host.

Even on TCP/IP-based networks, NetBIOS clients can still broadcast for the IP address of the destination host. The effectiveness of the broadcast method is limited because, by default, routers do not pass traffic over UDP Ports 137 and 138 (the NetBIOS name service and the NetBIOS datagram services, respectively). Therefore, NetBIOS name resolution via broadcast works only when destination clients are located on the same segment.

The LMHOSTS file is a static, manually updated text file that contains NetBIOS name and IP address mappings for NetBIOS hosts. The LMHOSTS file resolves NetBIOS names by reading the file from top to bottom. This means the most frequently accessed computers should have their names placed on top, whereas less frequently accessed files should have their names placed toward the bottom. Due to its static nature, the LMHOSTS file does not work well in networks that use dynamically assigned IP addresses or in large enterprise networks.

NetBIOS names can also be resolved from hostname resolution methods such as the HOSTS file or DNS server (discussed in the next section) if other NetBIOS name resolution methods have failed.

Hostname Resolution

Hostnames are used to identify computers on the Internet. Remember that any kind of name, whether a flat NetBIOS name or a hierarchical hostname, is just a convenience for human beings. Computers work only with numbers, so in order to be useful, hostnames, like NetBIOS names, must ultimately be resolved to IP addresses.

When the Internet was in its infancy, hostnames were resolved to IP addresses via a plain-text file named hosts.txt. This file was located at the Stanford Research Institute's Network Information Center (SRI-NIC). Whenever a machine was added to the network or an existing machine's IP address was changed, the hosts.txt file had to be edited. This hosts.txt file then had to be downloaded from SRI-NIC so that all machines on the network would have an accurate list of hostnames and IP addresses for hostname resolution.

There were several problems with using the hosts.txt file. First, it used a flat name space like that seen in NetBIOS. The flat name space required each computer to have a different name. Second, as more and more machines joined the network, traffic at SRI-NIC became a significant bottleneck to network communications. Third, the size of the hosts.txt file grew increasingly large, which led to long download times and reduced performance for lookups.

NOTE

Microsoft operating systems can still use a Hosts file for resolution of fully qualified domain names; however, this Hosts file does not use the .txt (or any) extension. A common mistake in creating a Hosts file in Notepad or other text editors is that the application saves it with the .txt extension, and it then will not work.

To solve these problems, in 1987 Paul Mockapetris developed and proposed the Domain Naming System (DNS). The DNS was designed to be a hierarchical naming system, with responsibility for the DNS database distributed rather than centralized. For that reason, today's hostnames are *hierarchical*. They have multiple parts, much as a person's name does in modern U.S. culture. Your last name identifies the family to which you belong, and your first and middle names identify an individual within that family. Hostnames work the same way, except that the "family" is a domain and there can be subdomains within a domain. Thus two computers can have the same computer name, as long as they are in different domains (just as there's no problem differentiating between two people named Bob when one is named Bob Smith and the other is named Bob Jones). There are thousands of machines on the Internet named www, although this is usually a name assigned to a virtual machine—the Web server function running on a computer that might have an entirely different name. Yet their "full names" are all unique; there is no problem differentiating between www.shinder.net and www.tacteam.net because their domain names are different.

At the top of the DNS hierarchy is the *root domain*. The root domain is sometimes represented as a period surrounded by quotation marks (".") or as a space surrounded by quotation marks. Just underneath the root domain are the *top-level domains*. The top-level domains consist of a two- or three-letter designation, such as .com, .net, .org (called *generic domains*) or .au, .us, .de (called *country codes*). The *second-level domains* lie below the top-level domains. These second-level domains are named for the organizations that own the domain names—for example, "BrandXDrugs.com." A second-level domain name can be obtained from a domain registrar, such as Network Solutions, Inc (NSI). The root domain, top-level domains, and second-level domains are the only centralized aspects of the DNS. After a company or an individual registers a second-level domain name with a domain registrar, they are free to create as many *subdomains* as they like—these subdomains are nested inside the second-level domain, as in "sedatives.BrandXDrugs."

NOTE

New domain name registrars are being approved on a continuous basis. For an up-to-date listing of authorized registrars, see ICANN's Web site at www.icann.org/registrars/accredited-list.html.

The combination of a hostname and its domain name is referred to as a *fully qualified domain name (FQDN)*. All hosts participating in the DNS are identifiable via their FQDNs. The servers that maintain a database mapping host and domain names to IP addresses are called *DNS servers*.

Computers on TCP/IP networks are configured with the IP address of a DNS server as part of setting up their TCP/IP properties. When a hostname needs to be resolved, the computer (called a *DNS client*) sends a request to the DNS server. The DNS server searches its database and either responds with the IP address associated with the hostname or, if the name is not in its database, the server can query other DNS servers to find the address.

Because DNS must work to resolve names all across the Internet, a number of standards govern its implementation. For example, hostnames must follow specified naming conventions. These are spelled out in RFCs 952 and 1123. According to these standards, names were limited to upper- and lowercase letters (A–Z and a–z), the numerals 0–9, and the hyphen (–).

DNS is also used by Microsoft's Active Directory (Windows 2000 and later domain controllers) for name resolution. Microsoft's DNS servers allow the use of other characters such as the underscore (_) in hostnames because they support UTF-8, a superset of the ASCII character set that allows you to use alphabets of other languages. However, these names will not be recognized by many of the UNIX-based DNS servers on the Internet.

TCP/IP Utilities

A number of software tools associated with the TCP/IP protocols can be useful to investigators. The TCP/IP stacks of different vendors are not identical, and neither are the diagnostic and information-gathering utilities that are included. In this section, we focus on the utilities that come with the Windows TCP/IP suite. We also mention their equivalents (when applicable) in UNIX/Linux implementations.

NOTE

The TCP/IP tools we discuss here are the command-line utilities that are included in the TCP/IP stacks of various operating systems. Third-party utilities are available (many of them free) that provide graphic interfaces to perform the same functions.

Connection Verification, Identification, and Tracing Utilities

Several command-line utilities can be used to test TCP/IP connectivity, gather information about the TCP/IP configuration, configure properties, and trace the route that a packet takes over the network. These tools include the following:

- PING
- NSLOOKUP
- IPCONFIG/IFCONFIG
- ROUTE
- TRACERT/TRACEROUTE
- ARP

PING, short for *Packet Internet Groper*, is used to determine whether a TCP/IP connection can be made to a particular address. You can PING a computer or router on the local network or a remote network, or you can test the configuration of the TCP/IP stack by PINGing the loopback address, 127.0.0.1. PING works by sending ICMP echo request messages to the destination computer, which then returns an echo reply message. The response shows you the number of packets sent and received (along with percentage of packet loss, if any) and the time in milliseconds that it takes for a packet to make the round trip. As shown in Figure 5.12, you can PING a computer by IP address or by name. If you PING by name, the response provides you with the computer's IP address.

PING includes a dozen switches that can be used to further control the behavior of the PING function. Available switches are shown in Table 5.3.

Table 5.3 PING switches

Switch	Function
-t	PINGs the specified host until stopped (continuous PING) by pressing Ctrl-C.
-a	Resolves addresses to hostnames.
-n count	Specifies number of echo requests to send.
-l size	Specifies send buffer size.
-f	Sets Don't Fragment flag in packet.
-i TTL	Time to live.
-v TOS	Type of service.

Continued

Table 5.3 Continued

Switch	Function
-r count	Records route for count hops.
-s count	Timestamp for count hops.
-j host-list	Loose source route along host list.
-k host-list	Strict source route along host list.
-w timeout	Timeout in milliseconds to wait for each reply.

Figure 5.12 The PING command provides TCP/IP connectivity information.

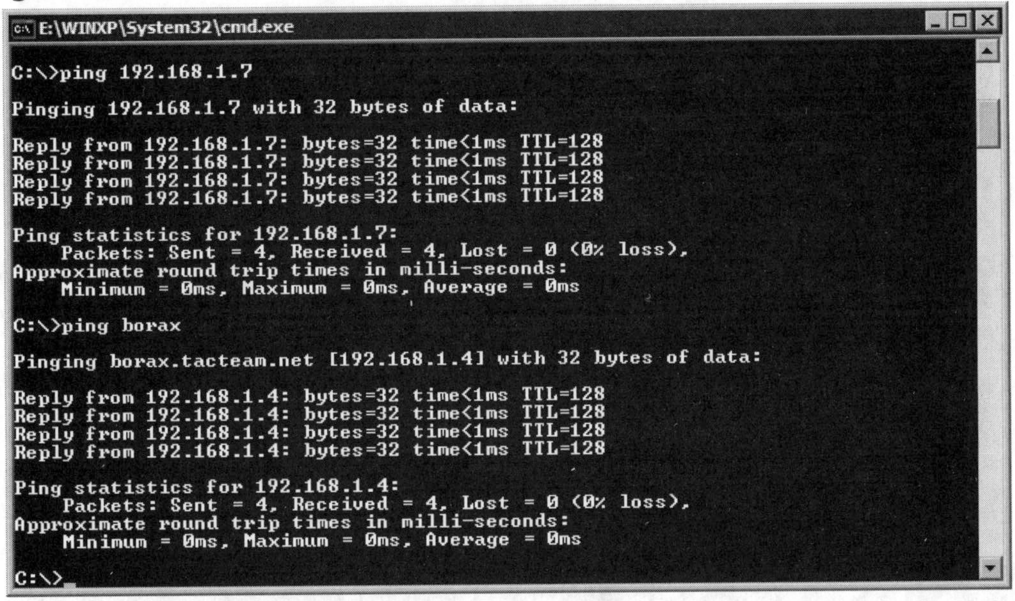

For more information about using PING and how the PING utility works, see www.cisco.com/warp/public/63/ping_traceroute.html#ping.

NSLOOKUP is used to find the hostname associated with an IP address (or vice versa), as shown in Figure 5.13. NSLOOKUP queries DNS servers for information about hosts and domains. NSLOOKUP can be a starting point for tracking cybercriminals using their IP addresses.

For more information on using NSLOOKUP, see the UNIX Shell Command manual page at www.stopspam.org/usenet/mmf/man/nslookup.html.

The **ipconfig** command (on Windows machines) provides basic TCP/IP configuration information. Figure 5.14 shows the results of **ipconfig** (run with the **/all** switch).

Figure 5.13 The NSLOOKUP utility can be used to discover the hostname associated with an IP address.

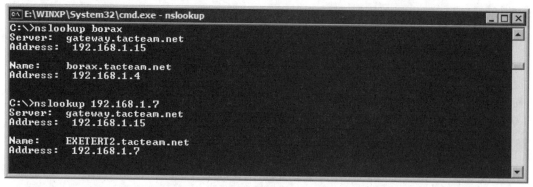

```
C:\>nslookup borax
Server:   gateway.tacteam.net
Address:  192.168.1.15

Name:     borax.tacteam.net
Address:  192.168.1.4


C:\>nslookup 192.168.1.7
Server:   gateway.tacteam.net
Address:  192.168.1.15

Name:     EXETERT2.tacteam.net
Address:  192.168.1.7
```

Figure 5.14 The ipconfig /all command in Windows provides configuration information.

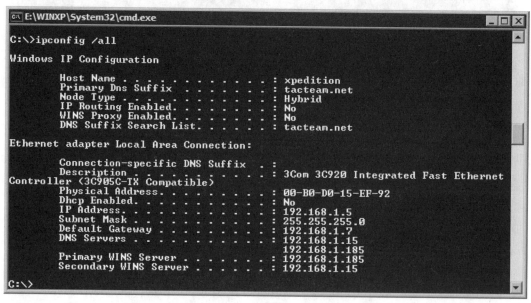

```
C:\>ipconfig /all

Windows IP Configuration

        Host Name . . . . . . . . . . . . : xpedition
        Primary Dns Suffix  . . . . . . . : tacteam.net
        Node Type . . . . . . . . . . . . : Hybrid
        IP Routing Enabled. . . . . . . . : No
        WINS Proxy Enabled. . . . . . . . : No
        DNS Suffix Search List. . . . . . : tacteam.net

Ethernet adapter Local Area Connection:

        Connection-specific DNS Suffix  . :
        Description . . . . . . . . . . . : 3Com 3C920 Integrated Fast Ethernet
Controller (3C905C-TX Compatible)
        Physical Address. . . . . . . . . : 00-B0-D0-15-EF-92
        Dhcp Enabled. . . . . . . . . . . : No
        IP Address. . . . . . . . . . . . : 192.168.1.5
        Subnet Mask . . . . . . . . . . . : 255.255.255.0
        Default Gateway . . . . . . . . . : 192.168.1.7
        DNS Servers . . . . . . . . . . . : 192.168.1.15
                                            192.168.1.185
        Primary WINS Server . . . . . . . : 192.168.1.185
        Secondary WINS Server . . . . . . : 192.168.1.15

C:\>
```

As you can see, this utility gives you a great deal of information about how this machine is configured, including the hostname and DNS suffix assigned to it, the Ethernet adapter installed (and its physical or MAC address), and the IP address, subnet mask, default gateway, and DNS and WINS servers assigned. We see that this information was manually assigned by the administrator, because DHCP is not enabled. We can also see that the machine is not acting as an IP router or a WINS proxy.

On UNIX/Linux machines, some basic configuration information is available using the **ifconfig** command with the **–a** switch. This is shown in Figure 5.15, using Macintosh OS X.

Figure 5.15 The command used to display configuration information in UNIX is **IFCONFIG –a**.

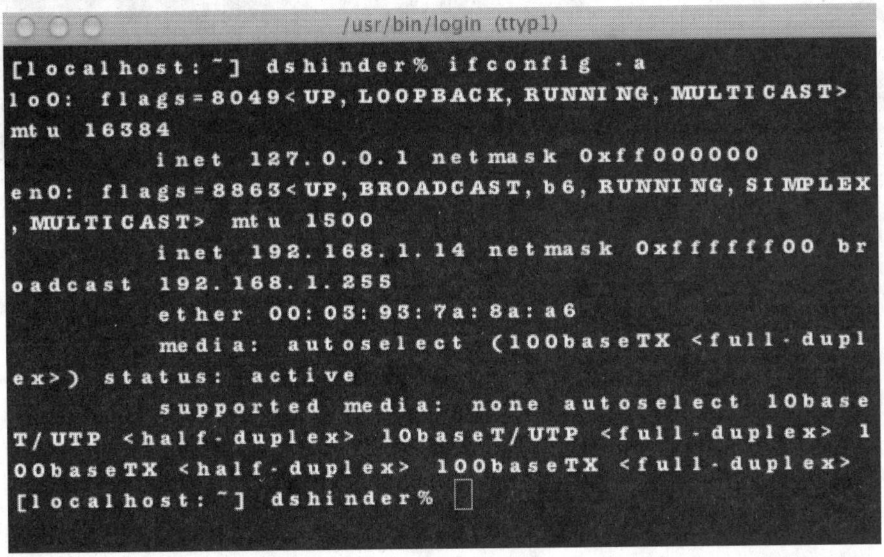

```
                        /usr/bin/login  (ttyp1)

[localhost: ~] dshinder% ifconfig -a
lo0:  flags=8049<UP, LOOPBACK, RUNNING, MULTICAST>
mtu 16384
        inet 127.0.0.1 netmask 0xff000000
en0:  flags=8863<UP, BROADCAST, b6, RUNNING, SIMPLEX
, MULTICAST> mtu 1500
        inet 192.168.1.14 netmask 0xffffff00 br
oadcast 192.168.1.255
        ether 00:03:93:7a:8a:a6
        media: autoselect (100baseTX <full-dupl
ex>) status: active
        supported media: none autoselect 10base
T/UTP <half-duplex> 10baseT/UTP <full-duplex> 1
00baseTX <half-duplex> 100baseTX <full-duplex>
[localhost: ~] dshinder% []
```

As you can see, the information is formatted differently, but you are still able to determine the computer's IP address, subnet mask (in hexadecimal rather than decimal), physical Ethernet address, and other basic information.

The *ROUTE* utility is used in both Windows and UNIX-based machines to view and manually manipulate the network routing tables. You can add, delete, or modify routes with this tool, although it is usually not necessary, since Windows can automatically builds a routing table using RIP or OSPF. In addition, on UNIX computers, system routing table daemons such as **routed(8)**, which uses RIP and the Internet Router Discovery Protocol (IRDP), handle this task. To view the routing table information, use the **ROUTE PRINT** command.

The **TRACERT** (in Windows) and **TRACEROUTE** (in UNIX) commands are used to trace the route taken by a packet to reach a remote host. You can specify either an IP address or a hostname as the destination machine. The results will show you the number of "hops" required to reach the destination, as well as the amount of time (in milliseconds) for each hop. You can see the names of the routers through which the packet passes. You can also specify a maximum number of hops to be used in searching for the target computer. Figure 5.16 illustrates a route trace that was completed in five hops.

Figure 5.16 The TRACERT and TRACEROUTE commands allow you to view the route taken by a packet to a remote destination.

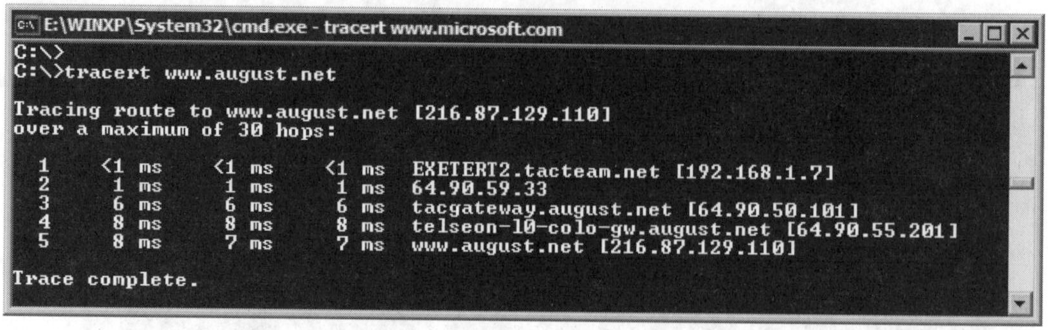

```
E:\WINXP\System32\cmd.exe - tracert www.microsoft.com                    _ □ ×
C:\>
C:\>tracert www.august.net

Tracing route to www.august.net [216.87.129.110]
over a maximum of 30 hops:

  1    <1 ms    <1 ms    <1 ms  EXETERT2.tacteam.net [192.168.1.7]
  2     1 ms     1 ms     1 ms  64.90.59.33
  3     6 ms     6 ms     6 ms  tacgateway.august.net [64.90.50.101]
  4     8 ms     8 ms     8 ms  telseon-10-colo-gw.august.net [64.90.55.201]
  5     8 ms     7 ms     7 ms  www.august.net [216.87.129.110]

Trace complete.
```

The **ARP** (Address Resolution Protocol) command allows you to view and manipulate the entries in the ARP cache. The ARP cache is a list of both the IP addresses and the corresponding MAC (physical) addresses for computers that have recently had a connection to the computer on which you're running the ARP utility. This utility also allows you to add and delete entries in the cache.

Network Statistic Utilities

Statistics utilities can provide you with information about network connections. These include:

- NETSTAT
- NBTSTAT

The **NETSTAT** command can be used on both Windows and UNIX-based computers to give you information about current active connections using different protocols (TCP, UDP, RAW, or UNIX socket). Running this command displays each connection on a separate line, showing the local address (computer and port) and the remote (or "foreign") address, as well as the status (state) of the connection. The output from **NETSTAT** is shown in Figure 5.17.

There are also switches that can be used with **NETSTAT** to provide different or additional information. Some of this information can be useful to investigators. For example, knowing that there are open and listening ports on the machine is an important security issue when the computer is connected to the Internet.

The **NETSTAT** switches are shown in Table 5.4.

Figure 5.17 The NETSTAT command can be used to display current active connections.

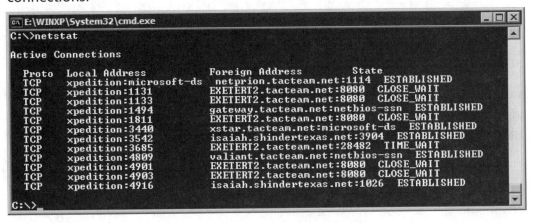

Table 5.4 NETSTAT switches

Switch	Function
-a	Shows all connections, including listening ports.
-e	Shows Ethernet statistics, such as the number of bytes of data received and sent (can be combined with the –s option).
-n	Shows addresses and port numbers in numeric form.
-o	Shows the owning process ID associated with each connection.
-p proto	Shows only the connections for the protocol specified by *proto* (for example, TCP).
-r	Shows the routing table (the same information you get with the **ROUTE PRINT** command in Windows).
-s	Shows per-protocol statistics.

Network Monitoring Tools

Many tools are available for monitoring network activity and even capturing transmitted packets and peeking inside them. Some of these tools are included with modern operating systems, some are distributed at no cost on the Internet as "freeware," and others must be purchased from third-party vendors.

The Simple Network Management Protocol

The Simple Network Management Protocol (SNMP) is not a utility in and of itself. Rather, it is a protocol used to communicate status messages from devices distributed throughout the network to machines configured to receive these status messages. Machines that report their status run SNMP *agent* software, and machines that receive the status messages run SNMP *management* software. One way to remember how this works is to think of the agent software as the "secret agent" that gets information about a network device and then reports the information to his or her "manager" at headquarters.

Although the name of the protocol would lead you to believe that the primary function is to allow you to "manage" objects on the network, management in this context is more related to monitoring rather than actually effecting any changes to the devices. SNMP allows you to audit the activities of servers, workstations, routers, bridges, intelligent hubs, and just about any network-connected device that supports the installation of agent software.

In order for agent software to collect information regarding a particular service, a *Management Information Base (MIB)* must be created. The MIB is a database and a collection of instructions about how and what information should be gathered from a system. The agent is responsible for reporting the information gathered by the MIB. However, agents don't usually volunteer information spontaneously. Rather, the agent must be queried by an SNMP management system before it gives up its knowledge. There is an exception to this rule, called a *trap message*. A trap message is sent spontaneously by an agent to SNMP management systems to which it has been configured to send.

Protocol Analyzers ("Sniffers")

Protocol analyzers allow network professionals to capture and analyze the traffic on the network. These can be hardware devices or software programs and are often referred to as *packet sniffers*. Microsoft's NT, 2000, and .NET operating systems come with a built-in protocol analyzer called *Network Monitor (NetMon)*.

The Microsoft NetMon is a software protocol analyzer that allows you to capture and analyze traffic on your network; it is included with the Windows NT and 2000 server operating systems. The version of NetMon that comes with the operating system is limited in scope; it does not allow you to place the network adapter in "promiscuous mode." When an adapter is placed in promiscuous mode, it is able to listen to all the traffic on the segment, even if that traffic is not destined for the machine running the Network Monitor software. A more robust version of NetMon is included in Microsoft's Systems Management Server (SMS).

Even with its limitations, the "lite" version of Network Monitor is a very useful tool for assessing the activity on the network. You can use the tool to collect network data and analyze it on the spot or save your recording activities for a later time. It allows you to monitoring network activity and set triggers for when certain events or data cross the wire, which could be useful if you are looking for certain keywords in e-mail communications moving through the network.

NOTE

Any person with administrative privileges can install the Network Monitor on a Windows server family computer and start "listening" to activity on the wire. This is one (among many) reasons that the number of persons in an organization who are assigned administrative privileges should be considered very carefully. The Network Monitor is also able to detect when someone else on the segment is using Network Monitor and provide you with their location.

The Network Monitor program allows you to capture only those frames that you are interested in, based on protocol or source or destination computer. You can apply even more detailed and exacting filters to data that you have finished collecting, which allows you to pinpoint the precise elements you might be looking for in the captured data. For more information about Microsoft's Network Monitor, see Q article 148942 on the Microsoft Web site.

On the Scene…

Finding Q Articles

You can find a great deal of information about Microsoft products, including detailed how-to instructions, in the Microsoft Technical Database (formerly called the Knowledge Base), which you can search at http://support.microsoft.com/default.aspx?ln=EN-GB&pr=kbinfo&.

Network analyzers are available from many different vendors, including the following:

- Sniffer Technologies, in partnership with Network Associates, makes a number of network analysis tools, including versions made specifically for wireless networks, enterprise-level networks, and portable solutions.

- Sniff-Tech markets a product called ANASIL that includes protocol capture and decoding for protocols used on Microsoft, UNIX, NetWare, and AppleTalk networks.

- Ethereal is a protocol analysis program for UNIX and Windows that can be downloaded free at www.ethereal.com.

Hackers often use sniffer software to covertly capture packets and read their contents (which can include network passwords). Protecting against unauthorized "sniff attacks" requires that data be encrypted while traveling across the network (as is done by the IP Security Protocol, IPSec). More information about sniffer programs for Windows and UNIX is available at www.packetattack.com/network_analysis_sniffers.html.

Why This Matters to the Investigator

An understanding of client/server networking and what goes on at the higher levels (above the physical) when computers communicate with one another is vital to understanding security vulnerabilities that allow hackers to access computers and networks without authorization. The TCP/IP protocols are the basis of Internet communication, and technically savvy cybercriminals are intimately familiar with how they work and how to exploit their characteristics to gain access or to attack and bring down servers and networks.

The information in this chapter forms the foundation for understanding the more detailed descriptions in Chapter 6, "Understanding Network Intrusions and Attacks," and will also help you understand the functions of the security mechanisms described in Chapter 7, "Understanding Cybercrime Prevention," and Chapter 8, "Implementing System Security."

Summary

Computer networking is a complex subject, in part due to the following reasons:

- There are many different ways to network computers at the physical level using different types of media and different layouts or topologies.

- There are many different methods of controlling access to the media and "directing traffic" at the link level.

- There are different ways to handle addressing and routing of messages between computers at the network level.

- There are different methods for dealing with the transfer of data at the transport level.

- There are a number of protocols and file-sharing mechanisms that can be used for computer communication at the higher levels.

A good understanding of networking requires knowledge of how data, converted to electrical or light pulses, is sent across cabling or over the airwaves, as well as the processes used on the sending and receiving ends to prepare that data for sending and to translate received data back into a form usable by applications and, ultimately, computer users.

For greater efficiency, data is broken into manageable chunks called *packets*, and it is these packets that are transmitted across a network. The packet structure and size vary, depending on the protocols in use. Network protocols are rules that govern the exact procedures computers follow when sending and receiving data. In order to standardize these processes so that systems using different hardware platforms and operating system software can communicate with one another, networking models and specifications are developed so that vendors can use them as guidelines to ensure compatibility.

The OSI and DoD models are layered to define specific tasks to be performed by protocols at different levels or steps in the network communication process. At the physical level, each computer that will communicate on a network requires at least one network interface, usually in the form of a network interface card, or NIC. The simplest networks require only NICs and cabling to enable communication. For more complex network configurations, a number of hardware devices operate at different layers to provide more efficient connectivity; these devices include hubs, switches, bridges, and routers. Gateways (usually implemented as software) operate at the highest levels and provide translation between different protocols.

Modern operating systems come with networking capabilities built in, and expensive server operating systems provide for many network services in addition to file and print sharing, including authentication, name resolution, remote access, and even the ability to function as a router. Authentication servers provide for centralized network security and management of resources. Different operating system platforms rely on different file-sharing protocols and authentication schemes, but most OS vendors provide for interoperability with other operating systems because many of today's networks are heterogeneous.

Regardless of operating system or hardware platform, the majority of networks today run on the TCP/IP protocols. TCP/IP is the most routable protocol stack and thus the most appropriate for large routed networks; it is required for connecting to the Internet. This chapter provides a basic overview of networking hardware and software and a high-level explanation of how TCP/IP communications are accomplished. You can consult many excellent books and Web resources for more details about each of these aspects of computer networking; some good references are listed in the Resources section at the end of this chapter.

Frequently Asked Questions

The following Frequently Asked Questions, answered by the authors of this book, are designed to both measure your understanding of the concepts presented in this chapter and to assist you with real-life implementation of these concepts. To have your questions about this chapter answered by the author, browse to **www.syngress.com/solutions** and click on the **"Ask the Author"** form.

Q: What's the difference between public and private IP addresses?

A: Public addresses are visible to the Internet. Public addresses must be unique across the global Internet. They are generally assigned to ISPs by the Internet Assigned Numbers Authority (IANA) and then assigned by ISPs to their customers. Public addresses are sometimes called *routable addresses* because they can be routed across the Internet. Private IP addresses are not routable on the Internet; they are used on private (internal) networks and come from one of the address ranges reserved for private addressing. Anyone can use the private addresses, and the address of each computer needs to be unique only within the private network. The private address ranges are 10.xxx.xxx.xxx (with a subnet mask of 255.0.0.0), 172.016.xxx.xxx (with a subnet mask of 255.255.0.0), and 192.168.xxx.xxx (with a subnet mask of 255.255.255.0).

Additionally, IP addresses in the range 169.254.xxx.xxx are reserved for the use of APIPA services. For more information, see RFC 1597 on private addressing at www.pku.edu.cn/academic/research/computer-center/tc/html/RFC1597.html.

Q: How can all the computers on a local network access the Internet through a single Internet connection?

A: There are several different ways that a LAN can share an Internet connection. If the ISP assigns multiple public IP addresses, the computers can be connected to a router, with the router connecting to the Internet via phone line, DSL cable, ISDN, or T-1. If the ISP allocates only a single public address for the connection, the computers can be connected to a Network Address Translation, or NAT, device—either a dedicated device or a computer running NAT. This NAT host connects to the Internet, and other computers (the NAT clients) go through it to access Internet resources. The client computers are assigned private IP addresses (either manually, via a DHCP server on the network, or through the NAT's IP allocation service). The NAT host translates the private addresses to the public address and maintains a table with which it keeps track of which Internet requests came from which internal computers. Microsoft servers include a full-fledged NAT service; Windows 98/ME, 2000, and XP Professional computers include a "lite" version of NAT called Internet Connection Sharing (ICS). In the Linux/UNIX world, address translation is often referred to as *IP masquerading*. NAT products such as Vicomsoft and IPNetRouter (from Sustainable Networks) are available for Macintosh systems. For more information about NAT, see RFC 2663 at www.ietf.org/rfc/rfc2663.txt?number=2663.

Q: What's the difference between the PPP and SLIP link protocols used for dialup networking?

A: SLIP was designed exclusively for TCP/IP and isn't appropriate if the LAN to which you are connecting uses a different network/transport protocol stack, such as IPX/SPX. Additionally, SLIP doesn't support DHCP, so when you configure it, you must enter a static IP address. Many ISPs don't assign customers static addresses (sometimes referred to as *"nailed" addresses*) but instead use DHCP to assign a new address each time you dial in. PPP is a more modern link protocol that addresses these problems; it supports non-TCP/IP protocols such as IPX/SPX and NetBEUI, and it allows use of multiple protocols. PPP supports automatic negotiation of IP addresses, so it works with

DHCP servers, and it also allows the use of checksums for error checking—something SLIP doesn't do. Basically, PPP was designed to replace SLIP, since it is much more flexible. Both of these protocols are not full networking protocols; they are used only for establishing a link across phone lines. Another protocol (such as TCP/IP or IPX/SPX) is required to communicate with applications on the remote computer or network.

Q: How do TCP and UDP use ports to distinguish between multiple applications using the protocols simultaneously?

A: Each application using TCP or UDP identifies itself by a 16-bit number called a *port number.* The UDP and TCP header information that is added to the data packets at the transport layer on the sending computer (prior to the packets being passed down to the IP layer) contains the port numbers for both source and destination computers. Thus, even if there are dozens of applications running at the same time using the TCP or UDP protocol, the correct packets are delivered to each application based on the destination port number, and responses are returned using the port number listed for the source in the received packet (which will become the destination port number in the reply message).

Q: Where can I find a complete list of the well-known TCP and UDP ports?

A: The Internet Assigned Numbers Authority (IANA) maintains lists of all types of numbers used on the Internet, including the list of well-known port numbers. For this information, see www.iana.org/assignments/port-numbers.

Q: If the current version of the Internet Protocol is version 4, why is the "next generation" called IPv6? Why did we skip IPv5?

A: An experimental real-time stream protocol called *ST,* or the *Internet Stream Protocol,* used the version number 5 in the IP header of its packets. ST was designed as a connection-oriented protocol operating at the network level like the connectionless IP. ST was never intended to replace IP but to operate as an adjunct to it as part of the IP family, for transmission of streaming audio, video, and the like. Because the v5 identification had already been used, the new version of IP was assigned the designation IPv6. (For more information about ST, see RFC 1819 at ftp://ftp.isi.edu/in-notes/rfc1819.txt).

Q: What are some sniffing tools that can be used to capture and analyze packets on UNIX networks?

A: Some common sniffing tools for UNIX include Ethereal (which we mentioned earlier, in versions for UNIX and Windows), tcpdump (included with the BSD operating systems), ipgrab (available at http://home.xnet.com/ ~cathmike/MSB/Software), tcpflow (capture only, but it stores data in a format convenient for protocol analysis; it is available free on the Web at www.circlemud.org/~jelson/software/tcpflow). There are also sniffer programs available for particular UNIX versions, such as Snoop for Solaris, Etherfind for Sun Osm, and nettle/ntfmt for HP-UX.

Resources

- Bell Labs: *Advantages of Digital Signals*
  www.bell-labs.com/technology/digital/advantages.html

- *Telecommunications Fundamentals: Analog and Digital Transmission*
  www.privateline.com/manual/three.html

- Explanation of multiplexing
  http://williams.comp.ncat.edu/Networks/multiplexing.htm

- Explanation of frequency division multiplexing
  www.cs.williams.edu/~cs105/f01/text/ch3/DigitalTrans_13.html

- Explanation of time division multiplexing
  www.cs.williams.edu/~cs105/f01/text/ch3/DigitalTrans_9.html

- Tutorial on DWDM from the International Engineering Consortium
  www.iec.org/online/tutorials/dwdm

- Bell Labs: *What Does Multiplexing Do for Communications*?
  www.bell-labs.com/technology/multiplex

- House Committee on National Security hearings on EMP
  http://commdocs.house.gov/committees/security/has197010.000/has197010_1.HTM

- Associated Press: *Experts cite electromagnetic pulse as terrorist threat*
  www.globalsecurity.org/org/news/2001/011001-attack03.htm

- *The Electromagnetic Pulse*
  http://home.swbell.net/kkmartin/emp.htm

- *Networking Tutorial*
  http://punch.engr.wisc.edu/~orchard/net-tutorial

- World of networking
  www.helmig.com

- Network primer
  www2.edc.org/cope/networkprimer

- Windows 2000 Server
  www.microsoft.com/windows2000/server/default.asp

- Novell NetWare Server
  www.novell.com

- Macintosh OS X Server
  www.apple.com/macosx/server

- UNIX operating systems
  www.cs.arizona.edu/people/bridges/os/unix.html

- Linux operating systems
  www.linux.org

- Windows Services for UNIX
  www.ehsco.com/reading/20000807ncr1.html

- MacWindows Web site for Macintosh–Windows Integration Solutions
  www.macwindows.com

- *Introduction to the Internet Protocols*
  http://oac3.hsc.uth.tmc.edu/staff/snewton/tcp-tutorial

- *TCP/IP and IPX Routing Tutorial*
  www.sangoma.com/fguide.htm

- *TCP/IP Resources List*
  www.private.org.il/tcpip_rl.html

Chapter 6

Understanding Network Intrusions and Attacks

Introduction

As we've discussed in earlier chapters, there are many different types of cyber-crime, committed by all kinds of cybercriminals—some of whom have very little technical knowledge or skill. However, thanks to the news media and a few pop-ular movies, most people associate the term *cybercrime* with a particular type of offense: hacking into a system or network from outside an organization. Included in this narrow definition are malicious attacks designed to crash computers and congest networks, even when no actual "illegal entry" takes place. In either case, the criminal is presumed to have a high level of knowledge about computers and networking.

Unlike the cyberscam artist who needs to know only enough about com-puters to send mass e-mailings, or the child pornographer whose technical know-how is limited to uploading and downloading files, the network intruder or attacker has traditionally been able to boast of a certain amount of skill. It takes knowledge (and sometimes talent) to circumvent security measures and slip through the holes programmers leave in applications and operating systems to gain access to someone else's servers. It takes a thorough understanding of how network protocols work to exploit their characteristics and bring down systems or entire networks. Or at least, it once did.

Dedicated hackers spend hundreds or even thousands of hours perfecting intrusion techniques and attacks. Today, however, many hackers who break into or bring down networks aren't really hackers at all—at least, not in the original sense of the word (which referred to computer "whiz kids" whose mastery of the technology was the key to their ability to penetrate and crack systems). This is because the "real" hackers have generously made available the fruits of their knowledge and labor in the form of scripts and executable programs that do all the work. The "script kiddies" who use them might be scorned as hacker "wannabes" by those with technical knowledge, but hacking tools still continue to proliferate, shared freely through "warez" newsgroups and Web sites, making intrusions and attacks easy. No longer does a would-be intruder or attack have to bother to learn the technical aspects of Windows vulnerabilities or TCP/IP secu-rity flaws. Now anyone, with no training at all, can "worm" his way into the net-work of a competing business or launch a massive denial-of-service attack against a company whose politics she doesn't like.

It is important for cybercrime investigators who build cases charging un-authorized access or breach of network integrity to understand the basics of how intrusion techniques and system attacks work, even though intruders and attackers need not necessarily understand the technicalities of what they're doing.

After all, the investigator could be required to testify in court about an important issue that must be established in every criminal case: whether probable cause existed to make the arrest. It might be difficult to convince a jury that you had enough evidence to believe the accused committed a crime if you're unable to explain exactly *what* the crime is and exactly *how* it was committed.

In this chapter, we provide overviews of the technical aspects of various types of intrusions and attacks. We start with a discussion of an intruder's preparatory activities that might precede an attack:

- Scanning for open ports on the targeted network

- Disguising the attacker's IP address and other identifying information

- Placing software constructs or hardware devices (such as Trojan programs or keystroke monitors) to gather preliminary data that will help the attacker carry out the attack

Next, we take a look at how intruders crack passwords to gain access to systems and networks. You'll learn about brute-force crack attacks, how passwords stored on a system can be discovered and exploited, and how hackers use social engineering to con authorized users into disclosing their passwords.

Then we discuss the many types of technical exploits that hackers use to access or attack networked computers, including application exploits, operating system exploits, and protocol exploits. We also address the "script kiddie" and "click kiddie" phenomena and show you how people with almost no technical expertise can use readily available tools to jumpstart their hacking careers. Finally, we discuss how companies put together incident response teams to deal with these intrusions and attacks when they occur and how the internal response team can work together with law enforcement to improve the likelihood that the intruder or attacker will be tracked down and successfully prosecuted.

NOTE

Some of the attacks and exploits discussed in this chapter might be considered by some to be "obsolete." However, this is true only if we assume that all systems are running the latest versions of software and that all security patches have been applied. Unfortunately, this is not the case; in a world where a substantial number of business and government computers still run MS-DOS and Windows 3.*x*, it would be naïve to assume that the vulnerabilities of older operating systems and applications are no longer relevant.

Understanding Network Intrusions and Attacks

Network intrusions and attacks come in many forms and from all directions. Although external threats (usually from across the Internet) get the most attention, attacks and intrusions can—and often do—come from employees, contractors, and others on site or within a local network. Remember that just because someone is authorized to access a network doesn't mean that he or she has authorization to access *all* its resources.

We can no longer assume that attackers are particularly knowledgeable about computers. At one time, an attacker had to have a minimal level of skill to launch an attack, but today readily available tools completely automate the attack process. An attack really can come from just about anyone who has the motivation and the mindset to launch it.

Crimestoppers...

Considering Internal Threats

All cybercrime by its very definition involves using a network to access systems. However, when investigators are confronted with theft or destruction of data or attacks that crash servers, the possibility of an "inside job" shouldn't be discounted. Not all attacks or unauthorized entries into systems come from the Internet; they can also come from somewhere on the LAN or via physical access to the affected machines.

Some intrusions and "attacks" can even be unintentional. Users with just enough technical knowledge to be dangerous could experiment with changing settings and crash the system or network; curious people could stumble on unsecured resources to which they shouldn't have access; and employees attempting to make things more convenient for themselves (for example, by installing wireless access points so they'll have network connectivity when they take their laptops to the conference room for meetings) can unknowingly open up security holes.

In the following sections, we examine the difference between an intrusion and an attack; discuss various types of attacks, including accidental ones; and provide some guidelines for preventing intentional internal security breaches.

Intrusions vs. Attacks

It is important for investigators to understand the difference between an intrusion and an attack because whether or not there was an actual unauthorized entry to the network or system can be an important factor in proving the elements of a criminal offense. Attacks can be committed without gaining entry to the network or system, as in the case of DoS attacks. These attacks overload network resources to make the network unavailable to legitimate users, but the attacker never gains access to any computer on the network.

If investigators and prosecutors don't understand this difference (which they can do only by understanding the technical aspects of how the attack works), they might file charges that won't stand up in court or bring the wrong charges against a cybercriminal. This would be similar to a situation in which no one on the law enforcement team understood the difference between the offenses of robbery and burglary. Robbery requires that a physical assault or threat of serious bodily injury take place during the commission or attempted commission of a theft. Burglary requires that the offender unlawfully enter the premises of another person to commit a theft. If law enforcement officers arrest a suspect for breaking into a home and stealing a television set while the residents are gone, and they charge the suspect with robbery (and if the prosecutor brings such a case to trial), the suspect will almost certainly be found not guilty, because the state doesn't have proof of the elements of the offense of robbery. This situation would never happen, because law enforcement officers are drilled in the technical differences between robbery and burglary from the time they attend the police academy, and all prosecuting attorneys are well versed in these differences. However, it's entirely plausible to imagine the wrong charges being filed in a computer crimes case simply because no one involved understands the technical aspects of these types of crimes.

CyberLaw Review…

CyberLaw Review: Analyzing the Law

As an example of how important it is to understand the elements of the offense, which vary from statute to statute and jurisdiction to jurisdiction, Texas Penal Code section 33.02 defines "Breach of Computer Security" as follows:

Continued

> A person commits an offense if the person knowingly accesses a computer, computer network, or computer system without the effective consent of the owner.
>
> At first glance, it would appear that this offense would not apply to attacks in which there is no entry to the network. The statute requires "access" as an element of the offense, and a standard dictionary definition of that word is "a means of entry." However, to understand what the legislature intended when this statute was passed, we have to look back to the *legal* definitions that apply to this particular chapter of the Penal Code, which are contained in section 33.01. There, the term "access" is defined as:
>
> > To approach, instruct, communicate with, store data in, retrieve or intercept data from, alter data or computer software in, or *otherwise make use of any resource of a computer, computer network, computer program, or computer system.*
>
> As you can see, this definition is broader. The key to bringing this charge against a DoS attacker is the phrase in italics. Because network bandwidth is a resource of a computer network, and because the attacker does indeed make use of that resource, the attacker could be charged under section 33.02.
>
> It is very important for law enforcement officers to carefully analyze the statutes under which they intend to file charges and, if in doubt, to consult the district attorney or state attorney general for clarification of the language in the statute.

It's important, then, to be precise when we refer to specific computer crimes. DoS attackers should not be referred to as *intruders* when no intrusion occurs. Likewise, not all intruders can accurately be classified as *attackers*—although those who gain access and then destroy data or plant viruses are properly called by both names.

Recognizing Direct vs. Distributed Attacks

There are two different ways that attackers can launch their attacks against a system or network. A *direct attack* is launched from a computer used by the attacker (often after pre-intrusion/attack tools, such as port scanners, are used to find potential victims).

A *distributed attack* is more complex. Distributed attacks use someone else's system(s), rather than the attacker's, to perform the tasks that directly launch the attack. In this type of attack, there are multiple victims, which include not only the target of the attack but intermediary remote systems from which the attack is launched that are controlled by the attacker. The intermediaries are referred to as *agents* or *zombies*. This type of attack, of course, makes it more difficult to track down the perpetrator, because the attack packets that reach the victim have multiple source addresses, and none of these is the address of the attack's originator. Commands from attacker to intermediary are often encrypted to further thwart tracing. Encrypted transmissions can't be read by a packet sniffer (a protocol analyzer).

A distributed attack works a little like the practical joke in which the jokester calls numerous pizza parlors, pretending to be a customer, and requests that pizzas be delivered to someone else's address. The primary victim is the resident at the target address who ends up with a flood of unwanted pizzas, but the pizza vendors are victims as well because their resources are used, without their prior knowledge or consent, to carry out the attack.

> **NOTE**
>
> To better understand the concept of DoS, the technicalities of which we discuss later in this chapter, let's take the pizza prank scenario described in this section a step further. If our attacker is really determined, he might call not only pizza parlors but also all the Chinese restaurants, florists, and other "we deliver" businesses in the area, coordinating the requests so that all the delivery persons converge on the victim at the same time. If there are so many delivery vans parked on the streets that the victim's family members are unable to get to their own driveway, this results in a *denial of service* to legitimate users of the driveway.

Attackers using the distributed method can launch their attacks simultaneously from dozens, hundreds, or even thousands of Internet hosts all over the world. This means that far more traffic can be generated than is possible with standard one-source attacks. A typical distributed attack model using UNIX-based computers, according to the CERT Distributed Systems Intruder Tools Workshop, has the attacker controlling several systems called *masters*. Each master controls a larger number of agents running *daemons*—the software that is used to launch the attack. The daemons are installed on the agent machines by exploiting operating system or protocol vulnerabilities. This entire process can be automated so that potential agents are discovered and penetrated and the daemon is installed on all of them, then steps taken to hide the fact that an intrusion occurred, using batch scripts. (We discuss attack automation in more detail in the next section.)

The distributed attack process (after installation of the daemons) is outlined in Table 6.1.

Table 6.1 The distributed attack process

Step	Component	Action
1	Daemon (or agent)	Announces itself to the "masters" that have been predefined
2	Master	Lists daemon as "ready and willing" to be used for attack
3	Attacker	Issues command to masters to launch attack
4	Master	Issues command to daemons on agents to launch attack (with specific parameters such as identity of target and duration of attack)
5	Daemon	Launches attack on specified victim

Because this model's components are arranged in a pyramid form, with one attacker controlling several masters, which in turn control numerous agent/daemons, it is easier to disable the attack system closer to the top, where there are fewer systems to deal with. If the masters are disabled, the agents and their daemon software will not be able to function. Of course, the most efficient disabling technique is to find the attacker, thus disabling the entire attack sequence.

Automated Attacks

An *automated attack* is one that's performed by a computer program rather than the attacker manually performing the steps in the attack sequence. For quite some time, hackers have distributed attack tools that make it easier to launch network attacks. However, prior to 2000, most of these tools would initiate only one attack sequence; launching additional attack sequences required the intervention of the human attacker. However, newer tools such as Nimda and Code Red are able to continually initiate new attack cycles on their own. This increasing level of automation makes these attacks more dangerous and more widespread. According to CERT, the increasing automation and sophistication of attack tools is one of the most significant trends in the "Black Hat" hacking community.

Today's attack tools can perform the entire attack process. Instead of a hacker being required to perform a port scan with one tool to identify vulnerable systems, then using a different tool to penetrate the victim network and yet another tool to propagate the attack, now one tool can do it all. This speeds up the process as well as making it easier for hackers who lack technical skills to mount a successful attack. Some attack tools are executed at the command line, but many of them have user-friendly graphical interfaces as well as detailed Help files to instruct attackers in their use. There might also be configuration files that allow users to customize the attack.

In order to avoid detection by IDS software that relies on pattern recognition, modern tools can employ different techniques—such as random selection— to interrupt patterns that would trigger detection by the IDS. In addition, many of the tools use common protocols such as HTTP and Internet Relay Chat (IRC), which disguise their packets by making them look like normal Internet traffic. These tools are widely available through anonymous FTP sites and hacker newsgroups on the Internet. Hackers can also modify legitimate network analysis tools if they have the source code, turning them into attack tools by adding code to exploit the vulnerabilities that they find.

> ## NOTE
>
> It is ironic that hackers make their attack tools available on anonymous FTP sites, since anonymous FTP and TFTP are themselves often exploited by attackers. Knowledgeable hackers can easily create tools and scripts that attempt an anonymous login; try various commands such as **pwd**, **mkdir**, and **rmdir** (to print the working directory, make a directory, and remove a directory on UNIX/Linux systems, respectively); and plant a Trojan in the FTP site that then enables the hacker to access the system remotely, without a password.

Accidental "Attacks"

Some intrusions and "attacks" might actually be unintentional. Server or network crashes can be caused by users experimenting, visiting Web sites that run malicious code, or unknowingly downloading and introducing a virus into the system. In fact, a large number of virus attacks are initiated accidentally or unknowingly. The user who appears to have sent the virus via e-mail is often a victim of the attack him- or herself, because many viruses and worms are written to spread themselves by accessing the victim's address book and sending infected mail to all the addresses found there.

Accidental attacks can be just as destructive as deliberate ones, and network security personnel must be just as vigilant in protecting against them. However, from the law enforcement perspective, the perpetrator's *intent* matters very much. Most criminal offenses require that an act be committed intentionally or at least knowingly, so the elements of the offense might not be present if an employee causes an intrusion or attack without intending to—even if his or her actions were careless. On the other hand, some acts are still considered criminal when a lower state of culpability (recklessness or negligence) is present. It is very important for investigators to be aware of the culpable mental state that is specified as an element of each offense to be charged. If no level of culpability is specified, the criminal code usually defines a "default" level of culpability that applies.

Preventing Intentional Internal Security Breaches

Users inside the network are in the best position to gain access to information or sabotage the network's integrity. According to most computer security studies, as documented in RFC 2196, actual loss (in terms of money, productivity, computer reputation, and other tangible and intangible harm) is greater for internal security breaches than for those from the outside. Internal attackers are more dangerous for several reasons:

- People inside the network generally know more about the company, the network, the layout of the building(s), normal operating procedure, and other information that makes it easier for them to gain access without detection.

- Internal attackers usually have at least some degree of legitimate access and could find it easy to discover passwords and holes in the current security system.

- Internal hackers know what information is on the network and what actions will cause the most damage.

Preventing such problems begins with the same methods used to prevent unintentional security compromises, but it goes a step further. To a large extent, unintended breaches can be prevented through education. This obviously will not have the same effect on network users who intend to breach security. The best way to prevent such breaches depends, in part, on the motivations of the employee(s) concerned.

Implementing auditing helps detect internal breaches of security by recording specified security events. Administrators are then able to track when objects such as files or folders are accessed, the user account used to access them, when users exercise user rights, and when users log onto or off the computer or network. Modern network operating systems include built-in auditing functionality. Methods of auditing security events are discussed in Chapter 8, "Implementing

System Security." Interpreting and using security audit log files are discussed in Chapter 9, "Implementing Cybercrime Detection Techniques."

Firewalls are helpful in keeping basically compliant employees from accidentally (or out of ignorance of security considerations) visiting dangerous Web sites or sending specific types of packets outside the local network. However, firewalls are of more limited use in preventing intentional internal security breaches. Simply limiting users' access to the external network cannot thwart insiders who are determined to destroy, modify, or copy data. Because they have physical access, insiders can copy data to removable media or to a portable computer (including tiny handheld machines) or perhaps even print it to paper and remove it from the premises. They can change the format of the data to disguise it, or they can even employ steganography to hide it inside seemingly innocent files and then upload the files to Web-based data storage services.

In a high-security environment, measures should be taken to prevent this sort of theft. For example:

- Install computers without floppy diskette drives—or even completely diskless workstations.

- Apply system or group policy that prevents users from installing software (such as that needed for a desktop computer to communicate with a Pocket PC or Palm OS device).

- Lock PC cases and cover physical access to serial ports, USB ports, and other connection points so that removable media devices can't be attached.

Intentional internal breaches of security constitute a serious problem, and company policies should treat them as such. We discuss this topic more in Chapter 7, "Understanding Cybercrime Prevention," under the section on designing and implementing security policies.

Preventing Unauthorized External Intrusions

External intrusions and attacks are the major concerns of many companies when it comes to network security issues. In a number of high-profile cases in recent years, the Web servers of prominent organizations such as Yahoo! and Microsoft have been hacked. Attempts to penetrate sensitive government networks, such as the Pentagon's systems, occur on a regular basis. Distributed denial-of-service (DDoS) attacks make front-page news when they crash servers and prevent Internet users from accessing popular sites.

The good news about external intrusions is that the area(s) that must be controlled are much more focused than with internal attacks. There are usually only a limited number of points of entry to the network from the outside. This is where a properly configured firewall can be invaluable, allowing authorized traffic into the network while keeping unauthorized traffic out. On the other hand, the popularity of firewalls ensures that dedicated hackers know how they work and spend a great deal of time and effort devising ways to defeat them.

> **NOTE**
>
> Psychological factors affect the ways in which companies handle various types of security breaches. Internal breaches are usually seen by companies as personnel problems and are handled administratively. External breaches might seem more like violations and are more often prosecuted in criminal actions. Because the external intruder can come from anywhere, at any time, the sense of uncertainty and fear of the unknown can cause organizations to react in a much stronger way to this type of threat. Thus, law enforcement officers are more likely to become involved when the breach is external. Officers might then (erroneously) conclude that the ratio of external to internal breaches is greater than it really is.

Planning for Firewall Failures

Organizations should never depend on the firewall to provide 100-percent protection, even against outside intruders. To be effective, a security plan must be both multifaceted and multilayered. Although administrators can hope that a firewall will keep intruders out of the network completely, their planning must take into consideration the possibility that the firewall will fail and address such questions as:

- If intruders *do* get in, what is the contingency plan?
- How can they reduce the amount of damage attackers can do?
- How can the most sensitive or valuable data be protected?

External Intruders with Internal Access

A special type of external intruder is the outsider who *physically* breaks into your facility to gain access to your network. Although not a true insider because he or she is not authorized to be there and does not have a valid account on the network, this intruder enjoys many of the same advantages as the true insider.

On the Scene...

Tactical Planning

In dealing with network intruders, network administrators should practice what police officers in defensive tactics training call *if/then thinking*. This strategy involves considering every possible outcome of a given situation and then posing the question: *"If* this happens, *then* what could be done to protect us from the consequences?" The answers to these questions should form the basis of the organization's security policy.

This tactic requires that administrators be able to plan responses in detail, which means thinking in specifics rather than generalities. The security threat assessment must be based in part on understanding the motivations of people initiating the attack and in part on the technical aspects of the type of attack that is initiated. In a high-security environment, these tasks should be the responsibility of an *incident response team*. We discuss deployment of such teams later in this chapter.

Recognizing the "Fact of the Attack"

If preventative measures don't work (and it's likely that sometimes they won't), the next step for network administrators is to shift into reactive mode and attempt to minimize the damage. Before they can do that, they must have a way to recognize that an attack is taking place.

Intrusion detection systems (IDSs) use two methods to identify that an attack is occurring:

- **Pattern recognition** Analyzing files, network traffic, sequences in RAM, or other data for repeated or recognizable signs of attack, such as unexplained increases in file size or particular character strings.

- **Effect recognition** Identifying the results of an attack, such as a system crash caused by overload or a sudden reboot for no reason.

It's easy to program an IDS to recognize specific patterns, but attackers can defeat it by making small changes to the pattern or by fragmenting the attack packets—that is, dividing the attack messages or code into fragmented packets. A number of TCP/IP exploits use fragmented packets; these exploits are called *frag attacks*. Effect recognition is more difficult because the "effects" often resemble normal network traffic or problems caused by hardware or software faults.

The problem with any IDS—indeed, with all computer software—is that it does only exactly what it is told to do. Thus far, true artificial intelligence (programs that can "think") hasn't been achieved. Law enforcement officers know that the human factor—intuition and the ability to make great leaps of logic—can be very important in detecting and solving crimes. Unfortunately, no device or program is able to observe the behavior of computer systems and network components and intuitively recognize that there's something wrong. Very specific criteria must be set and met before an IDS will recognize an attack. This explains why human administrators will always remain an important ingredient in creating a proper security posture in any organization and why eternal vigilance is more than just a watchword for people with security responsibilities.

Identifying and Categorizing Attack Types

The *attack type* refers to *how* an intruder gains entry to your computer or network (if, indeed, entry is actually gained at all) and *what the attacker does* once he or she has gained entry (or without gaining entry). Some of the more common types of hack attacks include social engineering attacks, DoS attacks, scanning and spoofing, "nuke" attacks, and dissemination of malicious code. When you have a basic understanding of how each type of attack works, you will be better armed to guard against them.

It is useful for us to sort these different intrusions and attacks into categories such as the following:

- Pre-intrusion/attack activities
- Password-cracking methods
- Technical exploits (taking advantage of characteristics of the applications, operating systems, or protocols)
- Malicious code attacks (Trojans, viruses, worms)

The following sections discuss specific types of attacks that fit into each category.

Recognizing Pre-intrusion/ Attack Activities

Hacker how-to documents often break the hack/attack process into steps, as follows:

1. Pre-attack

2. Initial access

3. Full system access

4. Planting "back doors" for future access

5. Covering tracks

The pre-attack phase focuses on gathering information. Experienced hackers tell newbies to learn as much about the targeted victim as they can before initiating an attack. This "intel" information is vitally important for a hacker who has a concrete goal, such as corporate espionage.

On the Scene...

Planning the Hack and Hacking the Plan

The most successful hackers plan their attack strategies in almost as much detail as a military unit or police SWAT team plans a strike or raid. Then they carry out the hack exactly according to plan. These are the real pros, and they are the most difficult to defend against or apprehend. The hackers who get caught are usually careless, hurried, or inexperienced. In contrast, amateur hackers "play it by ear," breaking into systems and wandering around looking for something of interest. The term *amateur* refers to someone who does something for fun, just for the love of it. Professional hackers (hackers for hire) know exactly what they're after, and they get in, get it, and get out quickly, like a master thief. The planning phase can last many times longer than the actual execution of the hack. When professional hackers get caught, it's usually because they're egotistical and brag about their exploits to the wrong people.

Pre-attack information gathering and planning involve determining the goal of the hack, determining the target of the attack (the network or system that must be compromised to achieve the goal), and identifying the weaknesses of the target that can be exploited to carry out the hack. Pre-attack planning can also include taking steps to disguise the attacker's identity or putting preliminary programs or devices in place to gather information or to make it easier to get into the system when the time comes to carry out the attack. Some specific pre-attack activities include:

- Port scanning to identify potential targets and their weaknesses

- IP spoofing to disguise the attacker's identity

- Placing Trojans on the target system

- Placing tracking devices and software (such as keystroke loggers) on the target system

- Putting protocol analyzers (sniffers) in place to capture transmissions to and from the target system

In the following sections, we look at each of these activities in more detail.

Port Scans

A *port* is, in its simplest meaning, a point where information enters or leaves a computer. The TCP and UDP protocols use port numbers to provide separate "subaddresses" to identify what service or application incoming information is destined for or from which outgoing information originates.

The term *port scanner*, in the context of network security, refers to a software program that hackers use to remotely determine what TCP/UDP ports are open on a given system and thus vulnerable to attack. Scanners are also used by administrators to detect vulnerabilities in their own systems, in order to correct them before an intruder finds them. Network diagnostic tools such as the famous Security Administrator's Tool for Analyzing Networks (SATAN), a UNIX utility, include sophisticated port-scanning capabilities.

Scanning is used for several purposes prior to penetration and/or attack:

- **Target enumeration** Locating host systems that are open to attack.

- **Target identification** Identifying the target system.

- **Service identification** Identifying the vulnerable services or ports on the target system.

NOTE

A common saying among hackers is, "A good port scanner is worth a thousand passwords."

A good scanning program can locate a target computer on the Internet (one that is vulnerable to attack), determine what TCP/IP services are running on the machine, and probe those services for security weaknesses. Nmap (www.insecure.org/nmap) is a popular open source port scanner available free on the Web. Many scanning programs are available as freeware on the Internet. For a good resource for information about scanning and some popular scanning techniques and software, see www.garykessler.net/library/is_tools_scan.html.

Port scanning refers to a means of locating "listening" TCP or UDP ports on a computer or router and obtaining as much information as possible about the device from the listening ports. TCP and UDP services and applications use a number of *well-known ports* (see "Who's Listening?," the "On the Scene" sidebar in this section), which are widely published. The hacker uses his knowledge of these commonly used ports to extrapolate information.

For example, Telnet normally uses port 23. If the hacker finds that port open and listening, he knows that Telnet is probably enabled on the machine. He can then try to infiltrate the system by, for example, guessing the appropriate password in a brute-force attack.

On the Scene...

Who's Listening?

The official well-known port assignments are documented in RFC 1700, available on the Web at www.freesoft.org/CIE/RFC/1700/index.htm. The port assignments are made by the Internet Assigned Numbers Authority (IANA). In general, a service uses the same port number with UDP as with TCP, although there are some exceptions. The assigned ports were originally those from 0–255, but the number was later expanded to 0–1023.

Some of the most used well-known ports include:

    TCP/UDP port 20: FTP (data)

    TCP/UDP port 21: FTP (control)

    TCP/UDP port 23: Telnet

    TCP/UDP port 25: SMTP

    TCP/UDP port 53: DNS

Continued

TCP/UDP port 67: BOOTP server

TCP/UDP port 68: BOOTP client

TCP/UDP port 69: TFTP

TCP/UDP port 80: HTTP

TCP/UDP port 88: Kerberos

TCP/UDP port 110: POP3

TCP/UDP port 119: NNTP

TCP/UDP port 137: NetBIOS name service

TCP/UDP port 138: NetBIOS datagram service

TCP/UDP port 139: NetBIOS session service

TCP/UDP port 194: IRC

TCP/UDP port 220: IMAPv3

TCP/UDP port 389: LDAP

Ports 1024–65,535 are called *registered ports*; these numbers are not controlled by IANA and can be used by user processes or applications. Some of these are traditionally used by specific applications (for example, SQL uses port 1433) and could be of interest to hackers.

A total of 65,535 TCP ports (and the same number of UDP ports) are available to be used for various services and applications. If a port is open, it responds when another computer attempts to contact it over the network. Port-scanning programs such as Nmap are used to determine which ports are open on a particular machine. The program sends packets for a wide variety of protocols, and by examining which messages receive responses and which don't, creates a map of the computer's listening ports.

Port scanning in itself does no harm to a network or system, but it provides hackers with information they can use to penetrate the network. Because people conducting port scans are often up to no good, they frequently forge the source IP address to hide their identity.

Half scans (also called *half open scans* or *FIN scans*) attempt to avoid detection by sending only initial or final packets rather than establishing a connection. A half scan starts the SYN/ACK process with a targeted computer but does not complete it. (See the description of this process in the following section on TCP/IP exploits.) Software that conducts half scans, such as Jakal, is called a *stealth scanner*. Many port-scanning detectors are unable to detect half scans.

CyberLaw Review...

Should Scanning Be Illegal?

Some in the IT industry argue that port scanning should not be illegal, because "no harm is done." They say port scanning is similar to ringing someone's doorbell to see if anybody is home—not in itself a crime. However, laws are enacted not just to protect from actual physical harm but also to protect people's privacy and their interests in their own property. Those on the other side of the argument say that port scanning is really more like the virtual equivalent of someone who goes from door to door in an apartment building, trying each one to find out whether it's locked and whether there is an easy way in. Although this practice might do no actual harm if the "door scanner" only collects information and doesn't enter the premises, and although the person might have the right to be in the public hallway, in most jurisdictions such behavior would, at the very least, cause discomfort to the apartments' residents and attract the attention of the police.

In 2000, in *Moulton v. VC3*, a U.S. District Court in Georgia ruled that port scanning does not damage a network and thus does not constitute a crime or create a cause of action for civil suit. Although the federal laws in regard to computer fraud and abuse were changed by the passage of the USA Patriot Act in 2001, there is still a requirement that loss or damage must occur in order to charge a violation. For more information on the ethics and legality of port scanning, see the article at http://rr.sans.org/audit/ethics.php on the SANS Institute's Web site. For an opinion paper that holds that scanning is not legal despite the Moulton ruling, see the article from the *Journal of Technology Law and Policy* at http://grove.ufl.edu/~techlaw/vol6/Preston.html.

NOTE

A good port-scanning resource for network administrators is www.doshelp.com/trojanports.htm, which details the ports that should be blocked for best security.

Address Spoofing

The dictionary defines a *spoof* as a good-humored hoax, but the definition of the verb *to spoof* indicates a less benign action: "to fool or deceive somebody"

(Microsoft's *Encarta World Dictionary 2001*). Hackers use spoofed addresses to deceive other computers and fool them into thinking a message originated from a different machine. Although IP spoofing is probably the most popular, it is not the only spoofing method used by hackers. Others include ARP spoofing, Web spoofing, and DNS spoofing. Let's take a quick look at how each of these works.

IP Spoofing

IP spoofing involves changing the packet headers of a message to indicate that it came from an IP address other than the true source. In essence, the sending computer impersonates another machine, fooling the recipient into accepting its messages. The spoofed address is normally a trusted port, which allows a hacker to get a message through a firewall or router that would otherwise be filtered out. When configured properly, modern firewalls protect against IP spoofing.

Spoofing is used whenever it is beneficial for one machine to impersonate another. It is often used in combination with one of the other types of attacks. For example, a spoofed address is used to hide the true IP address of the attacker in Ping of Death, Teardrop, and other attacks. Remote Procedure Call (RPC) services, the X Window system, the UNIX **r** services (rlogin, rsh, and so on) and any service that uses IP address authentication are all susceptible to IP spoofing.

After deciding on the targeted victim, the next step in spoofing is to find out the address of a trusted host. Legitimate communications between the trusted host and the target can be intercepted and examined. Often hackers use a DoS attack against the trusted host to prevent it from communicating on the network. Then the packet headers can be modified to make it look as though the attacker's messages are coming from the trusted host, and the packets are sent to a service or port that uses address authentication. One of the most difficult aspects of IP spoofing is the necessity of correctly guessing the sequence numbers of the trusted machine. This process is made easy for the attacker by the numerous spoofing tools that are available on the Web.

ARP Spoofing

The Address Resolution Protocol (ARP) maintains the *ARP cache*. This is a table that maps IP addresses to MAC (physical) addresses of computers on the network. This cache is necessary because the MAC address is used at the physical level to locate the destination computer to which a message should be delivered. If there is no cache entry for a particular IP address, a broadcast message is sent by ARP to all the computers on the subnet, requesting that the machine with the IP address in question respond with its MAC address. This mapping then gets added to the ARP cache. *ARP spoofing*, also called *ARP poisoning,* is a method of sending forged replies that result in incorrect entries in the cache. This results in subsequent messages being sent to the wrong computer (the machine whose MAC address is incorrectly matched with the IP address). Once again, this process has been automated by hacker tools such as ARPoison and Parasite.

DNS Spoofing

DNS spoofing refers to two methods of causing a DNS server to direct users incorrectly:

- "Poisoning" of the DNS cache (similar to ARP poisoning in that incorrect information is entered into the cache) of name resolution servers, resulting in those servers directing users to the wrong Web sites or e-mail being sent to the wrong mail servers.

- Using the recursive mechanism of DNS to predict the request that a DNS server will send and responding with forged information. (For more information on how recursion works, see the article *DNS Overview with a Discussion of DNS Spoofing* at http://rr.sans.org/DNS/DNS.php).

On the Scene...

What Makes DNS Spoofing So Dangerous?

Because the Domain Name System (DNS) is responsible for managing the resolution of domain names (such as www.microsoft.com) into an equivalent IP addresses (for example, 206.122.10.6), any successful replacement of a valid address with an alternate address causes people attempting to access the domain name to visit the wrong TCP/IP address. This gives attackers the chance to create their own Web site that masquerades as a legitimate site and to attempt to steal all kinds of information by getting between the user and the real site. Alternatively, the attackers can completely take over the apparent role of the real site. Because DNS helps mediate access to Web, FTP, e-mail, and other services, the opportunities for mischief inherent in DNS spoofing are serious and powerful.

Either of these methods allows the attacker to intercept the victim's mail or to set up spoofed Web pages that give users inaccurate information. This method can even be used to con the victim into providing personal information through Web forms. (See the section on Web spoofing in the discussion of browser exploits later in this chapter.)

Placement of Trojans

Trojans, or *Trojan horse software,* are programs that appear to be legitimate or innocent but actually do something else in addition to or instead of their ostensible purposes. We discuss Trojans in general later in the chapter, in the section "Attacking with Trojans, Viruses, and Worms." As part of the pre-attack phase, a hacker can plant on the victim's computer a Trojan program that installs keystroke-logging programs to gather information for the main attack or that sets up the means by which the attacker will later get into the system. An infamous case of the latter was the Back Orifice Trojan, which could be disguised as a component of some other innocuous software program and, once installed, created a "back door" in Windows 95/98 systems for attackers to take over control of the victim PC. For more information about Back Orifice, see www.nwinternet.com/~pchelp/bo/bobasics.htm.

Placement of Tracking Devices and Software

If an attacker has onsite access to the victim system, one way to collect passwords and other information prior to an attack is to place a physical tracking device (a *keystroke logger*) on the system. This is a very small device, about 2 inches long and a half-inch in diameter, that can be installed in less than a minute; you simply unplug the keyboard from the PC and plug the keyboard into the logger, then plug the logger into the PC's keyboard port. It is not noticeable to most users.

Inside the logger are a microchip and a nonvolatile memory chip (similar to a CompactFlash card or memory stick). Depending on the amount of memory in the device, it can record anywhere from a few to dozens of pages of keystrokes; for example, 64KB of memory will store about 32 pages. No software needs to be installed on the computer for the loggers to work, and they are compatible with a variety of PC operating systems. No battery or outside power source is required; the device draws power from the computer. Once the strokes have been captured, the attacker removes the device and attaches it to a different PC. The captured data can be password protected; once the correct password is entered, it can be read in Notepad or another text editor. Afterward, the data can be saved to a file and the memory in the device can be erased. An example of a keystroke-logging device is the KeyGhost (see www.keyghost.com).

Software programs can also perform keystroke logging, but the attacker needs to be able to log onto the system in order to install the software; the advantage of the physical device is that it can capture the passwords necessary to log on. Software-based loggers capture only the keystrokes made after booting into the operating system, whereas the hardware device can capture keystrokes made before the OS loads—for example, changes made to the system BIOS.

On the Scene...

Keystroke Logging as an Investigative or Monitoring Tool

Keystroke loggers and spyware programs are not used exclusively by criminals. Law enforcement investigators use logging devices and software to gather evidence of offenses. In early 2000, Nicodemo S. Scarfo, Jr., was charged with illegal gambling, racketeering, and loan shark activities based on evidence in a file on his computer, which had been encrypted with PGP. Investigators used a keystroke logger to get the information needed to break the encryption. Defense attorneys tried to get the evidence suppressed, arguing that the use of the tool amounted to an unconstitutional search. However, the court ruled against the petition to suppress, and Scarfo eventually pled guilty.

Vendors of these programs often market their products to law enforcement agencies, and some, such as Codex Data Systems, have begun offering their software free of charge to police, military, and intelligence agencies following the September 11, 2001, terrorist attacks.

Keystroke loggers and spyware have other legitimate purposes. Companies may use them to monitor employees' computer and Internet activities (according to company policy), and parents can use them to oversee what their children are doing on the Net.

Neither type of keystroke logger records screens that appear on the computer that are not typed in by the user—they do not record, for example, Web sites the user accesses, files the user opens, or mail the user reads. Other spyware programs can do much more than just log keystrokes. Many of these programs allow the person who installs and configures the software to specify criteria that will trigger capture of screenshots. Some of the programs can even rename themselves and change their locations on the disk to avoid detection. Examples of spyware programs include WinWhatWhere Investigator (www.winwhatwhere.com), Spector Pro (www.spectorsoft.com), and Data Interception by Remote Transmission, or D.I.R.T. (www.codexdatasystems.com).

Placement of Packet Capture and Protocol Analyzer Software

Network monitors, also called *protocol analyzers*, allow administrators to capture and analyze the traffic on their networks for troubleshooting purposes or to monitor network activity. Hackers can use these same tools to capture packets surreptitiously and read the information in those packets. Analyzers that allow for placing the network adapter in promiscuous mode are especially useful to hackers. In this mode, the adapter can capture traffic sent to or from any computer on the network segment. Some analyzers, such as the Network Monitor built into Microsoft's Windows 2000 Server, limit capture to packets sent to or from the machine that is running the analyzer software. However, a more robust version of Microsoft's NetMon comes with the company's Systems Management Server (SMS) product and permits the use of promiscuous mode.

These programs are network *sniffers*. Any person with Administrative privileges can install the Network Monitor on a Windows 2000 Server family computer and start "listening" to activity on the wire. Administrators—or hackers who have compromised an administrative account—can use the tool to collect network data and analyze it on the spot, or they can save the recorded activities to review at a later time. It is possible to set triggers for when certain events or data cross the wire, so the tool can be used, for example, when certain keywords in e-mail communications move through the network. The Network Monitor program allows its users to capture only those frames that they are interested in, based on protocol or the source or destination computer. Even more detailed and exacting filters can be applied to data that has been collected, allowing the monitoring person to pinpoint the precise elements that he or she is looking for in the captured data.

Figure 6.1 shows the contents of a captured packet. You can see the text message ("Windows 2000 is great!") that was sent across the network.

Figure 6.1 Packet sniffers such as Network Monitor can reveal the contents of messages sent on the network.

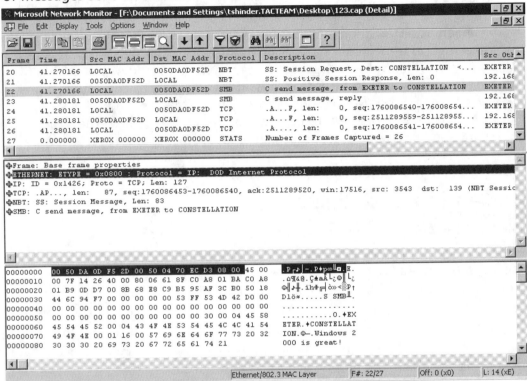

Dozens of commercial packet-sniffing programs are available. Sniffer Pro (www.sniffertechnologies.com) is probably the most popular. Others include LANSleuth from SSI (www.lansleuth.com) and Sniff'em (www.yasc.net/home2.html). In addition, many freeware/shareware sniffers are available, such as:

- PacketBoy (www.pro-soft.de/products/netboys/index.htm), which decodes TCP/IP protocols, NetWare protocols, and AppleTalk protocols

- Ethereal (www.ethereal.com), for both Windows and UNIX

- TraceWolf (www.simtel.net/pub/pd/16981.html), for Windows 9x/ME

Sniffing software usually has to be installed on the same local network as the victim computer; it doesn't work remotely across the Internet. However, hackers can exploit bugs such as those in SNMP to take over hubs, switches, and routers or use other tactics to take over control of a computer on the LAN to implement sniffing.

Prevention and Response

There is no way to prevent port scanning—but IT professionals can control whether or not the scanner finds open doors to their networks. An important security step for administrators is to use port-scanning software themselves to learn about their own networks' vulnerabilities and then plug the openings so others will be unable to use them to gain access. Most firewalls log port-scanning attempts, and freeware or shareware such as Jammer, Lockdown2000, or Nukenabber can be downloaded and installed to notify the administrator that ports are being scanned and provide the IP address from which the scan originates.

IP spoofing can be prevented using source address verification on the router, if it supports this function. Other steps that can be taken to protect against spoofing include:

- Use encrypted authentication.
- Configure the router to reject any messages from outside that appear to come from an internal (local) address.

Administrators can prevent ARP spoofing using static ARP tables. A static table is manually configured by the administrator, so broadcast responses don't result in automatic update of the cache. The problem with this solution is that it doesn't work well with large networks; the burden on the administrator to keep the tables current would be overwhelming. Another solution is *MAC binding*. This method is enabled on the network switches and allows automatic updating, but when a particular IP address has been associated with a MAC address, that association can't be changed except by an administrative action. Furthermore, some tools monitor changes to the cache, with automatic notification to administrators so they will be aware of any attempts to use ARP spoofing.

Administrators can prevent DNS spoofing by securing the DNS servers on the Internet and by using the latest version of the DNS software. For example, previous vulnerabilities have been fixed in BIND versions 8 and 9, and the vulnerabilities present in Windows NT DNS servers have been addressed in the Windows 2000 version.

Properly configured firewalls can help keep Trojans out of the network, and software such as Trojan Remover claims to be able to eliminate Trojan programs even when antivirus software cannot detect them. The usual virus protection guidelines (don't open unsolicited attachments, download files only from reputable sites, apply security patches diligently) can also help protect against Trojans.

Keystroke-logging devices are impossible to detect via software. Physical examination of the cable connecting the keyboard to the computer reveals the presence of such devices. Antikeystroke logger programs can scan for keystroke-logging activity and detect software-based loggers. An example is anti-keylogger, which is shareware that can be downloaded at www.webattack.com/get/antikey.shtml.

Protective measures against sniffers include limiting physical access to the network (because the sniffer software must be installed on a computer on the local subnet), using switches instead of hubs to prevent all packets from going to all the systems on the network, and using encryption. This last solution won't prevent sniffers from capturing network packets, but it will prevent the hacker from being able to read the data inside them. "Antisniffing" software can be used to scan the network for sniffers or for computers whose network adapters are running in promiscuous mode. Antisniff is available for both UNIX and Windows. For more information, see www.securitysoftwaretech.com/antisniff/overview.html.

Understanding Password Cracking

The best way to get into a system is to "trick" the system into thinking you're an authorized user. In many cases, you can do this simply by using a valid account name and password. This method is called *password cracking*. In this section, we look at the tools and resources hackers use to crack passwords. Investigators need to be aware of all the techniques and tools that can be used to impersonate a legitimate user and how they work. Understanding how a crack was accomplished provides valuable clues to the cracker's skill level and how determined he or she is to get into a particular network, as well as other characteristics that can help track down the culprit.

In computer security, there are three basic ways to validate user identity: the "what you know" method (with the password being what you know); the "what you have" method, which requires physical possession of some object such as a smart card; and the "what you are" method, which uses biometric data such as a fingerprint or retinal or iris scan. We discuss each of these methods in more detail in Chapter 7, "Understanding Cybercrime Prevention," in the section on authentication. For purposes of this discussion, it's important to know that the vast majority of networks rely solely on the first method, so anyone who knows or can guess the correct password that goes with a valid username can get in.

NOTE

Passwords are used for many purposes: to log onto the local computer or the network, to access password-protect Web sites or FTP sites, to access e-mail, to open password-protected documents, to get back to the desktop after the screensaver is activated, and even to enter the BIOS setup program. Many users, unable to remember dozens of different passwords, use the same password for everything. Although this strategy simplifies the user's life, it also simplifies the cracker's job. Once he or she has one password, it functions as an "open sesame" for everything the user has password-protected.

Password cracking involves acquiring valid passwords. This can be done in several ways, including:

- Brute force
- Recovery and exploitation of passwords stored on the system
- Use of password decryption software
- Social engineering

In the following sections, we look at each of these methods and ways to protect against them.

Brute Force

Brute force might not be the most elegant solution for a hacker in search of a password, but it can be very effective—especially if strong password policies aren't enforced. In its simplest form, a brute-force attacker tries one possible password after another until he or she hits on the right one. Although this process can be done manually by someone with a lot of time and patience, in practice it is usually done (much more efficiently) using a program that runs through all the words in a dictionary file, which is simply a large list of words (in what is some-times called a *dictionary attack)* and other possible character combinations.

Some of these cracking programs are very sophisticated and allow the cracker to implement rules or criteria. For example, if the cracker is able to obtain some information about the password—for example, the cracker knows that it consists of five alpha characters and three numeric—he or she can create a rule that will limit the program's attempts to passwords that fit the criteria (apple123, seven890, and so on). This strategy narrows the number of possible passwords and speeds the cracking process.

Password-cracking programs also have a legitimate use. An employee might leave a company or die suddenly without revealing passwords that were used to protect important files, which other employees now need to access. Even if they're still around, sometimes employees forget their passwords. Programs mar-keted for legitimate purposes are usually called *password recovery* programs, but of course the same software can be used by crackers for less-than-legitimate purposes. For example, Sunbelt Software's NTAccess works by creating a boot diskette, then using the tool to modify the boot disk to reset the Administrator password. Another program, Locksmith from Winternals, allows you to reset the password of any account remotely. Some companies do password recovery as a service. One such company is Password Crackers Inc. (www.pwcrack.com).

> **NOTE**
>
> Some recovery programs are focused on operating system passwords and others on application passwords. The Passware software at www.lostpassword.com is a modular system that lets you select modules according to your needs, to recover passwords in Windows NT, 2000, XP, Excel, Access, Outlook, Word, WinZip, WordPerfect, QuickBooks, ACT, and more. Their Passware Kit includes all the modules, and a demo version can be downloaded free from the site.

Some of these cracking programs won't work on Windows 2000/XP when file encryption (EFS) is used, and the programs we've discussed reset *local* pass-words—those stored on a specific computer—not network passwords such as those stored in Windows 2000 Active Directory and used to log onto the domain.

Some password protection schemes are more difficult to crack than others. The passwords on documents created with older versions of Microsoft Office and zipped files are notoriously easy to crack with readily available software. With any password scheme, the better (the longer and more complex) the passwords, the longer it takes to crack them. For difficult cracking jobs, some tools such as L0phtCrack versions 3 and above (shown in Figure 6.2) allow you to divide the task into parts and use multiple machines simultaneously to work on it in a method called *distributed cracking*.

Figure 6.2 Widely available tools such as L0phtCrack use comparative analysis to crack passwords.

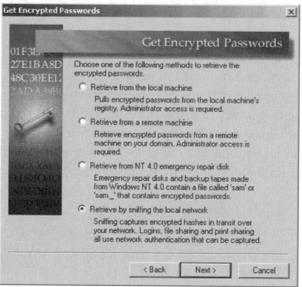

Cracking 101 on the Web

On hundreds of Web sites, would-be crackers can get information on how to defeat passwords and download tools such as L0phtCrack, NTcrack, Cracker Jack, and Dictionary Maker. Like all hacker sites, these sites come and go quickly and move from one domain to another to avoid scrutiny. A Web search on *password cracking tools* turns up thousands of hits, but you'll probably find that many of these return "File not found" messages when you try to access them. Nonetheless, if you're persistent, it's not hard to find all the information you need to start cracking. Dictionary files are available in many languages. A popular site for downloading dictionaries is ftp://ftp.cerias.purdue.edu/pub/dict.

Continued

None of these tools is illegal (yet), so there's not much that law enforcement can do about their easy availability. However, it's good for investigators to be aware of where cybercriminals get the tools they use to commit crimes, just as it's useful to know what outlets in an area (legally) sell poison, dynamite, guns, or other items that can be used for illegal purposes.

Exploitation of Stored Passwords

Trying to guess passwords, even with software to expedite the process, is a tedious business. It would be much easier if a cracker could just find a list of passwords lying around somewhere. Well, in some cases, that's exactly what happens—the list is right there for the taking on the computer's hard disk. Passwords have to be stored somewhere; after all, how else will the system know whether a user has entered the correct password? Additionally, most people have several different passwords in addition to their logon passwords; these are used for e-mail access, entry to restricted Web sites, and the like. Rather than memorizing all these secondary passwords, many users elect to have the system "remember" the password for them. Since computers have short memories (you'll recall that all the data in RAM is lost when the computer is rebooted), these "remembered" passwords must be stored in a file somewhere. All a cracker has to do is get his or her eager little hands on that file.

Thank goodness it's a little more complicated than that. In most cases, passwords are not stored in a plain-text file that the cracker can simply open and read, except in cases in which a forgetful user creates such a file, diligently recording passwords for various services and applications. Usually, stored passwords are *encrypted* or *hashed*.

For example, UNIX systems store passwords in the /etc/passwd file, along with other user information. The passwords are encrypted with a hash function. The computer doesn't compare the actual password you type in to a list to determine whether to log you in; instead, the password you enter is hashed and the resultant hash value is compared to that of the stored (hashed) password.

This system sounds foolproof, but it's not. The cracking software just needs to be a little more sophisticated. If the cracker can get the password file, the program uses whatever hash function the system uses and encrypts possible passwords (generating them via brute-force and dictionary methods), then compares the results with the encrypted passwords in the password file. This technique is called *comparative analysis*.

NOTE

UNIX and Linux systems can use *shadow passwords* to circumvent comparative analysis techniques. If shadow passwords are enabled, the encrypted password in the passwd file is replaced by an *x*. The real passwords are stored in another file, called /etc/shadow. What good does it do to store the information in a different file, especially when everyone familiar with UNIX knows the name and location of that file? The secret is that the /etc/shadow file can be accessed only by the root account. Although group accounts usually aren't assigned passwords, they can be. Group passwords can be shadowed like user passwords. In that case, the encrypted passwords are stored in a file called /etc/gshadow.

NetWare systems store passwords in the bindery files NETSBAL.SYS or NETSVAL.SYS (on older versions of NetWare) or the NDS database (on versions 4.*x* and above). The password is stored as an object attribute or property; the object might be a user account, printer, or the like.

Windows 9*x* machines store passwords in files named after the corresponding user account, with the extension .pwl, in the system root directory (called Windows by default). The passwords are encrypted, but a weak encryption algorithm is used, so it's easy to crack these passwords with software such as Glide. However, it's not even necessary to crack the passwords to get into a Windows 9*x* computer by booting into MS-DOS and renaming the password file. This system allows the cracker to enter any new password to log onto the system. The Windows 9*x* screensaver password is stored in the Registry file named user.dat, which is located in <*driveletter*>:\windows\profiles\<*username*>. The password is a string of hexadecimal values, with each two-digit hex value representing one ASCII character. To crack the password, you have to decrypt the hex values to ASCII.

Windows NT-based operating systems are much more secure. Like UNIX, they store a hash of the password in the Registry. This information is contained in the Security Accounts Manager (SAM) database, which hackers can sometimes obtain from the \<*systemroot*>\repair directory that is created when the rdisk utility is run with the **/s** switch to back up system configuration information to a diskette.

Windows 2000 uses Kerberos authentication, which is generally recognized as more secure than NTLM. However, Kerberos has vulnerabilities, too. Crackers can use sniffer software to capture network logon traffic and use the pre-authentication data used by Kerberos to verify a user's credentials. A discussion of how this is done is located on the Web at www.brd.ie/papers/w2kkrb/feasibility_of_w2k_kerberos_attack.htm. Information on cracking NT and Windows 2000 can be found on numerous Web sites, mailing lists, and newsgroups.

Why does all of this matter to the investigator? An investigator's knowledge of how various operating systems store passwords can be used, in some cases, to track criminals' actions. If security auditing is properly configured, investigators will be able to tell if and when various files have been accessed. Logs that record access to password files might indicate that passwords have been or will be compromised.

Interception of Passwords

Crackers don't always have to access password files or resort to guessing (brute force) to learn usable passwords. When passwords are sent across the network via local or remote access connections in plain-text form, they can be intercepted, as can other data traveling across the network, using sniffer software. Telnet sessions to UNIX computers can be intercepted and the plain-text password extrapolated if security measures haven't been taken. Use of non-secure authentication protocols such as Password Authentication Protocol (PAP) for remote access results in sending plain-text passwords across the link and should be avoided when possible. (We discuss authentication protocols in more detail in Chapter 7.)

Another means of intercepting passwords is to use a *keystroke logger*. As we discussed earlier in the chapter, this is a hardware device or software program that captures and records every character that is typed—including passwords.

It is often possible to detect an unauthorized packet sniffer on the wire using a device called a time domain reflectometer (TDR), which sends a pulse down the cable and creates a graph of the reflections that are returned. Users who know how to read the graph can tell whether and where unauthorized devices are attached to the cable.

Other ways of detecting unauthorized connections include monitoring hub or switch lights, using SNMP managers that log connections and disconnections, or using one of the many tools designed for the specific purpose of detecting sniffers on the network.

Furthermore, several techniques using PING, ARP, and DNS could help catch unauthorized sniffers. The use of these techniques is beyond the scope of this book, but you can find instructions for using them (and much more excellent information on packet sniffing) at Robert Graham's Sniffing FAQ located at www.secinf.net/info/misc/sniffingfaq.html.

Password Decryption Software

Most password-cracking programs don't actually decrypt anything. However, if the encryption algorithm is weak or implemented incorrectly, it is sometimes possible to use a technique called *one-byte patching,* which is able to decrypt the password by changing one byte in the program. Another technique used with weak algorithms requires that the cracker already have obtained one or more files in decrypted form; then they can be used to decrypt others that use the same algorithm. This is called the *known plain-text method.* This technique is popular as an attack against password-protected .zip, .rar, and .arj files. All of these are extensions used for compressed archive files.

When strong cryptography is used and complex passwords are chosen, it is much more difficult to use direct decryption; in these cases, a dictionary or brute-force attack is more often successful. PDF "decryptors" such as Guaranteed PDF Decryptor/Restrictions Remover (GuaPDF) use a type of brute force that involves testing all possible keys.

On the Scene...

The Weak Encryption Debate

Many security experts feel that weak, easily broken encryption is worse than no encryption at all because it gives users a false sense of security, leading them to be careless with sensitive data because they believe it is protected. Others argue that weak encryption is better than no encryption because it at least keeps out the casual, merely curious, or technically unsophisticated "snoop." The truth, as usual, lies between the extremes; weak encryption might be beneficial in some situations—for example, for a noncritical document such as a personal journal that a user wants to protect from other, nontechnical users who share the computer. On the other hand, weak security can be disastrous in the case of vitally important information such as trade secrets or military data that is likely to be targeted by technically sophisticated crackers. In this situation, the weak encryption actually *can* be worse than none at all because the fact that the file is encrypted draws the attention of the cracker, who might otherwise have ignored it.

Social Engineering

Unlike the other attack types, *social engineering* does not refer to a technological manipulation of computer hardware or software vulnerabilities, and it does not require much in the way of technical skills. Instead, this type of attack exploits *human* weaknesses—such as carelessness or the desire to be cooperative—to gain access to legitimate network credentials. The talents that are most useful to the intruder who relies on social engineering techniques are the so-called "people skills," such as a charming or persuasive personality or a commanding, authoritative presence.

Social engineering is defined as obtaining confidential information by means of human interaction (*Business Wire,* August 4, 1998). You can think of social engineering attackers as specialized con artists. They gain users' (or even better, administrators') trust and then take advantage of the relationship to find out user account names and passwords or have the unsuspecting users log them onto the system. Because it is based on convincing a valid network user to "open the door," social engineering can successfully get an intruder into a network that is protected by high-security measures such as biometric scanners.

Social engineering is, in many cases, the easiest way to gain unauthorized access to a computer network. The Social Engineering Competition at a Defcon annual hackers' convention in Las Vegas attracted hundreds of attendants eager to practice their manipulative techniques. Even hackers who are famous for their technical abilities know that *people* make up the biggest security vulnerability on most networks. Kevin Mitnick, convicted computer crimes felon and celebrity hacker extraordinaire, tells in his lectures how he used social engineering to gain access to systems during his hacking career.

NOTE

For more information on Mitnick's lectures, see *Mitnick Teaches Social Engineering,* at www.zdnet.com/filters/printerfriendly/ 0,6061,2604480-2,00.html.

These "engineers" often pose as technical support personnel—pretending to work as either in-house staff or for outside entities such as the telephone company, an ISP, the network's hardware vendor, or even the government. They often contact their victims by phone, and they usually spin a complex and plausible tale of why they need the users to divulge their passwords or other information (such as the IP address of the user's machine or the computer name of the network's authentication server).

> **NOTE**
>
> For more information about social engineering and how to tell when someone is attempting to pull a social engineering scam, see the preview chapter, *Everything You Wanted to Know About Social Engineering— But Were Afraid to Ask,* at the Happy Hacker Web site, located at www.happyhacker.org/uberhacker/se.shtml.

Prevention and Response

Because passwords are the first—and in some networks, the only—line of defense in protecting a network from intruders, it is extremely important that steps be taken to ensure the integrity of all users' passwords. We discuss password policies in more detail in Chapter 7; the following sections provide some general guidelines on protecting passwords and dealing with so-called social engineers.

General Password Protection Measures

Network administrators and users can take a number of measures to protect passwords, including the following:

- Follow guidelines for creating strong passwords, discussed in detail in Chapter 7 in the section on password policies.

- Configure settings so that user accounts are disabled or locked out after a reasonable number of incorrect password attempts.

- Use EFS on Windows 2000/XP/.NET computers to encrypt files.

- Store critical data on network servers rather than local machines.

- Don't rely on the password protection built into most applications.

- Enable password shadowing on UNIX/Linux systems.

- Disable LAN Manager Authentication on Windows networks. (NTLMv2 or Kerberos are much more secure.)

- Ensure that passwords are never sent across the network in plain-text form.

- Use antisniffer software and sniffer detection techniques to guard against crackers who try to intercept passwords traveling across the network.

Protecting the Network Against Social Engineers

Administrators find it especially challenging to protect against social engineering attacks. Adopting strongly worded policies that prohibit divulging passwords and other network information to anyone over the telephone and educating users about the phenomenon are obvious steps that administrators can take to reduce the likelihood of this type of security breach. Human nature being what it is, however, some users on every network will always be vulnerable to the social engineer's con game. A talented social engineer is a master at making users doubt their own doubts about his legitimacy.

The "wannabe" intruder might regale the user with woeful stories of the extra cost the company will incur if he or she spends extra time verifying his identity. He could pose as a member of the company's top management and take a stern approach, threatening the employee with disciplinary action or even loss of job if he doesn't get the user's cooperation. Or the social engineer could try to make the employee feel guilty by pretending to be a low-level employee who is just trying to do his job and who will be fired if he doesn't get access to the network and take care of the problem right away. A really good social engineer is patient and thorough. He will do his homework and will know enough about the company he targets or the organization he claims to represent to be convincing.

Because social engineering is a human problem, not a technical problem, prevention must come primarily through education rather than technological solutions.

Understanding Technical Exploits

A thief who is not able to forge an employee ID card to get in the front door of a company can, instead, come back at night and pick the locks on the back door to gain access. Likewise, if a cyberintruder or attacker is unable to come up with passwords to get into the network posing as a legitimate user, he or she has numerous methods for breaking in without credentials.

Generally, these methods exploit the characteristics of the protocols, operating system, or application software used on the targeted system or network, just as a master thief might exploit the fact that a building has ventilation shafts and use them to enter the premises. In the following sections, we discuss some popular technical exploits hackers use to gain access or interrupt communications on networks. Investigators should have a basic understanding of how these techniques work, for the same reasons that they need to know the technicalities of password cracking: Knowledge of how a cybercriminal commits the crime often provides valuable information for profiling that leads to apprehension.

Protocol Exploits

Protocol exploits use the characteristics of a protocol, such as the "handshake" method TCP uses to establish a communications session, to obtain a result that was never intended—for example, overwhelming the targeted system to the point where it is unable to communicate with legitimate users. There are many ways that the normal behavior of network protocols can be manipulated to congest the network or server to the point where no legitimate communications can get through. In this section, we discuss in detail what a DoS attack is and the many ways that the characteristics of TCP/IP can be used to launch DoS attacks. We also discuss source routing attacks and other protocol exploits.

DoS Attacks That Exploit TCP/IP

DoS attacks, mentioned previously in this chapter, are one of the most popular choices of Internet hackers who want to disrupt a network's operations. In February 2000, massive DoS attacks brought down several of the world's biggest Web sites, including Yahoo.com and Buy.com. Many such attacks exploit various characteristics of the TCP/IP protocol suite. This section goes into detail on how various DoS attacks work. Attack types we discuss include:

- DNS DoS attacks, which exploit the Domain Name System protocols
- SYN/LAND attacks, which exploit the way the TCP handshake process works
- The Ping of Death, which uses a "killer packet" to overwhelm a system
- Ping flood, fraggle, and smurf attacks, which use various methods to "flood" the network or server
- UDP bomb and UDP snork, which exploit the User Datagram Protocol
- Teardrop attacks, which exploit the IP packet header fields

- Exploits of SNMP, which is included with most TCP/IP implementations

What Is Denial of Service?

Although they do not destroy or steal data like some other types of attacks, DoS attackers have an objective bringing down a network, denying service to its legitimate users. DoS attacks are easy to initiate; software is readily available from hacker Web sites and warez newsgroups that allow anyone to launch a DoS attack with little or no technical expertise.

The purpose of a DoS attack is to render a network inaccessible by generating a type or amount of network traffic that crashes the servers, overwhelms the routers, or otherwise prevents the network's devices from functioning properly. DoS can be accomplished by tying up the server's resources by, for example, overwhelming the CPU and memory resources. In other cases, a particular user or machine can be the target of DoS attacks that hang up the client machine and require it to be rebooted.

Distributed DoS, or *DDoS,* attacks use intermediary computers, called *agents,* on which programs called *zombies* have previously been surreptitiously installed. The hacker activates these zombie programs remotely, causing the intermediary computers (which can number in the hundreds or even thousands) to simultaneously launch the actual attack. Because the attack comes from the computers running the zombie programs, which can be on networks anywhere in the world, the hacker is able to conceal the true origin of the attack.

Examples of DDoS tools hackers use are Tribe FloodNet (TFN), TFN2K, Trinoo, and Stacheldraht (German for *barbed wire*). Early versions of DDoS tools targeted UNIX and Solaris systems, but TFN2K can run on both UNIX and Windows systems.

Because DDoS attacks are so popular, many tools have been developed to help you detect, eliminate, and analyze DDoS software that might be installed on your network. It is important to note that DDoS attacks pose a two-layer threat. Not only could your network be the target of a DoS attack that crashes your servers and prevents incoming and outgoing traffic, but your computers could be used as the "innocent middlemen" to launch a DoS attack against another network or site.

DoS/DDoS attacks can be accomplished in a number of ways. Application exploits, operating system exploits, and protocol exploits can all be used to overload systems and create a denial of service. In the following sections, we address specific types of DoS and DDoS attacks and explain how they work.

DoS as a Weapon of Cyberwar

In November 2000, Lucent Technologies announced that a pro-Palestinian group named Unity had attacked its Web site using a tool called Defend, which creates a flood of messages designed to overwhelm the system and create a denial of service. Lucent was said to be targeted because it did business in Israel.

DNS DoS

The DNS DoS attack exploits the difference in size between a DNS query and a DNS response, in which all of the network's bandwidth is tied up by bogus DNS queries. The attacker uses the DNS servers as "amplifiers" to multiply the DNS traffic.

The attacker begins by sending small DNS queries that contains the spoofed IP address (see the "IP Spoofing" discussion earlier in this chapter) of the intended victim to each DNS server. The responses returned to the small queries are much larger in size so that if a large number of responses are returned at the same time, the link becomes congested and denial of service will take place.

One solution to this problem is for administrators to configure DNS servers to respond with a "refused" response, which is much smaller in size than a name resolution response, when they received DNS queries from suspicious or unexpected sources.

SYN/LAND Attacks

SYN attacks exploit the TCP "three-way handshake," the process by which a communications session is established between two computers. Because TCP (unlike UDP) is connection-oriented, a *session*, or direct one-to-one communication link, must be created prior to sending of data. The client computer initiates the communication with the server (the computer whose resources it wants to access).

The "handshake" includes the following steps:

1. The client machine sends a synchronization request (SYN) segment.

2. The server sends an acknowledgment (ACK) message and a SYN, which acknowledges the client machine's request that was sent in Step 1, and sends the client a synchronization request of its own. The client and server machines must synchronize each other's sequence numbers.

3. The client sends an ACK back to the server, acknowledging the server's request for synchronization. When both machines have acknowledged each other's requests, the handshake has been successfully completed and a connection is established between the two computers.

Figure 6.3 illustrates how the process works.

Figure 6.3 TCP uses a "three-way handshake" to establish a connection.

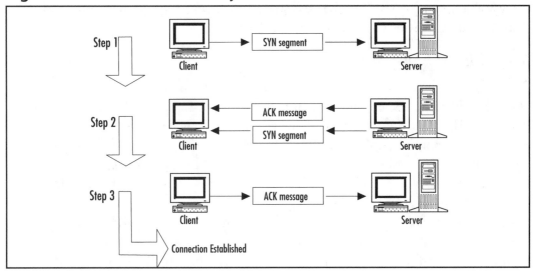

A SYN attack uses this process to flood the system targeted as the victim of the attack with multiple SYN packets that have bad source IP addresses. This causes the system to respond with SYN/ACK messages. The problem comes in when the system, waiting for the ACK message from the client that normally comes in response to its SYN/ACK, puts the waiting SYN/ACK messages into a queue. This is a problem because the queue is limited in the number of messages it can handle. When the queue is full, all subsequent incoming SYN packets will be ignored. In order for a SYN/ACK to be removed from the queue, an ACK must be returned from the client or an interval timer must run out and terminate the three-way handshake process.

Because the source IP addresses for the SYN packets sent by the attacker are no good, the ACKs that the server is waiting for never come. The queue stays full, and there is no room for valid SYN requests to be processed. Thus service is denied to legitimate clients attempting to establish communications with the server.

The LAND attack is a variation on the SYN attack. In the LAND attack, instead of sending SYN packets with IP addresses that do not exist, the flood of SYN packets all have the same spoof IP address—that of the targeted computer.

The LAND attack can be prevented by filtering out incoming packets whose source IP addresses appear to be from computers on the internal network.

The Ping of Death

Another type of DoS attack is the so-called *Ping of Death* (also known as the *large packet ping*). The Ping of Death attack is launched by creating an IP packet larger than 65,536 bytes, which is the maximum allowed by the IP specification (sometimes referred to as a *killer packet*). This packet can cause the target system to crash, hang, or reboot.

Ping Flood/Fraggle/Smurf

The *ping flood* or *ICMP flood* is a means of tying up a specific client machine. It is caused by an attacker sending a large number of ping packets (ICMP echo request packets) to the Winsock or dialer software. This flood prevents the software from responding to server ping activity requests, which causes the server to eventually time out the connection. A symptom of a ping flood is a huge amount of modem activity, as indicated by the modem lights. This type of attack is also referred to as a *ping storm*.

The *fraggle attack* is related to the ping storm. Using a spoofed IP address (which is the address of the targeted victim), an attacker sends ping packets to a subnet, causing all computers on the subnet to respond to the spoofed address and flood it with echo reply messages.

On the Scene...

Fraggle Attacks in Action

During the Kosovo crisis, pro-Serbian hackers frequently used the fraggle attack against U.S. and NATO sites to overload them and bring them down.

The *smurf* attack is a form of brute-force attack that uses the same method as the ping flood, but directs the flood of ICMP echo request packets at the network's router. The destination address of the ping packets is the broadcast address of the network, which causes the router to broadcast the packet to every computer on the network or segment. This can result in a very large amount of network traffic if there are many host computers and can create congestion that causes a denial of service to legitimate users.

NOTE

The broadcast address is normally represented by all 1s in the host ID (in the binary form of the address). This means, for example, that on Class C network 192.168.1.0, the broadcast address would be 192.168.1.255. The number 255 in decimal represents 11111111 in binary, and in a Class C network, the last, or *z*, octet represents the host ID. A message sent to the broadcast address is sent simultaneously to all hosts on the network.

In its most insidious form, the smurf attacker spoofs the source IP address of the ping packet. Then both the network to which the packets are sent *and* the network of the spoofed source IP address will be overwhelmed with traffic. The network to which the spoofed source address belongs will be deluged with responses to the ping when all the hosts to which the ping was sent answer the echo request with an echo reply.

Smurf attacks can generally do more damage than some other forms of DoS, such as SYN floods. The SYN flood affects only the ability of other computers to establish a TCP connection to the flooded server, but a smurf attack can bring an entire ISP down for minutes or hours. This is because a single attacker can easily send 40 to 50 ping packets per second, even using a slow modem connection. Because each packet is broadcast to every computer on the destination network, the number of responses per second is 40 to 50 times the number of computers on the network—which could be hundreds or thousands. This is enough data to congest even a T-1 link.

One way to prevent a smurf attack from using a network as the broadcast target is to turn off the capability to transmit broadcast traffic on the router. Most routers allow you to do this. To prevent the network from being the victim of the spoofed IP address, the firewall should be configured to filter out incoming ping packets.

UDP Bomb/UDP Snork

An attacker can use the User Datagram Protocol (UDP) and one of several services that echo packets on receipt to create service-denying network congestion by generating a flood of UDP packets between two target systems. For example, the UDP chargen service on the first computer, which is a testing tool that generates a series of characters for every packet that it receives, sends packets to another system's UDP echo service, which echoes every character it receives. UDP chargen is on port 19. By exploiting these testing tools, an endless flow of echoes goes back and forth between the two systems, congesting the network. This is sometimes called a *UDP packet storm* or *UDP bomb*.

In addition to port 7, the echo port, an attacker can use port 17, the quote of the day service (quotd), or the daytime service on port 13. These services also echo packets they receive. Disabling unnecessary UDP services on each computer (especially those mentioned earlier) or using a firewall to filter those ports or services protects you from this type of attack.

The *snork attack* is similar to the UDP bomb. It uses a UDP frame that has a source port of either 7 (echo) or 9 (chargen), with a destination port of 135 (Microsoft location service). The result is the same as the UDP bomb—a flood of unnecessary transmissions that can slow performance or crash the systems that are involved.

Teardrop Attacks

The *teardrop attack* works a little differently from the Ping of Death, but with similar results. The teardrop program creates IP fragments, which are pieces of an IP packet into which an original packet can be divided as it travels through the Internet. The problem is that the offset fields on these fragments, which are supposed to indicate the portion (in bytes) of the original packet that is contained in the fragment, overlap.

For example, normally two fragments' offset fields might appear as shown here:

```
Fragment 1:   (offset) 100 - 300
Fragment 2:   (offset) 301 - 600
```

This indicates that the first fragment contains bytes 100 through 300 of the original packet and the second fragment contains bytes 301 through 600.

Overlapping offset fields appear something like this:

```
Fragment 1: (offset)  100 - 300
Fragment 2: (offset)  200 - 400
```

When the destination computer tries to reassemble these packets, it is unable to do so and might crash, hang, or reboot.

Variations include:

- NewTear
- Teardrop2

- SynDrop

- Boink

All of these programs generate some sort of fragment overlap.

For more information about these variations, see *An Analysis of Fragmentation Attacks,* by Jason Anderson, at rr.sans.org/threats/frag_attacks.php.

SNMP Exploits

SNMP is used to monitor network devices and manage networks. It is a set of protocols that uses messages called *Protocol Data Units (PDUs)* over the network to various machines or devices that have SNMP *agent* software installed. These agents maintain Management Information Bases (MIBs) that contain information about the device. When agents receive the PDUs, they respond with information from the MIB.

Vulnerabilities have been discovered in some implementations of SNMP that provide a means for attackers to disable the devices or create a DoS.

NOTE

For more information about SNMP exploits, see the following articles:

- *SNMP Vulnerability Poses Major Threat* (www.vnunet.com/news/1129218)
- *SNMP Alert 2002: What Is It All About?* (http://rr.sans.org/protocols/SNMP_alert.php)

Source Routing Attacks

TCP/IP supports *source routing,* which is a means to permit the sender of network data to route the packets through a specific point on the network. There are two types of source routing:

- **Strict source routing** The sender of the data can specify the exact route (rarely used).

- **Loose source record route (LSRR)** The sender can specify certain routers (hops) through which the packet must pass.

The source route is option in the IP header that allows the sender to override routing decisions that are normally made by the routers between the source and destination machines. Network administrators use source routing to map the network or for troubleshooting routing and communications problems. It can also be used to force traffic through a route that will provide the best performance. Unfortunately, source routing can be exploited by hackers.

If the system allows source routing, an intruder can use it to reach private internal addresses on the LAN that normally would not be reachable from the Internet, by routing the traffic through another machine that is reachable from both the Internet and the internal machine Source routing can be disabled on most routers to prevent this type of attack.

Other Protocol Exploits

The attacks we have discussed so far involve exploiting some feature or weakness of the TCP/IP protocols. Hackers can also exploit vulnerabilities of other common protocols, such as HTTP, DNS, Common Gateway Interface (CGI), and other commonly used protocols.

Application Exploits

Application software exploits are those that take advantage of weaknesses of particular application programs; these weaknesses are often called *bugs*. Like protocol exploits, intruders use application exploits to gain unauthorized access to computers or networks or to crash or clog up the systems to deny service to others.

Bug Exploits

Common "bugs" can be categorized as follows:

- **Buffer overflows** Many common security holes are based on buffer overflow problems. Buffer overflows occur when the number of bytes or characters input exceeds the maximum number allowed by the program.

- **Unexpected input** Programmers might not take steps to define what happens if invalid input (input that doesn't match program specifications) is entered. This could cause the program to crash or open a way into the system.

- **Configuration bugs** These are not really "bugs," per se; rather, they are ways of configuring the software that leaves it vulnerable to penetration.

Popular software such as Microsoft Internet Information Server (IIS), Internet Explorer (MSIE), and Outlook Express (MSOE) are the favorite targets of hackers looking for software security holes to exploit. ActiveX controls, JavaScript, and VBScript can be used to add animations or applets to Web sites or e-mail messages, but hackers can exploit these features to write controls or scripts that allow them to remotely plant viruses, access data, or change or delete files on the hard disk of unaware users who visit the page or open the mail and run the script.

Major software vendors regularly release security patches to fix exploitable bugs. It is very important for network administrators to stay up to date in applying these fixes to ensure that their systems are as secure as possible. The following sections take a closer look at some popular attacks that exploit application software.

Mail Bombs

A *mail bomb* is a means of overwhelming a mail server, causing it to stop functioning and thus denying service to users. A mail bomb is a relatively simple form of attack, accomplished by sending a massive quantity of e-mail to a specific user or system. Programs available on hacking sites on the Internet allow a user to easily launch a mail bomb attack, automatically sending floods of e-mail to a specified address while protecting the attacker's identity. A number of types of mail-bombing techniques can be used against the popular Sendmail program, including chain bombs, error message bombs, covert distribution channels, and abuse-of-mail exploders. For detailed technical explanations of these techniques, see www.silkroad.com/papers/html/bomb.

One variation on the mail bomb automatically subscribes a targeted user to hundreds or thousands of high-volume Internet mailing lists, which fill the user's mailbox and/or mail server. Bombers call this attack *list linking*. Examples of these mail bomb programs include Unabomber, Extreme Mail, Avalanche, Voodoo, and Kaboom.

The solution to repeated mail bomb attacks is to block traffic from the originating network using packet filters. Unfortunately, this solution does not work with list linking because the originator's address is obscured; the deluge of traffic comes from the mailing lists to which the victim has unknowingly been subscribed.

Browser Exploits

Web browsers are client software programs such as MSIE, Netscape, and Opera that connect to servers running Web server software such as IIS or Apache and request Web pages via a URL, which is a "friendly" address that represents an IP address and particular files on the server at that address. The browser receives files that are encoded (usually in HTML) and must interpret the code or "markup" that determines how the page will be displayed on the user's monitor. Browsers are open to a number of types of attack.

Exploitable Browser Characteristics

Early browser programs were fairly simple, but today's browsers are complex; they are capable of not only displaying text and graphics but of playing sound files and movies and running executable code. The browser software also usually stores information about the computer on which it is installed and even about the user (data stored as cookies on the local hard disk), which can be uploaded to Web servers—either deliberately by the user or in response to code on a Web site.

These characteristics all serve useful purposes. Support for running code (as "active content" such as Java, JavaScript, and ActiveX) allows Web designers to create pages that interact with users in sophisticated ways. Cookies allow users to set preferences on sites that will be retained the next time they visit the site. However, hackers can exploit these characteristics in many ways. For example, a hacker can program a Web site to run code that transfers a virus to the client computer through the browser, erases key system files, or plants a "back door" program that then allows the hacker to take control of the user's system. Chapter 8, "Implementing System Security," discusses active content and other browser security issues and provides tips on how to disable these features when they aren't needed and make popular browsers more secure.

Web Spoofing

Web spoofing is a means by which an attacker is able to see and even make changes to Web pages that are transmitted to or from another computer (the target machine). These pages include confidential information such as credit card numbers entered into online commerce forms and passwords that are used to access restricted Web sites. JavaScript can be used to route Web pages and information through the attacker's computer, which impersonates the destination Web server. The attacker can send e-mail to the victim that contains a link to the forged page or put a link into a popular search engine. SSL doesn't necessarily prevent this sort of "man in the middle" attack; the connection appears to the victim user to be secure because it *is* secure. The problem is that the secure connection is to a different site than the one the victim thinks he or she is connecting to. *Hyperlink spoofing* exploits the fact that SSL doesn't verify hyperlinks that the user follows, so if a user gets to a site by following a link, the user can be sent to a spoofed site that appears to be a legitimate site.

Web spoofing is a high-tech form of con artistry. The point of the scam is to fool the user into giving confidential information such as credit card numbers, bank account numbers, or Social Security numbers to an entity that the user thinks is legitimate and then using that information for criminal purposes such as identity theft or credit card fraud. The only difference between this and the "real-world" con artist who knocks on a victim's door and pretends to be from the bank, requiring account information, is in the technology used to pull it off.

NOTE

For more technical details about Web and hyperlink spoofing, see the paper by Frank O'Dwyer at www.brd.ie/papers/sslpaper/sslpaper.html and the paper by Felten, Balfanz, Dean, and Wallach at www.cs.princeton .edu/sip/pub/spoofing.pdf.

There might be clues that will tip off an observant victim that a Web site is not what it appears to be, such as the URL or status line of the browser. However, the attacker can use JavaScript to cover his or her tracks by modifying these elements. An attacker can even go so far as to use JavaScript to replace the browser's menu bar with one that looks the same but replaces functions that provide clues to the invalidity of the page, such as the display of the page's source code.

Later versions of browser software have been modified to make Web spoofing more difficult. However, many people in the business world are still using MSIE or Netscape versions 3, both of which are highly vulnerable to this type of attack.

Web Server Exploits

Web servers host Web pages that are made available to others across the Internet or an intranet. Public Web servers (those accessible from the Internet) always pose an inherent security risk because they must be available to the Internet in order to do what they're supposed to do. Clients (Web browser software) must be able to send transmissions to the Web server for the purpose of requesting Web pages. However, allowing transmissions to come into the network to the Web server makes the system—and the entire network, unless measures are undertaken to isolate the Web server from the rest of the internal network—vulnerable to attackers.

Web server applications, like other software, can contain bugs that can be exploited. For example, in 2001 a flaw was discovered in Microsoft's IIS software (included with Windows NT, 2000, and XP) that exploited the code used for the indexing feature. The component was installed by default. When it was running, hackers could create buffer overflows to take control of the Web server and change Web pages or attack the system to bring it down. Microsoft quickly released security patches to address the problem, but many companies don't upgrade their software or update it with available fixes, and new, different security holes are being found all the time in all major Web server programs. Major flaws have been found in Apache Web servers' PHP scripting language that, if exploited by an attacker, can result in the attacker running arbitrary code on the system. Security patches are available to address this issue. These are just a few examples of the ways that Web servers can be exploited, making it vitally important that these machines be secured.

We discuss the implementation of Web server security in more detail in Chapter 8.

Buffer Overflows

A *buffer* is a sort of holding area for data. To speed processing, many software programs use a memory buffer to store changes to data, then the information in the buffer is copied to the disk. When more information is put into the buffer than it is able to handle, a *buffer overflow* occurs. Overflows can be caused deliberately by hackers and then exploited to run malicious code.

There are two types of overflows: *stack overflows* and *heap overflows*. The *stack* and the *heap* are two areas of the memory structure that are allocated when a program is run. Function calls are stored in the stack, and dynamically allocated variables are stored in the heap. A particular amount of memory is allocated to the buffer. Attackers can use buffer overflows in the heap to overwrite a password, a filename, or other data. If the filename is overwritten, a different file will be opened. If this is an executable file, code will be run that was not intended to be run. On UNIX systems, the substituted program code is usually the command interpreter, which allows the attacker to execute commands with Superuser privileges. On Windows systems, the overflow code can be used to send an HTTP request to download malicious code of the attacker's choice.

Buffer overflows are based on the way the C programming language works. Many function calls don't check to ensure that the buffer will be big enough to hold the data copied to it. Programmers can use calls that do this check to prevent overflows, but many do not.

Creating a buffer overflow attack requires that the hacker understand assembly language as well as technical details about the operating system to be able to write the replacement code to the stack. However, the code for these attacks is often published so that others, who have less technical knowledge, can use it. Some types of firewalls, called *stateful inspection* firewalls, allow buffer overflow attacks through, whereas *application gateways* (if properly configured) can filter out most overflow attacks. We discuss firewalls in detail in Chapter 7, "Understanding Cybercrime Prevention."

Operating System Exploits

Some exploits are unique to a particular operating system or family of operating systems. These hacks exploit specific characteristics of the operating system code to carry out the attack. All operating systems have their own vulnerabilities.

The WinNuke Out-of-Band Attack

The *out-of-band (OOB) attack* is one that exploits a vulnerability in some Microsoft networks, so it is sometimes called the *Windows OOB bug*. The WinNuke program and variations such as Sinnerz and Muerte create an OOB data transmission that crashes the machine to which it is sent. It works like this: A TCP/IP connection is established with the target IP address, using port 139 (the NetBIOS port). Then the program sends data using a flag called MSG_OOB (or Urgent) in the packet header. This flag instructs the computer's Winsock to send data called *out-of-band data*. Upon receipt of this flag, the targeted Windows server expects a pointer to the position in the packet where the Urgent data ends, with normal data following, but the OOB pointer in the packet created by WinNuke points to the end of the frame, with no data following.

The Windows machine does not know how to handle this situation and ceases communicating on the network. Service is denied to any users who subsequently attempt to communicate with it. A WinNuke attack usually requires a reboot of the affected system to reestablish network communications.

Windows 95 and NT 3.51 and 4.0 are vulnerable to the WinNuke exploit, unless the fixes provided by Microsoft have been installed. Windows 98/ME and Windows 2000/XP are not vulnerable to WinNuke. Unfortunately, many networks still use older Microsoft operating systems, sometimes without updating patches and service packs.

Windows Registry Attacks

The Windows Registry in Windows 9*x*/ME and NT/2000/XP (that is, all Windows operating systems later than Windows 3.*x*) is a database in which critical system and application configuration and initialization information is stored. Having this information in one centralized location instead of scattered in multiple initialization and configuration files offers many benefits, but it also makes the Registry vulnerable to hackers and attackers.

The Regedit and Regedt32 tools in Windows allow the user to connect to the Registry on a remote system across the network and make changes to Registry settings, as shown in Figure 6.4. A hacker can exploit this ability and alter important information that could bring down the system. Administrative privileges are needed to edit remote registries, and you cannot edit a Windows 95/98 computer's Registry unless remote administration has been explicitly enabled by installing the remote Registry service. This can be done by administrators using a batch file during the rollout of a number of Windows 9*x* machines.

It can be difficult to detect registry attacks, because the system accesses the registry often, complicating the monitoring process. However, utilities such as RegMon can be used to track registry access data, which can be compared with common attack models.

Figure 6.4 The Regedit utility can be used to connect to and edit a remote system's Registry.

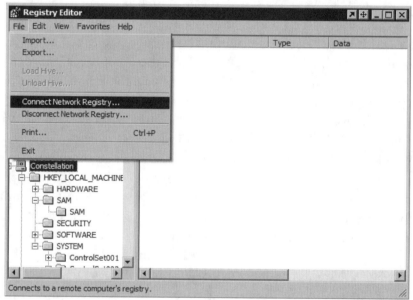

Other Windows Exploits

Many vulnerabilities have been discovered in the Windows operating systems. Microsoft is generally quick to patch these vulnerabilities once they become known. Many of the operating system vulnerabilities are caused by buffer overflows in built-in applications such as Network Monitor, the SNMP service, and the Universal Plug and Play (UPnP) service. Others are created by installing particular software programs in Windows or stem from security flaws in the MSIE Web browser. Here are a few of the more interesting security flaws that have been discovered in Windows 2000:

- Renaming the CD-ROM or other removable drive automatically creates an administrative share for the new drive letter. Although this share is not visible in the network browser, no password is required to access the share if its name is known. The problem was fixed in Service Pack 2, but users running Windows 2000 without this service pack are vulnerable.

- The Network News Transport Protocol (NNTP) service in Windows NT 4.0 and 2000 has a programming flaw that causes a memory leak that an attacker can exploit to use up all the server's memory and create a DoS. Microsoft released a patch to fix this problem.

- A programming flaw allowed hackers to start an NTLM challenge-response authentication process with a remote Telnet server, causing user credentials to be sent across the network when a user clicked a link in an HTML document. A patch was released to address this problem.

NOTE

For a good list of known Windows 2000 security vulnerabilities, see the LabMice Web site at www.labmice.net/articles/win2000securityholes.htm. For lists of exploits that can be used with Linux, Macintosh, and various flavors of UNIX (as well as Windows), see the Exploit World Web site at www.insecure.org/sploits.html.

UNIX Exploits

Many UNIX/Linux exploits aim at gaining root access. In UNIX, the root account is the equivalent of the Administrator account on a Windows system. A user logged on with the root account has full control of the system and is able to clear the logs to cover his or her tracks. "Getting root" often involves finding a file that has Superuser ID (SUID) permissions and running a script (downloadable from hacker sites on the Web) or exploiting bugs in Sendmail or some other service.

Rootkit Attacks

Despite its name, a *rootkit attack* is not a method of obtaining root account privileges—at least, not directly. It is a group of programs that install a Trojan login replacement with a back door, along with a packet sniffer, on UNIX boxes. The sniffer can then be used to capture network traffic, including user credentials, thus giving the user access to the root account by logging in with legitimate credentials. Software such as Rkdet is available to detect rootkit installation or packet sniffers running on a UNIX system.

NFS Exploits

The Network File System (NFS) allows users to remotely mount disks on other computers in order to access the files on the remote system. This makes the files on the remote disk available across the network. A program called nfsbug can be used to try out different methods of mounting an NFS disk to determine if the remote computer is configured in such a way as to allow remote mounting. If it works, this allows the attacker full access to the remote file system. The attacker can then read or write to all the files.

Other UNIX Exploits

The *nix operating systems, like their Windows cousins, are vulnerable to a variety of buffer overflow exploits, insecure default configurations, and programming flaws that hackers can use to compromise the systems and networks. For an incomplete but fairly comprehensive list of vulnerabilities in specific distributions of UNIX and Linux, see the UNIX security Web site at www.cs.iastate.edu/%7eghelmer/unixsecurity/unix_vuln.html.

Router Exploits

Many hackers now target routers instead of computers for their attacks. The growing popularity of DSL and cable Internet connectivity has brought routers to home networks as well as business networks. This, in turn, has created a new point of vulnerability.

Many of the new, relatively inexpensive routers designed for broadband connections come with default administrator passwords that can be used on any of the vendor's devices if the administrator does not change the password. This means a hacker with knowledge of the default password could log on and make changes to the routing table or router configuration. This differs from most operating systems that do not come with a default password but require the user to create one during installation. In addition to the administrator password, some router vendors have created special so-called "back door" passwords for their systems, intended to be used by the vendor's tech support personnel so that if an administrator forgot the admin password, the vendor could help the administrator get back in. Of course, this system could also be exploited by hackers with knowledge of the secret "master" password.

Hackers can also obtain router passwords the same way they get the passwords for computers: using sniffer or spyware software, brute-force attacks, or social engineering tactics. Whichever method the hacker uses to access the router, he or she can then create DoS attacks by changing routing table entries to send all messages to the same destination. In fact, if the router uses the Routing Information Protocol to dynamically update its routing tables, the attacker can send spoofed RIP messages to make the changes to the routing table without even needing to access the router directly.

DoS attacks can also target routers. Shutting down the router effectively stops communication between the subnet and the outside world. Cisco announced in 2001 that its 12000 series routers were vulnerable to DoS attacks.

For more information about the growing popularity of router exploits, see www.vnunet.com/News/1126398.

Prevention and Response

Administrators can take a number of steps to help prevent protocol, application, and operating system exploits, including the following:

- Ensure that all systems have the latest security patches. Applying the patches protects against many DoS attacks, which rely on operating system or protocol "bugs."

- Linux systems can be protected from SYN attacks by building the kernel with SYN cookies. Some versions of UNIX (such as Solaris 2.6 and above) have built-in protection against SYN attacks. In Windows 2000, the Registry can be edited to protect against SYN attacks. For information and how-to instructions, see http://security.uchicago.edu/seminars/DDoS/netprot.shtml.

- Routers can be configured to respond to directed broadcasts instead of passing them on to the subnet to guard against smurf attacks.

- DNS servers can be configured to respond with a "refused" response when they received DNS queries from suspicious or unexpected sources to protect from DNS DoS attacks.

- The router can be configured to filter out incoming packets with a source IP address that appears to be from the local network.

- Configure the system to ignore router redirects.

- Disabling SNMP, if it is not needed, protects against exploits that rely on the protocol.

- Disabling Java, JavaScript, ActiveX, and other active content in the Web browser thwarts many common browser exploits.

- Use application gateway firewalls to protect against buffer overflow attacks.

- Change default passwords on routers and disable "back door" passwords.

Attacking with Trojans, Viruses, and Worms

Intruders who access networks and systems without authorization or inside attackers with malicious motives can plant various types of programs to cause damage to the network. These programs—often lumped together under the general term *viruses,* although there are other varieties—have cost companies and individuals billions of dollars in lost data, lost productivity, and the time and expense of recovery. Some of the more destructive examples of malicious code, also sometimes referred to as *malware,* over the past decade are:

- **CIH/Chernobyl** In the late 1990s, this virus caused a great deal of damage to business and home computer users. It infected executable files and was spread by running an infected file on a Windows 95/98 machine. There were several variants of CIH; these were "time bomb" viruses that activated on a predefined date (either April 26—the anniversary of the Chernobyl disaster—or every month on the twenty-sixth). Until the trigger date, the virus remained dormant. Once the computer's internal clock indicated the activation date, the virus would overwrite the first 2048 sectors of every hard disk in the computer, thus wiping out the file allocation table and causing the hard disk to appear to be erased. However, the data on the rest of the disk could be recovered using data recovery software; many users were unaware of this capability. The virus also attempted to write to the BIOS boot block, rendering the computer unbootable. (This did not work on computers that had been set to prevent writing to the BIOS.) This virus started to show up again in the spring of 2002, piggybacking on the Klez virus, described later in this list.

- **Melissa** This was the first virus to be widely disseminated via e-mail, starting in March 1999. It is a macro virus, written in Visual Basic for Applications (VBA) and embedded in a Microsoft Word 97/2000 document. When the infected document is opened, the macro runs (unless Word is set not to run macros), sending itself to the first 50 entries in every Microsoft Outlook MAPI address book. These include mailing list addresses, which could result in very rapid propagation of the virus. The virus also made changes to the Normal.dot template, which caused newly created Word documents to be infected. Because of the huge volume of mail it produced, the virus caused a denial of service on some e-mail servers. The confessed author of the virus, David Smith, was sentenced to 20 months in federal prison and fined $5000.

- **Code Red** In the summer of 2001, this self-propagating worm began to infect Web servers running Internet Information Server (IIS). On various trigger dates, the infected machine would try to connect to TCP port 80 (used for Web services) on computers with randomly selected IP addresses. When successful, it attempted to infect the remote systems. Some variations also defaced Web pages stored on the server. On other dates, the infected machine would launch a DoS attack against a specific IP address embedded in the code. CERT reported that Code Red infected over 250,000 systems over the course of nine hours on July 19, 2001.

- **Nimda** In the late summer of 2001, the Nimda worm infected numerous computers running Windows 95/98/ME, NT, and 2000. The worm made changes to Web documents and executable files on the infected systems and created multiple copies of itself. It spread via e-mail, via network shares, and through accessing infected Web sites. It also exploited vulnerabilities in IIS versions 4 and 5 and spread from client machines to Web servers through the back doors left by the Code Red II worm. Nimda allowed attackers to then execute arbitrary commands on IIS machines that had not been patched, and denials of service were caused by the worm's activities.

- **Klez** In late 2001 and early 2002, this e-mail worm spread throughout the Internet. It propagates through e-mail mass mailings and exploits vulnerabilities in the unpatched versions of Outlook and Outlook Express mail clients, attempting to run when the message containing it is previewed. When it runs, it copies itself to the System or System32 folder in the system root directory and modifies a Registry key to cause it to be executed when Windows is started. It also tries to disable any virus scanners and sends copies of itself to addresses in the Windows address book, in the form of a random filename with a double extension (for example, file.doc.exe). The payload executes on the thirteenth day of every other month, starting with January, resulting in files on local and mapped drives being set to 0 bytes in length.

These are only a few examples of the damage and inconvenience caused by various forms of malicious code. There are three broad categories of this type of code, identified as *Trojans* or *Trojan horse programs, viruses,* and *worms.* We take a brief look at each of these attack types in the following sections.

Trojans

The name *Trojan* is short for *Trojan horse* and refers to a software program that appears to perform a useful function but in fact performs actions that the program's user does not intend or is not aware of. Trojan horses are often written by hackers to circumvent a system's security. Once the Trojan is installed, the hacker can exploit the security holes it creates to gain unauthorized access, or the Trojan program may perform some action such as:

- Deleting or modifying files
- Transmitting files across the network to the intruder
- Installing other programs or viruses

Basically, the Trojan can perform any action that the user has privileges and permissions to do on the system. This means that a Trojan is especially dangerous if the unsuspecting user who installs it is an administrator and has access to the system files.

WARNING

Although Microsoft Office documents are not executable files themselves, they can contain *macros,* which are small programs that are embedded into the documents and can be used to spread malicious code. Thus, Office documents should be treated as though they are executables unless running macros is disabled in the Office program.

Trojans can be very cleverly disguised as innocuous programs, utilities, or screensavers. A Trojan can also be installed by an executable script (JavaScript, a Java applet, ActiveX control, or the like) on a Web site. Accessing the site can initiate the program's installation if the Web browser is configured to allow scripts to run automatically. Trojans can use Windows' default behavior to disguise their true nature. Because the file extension (the characters that appear after the last dot in a filename) are hidden by default, a hacker can name a file something like vacation.jpg.exe and it will be shown in Windows Explorer as vacation.jpg, seeming to be an innocent graphics file when it is really an executable program.

Of course, double-clicking it to open the "picture" will run the program. Trojans that are designed to allow a hacker unauthorized access across the network (such as Back Orifice and NetBus) are sometimes called *remote access Trojans,* or *RATs.*

For more information about Trojans in general and links to specific fixes for Trojan attacks, see www.irchelp.org/irchelp/security/trojan.html.

Viruses

Viruses are programs that are usually installed without the user's awareness and perform undesired actions that are often harmful, although sometimes merely annoying. Viruses can also replicate themselves, infecting other systems by writing themselves to any diskette that is used in the computer or sending themselves across the network. Viruses are often distributed as attachments to e-mail or as macros in word-processing documents. Some activate immediately on installation, and others lie dormant until a specific date or time or a particular system event triggers them. For more information, see the article *How Computer Viruses Work* at www.howstuffworks.com/virus.htm.

Viruses come in thousands of varieties. They can do anything from popping up a message that says "Hi!" to erasing the entire contents of a computer's hard disk. The proliferation of computer viruses has also led to the phenomenon of the *virus hoax,* which is a warning—generally circulated via e-mail or Web sites—about a virus that does not exist or that does not do what the warning claims it will do.

Real viruses, however, present a real threat to your network. Companies such as Symantec and McAfee make antivirus software that is aimed at detecting and removing virus programs. Because new viruses are created daily, it is important to download regularly new *virus definition files,* which contain information required to detect each virus type, to ensure that your virus protection stays up to date.

The types of viruses include:

- **Boot sector viruses** These are often transmitted via a diskette. The virus is written to the master boot record on the hard disk, from which it is loaded into the computer's memory every time the system is booted.

- **Application or program viruses** These are executable programs that, when run, infect your system. Viruses can also be attached to other, harmless programs and installed at the same time the desirable program is installed.

- **Macro viruses** These are embedded in documents (such as Microsoft Word documents) that can use macros, small applications or "applets" that automate the performance of some task or sequence.

On the Scene...

Understanding the Virus Threat

The most dangerous aspect of computer viruses (as is true of their biological counterparts) is their ability to "mutate" into something else. Of course, this mutation doesn't happen spontaneously, but virus writers build on the code of others to make relatively benign viruses more destructive—and to avoid detection by antivirus software.

Viruses that are programmed to "go off" (activate and destroy data or files) on a certain date are called *time bombs* or *logic bombs*. One of the first of this type to gain worldwide attention was the Michelangelo virus in the early 1990s, which attempted to erase the hard disks of infected PCs on March 6, the birthday of the famous painter. A few years later, a disgruntled ex-employee of Omega Engineering planted a time-bomb virus on the company's network that resulted in approximately $10 million in loss and damage. He was convicted of the crime and sentenced to 41 months in prison.

Worms

A *worm* is a program that can travel across a network from one computer to another. Sometimes different parts of a worm run on different computers. Worms make multiple copies of themselves and spread throughout a network. The distinction between viruses and worms has become blurred. Originally the term *worm* was used to describe code that attacked multiuser systems (networks), whereas *virus* described programs that replicated on individual computers.

The primary purpose of the worm is to replicate. These programs were initially used for legitimate purposes in performing network management duties, but their ability to multiply quickly has been exploited by hackers who create malicious worms that replicate wildly and can also exploit operating system weaknesses and perform other harmful actions.

NOTE

One of the first widely disseminated worm programs was the Internet Worm of 1988, which practically shut down the entire Internet. For a detailed paper on how it happened, see *A Tour of the Worm* at http://world.std.com/~franl/worm.html.

Prevention and Response

Protecting systems and networks from the damage caused by Trojans, viruses, and worms is mostly a matter of common sense. Practices that can help prevent infection include these:

- Don't run executable (.exe) files from unknown sources, including those attached to e-mail or downloaded from Web sites.

- Turn off the Preview and/or HTML mail options in your e-mail client program.

- Don't open Microsoft Office documents from unknown sources without first disabling macros.

- Be careful about using diskettes that have been used in other computers.

- Install and use firewall software.

- Install antivirus software, configuring it to run scans automatically at pre-defined times and updating the definition files regularly.

- Use intrusion prevention tools called *behavior blockers* that deny programs the ability to execute operations that have not been explicitly permitted.

- Use *behavior detection* solutions such as Finjan's SurfinGate and SurfinShield that can use heuristic techniques to analyze executable files and assess whether they are likely to be hostile.

- Use *integrity checker* software (such as Tripwire) to scan the system for changes.

Recognizing the presence of malicious code is the first-response step if the system does get infected. Administrators and users need to be on the alert for common indications that a virus might be present, such as missing files or programs; unexplained changes to the system's configuration; unexpected and unexplained displays, messages, or sounds; new files or programs that suddenly appear with no explanation; memory "leaks" (less available system memory than normal) or unexplained use of disk space; and any other odd behavior of programs or the operating system. If a virus is suspected, a good antivirus program should be installed and run to scan the system for viruses and attempt to remove or quarantine any that are found. Finally, all mission-critical or irreplaceable data should be backed up on a regular basis in case all these measures fail.

Some virus writers create "proof of concept" viruses that do not cause damage and are designed merely to demonstrate that a particular type of virus can be written. For example, it was once thought that viruses could not be spread by simply reading e-mail; users were told that as long as they didn't open attachments, they were safe. The first viruses exploiting HTML e-mail to run and infect systems when a user opened the e-mail message (not an attachment) proved the concept of a virus that could spread via e-mail alone. In June 2002, researchers at McAfee received a proof-of-concept virus called Perrun that is claimed to be embedded in a JPEG image file. If genuine, this was the first known case of a virus embedded in a picture file that runs automatically when the graphic is viewed. That same month, Symantec reported the first cross-platform virus; it could infect both Linux and Windows systems.

Some technical commentators have questioned the feasibility of these new viruses, but many technical types also once assured users that viruses couldn't spread via e-mail. The moral of the story is that virus writers are a creative and persistent bunch and will continue to come up with new ways to do the "impossible," so computer users should never assume that any particular file type or operating system is immune to malicious code. The only sure way to protect against viruses is to power down the computer and leave it turned off.

> **NOTE**
>
> Information about specific viruses and instructions on how to clean an infected system are available at www.symantec.com and www.mcafee.com. Both antivirus vendors provide detailed databases that list and describe known viruses.

Hacking for Nontechies

As we've mentioned, highly developed technical skills are no longer necessary for people who want to break into computer systems and networks. Some say that hacking was originally an art that required great talent, later required only a bit of skill, and today can be done by anyone who has enough hand/eye coordination to click a mouse. To put it more eloquently, "Hacking has devolved from a labor of love to unskilled labor." This process of deterioration began with the phenomenon of the *script kiddie.*

The Script Kiddie Phenomenon

You'll find a dozen definitions of *script kiddie,* depending on the source you consult. Webopedia (www.webopedia.com) defines the term as someone who "randomly seeks out a specific weakness over the Internet in order to gain root access to a system without really understanding what it is s/he is exploiting because the weakness was discovered by someone else." The Jargon Lexicon at www.tuxedo.org/~esr/jargon is a bit more judgmental: "The lowest form of cracker … People who cannot program but who create tacky HTML pages by copying JavaScript routines from other tacky HTML pages."

Regardless of the precise definition, most agree on one thing: Script kiddies don't have much technical expertise themselves, but they use code written by others to wreak havoc. In the hacker culture, they are generally regarded with contempt or at least with a lack of respect. Nonetheless, hackers who *do* understand the technology continue to distribute scripts and programs that the script kiddies use to do their dirty work.

According to the SANS Institute (http://rr.sans.org/hackers/monkeys.php), script kiddies and their cousins, *packet monkeys* (defined as people who launch DoS attacks against Web sites for "no apparent reason"), are the new generation of hackers who are responsible for many of the large-scale DDoS attacks of recent years, including those that brought down Yahoo!, eBay, ZDNet, and CNN. The Yahoo! attack was launched by a Canadian teenager called "Mafiaboy" who used a utility called Stacheldraht that was written by a German hacker.

The "real" hackers spend years playing with computer systems and learning the intricacies of complex operating systems, often preferring to work with UNIX. They take pride in their knowledge and in the "elegance" of their attacks. They regard script kiddies, who rely on scripts written by others and even stoop to using hacking tools with graphical interfaces, in much the way a master jewel thief regards a street thug. Because script kiddies are unskilled (and thus less able to cover their tracks) and because they tend to crave attention (whereas most skilled hackers take pride in being able to stealthily invade a system and get out without anyone knowing), script kiddies make up a large proportion of the network intruders and attackers who are caught and prosecuted.

Despite their disrespectful nickname and the low level of regard they're given in the hacker community, script kiddies can do a lot of damage, and the randomness of their attacks makes them especially dangerous. As with drive-by shootings that target random victims, script kiddies' actions are impossible to predict and they place everyone at risk.

The "Point and Click" Hacker

As unsophisticated as script kiddies are, another variety of "wannabe" hacker is even less technically savvy. At least the average script kiddie knows enough to type a few commands to launch the script he or she got from somebody else. The newest incarnation of "do it the easy way" attackers is too unknowledgeable—or too lazy—to do even that. Instead, this new breed uses "point and click" utilities with pretty graphical interfaces or "fill in the blank" Web sites that serve as front ends to launch the chosen attack(s) against specified targets without the so-called hacker even needing to know how to download a file.

David Rhoades of Maven Security came up with the term *click kiddies* to describe these "rebels without a clue." Rhoades travels to computer security conferences around the world with his presentation, called "Hacking for the Masses." In his talk, he outlines just how easy it is for literally anyone to commit online breaking and entering—and much worse—with readily available tools that, to paraphrase Rhoades, are so user-friendly even your grandmother can bring down several servers before dinner.

Use of the Web-based attack tools favored by click kiddies also makes it more difficult to trace the origin of the attack, since the attack is coming from an intermediary (the Web site that provides the tool) instead of directly from the attacker.

NOTE

An online version of Rhoades' "Hacking for the Masses" presentation, complete with examples of the Web-based tools he discusses, is available for viewing or download at his Web site, http://www.clickkiddie.net.

Prevention and Response

The same preventative measures that we've already discussed apply to protecting a network from nontechie hackers. In addition, script kiddies can sometimes be lured in and caught by setting up a *honeypot*, which is a system designed specifically for the purpose of trapping attackers. The honeypot is a system or network that acts as an "open invitation" to hackers. It is connected to the Internet with minimal protection, running unpatched operating systems and application software that can be easily exploited. The systems are constantly monitored so that the attacker can be identified and traced before he or she has a chance to destroy evidence.

We discuss honeypots in more detail in Chapter 9, "Implementing Cybercrime Detection Techniques."

Summary

The sheer number of ways that a hacker can intrude or attack a network can be overwhelming. As soon as one security "hole" is plugged, dozens more are discovered or created. Some of these methods are so subtle that no one might ever realize the network's security has been compromised. Others are so blatant that *everyone* will know instantly.

Attackers range from charmers with lots of "people skills" who can persuade legitimate users to provide the credentials they need to break into the system to technical "whiz kids" who can exploit the characteristics of network protocols, applications, and operating systems and technically unsophisticated hacker "wannabes" who use scripts, GUI tools, and Web sites created by others to carry out their attacks. The attacks themselves can range from denials of service that disrupt communications on the entire network to "benign" viruses that do no more than pop up an annoying message window. In many cases, the goal of an attack is to plant a "back door" in the system that will allow the hacker to reenter later at will.

The good news is that network professionals can take many steps to prevent technical exploits on their systems. In fact, applying all the current patches, fixes, service packs, and other upgrades and running good antivirus software with updated virus file definitions will go a long way toward keeping intruders out and attackers at bay. The bad news is that administrators must be constantly vigilant to guard against new threats that appear on a daily basis. The state of hacking has reached the point at which anyone and everyone who wants to launch an attack can do so, and the incidence of "drive-by hacking" has increased with the advent of easy-to-use hacking tools.

Frequently Asked Questions

The following Frequently Asked Questions, answered by the authors of this book, are designed to both measure your understanding of the concepts presented in this chapter and to assist you with real-life implementation of these concepts. To have your questions about this chapter answered by the author, browse to **www.syngress.com/solutions** and click on the **"Ask the Author"** form.

Q: Why aren't the tools described in this chapter—port-scanning utilities, packet sniffers, keystroke-logging devices, and so on—illegal to create or download?

A: Many of these tools have legitimate uses. It is especially important for network administrators and security consultants to be able to use scanning tools to determine where the vulnerabilities are in their own or their clients' networks in order to take the appropriate steps to "harden" the systems. After all, if scanning tools were outlawed, only outlaws would have scanning tools. These utilities—like many other things—can be used either offensively or defensively. Keystroke-logging devices and other "spyware" can be useful in situations in which monitoring users' activities is legal and appropriate—for example, for employers to keep tabs on what employees are doing on the network (especially when the employer could be held liable for those activities) and for parents to exercise control over children's online activities.

Q: If a company has a good firewall installed, won't that protect from all these attacks?

A: No. Firewall products are very useful for controlling what comes into or goes out of a network. But a firewall is like a computer (in many cases, a firewall *is* a specialized computer); it does only what the person who configures it tells it to do. Some types of attacks are recognized and can be stopped by firewalls, but others exploit the characteristics of the protocols commonly used for legitimate network communications, and packets might appear to be nothing more than a benign bit of data destined for a computer on the internal network. Trojans, viruses, and worms piggyback into the network as e-mail attachments or through remote file sharing. Firewalls won't catch them, but a good antivirus program, frequently updated and set to scan all incoming e-mail, might be able to do so. Many companies seem to operate under the assumption that installing a firewall is akin to invoking a magic spell that casts a force field of protection around their networks, rendering them completely immune to attack. Even the best firewall won't protect against social engineering attacks, nor will it do any good against internal attackers who have physical access to the network. Studies have shown that a large number of network-related crimes are actually "inside jobs." In the next chapter, you'll learn in detail how firewalls work, which will make it easier to understand why they are not the "cure all" solution to network security that they're sometimes made out to be.

Q: Exactly how does social engineering work? Why would anyone reveal his or her password to a stranger? Does this really happen?

A: Yes, it really happens—and more often than you might think. Skilled social engineers are good con artists; they are masters at making other people trust them. In large companies, employees often aren't personally familiar with all the other employees, so it's relatively easy for the social engineer to come strolling in or even call on the phone and persuade a user that he or she is a member of the IT department and needs the user's password. The social engineer might have a convincing story, saying, for instance, that a hacker has gotten into the system and discovered all the password files, and now the IT department needs to know everyone's old password so they can reset them and issue new ones to protect against the hacker. Like all con artists, the social engineer usually plays on common human emotions. For example, the engineer will play up the danger that the hacker can access and destroy all of the user's data if the "IT worker" doesn't get the password immediately and make the change. In other cases, the engineer might exploit other emotions, such as people's natural desire to help, claiming that the "IT worker" will get in trouble with the "big boss," maybe even lose the job, if he or she is unable to get the password information needed. Social engineers are not above appealing to the user's ego or pretending sexual/romantic interest in the user to get the password, either. Although some might not categorize it as social engineering, another technique involves simply spying on the user to obtain the password ("shoulder surfing" or looking over the user's shoulder as it is typed) or going through the user's papers to find a written record of the password. Infamous hacker Kevin Mitnik is quoted as saying, "You can have the best technology, firewalls, intrusion-detection systems, biometric devices. All it takes is a call to an unsuspecting employee, and that's all she wrote, baby. They got everything." Visit http://searchsecurity.techtarget.com/originalContent/0,289142,sid14_gci771517,00.html for more on this topic.

Q: I think I understand the differences between a virus, a Trojan, and a worm. But what are all these other types of viruses I hear about: stealth viruses, polymorphic viruses, armored viruses, and cavity viruses?

A: *Stealth viruses* are able to conceal the changes they make to files, boot records, and the like from antivirus programs. They do so by forging the results of a program's attempt to read the infected files. A *polymorphic virus* makes copies of itself to spread, like other viruses, but the copies are not exactly like the original. The virus "morphs" into something slightly different in an effort to avoid detection by antivirus software that might not have definitions for all the variations. Viruses can use a "mutation engine" to create these variations on themselves. An *armored virus* uses a technique that makes it difficult to understand the virus code. A *cavity virus* is able to overwrite part of the infected (host) file while not increasing the length of the file, which would be a tip-off that a virus had infected the file. All of these and more virus classifications are described in Nick FitzGerald's Virus FAQ sheet located at www.safetynet.com/support/kbvfaq.asp#SB. Although somewhat out of date in regard to specific viruses, this site contains some good basic information that forms a foundation for modern virus studies.

Resources

- *Strategies for Defeating Distributed Attacks*
  http://razor.bindview.com/publish/papers/strategies.html

- *CERT Warns of Automated Attacks*
  www.vnunet.com/News/1130755

- Russian PaSsWord Crackers: examples of free cracking software
  www.password-crackers.com/crack.html

- *Everything You Wanted to Know About Social Engineering—But Were Afraid to Ask*
  www.happyhacker.org/uberhacker/se.shtml

- *The Unofficial NetWare Hack FAQ*
  http://nmrc.org/faqs/netware/nw_sec02.html#02-1

- *Web Spoofing: An Internet Con Game* (the Princeton paper)
  www.cs.princeton.edu/sip/pub/spoofing.pdf

- SANS Institute: *DNS Overview with Discussion of DNS Spoofing*
  http://rr.sans.org/DNS/DNS.php

- *Port Scanning: It's Not Just an Offensive Tool Anymore,* by Gary Kessler
  www.garykessler.net/library/is_tools_scan.html

- *The Ethics and Legality of Port Scanning,* by Shaun Jamieson
  http://rr.sans.org/audit/ethics.php

- *Finding Fences in Cyberspace: Privacy, Property and Open Access on the Internet,* by Ethan Preston
  http://grove.ufl.edu/~techlaw/vol6/Preston.html

- *Back Orifice Basics*
  www.nwinternet.com/~pchelp/bo/bobasics.htm

- *E-Mail Bombs and Countermeasures: Cyber Attacks on Availability and Brand Integrity*
  www.silkroad.com/papers/html/bomb/

- *Known Windows 2000 Security Vulnerabilities*
  www.labmice.net/articles/win2000securityholes.htm

- Exploit World: Exploits for various operating systems
  www.insecure.org/sploits.html

- *Routers Surpass Servers for Hacker Attacks,* by James Middleton
  www.vnunet.com/News/1126398

- *How Computer Viruses Work,* by Marshall Brain
  www.howstuffworks.com/virus.htm

- *The Internet Worm of 1988: A Tour of the Worm*
  http://world.std.com/~franl/worm.html

- *Script Kiddies and Packet Monkeys—The New Generation of "Hackers,"* by Denis Dion
  http://rr.sans.org/hackers/monkeys.php

- *Know Your Enemy: The Tools and Methodologies of the Script Kiddie,* from the Honeynet Project
  http://project.honeynet.org/papers/enemy

- *Hacking for the Masses,* presentation by David Rhoades, Maven Security
  www.clickkiddie.net

- *Script Kiddies: Who Are They and What Are They Doing?*
  by Andrew Stephens
  http://rr.sans.org/hackers/kiddies.php

- *UNIX Forensics Techniques for Incidence Response*
  www.incident-response.org

- *Computer Forensics: Introduction to Incident Response and Investigation of Windows NT/2000*
  http://rr.sans.org/incident/comp_forensics3.php

Chapter 7

Understanding Cybercrime Prevention

Topics we'll investigate in this chapter:

- **Understanding Security Concepts**

- **Understanding the Technical Aspects of Network Security**

- **Making the Most of Hardware and Software Security**

- **Understanding Firewalls**

- **Deploying an Incident Response Team**

- **Designing and Implementing Security Policies**

☑ **Summary**

☑ **Frequently Asked Questions**

☑ **Resources**

Introduction

Understanding what cybercrime is and how cybercrimes can be committed only gives an investigator half the picture. Just as every police officer needs a good grasp of physical defensive tactics, the cybercrime investigator must be aware of the tactics that are commonly used to defend a network from criminal intrusion or attack. In this chapter, we discuss the basic concepts involved in computer and network security. This includes the importance of multilayered security and the components that make up a multilayered security plan. We also emphasize the need for investigators to "talk the talk" by learning computer security terminology.

We discuss physical security, the first (and often-overlooked) line of defense. We show you how network administrators keep workstations and servers secure and how a good security plan goes a step further to protect the network's routers, switches, hubs, and other connectivity devices, as well as the cable over which the signal travels (and from which it can be intercepted). We also look at special problems involved in physically securing portable computers and some innovative products that can be used to protect these computers and the data they contain.

Next, we delve into the fascinating and complex world of *cryptography,* the study of "hidden writing." We look at encryption technologies and algorithms and the many ways in which encryption can be used to protect data stored on computers or traveling across the network. You learn about the purposes of encryption in the context of network security and how it can provide for authentication, data confidentiality, and data integrity. We provide a brief history of cryptography and discuss common encryption protocols in use today. We also explain the differences between *encryption* and *steganography* and how these two techniques are used together for stronger security—by both the good guys and the cybercriminals. Finally, we discuss cryptanalysis and decryption techniques and how cryptographic software is being used today as a terrorist tool.

Moving from theory to implementation, we next discuss how organizations can make the most of both hardware- and software-based security products to protect their networks. First, we look at hardware devices, including firewall appliances and authentication devices such as smart card readers, fingerprint scanners, retinal and iris scanners, and voice analysis devices. Then we discuss software-based security solutions, including cryptographic software, digital certificates, and the public key infrastructure.

The next section takes us into how firewalls—both hardware- and software-based—work "under the hood." You learn about layered filtering and how the best firewalls provide protection at the packet, circuit, and application levels. Then we discuss integrated intrusion detection and the way that many firewall products can be configured to perform predefined attacks when an attack occurs.

After covering the specifics of available security products, we turn to another aspect of creating an overall security plan—the issue of how to form an incident response team to deal quickly and effectively with attacks when they occur. But having a team in place will not provide the protection that an organization needs unless the team—and the users and IT professionals who make up the "human side" of the network—are governed by specific, detailed security policies that bring the organization's security plan into focus and incorporate it into the everyday use of the systems and network. Thus the last section of this chapter deals with why and how solid security policies can be developed and put in place, creating a foundation for the implementation of all the security measures that we've addressed as well as laying the cornerstone of the organization's cybercrime prevention plan.

Understanding Network Security Concepts

In Chapter 6, you learned about "technical" intrusions and attacks on networks and how hackers (and hacker wannabes) can exploit the protocols, operating systems, and applications to commit the criminal acts of unauthorized access, interrupting network communications, and destroying or damaging computer data. It is important for investigators to have at least a basic understanding of how these attacks are carried out. It is also important for investigators to be aware of how networks can be defended from further attacks, for several reasons:

- In the course of investigating an intrusion or attack, knowing what security measures were in place at the time of the incident might help narrow down the exact nature of the attack and even who could have perpetrated it.

- Understanding how various security measures work can lead investigators to log files and other sources of information useful in the investigation.

- Knowledge of security measures and concepts allows investigators to make suggestions to victims as to how they might prevent further incidents.

- Some of the measures used by the "good guys" to protect their networks and data (such as encryption) can also be used by the "bad guys" to cover their criminal activities.

Knowledge is power. That's a famous hacker motto, (along with such other gems as "Information wants to be free" and the simplistic but optimistically ambitious

"Hack the world!"). However, it is a truism that applies not only to people attempting to gain access to data they aren't supposed to see, but also to those who are trying to protect themselves from the intruders. The first step in winning any battle—and network security *is* a battle over the ownership and control of your computer files—is the same as it's always been: "Know thine enemy."

To protect a network's resources from theft, damage, or unwanted exposure, administrators must understand who initiates these things, why, and how they do it. Knowledge will make *you,* the investigator, powerful, too—and better able to track down and prosecute unauthorized intruders and attackers.

Applying Security Planning Basics

Securing a company's electronic assets from cybercriminals must involve much more than the IT department; it must involve the entire organization—just as a community policing effort, to be effective, must involve the police department as a whole and not just an isolated "community service division." For cyberinvestigators to understand the security planning and implementation process, they need to start at the beginning, with the very basics of computer security. The following sections illustrate how some of the most basic tenets of traditional security can be applied to the context of computer networking.

Defining Security

A generic dictionary definition of *security* (taken from the *American Heritage Dictionary*) is "freedom from risk or danger; safety." This definition is perhaps a little misleading when it comes to computer and networking security, because it implies a degree of protection that is inherently impossible in the modern connectivity-oriented computing environment.

This is why the same dictionary provides another definition, specific to computer science: "The *level to which* a program or device is safe from unauthorized use" [emphasis added]. Implicit in this definition is the caveat that the objectives of *security* and *accessibility*—the two top priorities on the minds of many network administrators—are, by their very natures, diametrically opposed. The more accessible the data, the less secure it is. Likewise, the more tightly you secure the data, the more you impede accessibility. Any security plan is an attempt to strike the proper balance between the two objectives.

The first step is to determine *what* needs to be protected, and to what degree. Because not every asset is equally valuable, some assets need stronger protection than others. This determination leads to the concept of instituting multiple layers of security.

The Importance of Multilayered Security

An effective security plan does not rely on one technology or solution but instead takes a multilayered approach. Compare this approach to a business's physical security measures; most companies don't depend on just the locks on the buildings' doors to keep intruders and thieves out. Instead, they might also have perimeter security (a fence), perhaps additional external security such as a guard or guard dog, external and internal alarm systems, and to protect special valuables, further internal safeguards such as a vault. IT security should be similarly layered. For example:

- Firewalls at network entry points (and possibly a DMZ or screened subnet between the LAN and the network interface connected to the Internet) that function as perimeter protection

- Password protection at local computers, requiring user authentication to log on, to keep unauthorized persons out

- Access permissions set on individual network resources to restrict access of those who are "in" (logged onto the network)

- Encryption of data sent across the network or stored on disk to protect what is especially valuable, sensitive, or confidential

- Servers, routers, and hubs located in locked rooms to prevent people with physical access from hijacking data without authorization

The Intrusion Triangle

Crime prevention specialists use a model called the Crime Triangle to explain that certain criteria must exist before a crime can occur. We can adapt this same familiar law enforcement concept to network security: The same three criteria in the Crime Triangle must exist before a network security breach can take place. The three "legs," or points of the triangle, are shown in Figure 7.1.

Let's look at each point on the triangle individually:

- **Motive** An intruder must have a reason to want to breach the security of the network (even if the reason is "just for fun"); otherwise he or she won't bother.

- **Means** An intruder must have the ability (either the programming knowledge or, in the case of script kiddies, the intrusion software written by others) or he or she won't be able to breach your security.

- **Opportunity** An intruder must have the chance to enter the network because of flaws in the security plan, holes in a software program that open an avenue of access, or physical proximity to network components. If there is no opportunity to intrude, the would-be hacker will go elsewhere.

Figure 7.1 All three legs of the Crime Triangle must exist for a network intrusion to occur.

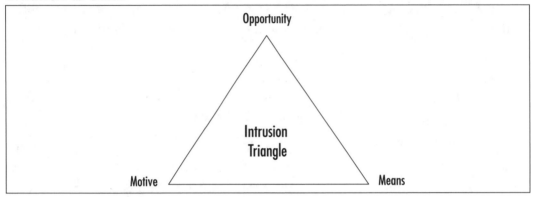

If you think about the three-point intrusion criteria for a moment, you'll see that there is really only one leg of the triangle over which the network administrator or security specialist has any control. It is unlikely that anyone can do much to remove the intruder's *motive*. The motive is likely to be built into the type of data that's on the network or even the personality of the intruder him- or herself. It is also not often possible to prevent the intruder from having or obtaining the *means* to breach your security. Programming knowledge is freely available, and many experienced hackers are more than happy to help less sophisticated ones. The one thing that people who strive to prevent cybercrime *can* affect is the *opportunity* afforded the hacker.

Removing Intrusion Opportunities

Crime prevention officers tell members of the community that they probably can't keep a potential burglar from wanting to steal, and they certainly can't keep the potential burglar from obtaining burglary tools or learning the "tricks of the trade." What they *can* do is take away, as much as possible, the opportunity for the burglar to target their own homes.

This means putting dead-bolt locks on house doors (and using them); getting a big, loud dog who is unfriendly to strangers; and installing an alarm system. In other words, the homeowner's goal is not to prevent the burglar from burglarizing but to make his or her own home a less desirable target. For network "owners," the objective is to "harden" the network, so that all those hackers out there who already have the motive and the means will look for an easier victim.

The best and most expensive locks in the world won't keep intruders out of your house if you don't use them. And if those locks are difficult to use and cause you inconvenience in your everyday comings and goings, you probably *won't* use them—at least, not all the time. A poorly implemented network security system that is difficult to administer or that unduly inconveniences network users might end up similarly; eventually the person burdened with maintaining it will throw his or her hands up in frustration and just turn the darn thing off. And that will leave the network wide open to intruders.

Talking the Talk: Security Terminology

Every industry has its own "language," the jargon that describes ideas, items, concepts, and procedures that are unique to the field. Lawyers speak "legalese," rife with *wherefores* and *hereuntos;* doctors and nurses use terms like *crash cart* and *defib*, and police reports are sprinkled with references to *perps* and *vics* and *MVAs*. Computer networking is infamous for its "technotalk" and the proliferation of acronyms that often mystify outsiders. Specialty areas within an industry often have their own brands of jargon as well, and the computer security subfield is no exception.

It might not be absolutely necessary for the cybercrime investigator to understand all the technical aspects of how security measures work—but knowledge of the technical language used to describe security concepts and devices will serve a couple of important purposes:

- It will make you aware of what can and can't be accomplished by a hacker in particular network environment.

- If you are able to "talk the talk"—to converse intelligently about security issues and measures—you will be better able to win the trust of and communicate with the IT professionals who provide much of the information necessary to your investigation.

It is not possible to provide a complete glossary of security-related terms within the scope of this chapter, but in this section, we define some of the more common words and phrases that you might encounter as you begin to explore the fascinating world of computer security:

- **Authentication** Verification of identity of a user, computer, or process.

- **Authorization** The actions that a user, computer, or process, once identified, is permitted to do.

- **Audit** To track security-related events, such as logging onto the system or network, accessing objects, or exercising user/group rights or privileges.

- **Breach** Successfully defeating security measures to gain access to data or resources without authorization, to make data or resources available to unauthorized persons, or to delete or alter computer files.

- **Cipher** A method used to encrypt data.

- **Cipher text** Data in encrypted form.

- **Confidentiality of data** Ensuring that the contents of messages will be kept secret. See also *integrity of data*.

- **Cryptography (crypto)** The science of hiding information.

- **Encryption** The process of converting data (plain text) into a format (cipher text) that cannot be read or understood by anyone except those authorized to receive it.

- **Encryption algorithm** A formula or calculation that is applied to data to encrypt, or scramble, it.

- **Integrity of data** Ensuring that data has not been modified or altered, that the data received is identical to the data that was sent.

- **Key** A variable that is used in conjunction with an algorithm to encrypt or decrypt data.

- **Penetration testing** Evaluating a system by attempting to circumvent the computer's or network's security measures.

- **Reliability** The probability of a computer system or network continuing to perform in a satisfactory manner for a specific time period under normal operating conditions.

- **Risk** The probability that a specific security threat will be able to exploit a system vulnerability, resulting in damage, loss of data, or other undesired results.

- **Risk management** The process of identifying, controlling, and either minimizing or completely eliminating events that pose a threat to system reliability, data integrity, and data confidentiality.

- **TCSEC** Trusted Computer System Evaluation Criteria, a system for evaluating a system's level of security.

- **Technical vulnerability** A flaw or bug in the hardware or software components of a system that leave it vulnerable to security breach.

- **Vulnerability** A weakness in the hardware, software, or security plan that leaves a system or network open to threat of unauthorized access or damage or destruction of data.

NOTE

For definitions of many more security-related terms, see the following Web sites:

www.securitypanel.org/glossary.html
www.mobrien.com/terminology.shtml
www.whatis.com

Importance of Physical Security

One of the most important, and at the same time most overlooked, aspects of a comprehensive network security plan is physical access control. This matter is often left up to facilities managers and plant security departments or outsourced to security guard companies. Network administrators concern themselves with sophisticated software and hardware solutions that prevent intruders from accessing internal computers remotely while doing nothing to protect the servers, routers, cable, and other physical components of the network from direct access.

In far too many supposedly security-conscious organizations, computers are locked away from employees and visitors all day, only to be left open at night to the janitorial staff—who usually have keys to all offices. It is not at all uncommon for computer espionage experts to pose as members of a cleaning crew to gain physical access to machines that hold sensitive data. This is a favorite ploy for several reasons:

- Cleaning services are often contracted to outside firms; thus company management has minimal control over the screening of the individuals who are hired by the contractor and who are given access to the offices and other parts of the building.

■ Workers in the cleaning industry are often transient, so company employees might not be easily aware of who is or isn't a legitimate member of the cleaning crew.

■ Cleaning is usually done late at night, when all or most company employees are gone, making it easier to surreptitiously steal data.

■ Cleaning-crew members are often paid little or no attention by company employees, who take their presence for granted and think nothing of cleaners being in areas where the presence of others would be questioned.

Physically breaking into the server room and stealing the hard disk on which sensitive data resides may be a crude method of committing cybercrime; nonetheless, it happens. In some organizations, it could be the easiest way to gain unauthorized access, especially for an intruder who has help "on the inside." One of the first things an investigator will want to do in a network intrusion case is to review the physical security measures in place to determine whether access could have been gained this way. Knowledge that the intruder was physically on the site narrows your list of possible suspects from "all hackers, all over the world" to persons who are or have been in the immediate vicinity.

It is beyond the scope of this book to go into great detail about how to physically secure a network, but it is important to understand that physical access control is the "outer perimeter" of any organization's security plan. Ensuring physical access control means:

■ Controlling physical access to the servers

■ Controlling physical access to networked workstations

■ Controlling physical access to network devices

■ Controlling physical access to the cable

■ Being aware of security considerations with wireless media

■ Being aware of security considerations related to portable computers

■ Recognizing the security risk of allowing data to be printed

■ Recognizing the security risks involving diskettes, CDs, tapes, and other removable media

Let's look at why each of these is important and how a physical security plan can address all these factors.

Protecting the Servers

File servers on which sensitive data is stored, as well as infrastructure servers that provide mission-critical services such as logon authentication and access control, should be placed in a highly secure location. At the minimum, servers should be in a locked room to which only employees who need to work directly with the servers have access. Keys should be distributed sparingly, and records should be kept of keys' issuance and return.

If security needs are high due to the nature of the business or the data, access to the server room could be controlled by magnetic card, electronic locks requiring entry of a numerical code, or even biometric access control devices such as fingerprint or retinal scanners. Other security measures include monitor detectors or other alarm systems, activated during nonbusiness hours, and security cameras. A security guard or company should monitor these devices.

Keeping Workstations Secure

Many network security plans focus on the servers but ignore the risk posed by workstations that have network access to those servers. It is not uncommon for employees to leave their computers unsecured when they leave for lunch or even when they leave for the evening. Often there will be a workstation in the receptionist area that is open to visitors who walk in off the street. If the receptionist manning the station must leave briefly, the computer—and the network to which it is connected—is vulnerable unless steps have been taken to ensure that it is secure.

A good security plan includes protection of all unmanned workstations. A secure client operating system such as Windows NT or Windows 2000 requires an interactive logon with a valid account name and password in order to access the operating system (unlike Windows 9x). These systems allow users to "lock" the workstation when they are going to be away from it, so someone else can't just step up and start using the computer. Organizations must not depend on access permissions and other software security methods alone to protect the network. If a potential intruder can gain physical access to a networked computer, he or she is that much closer to accessing valuable data or introducing a virus onto the network.

Many modern PC cases come with some type of locking mechanism that will help prevent an unauthorized person from opening the case and stealing the hard disk. Locks are also available to prevent use of the diskette drive, copying of data to diskette, or rebooting the computer with a diskette.

Protecting Network Devices

Hubs, routers, switches, and other network devices should be physically secured from unauthorized access. It is easy to forget that just because a device doesn't have a monitor on which you can *see* data, this does not mean the data can't be captured or destroyed at that access point.

For example, a traditional Ethernet hub sends all data out every port on the hub. An intruder who has access to the hub can plug a packet-sniffing device (or a laptop computer with sniffer software) that operates in "promiscuous mode" into a spare port and capture data sent to any computer on the segment, as shown in Figure 7.2.

Although switches and routers are somewhat more secure than hubs, any device through which the data passes is a point of vulnerability. Replacing hubs with switches and routers makes it more difficult for an intruder to "sniff" on your network. However, it is still possible to use techniques such as *router redirection* via ARP spoofing, in which nearby machines are redirected to forward traffic through an intruder's machine, by sending ARP packets that contain the router's IP address mapped to the intruder's machine's MAC address. This results in other machines believing the intruder's machine is the router, and so they send their traffic to it. A similar method uses ICMP router advertisement messages.

Figure 7.2 An intruder who has access to the hub can easily intercept data.

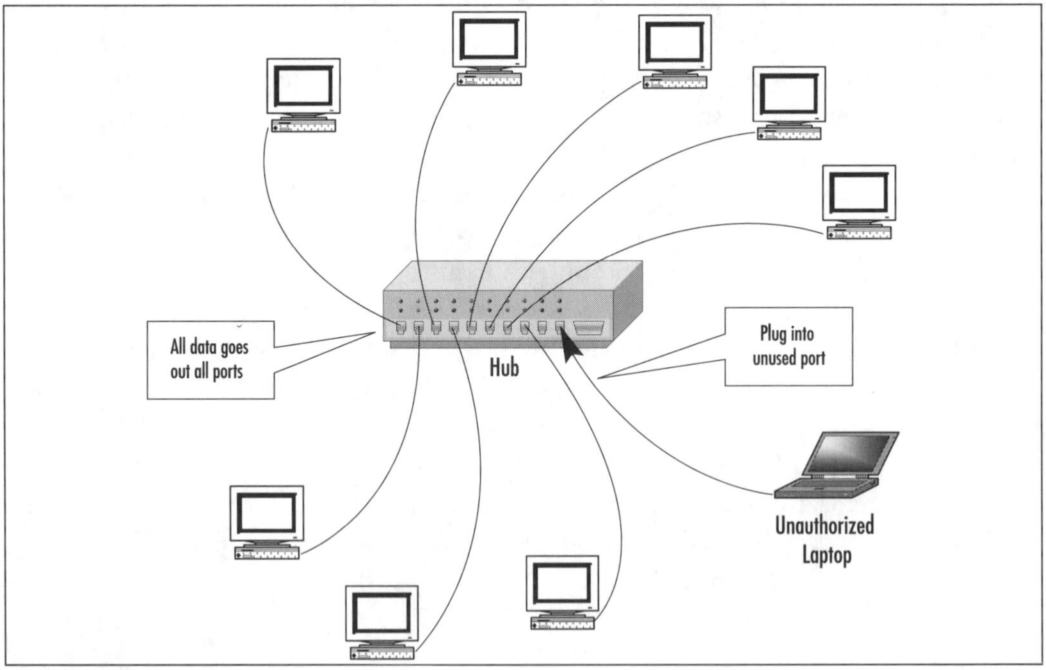

With certain switches, it is also possible to overflow the address tables with multiple false MAC addresses or send a continuous flow of random garbage through the switch to trigger it to change from bridging mode to repeating mode. This means all frames will be broadcast on all ports, giving the intruder the same opportunity to access the data that he would have with a regular hub. This activity is called *switch jamming*. If the switch has a special monitor port designed to be used with a sniffer for legitimate (network troubleshooting) purposes, an intruder who has physical access to the switch can simply plug into this port and capture network data. For these reasons, all network devices should be placed in a locked room or closet; administrators should protect these devices in the same manner as the servers.

Securing the Cable

The next step in protecting the network and its data is to secure the cable across which that data travels. Twisted-pair and coaxial cable are both vulnerable to data capture; an intruder who has access to the cable can tap into it and eavesdrop on messages being sent across it. A number of companies make "tapping" devices. Fiber optic cable is more difficult to tap into because it does not produce electrical pulses but instead uses pulses of light to represent the 0s and 1s of binary data. It is possible, however, for a sophisticated intruder to use an optical splitter and tap into the signal on fiber optic media. Cable taps can sometimes be detected using a time domain reflectometer (TDR) or optical TDR to measure the strength of the signal and determine where the tap is located.

Compromise of security at the physical level is a special threat when network cables are not contained in one facility but span a distance between buildings. There is even a name for this risk: *manhole manipulation,* referring to the easy access intruders often have to cabling that runs through underground conduits.

NOTE

Wireless connections are even more susceptible to interception than cabled ones. At least the cabling can be hidden within the infrastructure, making it difficult to access. Wireless transmissions go over the airwaves and can be "grabbed" by anyone with the desire and the proper equipment. We discuss how to secure wireless connections in Chapter 8, "Implementing System Security."

Have Laptop, Will Travel

Portable computers—laptops, notebooks, and new fully functional handheld computers such as the Pocket PC and Palm OS machines—present their own security problems based on the very features that make them popular: their small size and mobility. Physical security for portable computers is especially important because it is so easy to steal the entire machine, data and all.

Luckily, a large number of companies make theft protection devices and security software for laptops. Locks and alarms are widely available, along with software programs that will disable the laptop's functionality if it is stolen or even help track it down by causing the computer to "phone home" the first time the portable computer is attached to a modem (see Figure 7.3). In addition, data on portables can be encrypted to protect it from access if the devices are stolen.

Figure 7.3 Tracking programs can help recover stolen portable computers.

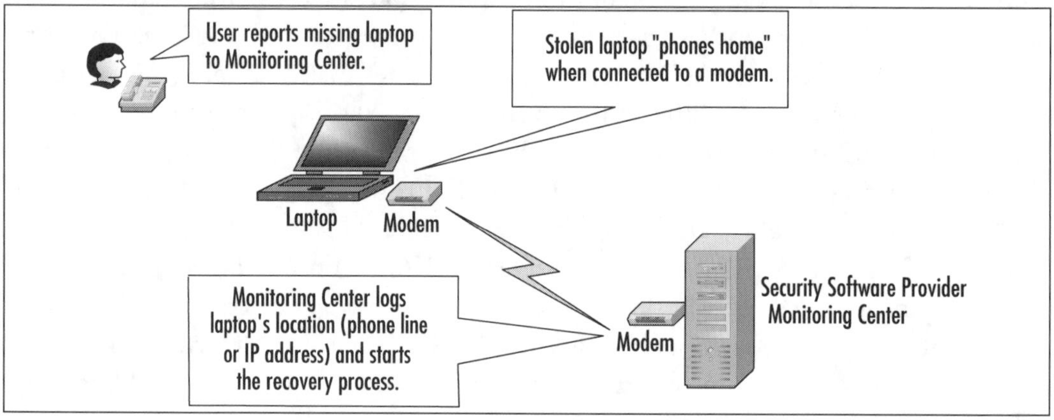

An example of theft recovery and tracking software for laptops is Cyber Angel (www.sentryinc.com) from Computer Sentry Software. Another product, TrackIT (www.trackitcorp.com), is a hardware antitheft device for computer cases and other baggage.

Some laptops come with removable hard disks. If users have highly sensitive data that must be accessed with a laptop, it's a good idea to store it on a removable disk (PC Card disks and those that plug into the parallel port are widely available) and encrypt it. The user should also separate that disk from the computer when it is not in use.

> **NOTE**
>
> The possibility of theft is not the only way in which laptops present a security risk. Another threat to the network is that a data thief who is able to enter the physical premises might be able to plug a laptop into the network, crack passwords or obtain a password via social engineering, and download data to the portable machine, which he or she can then easily carry away.

The Paper Chase

Network security specialists and administrators tend to concentrate on protecting data in electronic form, but intruders can also steal confidential digital information by printing it or locating a hard copy that was printed by someone else. It does little good to implement strong password policies and network access controls if employees can print sensitive material and then leave it lying on desks, stored in unlocked file cabinets, or thrown into an easily accessed trash basket. "Dumpster diving" (searching the trash for company secrets) is a common form of corporate espionage—and one that surprisingly often yields results.

If confidential data must be printed, the paper copy should be kept as physically secure as the digital version. Disposal should require shredding, and in cases of particularly high-security information, the shredded paper can be mixed with water to create a pulp that is impossible to put back together again.

Removable Storage Risks

Yet another potential point of failure in the network security plan involves saving data to removable media. Diskettes, Zip and Jaz disks, tapes, PC cards, CDs, and DVDs containing sensitive data must be kept physically secured at all times. As you will see in Chapter 10, "Collecting and Preserving Digital Evidence," deleting the files on a disk, or even formatting the disk, does *not* completely erase the data; the data is still there and can be retrieved using special software until it has been overwritten.

Although removable media can present a security threat to the network, it can also play an important part in the overall security plan, when used properly. Removable disks (including fully bootable, large-capacity hard disks installed in mobile "nesting" racks) can be removed from the computer and locked in a safe or removed from the premises to protect the data that is stored there.

Understanding Basic Cryptography Concepts

Cryptography is a word derived from the Greek *kryptos* ("hidden"), and the use of cryptography pre-dates the computer age by hundreds of years. Keeping secrets has long been a concern of human beings, and the purpose of cryptography is to hide information or change it so that it is incomprehensible to people for whom it is not intended. Cryptographic techniques include:

- **Encryption,** which involves applying a procedure called an *algorithm* to plain text to turn it into something that will appear to be gibberish to anyone who doesn't have the *key* to decrypt it.

- **Steganography,** which is a means of hiding the existence of the data, not just its contents. This is usually done by concealing it within other, innocuous data.

NOTE

The words *cryptography* and *encryption* are often used interchangeably, but cryptography is a much broader term than encryption; encryption is a form of cryptography. In other words, all encryption is cryptography, but not all cryptography is encryption.

Understanding the Purposes of Cryptographic Security

Cryptographic techniques are an important part of a multilayered security plan. Some security measures, such as implementation of a firewall and use of access permissions, attempt to keep intruders out of the network or computer altogether, much like fences and door locks attempt to keep burglars off the grounds or out of the house. Cryptography provides an inner line of defense. Like a wall safe that is there in case the burglars *do* make it inside your house—and to protect valuables from people who are authorized to come into your house—cryptography protects data from intruders who are able to penetrate the outer network defenses and from those who are authorized to access the network but not *this* particular data.

Cryptographic techniques concern themselves with three basic purposes:

- **Authentication** Verifying the identity of a user or computer.

- **Confidentiality** Keeping the contents of the data secret.

- **Integrity** Ensuring that data doesn't change between the time it leaves the source and the time it reaches its destination.

One or more of these goals may be a priority, depending upon the situation. For example, if an investigator receives a message from the Chief to fly to the West Coast to interview a witness in a case, the overriding concern might be knowing that it was, indeed, the Chief of Police who sent the message and not a fellow officer playing a practical joke. In this case, *authentication* of the message sender's identity is of utmost importance. If the case relates to an internal affairs investigation and it is important that no one else in the department know where the investigator is going, *confidentiality* of the data might be important as well. And if the message states that the investigator is authorized to spend $3000 on the trip, it might be important to ensure that the message has not been changed (after all, chiefs are not usually this generous) in transit—in other words, that the message's *integrity* has not been compromised.

All three mechanisms can be used together, or they can be used separately when only one or two of these considerations are important. In the following sections, we look more closely at how each one works in relation to network security.

On the Scene...

An Historical Perspective on Cryptography

Cryptography has probably been around almost as long as written language. According to *A Short History of Cryptography*, by Fred Cohen (www.all.net/books/ip/Chap2-1.html), the study of cryptography has been around for 4000 years or more. Whenever communications are recorded, the issue of protecting those recorded communications arises.

In both business and personal communications, it is often not desirable to share the contents with everyone—in fact, in many cases doing so could have disastrous results. Thus, early civilizations looked for ways to conceal the contents of messages from prying eyes. In ancient Egypt, deviations on the hieroglyphic language in use were developed for that purpose. The Greeks used a "transposition code" in which each letter of the alphabet was represented by another that indicated where, in a grid,

Continued

the original letter was located. In early India, spies employed by the government used phonetic-based "substitution codes" (the same concept children use for pig Latin). In biblical times, a substitution cipher called *atbash*, which worked by replacing the last letter of the Hebrew alphabet with the first and so on, was used to encrypt writings. Encryption methods were used by such diverse historical figures as Julius Caesar (after whom the "Caesar cipher" was named), Thomas Jefferson (who invented the cipher wheel), and Sir Francis Bacon. Governments have long used encryption to protect sensitive military messages.

Authenticating Identity

Many different methods can be used to authenticate a user's (or in some cases, a computer's) identity. In general, the user is asked to provide something that is associated with his or her user account that could not easily be provided by someone else. The requested credential is generally one (or more) of the following:

- **Something you know** One way to determine that a person is really who he or she claims to be is to ask a question that only the "real McCoy" is likely to be able to answer. If you are engaging in online messaging with someone who purports to be your brother, before discussing personal or sensitive subjects, you might ask him what your mother's oldest sister's name is, or ask him to name the song that the two of you played in a piano duet as children. In information security, the "something you know" is usually a password or personal identification number (PIN).

- **Something you have** Passwords can be compromised—as you learned in Chapter 6. For example, someone can discover passwords through a brute-force attack or by watching over a user's shoulder as he or she types the password. In many of these cases, the user doesn't know that someone else now knows the password. A better authentication method is to require that the user provide a physical object, such as a "smart card" (a credit-card-sized device with an embedded chip that contains authentication information). If the card is lost or stolen, the user is likely to know about it. Smart cards are used to log onto computer networks and to access bank accounts and make purchases.

- **Something you are** Although a card or other physical object that must be in the user's possession is a step up from password authentication, cards can be lost or stolen or perhaps even duplicated. An even more secure method of proving identity is via what you are, that is, biological data such as a fingerprint, voice print, or retinal or iris scan. Biometric methods are much more difficult to defeat than other identification methods.

NOTE

Some security literature mentions a fourth means of proving identity: *something you do.* An example would be a sample of your handwriting, and voice prints might also be considered to be in this category.

On the Scene...

Defeating "Foolproof" Authentication Mechanisms

In 2000, a French engineer/hacker named Serge Humpich (and known as "the Count of Monte Crypto") was able to defeat the 640-bit encryption key used by smart cards issued by banks in France, which millions of French consumers used for purchasing items. The equipment he used to break the encryption key cost only US$250.

Even supposedly "foolproof" biometric methods aren't. This is because the biometric data must be analyzed by a software program, and everyone who has worked with computers knows that there is no such thing as a software program that works perfectly. Thus the vendors of biometric solutions establish fault-tolerance limits that are based on a certain level of false rejection and false acceptance rates (called FRRs and FARs, respectively). *False rejection* occurs when an authorized user is rejected by the system, and *false acceptance* occurs when an unauthorized user is "passed" by the software and allowed access. In fact, fingerprint scanners have been defeated by such simple methods as blowing on the sensor surface to reactivate a fingerprint previously left there or by dusting a latent fingerprint on the sensor with graphite and then applying adhesive film to the surface and pressing on it gently. These techniques are examples of *latent image reactivation*. In a well-publicized case in May 2002, a cryptographer in Japan was able to create a phony fingerprint using gelatine, which he claimed fooled fingerprint scanners approximately 80 out of 100 times.

Continued

For more information about the reliability of biometric devices, see the following articles: www.heise.de/ct/english/02/11/114/ and http://theregister.co.uk/content/55/25300.html.

Because none of these authentication methods (or any other) is absolutely foolproof, it makes sense in a high-security environment to use a multifactor authentication system (sometimes called *two-way* or *three-way authentication,* depending on the number of authentication methods used) by combining two or more of them. That is, a user is required to provide both something he has *and* something he knows (in fact, most smart card implementations require that the user not only insert the card in a reader but also enter a PIN), or he must both undergo a biometric scan and provide a password before being granted access.

Another method of implementation is *layered authentication,* in which one form of authentication is accepted to provide a lower level of access, and additional authentication is required for a higher level of access. For more information about this concept, see Jeff Parker's article titled *Layered Authentication* at http://rr.sans.org/authentic/layered.php.

When Is Authentication Necessary?

There are a number of different circumstances in which authentication is necessary, and different authentication methods are used in different circumstances. For example:

- **Logon authentication** When users initially access the computer or network (log on), a secure operating system will require that the user authenticate to a security accounts database. When logging onto the local computer, the user must enter an account name and password that are stored in a local security database on that machine's hard disk. When logging onto a server-based network (such as a Windows NT/2000/ .NET domain or a NetWare NDS network), the user must enter an account name and password that is in the authentication server's database. Additionally, Windows domains require that NT/2000/XP Pro/.NET computers have a computer account in order to join the domain. (The computer's credentials are sent to the domain controller automatically, without any user intervention.) However, a user with a domain account can log on from an insecure computer, such as a Windows 9*x*/ME/XP Home machine. Windows NT uses NTLM authentication, whereas Windows 2000—although it supports NTLM for backward compatibility—uses Kerberos authentication by default. (NTLM, Kerberos, and other protocols are described in the next section, "Authentication Protocols.")

■ **Remote access authentication** When users access the network over a remote connection (dialup or VPN), security is especially important because the computer from which the user is logging on isn't physically wired to the local network. Different, additional protocols are used for remote access authentication. When a remote logon is initiated, the remote client and the remote access server generally negotiate an authentication method and protocols that both are configured to support. There are a number of different methods for authenticating remote users, some of which we discuss in the following section, "Authentication Protocols."

NOTE

In a network that uses an authentication server, users are authenticated when they log onto the network, and then access to individual network resources is controlled based on the permissions granted to the account with which the user logged on. In workgroup (peer-to-peer) networks, there is no authentication server, but access to resources can be protected using *file-level security.* Passwords are assigned to individual resources, and those passwords are shared with users who are authorized to access them. Every time a user wants to open a particular file or use a particular printer, he or she must enter the correct password. This is not really authentication, because the user's identity isn't verified (the password is not associated with a user account), although entering the password does verify that the user is authorized to access the resource.

Authentication Protocols

The protocols used for authenticating identity depend on the authentication type. Some common protocols used for authentication include the following:

■ **Kerberos** is a logon authentication protocol that is based on secret key (symmetric) cryptography. It usually uses the DES or Triple-DES (3DES) algorithm, although with the latest version, Kerberos v5, algorithms other than DES can be used. Kerberos uses a system of "tickets" to provide verification of identity to multiple servers throughout the network. This system works a little like the payment system at some amusement parks and fairs where, instead of paying to ride each individual ride, customers must buy tickets at a central location and then use those tickets to access the rides. Similarly, with Kerberos, a client who wants to access resources on network servers is not authenticated by each server; instead, all the servers rely on "tickets" issued by a central server, called the Key Distribution Center (KDC). The client sends a request for a ticket (encrypted with the client's key) to the KDC. The KDC issues a ticket called a Ticket-Granting Ticket (TGT), which is encrypted and submitted to the Ticket-Granting Service (TGS). The TGS can be running on the same physical machine that is running the KDC. The TGS issues a session ticket to the client for accessing the particular network resource that was requested (which is usually on a different server). The session ticket is presented to the server that hosts the resource, and access is granted. The session key is valid only for that particular session and is set to expire after a specific amount of time. Kerberos allows mutual authentication; that is, the identities of both the client and the server can be verified. For a more detailed explanation of how Kerberos works, see the *Kerberos v5 Administrators Guide* at www.lns.cornell.edu/public/COMP/krb5/admin/admin_2.html.

- **NT LanMan, or NTLM,** is another Microsoft logon authentication method, used by Windows NT domains and supported by Windows 2000 in case "down-level" client computers (those running NT or Windows 9x) want to log onto the network. NTLMv2, the current version, provides more security than NTLMv1. Version 2 is supported by Windows 2000 and NT 4.0 with SP4 or higher. If the Directory Services client software (which is available on the Windows 2000 Server CD-ROM) is installed on Windows 9x computers, NTLMv2 can be used; however, it is necessary to edit the registry to enable it. Unlike Kerberos, with NTLM, when a client wants to access a server's resources, that server must contact the domain controller to have the client's identity verified. The client doesn't have credentials already issued (the session ticket in Kerberos) that the file or application server knows it can trust.

- **Password Authentication Protocol (PAP)** is a remote access authentication protocol used for PPP (dialup) connections. Its distinguishing characteristic (and the reason it should not be used on secure networks) is the fact that it sends passwords in plain text. This means the passwords can be intercepted during transmission and used by an unauthorized person. The only good reason to use PAP is if you face a situation where the remote server doesn't support other, more secure authentication methods. Shiva PAP (S-PAP) addresses this problem by using a two-way reversible authentication method that encrypts passwords so they will not be subject to interception and misuse.

- **Challenge Handshake Authentication Protocol (CHAP)** uses a hashing algorithm and a shared secret (more about that later in the chapter, in the section on encryption) to protect the password. CHAP provides more security than PAP. Microsoft developed its own version of the protocol, called MS-CHAP, which uses the DES encryption algorithm and LM/NTHASH.

- **The Remote Authentication Dial-In User Service (RADIUS)** is another means of authenticating remote connections that takes the authentication responsibility off each individual remote access server by providing a centralized server to authenticate clients securely. Exchanges are encrypted using a shared key, and multiple RADIUS servers can communicate with each other and exchange authentication information.

- **The AppleTalk Remote Access Protocol (ARAP)** is a two-way authentication protocol that uses DES encryption for remote access connections on AppleTalk networks.

- **Secure Shell (SSH)** allows users to log into UNIX systems remotely. Both ends of the connection (client and server) are authenticated, and data—as well as passwords—can be encrypted. 3DES, Blowfish, and Twofish are encryption algorithms that are supported by SSHv2, which also allows the use of smart cards.

NOTE

There are also versions of SSH made for Windows and Mac machines. Freeware SSH client software for these operating systems is available at www.openssh.org/windows.html.

A concept that is closely related to authentication is *nonrepudiation*. This is a means of ensuring that whoever sends a message cannot later claim that he or she didn't send it. Nonrepudiation is sometimes considered to be a fourth, separate purpose of cryptography, but we include it here in the discussion of authentication because the two concepts go together; nonrepudiation just goes a step further than authentication.

On the Scene...

Identity Confirmed; Now What?

Once a user's identity has been established, the next step in the security process is *authorization,* which is concerned with what that user is permitted to do. Authentication and authorization work together to provide a security system that takes into account the need for different users to have different capabilities on the network.

Administrators can control which files and other objects a user can access and the level of access (read only, change, and so on) by setting *permissions.* Most network operating systems provide a mechanism for associating specific permissions on an object with certain user accounts or groups. For example, Windows NT/2000/XP provide for two levels of permissions: *share permissions* that apply only to users accessing the resource across the network, and *file-level permissions* (also called NTFS permissions) that apply both across the network and to users accessing the resource from the local machine.

Administrators can also control which system-wide actions a particular user (or group of users) can perform by setting *user rights.* User rights differ from permissions in that permissions apply to access of individual files, folders, printers, and other objects.

Providing Confidentiality of Data

Confidentiality refers to any method that keeps the contents of the data secret. Usually this means encrypting it to prevent unauthorized persons from understanding what the data says even if they intercept it. In a high-security environment, where network communications necessarily involve information that should not be shared with the world, it is important to use strong encryption to protect the confidentiality of sensitive data. We discuss exactly how that is done in the "Basic Cryptography Concepts" section later in the chapter.

Ensuring Data Integrity

Data integrity, in the context of cryptography, means that there is a way to verify that the data was not changed after it left the sender, that the data that was sent is exactly the same as the data that is received at the final destination. It is essential to be able to count on data integrity in network transactions such as e-commerce.

NOTE

The term *data integrity* has a broader meaning in terms of general computing and networking than it does in the context of cryptography. In this sense, it refers to protection of data from damage or destruction; the integrity of data can be threatened by a power surge, a magnetic field, fire, flood, or the like as well as by persons who would deliberately modify it. You can install utilities such as Tripwire (www.tripwire.org) to monitor changes to system data on the hard disk.

Basic Cryptography Concepts

Cryptographic techniques such as encryption are the basis of *digital certificates, digital signatures,* and the *public key infrastructure,* or *PKI.* All of these technologies are important components of an enterprise-level security plan, and we discuss the use of each later in this chapter. Now that you understand the purposes of cryptography, we can look at the mechanics of how these technologies are implemented.

Scrambling Text with Codes and Ciphers

There are many different ways to "scramble" text or hide its meaning in such a way that only authorized persons (at least in theory) are able to read it. This scrambled (encrypted) text is called *cipher text.* A method for encrypting text is called a *cipher* or a *code.* Technically, a code uses substitution at the word or phrase level, whereas a cipher works at the level of individual letters or digits. The two words are often used interchangeably, but computerized cryptographic techniques generally rely on ciphers that operate on the binary form of the data by applying an *algorithm* (a mathematical calculation). Some common cipher/code types are:

- Substitution
- Transposition
- Obscure languages

Substitution Ciphers

Simple substitution is a method often used by children in their first experiments with secret code. A substitution cipher merely substitutes different letters, numbers, or other characters for each character in the original text. The most straightforward example is a simplistic substitution in which each letter of the alphabet is represented by a numerical digit, starting with 1 for A. The message *goodbye* then becomes 7-15-15-4-2-25-5. This code is obviously extremely easy to break.

The Caesar Cipher used a simple shifting method, in which each letter of the message is represented by the letter two places to the right in the alphabet (A becomes C, B becomes D, and so on). Other substitution methods can be much more difficult to crack. For example, if two parties exchanging communications have an identical copy of a particular book, they might create a message by referencing page, line, and word numbers (e.g., 73-12-6 tells you that the word in the message is the same as the sixth word in the twelfth line on page 72 of the code book). In this case, anyone who doesn't have a copy of the book (and to cite the correct pages, it must be the exact same edition and print run) will not be able to decipher the message.

Some types of substitution ciphers are:

- **Monoalphabetic substitution** Each letter is represented by another letter or character in a one-to-one relationship.

- **Polyalphabetic substitution** Different cipher-text characters can represent the same plain-text letter, making it more difficult to decrypt messages using the frequency analysis technique. Renaissance architect and art theorist Leon Battista Alberti is credited with developing this technique, earning him recognition as the "father of Western cryptography."

- **Polygraphic (block) cipher** Several letters (or digits when dealing with binary data) are encrypted at the same time, using a system that can handle all the possible combinations of a set number of characters.

- **Fractionation** Multiple symbols are substituted for each plain-text letter, then the letters or digits are transposed.

Transposition Ciphers

Transposition ciphers use tables in which the plain text is entered one way, then read another way to create the encrypted text. For example, each character of text is entered into the table cells going across from left to right, then the cipher text is produced by reading the characters in columns. A variation uses a square grid with holes that is placed on top of a sheet of paper, then the message is written, rotating the grid at intervals.

Obscure Languages as Code

Obscure languages have been used as code by governments for military communications. Ancient ("dead") languages have been used in this way. The U.S. military even used Navajo "code talkers" (speakers of the complex and little known Navajo language) in World War II to send secret communications. This language was chosen because it was hard to learn, and only a few people in the world knew it. The Navajo language had never been written, which made it even more obscure. Members of the Navajo tribe were recruited to develop a code based on the language. For more information about this project, see the article *Navajo Code Talkers* at http://raphael.math.uic.edu/~jeremy/crypt/contrib/mollo2.html.

Mechanical and Electrical Cipher Devices

Cipher devices such as cipher wheels and cylinders can be used to encrypt and decrypt text. An early example of this technique was the *skytale cipher* or *staff cipher* used by the Spartans. They wrapped a sheet of papyrus around a staff and wrote their message down the length of the staff. When the sheet was unwrapped, the message couldn't be easily read unless it was wrapped around a staff of the same diameter as the original one.

Leon Battista Alberti used a set of disks that both had the alphabet etched on them to employ his polyalphabetic ciphering system. He lined up the two disks to determine what cipher-text character would represent each plain-text letter. By rotating the disks at set intervals, he caused different cipher-text letters to represent the same plain-text letters at different places in the message.

Many different cipher machines have been developed by government and military entities. Most use multiple rotating disks to create letter substitutions, and they can be operated either mechanically or electrically. Thomas Jefferson invented a cipher wheel of this type. During World War II, the Japanese used cipher machines called RED and PURPLE, and the German Enigma machine (a wired rotor machine that has equally spaced electrical contacts on each side of a disk, which are connected to one another in scrambled order) is perhaps the most famous—or infamous—of the cipher devices.

Computerizing the Ciphering Process

The availability of computer technology made it much easier to encrypt messages using very complex methods that would be difficult or impossible to use by hand or with mechanical and electrical devices. As we discussed in Chapter 4, "Understanding Computer Basics," when you get down to the heart of the system, computers really do only one thing: perform calculations on numbers. However, they can do an incredible number of such calculations incredibly quickly. This is exactly what is needed for complex encryption algorithms. Of course, computers also make it much easier to *decrypt* encrypted data. Ciphers that would take hundreds or thousands of years to break with a team of top cryptanalysts working on them manually can be cracked in hours, days, or weeks using high-powered computers.

One of the first well-known computer ciphering systems was LUCIFER, an IBM project that formed the foundation of the popular Data Encryption Standard (DES) cipher that is still widely used (along with its more secure version, 3DES). LUCIFER was a block cipher, as is DES. It used a 128-bit key to encrypt blocks of binary data that were 128 bits in length. The cipher was applied to each block several times. Even though LUCIFER uses a larger block and key than DES, it is less secure. That's because its key schedule is regular and thus more predictable. In the "Encryption Algorithms" section later in this chapter, we discuss DES and other modern ciphers used by computerized encryption schemes.

NOTE

For much more detailed information about how different types of ciphers and cipher devices work, see http://pardus-larus.student .utwente.nl/librarilo/texts/computers/crypto.

What Is Encryption?

Encryption is a form of cryptography that "scrambles" plain text into unintelligible cipher text. Encryption is the foundation of such security measures as digital signatures, digital certificates, and the public key infrastructure that uses these technologies to make computer transactions more secure. Computer-based encryption techniques use keys to encrypt and decrypt data. A *key* is a variable (sometimes represented as a password) that is a large binary number—the larger, the better. Key length is measured in bits, and the more bits in a key, the more difficult the key will be to "crack."

The key is only one component in the encryption process. It must be used in conjunction with an encryption *algorithm* (a process or calculation) to produce the cipher text. Encryption methods are usually categorized as either symmetric or asymmetric, depending on the number of keys that are used. We discuss these two basic types of encryption technology in the following sections.

Symmetric Encryption

Symmetric encryption is also called *secret key encryption*, and it uses just one key, called a *shared secret,* for both encrypting and decrypting. This is a simple, easy-to-use method of encryption, but there is one problem with it: the key must be shared between the sender and the recipient of the data, so a secure method of *key exchange* must be devised. Otherwise, if a third party intercepts the key during the exchange, an unauthorized person can easily decrypt the data.

Asymmetric Encryption

To address the problem of key exchange, another type of encryption was developed. *Asymmetric encryption* is also called *public key encryption*, but it actually relies on a *key pair*. Two mathematically related keys, one called the *public key* and another called the *private key*, are generated to be used together. The private key is never shared; it is kept secret and used only by its owner. The public key is made available to anyone who wants it. Because of the time and amount of computer processing power required, it is considered "mathematically unfeasible" for anyone to be able to use the public key to recreate the private key, so this form of encryption is considered very secure.

The primary advantage of asymmetric encryption is that there is no need to securely transmit a secret key. Instead, the public key is published openly, made available to the entire world. There is no need to keep it secret, because it can't be used alone. The encryption process works like this:

1. The sender of a message uses the intended recipient's public key, which is freely available, to encrypt a message.

2. The recipient decrypts the message using his or her private key. Only the private key associated with the public key that encrypted it can be used to decrypt the message.

This key pair can also be used to provide for authentication of a message sender's identity using the keys a little differently: This time the sender uses his or her own *private* key to encrypt the message. This system provides no confidentiality, because anyone can decrypt the message using the owner's public key. However, it does verify the sender's identity, because if the associated public key will decrypt the message, it could only have been encrypted with that person's private key.

Obviously, the most important issue in public key cryptography is the protection of the private keys. This concept is especially important because compromise of a private key not only allows the unauthorized person to read private messages sent to the owner, but it also allows the key thief to "sign" transactions emulating the owner, thus stealing the owner's identity. When the key pair is used for secure credit card or banking transactions, the result can be disastrous.

Securing Data with Cryptographic Algorithms

Literally thousands of different cryptographic algorithms have been developed over the years. Crytographic algorithms can be classified as follows:

- **Encryption algorithms** that are used to encrypt data and provide confidentiality

- **Signature algorithms** that are used to digitally "sign" data to provide authentication

- **Hashing algorithms** that are used to provide data integrity

Algorithms (ciphers) are also categorized by the way they work at the technical level (stream ciphers and block ciphers). This categorization refers to whether the algorithm is applied to a stream of data, operating on individual bits, or to an entire block of data. *Stream ciphers* are faster because they work on smaller units of data. The key is generated as a *keystream,* and this is combined with the plain text to be encrypted. RC4 is the most commonly used stream cipher. Another is ISAAC.

Block ciphers take a block of plain text and turn it into a block of cipher text. (Usually the block is 64 or 128 bits in size.) Common block ciphers include DES, CAST, Blowfish, IDEA, RC5/RC6, and SAFER. Most Advanced Encryption Standard (AES) candidates are block ciphers.

NOTE

AES is a standard for cryptography used by the U.S. federal government to protect sensitive but unclassified information. A number of different algorithms were considered candidates for this standard. The National Institute of Standards and Technology (NIST) selected the Rijndael algorithm for the AES. For more information about the Advanced Encryption Standard, see http://csrc.nist.gov/encryption/aes/aesfact.html.

Encryption Algorithms

Some popular encryption algorithms (many of which were AES candidates) are:

- **Rijndael (AES standard)** www.tcs.hut.fi/~helger/crypto/link/block/rijndael.html

- **DES and 3DES** www.rsasecurity.com/rsalabs/faq/3-2-1.html

- **SAFER** www.cylink.com/news/press/pressrels/92000.htm

- **IDEA** http://home.ecn.ab.ca/~jsavard/crypto/co0404.htm

- **DEAL** www.ii.uib.no/~larsr/newblock.html

- **CAST-256** www.entrust.com/resources/pdf/cast-256.pdf

- **MARS** www.research.ibm.com/security/mars.html

- **Blowfish and Twofish** www.counterpane.com/blowfish.html and www.tcs.hut.fi/~helger/crypto/link/block/twofish.html

Other encryption algorithms include SERPENT, RC4/RC5/RC6, LOKI-97, FROG, and Hasty Pudding.

Signature Algorithms

Signature algorithms are used to create digital signatures. A *digital signature* is merely a means of "signing" data (as described earlier in the section on asymmetric encryption) to authenticate that the message sender is really the person he or she claims to be. Digital signatures can also provide for data integrity along with authentication and nonrepudiation. Digital signatures have become important in a world where many business transactions, including contractual agreements, are conducted over the Internet. Digital signatures generally use both signature algorithms and hash algorithms.

When a message is encrypted with a user's private key, the hash value that is created becomes the signature for that message. Signing a different message will produce a different signature. Each signature is unique, and any attempt to move the signature from one message to another would result in a hash value that would not match the original; thus the signature would be invalidated.

Hashing Algorithms

Hashing is a technique in which an algorithm (also called a *hash function*) is applied to a portion of data to create a unique digital "fingerprint" that is a fixed-size variable. If anyone changes the data by so much as one binary digit, the hash function will produce a different output (called the *hash value*) and the recipient will know that the data has been changed. Hashing can ensure integrity and provide authentication as well.

The hash function cannot be "reverse-engineered"; that is, you can't use the hash value to discover the original data that was hashed. Thus hashing algorithms are referred to as *one-way hashes*. A good hash function will not return the same result from two different inputs (called a *collision*); each result should be unique.

There are several different types of hashing, including division-remainder, digit rearrangement, folding, and radix transformation. These classifications refer to the mathematical process used to obtain the hash value. Standard hashing algorithms include:

- **MD2, MD4, and MD5** These methods use a *message digest* (the hash value) that is 128 bits in length. They were created by Ron Rivest and are popularly used for digital signatures.

- **Secure Hash Algorithm (SHA)** There are several variations on this algorithm, including SHA-1, SHA-256, SHA-384, and SHA-512. The differences between them lie in the length of the hash value. SHA was created by a cooperative effort of two U.S. government agencies, NIST and the NSA.

How Encryption Is Used in Information Security

Encryption is used for a number of different purposes in organizations that deal in sensitive data of any type. In the "Designing and Implementing Security Policies" section later in this chapter, we discuss the types of information that should be protected. In this section, we look at the different ways encryption technologies can be used to protect that information.

Encrypting Data Stored on Disk

Disk encryption refers to encrypting the entire contents of a hard disk, diskette, or removable disk. *File encryption* refers to encrypting data stored on disk on a file-by-file basis. In either case, the goal is to prevent unauthorized persons from opening and reading files that are stored on the disk.

Support for disk/file encryption can be built into an operating system or file system. NTFS v5, the native file system for Windows 2000/XP/.NET, includes the Encrypting File System (EFS), which can be used to protect data on a hard disk or large removable disk. (EFS can't be used to protect data on floppy diskettes because they cannot be formatted in NTFS format.) EFS allows encryption of individual files and/or folders.

Third-party programs—such as ScramDisk, PGPdisk, and SafeDisk for Windows operating systems and the Crypto File System and Transparent Cryptographic File System (TCFS) for UNIX/Linux—can be installed to provide encryption on file systems that don't natively support encryption or to provide partition-level or virtual drive encryption.

With partition-level and virtual drive encryption, a user does not have to explicitly set encryption properties on individual files and folders (as is true with file-level encryption). Instead, an entire partition is marked as encrypted or an encrypted virtual drive is created, and all data that is stored there will be automatically encrypted. Many users choose these methods because performance is better than with file-level encryption. Some file/disk encryption methods use a password to protect encrypted data; when someone wants to access an encrypted file, he or she must enter a password. Other methods rely on the user account that is logged on to determine whether access will be granted. EFS, for example, uses digital certificates that are associated with the user account. These later methods require less user interaction, but they have their drawbacks. It might not be possible to share encrypted files with others without decrypting them in cases where only one particular account is allowed access. In addition, there is a security risk if the user leaves the computer while logged on; then anyone who sits down at the machine can access the encrypted data.

Encrypting Data That Travels Across the Network

Early in this chapter, in the section addressing physical security, we discussed how data can be intercepted and captured as it travels across a network and its contents revealed with a "sniffer," or protocol analyzer. When sensitive data is transmitted across the network, users can protect against its decoding by ensuring that it is encrypted so that if unauthorized persons *do* intercept it, they won't be able to read it. The industry standard method for doing this on a TCP/IP network is to use the Internet Protocol Security (IPSec) encryption mechanism.

Specifications for IPSec are laid out in RFC 2401. (A number of additional RFCs pertain to different protocols used by IPSec.) IPSec can be used with different operating systems and platforms. Windows 2000/XP/.NET include built-in support for IPSec. IPSec can provide machine-level authentication (verification of the identity of the computer from which a network transmission originated). It can be configured to work in one of two modes:

- **Transport mode** This mode provides end-to-end security, from the source computer to the destination computer. It is also called *host-to-host mode*.

- **Tunnel mode** This mode provides for encryption between two secure gateways (the computers that act as gateways between an internal network and the Internet or other internetwork).

Because it is capable of tunneling, IPSec can be used to create virtual private networks on its own, and it is also used in conjunction with the Layer 2 Tunneling Protocol (L2TP) to provide encryption in an L2TP VPN tunnel.

Although often referred to as a protocol, IPSec is actually a security scheme that incorporates several different protocols. These include the following:

- **Authentication Header (AH) protocol** This protocol is used for authentication and to ensure data integrity by signing each data packet. AH signs the entire packet (including the IP headers) but does not provide data confidentiality.

- **Encapsulating Security Payload (ESP) protocol** This protocol is used to encrypt data for confidentiality. It also signs the data portion of the packet for authentication and integrity, but it doesn't sign the entire packet.

These two protocols can be used separately or together (in the latter case, when both data confidentiality and signing of the entire packet are desired). Other protocols used by IPSec include:

- **The Internet Security Association and Key Management Protocol (ISAKMP)** This protocol creates security associations between two computers that communicate using IPSec, to define the process of exchanging information.

- **The Oakley Key Generation Protocol** This protocol creates the keys used during the transaction. These are temporary keys that are discarded after the communication session is terminated.

Because IPSec uses shared keys (symmetric encryption), it is important that there be a way to exchange keys securely across the network. The *Diffie-Hellman Key Exchange algorithm* provides a way for the computers on both sides of the transaction to generate identical keys without ever actually sending the key itself across the network and exposing it to possible interception. The encryption algorithms used by IPSec are standard ciphers such as DES/3DES, IDEA, Blowfish, RC-5, and CAST-128.

Another important feature of IPSec is its ability to provide *antireplay*—protection against hackers who might try to capture transmissions and replay them to create a communication session, emulating one of the parties to the original transaction. IPSec is an important mechanism for protecting data during the vulnerable period when it is being sent across a network. The current version of the Internet Protocol, IPv4, allows the use of IPSec as an option; the next generation, IPv6, will require it.

Encrypting E-Mail Communications

More and more people are using e-mail for communications of all kinds, including messages that contain sensitive personal or business information. Several software programs encrypt e-mail; the most popular is Pretty Good Privacy (PGP), which was created by Phil Zimmermann in the early 1990s. Since then, PGP has become widely distributed, and versions are available for most common operating systems—even more outdated or obscure OSs such as OS/2 and Amiga.

PGP first compresses and then encrypts the plain-text data using a one-time secret key (or *session key*), which is itself then encrypted with the public key of the intended recipient. The encrypted session key is sent to the recipient along with the encrypted data, and the recipient uses his or her private key to decrypt the session key so it can be used to decrypt the message itself. Because both symmetric and asymmetric encryption are used in this process, PGP is called a *hybrid cryptosystem*. Different versions of PGP use different encryption algorithms. Version 2.6.*x* (sometimes called "classic PGP" and considered by some to be more secure than newer versions) uses a combination of the RSA asymmetric cipher and the IDEA symmetric cipher. The MD5 hash algorithm is also used to create a fixed-length replacement for very long text strings in digital signatures.

Public keys and private keys are stored in separate files called *keyrings* on the hard disk of the computer where PGP is installed. Both the sender and recipient must have PGP installed to use the program for secure communications.

PGP's biggest vulnerability is related to the fact that users have to use a passphrase to perform actions such as signing documents and decrypting messages (anything for which the private key is used). Protecting this passphrase is a big security issue; good security practices require that the passphrase not be revealed to anyone else or stored on the system for "automatic" entry. Anyone who knows the passphrase can read the encrypted messages or send messages that purport to be from the legitimate user. If the passphrase does become compromised, a key revocation certificate can be generated and issued to render the associated public key null and void. PGP also includes a wipe option (**-w**) that can be used to overwrite the contents of an encrypted file when you delete it, so that it can't be easily recovered using data recovery utilities.

NOTE

For more information about PGP, see the International PGP Home Page at www.pgpi.org.

What Is Steganography?

Steganography (from the Greek word for *covered writing*) refers to a method of hiding data—not just concealing its contents as encryption does, but concealing its very existence. Steganography is usually used in conjunction with encryption for added protection of sensitive data. This method ameliorates one of the biggest problems of encrypting data—the fact that it is encrypted draws the attention of people who are looking for confidential or sensitive information.

The concept of steganography has been around for a long time. The ancient Greeks are said to have sent secret messages by shaving the head of the messenger and writing the message on his scalp, then letting the hair grow back over it before sending him on his way to deliver the message. Early methods of steganography involved using "invisible ink" or concealing a message inside another message using a code whereby only every fifth word, for example, "counts" as part of the real, hidden message. One of the earliest books on the subject, *Steganographica,* by Gaspari Schotti, was published in the 1600s.

Steganography in the computer world also hides data inside other data, but the way it does so is a little more complex. Because of the way data is stored in files, there are often unused (empty) bits in a file such as a document or graphic. A message can be broken up and stored in these unused bits, and when the file is sent it will appear to be only the original file (called the *container file*). The hidden information inside is usually encrypted, and the recipient will need special software to retrieve it (and then decrypt it, if necessary). Messages can be concealed inside all sorts of other files, including executables and graphic and audio files. Another form of steganography is the hidden watermark that is sometimes used to embed a trademark or other symbol in a document or file.

A number of different software programs can be used for this purpose, including JP Hide and Seek, which conceals data inside .jpg files, and MP3Stego, which conceals data in .mp3 files. Steganos Security Suite is a package of software programs that provide steganography, encryption, and other services.

Other programs, such as StegDetect, are designed to look for hidden content in files. The process of detecting steganographic data is called *steganalysis.*

NOTE

For more information and links to lots of good steganography Web sites, see *Information Hiding* at www.jjtc.com/steganography.

Modern Decryption Methods

The use of cryptography naturally led to the science of *cryptanalysis*, the process of decrypting encrypted messages. One of the early methods for "cracking" polyalphabetic substitution ciphers was *frequency analysis,* which involved examining the encrypted text for repeated character strings and using the distance between the repeated strings to calculate the key length. (Repetitions of identical plain-text characters that are ciphered in the same way will occur at intervals that are a multiple of the key length.) Then statistical methods can be used to painstakingly determine which plain-text character each cipher-text character represents.

Cryptanalysts throughout history have used a number of different methods to break encryption algorithms, including the following:

- **Known plain-text analysis** If the analyst has a sample of decrypted text that was encrypted using a particular cipher, he or she can sometimes deduce the key by studying the cipher text.

- **Differential cryptanalysis** If the analyst can obtain cipher text from plain text but is unable to analyze the key, it can be deduced by comparing the cipher text and the plain text.

- **Ciphertext-only analysis** Used when only the cipher text is available and the analyst has no sample of plain text.

- **Timing/differential power analysis** A means of measuring the differences in power consumption over a period during which a computer chip is encrypting information to analyze key computations.

- **Key interception (man in the middle)** The analyst tricks two parties to an encrypted exchange into sending their keys by making them think they're exchanging keys with each other.

Mathematician Claude Shannon (see the sidebar in this section) put forth the theory of *workload.* This term refers to the fact that increasing the amount of work (and the time required to do it) necessary to crack an encryption system increases the strength of the encryption and is an alternative to increasing the unicity distance (the amount of cipher text needed to crack the encryption).

Computer encryption ciphers are difficult to crack, but it can be done. With enough time and patience, a brute-force attack that tries every possible key will be successful. The goal of cryptographers is to create ciphers for which this process will take such a long time—even using supercomputers or distributed processing methods—that the effort will not be worthwhile. Today's popular encryption algorithms rely on this deterrent effect.

Crimestoppers...

A Perfect Cipher?

A *perfect cipher* is one in which every possible cipher text is equally likely for every method, thus rendering the encryption unbreakable without the key.

In his paper *A Communications Theory of Secrecy Systems*, published in 1948, Claude Shannon, a Bell Labs mathematician sometimes called the "father of information theory", postulated that given enough time and a large enough sample of the cipher text, every cipher can be broken. He held that a number he called the *unicity distance*, which represented the amount of cipher text that is needed to be able to decrypt a message, could be used as a measurement of how strong a cipher is. If the unicity distance is infinite (the sequence of numbers in the key is genuinely random and is at least as long as the message, and the key is used only for that one message), the cipher is called a *one-time pad* and the message is undecipherable.

Another example of an undecipherable message is one in which the length of the entire message is shorter than the amount of cipher text needed to break the key. If an alphabetical substitution cipher has a key length that is greater than the message length, the message can't be decrypted by analyzing the cipher text.

Cybercriminals' Use of Encryption and Steganography

We have been discussing the legitimate use of cryptographic techniques as part of an organization's security plan. There are many reasons to take steps to provide extra protection for data such as trade secrets, customer and client personal information, and so forth. However, these same technologies can be—and often are—also used by cybercriminals to conceal the self-incriminating information in messages they send to one another. Terrorists are believed to use steganography and encryption (as well as less technical code words inserted in seemingly innocuous e-mails or Web pages) to communicate with one another and coordinate their financial activities and attacks.

In cases of serious crimes, investigators might need to employ the services of a cryptanalyst to help decipher encrypted data that could contain information essential to identifying criminals or preventing future criminal activities.

On the Scene...

Cryptography as a Terrorist Tool

According to an article in *USA Today* and later reported on the Wired Web site at www.wired.com/news/print/0,1294,41658,00.html, government officials believe al Qa'ida terrorists use steganography to hide their secret communications "in plain sight" in messages and files posted on bulletin board Web sites and exchanged in Internet chat rooms and encryption technologies to conceal the true content of e-mail messages. Encrypted files containing terrorist plans have been found on the computers of various terrorist suspects, including Pakistani terrorist Khalil Deek and the terrorist convicted of plotting the first World Trade Center bombing in 1993, Ramzi Yousef. In both cases, mathematicians working for the FBI were able to use supercomputers to decrypt the files, although in the case of some files, it took more than a year to do so.

For more information, see www.usatoday.com/life/cyber/tech/2001-02-05-binladen.htm.

Making the Most of Hardware and Software Security

A multilayer security plan will incorporate multiple security solutions. Security is not a "one size fits all" issue, so the options that work best for one organization are not necessarily the best choice for another. Security solutions can be generally broken down into two categories: hardware solutions and software solutions.

Implementing Hardware-Based Security

Hardware security solutions can come in the form of network devices: Firewalls, routers, even switches can function to provide a certain level of security. In general, these devices are dedicated computers themselves, running proprietary software.

Hardware-Based Firewalls

Many firewall vendors provide hardware-based solutions. Some of the most popular hardware firewalls include the Cisco PIX firewall, SonicWall, the Webramp 1700, the Firebox from WatchGuard Technologies, and the OfficeConnect firewalls from 3Com. Hardware solutions are available for networks of all sizes. For example, the

3Com products focus on small office/home office (SOHO) users, whereas the Cisco PIX comes in configurations that support up to 250,000 connections.

Hardware-based firewalls are often referred to as *firewall appliances*. A disadvantage of hardware-based firewalls is the proprietary nature of the software they run. Another disadvantage of many of these products, such as Cisco's highly respected PIX, is the high cost. Hardware-based firewalls perform basically the same functions as software-based firewalls. Later in this chapter, in the section "Understanding Firewalls and Proxies," we discuss how both of these work.

Authentication Devices

Other hardware-based components of your network security plan may include devices that provide extra security for authentication, such as:

- Smart card readers
- Fingerprint scanners
- Retinal and iris scanners
- Voice analysis devices

These devices can be used in environments that require a high level of security for secure and reliable network authentication. Microsoft has acquired Biometric API (BAPI) technology from I/O Software and plans to incorporate support for biometric authentication devices into future versions of its operating systems. Windows 2000 already supports smart card authentication.

Smart Card Authentication

The term *smart card* has several different meanings. In a broad sense, it refers to any plastic credit-card-sized card that has a computer chip (a memory chip and/or a tiny microprocessor) embedded in it to hold information that can be changed (as opposed to less "smart" cards that use a magnetic strip that holds static information). A smart card *reader*—a hardware device—is needed to write to and read the information on the card. Smart cards can be used for different purposes, but one of the most popular is for authentication. Satellite television services use smart cards in the SATV receiver to identify the subscriber and that subscriber's service level. Banks use smart cards for conducting transactions. These cards are especially popular in Europe.

Smart cards can also be used for network logon authentication. This provides an extra level of security, the "something you have" factor described in the "Authenticating Identity" section earlier in this chapter. The cards are generally resistant to tampering and relatively difficult for a hacker to compromise, since they are self-contained. They're also inexpensive in comparison with biometric authentication devices.

Smart cards used for logon authentication generally store a *digital certificate* that contains user identification information, the user's public key, and the signature of the trusted third party that issued the certificate, as well as a time for which the certificate is valid. The certificates are stored on the cards by an authorized administrator. To log on with a smart card, a user must insert the card in the reader or swipe it through and enter a PIN that is associated with the card. If the PIN is compromised, an administrator can change it or issue a new card. To use smart cards for network logon, the computer must run an operating system that supports smart card authentication, such as Windows 2000 or XP, or use add-on software such as Sphinx (www.securetech-corp.com/sphinx.html).

On the Scene...

The Future of Smart Cards

In the future, if smart card authentication becomes more popular, computers might come with smart card readers built in as a matter of course. Several thin-client devices (such as those made by Sun Ray and Acer) already have smart card readers built in. Currently, you can buy both internal and external readers. The ChipDrive (www.towitoko.com/datintrn.html) is an example of the former.

Standards for smart cards have been specified in ISO 7816, issued by the International Organization for Standardization. These standards define specifications only for lower-level protocols. There are two major standards for smart card programming: the PC/SC standard and the OpenCard Standard. For more information about smart card technology, see the Smart Card Alliance Web site at www.smartcardalliance.org/industry_info/index.htm.

A number of companies manufacture smart cards and readers. Some vendors make keyboards that have built-in smart card readers, and there are combination fingerprint scanner/smart card readers for providing both card-based and biometric security.

Although smart cards provide for extra security, they (like all authentication methods) are not foolproof. Many cryptographers have been able to "break" smart card encryption. In general, there are two methods for defeating smart cards:

logical and physical. An example of the logical attack is erasing parts of the data on the embedded microchip by raising or dropping the voltage; in some cases, this activity "unlocks" the security without deleting the data. A physical attack might involve actually cutting the chip out of the card and using a laser-cutter micro-scope to examine it. Although a determined attacker might be able to crack the smart card in this way, these methods are not easy and they don't always work.

Biometric Authentication

Biometric authentication devices rely on physical characteristics such a fingerprint, facial patterns, or iris or retinal patterns to verify user identity. Biometric authentication is becoming popular for many purposes, including network logon. A biometric template or identifier (a sample known to be from the authorized user) must be stored in a database for the device to compare to a new sample given during the logon process. Biometrics are often used in conjunction with smart cards in high-security environments. The most popular types of biometric devices are the following:

- **Fingerprint scanners** These are widely available for both desktop and portable computers from a variety of vendors, connecting via a USB or PCMCIA (PC Card) interface.

- **Facial pattern recognition devices** These devices use facial geom-etry analysis to verify identity.

- **Hand geometry recognition devices** These are similar to facial pat-tern devices but analyze hand geometry.

- **Iris scan identification devices** Iris scanners analyze the trabecular meshwork tissue in the iris, which is permanently formed during the eighth month of human gestation.

- **Retinal scan identification devices** Retina scanners analyze the pat-terns of blood vessels on the retina.

A large number of physiological characteristics can be used as identifiers, and devices have been developed that verify identity based on knee scans, ear geom-etry, vein pattern recognition, and even body odor recognition. In addition, some devices analyze and compare behavioral traits using methods such as voice pat-tern recognition, signature verification, keystroke pattern recognition, breathing pattern recognition, gait pattern recognition, and even brainwave pattern recogni-tion, although many of these are only in experimental stages.

Biometrics are considered to be among the most reliable authentication methods possible. However, these methods are proving to be less reliable than previously believed. For example, in May 2002, according to the British Broadcasting Corporation (BBC) News (http://news.bbc.co.uk/hi/english/sci/tech/newsid_2016000/2016788.stm), studies of the facial recognition system used at some airports showed that it was accurate less than 50 percent of the time. Some fingerprint sensors can be defeated by breathing on the sensors or placing a bag of water on them, to reconstitute the print previously left behind. It's also possible to construct fake "fingers" that have an authorized fingerprint and can be used to fool the fingerprint scanner. A Japanese cryptographer demonstrated this technique using liquid gelatin to make a "gummy" fingerprint (www.esecurityplanet.com/trends/article/0,,10751_1379041,00.html). Inexpensive chips and/or badly written software can also cause both false rejections and false acceptances with biometric devices.

> **NOTE**
>
> For more information about the security flaws in biometric recognition systems, see the article *Body Check* at www.heise.de/ct/english/02/11/114.

Implementing Software-Based Security

Software security solutions cover a much broader range than do hardware-based solutions. These solutions include the security features built into the network operating system as well as additional security software made by the operating system vendors or third-party vendors. Software security has its advantages: It is often less expensive than hardware-based solutions and integrates more easily into the system and network. However, software security often suffers from decreased performance, compared to hardware-based security implementations, and security applications that run on popular operating systems can be easier to hack than the proprietary programs that run on dedicated hardware devices. Nonetheless, software security is popular and provides a full range of methods for protecting data and providing authentication, confidentiality, and integrity.

Cryptographic Software

Thousands of cryptographic products are available for different purposes: disk/file encryption, e-mail encryption, steganography, and more. We have mentioned some of these in the sections addressing how the technologies work. In addition to the commercial products, many encryption and authentication software programs are available as freeware. For a list of some of these products and links to download sites, see www.alw.nih.gov/Security/prog-auth.html.

Digital Certificates

As mentioned earlier, public key encryption is more secure than secret key encryption because there is no need to transmit a key across unsecured channels, but public key cryptography is also more complex, and it's more difficult to implement on a large scale. There must be a system that ensures that public keys that are posted to the Internet are not forgeries posted by someone who purports to be another user. If this happens, the data that is encrypted with that public key (and intended to be sent to the user whose name was associated with it) could be intercepted by the unauthorized user who posted the key. That unauthorized person would then be able to decrypt the data and read the message.

We need a mechanism that will provide a way for a trusted third party to confirm that the user who publishes the public key is in fact who he or she claims to be. A digital certificate provides this assurance. To understand how a digital certificate works, think of the way a driver's license or state ID card is used for identity verification. If a store or bank requires that you prove your identity by producing a license or state ID card, that entity is relying on the word of a trusted third party (in this case, the Department of Motor Vehicles) that you are who you say you are. The store or bank presumes that the DMV has checked you out and would not have issued the official identification document unless your identity was confirmed.

Just as the store or bank accepts your driver's license as proof of your identity, another computer with which you want to exchange data or make transactions will accept the digital certificate issued by a trusted third party. In the case of digital certificates, the trusted third party is a *certification authority (CA)*. The CA verifies that a particular identity is bound to the public key that is included in the certificate.

Some public CAs, such as VeriSign, issue certificates to persons on the Internet. Private (internal) CAs are set up by organizations to issue certificates to users within the local network. The CA is a server that runs special software that allows it to issue, manage, and revoke digital certificates. The CA's role is to guarantee to other users, computers, and applications that a particular public key really belongs to the entity with whose name it is associated.

The Public Key Infrastructure

A *public key infrastructure,* or *PKI,* is a security framework based on digital certificates. The PKI provides a system for users to request certificates and for CAs to issue, manage, and revoke certificates and disseminate certificate revocation lists

(CRLs) so that other entities will know when a particular entity's certificate is no longer valid. The PKI is based on the X.509 standards established by the ISO.

An important component of the PKI is the set of security policies that govern it. These policies should define the rules for issuance and use of digital certificates and the keys that are associated with them. Public certification authorities like VeriSign are required to provide a certificate practice statement (CPS). This is a document that outlines in detail the procedures for implementing the PKI.

When there are multiple CAs in the same PKI, as is the case in most large organizations, they are arranged in a hierarchical manner. The *root CA* is the most trusted CA in the PKI. Its certificate is self-signed, and it is responsible for issuing certificates to all the other CAs in the PKI, which are called *subordinate CAs*. The subordinate CAs issue certificates to users and computers, whereas the root CA generally issues certificates only to subordinate CAs. Public CAs are published in the Global Trust Register, which acts like a root CA for public CAs (albeit in printed form).

Certificates can be issued by a CA for many different purposes, including file encryption, smart card authentication, e-mail, IP security, and network logon. Users can export or import certificates, moving them from one computer to another. The export function is also used to create a backup of a certificate, which can then be restored to the *certificate store,* the location on the hard disk where certificates are kept, if the original certificate is destroyed. Certificates are issued automatically in some cases; in other cases, they must be explicitly requested by the user. There are different ways to request a certificate, depending on the CA software and the PKI policies. Requesting a certificate from a public CA usually involves filling out an application form on the CA's Web site.

It is very important that a PKI contain a mechanism for publishing certificate revocations so that other entities won't mistakenly rely on a certificate that is no longer valid. Certificates are revoked when the public key is compromised or when users leave the company or for some reason are no longer trusted. A CRL lists certificates that have been revoked and is updated regularly and distributed throughout the organization by the CA.

Software-Based Firewalls

In addition to the PKI software that provides for verification of identity, a vitally important type of software-based security is the *software firewall*. In reality, all firewalls are software-based. The hardware devices sold as firewalls run proprietary software that performs basically the same functions as a software program that can be installed on a regular PC. We use the term *software-based firewall* to describe firewall products such as Microsoft ISA Server or IBM SecureWay, as opposed to hardware/software (or firmware) combination appliances such as those produced by Cisco Systems. Some vendors, such as Check Point, market both types of product. In the next section, we discuss in detail how firewalls work.

On the Scene...

The Difference Between a Firewall and a Proxy

Proxy servers have been around for quite a while. The original meaning of the term *proxy* was "one who is authorized to act for another." Perhaps the most famous—or infamous—use of the word came about in relation to the practice of marriage by proxy, in which a substitute would stand in for one of the parties, allowing a wedding ceremony to be performed even though the groom (or less commonly, the bride) was not physically present. Proxy weddings at one time were a popular way for a couple to get "hitched" while the groom was serving in the military.

Proxy servers are so named because, like the hapless stand-in who says "I do" when it's really someone else who does, they act as go-betweens to allow something to take place (in this case, network communications) between systems that must remain separate.

Proxy servers "stand in" between the computers on a LAN and those on the public network outside. Another good analogy is a gatekeeper who is stationed at the entrance to an estate to check all incoming visitors to ensure that they are on the list of invited guests. The proxy can actually hide the computers on the LAN from outsiders. Only the IP address of the proxy server is "visible" to others on the Internet; internal computers use private IP addresses (nonroutable over the Internet) that cannot be seen from the other side of the proxy.

In fact, a proxy can go further and function more like a prison guard, who not only makes certain that only authorized persons get in but also sees that only those who have permission to go out are allowed to leave. Just as the guard checks his list before letting anyone in or out, the proxy *filters* outgoing and incoming data according to predefined criteria. At this point, the proxy is behaving like a *firewall*.

Understanding Firewalls

A firewall goes a bit further than just "standing in" for the local computers and hiding them from view on the global network, as a proxy server does. Firewalls are specifically designed to control inbound and outbound access, preventing unauthorized data from entering the network and restricting how and what type of data can be sent out.

The firewall gets its name from the building industry. In commercial structures, it is common to build a barrier wall made of fireproof material between two areas of a building. This wall is designed to prevent fire from spreading from one part of the building to the other. Another example is the heat barrier between the engine of an automobile and the passenger compartment, also called a firewall. Likewise, a network firewall acts as a barrier to prevent "bad data"—whether that be virus code or simply messages to or from unauthorized systems—from spreading from the outside network (usually the Internet) to the internal network. It also prevents packets of a particular type or to or from a particular user or computer from spreading from the LAN to the outside network.

In choosing between different firewall solutions, organizations encounter two basic firewall design options:

- A firewall can be designed to *permit* all packets to pass through unless they are expressly denied.

- A firewall can be designed to *deny* all packets unless they are expressly permitted.

Obviously, the second method is more secure, but it can result in the denial of access that administrators actually want to allow. The first method is easier to implement but is also more easily penetrated or circumvented.

How Firewalls Use Layered Filtering

Firewall products support the filtering of messages to either allow data to pass through or prevent it from doing so, according to specified criteria. The best firewalls support *layered filtering*. This means they can perform filtering at the packet layer, the circuit layer, or the application layer; some firewalls support only one of these filtering types, but most advanced firewall products, such as Microsoft ISA Server or Check Point's Firewall-1 product, support all three types. Firewalls that combine packet filtering, circuit filtering, and application layer filtering provide the highest level of security. These types of firewall also tend to be the most expensive. In the following sections, we look briefly at how each filtering method works.

Packet Filtering

Packet filtering does most of its work at the network layer of the OSI networking model (equivalent to the internetwork layer of the DoD model), dealing with IP packets. Packet filters examine the information contained in the IP packet header of a message and then either permit the data to cross the firewall or reject the packet based on that information. When IP packet filtering is enabled, the firewall will intercept and evaluate packets before passing them on to a higher level in the firewall or to an application filter.

The information that the packet filter uses to make its decision includes the IP address of the source and/or destination computer(s) and the TCP or UDP port number. (Yes, the port numbers are in the transport layer header, so technically, although packet filtering generally operates at the network layer, it also processes some higher-layer information.) Packet filtering allows the data to proceed to the transport layer only if the packet-filtering rules allow for it to do so.

Packet filtering lets administrators block packets that come from a particular Internet host or those that are destined for a particular service on the network (for example, the Web server or SMTP server). *Dynamic packet filtering* provides higher security because it opens the necessary port(s) only when required for communication to take place, then closes the port(s) immediately after the communication ends. *Static packet filters* are configured to allow inbound and outbound access to a predefined IP address (or group of IP addresses) and port number (or groups of ports).

It is important to note that packet filters cannot perform filtering based on anything that is contained in the data field of the packet, nor can they use the state of the communication channel to aid in making their decision to accept or reject the packet. If filtering decisions need to be made on the basis of either of these criteria, the firewall must be configured to use filtering that operates at a different layer (circuit or application filtering).

Circuit Filtering

Circuit filters operate at a higher layer of the OSI model, the transport layer (the host-to-host layer in the DoD model). Circuit filters restrict access on the basis of host machines (not users) by processing the information found in the TCP and UDP packet headers. This allows administrators to create filters that would, for example, prohibit anyone using Computer A from using FTP to access Computer B.

When circuit filters are used, access control is based on TCP data streams or UDP datagrams. Circuit filters can act based on TCP and UDP status flags and sequencing information, in addition to source and destination addresses and port numbers. Circuit-level filtering allows administrators to inspect sessions rather than packets. A session is sometimes thought of as a connection, but actually a session can be made up of more than one connection. Sessions are established only in response to a user request, which adds to security.

Circuit filters don't restrict access based on user information; they also cannot interpret the meanings of the packets. That is, they cannot distinguish between a **GET** command and a **PUT** command sent by an application program. To do this, application filtering must be used.

Application Filtering

At times, the best tactic is to filter packets based on the information contained in the data itself. Packet filters and circuit filters don't use the contents of the data stream in making filtering decisions, but this *can* be done with *application filtering*. An application filter operates at the top layer of the networking model, the appropriately named application layer. Application filters can use the packet header information but are also able to allow or reject packets on the basis of the data contents and the user information.

Administrators can use application filtering to control access based on a user's identity and/or based on the particular task the user is attempting to perform. With application filters, criteria can be set based on commands issued by the application. This means that, for example, the administrator could restrict a particular user from downloading files to a specified computer using FTP. At the same time, the administrator could allow that user to upload files via FTP to that same computer. This is possible because different commands are issued depending on whether the user is retrieving files from the server or depositing them there.

Many firewall experts consider application gateways to be the most secure of the filtering technologies. This is because the criteria they use for filtering covers a broader span than the other methods. Sometimes hackers write malicious programs that use the port address of an authorized application, such as port 53, which is the DNS address. A packet or circuit filter would not be able to recognize that the packet is not a valid DNS request or response and would allow it to pass through. An application filter, however, is able to examine the contents of the packet and determine that it should *not* be allowed.

There are drawbacks to this filtering type. The biggest problem is that there must be a separate application gateway for every Internet service that the firewall needs to support. This makes for more configuration work; however, this weakness is also a strength that adds to the security of the firewall. Since a gateway for each service must be explicitly enabled, an administrator won't accidentally allow services that pose a threat to the network. Application filtering is the most sophisticated level of filtering performed by the firewall service and is especially useful in protecting the network against specific types of attacks, such as malicious SMTP commands or attempts to penetrate the local DNS servers.

Integrated Intrusion Detection

Many firewalls also incorporate an *intrusion detection system* that can actually recognize that an attack of a specific type is being attempted and can perform a predefined action when such an intrusion is identified, such as one of the following:

- Send an e-mail message to the administrator
- Send a network message to the administrator
- Page the administrator
- Write an event entry to the event log
- Run a previously specified program or script
- Stop the firewall service

Intrusion detection systems can recognize many different common forms of network intrusion, such as port scans, LAND attacks, Ping of Death, UDP bombs, out-of-band attacks, and others. Special detection filters may also be built in, such as a Post Office Protocol (POP) intrusion detection filter that analyzes POP mail traffic to guard against POP buffer overflows, or a DNS intrusion detection filter that can be configured to look for DNS hostname overflow or length overflow attacks.

Forming an Incident Response Team

An intrusion or attack can be scary, frustrating, maddening—as with a physical attack on one's person, the emotional reactions can make it difficult to exercise good judgment and make the correct decisions about how to respond. This situation is made easier if you have properly prepared for it. Many companies, taking the proactive approach, form incident response teams—called *computer incident response teams,* or *CIRTs*—made up of individuals who train together (much like a military unit or police SWAT team) in how to handle anticipated incidents. The goal is to be able to swing into action when an actual incident occurs, with each team member covering a preassigned area of responsibility and thus decreasing the amount of damage and increasing the likelihood of apprehending the perpetrator of the incident.

In their book *Incident Response: Investigating Computer Crime,* Chris Prosise and Kevin Mandia define an incident as "an event that interrupts normal operating procedure and precipitates some level of crisis." The CERT guidelines define specific incidents, including violation of security policy, attempts to gain unauthorized access, unwanted denial of service/resources, unauthorized use, and changes made to system or data without the owner's knowledge, instruction, or consent. An incident can be anything from an attack that crashes all the servers and cuts off all network communications to an intrusion that causes no actual damage but demonstrates the vulnerability of the organization's systems. The various types of attacks described in Chapter 6 (for example, the many varieties of DoS/DDoS attacks) certainly qualify as incidents.

The response team should have its own hardware and software to use in conducting the investigation. It is important that the victim systems be preserved in the state they were in when the incident was discovered. Any changes made to these systems can compromise the integrity of the evidence and affect its admissibility in court.

Response team members may be called to testify in court if criminal charges or civil lawsuits are brought in relation to the incident. This is another reason to create extensive documentation that can be reviewed prior to giving testimony. Often, a case doesn't come to trial until months or even years after the incident, and the human memory often isn't reliable after so long a time without a little help. The team member who creates the documentation should be the one to testify to its authenticity if it is to be entered into evidence.

NOTE

It is important for team members to understand that their reports regarding the incident may end up being entered into evidence at trial. For this reason, such documentation should be kept in a special notebook with numbered pages, and the notebook should not contain any personal information, since the entire notebook may become part of the official record.

The steps involved in incident response include:

- **Training** Once versed in the theory of incident response, the team should train together in realistic scenario-based drills until response actions become automatic. Training should also address the law relating to privacy considerations and other issues that could affect or restrict team members' activities during the response.

- **Incident recognition** Monitoring should be conducted to ensure that team members are alerted to the possibility that an incident is occurring in its earliest stages.

- **Incident verification** This step involves examining logs, observing system/network behavior, interviewing witnesses, and so on to verify that an incident has in fact occurred.

- **Incident classification** An assessment should be conducted to determine the nature of the incident and the threat level.

- **Incident containment** Immediate steps should be taken to stop the incident and prevent any more damage.

- **Evidence preservation** Immediate steps should be taken to preserve all evidence of the incident for the purposes of tracking the offender and possible prosecution or civil litigation.

- **Incident analysis** A thorough investigation should be conducted to determine exactly what happened and how.

- **Restoration** Systems should be brought back to a working state as soon as possible, to minimize loss of productivity.

- **Followup activities** New security measures should be established to ensure that the same type of incident doesn't occur again.

- **Documentation** Each step of the response process should be documented and preserved for later review and use.

NOTE

Documentation may include "crime scene photographs"; photos or screenshots to preserve the information on the monitor might be desirable in some cases. A digital camera should be part of the investigative team's response kit.

It is not necessary for every member of the team to participate in every step of the response process. All team members should know their own roles and allow other team members to perform as assigned. Team member roles should be assigned according to each individual's area of expertise. Teams often include persons from the IT department, corporate security, management, legal department, and even the financial, human resources, and public relations departments. Response team members should be on call and able to respond to incidents at all hours and on any day of the week. Chapter 10, "Collecting and Preserving Digital Evidence," addresses in detail the steps involved in conducting the investigation and the equipment that is needed.

Incident response is the culmination of everything we've discussed in this book and the first step in the investigative process. In this chapter, we've moved from security theory and concepts to the "hands-on" aspects of a security plan: implementation of security measures and finally, should those fail, planning to respond to an attack. However, the document that brings all these topics together is the organization's *security policy,* which governs everything from the way security technologies are to be used to the procedures prescribed for the incident response team. The next section provides an overview of security policies: what they are (and aren't) and how they're developed. We include examples of some specific policy issues that every organization should address.

Designing and Implementing Security Policies

Security issues are at the forefront of organizational priorities today. Companies lose millions of dollars and untold hours of worker productivity due to lax security. Companies realize that protection of their assets—digital as well as physical—is no longer a luxury; in the twenty-first century, it has become a necessity.

An enormous amount of a company's most crucial information, including financial data, personnel records, customer information, and trade secrets, is concentrated in one virtual "place": the organization's network. This centralization renders this information vulnerable to unauthorized access and accidental or intentional destruction, both from within and (assuming the local network is connected to the Internet, as most today are) from outside intruders. Implementation of security measures, to be effective, must be based on an organized plan that takes into account all aspects of the organization's security needs. There must be rules and guidelines governing how the plan is put into action. These are disseminated throughout the organization as *policies.*

Understanding Policy-Based Security

Those of us in the security field often stress the need for detailed policies that are customized to fit the needs of each particular organization—sometimes to the point of sounding like a broken record. However, there's a good reason for this: The security policy is the foundation of an organization's security plan. It is the governing document, much like a police department's general orders, a city's charter, or a corporate board's mission statement. The following sections discuss the purpose and function of an IT *security policy* and the process of evaluating and defining security needs, developing the policy, and implementing it throughout the organization.

What Is a Security Policy?

A *security policy*, as the term is used here, refers to a written document that defines an organization's approach to security or a specific security area (in this case, computer and network security) and lays down a set of rules to be followed in implementing the organization's security philosophy.

Organizations may establish both written and unwritten rules pertaining to security matters and may issue a number of different types of documents dealing with these issues. How does the security policy differ from security-related memoranda and directives, standards, specifications, guidelines, and procedural documents?

Security Memoranda

Generally, a *security memorandum* or freestanding *security directive* is issued in response to a particular incident and may be used as a way to establish a rule that is not covered in the policy. If the rule applies only to a specific one-time situation or will be in effect for only a limited time, a memorandum might be all that's needed. If the rule will be permanent or long-term and is applicable to a broader spectrum of situations, it should be incorporated into the organization's formal policy as soon as possible. A memorandum can also be informational only, its purpose to make users aware of security considerations without laying out specific rules or guidelines.

Security Standards and Specifications

Standards and *specifications* are generally requirements that are to be met in implementing system-specific security procedures and may be used to measure or rate the overall reliability, compatibility, or other characteristics of the system. For example, the U.S. government has developed criteria, defined in the *Department of Defense Trusted Computer System Evaluation Criteria* handbook (also called the "orange book") and the *Trusted Network Interpretation of the TCSEC* (the "red book"), for rating security implementations. Other countries have similar rating systems. The ISO has developed ISO 17799 as an internationally recognized set of "best practices" regarding IT security. The security policy might specify adherence to particular standards or specifications.

Security Procedures

Procedural documents supplement the policy and may be incorporated into it as part of a policies and procedures manual. The procedural document gives step-by-step technical instructions for tasks that are required to implement the policies. For example, if the policy states that users must change their passwords every 30 days, you might have two associated procedural documents: one directed to network administrators that details how to set password requirements on the Windows domain controller to force users to change passwords at 30-day intervals, and another directed to users detailing how to change their passwords. When contained in separate documents, the policy section and associated procedural document(s) should reference one another.

Why This Information Matters to the Investigator

Investigators responding to cybercrimes that involve a corporate network need to have a thorough understanding of how security is implemented within the organization, just as an investigator responding to a home invasion needs to know the layout of the house, how and where commercial security devices are in place, what the family's security philosophy is, and so forth. Unlike most residential situations, corporations will often have formal, written documentation that lays out all the guidelines followed in implementing the security plan.

However, these documents aren't always easy to understand—unless you also understand the process by which they're created, adopted, and implemented. In the following sections, we provide an overview of that process: how organizations assess their security needs based on known risk factors, threat levels, and other factors that determine how much and what types of security will be implemented; how policy areas are defined; and how the document itself is developed (usually by a policy development team).

This background will make it easier for investigators to come into an organization and analyze its role as the victim or source of cybercrimes based on information contained in the policy document. For example, if an examination of the policies shows that the organization has an extremely strong password policy, and further investigative techniques such as interviewing employees reveal that the policies are universally enforced, this could indicate that intruders used techniques other than password cracking to gain access, or it could indicate that there is a "leak" inside the organization. In other words, understanding the policies can help to narrow the focus of the investigation. This is often one of the most diffi-cult and most vital steps in the investigative process.

Evaluating Security Needs

If we accept the stated definition of security policy, it becomes obvious that there is not and cannot be a one-size-fits-all IT security policy that will work equally well for all organizations. Security needs differ, based on:

- Risk factors
- The perceived and actual threat level
- Organizational vulnerabilities
- The organization's philosophy (open versus closed system)
- Legal factors
- Available funds

It is important to analyze all these factors carefully in developing a policy that offers both adequate protection and a desirable level of access.

Components of an Organizational Security Plan

Security features are now built into operating system software; Windows NT, 2000, XP, and—coming soon to a server near you—.NET include numerous security features. Microsoft recently announced that its developers will focus even more closely on security issues. UNIX and Linux distributions come with built-in security features. IT security products, both hardware and software, abound. Security training and numerous security certifications are available, and IT profes-sionals are seeking them out.

These are all important components of an organization's overall security plan, but they are not enough. Effective coordination and interaction of all these parts requires one more thing: a comprehensive security policy.

Defining Areas of Responsibility

To assess security needs accurately, someone should review the company's infras-tructure, processes, and procedures and involve personnel at all levels of the orga-nization and from as many different departments as possible. Ideally, the following tasks will be performed by a carefully selected team that includes, at a minimum, members of management, IT personnel, and a company legal representative. Each team member should be assigned specific areas of responsibility, and deadlines for completion should be assigned.

Responsibility for Developing the Security Plan and Policies

The initial creation of a good security plan requires a great deal of thought and effort. The policy will impact those at all levels of the organization, and it is desirable to solicit input from as many representatives of different departments and job descriptions as is practical. An effective approach is to form a committee consisting of people from several areas of the organization to be involved in creating and reviewing the security plan and policies. A security planning committee of this type might include some or all of the following:

- The network administrator and one or more assistant administrators
- The site's security administrator
- Department heads of various company departments or their representatives
- Representatives of user groups that will be impacted by the security policies (for example, the secretarial staff, the data processing center)
- A member of the legal department who specializes in computer and technology law
- A member of the finance or budget department
- A member of upper management

Responsibility for Implementing and Enforcing the Security Plan and Policies

Security policies will generally be implemented and enforced by network administrators and members of the IT staff. Job descriptions and policies should designate exactly who is responsible for the implementation of which parts of the plan. There should be a clear-cut chain of command that specifies whose decision prevails in case of conflict. In some cases—such as physical penetration of the network—the company security staff will become involved. Written, clearly formulated policies should be in place that stipulate which department has responsibility for which tasks in such situations.

The security plan should also address the procedures for reporting security breaches, both internally and if the police or other outside agencies are to be brought in. In addition, it should be specified who is responsible for or has the authority to call in outside agents.

One of the most important factors in a good security policy is that it must be enforceable. If the policy can be enforced through security tools, this method is preferred. If the policies must be enforced through reprimand or other actions against employees who violate them, there should be clearly worded, universally distributed written documentation of what constitutes a violation and what sanctions will result, as well as who is responsible for imposing such sanctions.

Analyzing Risk Factors

Before the policy development team can set policies, they need to determine both the nature and the level of the security risks to the organization. Traditionally, risk analysis involves:

- Determining to what types of security breaches the organization is vulnerable

- For each type, determining the probability of such a breach occurring

- For each type, determining the extent of the loss that would be suffered if the breach did occur

This process is known as *quantitative risk analysis.*

Another type of risk analysis, *qualitative risk analysis,* disregards the probability element and instead focuses on potential threats and the characteristics of the system or network that make it vulnerable to these threats. Then methods are developed for preventing or reducing the likelihood of breaches, detecting when breaches do occur, and decreasing and repairing the damage done if a breach does occur.

Risk analysis tools are available to help identify threats and vulnerabilities, rate the threat level, estimate the impact on the organization, and recommend solutions. An example is the COBRA Risk Consultant from C&A Systems Security Ltd. COBRA methodology is used by major corporations and governmental entities.

Why is a risk analysis necessary? There are several reasons, including the following:

- From the IT professional's point of view, a detailed risk analysis is the first and perhaps most important step in justifying to management the cost to implement needed security measures.

- From the business manager's point of view, the risk analysis document provides a solid, objective basis for making budgetary and personnel-impacting decisions.

- Data collected during the risk analysis process forces both IT and management to face and acknowledge threats and vulnerabilities of which they might not have been aware or which they previously might have been able to ignore.

- Risk analysis allows the organization to focus resources on the existing threats and vulnerabilities and avoid wasting time and funds on unnecessary measures.

Because the risk analysis process involves personnel throughout the organization, it can raise security awareness and help make appropriate security practices the responsibility of everyone who uses the computers and network. This is a basic tenet of crime prevention.

Assessing Threats and Threat Levels

The dictionary defines a *threat* as "somebody or something likely to cause harm." The threat assessment portion of the risk analysis should include:

- Sources of potential threats

- The nature of potential threats

- The likelihood of occurrence of each potential threat type

- The estimated impact of each potential threat type

Sources of potential threats can be divided into internal and external categories. Although many security policies focus on the threat of a security breach from outside the network or organization (across the Internet), in actuality many organizations find that their biggest potential losses come from inside—the deliberate or unintentional actions of employees, contractors, and others who have legitimate access to the network. It is important to address both categories when performing a threat assessment.

Further defining threat sources requires that the assessment team determine both *who* and *what* could pose a threat to the network. For example, people who could pose a threat include most of the cybercriminal types discussed in Chapter 3—for example:

- Random hackers, motivated by fun, the personal challenge of breaking into the network, or competition with other hackers

- Data thieves who target the organization and information specifically; this type includes corporate espionage

- Emotionally motivated people, such as ex-employees out for revenge, business competitors who want to damage the company's ability to do business, or people with a grudge against the company, its personnel, or the industry to which it belongs

- People who accidentally or inadvertently cause damage or data loss (most often internal threats, such as the employee who is "experimenting" and unintentionally deletes important files from the server)

The nature of possible threats is the *what* in this equation. Any of these people could initiate threats of one or more of the following natures:

- Unauthorized access to data

- Unauthorized disclosure of information

- Destruction of data

- Modification or corruption of data

- Introduction of viruses, worms, or Trojans

- Denial or interruption of service or network congestion/slowdown

---

NOTE

A thorough threat assessment program will not overlook the threats posed by events such as fire, flood, and power loss as well as those caused by human agents.

The next step in threat analysis consists of assigning a likelihood or probability to each type of threat event. A high probability indicates that the threat event is more likely than not to occur, as when there is a history of its occurrence in the past. A medium probability indicates that the threat event might or might not occur. A low probability indicates that the threat event is not likely to occur, although it is possible. Finally, the assessment team must evaluate the probable impact on the organization for each potential threat event. For example:

- If the company's customer database were destroyed, how would this affect such activities as sales, billing, and so on?

- If the company network were down for one day, what is the potential cost to the company in lost sales, lost employee productivity, and the like?

- If the company's client records were made public, what is the potential loss in terms of lawsuits, withdrawal of client business, or similar actions?

Once all these questions have been asked and answered, it is a relatively simple matter to construct a threat assessment matrix that will put this information into perspective and help the policy development team focus the company's security policies on the threat areas of highest likelihood and most significant impact.

Analyzing Organizational and Network Vulnerabilities

In Chapters 5 and 6, we discussed how to analyze a network's *technical vulnerabilities*. These vulnerabilities are those characteristics or configurations that an attacker can exploit to gain unauthorized access or misuse your network and its resources. Network vulnerabilities are often referred to as *security holes*. Security holes should be identified as part of the policy development process. These vulnerabilities can be caused by a programming characteristic or (mis)configuration of the operating system, a protocol or service, or an application. Examples might include:

- Operating system code that allows hackers to crash a computer by accessing a file whose path contains certain reserved words

- Unnecessarily open TCP/UDP ports that hackers can use to get into or obtain information about the system

- A Web browser's handling of JavaScript that allows malicious code to execute unwanted commands

The network's connections to the Internet and other networks obviously affect vulnerability. Data on a network that is connected 24/7 via a high-speed link is more vulnerable than on a network that is only intermittently connected to the outside. A network that allows multiple outside connections (such as modems and phone lines on a number of different computers) increases vulnerability to outside attack. Dialup modem connections merit special consideration. Although a dialup connection is less open to intrusion than a full-time dedicated connection—both because it is connected to the outside for a shorter time period, reducing the window of opportunity for intrusion, and because it usually has a dynamic IP address, making it harder for an intruder to locate it on multiple occasions—allowing workstations on the network to have modems and phone lines can create a huge security risk.

If improperly configured, a computer with a dialup connection to the Internet that is also cabled to the internal network can act as a router, allowing outside intruders to access not just the workstation connected to the modem, but other computers on the LAN. One reason for allowing modems at individual workstations is to allow users to dialup connections to other private networks. A more secure way to do this is to remove the modems and have the users establish a VPN connection with the other private network through the LAN's Internet connection. The best security policy is to have as few connections from the internal network to the outside as possible and control access at those entry points (the *network perimeter*).

NOTE

Third-party software tools known as *vulnerability scanners* are designed to discover the vulnerabilities on a network, using a database of known commonly exploited weaknesses and probing for those weaknesses on your network.

Organizational vulnerabilities are those areas and data that are open to danger or harm if exposed to an attack. In order to determine these vulnerabilities, the policy team should first identify the assets that could be exposed to the types of threats previously identified. For example:

- The company's financial records
- Trade secrets
- Personnel information
- Customer/client information
- Private correspondence
- Intellectual property
- Marketing and business strategy documents
- Network integrity
- System and program files

A number of factors should be considered when the team is assessing vulnerabilities, including the nature of the data that goes through the organization's network. The vulnerability of data that is highly confidential (such as trade secrets) or irreplaceable (such as original artwork or writing) should be of highest priority. Vulnerability is also affected by the size of the organization and network. A larger number of people who have access to the network indicates a greater chance of exposure to someone who will want to do harm.

CyberLaw Review...

Policy Development in the High-Security Environment

Certain fields have inherent high-security requirements. An obvious example is the military or other government agencies that deal with defense or national security issues. Private companies with government defense contracts also fall into this category. Others might be less obvious:

Law firms are bound by law and ethics to protect client confidentiality; medical offices must protect patient records; law enforcement agencies, courts, and other governmental bodies must protect sensitive data; educational institutions must protect the privacy of student records. Any company that gathers information from individuals or organizations under guarantee that the data will be kept confidential has an obligation to protect that data.

The competitive nature of a business is also a consideration. In a field such as biogenetic research, which is a "hot" market, new developments are being made on a daily basis. Any of these could involve huge profits for the company that patents an idea, so protecting trade secrets becomes vitally important. Most businesses have *some* data of a confidential nature on the network's computer systems, but the security requirements in some fields are much higher than in others. This level of requirement should be considered in developing the security plan.

Generally, payroll and human resource records (personnel files, insurance claim documents, and the like), company financial records (accounting documents, financial statements, tax documents), and a variety of other common business records need to be protected. Even in cases where these documents are required to be made public, steps must be taken to ensure that they can't be modified or destroyed. Remember that *data integrity*, as well as *data confidentiality*, is protected by a good security plan.

In the United States, laws governing privacy protections in specific industries affect an organization's security plan and policies. For example, the Health Insurance Portability and Accountability Act (HIPAA) governs electronic storage and transmission of patient information and

Continued

requires that physicians and other health care providers implement certain security standards, provide notification to patients of the privacy measures in place, and document every disclosure of patient information to outside entities (with some exceptions). All medical practices are required to comply with HIPAA by April 2003. Violation of the HIPAA regulations can result in fines ranging from $100 (per violation) to $250,000 and up to 10 years in prison in cases of deliberate disclosure of patient information with the intent to sell, transfer, or use it for personal gain or commercial or malicious purposes.

HIPAA is federal law; some states also have laws that impose even more stringent privacy protections on the health care industry. Other industries are governed by similar laws. For example, the Gramm-Leach-Bliley (GLB) Act imposes restrictions on financial institutions regarding disclosure of clients' personal information, with similar penalties for violation.

Analyzing Organizational Factors

The next step in evaluating security needs is to determine the philosophy of the organization's management regarding security versus accessibility. It is important to remember that the two are conflicting characteristics; the more of one that a system has, the less of the other it will have. The organizational philosophy determines where on the security-access continuum a particular network falls (and thus determines its policies).

Some companies institute a highly structured, formal management style. Employees are expected to respect a strict chain of command, and information is generally disseminated on a "need to know" basis. Governmental agencies, especially those related to law enforcement, such as police departments and investigative agencies, often follow this philosophy, sometimes referred to as the *paramilitary model*.

Other companies, particularly those in "creative" industries and other fields that are subject to little state regulation, are built on the opposite premise: that all employees should have as much information and input as possible, that managers should function as "team leaders" rather than authoritarian supervisors, and that restrictions on employee actions should be imposed only when necessary for the efficiency and productivity of the organization. This is sometimes called the *"one big happy family" model*. Creativity is valued more than "going by the book," and job satisfaction is considered to be an important aspect of enhancing employee performance and productivity.

In business management circles, these two diametrically opposed models are called *Theory X* (traditional paramilitary style) and *Theory Y* (modern, team-oriented approach). Although numerous other management models have been popularized in recent years, such as management by objective (MBO) and total quality management (TQM), each company's management style falls somewhere on the continuum between Theory X and Theory Y. The management model is based on the personal philosophies of the company's top decision makers regarding the relationship between management and employees.

The management model can have a profound influence on what is or isn't acceptable in planning security for the network. A "deny all access"-based security policy that is viewed as appropriate in a Theory X organization could meet with so much resentment and employee dissatisfaction in a Theory Y company that it disrupts business operations. Policy makers must always consider the company "atmosphere" as part of security planning. If there are good reasons to implement strict security in a Theory Y atmosphere, the restrictions will probably have to be justified to management and "sold" to employees, whereas those same restrictions might be accepted without question in a more traditional organization.

Considering Legal Factors

Security needs are dependent not only on the wishes of company managers, but they may also be dictated or at least guided by the criminal and civil law in a particular jurisdiction. If the company's industry is subject to government regulations, the information on its network falls under privacy protection acts, or company contracts prohibit disclosure of information on the company network, these are legal factors that must be considered in establishing security policies.

It is important to protect the company from liability that might be incurred if employees or others using the network violate laws. For this reason, it is essential that the security policy development team include one or more attorneys who are well versed in applicable laws (for example, the Data Protection Act in the United Kingdom or the Digital Millennium Copyright Act in the United States) and who are familiar with the terms of the company's contracts with partners, vendors, clients, and others.

Analyzing Cost Factors

Finally, but rarely of least concern, the needs evaluation must take into account the monetary cost of implementing heightened security. Determining the funds available for security upgrades will affect security policies by forcing the development team to differentiate the organization's security *needs* from security *wants*.

Cost factors can also force the team to prioritize security needs so that those threats that are most likely or most imminent can be addressed, those assets that are most important can be protected, and those vulnerabilities that are most egregious can be closed first.

Assessing Security Solutions

Once the company has identified and documented its security needs and established a working budget for addressing those needs, it is possible to assess solutions and determine which one(s) meet those needs within that budget. Network security solutions can be generally divided into three broad categories: hardware, software, and policy-only solutions.

Hardware Solutions

Hardware-based security solutions involve adding some physical device such as a dedicated firewall to protect the network or a smart card reader for logon authentication. Removal of diskette and CD drives from desktop computers to prevent unauthorized copying of files to removable media or introduction of viruses is also a hardware-based solution. Other security hardware devices include:

- Keystroke capture devices for monitoring computer use
- Hardware tokens for storing security keys
- Cryptographic hardware devices for offloading the processing of crypto operations
- Biometric authentication devices such as fingerprint or retina scanners

Hardware solutions can be more costly than software-only solutions, but they offer several advantages. Hardware security is usually more secure because there is less exposure of security information such as private keys, and it is more difficult to tamper with hardware than software. Hardware solutions also often offer faster performance.

Software Solutions

Software solutions include intrusion detection systems, packet/circuit/application filtering software, and security auditing software, as well as software firewall packages such as Microsoft's Internet Security and Acceleration (ISA) Server, which combine these functions. Other software security solutions are antivirus programs such as those made by Symantec and McAfee, "spyware" used to monitor how computers are being used (including packet sniffer software that can capture and analyze network traffic), and network management packages that incorporate security features. Operating system and application "fixes" that patch security holes can also be placed in this category.

Policy Solutions

Most hardware and software security measures have accompanying policies that prescribe when and how they are to be deployed and used, but many security measures consist of policy only. For example:

- Policies that prohibit users from disclosing their passwords to anyone else

- Policies that require users to lock their workstations when they leave their desks

- Policies that require users to get permission before installing any software on their machines

- Policies that prohibit users from allowing anyone else to use the computer after they've logged in

Of course, in many cases policies will be enforced via software or hardware. For example, a policy that prohibits users from copying network files to their local disks can be enforced by permissions that allow read-only access. A policy that requires users to change their passwords every 30 days can be enforced by setting passwords to expire after that time period.

Complying with Security Standards

The security policy document should lay out standards regarding such issues as confidentiality and integrity of data, authorization and authentication, access, appropriate use of network resources, and employee privacy issues. If compliance with federal standards (such as a C2 rating) or industry-specific standards (such as HIPAA for health care organizations) is required, then the specifications should be included and mandated in the policy document.

Policies should be reviewed for compliance with international standards such as ISO 17799. You might want to reference related sections of ISO 17799 in individual policies similarly to the reference to related policies.

Government Security Ratings

Security ratings might be of interest in the development of a company's security policy, although they are not likely to be important unless the organization works under government contract requiring a specified level of security. The U.S. government provides specifications for the rating of network security implementations in a publication often referred to as the *orange book,* formally called the *Department of Defense Trusted Computer System Evaluation Criteria,* or *TCSEC.* The *red book,* or *Trusted Network Interpretation of the TCSEC (TNI),* explains how the TCSEC evaluation criteria are applied to computer networks.

Other countries have security rating systems that work in a similar way. For example:

- CTPEC (Canada)

- AISEP (Australia)

- ITSEC (Western Europe)

To obtain a government contract in the United States, companies are often required to obtain a C2 rating. A C2 rating has several requirements:

1. That the operating system in use be capable of tracking access to data, including both who accessed it and when it was accessed (as is done by the auditing function of Windows NT/2000)

2. That users' access to objects be subject to control (access permissions)

3. That users are uniquely identified on the system (user account name and password)

4. That security-related events can be tracked and permanently recorded for auditing (audit log)

> **NOTE**
>
> These are general guidelines, and the requirements must be implemented in specific ways to obtain the rating. If an organization needs a C2 rating for its systems, the policy development team should consult the National Computer Security Center (NCSC) publications to ensure that they meet all requirements.
>
> The DoD Trusted Computer System Evaluation Criteria (the *orange book*) can be accessed at www.radium.ncsc.mil/tpep/library/rainbow/ 5200.28-STD.html.

Utilizing Model Policies

Model security policies can be used to guide the policy development team in preparing a comprehensive policy document. Policy templates can be purchased from various sources (for example, RUSecure Information Security Policies), and sample policies are available for download from such organizations as the SANS Institute.

An advantage is that purchased model policies may be guaranteed to be ISO 17799 compliant, HIPAA compliant, or the like. However, policy makers should beware of simply copying a sample policy without an extensive review to ensure that the policies fit the organization's philosophy, budget, and business model. Sample policies are usually "sanitized"—that is, organization-specific issues have been removed to provide a generic policy that is designed to serve as a starting point in creating customized policies.

Defining Policy Areas

An important part of policy development involves defining the areas that will be addressed by the organization's security policies. This process will vary from one organization to another, but some common policy areas are always of concern. An example is the password policy. In the following section, we discuss some of the most important factors in setting password policies.

Password Policies

In the networking world, passwords (in combination with user account names) are normally the "keys to the kingdom" that provide access to network resources and data. It might seem simplistic to say that a comprehensive security plan should include an effective password policy, but it is a basic component that is more difficult to implement than it might appear at first glance. In order to be effective, a password policy must require users to select passwords that are difficult to "crack" yet easy for them to remember so they don't commit the common security breach of writing the password on a "sticky note" that will end up stuck to the monitor or sitting prominently in the top desk drawer.

A good password policy is the first line of defense in protecting the network from intruders. Careless password practices (choosing common passwords such as *god* or *love* or the user's spouse's name; choosing short, all-alpha, one-case passwords; writing passwords down or sending them across the network in plain text) are like leaving your car doors unlocked with the keys in the ignition. Although some intruders might target a specific system, many others are just "browsing" for a network that's easy to break into. Lack of a good password policy is an open invitation to them.

Policy developers must remember that expensive, sophisticated firewalls and other strict security measures (short of biometric scanning devices that recognize fingerprints or retinal images) will not protect the network if an intruder has knowledge of a valid username and password. It is particularly important to use strong passwords for administrative accounts.

Best practices for password creation require that you address the following, each of which is discussed in the sections that follow:

- Password length and complexity
- Who creates the password?
- Forced changing of passwords

Password Length and Complexity

It's easy to define a "bad" password—it's one that can be easily guessed by someone other than the authorized user. You'll recall from Chapter 6 that one way in which "crackers" do their work is via the *brute-force attack*. In this kind of attack, the cracker manually or, more often using a script or specially written software program, simply tries every possible combination of characters until he finally hits upon the right one. It goes without saying that using this method, it will be easier to guess a short password than a longer one because there are fewer possible combinations. For this reason, most security experts recommend that passwords have a minimum required length (for example, eight characters). Modern network operating systems such as Windows 2000 allow domain administrators to impose such rules so that if a user attempts to set a password that doesn't meet the minimum length requirement, the password change will be rejected.

Who Creates the Password?

Network administrators might be tempted to institute a policy whereby they create all passwords and issue them to the users. This policy has the advantage of ensuring that all passwords meet the administrator's criteria in regard to length and complexity. However, it has a few big disadvantages as well:

- It places a heavy burden on administrators, who must handle all password changes and be responsible for letting users know what their passwords are. Of course, an administrator would not want to notify a user of his or her password via e-mail or other insecure channels. In fact, the best way to do so is to personally deliver the password information. In a large organization, this becomes particularly taxing if there is a policy requiring that passwords be changed on a regular basis.

- Users will have more difficulty remembering passwords that they didn't choose themselves. This means they are more likely to write the passwords down, resulting in security compromises. Otherwise, they might have to contact the administrator frequently to be reminded of their passwords.

- If the administrator creates all passwords, this means the administrator *knows* everyone's password. This might or might not be acceptable under the overall security policy. Some users (including management) could be uncomfortable with the idea that the administrator knows their passwords. Even though an administrator can generally access a user's account and/or files without knowing the password, it is less obvious to the users and thus less a concern.

Allowing users to create their own passwords within set parameters (length and complexity requirements) is usually the best option. The user is less likely to forget the password because he can create a complex password that is meaningless to anyone else but has meaning to him. For example, it would be difficult for others to guess the password Mft2doSmis. It has 10 characters, combines alpha and numeric characters, and combines upper and lower case in a seemingly random manner. To a user, it might be easy to remember because it stands for "My favorite thing to do on Sunday morning is sleep."

Password Change Policy

Best practices dictate that users change their passwords at regular intervals and after any suspected security breach. Modern network operating systems such as Windows 2000 allow the administrator to set a maximum password age, forcing users to change their passwords at the end of the specified period (in days). Password expiration periods can be set from 1 to 999 days. Individual user accounts that need to keep the same passwords can be configured so that their passwords never expire. This overrides the general password expiration setting.

Because it is the nature of most users to make their passwords as easy to remember as possible, policies should strive to prevent the following practices, all of which can present security risks:

- Changing the password to a variation of the same password (for example, changing from Tag2mB to Tag3mB)

- Changing the password back and forth between two favored passwords each time a change is required (that is, changing from Tag2mB to VERoh9 and back again continuously)

- "Changing" the password to the same password (entering the same password for the new password as was already being used)

Administrators can use operating system features to prevent these practices. For example, in Windows 2000, you can configure the operating system to remember the user's password history so that up to a maximum of the last 24 passwords will be recorded and the user will not be able to change the password to one that has been used during that time.

Summary of Best Password Practices

Here is a short overview of the best password practices:

- Passwords should have a minimum of eight characters.
- Passwords should not be "dictionary" words.
- Passwords should consist of a mixture of alpha, numeric, and symbol characters.
- Passwords should be created by their users.
- Passwords should be easy for users to remember.
- Passwords should never be written down.
- Passwords should be changed on a regular basis.
- Passwords should be changed anytime compromise is suspected.
- Password change policies should prevent users from making only slight changes.

Other Common Policy Areas

Password policies are important to almost every organization, but other policy areas that often need to be addressed include the following:

- **Server and workstation security policies** define rules governing physical security of network-connected computers, mandating logoff or password-protected screensavers when leaving a station unattended, system shutdown policies, sharing of workstations, and so forth.
- **Encryption policies** define when encryption should or shouldn't be used and the encryption technologies or algorithms that are acceptable. For example, a policy might mandate that specific proven algorithms such as 3DES, RSA, or IDEA be used and prohibit use of proprietary or nonstandard algorithms.

- **E-mail policies** govern such matters as opening e-mail attachments, using e-mail clients configured to display HTML mail, forwarding internal e-mail to people outside the organization, and so forth.

- **Remote access policies** define rules for connecting to the company network from outside using dialin or VPN connections, specify what remote authentication methods can be used, prohibiting "dual homing" (being connected to another network while simultaneously being connected to the company network), and so forth.

- **Wireless access policies** set forth standards for connecting to the corporate network using wireless equipment, requiring use of WEP or other encryption technologies, prohibiting connection of unauthorized wireless access points to the network, and so forth.

- **Acceptable use policies** define what users are allowed to do or are prohibited from doing on the network, governing personal use (such as Web surfing, sending personal e-mail), downloading files, posting to newsgroups, prohibiting installation of unauthorized software applications, and so forth.

Many other policy areas could be applicable to specific organizations; defining policy areas to be addressed is an important task for the policy development team. Examples of policy documents that cover the areas mentioned (and others) can be viewed on the SANS Institute's Security Policy Project resource page at www.sans.org/newlook/resources/policies/policies.htm#template.

Developing the Policy Document

The policy development team should ideally be chosen prior to and involved in the needs evaluation process. The team should comprise management and IT personnel, along with someone from each department within the organization. The team should include a legal advisor. As they begin to solidify and codify your policies, the team members must work closely together to:

- Establish security priorities based on the threat assessment matrix.

- Consider and incorporate security standards as needed.

- Determine the practices and procedures that are necessary to achieve the desired level of security at both the administrative and user levels.

- Clearly define both required and prohibited behaviors.

- Determine and define consequences for violations.

- Determine that policies are enforceable and methods for enforcement.

Policies should represent a consensus as to what is and is not appropriate computer-related behavior.

Establishing Scope and Priorities

The policy development team should determine the scope of the policy document. For example, will policies regarding telephone, mobile phone, and fax use be included in the IT security policy or be part of a separate policy document? Will procedures for purchasing hardware and software be covered, or will this area be addressed in an overall organizational purchasing policy document? The easiest way to create a policy nightmare is to have two policy documents with conflicting directives.

There might not be funds available to address all security needs. Even if enough funds are allocated, most organizations will not be able to implement all security measures simultaneously. Thus the team must establish priorities to determine which policies will be implemented first. Prioritization will be based on such factors as:

- Immediacy of the threat
- Potential loss
- Ease of implementation
- Available funding

We discussed immediacy of the threat and potential loss in the threat assessment section. Ease of implementation can also be a factor in prioritizing. Policies that can easily and quickly be implemented can be put in place first, while work begins on those that require more time and effort. Policies generally mandate one or more of the following: physical safeguards, technical security mechanisms, or administrative procedures. Changing administrative procedures can often be done more quickly and easily than implementing physical safeguards (which could require purchase and setup of equipment or modifications to the facilities) or technical mechanisms (which could require purchase of software as well as a learning curve for IT personnel and users).

Policy Development Guidelines

Policies can be divided into different policy types: *regulatory policies,* which must be implemented to comply with the law or regulatory agency requirements; *advisory policies,* which are strongly recommended though not mandated, and *information policies,* which provide information but do not prescribe or proscribe any action.

Security policies canserve a number of secondary purposes in addition to the primary purpose of preventing unauthorized use of the network. For example, the policies can be the basis for personnel action (discipline or termination), can be used in the company's defense (or against it) in a civil lawsuit, and can even be instrumental in building a criminal case for prosecution. Thus it is imperative that the policies that are finally published be well thought out, reasonable, and clearly articulated.

Policy writers should avoid technical jargon insofar as is possible; the security policies must be understandable to and usable by company managers, human resources personnel, and the users to whom they apply, as well as IT personnel. It's a good idea to include a glossary to define the technical terminology that is unavoidable. It is also important to create accountability; the person(s) responsible for each area of network/computer security and that person's scope of responsibility should be identified in the policy document.

Policies should state what actions are required, recommended, or prohibited. In addition to defining the action, they should give an example of behavior that would constitute that action, or a violation. For example, if the policy states, "Each user is required to protect the secrecy of his or her network logon password," it should give concrete examples such as, "Users are required to memorize their passwords. Users are prohibited from possessing any written record of their passwords anywhere on company property and are prohibited from divulging their passwords to any other person. If any person asks a user to divulge his or her password, the user is required to report the request to the network administrator immediately."

Policies should clearly state the consequences for violation. Consequences should be based on the severity of the violation, damage/loss caused, intent or lack thereof, and history of past violations. It's always important to ensure that the policies are consistent—not just with one another within the IT security policy document, but with other company and departmental policies. Finally, it's imperative to make sure that policies don't conflict with any local, state, or federal laws.

Policy Document Organization

The policy document should not be a hodgepodge collection of security directives. It should be logically organized so that related policies are brought together under broadly defined areas. For example, sections might include:

- Physical security (e.g., placement of servers, installation of hardware, securing cabling, securing printers, location of backup tapes, access to rooms/buildings where computer equipment is located)

- Local system security (e.g., users' responsibilities in regard to securing their own workstations, installation of software, copying files)

- Password security (e.g., policies governing length of passwords, complexity of passwords, changing passwords, and protection of passwords)

- Network security (e.g., policies governing use of firewalls, downloading/uploading of files, Web access, using instant messaging software)

- Server security (e.g., access to servers, protection of Web servers, file servers, DNS servers, authentication servers)

- Remote access security (e.g., policies governing telecommuters, on-the-road executives, after hours access from home, designated VPN software and configurations)

- Data management and document-handling policies (e.g., policies that govern transferring and exchanging data, securing databases, modifying directory structures, creating/deleting files, filename policies, classification of data sensitivity)

- E-mail security (e.g., policies governing sending/receiving attachments, use of HTML mail, e-mail client configuration settings)

- Software development policies (e.g., governing security and control over in-house software code)

- E-commerce security (e.g., governing online sales and purchases)

- Wireless communication security (e.g., policies governing standards for use of wireless devices on the network)

- Intranet and extranet policies (e.g., governing terms of access, acceptable use)

- Backup policies (e.g., scheduling, responsibility, retention, storage)

- Disaster prevention and recovery policies (e.g., continuity of service, power backup)

- Policies governing security violations (e.g., responsibility to report, response handling)

- Policies governing employees who leave the company, both on friendly and hostile terms (e.g., turning over equipment and access cards, deactivation of network accounts)

The policy document should contain a detailed table of contents. Each individual policy should have the following components:

- A title that describes clearly what the policy pertains to and a notation of any policy that it supercedes or replaces

- The effective date of the policy (and duration or expiration date if the policy is temporary)

- Reference to related policies

- A section stating the purpose or objective of the policy

- A section identifying the threat or vulnerability being addressed

- A brief summary of the policy

- A section that lays out in detail the policy itself—that is, defining the act or acts that are required or prohibited; this should include identification of people responsible for implementing the policy, to whom the policy applies, and any exceptions to the policy

- Signature of the authority issuing the policy

Educating Network Users on Security Issues

The best security policies in the world will be ineffective if the network users are not aware of them or if the policies are so restrictive and place so many inconveniences on users that they go out of their way to attempt to circumvent them. The security plan itself should contain a program for educating network users— not just as to what the policies are, but *why* they are important and how the users benefit from them. Users should also be instructed in the best ways to comply with the policies and what to do if they are unable to comply or if they observe other users deliberately violating the policies. If users are involved in the planning and policy-making stages, it will be much easier to educate them and gain their support for the policies at the implementation and enforcement stages.

Policy Enforcement

In order to be effective, policies must be enforceable, and they must be enforced consistently. Policies that are unenforceable (perhaps because you don't have the means to detect violations) or that you are not willing to enforce are worse than useless; their existence undermines the credibility of the rest of the policies. Enforcement must not be selective; if exceptions to the policies are necessary for certain people or in certain circumstances, those exceptions should be laid out in the policy itself.

Enforcement authority should be divided among a number of people to provide a system of checks and balances. Employees should be made aware of whom is responsible for policy enforcement, and the enforcement team must be given the authority to carry out the job (for example, the authority to monitor e-mail and Web access). Employees should be informed, within the policy document, that they may be subject to such monitoring.

Policy Dissemination

Copies of the IT security policy should be distributed to all personnel to whom the policies apply. All employees should be required to sign a statement acknowledging that they have received, have read, and agree to abide by the terms of the policy. Amendments to the policy should be distributed, and the distribution documented in the same way. This is important in the event that disciplinary action is taken against an employee for violation of the policy.

Copies of the policy can also be made available to organizational personnel in electronic format. This should be in addition to, not instead of, the procedure recommended above. One of the easiest ways to do this is on the intranet in HTML format. This allows the policy maker to create hyperlinks to reference documents and cross-reference related policies and makes it easy for users to search the document(s) for keywords and phrases. Security awareness and training policies might also be included and should specify required training for different levels of personnel (permanent staff, temporary staff, contractors, management, technical personnel, users of new systems, and so on).

Ongoing Assessment and Policy Update

The security policy is not a static document. Company business practices and priorities change, and new types of threats emerge as hackers learn new ways of accessing or attacking networks. The policy document should be reviewed on a regular basis and revised when necessary to meet new challenges and adapt to changing circumstances. The document itself should include a policy outlining the schedule for review, who is responsible for conducting the review, and the procedure for amending the document, as well as the procedure for disseminating changes to all affected personnel throughout the organization.

Summary

An understanding of basic security concepts gives a cybercrime investigator a distinct advantage in communicating intelligently with IT personnel and a better idea of exactly how a cybercrime was committed, based on the security measures in place at the time. Additionally, investigators should be proactive in helping the victims of cybercrime protect themselves against subsequent attacks. Although the investigator probably cannot and will not be expected to provide in-depth advice about the technical implementation of security systems, he or she should be able to discuss options in a general way and point crime victims in the right direction with some general suggestions.

A good investigator, like a good network security specialist or a good crime prevention officer, realizes that any security plan must be multilayered in order to be effective. It is important that all major security areas be addressed. These include physical security, perimeter security (through placement of firewalls at the network's entry points), security of data stored on disks (through file/disk encryption), security of data traveling across the network (through IP Security), and a means of verifying the identities of users, computers, and other entities that have access to network resources (through the building of a PKI).

Many security technologies are based on or use cryptographic techniques. An investigator might encounter encrypted data or even suspect that the existence of additional data is being concealed using steganography. An understanding of how cryptography developed and how it works in the computerized environment can be invaluable in investigating many types of cybercrime. Knowing a little about different encryption types and the algorithms they use allows the investigator to assess just how secure a particular system is—whether it belongs to a cybercrime victim or to a cybercrime suspect.

Finally, it's useful for the investigator to understand the process involved in creating and deploying organizational security policies and to see samples of such policies in order to understand the "big picture" of where the policies came from (revealing the organization's overall security philosophy) and exactly how security is deployed within the organization to help narrow the focus of the investigation. A good cybercrime investigator has at least a surface knowledge of all aspects of information technology security. He or she need not be a hands-on IT professional but should be able to "talk the talk" and understand what's being said when the real IT pros offer information about their organization's network.

Frequently Asked Questions

The following Frequently Asked Questions, answered by the authors of this book, are designed to both measure your understanding of the concepts presented in this chapter and to assist you with real-life implementation of these concepts. To have your questions about this chapter answered by the author, browse to **www.syngress.com/solutions** and click on the **"Ask the Author"** form.

Q: Is it a good idea for an organization to buy encryption software that uses "secret" algorithms?

A: No. Most security experts advise that only well-known, trusted, and tested algorithms be used. Although a vendor may claim that its product is more secure because the algorithms it uses are proprietary or secret, in reality proprietary algorithms are considered to be generally unsafe. Most of the best algorithms are public ones; knowing the algorithm doesn't help a hacker crack the encryption if the cipher is a strong one. If a vendor doesn't want to make its algorithm public, that might mean the vendor isn't confident that the algorithm can stand up to public scrutiny. An excellent discussion of open standardized encryption versus proprietary technologies is available in *Secrets and Lies: Digital Security in a Networked World,* by Bruce Schneier.

Q: Are digital signatures legally binding for signing documents such as contracts?

A: The short answer is: It depends. National and state governments in many jurisdictions have enacted laws governing the use of digital signatures for various types of transactions. In 1998, the U.S. Congress passed the Digital Signature and Electronic Authentication Law (SEAL), which amended the Bank Protection Act of 1968 to allow use of digital signatures to facilitate the use of electronic authentication by financial institutions (for more information about the Act, see http://thomas.loc.gov/cgi-bin/query/z?c105 :S.1594.IS:.).

   In 2000, the Electronic Signature in Global & National Commerce Act (ESIGN) was signed into law by President Bill Clinton, making digital signatures legal for most contracts entered into electronically (including mortgages). Some contractual agreements between private parties in the United States are governed by state laws. Most states have enacted legislation that specifies circumstances under which digital signatures are considered legally binding. For example, the state of Texas passed a digital signature law that went into effect in 1997, amending the Uniform Commercial Code to allow electronic communications sent from within or received in Texas in connection with the sale of merchandise to be digitally signed. It also specified that use of digital signatures be subject to the criminal laws in the Texas Penal Code that pertain to fraud and computer crimes. Outside the United States, the laws vary greatly. In July 2001, a European Commission directive went into effect in the 15 European Union member states, making digital signatures as legally binding for signing contracts as handwritten signatures.

Q: Is a firewall a foolproof, all-encompassing security method?

A: There is *no* foolproof, all-encompassing security method; the only effective security plan is one that uses multiple layers of security. A firewall is an important part of such a plan. It provides protection at the perimeter of the network, but firewalls don't protect against many types of security breaches, such as internal breaches, physical breaches, or intrusions caused by compromise of user passwords. The Firewall FAQ site (www.faqs.org/faqs/firewalls-faq) notes that many organizations place a firewall on the network and think they're protected when there are numerous other vulnerabilities (such as dialup modems on individual computers), similar to a person who has a 6-foot thick steel door installed in a wooden house with unlocked windows. Firewalls also don't usually do a very good job of protecting against viruses and Trojans. On the other hand, the better firewalls *do* allow for very granular filtering of both incoming and outgoing data at different levels, based on the organization's needs. Every business network (and home computers that are connected to the Internet) should have some sort of firewall. Firewall products range from proprietary hardware appliances that cost thousands of dollars or high-end software firewalls that cost hundreds of dollars to simple freeware and shareware products that are suitable for home use. Windows XP even comes with a built-in firewall, although it is a simple one that shouldn't be relied on to protect mission-critical systems.

Resources

- Cyber Angel (Computer Sentry Software)
  www.sentryinc.com

- Body Check: *Biometric Access Protection Devices and Their Programs Put to the Test*
  www.heise.de/ct/english/02/11/114

- The Register: *Gummi Bears Defeat Fingerprint Sensors*, by John Leyden
  http://theregister.co.uk/content/55/25300.html

- ISO 17799 Security Standard
  www.iso17799-web.com

- COBRA Risk Consultant (evaluation version)
  www.ca-systems.zetnet.co.uk/cobdown.htm

- Health Insurance Portability and Accountability Act (HIPAA) standards
  www.smed.com/hipaa/overview-fastfacts.php

- RUSecure Information Security Policies
  www.information-security-policies.com/index.htm

- SANS Institute Security Policy Project
  www.sans.org/newlook/resources/policies/policies.htm

- *Kerberos v5 System Administrator's Guide*
  www.lns.cornell.edu/public/COMP/krb5/admin/admin_2.html

- SANS Institute: *Layered Authentication*, by Jeff Parker
  http://rr.sans.org/authentic/layered.php

- *A Short History of Cryptography*, by Fred Cohen
  www.all.net/books/ip/Chap2-1.html

- *A Cryptographic Compendium*
  http://pardus-larus.student.utwente.nl/librarilo/texts/computers/crypto

- *Protection of Your Secret Key: How Secure Is PGP?*, by Ralf Senderek
  http://senderek.de/security/secret-key.protection.html#summary

Chapter 8

Implementing System Security

Topics we'll investigate in this chapter:

- Implementing Broadband Security Measures

- Implementing Browser Security

- Implementing Web Server Security

- Understanding Security and the Microsoft OSs

- Understanding Security and UNIX/Linux OSs

- Understanding Security and Macintosh OSs

- Understanding Mainframe Security

- Understanding Wireless Security

☑ Summary

☑ Frequently Asked Questions

☑ Resources

Introduction

In preceding chapters, we defined cybercrime and discussed the people who perpetrate it, and we explored the computer and networking basics that form the foundation required to understand technically sophisticated cybercrimes. Then we looked at the various types of network intrusions and attacks and discussed basic computer and network security concepts. Security is the key to preventing—or, failing that, detecting—network-related criminal activity.

Cybercrime is possible because computers and networks are not properly secured. Law enforcement officers know that most criminals look for "easy" prey—that is, pickpockets look for victims who fail to secure their wallets or purses, and burglars hit the residences and businesses that take fewer steps to secure their property. It should come as no surprise that cybercriminals do the same. Most attacks against computer systems and networks exploit well-known vulnerabilities—vulnerabilities that, in many cases, can be fixed with a simple patch or configuration change. Often, applying these simple security measures costs nothing. Yet computer users and network administrators are as lax in protecting their valuable data as many citizens are in protecting their personal property. The fact that these known exploits still work most of the time shows that most individuals and companies are not performing due diligence in protecting their IT assets before connecting them to the Internet.

There are many reasons for this behavior, including:

- The average computer user's lack of knowledge of security issues

- Busy network professionals' lack of time (the "I really meant to get around to it" syndrome)

- Psychological denial that leads people who are aware of the risk to think that even though such things happen, "it can't happen to me"

Of course, none of these reasons is good enough to justify the potential loss due to cybercrime, and that fact hits home with a vengeance *after* the network and its data have been compromised. It's important to realize that it's not just naïve individuals or small businesses on tight budgets that neglect their security needs. Unfortunately, many companies are like the police agencies that "can't afford" to buy body armor for their officers—until one of their own is killed in a shooting. Human nature is such that it often takes a tragedy to motivate people in charge to take action.

How Can Systems Be Secured?

System security is not a thing; it's a process—the process of building a barrier between the network and those who would do it harm. The key is to make your barrier more difficult to cross than someone else's. In other words, IT security involves creating a deterrent to convince a would-be–intruder or attacker that your system is more difficult to breach than some other system. However, if an attacker specifically wants to breach your security perimeter, given enough time, he or she will be able to do so.

Crime prevention officers tell residents at neighborhood watch meetings that there is no way to make a home completely impervious to burglars—and if you could, it would be a windowless fortress that would be unpleasant to live in. No lock will keep out someone who's determined to break in, but what good locks *will* do is slow an intruder. If you make it difficult enough to get in, a typical burglar will go elsewhere, looking for quicker and easier pickings. Likewise, no computer or network can ever be 100-percent secure unless it is disconnected from every communication interface and completely powered off—and of course, such a fully secured system is also completely useless to the user. What system security methods *can* do is raise the break-in difficulty level to the point where most would-be intruders will take their attacks somewhere else—especially since they'll find no shortage of networks that can be broken into with little effort.

NOTE

Understanding that IT security cannot be 100-percent effective should focus your efforts on establishing the best security you can afford, rather than wasting your time and money searching for the "perfect" security solution.

The Security Mentality

Stuart McClure and Joel Scambray, authors of the weekly Security Watch column in *InfoWorld Magazine*, have pointed out that "Security is not a goal, it is a process; security is not a product, it's a mentality." This sums up the necessary mindset to practice security.

If we expand on this philosophy a bit, there's a good deal more to say: Security is not something you can install right off the shelf, nor is it something you can ever achieve or complete. Security is an ongoing course of action that involves continually improving, tuning, and adjusting your systems to protect against new vulnerabilities and attacks. You cannot view security as a characteristic limited to computers, either; security must be an end-to-end solution. For your enterprise to be secure, you must address everything: computers, networking devices, connectivity media, boundary devices, communication devices, operating systems, applications, services, protocols, people, physical access, and the relationships among all these components of your business.

A good network security specialist has at least one thing in common with a good law enforcement officer: Both are naturally suspicious—sometimes almost to the point of paranoia. Both subscribe to the philosophy that it's better to be safe than sorry. A security-conscious network professional sees a potential attack in every security hole. This can be annoying to other network users, just as a police officer's insistence on sitting with a clear view of the door can be annoying to civilian friends and family members. However, considering every possible threat is part of the job—both jobs. After all, just because you're paranoid doesn't mean they *aren't* out to get you—or your data!

On the Scene...

Developing a Defensive Mindset

Early in their training, most law enforcement officers become familiar with the color codes that identify differing mental states of alertness. This color system is usually attributed to Colonel Jeff Cooper, a legendary firearms and personal defense expert, and is used to represent mental "conditions" as follows:

Condition White Describes the mindset of most people as they go about their daily business, oblivious to possible danger and wrapped up in their own thoughts and activities.

Condition Yellow Describes the optimum mindset for self-protection under ordinary circumstances—relaxed but alert and looking for signs of potential danger.

Condition Orange Describes the mindset a person should be in when known dangers exist (for example, when walking down a street at night in a high-crime area), constantly scanning for possible threats and ready to escalate to a higher state if necessary.

Continued

Condition Red Describes the mindset of a person who has encountered a threat (or, as police officers put it, when the proverbial waste byproducts have already hit the oscillating instrument); in this condition, the body experiences an adrenaline rush and the person reacts—usually—in one of two ways: fight or flight.

We can borrow these "mindset" codes to describe the state of our network's security. Unfortunately, too many networks operate in Condition White, with administrators and users oblivious to the many threats that exist. For our purposes, Condition Yellow is probably not enough to adequately protect computer systems and networks; any network that is connected to the Internet must be considered to be in a known high-crime area. Thus network security professionals should remain in Condition Orange, a heightened state of alertness, constantly on the lookout for threats and ready to respond when (not if) intrusions or attacks occur.

Elements of System Security

System security is about much more than just keeping out malicious users and preventing attacks. It is also about maintaining and providing access to resources for authorized users, and it is about maintaining the integrity of the data and the infrastructure. These related but separate elements of system security are described using four terms: *authentication*, *confidentiality*, *integrity*, and *availability*. If network administrators fail to properly manage any one of these elements, they will fail in the task of providing security for the IT infrastructure.

Successfully designing, deploying, and maintaining security requires mastery of an ever-expanding body of knowledge. This book couldn't possibly provide you with all the details of locking down even a *single* operating system, much less the entire IT infrastructure of a small company or enterprise corporation. However, we can highlight some of the big issues you face in your security efforts and point you in the direction of additional resources that address each of these topics in much more detail.

In this chapter, we take a look at the following security concerns:

- How to implement security on broadband connections

- How to implement and maintain Web browser security

- Special problems with implementing security on a Web server

- An overview of how to secure Microsoft operating systems

- An overview of how to secure UNIX/Linux operating systems

- An overview of how to secure Macintosh operating systems

- An overview of how to secure mainframe systems

- The importance and challenges of managing wireless security

Implementing Broadband Security Measures

Broadband is one of the buzzwords in Internet connectivity today. Broadband technologies have made it possible for both home users and small office networks to obtain reasonably high data-throughput rates at relatively low cost. No longer are high-speed connections limited to enterprises with deep pockets. The widespread availability and implementation of broadband connectivity has brought at least 10 percent of the U.S. and 22 percent of the Canadian online community into the Internet fast lane, according to *Cable Datacom News* (March 2002). As more end users (i.e., customers) gain access to greater bandwidth, Web sites can offer them more resources, more multimedia content, and more volume than was feasible for slower modem connections. However, a great deal of confusion, even among IT professionals, has arisen about what broadband really is. The term is sometimes used to refer to any high-speed connection, but it has a specific technical meaning. *Broadband* refers to a connection technology that uses multiple frequencies over a common networking medium (like the coaxial cable used for cable television, or CATV) to exploit all available bandwidth. This allows data to be *multiplexed* so that it can travel on different frequencies (or channels) simultaneously and more data can be transmitted in a specified period of time than with *baseband* (one channel) technologies such as Ethernet. Broadband is also sometimes called *wideband*.

NOTE

In addition to *broadband* and *baseband*, you'll sometimes hear the term *narrowband.* This term is often used to refer to technologies that carry only voice communications. In radio communications, narrowband refers to the 50cps to 64Kbps frequency range allocated by the Federal Communications Commission (FCC) for paging and mobile radio services.

Some factors that affect the data transmission capacity of a communications medium include its frequency range and the *quality* (or signal-to-noise ratio) of the connection. A single channel has a fixed capacity within those parameters, but capacity can be increased by increasing the number of communications channels. This is how broadband works.

Cable modems deliver the most common form of broadband Internet connectivity. And in fact, cable has many advantages as an Internet technology. Cable companies have extensive network infrastructures in place for transmission of television programming. Because it is a broadband technology, computer data signals can be sent over the cable on their own frequency, just as each TV channel's signal travels over its own frequency. Cable Internet typically offers speeds ranging from 500Kbps to 1.5Mbps (roughly equivalent to T-1, at prices at least 10 times lower), and the technology is capable of much higher speeds—up to 10Mbps or more.

Despite its advantages, cable has some significant disadvantages, including the following:

- Some cable companies' lines are capable of only one-way transmission (which, after all, is all that's needed for transmitting TV programs). In this case, users must send upstream messages via a regular analog phone line; only the downstream data comes over the cable. Fortunately, most cable companies have upgraded their infrastructures to support two-way transmission.

- Even with two-way cable, many cable companies throttle upstream bandwidth to 128Kbps. This is to prevent users from running Internet servers (which is also often prohibited by subscribers' terms-of-service agreements).

- Another disadvantage, in some areas, is lack of reliability. The cable network might be "down" a lot, leaving users without an Internet connection for periods of time. Unlike expensive business solutions such as leased lines, there is no guaranteed uptime (nor is there guaranteed bandwidth) included in a typical cable contract for Internet access.

- Perhaps the most serious disadvantage comes from the fact that cable is a "shared bandwidth" technology. This means that all subscribers in any immediate area share the same connection medium. In other words, everyone in a neighborhood is connected to the same subnet and therefore has the potential to become a security threat to any other system in that neighborhood. This is the primary weakness of cable Internet technology. Keep in mind that to launch an attack against a computer you must be able to communicate with that computer. Being connected to the same network medium facilitate—some might even argue it enables—malicious communications among those computers.

Digital Subscriber Line (DSL) technology provides broadband Internet connectivity over telephone lines. Asymmetric DSL (ADSL), the most widely available form of DSL, uses a signal coding technique called *discrete multitone* that divides a pair of copper wires in an ordinary telephone line into 256 sub-channels. Via this technique, data can be transmitted at over 8Mbps—but only for a relatively short distance, due to attenuation. The frequencies used are above the voice band; this means that both voice and data signals travel over the same phone line at the same time.

NOTE

For more information about how DSL works, see www.howstuffworks .com/dsl.htm.

Broadband Integrated Services Digital Network (B-ISDN) is another broadband technology that uses telephone lines. In this case, however, these are fiber optic phone lines rather than copper wiring. B-ISDN provides data transmission speeds of up to 1.5Mbps. The original ISDN technology was once intended to replace analog voice lines with digital lines, which are more reliable and less vulnerable to "noise" (interference). There are two types of ISDN service: Basic Rate Interface (BRI) and Primary Rate Interface (PRI). BRI is more often used by consumers and small businesses. It provides two channels (called *B channels* or *bearer channels*) on which data or voice can be transmitted at 64Kbps. These two channels can be used separately so that you can connect to the Internet at 64Kbps and use the other line for voice calls at the same time, or they can be aggregated to give you a 128K data transmission rate. Another channel, called the *D channel* or *data channel*, is 16Kbps and manages signaling. PRI is much more expensive than BRI but provides more bandwidth: twenty-three 64Kbps B channels plus one 64Kbps D channel, for a total capacity of 1.5Mbps (this applies to the United States; in Europe, PRI provides 1.98Mbps).

DSL and ISDN connections are not shared connections. Instead, the connection medium is used only by the two endpoints of the connection. Since there are only two parties in these connections, they offer a more secure means of communication than cable modem. Those to whom security is important—and that should include everyone who uses the Internet—should opt for an unshared connectivity option if it is available and affordable. Satellite Internet technologies can provide always-on Internet access at speeds up to about 500Kbps in areas where cable and DSL aren't available. Satellite is available almost anywhere, as long as you have an unobstructed view of the sky where the satellite is located. (This is required because satellite is a line-of-sight technology.) First-generation satellite was a one-way technology, like early cable modem services, but this has changed. Starband has partnered with Echostar and Microsoft to offer two-way satellite access, and Hughes Networks' DirecPC now provides two-way service with its DirecWay systems.

Broadband Security Issues

The benefits of high-speed broadband connectivity are complicated by problems and vulnerabilities unique to broadband. These issues arose directly out of the broadband implementation and were not palpable threats to the dialup modem community. One threat is the always-connected aspect of broadband. No longer do users have to manually initiate a connection when they want to surf the Web or access e-mail, since broadband connections are always on. In the past, modem users typically disconnected from the Internet once they completed their online sessions. This removed their computers from the Internet and prevented crackers from accessing their systems or mounting attacks against them. With broadband connections that remain up 24/7 and automatically reconnect when interrupted, a computer is now available to be attacked on an ongoing basis.

A second aspect of this always-connected issue is the IP address assigned to a system. With dialup modem connectivity, a PC is usually configured to use Dynamic Host Configuration Protocol (DHCP) to obtain its address and is assigned a different IP address each time the connection is established. Thus, a modem-connected PC that has one address today will usually have a different address tomorrow, and the address it used yesterday will be assigned to a different system today. This makes tracking individual systems difficult. However, with broadband connectivity, systems are often assigned a dedicated IP address or are able to continually renew their DHCP-assigned IP addresses so that their online identifiers remain consistent over a long period of time (if not indefinitely). This makes tracking a specific system extremely easy.

Law enforcement officers can easily understand the impact on detection and apprehension; many traditional criminals—especially scam artists—are always on the move, living in motel rooms or with friends and changing addresses every few weeks or months. These offenders are much more difficult to track down than those who have established a permanent residence and a fixed address. The same is true of cybercriminals. The ones who use static (consistent) IP addresses are easier to find than those with ever-changing addresses. Although there are ways for technically savvy criminals to disguise their IP addresses, the advent of broadband, with a greater likelihood of static addressing, makes the investigator's job easier when dealing with cybercriminals who are less knowledgeable about the technology.

On the other hand, the longer a system remains online, especially when it retains the same IP address, the more vulnerable that system is to repeated brute-force and port-scanning attacks. Given enough time, every system can be breached, even if security-conscious administrators have taken standard pre-cautions such as deploying a firewall, installing patches, and assigning strong passwords. Remember, security is a deterrent—it is not an impenetrable barrier. Given enough time and determination, any security measure can be breached.

Simply powering down the computer when it's not in use isn't enough to protect against these threats. Through the power of automation, crackers can con-tinuously scan an IP address to determine when the computer is on or off. Yes, it is possible to prevent the attack from progressing while the PC is powered down, but the attack can resume right where it left off once the system boots back up. Instead of relying on "security through obscurity" (attempting to hide the exis-tence of a system or data from an attacker), you can take numerous proactive steps to reduce your vulnerability to broadband-specific attacks. We discuss these steps in the next section.

It might sound strange, but another flaw in broadband security is the speed at which it allows data to flow. First, this speed allows a faster attack against your system. A malicious user can send a significantly greater amount of data to your system over a broadband connection than is possible over a dialup modem con-nection. Second, once your system is compromised, it takes an attacker less time to download or upload files.

Obviously, broadband connectivity has its drawbacks. But for many Internet users, it still offers an irresistible promise of lightning-fast connectivity at very low cost. It's important to first recognize that there is a problem and then take specific risk reduction measures, so in this section, we not only point out the flaws but offer guidance on reducing the risks associated with using broadband connectivity.

When implementing risk-reducing strategies such as improving security, you must take into account the specific hardware and software configuration of each computer. This includes the operating system in use, the applications installed, and the services used on the connected computer. Implementing security precautions on just one aspect of your system does not provide adequate security. You must deploy a multilayered security solution so that there will be numerous barriers to unauthorized access.

> **NOTE**
>
> We discuss the concept of multilayered security in Chapter 7, "Understanding Cybercrime Prevention."

When a large company contracts with an ISP for a high-speed bandwidth connection, security is probably the most important item in the service contract. However, individual customers (and many small businesses) who obtain low-cost broadband connections often overlook security. This oversight primarily stems from the fact that few individuals or small company employees are trained security professionals, and they simply don't know any better. Even when they have a vague idea that there are security risks they should be addressing, they might be overwhelmed by the complexity of the topic and the sheer number of competing security "solutions" available, as well as the high cost of implementing many such recommended solutions. The promise of fast Internet downloads for little cost blinds many users to other important issues, such as security and privacy, that should be carefully considered before broadband deployment.

In the following sections, we discuss specific risk-reducing strategies you can employ to improve the security of your computer or network using broadband connectivity. Individuals and companies who are implementing broadband must also consider the issues raised later in this chapter, when we discuss how to secure specific operating systems.

Deploying Antivirus Software

Security has many facets, two of which are the need to prevent *unauthorized* access and the need to support *authorized* access. All too often, the prevention of attacks comes at the expense of ensuring access to data by valid users. It is important to keep a balanced perspective when deploying any security measure. Think of security in terms of the popular policing motto, "To protect and to serve." If your security implementation fails to adequately support either of these elements, protecting your data and serving your authorized users, you have failed to implement a truly effective security plan.

On the Scene...

How High Security Can Turn into High Risk

Paradoxically, overly restrictive security policies can even result in *lowered* security (while creating a false sense of high security) because frustrated employees will look for ways to circumvent security measures, intentionally or unintentionally. Gung-ho security enthusiasts who march in and "tighten up" a network without taking user needs into account can do more harm than good in the long run, despite the best of intentions.

The simplest example is the imposition of a policy that requires employees to use randomly generated 20-character passwords that change every week. Because they are unable to remember such passwords, employees are much more likely to resort to writing them down (even if that is a violation of policy) than if the employees themselves chose their own passwords so that the passwords would have meaning to the people who must remember them. Writing down the passwords (especially since people tend to keep that little note close to the computer, for convenience) poses a much greater security risk than the possibility that user-selected passwords might be a little easier to crack. A compromise solution here is to allow users to select their own passwords, but also to set policies (which can be enforced using appropriate software) requiring that user passwords meet a minimum length and complexity—for example, stipulating that both alpha and numeric characters must be included, and the password must be at least 8 characters long.

This is a challenge because security and availability will always be at opposite ends of the continuum. The more you have of one, the less you have of the other. However, you *must* strike a balance, because a security policy that is too restrictive could have the same result as one that is too lax—that is, a negative (perhaps even catastrophic) impact on the company's bottom line.

Maintaining the *integrity* of your data so that it can be served to authorized users is just as important as preventing unwanted outsiders from stealing it. Many things—including human error, disgruntled employees, and even hardware failure—can threaten your data's integrity. But the most serious, prevalent, and imminent threat is corruption, destruction, or alteration of data by virus infection. A broadband connection is just as likely as a LAN link or a dialup connection to be a pathway for virus infection. No matter how your computer is connected to the Internet or other systems, you must protect it from viruses.

According to a study being performed by Message Labs (www.messagelabs .com), the rate at which viruses are spreading through e-mail is increasing exponentially. Reports generated from data collection indicate that starting in 1999, e-mail–borne viruses were detected about once per hour. In 2000, the detection rate jumped to once every three minutes. In 2001, a virus was detected every 30 seconds. By mid-2002, this rate had accelerated to one virus detection every 10 seconds. And that rate continues to increase.

When striving to protect your data's integrity, you can obtain no greater bang for your buck than that gained by deploying reliable antivirus software. When selecting such a product, look for the following:

- The product should originate from a well-known, reputable company.

- The product should automatically update its virus definitions.

- The product should scan stored files, memory (RAM), removable media, e-mail, and Web-transmitted data.

- The product should clean or quarantine any infected files it detects.

Whenever possible, deploy two or more virus solutions together on the network, to work as a layered system. However, do not install two antivirus tools on the same computer, because doing so can often cause the system to crash or behave erratically. Many organizations opt to place an antivirus product on each border system (firewall, gateway, proxy, and so on), on each server, and on each client. This multilayered approach provides more thorough protection and eliminates the problems that can come with reliance on a single vendor's solution.

Crimestoppers…

One Hundred Percent Virus-Free E-Mail

E-mail is the number-one virus delivery mechanism today, so it is essential to keep as much malicious e-mail out of your network as possible. With the increasing reliance on e-mail for commercial and private communications, balancing security against availability can be especially difficult in regard to electronic mail.

Some companies provide solutions to this problem. For example, Message Labs offers a service that guarantees 100-percent virus-free e-mail delivered to your e-mail servers. This guarantee is based on

Continued

Message Labs' ability to adequately screen inbound e-mail for any possible virus infection or carrier agent. This task is accomplished by routing your inbound e-mail to one of the company's control tower systems. There each message is inspected by at least three antivirus solutions from reliable vendors as well as an artificial intelligence search tool that relies on heuristics, pattern matching, signature matching, and traffic flow analysis to detect unknown viral threats. After a delay of about 1.5 seconds, your e-mail is then delivered to your internal e-mail servers for distribution on your network. Message Labs maintains an excellent track record for making good on promises. For more information, visit the company's Web site at www.messagelabs.com.

NOTE

We discuss viruses, Trojans, and other malicious code and provide more detailed information on how to protect systems from these threats in Chapter 6, "Understanding Network Intrusions and Attacks."

Defining Strong User Passwords

Only two elements are necessary to gain access to most computer systems: a user identity (username) and its associated password. Most usernames are obvious or very easy to guess—a person's first name, first initial and last name, or the like—and are therefore not confidential. Thus access authorization is likely to be based solely on the password. Passwords must be very strong and kept secured to maintain control over access. This is true whether your system is linked to a broadband connection, a LAN cable, or a dialup link. Because broadband connections are always on, however, they offer a potential intruder much more time than a dialup connection to carry out a brute-force attack (which is essentially a trial-and-error method that attempts various character combinations until the attacker stumbles onto one that works).

In Chapter 7, "Understanding Cybercrime Prevention," we discuss in detail how to create strong passwords that are difficult to crack and how to set and enforce password policies to ensure that none of the passwords in use in your organization creates an "easy in" for intruders.

Setting Access Permissions

Controlling access is an important element in maintaining system security. The most secure environments follow the "least privileged" principle. This principle states that users are granted the least amount of access possible that still enables them to complete their required work tasks. Expansions to that access are carefully considered before being implemented. Law enforcement officers are familiar with this principle in regard to noncomputerized information; this concept is usually termed *need to know*. Generally, following this principle means that the network administrators hear more complaints from users about being unable to access resources. However, hearing complaints from authorized users is better than hearing about access violations that damage an organization's profitability or its capability to conduct business.

In practice, maintaining the least privileged principle directly affects the level of administrative, management and auditing overhead, increasing the levels required to implement and maintain the environment. One alternative, the use of user groups, is a great time saver, but it also invites administrators to be lazy. Instead of assigning individual access controls, groups of similar users are all assigned the same access. In cases where all users in the group have exactly the same access needs, this method works. However, in many cases, some individual users need more or less access than other group members. Unfortunately, in the past operating system vendors such as Microsoft and Novell have advised that administrators always assign permissions to groups rather than individual user accounts. When security is important, however, the extra effort to fine-tune individual user access provides greater control over what users can and cannot access.

Keeping individual user access as specific as possible limits the threat of a single compromised user account granting a malicious person unrestricted access. It does not prevent the compromise of more privileged accounts, such as those of administrators or specific service operators. However, it does force intruders to focus their efforts on those more privileged accounts, where stronger passwords are usually enforced and more account use auditing and monitoring occurs.

We discuss establishing and enforcing access policies in more detail in Chapter 7.

Disabling File and Print Sharing

The ability to share files and printers with other members of your network can make many tasks simpler and, in fact, was the original purpose for networking computers in the first place. However, this ability also has a dark side—especially when users are unaware that they're sharing resources. If a trusted user can gain access, the possibility exists that a malicious user can obtain access as well. On systems linked by broadband connections, crackers have all the time they need to connect to your shared resources and exploit them.

On Windows operating systems, there is a service called File and Print Sharing (or, in Windows NT, the Server service). This service, when enabled, allows others to access your system across the network. Other operating systems have similar services (and thus similar weaknesses). The Microsoft File and Print Sharing service uses Network Basic Input/Output System (NetBIOS) Server Message Block (SMB) traffic to advertise shared resources ad but does not offer security to restrict who can see and access those shares. Such security is controlled by setting permissions on the shares. The problem is that when a share is created, by default the permissions are set to give full control over the resource to the Everyone group—which includes literally everyone who accesses that system. By default, the File and Print Sharing service is bound to all interfaces (see the "NIC Bindings" section later in this chapter). This means that when sharing is enabled with the purpose of sharing resources with the trusted internal network over a NIC, the system is also sharing those resources with the entire Internet over the broadband connection. Many users are completely unaware of these defaults and don't realize their resources are available to anyone "out there" who knows enough about Windows to find them.

At the very least, the File and Print Sharing service should be unbound from the broadband connection adapter. Another solution (or a further precaution to take in addition to unbinding the broadband adapter) is to use a different protocol on the internal network. For example, computers could communicate over NetBIOS Extended User Interface (NetBEUI) over a small local, unrouted network. If File and Print Sharing is bound to NetBEUI and unbound from the Transmission Control Protocol/Internet Protocol (TCP/IP) used over the Internet, internal users can still share resources, but those resources will be unavailable to "outsiders" on the Internet.

If the user doesn't need to share resources with anyone on the internal (local) network, the File and Print Sharing service should be completely disabled. On most networks where security is important, this service is disabled on all clients. This action forces all shared resources to be stored on network servers, which typically have better security and access controls than end-user client systems.

Using NAT

Network Address Translation (NAT) is a feature of many firewalls, proxies, and routing-capable systems. NAT has several benefits, one of which is its ability to hide the IP address and network design of the internal network. The ability to hide your internal network from the Internet reduces the risk of intruders gleaning information about your network and exploiting that information to gain access. If an intruder doesn't know the structure of a network, the network layout, the names and IP address of systems, and so on, it is very difficult to gain access to that network.

NAT enables internal clients to use nonroutable IP addresses, such as the private IP addresses defined in RFC 1918, but still enables them to access Internet resources. NAT restricts traffic flow so that only traffic requested or initiated by an internal client can cross the NAT system from external networks.

If only a single system is linked to the Internet with a broadband connection, NAT is of little use. However, for local networks that share a broadband connection, NAT's benefits can be utilized for security purposes. When using NAT, the internal addresses are reassigned to private IP addresses and the internal network is identified on the NAT host system. Once NAT is configured, external malicious users are only able to access the IP address of the NAT host that is directly connected to the Internet, but they are not able to "see" any of the internal computers that go through the NAT host to access the Internet.

On the Scene...

Deploying a NAT Solution

NAT is relatively easy to implement, and there are several ways to do so. Many broadband hardware devices (cable and DSL modems) are called cable/DSL "routers" because they allow you to connect multiple computers. However, they are actually combination modem/NAT devices rather than routers because they require only one external (public) IP address. You can also buy NAT devices that attach your basic cable or DSL modem to the internal network. Alternatively, the computer that is directly connected to a broadband modem can use NAT software to act as the NAT device itself. This can be an add-on software program such as Sygate (www.sygate.com) or the NAT software that is built into some operating systems. For example, Windows 2000 Server includes a fully configurable NAT as part of its Routing and Remote Access services. Windows 98SE, 2000 Professional, ME, and XP include a "lite" version of NAT called Internet Connection Sharing (ICS).

For a quick, illustrated explanation of how NAT works with a broadband connection, see the HomeNetHelp article at www.homenethelp.com/web/explain/about-NAT.asp.

When NAT is used to hide internal IP addresses, it is sometimes called a *NAT firewall*; however, don't let the word *firewall* give you a false sense of security. NAT by itself solvesonly one piece of the security perimeter puzzle. A true firewall does much more than hide internal IP addresses.

Deploying a Firewall

As we discussed in Chapter 7, a firewall is a device or a software product whose primary purpose is to filter traffic crossing the boundaries of a network. That boundary can be a broadband connection, a dialup link, or some type of LAN or WAN connection. The network can be an enterprise LAN, a single system, or anything in-between.

The most typical use for firewalls is to restrict what types of traffic can traverse the boundary connections of your network. There are several types of firewalls or filtering mechanisms available to handle this job: packet filters, stateful inspection systems, proxy systems, and circuit-level filtering.

You will recall that *packet filters*, also known as *screening routers*, decide what traffic is allowed or blocked based on information found in TCP headers. The information used from the TCP header is typically the source or destination IP address and the corresponding TCP or User Datagram Protocol (UDP) port. Packet filters are static, always open, and therefore unable to properly manage dynamic port applications. Furthermore, packet filters are unable to monitor or traffic content.

Stateful inspection systems inspect the ongoing activities within active communication sessions to ensure that the type of traffic detected is valid. Stateful inspection was designed to address deficiencies in packet filters, specifically to ensure that traffic over dynamic ports is valid and authorized.

Proxy systems, also known as *application gateways* or *application firewalls*, are able to filter traffic based on high-level protocols (such as Hypertext Transfer Protocol, or HTTP; File Transfer Protocol, or FTP; Simple Mail Transfer Protocol, or SMTP; and Telnet), applications, or even specific control commands. Proxy systems work well with dynamic port applications. The downside to proxy systems is that a unique proxy service is required for each Internet service or application. Unfortunately, some services and applications don't lend themselves well to being proxied. Proxy systems also lower the network performance due to the amount of processing involved with fully inspecting each packet.

Circuit-level filtering makes traffic decisions based on the content of the session rather than individual packets. Circuit-level filters open ports only when internal clients make requests, thus supporting dynamic port applications such as FTP. This type of filter supports a wider range of protocols than a proxy system, but it does not provide the detailed controls that a proxy system does.

When selecting a firewall to protect broadband connections, the user should seek a product with all these filtering capabilities as well as extensive logging and auditing features and alarms and alerts (the reasons these latter features are important are covered in Chapter 9). Another good idea is to seek out products with NAT and intrusion-detection capabilities (also covered in Chapter 9).

For individual, standalone, or home systems, several fairly inexpensive personal firewall products provide adequate security for nonprofessional computer use, such as ZoneAlarm from Zone Labs. Microsoft's newest operating system, Windows XP, also includes a built-in personal firewall feature. However, to protect a business network, administrators cannot rely on "personal" firewalls. Companies should invest in a heavy-duty firewall that provides a higher level of security and greater configurability. Deployment might be simplified if you contract with a security outsourcing company to install, configure, maintain, and administer your firewall.

Disabling Unneeded Services

One of the primary tenets for maintaining physical security in a residence or business property is to reduce the number of pathways an intruder can take to gain access to it. This reduction typically involves locking doors and windows, sealing off access tunnels, and securing ventilation shafts. Administrators should apply the same perspective in regard to the electronic pathways into the network. Any means by which valid data can reach the network or computer is also a potential path for a malicious intruder or attack.

Systems linked to the Internet by broadband connections should have any unneeded protocols, applications, and services either disabled or completely removed or uninstalled. With the proliferation of poor programming practices that often lead to security vulnerabilities, it is essential to limit exposure to potential threats simply by removing unessential software from the network's computer systems. For example, many versions of Windows automatically install a Web server during default OS installation. If a system is not specifically intended for use as a Web server, that component of the OS should be disabled.

Configuring System Auditing

When a system is compromised, one of two things occurs:

- Bad things happen and you are clearly aware of them (system crash, deleted files, or the like).

- Bad things happen and you are unaware of them (a hacker toolkit is downloaded to your system, a user account is compromised, or a similar security breach).

Waiting for clear indications of system violations to appear is a poor security practice, especially since unseen compromises usually result in more severe consequences. Law enforcement officers can relate this concept to the difference between *reactive policing*, in which a law enforcement agency waits until a crime is reported to go into action, and *proactive policing*, which involves activities designed to prevent crimes from occurring in the first place. We all know that the proactive method is more effective in fighting crime, but it has one drawback: It's a lot more work. Unfortunately, system administrators, police officers, and other human beings are often tempted to take the path that requires the least amount of effort, and that's why preventable crimes—including network security breaches—proliferate.

The only way to know when your system has been breached or when an unsuccessful attempt to penetrate your security has occurred is to monitor or audit for unusual or abnormal activity—just as patrol officers drive through the neighborhoods on their beats, looking for anything out of the ordinary. Most OSs include native auditing capabilities. For example, Windows servers and business-oriented client operating systems such as NT Workstation and Windows 2000/XP Professional provide for security auditing that is tracked through a security log available to administrators through the Event Viewer administrative tool. At a minimum, administrators should audit logons and logoffs, changes to user accounts and privileges, and use of administrative-level functions. These are activities that are often involved in a security breach and can serve as indicators when the computer or network has been compromised.

If the amount of data the auditing system gathers is too much to manage manually, as might be the case on enterprise networks, it could be beneficial to invest in an intrusion detection system (IDS). An IDS automates the tedious task of looking for abnormal or suspicious system activity. IDS uses pattern recognition and heuristic learning to detect suspect activities by authorized user accounts as well as external malicious users.

On the Scene…

Securing Remote Connectivity

Connecting to a home system from the office or connecting to the office LAN while traveling are often essential capabilities for employees in today's network-centric business world. Unfortunately, many of the tools and protocols native to operating systems, such as Telnet, FTP, and the remote or **r** commands, are inherently insecure. All these services transmit authentication credentials and data in clear, unencrypted form. For secure remote communications, users must employ services and protocols that not only support data encryption but also protect authentication credentials. If users plan to establish remote connections over broadband links, using secure communication mechanisms is essential.

When working with a Windows 9*x*, NT, 2000, XP, or .NET system on both ends of the connection, users can employ the Point-to-Point Tunneling Protocol (PPTP). There is also some modest support for PPTP on some UNIX and Linux systems. PPTP is used to create a *virtual private network (VPN)* over the Internet or a direct dialup connection. A VPN connects one system to another just as though they were linked by a typical network cable. The network interactions are exactly the same as a typical LAN connection, except for speed, which is limited by the bandwidth of the slowest interface between the two connected systems. PPTP establishes a virtual "tunnel" between two systems. Within that tunnel, PPP provides support for the actual networking protocol (such as TCP/IP) used by the two connected systems. PPTP does not itself provide encryption; rather, it relies on the encryption protocols of PPP. The Microsoft Point-to-Point Encryption (MPPE) Protocol is used for encryption in a PPTP tunnel between two Windows systems. Only when MS-CHAP-2 is used are both data and authentication encryption possible. PPTP VPN tunnels do offer some security, but they are considered weaker than other solutions.

If the end systems are running Windows 2000, XP, or .NET, then administrators can use the Layer 2 Tunneling Protocol (L2TP) to establish the VPN tunnel. L2TP is an industry-standard tunneling protocol developed by a cooperative effort of Microsoft and Cisco Systems; it combines elements of Microsoft's PPTP and Cisco's Layer 2 Forwarding (L2F) protocols. L2TP is supported by Linux operating systems, using the L2TP Daemon (l2tpd). The TunnelBuilder VPN client for Macintosh supports both PPTP and L2TP tunnels.

Continued

www.syngress.com

The specifications for L2TP are laid out in RFC 2661, available on the Web at www.ietf.org/rfc/rfc2661.txt?number=2661. L2TP, like PPTP, does not provide encryption itself but relies on the IP Security Protocol, IPSec, to provide encryption. Administrators can also use IPSec as a tunneling protocol by itself (in "tunnel mode") for interoperability with routers and gateways that don't support L2TP or PPTP. Microsoft's IPSec tunnel mode supports only gateway-to-gateway tunnels and is not used between two endpoints.

When using multiple OSs from various vendors, there is yet another option for remote connectivity: Secure Shell (SSH). SSH is a utility that is used to log onto, execute commands on, transfer files between, or remap services from remote systems. SSH offers both authentication and data encryption. On UNIX and Linux systems, the SSH replaces numerous insecure utilities such as Telnet, RLOGIN, RSH, RCP, and FTP. Versions of SSH are available for various versions of UNIX, Linux, Windows, Macintosh, Palm, and Java. SSH tunnels differ from VPN tunnels in that SSH clients do not connect to the remote system as network clients. Instead, SSH clients simply connect to individual services to perform service-specific activities. One common use for SSH is to remap remote services to local ports or addresses, such as mapping an e-mail server from your office to a local system address for easy access while traveling or telecommuting. One popular SSH product is OpenSSH, developed by the OpenBSD project. You can read more about this utility and download the program from the OpenSSH Web site at www.openssh.com.

Implementing Browser and E-Mail Security

No matter what type of Internet connection a company or individual uses, whether broadband, dialup, or LAN, it is important to address the security vulnerabilities that Web browsers introduce to the systems and network. Many of the most commonly used Internet service client software programs, such as Web browsers and e-mail utilities, are vulnerable to an ever-expanding list of malicious attacks. Most of these attacks are made possible by the dynamic and automated capabilities that these tools have acquired over the years. The inclusion of scripting and programming languages in these utilities (for example, JavaScript, Java, and ActiveX) has introduced new and easily exploited security vulnerabilities to an already imperfect environment. In an effort to maintain browser market share by offering the widest range of capabilities and features, Microsoft's Web browser Internet Explorer and e-mail clients Outlook and Outlook Express have become immensely popular and consequently are the most commonly attacked Internet service clients.

It is important to remember that Microsoft is not the only vendor whose Internet service products are susceptible to attacks—it's merely because this company's products are the most popular that they have become the favorite target of attackers. Some users—including networking professionals who should know better—operate under a false sense of security (we might say they're operating in Condition White) because they use non-Microsoft products. Each time a security flaw in Internet Explorer, Outlook, or a Microsoft operating system is announced, they proudly boast that they would never use such an insecure product. Meanwhile, a Web search for UNIX or Linux security vulnerabilities turns up thousands of pages detailing security holes in various UNIX/Linux versions. It bears repeating once again that there is *no* truly secure network-connected computer.

When it comes to Web browsers, the truth is that any utility that supports the execution of scripts or programming code downloaded from a Web page or an e-mail message is vulnerable. Netscape, in its efforts to keep up with Microsoft in terms of features, supports the same types of scripting and thus suffers from the same vulnerabilities. Opera, a small alternative browser popular with many users, now supports Java, although early versions didn't. The proliferation of these vulnerabilities is the result of pursuing functionality in hopes of obtaining market share instead of thoroughly investigating and dealing with the security implications.

Most vulnerabilities found in Web and e-mail clients relate to buffer overflow errors or arbitrary code execution. Both of these vulnerabilities enable a remote system, whether a Web site or a sender of an e-mail message, to execute malicious code on your computer. In most cases, the executed code is granted system-level privileges, meaning that there are literally no restrictions on what actions such code can take.

The same technologies that create vulnerabilities in Web browsers can also be used in HTML e-mail. Many popular e-mail clients, including Outlook and Outlook Express, Eudora, and Netscape Mail, can allow active content to run, leaving a system open to malicious coders. Pegasus Mail is somewhat more secure because its HTML handler doesn't run scripts, Java applets, or ActiveX controls. (However, Pegasus does allow opening of attached documents that could contain malicious macros.)

Securing E-Mail Clients

The following Web resources give you more specific information about securing various e-mail clients:

Outlook/Outlook Express: http://antivirus.about.com/library/bloutlook.htm

Pegasus: http://antivirus.about.com/library/blpegasus.htm

Eudora: http://antivirus.about.com/library/bleudora.htm

Netscape: http://antivirus.about.com/library/blnetscape.htm

In the next sections, we take a look at the technologies that create security risks in Web browsers and e-mail, and then we discuss how to make each of the popular browser programs more secure.

Types of Dangerous Code

Several different types of code can be used to both enhance Web pages and e-mail and to perform unwanted and even dangerous actions on a computer. The following sections provide an overview of the most popular of these types of code: JavaScript, ActiveX, and Java.

JavaScript

JavaScript is a scripting language developed by Netscape to allow executable code to be embedded in Web pages. All major Web browsers support JavaScript. JavaScript is used to manipulate browser window size, open and close windows, manage forms, and alter browser settings. JavaScript itself is relatively secure. However, improper implementations (such as vendor programming errors) have enabled numerous attacks. Each vendor has patched most of these vulnerabilities, but it is still possible to use JavaScript to perform a malicious activity if you can trick Web surfers into doing something they shouldn't. Unfortunately, it is usually easy for a malicious Web site to trick visitors into providing access or enabling code execution when they shouldn't. For information about specific exploits that use JavaScript, see the JavaScript for Beginners Web site at http://polaris.umuc.edu/~mgaylor/Issues.html.

> **NOTE**
>
> JavaScript is completely different from Java. Their only similarity is in the first four letters of their names.

ActiveX

ActiveX is a code-embedding technology developed by Microsoft. It employs a security control known as *code signing*. Each ActiveX program is called a *control*. When a control is downloaded to a Web browser, it is scanned for a digital signature using the Authenticode technology to verify the signature with a certification authority and ensure that it hasn't been altered before downloading the control. A dialog box is displayed, indicating that the ActiveX control is signed by a specific company or individual, and prompts the user to indicate whether to accept this control, always accept controls from this entity, or deny this control. Once an ActiveX control is on a system, it can do anything it is programmed to do, whether benign or malicious. Knowing the identities of the authors of a control doesn't guarantee that the control is secure nor that its interactions with other controls will not introduce new vulnerabilities to your system.

One of the first well-known exploits of ActiveX was the Exploder control developed by Fred McLain to illustrate the dangers of ActiveX. For more information about this exploit, which can shut down a computer from a Web page, see www.halcyon.com/mclain/ActiveX/Exploder/FAQ.htm.

Java

Java is a programming language developed by Sun Microsystems. It is fundamentally different from JavaScript in that it uses a technique known as *sandboxing* to restrict its capabilities. Java programs that execute locally are called *applets*. Each applet is checked to make sure it is coded properly and is not corrupted before it is allowed to execute. Then a security monitor oversees the applet's activity to prevent it from performing actions that it should not be able to do, such as reading data, opening network connections, or deleting files.

Unfortunately, some implementations of Java have been compromised using various exploits. For example, in August 2000, CERT released a security advisory warning that some versions of Netscape Communicator contained Java classes that allowed unsigned Java applets to access local and remote resources in violation of the security policies for applets. Hostile applets can crash browsers and systems, kill other applets, extract your e-mail address and send it to the applet's distributor, and perform other nasty acts. See the Hostile Applets page at www.cigital.com/hostile-applets/index.html.

> **NOTE**
>
> An excellent paper on Java security issues is located at http://ei.cs.vt.edu/ ~wwwbtb/fall.96/book/chap14/index.html. The transcript of a good discussion comparing ActiveX and Java in terms of security issues is available from the Princeton Secure Internet Programming team at www.cs.princeton.edu/sip/faq/java-vs-activex.html.

Making Browsers and E-Mail Clients More Secure

There are several steps network administrators and users can take to make Web browsers and e-mail clients more secure and protect against malicious code or unauthorized use of information. These steps include restricting the use of programming languages, keeping security patches current, and becoming aware of the function of cookies.

Restricting Programming Languages

Most Web browsers have options settings that allow users to restrict or deny the use of Web-based programming languages. For example, Internet Explorer can be set to always allow, always deny, or prompt for user input when a JavaScript, Java, or ActiveX element appears on a Web page. Restricting all executable code from Web sites, or at least forcing the user to make choices each time it's downloaded, reduces security breaches caused by malicious downloaded components.

A side benefit of restricting these programming languages for a Web browser is that those restrictions often apply to the e-mail client as well. This is true when the browser is Internet Explorer and the e-mail client is Outlook or Outlook Express, and Netscape and Eudora also depend on the Web browser for HTML handling. The same malicious code that can be downloaded from a Web site could just as easily be sent to a person's e-mail account. If you don't have such restrictions in place, your mail client could automatically execute downloaded code.

Keep Security Patches Current

New exploits for Web browsers and e-mail clients seem to appear daily. Product vendors usually address significant threats promptly by releasing a patch for their products. In order to maintain a secure system, you must remain informed about your software and apply patches for vulnerabilities when they become available.

However, you must consider a few caveats when working with software patches:

- Patches are often released quickly, in response to an immediate problem, so they may not have been thoroughly tested. This can result in failed installations, crashed systems, inoperable programs, or additional security vulnerabilities.

- It is extremely important to test new patches on nonproduction systems before deploying them throughout your network.

- If a patch cannot be deemed safe for deployment, you should weigh the consequences of not deploying it and remaining vulnerable to the threat against the possibility that the patch might itself cause system damage. If the threat is minimal, it is often safer to wait until you experience the problem a patch is designed to address before deploying such a questionable patch.

Cookie Awareness

A *cookie* is a kind of token or message that a Web site hands off to a Web browser to help track a visitor between clicks. The browser stores the message on the visitor's local hard disk in a text file. The file contains information that identifies the user and his or her preferences or previous activities at that Web site. If the user revisits the same Web site, the user's browser sends the cookie back to the Web server. Cookies are extremely useful in allowing a Web site to provide a seemingly continuous communications session with a visitor, such as maintaining a shopping cart, remembering search keywords, or customizing displayed data based on the user's preferences. However, because cookies contain identifying information, they might be used for less noble purposes.

Cookies have been discussed extensively in the popular press. These stories sometimes grant cookies more power than they really have and assign them more regard than they deserve. Cookies raise questions about privacy, but they are unable to execute code or access files. Instead, cookies simply store data from Web browsing sessions and send that same data back to a Web server. Cookies can be delivered to a computer via Web pages or HTML-enabled e-mail. Malicious, or at least unscrupulous, use of cookies occurs when they are used to track a user's surfing habits from one system to another, grab a user's logon information from one site and send it to another, or even to capture a user's e-mail address and add the user to mailing lists without the user's knowledge. Fortunately, cookies can be disabled in the same manner as programming languages.

Securing Web Browser Software

Although the same general principles apply, each of the popular Web browser programs has a slightly different method to configure its security options. The following sections demonstrate how to make changes to the settings of the three most popular browsers—Microsoft Internet Explorer, Netscape, and Opera—and turn off features that allow security holes to be exploited.

Securing Microsoft Internet Explorer

Securing Microsoft Internet Explorer (IE) involves applying the latest updates and patches, modifying a few settings, and practicing intelligent surfing. Microsoft seems to release an IE-specific security patch just about every week. This constant flow of patches is due to both the oversights of the programmers who wrote the code and to the focused attacks on Microsoft products by the malevolent hacker community. In spite of this negative attention, IE can still be employed as a relatively secure Web browser—when it is configured correctly.

The first step in securing IE is to install the latest patches and updates. Users can do so automatically through Windows Update or manually. Either way, only through patch application will most of the known vulnerabilities of IE programming be resolved. For information about security patches available for Microsoft's latest browser software, see www.microsoft.com/windows/ie/security/default.asp.

The second step is to configure IE for secure surfing. Users can do this through the Internet Options applet. In IE version 6 (the current browser at the time of this writing), this applet is accessed through the Windows Control Panel or through the Tools menu of IE. If the default settings are altered on the Security, Privacy, Content, and Advanced tabs, as shown in Figure 8.1, IE security is improved significantly.

Zones are defined on the Security tab. A *zone* is nothing more than a named collection of Web sites (from the Internet or a local intranet) that can be assigned a specific security level. IE uses zones to define the threat level a specific Web site poses to the system. IE offers four security zone options:

- **Internet** Contains all sites not assigned to other zones.

- **Local intranet** Contains all sites within the local intranet or on the local system. This zone is maintained automatically by the OS.

- **Trusted sites** Contains only sites manually added to this zone. Users should add only fully trusted sites to this zone.

- **Restricted sites** Contains only sites manually added to this zone. Users should add any sites that are specifically not trusted or that are known to be malicious to this zone.

Figure 8.1 Settings on the Security tab in IE's Internet Options define security zones.

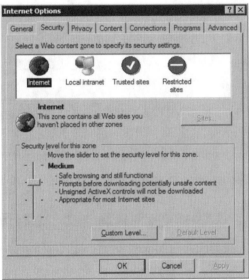

Each zone is assigned a predefined security level or a custom level can be created. The predefined security levels are offered on a slide controller with four settings—Low, Medium-Low, Medium, and High—with a description of the content that will be downloaded under particular conditions (see the description for Medium in Figure 8.1).

You can define custom security levels to exactly fit the security restrictions of your environment. There are over 20 individual security controls related to how ActiveX, downloads, Java, data management, data handling, scripting, and logon are handled. The most secure configuration is to set all zones to the High security level. However, keep in mind that increased security means less functionality and capability.

The Privacy tab, shown in Figure 8.2, defines how IE manages personal information through cookies.

Figure 8.2 Cookie options can be set in IE via the Privacy tab in Internet Options.

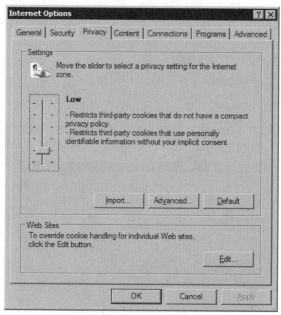

Figure 8.3 You can configure certificate options in IE using the Content tab in Internet Options.

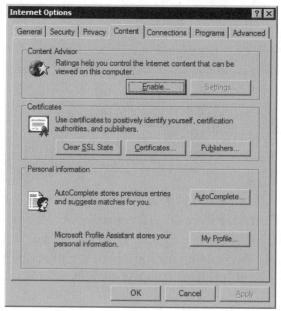

Figure 8.4 The Advanced tab in IE's Internet Options allows you to configure security settings.

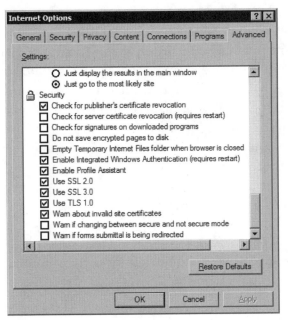

The Privacy tab offers a slide controller with six settings ranging from full disclosure to complete isolation. You can also define a custom set of cookie controls by deciding whether first-party and third-party cookies are allowed, denied, or initiate a prompt and whether session cookies are allowed. You can define individual Web sites whose cookies are either always allowed or always blocked. Preventing all use of cookies is the most secure configuration, but it is also the least functional. Many Web sites will not function properly under this setting, and some will not even allow you to visit them when cookies are disabled.

The Content tab, shown in Figure 8.3, gives you access to the certificates that are trusted and accepted by IE. If you've accepted a certificate that you no longer trust, you can peruse this storehouse and remove it.

The Content tab also gives you access to IE's AutoComplete capability. This feature is useful in many circumstances, but when it is used to remember usernames and passwords to Internet sites, it becomes a security risk. The most secure configuration requires that AutoComplete be turned off for usernames and passwords, that prompting to save passwords is disabled, and that the current password cache is cleared.

On the Advanced tab, shown in Figure 8.4, several security-specific controls are included at the bottom of a lengthy list of functional controls. These security controls include checking for certificate revocation, don't save encrypted pages to disk, delete temporary Internet files when the browser is closed, using Secure Shell/Transport Layer Security (SSL/TLS), and warn when forms are submitted insecurely. The most secure configuration has all these settings enabled.

A final step in maintaining a secure IE deployment is to practice safe surfing habits. Common sense should determine what users do, both online and off. Unfortunately, as many law enforcement officers have observed in the course of their duties, common sense isn't all that common. Most of us wouldn't walk down a dark alley in the middle of the city at 3:00 A.M., but people do it—and unfortunately, they sometimes learn a lesson the hard way. Visiting Web sites of questionable design is the virtual equivalent of putting yourself in harm's way in a dark alley, but Internet users do it all the time. Here are some guidelines that should be followed to ensure safe surfing:

- Download software only from original vendor Web sites.

- Always attempt to verify the origin or ownership of a Web site before downloading materials from it.

- Never assume anything presented online is 100-percent accurate.

- Avoid visiting suspect Web sites—especially those that offer cracking tools, pirated programs, or pornography—from a system that needs to remain secure.

- Always reject certificates or other dialog box prompts by clicking **No**, **Cancel**, or **Close** when prompted by Web sites or vendors with which you are unfamiliar.

Securing Netscape Navigator

Securing Netscape Navigator is similar to securing Internet Explorer. You should keep the software up to date by installing security-related patches from Netscape, and you should practice safe surfing habits. Security settings specific to Netscape Navigator are defined through the Preferences dialog box under the Privacy & Security and Advanced sections.

The Cookies subsection of Privacy & Security defines how cookies are handled. You can elect to enable all cookies, enable only first-party cookies, or disable all cookies. Through the Cookie Manager (accessed by pressing the **View Stored Cookies** button), you can inspect individual cookies and elect to remove all or just specific cookies. The most secure configuration is to disable all cookies. A less secure but more functional configuration is to allow first-party cookies but to display a warning before storing a cookie.

The Web Passwords subsection of Privacy & Security defines whether usernames and passwords for Web sites are stored on your system so they can be automatically reused on subsequent site visits. This capability can be turned on or off, plus you can individually delete any stored logon credentials. The most secure configuration is to disable automatic storage and delete any currently stored credentials. The Macintosh version of Netscape, running on OS X, is shown in Figure 8.5.

Figure 8.5 Netscape's Privacy & Security options allow you to manage cookies and passwords.

Users can use the Certificates subsection of Privacy & Security (in the Windows version of Netscape) to view and manage certificates. Similar to IE's manager, it allows you to view accepted certificates and even delete them. It is a good security practice to review your accepted certificates on a regular basis.

The Advanced section offers check boxes to enable or disable Java and JavaScript. Netscape Navigator does not support ActiveX. The most secure configuration is to disable both of these programming languages.

Securing Opera

Securing the Opera Web browser is similar to the process for IE and Netscape. First, update the software with the latest patches available from the vendor. Next, secure the browser itself. Then practice safe surfing habits.

Securing the Opera browser is performed through the Preferences dialog box, which is accessed from the File menu. Opera natively supports JavaScript but not ActiveX. Java support can be added to Opera if desired. JavaScript can be disabled through the Multimedia section of Opera's Preferences section. If Java is installed, Java can be enabled or disabled here as well. The Privacy section, shown in Figure 8.6, controls the use of cookies. Cookies can be enabled, disabled, or accepted only from first parties.

The Security section of Preferences, shown in Figure 8.7, is used to control certificates, password caching, and form insecurity. Users can choose the security protocols (SSL 2, SSL 3, and TLS 1) that will be enabled, and can configure the properties of each.

Figure 8.6 The Privacy section of Opera's Preferences allows you to control the behavior of cookies.

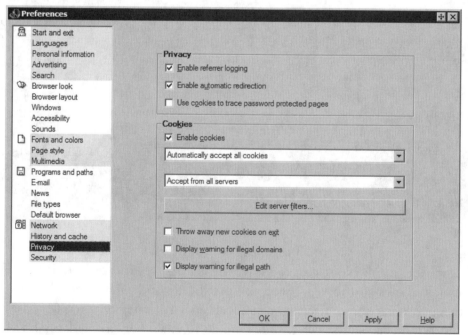

Figure 8.7 The Security section in Opera's Preferences allows you to control certificates, protocols, passwords, and form submission.

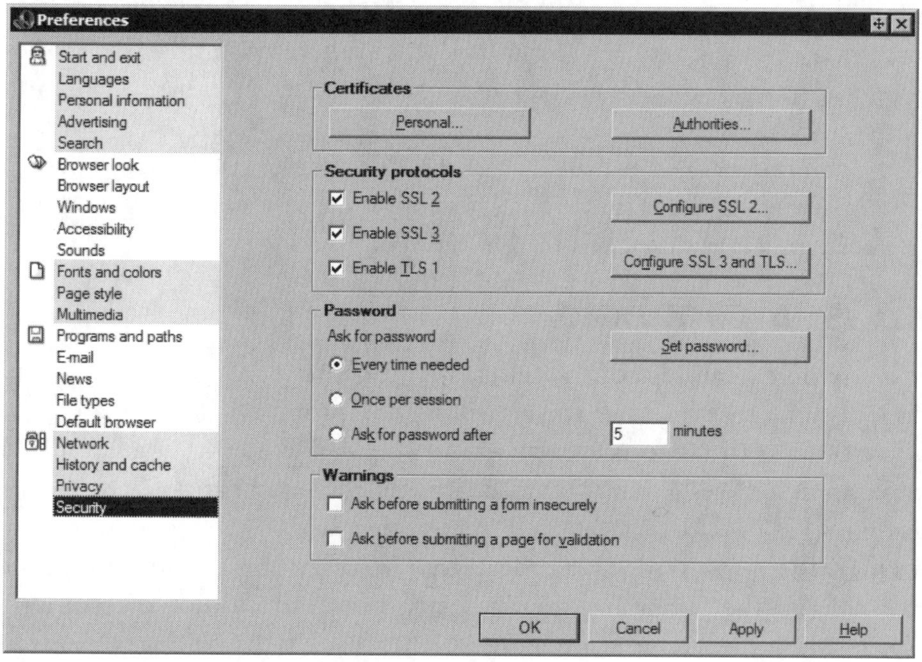

Implementing Web Server Security

Most companies and organizations today have a Web presence on the Internet. An Internet presence offers numerous business advantages, such as the ability to reach a large audience with advertising, to interact with customers and partners, and to provide updated information to interested parties.

Web pages are stored on servers running Web services software such as Microsoft's Internet Information Server (IIS) or Apache (on Linux/UNIX servers). Web servers must be accessible via the Internet if the public is to be able to access their Web pages. However, this accessibility provides a point of entry to Internet "bad guys" who want to get into the network, so it is vitally important that Web servers be secured. Protecting a Web server is no small task. Systems attached to the Internet before they are fully "hardened" are usually detected and compromised within minutes. Malicious crackers are always actively searching for systems to infiltrate, making it essential that you properly lock down a Web server before bringing it online.

First and foremost, administrators should lock down the underlying operating system. This process includes applying updates and patches, removing unneeded protocols and services, and properly configuring all native security controls. Some of the important issues related to specific OS lockdown procedures are discussed later in this chapter.

Second, it is wise to place the Web server behind a protective barrier, such as a firewall or a reverse proxy. Anything that will limit, restrict, filter, or control traffic into and out of the Web server reduces the means by which malicious users can attack the system.

Third, administrators must lock down the Web server itself. This process actually has numerous facets, each of which is important to maintaining a secure Web server. These topics are discussed in the following sections.

DMZ vs. Stronghold

There are two general lines of thought when it comes to Web server security. One is to assume that the Web server will be compromised and to plan accordingly. The other is to try to prevent any and all possible attacks at all costs. The first philosophy utilizes a deployment design called a *demilitarized zone (DMZ);* the second relies on a design referred to as a *stronghold.*

A DMZ is a networking area where your Web server (and other servers that are accessible via the public Internet) is secured from most known common exploits, but it is known to be insecure at some level. Because the DMZ is a separate network, the internal network remains more secure. A DMZ assumes that the time and money required to protect against every possible attack are too great an expense to offset the value of the data hosted on the Web server.

> **NOTE**
>
> Microsoft uses the term *screened subnet* to refer to the DMZ in some of its documentation. You'll also hear the same concept called a *perimeter network.*

To compensate for the lack of front-line security, organizations that deploy a DMZ configuration typically have a duplicate Web server positioned on their internal LAN that maintains a mirror image of the publicly accessible Web server. In the event that the primary Web server is compromised, the mirror backup can be repositioned to act as the public Web server until the primary system is repaired. Other companies employ an even less expensive solution by maintaining only tape backups of the primary Web server. Such a company might assume the time and money lost while its Web server is offline will not significantly impact the organization. It also might assume that the value of its Web presence does not justify a more fault-tolerant solution, such as the expense of creating and maintaining a backup system.

A *stronghold* is a networking area where the Web server is protected from all known exploits and significant effort is expended to protect against unknown new exploits. A stronghold assumes that the data hosted on the Web server is valuable enough to spare no expense in protecting it. This type of configuration is often deployed by organizations whose Web server integrity and availability are essential to doing business, such as e-commerce sites.

Each organization must choose the protection policy that is appropriate to its situation and that fits its needs best. A DMZ deployment is cheaper but more prone to attack than a stronghold. A stronghold deployment is more expensive than a DMZ but will repel most attacks.

Isolating the Web Server

For security purposes, the Web server should be separated and isolated from the internal LAN. Otherwise, if the Web server is compromised, the attacker could get a free ticket into the entire network. Separating the Web server from the production internal network prevents Web attacks from becoming organization killers.

Separating the Web server from the LAN can take many forms, such as:

- Deploying a separate domain just for the Web server and its supporting services

- Using a Web-in-a-box solution that has no other capabilities than Web page service

- Colocating Web servers at an ISP

- Outsourcing Web services to an ISP or other third party

No matter what method an organization chooses, it is also wise to consider creating a sideband communication channel for all management, administration, and file transfer activities. A sideband communication channel can be as simple as using a unique protocol between your LAN and the Web server and preventing (blocking via unbinding) TCP/IP from crossing that link. A sideband channel could be a dialup link, a dedicated ISDN line, or even a direct-connect serial port link. Using a sideband channel restricts the traffic that can flow between the Web server and the internal network. This system could dampen the speed or the capabilities of remote administration; however, it greatly reduces the possibility that a malicious user can cross over from a compromised Web server to the LAN.

If security is of utmost importance, organizations can deploy a firewall on the sideband channel or eliminate direct communication completely. If the administrator must be physically present at the Web server and must transfer data to and from it using removable media (CD-Rs, CD-RWs, Zip or Jaz drives, or the like), this completely eliminates the possibility of a malicious user employing the Web server as a bridge into the LAN.

Web Server Lockdown

Locking down the Web server itself follows a path that begins in a way that should already be familiar to you: applying the latest patches and updates from the vendor. Once this task is accomplished, the network administrator should follow the vendor's recommendations for securely configuring Web sites. The following sections discuss typical recommendations made by Web server vendors and security professionals.

Managing Access Control

Many Web servers, such as IIS on Windows NT and Windows 2000, use a named user account to authenticate anonymous Web visitors. When a Web visitor accesses a Web site using this methodology, the Web server automatically logs that user on as the IIS user account. The visiting user remains anonymous, but the host server platform uses the IIS user account to control access. This account grants system administrators granular access control on a Web server.

These specialized Web user accounts should have their access restricted so they cannot log on locally nor access anything outside the Web root. Additionally, administrators should be very careful about granting these accounts the ability to write to files or execute programs; this should be done only when absolutely necessary. If other named user accounts are allowed to log on over the Web, it is essential that these accounts not be the same user accounts employed to log onto the internal network. In other words, if employees will log on via the Web using their own credentials instead of the anonymous Web user account, administrators should create special accounts for those employees to use just for Web logon. Authorizations over the Internet should be considered insecure unless strong encryption mechanisms are in place to protect them. SSL can be used to protect Web traffic; however, the protection it offers is not significant enough to justify using internal accounts on the Internet.

Handling Directory and Data Structures

Planning the hierarchy or structure of the Web root is an important part of securing a Web server. The root is the highest level web in the hierarchy that consists of webs nested within webs. Whenever possible, Web server administrators should place all Web content within the Web root. All the Web information (the Web pages written in HTML, graphics files, sound files, and so on) is normally stored in folders and directories on the Web server. Administrators can create *virtual directories,* which are folders that are not contained within the Web server hierarchy (they can be on a completely different computer) but appear to the user to be part of that hierarchy. Another way of providing access to data that is on another computer is *mapping* drives or folders. These methods allow administrators to store files where they are most easily updated or take advantage of extra drive space on other computers. However, mapping drives, mapping folders, or creating virtual directories can result in easier access for intruders if the Web server's security is compromised. It is especially important not to map drives from other systems on the internal network.

If users accessing these webs must have access to materials on another system, such as a database, it is best to deploy a duplicate server within the Web server's DMZ or domain. That duplicate server should contain only a backup, not the primary working copy of the database. The duplicate server should also be configured so that no Web user or Web process can alter or write to its data store. Database updates should come only from the protected server within the internal network. If data from Web sessions must be recorded into the database, it is best to configure a sideband connection from the Web zone back to the primary server system for data transfers. Administrators should also spend considerable effort verifying the validity of input data before adding it to the database server.

Scripting Vulnerabilities

Maintaining a secure Web server means ensuring that all scripts and Web applications deployed on the Web server are free from Trojans, backdoors, or other malicious code. Many scripts are available on the Internet for the use of Web developers. However, scripts downloaded from external sources are more susceptible to coding problems than those developed in house. If it is necessary to use external programming code sources, developers and administrators should employ quality assurance tests to search for out-of-place system calls, extra code, and unnecessary functions. These hidden segments of malevolent code are called *logic bombs.*

One logic bomb to watch out for occurs within Internet Server Application Programming Interface (ISAPI) scripts. The command **RevertToSelf()** allows the script to execute any following commands at a system-level security context. In a properly designed script, this command should never be used. If this command is present, the code has been altered, or was designed by a malicious or inexperienced coder. The presence of such a command enables attacks on a Web server through the submission of certain URL syntax constructions to launch a logic bomb.

Logging Activity

Logging, auditing, or monitoring the activity on your Web server becomes more important as the value of the data stored on the server increases. The monitoring process should focus on attempts to perform actions that are atypical for a Web user. These actions include, among others:

- Attempting to execute scripts
- Trying to write files
- Attempting to access files outside the Web root

The more traffic your Web server supports, the more difficult it becomes to review the audit trails. An automated solution is needed when time required to review log files exceeds the time administrators have available for that task. Intrusion detection systems are automated monitoring tools that look for abnormal or malicious activity on a system. An IDS can simply scan for problems and notify administrators or actively repel attacks once they are detected.

Backups

Unfortunately, every administrator should assume that the Web server will be compromised at some point and that the data hosted on it will be destroyed, copied, or corrupted. This assumption will not become a reality in all cases, but planning for the worst is always the best security practice. A reliable backup mechanism must be in place to protect the Web server from failure. This mechanism can be a real-time mirror server to back up the primary Web server or just a daily backup to tape. Either way, a backup is the only insurance available that allows a return to normal operations within a reasonable amount of time. If security is as much maintaining availability as it is maintaining confidentiality, backups should be part of any organization's security policy.

Maintaining Integrity

Locking down the Web server is only one step in the security process. It is also necessary to maintain that security over time. Sustaining a secure environment requires monitoring the system for anomalies, applying new patches when they are available, and adjusting security configurations to match the ever-changing needs of the internal and external Web community. If a security breach occurs, the organization should reevaluate previous security decisions and implementations. Administrators could have overlooked a security hole because of ignorance, or they might have simply misconfigured some security control.

Rogue Web Servers

There is one thing worse for a network administrator than having a Web server and knowing that it is not 100-percent secure, even after locking it down, and that is having a Web server on the network that you're not aware exists. These are sometimes called *rogue Web servers,* and they can come about in two ways. It is possible that a technically savvy user on the network has configured Web services on his or her machine. More often, however, rogue Web servers are deployed unintentionally. Many operating systems include Web server software and install it as part of the default OS installation. If administrators aren't careful, when they install Windows (especially a member of the Server family) on a network computer, they can create a new Web server without even realizing it's there. When a Web server is present on a network without the knowledge of network administrators, no one will take all the precautions necessary to secure that system. This makes the system (and through it, the entire network) vulnerable to every out-of-the-box exploit and attack for that Web server.

Crimestoppers...

Hunting Down Rogue Web Servers

To check a system to see if a local Web server is running without your knowledge, you can use a Web browser to access http://localhost/. If no Web server is running, you should see an error stating that you are unable to access the Web server. If you see any other message or a Web page (including a message advising that the page is under construction or coming soon), you are running a Web server locally. Once you discover the existence of such a server, you must either secure it or remove or disable it. Otherwise, the system will remain insecure.

Understanding Security and Microsoft Operating Systems

Microsoft is one of the leading vendors of server and desktop operating systems. Almost everyone has heard of or used some version of Windows. However, even with Microsoft's widespread use, the company's track record for security has been less than spotless. (Of course, the same is true for every other operating system.)

Fortunately, Microsoft has initiated several programs to improve its security structure and to help end users deploy its products more securely.

In late 2001, Microsoft launched its Strategic Technology Protection Program (STPP), which focuses on training end users to securely deploy Microsoft products. STPP has improved reporting of security issues to the user community and produced a security toolkit. This toolkit includes all the service packs and security-related hot fixes as well as security utilities and documentation for Windows NT 4.0 and Windows 2000. Once Windows .NET is available, the toolkit will be expanded to include .NET materials as well.

In early 2002, Microsoft initiated its internal Trustworthy Computing campaign. This campaign focuses on availability, security, and privacy. The company's initial goal is to review the code for all its current products and to develop processes to ensure better security in future products and upgrades.

General Microsoft Security Issues

Before discussing Windows version-specific issues, we need to look at several security problems that exist across most, if not all, of Microsoft's current product line: Windows 95, Windows 98/SE/Me, Windows NT 4.0, Windows 2000, and Windows XP.

NetBIOS

Sytek developed NetBIOS for IBM to enable PCs to communicate over a LAN. Microsoft adopted NetBIOS as its primary intranetwork (LAN) communication mechanism. NetBIOS uses low overhead and operates very efficiently, but it cannot be routed and offers no security. Early versions of Windows depended on NetBIOS for name resolution. Windows XP and Windows 2000 can both operate without NetBIOS in a Windows 2000 native-mode domain (using Active Directory), but NetBIOS is still enabled by default to ensure backward compatibility with Windows 9x and Windows NT systems.

When NetBIOS is removed from a system that does not have support for or access to an Active Directory domain, such systems lose most of their abilities to share resources. For this reason, it might be necessary to enable NetBIOS on internal network interfaces on most Windows systems. When securing a Microsoft Windows system, an important step in implementing security is to disable or unbind NetBIOS from any Internet or external interfaces, if not from entire systems. When in doubt, test your changes in a lab environment before making wholesale changes to production systems and networks.

Widespread Automated Functionality

Microsoft is often a leader in innovation in regard to the features and capabilities it packs into Windows. Unfortunately, many such capabilities and features increase usability and convenience but don't offer security or are inherently insecure. Microsoft has taken steps on some features to provide secure alternatives. For example, New Technology File System (NTFS), a securable file system, is available on Windows NT, 2000, and XP. Only the file allocation table (FAT) file system, which is much less secure, is available on Windows 9*x* systems.

Some capabilities included in Windows open significant security holes that are difficult to fill. For example, Windows XP is vulnerable to at least two serious security problems. One is related to Universal Plug and Play (UPnP) and the other to raw sockets. UPnP was designed to allow automatic detection, installation, and configuration of hardware devices, both local and over the network. However, the process involved in doing this opens connection ports that a malicious Internet user could exploit. For more information about this vulnerability and to download the patches, see the Microsoft Web site at www.microsoft.com/technet/treeview/default.asp?url=/technet/security/bulletin/MS01-059.asp.

> **NOTE**
>
> Raw sockets are not a "feature" unique to Windows or to XP. UNIX, VMS, Linux, and Mac OS X also have raw sockets capability. In fact, Windows 2000 included raw sockets as well. One reason so much attention has been paid to raw sockets in XP is the fact that XP Home Edition is aimed at consumers, whereas the other operating systems are used primarily in business environments. Another reason is the fact that XP makes the feature available to all users. (with Windows 2000 and non-Windows operating systems, only administrators have raw socket access.) This became such a public issue that in 2001, the State of New York passed a law banning the use of raw sockets when using the Internet (see www.kumite.com/rsnbrgr/rob/grcspoof/cnn).

Raw sockets are a feature of the TCP/IP stack that was originally developed as a research tool, and was never intended for real-world production environment systems. Basically, raw sockets allow a TCP/IP stack to be bypassed and grant direct access to the network's data transport layer. This capability makes possible IP address spoofing and SYN floods (both common Internet attacks). Microsoft included raw sockets in its TCP/IP stack for Windows 2000 and XP, because this feature is used by XP's new Internet Connection Firewall. This addition opened up a firestorm of controversy. For information about the security risks inherent in raw sockets, see Steve Gibson's article at http://grc.com/dos/xpsummary.htm. For Microsoft's response to critics regarding its implementation of raw sockets, see its Web site at www.microsoft.com/technet/treeview/default.asp?url=/TechNet/security/news/raw_sockets.asp.

These are two examples of problems created by adding features to Windows. Some of these feature-caused security issues have been resolved by patches from Microsoft. Others require third-party solutions or the deployment of a firewall to restrict access to the vulnerable systems.

IRDP Vulnerability

The Internet Control Message Protocol (ICMP) Router Discovery Protocol (IRDP) is used to detect and configure default gateway addresses on DHCP clients. It is enabled by default on Windows 9*x* DHCP clients and is present but disabled by default on Windows 2000 DHCP clients. IRDP does not use any type of authentication, so attackers can exploit this protocol. The most common attack using IRDP is to send a default route entry to the victim. This attack can then be used to facilitate traffic logging (routing traffic through a system that records every packet that passes it), man-in-the-middle attacks (acting as an imposter or as a proxy for a secured connection), and denial-of-service attacks (routing all traffic to wrong addresses).

The IRDP exploitation is prevalent on broadband connections such as cable modems. Protection from IRDP attacks include:

- Blocking ICMP Type 9 and 10 packets with a firewall
- Disabling IRDP through the registry (for Windows 95/98, see the Q216141 article at http://support.microsoft.com/default.aspx?scid=kb;EN-US;q216141; for Windows 2000, see the Q269734 article at http://support.microsoft.com/default.aspx?scid=kb;EN-US;q269734)

NIC Bindings

Microsoft Windows operating systems use a mechanism known as *binding* to associate specific services and protocols with particular network interfaces. A network interface can be any port into or out of the computer, including a NIC, a modem, or even a serial port. By default, Windows enables every possible binding when the OS is first installed and when a new interface or new service or protocol is installed. This is done to ensure that everything "just works"—it's easier and more convenient for less knowledgeable users than having to troubleshoot communications problems and enable the correct bindings. However, it also opens up security holes, so each time a significant change is made to a system, you should reinspect the bindings to make sure no unwanted bindings are enabled.

One of the most common problems arising from this situation occurs when a system is connected to a broadband communication device for the first time. Windows automatically binds TCP/IP to the new interface as well as the Microsoft Networking service and File and Print Services. This effectively transforms a "standalone" system into a member of a network comprising other systems on the local broadband segment. This situation poses a significant security risk. To return the system to a more secure configuration, you must disable the bindings for every service and protocol other than TCP/IP on the new Internet interface.

NOTE

It is important to educate users in regard to the fact that any computer with an Internet connection—even a standard analog dialup connection—is no longer truly a standalone system; it is a member of a network—the biggest network of them all.

Securing Windows 9x Computers

Maintaining a secure environment requires the use of secure clients as well as servers. For networks using Windows 9x clients, creating a secure environment can be difficult, if not impossible. Windows 9x was intended as a consumer (home) operating system and includes few significant security controls and features. However, because the cost is lower than for Microsoft's business-oriented client operating systems (NT Workstation and 2000 and XP Professional), many businesses use Windows 9x machines as desktop clients. To maintain a semblance of security with Windows 9x systems, you must maintain absolute control over physical access. If physical access is controlled, reasonable online communications security can be implemented. Here are some steps administrators should take after physically securing the systems:

1. Install the latest patches and upgrades from Microsoft.

2. Configure the systems to use Windows Family Logon. Windows Family Logon restricts logons to only existing user accounts.

3. Configure the system *not* to store passwords locally. By default, passwords are stored in a password cache (a .pwl file).

4. Use System Policies to restrict access to Control Panel applets, especially those used to install new protocols and services or to alter the configuration of the system.

Since Windows 9x systems are fairly insecure, they are a poor client choice for environments that handle highly confidential data. If they must be used in these environments, administrators should restrict users on these clients to the minimal access necessary to complete their work tasks. (Actually, this is the best policy in a high-security environment, regardless of the client OS.) Keep in mind that Windows 9x uses an insecure encryption algorithm for authentication (LAN Manager authentication) and uses only the insecure FAT file system. If confidential information is stored on a Windows 9x client, even in the paging file, it can be easily extracted.

Crimestoppers...

Encrypting Data on Windows 9x Computers

Although Windows 9x and FAT do not support EFS, the file encryption scheme used by Windows 2000/XP, third-party products are available that allow you to encrypt data stored on a Windows 9x computer. These include the following:

- SecureAction Advanced Encryption Package 2002: www.secureaction.com/encryption_pro

- Cryptainer PE: www.sharewarejunkies.com/02zwd5/cryptainer.htm

- EasyCrypt: www.easycrypt.co.uk

Many shareware and freeware programs are available that provide file encryption for 9x systems. See www.tucows.com/system/fileencryption95.html for more information.

If a Windows 9*x* client is deployed in a Windows 2000 Active Directory domain, you can elect to disable NetBIOS on the client if you install the Active Directory Client Extensions for Windows 95/98. This security upgrade is found on the Windows 2000 Server distribution CD and the Microsoft Web site (www.microsoft.com/windows2000/server/evaluation/news/bulletins/ adextension.asp). This add-on grants Windows 9*x* systems Active Directory site awareness, Windows 2000 domain logon, Active Directory service interfaces, distributed file system (Dfs) client, access to Windows Address Book, and NT Lan Manager (NTLM) v.2. This add-on does not add Kerberos, support for Group Policy, support for Intellimirror, IPSec, L2TP, service provider naming, or mutual authentication.

The measures that must be taken for securing a Windows 9*x* system are as follows:

- Apply the latest service pack and related hot fixes.

- Disable the Dial-Up Server to prevent incoming connection attempts over dialup modems or an Internet link.

- Disable file and printer sharing.

- Unbind or remove extraneous protocols.

- Use strong passwords.

- Enable Windows Family Logon.

- Do not elect to save passwords, disable password caching, and delete the .pwl password file.

- Do not download and install drivers or software that are not digitally signed.

- Perform regular backups and secure the backup media.

- Install and update antivirus software.

- Use third-party add-ons or hardware to provide additional security.

The actual process of securing Windows 9*x* clients is even more detailed. Fortunately, Microsoft maintains a useful security checklist for Windows 95, 98, 98 SE, and Me clients at www.microsoft.com/Education/?ID=Windows9xSecurity. It is highly recommended that all administrators review this checklist before deploying Windows 9*x* in a production network where security is a concern.

Securing a Windows NT 4.0 Network

The good news is that Windows NT 4.0 is significantly more secure than Windows 9*x* systems. Windows NT employs NTLM to protect logon authentication, which is reasonably secure, and it supports the NTFS file system, system policies, password policies, user rights policies, auditing, and other security features. However, the bad news is that Windows NT is not without its own security problems. For example, all Windows NT systems have two well-known user accounts: administrator and guest. Neither of these accounts can be deleted (although the guest account can be disabled and in fact is disabled by default in NT Workstation but not in NT Server). Both default accounts can be renamed; this should be done immediately after installing the OS. Otherwise, hackers already have half the information (user account name and password) they need to access the system. Another problem is that the default guest account is assigned a blank password by default. Both of these built-in accounts should be assigned strong passwords, and the Guest account should be disabled if it is not needed.

Right out of the box, Windows NT is vulnerable to hundreds of attacks, including denial of service, privilege elevation, and code execution. Fortunately, many of these vulnerabilities are removed through the application of Service Pack 6a and the subsequent post-SP6a hot fixes.

The measures that must be taken to secure a Windows NT system include:

- Format all partitions with NTFS to allow administrators to assign file-level access permissions and take advantage of the security advantages of NTFS.

- Assign strong passwords to Administrator and Guest accounts and disable the Guest account if it is not needed.

- Disable unnecessary protocols and services (see the "On the Scene" sidebar later in this section for a list of services that may be disabled).

- Disable unneeded accounts, including the Guest account.

- Tighten permissions on system directories.

- Prevent anonymous Registry access.

- Set access control lists (ACLs) in the registry.

- Restrict access to Local Security Authority (LSA) information.

- Enable SYSKEY to protect the Security Accounts Manager (SAM) database, which includes account passwords.

- Disable LAN Manager authentication.

- Set the paging file to clear during shutdown.

- Set strong password policies.

- Set an account lockout policy to shut users out after a reasonable number of failed logon attempts (three to five) due to incorrect password entry.

- Create Administrator account decoys by renaming the real default Administrator account to something innocuous, and create an account called Administrator that has highly restricted access and privileges.

- Remove unneeded resource shares and change the default permissions (which give the Everyone group full control) on newly created shares.

- Use the "least privileged" axiom on all ACLs.

- Restrict access to removable media to interactive users only (those logged on locally, physically sitting at the computer).

- Restrict user rights. This is a different issue from permissions; permissions are assigned to control access to individual resources such as files or printers, whereas user rights control what users can do systemwide, such as the right to create shares or the right to shut down the system.

- Configure security auditing. Many activities can be audited, including logon attempts, changes made to user/group accounts, system shutdowns, and even access to individual files and objects. Auditing everything would use a great deal of resources and create an audit log that would be huge and difficult to review, so it's important to carefully consider which events to audit.

- Hide the last username at logon. This is done by editing the Registry; instructions for doing so are at www.winguides.com/registry/display.php/1.

- Remove network access for all users if the machine is a client that does not need to share its resources. This is done through the User Manager tool, by editing user rights policies.

- Maintain the emergency repair disk (ERD) and keep it secure.

- Perform regular backups and secure the backup media (including off-site storage of backups).

- Install and update antivirus software.

- Apply the latest service packs and applicable hot fixes.

For details on these security issues, see the security checklists for Windows NT maintained by Microsoft. These checklists are designed to simplify the tedious task of locking down new and existing deployments of Windows NT 4.0 Workstation and Server (member server and domain controller). These checklists can be found on the Microsoft Web site at www.microsoft.com/technet/ treeview/default.asp?url=/technet/security/tools/tools.asp (located halfway down the page under the Security Checklists heading).

On the Scene...

Which Network Services Can Be Disabled?

Some of the NT services that can present security vulnerabilities are listed here. Services that are not needed can be stopped and disabled through Services applet in Control Panel:

- Alerter Service
- ClipBook Server
- Computer Browser
- DHCP Client (if the system has a static IP address)
- Directory Replicator
- FTP Publishing Service
- IIS Admin Service
- IPSec Policy Agent
- Messenger
- Net Logon
- Network DDE
- Network DDE: DSDM
- Plug and Play
- Remote Procedure Call (RPC) Locator
- Remote Registry Service
- RIP Service
- RunAs Service

Continued

- Server Service
- Simple TCP/IP Services (if installed)
- SNMP Trap Service
- Spooler
- TCPIP NetBIOS Helper
- Telephony Service
- Tracking Client
- Workstation
- World Wide Web Publishing Service

Some of these services are needed for connecting the NT computer to a Windows 2000 domain, and some are required by certain applications, so disable only those that are not being used.

Securing a Windows 2000 Network

Windows 2000 is a significant step forward for Microsoft in terms of operating system security. Windows 2000 boasts more security features than all previous versions of Windows combined. It includes support for Kerberos and smart cards for secured authentication and supports various encryption services, such as SSL, Private Communication Technology (PCT), Distributed Password Authentication (DPA), TLS, IPSec, L2TP, and others, for secured communications. However, just as with Windows NT, Windows 2000 has numerous security flaws right out of the box. Many of these flaws have been addressed in service packs and hot fixes. So, once again, a key element in securing the OS includes application of the latest service packs and hot fixes.

Many of the security features from Windows NT that required registry editing are now defined security controls within Windows 2000 Group Policy. The use of Group Policy has greatly simplified security management for large networks by centralizing security controls and application mechanisms.

Many of the security lapses in Windows NT, such as insecure ACLs on system folders, are corrected in Windows 2000. In many cases, locking down Windows 2000 requires less overall effort than was required to do so for Windows NT.

The measures that must be taken to secure a Windows 2000 system include:

- Format all partitions with NTFS.
- Assign strong passwords to Administrator and Guest accounts.

- Disable unnecessary services.

- Disable unneeded accounts, including the Guest account.

- Set ACLs on files and folders.

- Set ACLs in the Registry.

- Set paging file to clear during shutdown.

- Set strong password policies

- Set the account lockout policy. Both password and lockout policies are now set through a Group Policy object; if the computer is a member of a Windows 2000 domain, domain policies override local security policies.

- Create Administrator account decoys.

- Remove unneeded resource shares.

- Use the "least privileged" axiom on all ACLs.

- Restrict access to removable media to local interactive users only.

- Restrict user rights (set through Group Policy; as with account and password policies, domain policies override local settings).

- Configure auditing. Security auditing must be enabled through Group Policy on Windows 2000 machines.

- Hide the last username at logon.

- Perform regular backups and secure the backup media.

- Install and update antivirus software.

- Apply the latest service packs and applicable hot fixes.

For details on these security issues, see the security checklists for Windows 2000 maintained by Microsoft. These checklists are designed to simplify the tedious task of locking down new and existing deployments of Windows 2000 Professional and Server (member server and domain controller). These checklists can be found on the Microsoft Web site at www.microsoft.com/technet/treeview/default.asp?url=/technet/security/tools/tools.asp (located halfway down the page under the Security Checklists heading).

The National Security Agency (NSA) provides a set of guidelines for securing Windows NT and Windows 2000 servers. See http://nsa2.www.conxion.com/index.html.

Windows .NET: The Future of Windows Security

Windows .NET promises to be another significant step forward for Microsoft when it comes to system security. It builds on the security foundations laid by Windows 2000 and then goes further. Although Windows .NET is still in beta development at the time of this writing, Microsoft is boasting about several improvements that are to be included in this new operating system, such as:

- Common Language Runtime (CLR), which is a software engine that checks digital signatures, source code origins, and code alterations to prevent malicious code from executing or prevent programming or corruption errors from causing problems

- Secured wireless and Ethernet LANs through authentication and authorization of connected systems and users based on the IEEE 802.1*x* protocols

- Software restriction policies to control what software can be executed on a system

- A default locked-down configuration for installations of IIS 6.0

- Encryption of the Offline Files database and cached files

- A FIPS-compliant kernel-mode Crypto module to facilitate the use of high-end encryption services

Because of the new focus on security through Microsoft's STPP and Trusted Computing initiatives, Windows .NET Server is well on its way to providing a reasonably secure environment right out of the box. For more information on the security features of Windows .NET Server, please see the Microsoft Web site at www.microsoft.com/windows.netserver/evaluation/overview/technologies/security.asp.

Understanding Security and UNIX/Linux Operating Systems

UNIX and Linux systems seem to have a reputation for being more secure than Windows operating systems. To some extent, this reputation might be justified, but UNIX and Linux have a significant number of unique security vulnerabilities as well as sharing some common vulnerabilities with Windows OSs. Remember: No operating system is without security problems. Since UNIX has been around for more than 20 years, it has already been through numerous attack and repair cycles. For that reason, its current manifestations are generally more secure than many Windows OSs. Linux is based on UNIX architecture and is a fairly new OS (it's a little over 10 years old; version 0.02 was released in 1991). It is generally more secure than Windows for two reasons: It lacks several of the biggest pitfalls of Windows (such as support for NetBIOS) and it is less a target for attackers who prefer to concentrate on developing attacks for the mostly widely deployed operating systems, which means Windows. Nonetheless, both UNIX and Linux still have security problems.

For example, the passwd program used by some versions of UNIX *appears* to require somewhat secure passwords: that is, it requires passwords that contain at least five letters (or four characters if numerals or symbols are included). But this requirement is an illusion, because the program will accept a shorter password if the user enters it three times—thus overriding the "requirement."

Many UNIX machines use accounts with names such as *lpq* or *date* that are used to execute simple commands without requiring users to log in. Often such accounts have blank passwords and a user ID of 0, which means they execute with superuser permissions. This is a big security hole because anyone can use these accounts, including hackers who might replace the command that is supposed to be run by the account with one of his or her own commands.

When securing a deployment of UNIX or Linux, the following measures must be taken. This list is not exhaustive and does not apply to every version of UNIX or Linux:

- Apply the latest updates and security patches.

- Use strong passwords.

- Implement password aging.

- Implement a shadow password file.

- Eliminate unused accounts, and set expiration dates on temporary accounts.

- Disable unused guest accounts.

- Eliminate shared accounts. This is a type of "group account" that differs from the security groups used on Windows, NetWare, and UNIX systems. The latter contains user accounts; the UNIX shared group account is a single account that many different people use—often members of a team working together on a particular project. Instead of using group accounts, the user accounts should be placed in groups by editing the /etc/group file.

- Be careful about implementing the "trusted hosts" concepts. They allow users to designate host computers that are to be considered trusted, so the users will not have to enter a password every time they use the network. This system can be exploited, so the best security practice is to disallow trusted hosts. If trusted hosts are allowed, only local hosts should be trusted; remote hosts should never be trusted. (Trusted hosts are listed in the /etc/hosts.equiv file.)

- Remove the "secure" designation from all terminals, so that the root account can't log in from unsecure terminals, even with the password. Authorized users will still be able to use the **su** command to become a superuser.

- Ensure that NFS security is enabled. Some UNIX implementations have no NFS security features enabled by default, which means that any Internet host (including untrusted hosts) can access files via NFS.

- Disallow anonymous FTP unless it is necessary.

- Disallow shell scripts that have the *setuid* or *setgid* permission bits set on them. (See the "The Dangers of SetUID and SetGID" sidebar in this section for information about these permission bits.)

- Set the sticky bit on directories to prevent users from deleting or renaming other users' files.

- Set default file permissions so group/world read/write access is not granted.

- Write-protect the root account startup files and home directory.

- Use only secured applications and service daemons. Secure NFS, NIS, X Window, and so on. Disable the **r** commands if they are not used.

- Remove unnecessary services and protocols. You can remove unneeded services by editing the /etc/inetd.conf and /etc/rc.conf files.

- Log all connections to network services, and use TCP wrapper to track connections.

- Prevent DNS hostname spoofing.

- Set appropriate permissions on all files.

- Employ packet filtering.

- For remote logins, use a secured shell instead of Telnet, FTP, RLOGIN, RSH, and so on.

- For file encryption, use add-on programs that use strong algorithms (such as 3DES) rather than the standard UNIX **crypt** command, which is easily broken.

- Ensure that device files such as /dev/kmem, /dev/mem and /dev/drum cannot be read by the world. Most device files should be owned by user "root."

- Use the **who** command to determine who is currently logged into the system. This command displays the contents of the /etc/utmp file, which lists login name, terminal, login time, and remote host of each logged-in user. Use the **last** command to display a log of each login session (including FTP sessions) as well as the time of each shutdown and reboot. The /etc/security scripts that run daily can be used to monitor security-related events.

- Run the syslog daemon (syslogd) in secure mode to prevent receiving forged UDP datagrams from other systems.

- If you are not using programs that require RPC, disable the port daemon.

- Sendmail is enabled by default on some UNIX systems. Turn it off if you don't need it. If you are using Sendmail, be sure it has the latest patches and ensure that spammers can't use your system to relay spam.

On the Scene…

The Dangers of SetUID and SetGID

SetUID and SetGID are UNIX programs that allow programs to run with additional permissions that the user running the program doesn't have. (Generally, an application runs with the same permissions as the user who executes it.) When a program is given the SetUID or SetGID permissions, it runs as the user or group that owns the program file. Usually this means the program runs with the permissions of the root user. Root is the master user account on a UNIX system that has complete control over the system (similar to the Administrator account on Windows computers). Hackers can exploit SetUID and SetGID to access resources they shouldn't be able to access.

For a detailed step-by-step description of locking down a UNIX or Linux system, see the excellent UNIX security checklist on the CERT Web site at www.cert.org/tech_tips/unix_security_checklist2.0.html. A good Linux security checklist can be found on the University of Georgia Web site at www.eits.uga .edu/wsg/security/linuxdetails.html.

If the X Window graphical interface is used on UNIX systems, it should be secured. See http://ciac.llnl.gov/ciac/documents/ciac2316.html for information on securing X Window.

Understanding Security and Macintosh Operating Systems

Over 85 percent of computers in the world are Windows-based. Macintosh systems make up a few percentage points of the 15 percent that remain. This means that most of the malicious activity on the Internet and elsewhere is focused on systems other than Macintosh, so Macintosh systems enjoy an unintended form of security through obscurity. In addition, versions of Macintosh prior to OS X did not have an easily accessible (or easy to use) command-line interface, nor did they use standard networking services with which hackers are familiar. However, that does not mean a Macintosh user can rest on Apple's laurels. Macintosh systems are still vulnerable to several security exploits, such as denial of service, port scanning, and viruses.

Protecting from these exploits requires following security practices that are common to all operating systems, including taking the following measures:

- Apply the latest updates and security patches.

- Use strong passwords.

- Eliminate unused accounts, and set expiration dates on temporary accounts.

- Remove unnecessary services and protocols (by editing the inetd.conf file or using the NetInfo GUI).

- Log all connections to network services.

- Set access permissions on files and folders.

- Disable file sharing.

- Remove unneeded resource shares.

- Configure auditing.

- Perform regular backups and secure the backup media.

- Install and update antivirus software (Symantec and McAfee make OS X versions).

- Use nonadministrative accounts for nonadministrative activities.

- Use a firewall to filter traffic.

In 2001, Apple released the new Macintosh operating system, OS X. More than just the latest version of the Macintosh operating system in a string of upgrades, OS X is a completely rewritten OS based on the UNIX OS FreeBSD. Apple calls its implementation of BSD *Darwin* and has made it an open source project. OS X is more like UNIX than it is like OS 8 or 9. This is a positive move in terms of stability and security, but it also means Mac users will encounter new security issues. In addition, many utilities, programs, and services previously available only on UNIX systems are now or will soon be available for OS X. Thus, maintaining vigilance is essential to the long-term security of an OS X system.

OS X has some security advantages compared with many other UNIX implementations. Many of its network services (Telnet, HTTPD, Sendmail, and the like) are turned off by default, and the root account has to be specifically enabled before it can be used. However, some security measures should be taken specific to OS X, including:

- Deselect the "Automatically log in" option in the System Preferences | Login panel (on the Login Window tab) and ensure that the Login window is set to display as "name and password entry fields," rather than displaying a list of the user accounts on the computer.

- Set the screen saver to ask for authentication information (through the Screen Savers panel of System Preferences).

- Remove the SetUID and SetGID permission bits from the RCP, RDUMP, RRESTORE, RLOGIN, and RSH utilities, or remove these utilities if they aren't used.

- Review the files in legacy directories (those that were already on a Mac OS 9 machine prior to upgrading to OS X) and change the permissions; by default, files and folders used by the Classic environment have read and write permissions assigned to the world.

- Upgrade inetd, the "super server" that listens for attempts to connect to Internet services that are in the NetInfo database, to a more secure service such as xinetd (freeware available from Xindetd.org).

- Configure the IPFW firewall included in OS X; for easier configuration, install Brickhouse, a graphical interface for creating rule sets.

- Use a file integrity checker that supports OS X (such as Osiris) to track system changes.

To stay abreast of the security concerns for Macintosh systems, visit the Apple Web site at www.info.apple.com/usen/macosx and the Macintosh Security Site at www.securemac.com.

Understanding Mainframe Security

Mainframes remain a significant presence in many educational and research environments. Mainframes offer significant computing power, rigid access controls, and the ability to employ thin clients in a host-terminal configuration. Traditionally, mainframes have been less vulnerable than personal computers to security breaches, but that was when access to the mainframe was only through in-house terminals. Now Internet connectivity and the addition of more features (such as Web server and e-commerce capabilities) has opened up mainframe systems to many of the same problems that plague administrators of PC-based networks. To maintain the security of a mainframe environment, the following measures must be taken:

- Apply the latest updates and security patches.

- Use strong passwords.

- Eliminate unused accounts, and set expiration dates on temporary accounts.

- Remove unnecessary services and protocols.

- Log all connections to network services.

- Set access permissions on files and folders.

- Configure auditing.

- Perform regular backups and secure the backup media.

- Install and update antivirus software.

- Use nonadministrative accounts for nonadministrative activities.

- Use a firewall to filter traffic.

- Secure the links between the mainframe and remote clients.

Mainframe security products include Computer Associates' Top Secret and IBM's Resource Access Control Facility (RACF). For more information about Top Secret, see http://rr.sans.org/main/top_secret.php. For information about RACF, see www-1.ibm.com/servers/eserver/zseries/zos/racf/overview.html.

Understanding Wireless Security

The ability to stay connected to your network while roaming around the office, not tied down by a cable, has gained widespread popularity very quickly. Wireless networking technologies have been around for nearly a decade, but only recently have wireless capabilities and throughput begun to approach that of traditional wirebound networking solutions. This surge in efficacy has convinced many network administrators to deploy this simple and reasonably priced technology. The cost of wireless NICs has fallen below $100 and access ports are only about twice that. This means anyone, even home users, can plug a port into an Ethernet jack on a hub, install a wireless NIC, and have fully functional wireless networking with little or no additional configuration.

The goals of wireless security are the same as within a wired network: authentication of users and computers: providing confidentiality of data and ensuring data integrity. However, wireless presents special challenges because the signals pass through the airwaves, using radio frequencies. This makes eavesdropping easier in a wireless LAN (WLAN) than in a cabled network.

Most wireless networking technologies are based on the 802.11b standard. Although this standard does define several security mechanisms to protect wireless traffic, there are numerous exploits to circumvent or crack the restrictions. Unfortunately, the wireless access ports are usually connected to an internal network behind the firewall. This effectively grants external users with the right equipment nearly the same type of access as they would enjoy if they were able to plug into an open port in the company's wiring closet.

One form of eavesdropping, called *war driving*, is the act of driving around with an antenna to locate insecure wireless networks. This activity has become a popular hacker pastime. The really alarming part of war driving is that anyone can build an antenna with parts that cost less than $5, and often homemade antennas are more sensitive and directional than commercial devices. Organizations using wireless networking solutions might assume that the signals are contained within the walls of the office, but this assumption is not based on fact. Signals strong enough to support connectivity can be detected blocks away, even around corners and on the other side of line-of-sight blocking structures.

Once a malicious user has discovered a wireless connection, it is only a matter of time before he or she gains access to any and every part of the network. Hackers can use packet sniffing, brute-force attacks, and other information discovery attacks to find weaknesses in order to exploit them. Fortunately, the goal of most war driver efforts is to tap into high-speed corporate Internet access for free rather than to infiltrate the internal network. However, unauthorized use of company equipment and services costs money, time, and productivity, so their actions can't be regarded as benign.

Until secured wireless solutions are available and deployed, existing wireless technologies must be used intelligently. One common way to improve the security of wireless connectivity is to use a VPN link over the wireless network. Such a link is typically deployed by attaching the wireless portal directly to a VPN server that serves as a gateway for authorized clients and a firewall for unauthorized clients. This setup forces the client systems to properly authenticate before being granted access to the network and encrypts all data passing over the wireless link. Additionally, it removes the wireless port from the internal network so its traffic cannot be intercepted by a sniffer and internal systems cannot be directly accessed without successful VPN authentication.

Other options to improve the security of wireless technologies include taking the following actions:

- Isolate all wireless access points from the internal network. Require additional authentication or connection mechanisms before access to the internal network or Internet gateway is granted.

- Disable wireless network broadcasting of Service Set Identifiers (SSIDs). This action disables many of the automatic configuration features for clients, but manual configuration greatly reduces unauthorized clients' ability to connect.

- Require specific MAC addresses from authorized wireless cards to establish connectivity.

- Be on the lookout for "rogue WLANs," unauthorized wireless access points set up by employees within the company for their own convenience. For example, a member of the firm who wants to be able to take his or her laptop to meetings and maintain network connectivity might buy an inexpensive access point and plug it into the Ethernet jack in the office, unaware of the security risks involved.

- Enable Wired Equivalent Privacy (WEP) on the wireless system. Although it has some security flaws, WEP does provide some measure of security. By default, most wireless systems have WEP disabled, which leaves the network completely vulnerable.

For more information on the vulnerabilities of wireless networking and how to secure your wireless network, see the following Web sites:

- Security of the WEP algorithm
  www.isaac.cs.berkeley.edu/isaac/wep-faq.html

- Security Administrator: *802.11 Wireless Networks: Is Yours Really Safe?*
  www.secadministrator.com/articles/index.cfm?articleid=22147

- Gregory Rehm's *802.11b Homebrew Antenna Shootout, 2/14/2*
  www.turnpoint.net/wireless/has.html

- BBC: *Hacking with a Pringles Tube*
  http://news.bbc.co.uk/hi/english/sci/tech/newsid_1860000/1860241.stm

- Vnunet.com: *Wireless LANs Can Be Secure*
  www.vnunet.com/Features/1131228

Summary

Why does all this matter to the cybercrime investigator? Only by understanding how computer security works—and how it sometimes doesn't—can you predict where and how network attacks and intrusions will occur, track the actions of cybercriminals who break into systems, build evidence based on those break-ins, and help the victims of cybercrime protect themselves from future attacks.

The first step in preventing cybercrime is to secure computer systems and networks against attacks. No system can be completely secure, but the goal of security is to present a barrier significant enough to repel most—if not all—attackers. Generally, the elements or issues that must be addressed to create a secure environment are the same for any type of system. But the specifics of how to implement a security policy and how to make individual security changes vary from one operating system to the next, and different technologies such as broadband, mainframe systems, and wireless network present their own unique challenges.

With the widespread use of inexpensive high-speed broadband connections, more home and professional systems than ever before are vulnerable to sustained Internet attacks. Proper security precautions must be taken to protect these 24/7 connections against attacks from the Internet, including deploying antivirus software, using strong passwords, disabling file and print sharing, and using a firewall.

When planning security, you must take into consideration not only the method by which Internet access is brought to a system but also the software programs used to interact with Internet-based resources. Web browsers are notoriously vulnerable to numerous attacks. However, with a bit of effort to keep the software up to date and configure settings for the best security, most common attacks can be avoided.

Organizations that host Web sites for public consumption provide useful content for visitors, but they must also take steps to protect the Web server from malevolent intruders. Protecting a Web server involves securing the host OS as well as the Web server software itself. When securing a Web server, administrators must choose between a modest effort and an all-out effort to protect against security incidents, based on the importance of the data that stands to be compromised. In any case, isolating the Web servers from the organization's internal LAN is an essential part of keeping the network secure.

When locking down individual systems, the operating system deployed on that system determines the specific steps that must be taken. Each OS has unique vulnerabilities and security solutions. Understanding these idiosyncrasies and staying informed about new patches and vulnerabilities are essential to the prevention of many types of cybercrime.

Frequently Asked Questions

The following Frequently Asked Questions, answered by the authors of this book, are designed to both measure your understanding of the concepts presented in this chapter and to assist you with real-life implementation of these concepts. To have your questions about this chapter answered by the author, browse to **www.syngress.com/solutions** and click on the **"Ask the Author"** form.

Q: Why are so many computer technologies so insecure?

A: Unfortunately, many computer technologies that are widely deployed today were designed 20 years or more ago (for example, the TCP/IP protocols and the UNIX operating system). At that time, the phenomenon of network attacks wasn't even an issue. This is an example of how the creators, designers, or originators of a technology or concept are unable to fully understand the impact their creation will have in the future. Alexander Graham Bell invented the telephone, but he envisioned it being used to forewarn the recipients of telegrams, not as a *replacement* for the telegraph. Likewise, many IT technologies were created to ease communications, enable capabilities, or perform new functions, but security wasn't an essential concept in their design. Today, most technologies include extensive security review and testing. Nevertheless, it is likely that issues are being overlooked today that will become important in the future.

Q: How can I stay informed about security issues specific to a product, OS, or hardware device I have on my network?

A: To stay informed, you must seek out resources where the information you want is gathered and presented. Most product vendors provide this information on a Web site and in newsletters. Taking the time to browse a vendor's Web site or even to search vendor sites using keywords such as *security* often reveals a wealth of information. However, don't rely solely on a vendor for an unbiased and complete perspective on its security issues. Seek third-party sources for information as well. Numerous Web sites, mailing lists, and newsgroups are supported by security professionals, industry watch groups, magazines, and security products and services. Several excellent sites are included in the resource list at the end of this chapter. You can also find other sites by searching the Web using keywords such as *security, vulnerabilities,* or a product name.

Q: I've heard that understanding the mindset of a hacker or cracker can help thwart their attempts to infiltrate your network. How can I accomplish this without putting my systems or myself at additional risk?

A: Just as there are numerous reputable security companies on the Internet that offer tools and utilities to test and improve the security of your systems, there are groups of crackers or hackers with a Web presence. These "underground" community resources are often invaluable collections of documentation and tools that you can't find anywhere else, especially from commercial sites. However, you should take the precaution of visiting these sites only from a secured system that is not connected to your production environment. If you download any materials from such sites, take extra precautions to test for viruses and Trojans before moving the material to a production system.

Q: How can I verify that the security barriers I've erected and the patches I've applied have successfully eliminated specific security vulnerabilities?

A: The best way to do this is to attack your own system. Using a corruption of the Golden Rule, Ed Tittel, author of numerous IT books and articles and technical editor of this book, often states, "Do unto yourself, before others do unto you." Basically, you should employ common attack methods used by crackers and hackers to see whether their exploits are successful against your hardened system. In addition to deploying manual attacks against your own systems, you can refer to several Web sites, service groups, and products that can perform automated security auditing and stress-testing against your network. Several of these sites are included in the resource list that follows.

Resources

- BBC News: *Hacking with a Pringles Tube*
  http://news.bbc.co.uk/hi/english/sci/tech/newsid_1860000/1860241.stm

- CERT: Unix Security Checklist
  www.cert.org/tech_tips/unix_security_checklist2.0.html

- CIAC: *Securing X Windows*
  http://ciac.llnl.gov/ciac/documents/ciac2316.html

- Gregory Rehm's *802.11b Homebrew Antenna Shootout, 2/14/2*
  www.turnpoint.net/wireless/has.html

- How Stuff Works: *How DSL Works*
  www.howstuffworks.com/dsl.htm

- InterSect's Windows 2000 Security Configuration document
  www.intersectalliance.com/projects/Win2kConfig/index.html

- JavaScript for beginners
  http://polaris.umuc.edu/~mgaylor/Issues.html

- Linux security checklist from University of Georgia
  www.eits.uga.edu/wsg/security/linuxdetails.html

- Microsoft's *Security Operations Guide for Windows 2000 Server*
  www.microsoft.com/downloads/release.asp?releaseid=37123

- OpenSSH
  www.openssh.com

- SANS Institute
  www.sans.org

- SANS Windows 2000 security papers
  www.sans.org/infosecFAQ/win2000/standalone.htm
  www.sans.org/infosecFAQ/win2000/win2000_sec.htm

- Security Administrator: *802.11 Wireless Networks: Is Yours Really Safe?*
  www.secadministrator.com/articles/index.cfm?articleid=22147
  www.secadministrator.com

- Gibson Research: *Shields UP!*
  www.grc.com

- UNIX security checklist from CERT
  www.cert.org/tech_tips/unix_security_checklist2.0.html

- *Wireless LANs Can Be Secure*
  www.vnunet.com/Features/1131228

- *Hack Proofing Your Wireless Network,* by Christian Barnes et al.
  Syngress Publishing, 2002. ISBN 1928994598

- *Configuring Windows 2000 Server Security,* by Thomas Shinder et al.
  Syngress Media, 1999. ISBN 1928994024

- Computer Associates' Virus Information Center
  www3.ca.com/virus

- Computer Incident Advisory Capability (CIAC)
  www.ciac.org

- Peter Gutmann's Web site on security weaknesses
  www.cs.auckland.ac.nz/~pgut001

- Evaluation of vulnerability scanners:
  http://img.cmpnet.com/nc/1201/graphics/f1-detect-results.pdf

- Federal Computer Incident Response Capability (FedCIRC)
  www.fedcirc.gov

- Foundstone's Free Tools
  www.foundstone.com/knowledge/free_tools.html

- Global Networking & Computing (GNAC)
  http://lists.gnac.net/firewalls

- *Home PC Firewall Guide*
  www.firewallguide.com

- TechWeb/Network Computing: *Hammering Out a Secure Framework*
  www.networkcomputing.com/1101/1101f3.html

- Internet Security Systems' BlackICE, ICEcap, advICE
  www.iss.net

- Microsoft Security Advisor & Notification Service
  www.microsoft.com/security

- Microsoft TechNet
  www.microsoft.com/technet

- Network Associates' CyberCop and Anti-Virus
  www.nai.com

- HomeNetHelp: *NAT Basics*
  www.homenethelp.com/web/explain/about-NAT.asp

- NFR security
  www.nfr.net

- NSA's Security Recommendation Guides
  www.nsa.gov

- NTBugTraq
  www.ntbugtraq.com

- NTSecurity.nu's Security Toolbox
  www.ntsecurity.nu/toolbox

- Snort–win32: Open Source, full–function intrusion detection product
  www.snort.org

- Security mailing lists
  http://oliver.efri.hr/~crv/security/mlist/mlist.html

- Security Space: Security audits
  www.securityspace.com/smysecure/index.html

- Simovits Consulting: Ports used by Trojans
  www.simovits.com/nyheter9902.html

- Somarsoft
  www.somarsoft.com

- Sunbelt Software (nt-admin list)
  www.sunbelt-software.com

- Symantec's Norton Anti-Virus
  www.symantec.com/avcenter

Chapter 9

Implementing Cybercrime Detection Techniques

Topics we'll investigate in this chapter:

- **Security Auditing and Log Files**

- **Firewall Logs, Reports, Alarms, and Alerts**

- **Understanding E-Mail Headers**

- **Tracing a Domain Name or IP Address**

- **Commercial Intrusion Detection Systems**

- **IP Spoofing and Other Antidetection Tactics**

- **Honeypots, Honeynets, and Other "Cyberstings"**

☑ **Summary**

☑ **Frequently Asked Questions**

☑ **Resources**

Introduction

In the preceding chapter, we turned our focus from an analysis and explanation of cybercrime, who's involved in perpetrating such crimes, and underlying computer and networking security basics to investigate what's involved in countering potential threats—namely, we covered various aspects and areas in which it's essential to implement system, network, and communications security. Unfortunately, our security measures won't always work. Another important part of preparing for potential threats and related risks of criminal mischief, intrusion, or attack is being prepared to deal with the aftermath of a cybercrime and to start gathering the information that will be necessary to build a case for prosecution.

Once an attack has occurred or a system or network has been compromised, it's essential to be able to sift through the evidence of what's happened. From a technical information technology perspective, this means knowing how to find, recognize, and locate the visible evidence of a cybercrime. From a law enforcement perspective, this means knowing how to handle such evidence to make sure it will be admissible in court if necessary. However, these roles overlap somewhat. A good investigator also needs to know the technicalities of where and how evidence can be located, to properly put together the offense report and help the prosecutor formulate questions for witnesses. Likewise, the IT professional needs an understanding of how evidence must be treated to preserve its integrity in the eyes of the law.

In this chapter, we focus primarily on the former activity; we introduce various sources and potential types of evidence that investigators can gather to provide evidence of attempts to perpetrate cybercrimes. In some cases, this evidence may be collected whether the attempted crime succeeds or fails; in other cases, such evidence may only be available as a byproduct of a successful attack.

To some extent, computers and other network devices are capable of recording information about activity that occurs within them or passes through them. When evidence of cybercrime is needed, this kind of data can be an essential element in making a successful case or in making a decision to prosecute the people responsible. But as with so many other aspects of system and network security, it's necessary to understand the underlying technologies and software that must be put to work to make it possible to produce such evidence. It's also necessary to understand what this evidence looks like, how it may be interpreted, and what kinds of telltale signs or data to look for that could not only help document that a cybercrime was committed but also help identify the responsible party or parties involved and prove to the satisfaction of a jury that they did it.

As we've noted elsewhere in this book, a lack of due diligence in protecting IT assets and information is very often involved in exposing companies and organizations to loss or harm. This loss or harm may occur as a result of either an insider attack (from an employee, consultant, or other person "in the know") or of an attack mounted from outside the network boundary. We've also mentioned that there is no such thing as perfect security, so it's also necessary to concede that even a remote chance of successful attack, penetration, or compromise means that it's necessary to be able to monitor, detect, and react to security incidents if and when they occur.

Thus, an important part of the due diligence necessary in dealing with security matters is to be ready to perform subsequent analysis and investigations to determine causes and to identify perpetrators whenever possible. Whether or not an organization decides to prosecute a security incident is almost beside the point. To the organization and its IT professionals, the real value of understanding how to gather and interpret evidence of cybercrimes comes from the ability it confers to improve or harden security after the fact, to prevent any recurrence of the attacks or circumstances that permitted such crimes to occur in the first place.

Even if the company or organization never actually decides to pursue legal remedies for attempted or successful attacks, the ability to gather, interpret, and respond to the information inherent in the tracks and traces of such events is an essential part of a proper security regime. Finally, it's important to realize that maintaining proper system and network security requires active checks on how security policy is implemented and how well it's working to determine if potential or actual vulnerabilities exist.

Think of this as a "how are we doing?" kind of check, security-wise, that acts not only to make sure that whatever security controls have been implemented match what a security policy requires, but also to repeatedly assess vulnerabilities to new security exploits and attack techniques as they occur. This is not unlike the continuous training and preparation for a violent confrontation that most police officers undergo on a regular basis. Even if there is no reason to expect violence, officers are always prepared for a situation to turn bad, and during and after any contact related to a call, officers are constantly monitoring the situation. Likewise, a savvy security professional knows that he or she must check the status of the network on a regular basis, if only to be sure nothing untoward or unexpected is in progress or has already happened. This empirical form of assessing security posture is a key ingredient in maintaining strong security at all times and is the first step in incident response.

Security Auditing and Log Files

An important concept in system and network security is what's often called the AAA, or "triple-A" model of security. In this case, the acronym is subject to several interpretations, including:

- Administration, authorization, and authentication
- Authentication, authorization, and accounting

Although both expansions of the acronym are pretty widespread, the second is the one that we use in this chapter.

The idea behind AAA is that strong security rests on a three-legged foundation in which:

- **Authentication**, as discussed in detail in Chapter 7, ensures that users, processes, and services that seek to consume system resources or access their contents provide sufficient proof of identity to enter systems and networks before any such requests may be issued.

- **Authorization** (sometimes also called *access control*) ensures that requests for resources will not be granted unless requesters have the permissions necessary not only to read or otherwise inspect the contents of the resources they want to access, but also that they have explicit permissions to perform the kind of operation they seek to perform on the resource. Some individuals may be granted read-only access to information to which they have no permissions to make changes (or to delete such information altogether), whereas other individuals may be granted the ability to modify or delete such information at will.

- **Accounting** relates to monitoring and tracking system activity. Some companies or organizations put a monetary value on computer resources, usage, and access. In this situation, accounting tracks such activity to assess so-called "chargebacks" for use of computer or network services based on actual consumption. But from a security standpoint, the other form of monitoring or tracking involved under the general heading of accounting is called *auditing*. As in its formal meaning in financial accounting, auditing means tracking access and use of resources—in this case, communications links, systems, networks, and related resources, so that activity may be logged. This auditing deposits tangible data into various kinds of computerized records so they may be analyzed for all kinds of purposes after the fact. Such logs provide a key source of evidence in detecting and analyzing cybercrimes, whether only attempted or successfully completed.

Note that both authentication and authorization put various kinds of barriers or checks between users (or consumers) and the resources they seek to utilize. Only accounting tracks what actually happens on the networks and systems it monitors. Thus, accounting—or, more properly, auditing—is the essential activity that closes the loop between what is supposed to happen from a security stand-point and what actually occurs on the systems and networks to which authentication and authorization controls apply.

Auditing is a capability that's built into most computer operating systems and network devices. But since creating audit trails means generating files in which activity records may be stored, auditing is generally viewed as a discretionary form of tracking and monitoring, rather than something to be applied to all user activity and resource access across the board. A good general principle to apply when deciding whether or not to audit certain kinds of activity or access to specific resources is based on a careful assessment of the risks involved. In other words, it's wise to audit for potentially harmful or dangerous activities and for access to sensitive files and other resources. But it's also important to recognize that auditing everything is just as impractical as auditing nothing. These general exhortations will make more sense if we look at how certain operating systems handle auditing and what kinds of activities and accesses they can track and monitor. Following that discussion, we can generalize further about auditing and the trails that auditing leaves behind (usually called *logs* or *log files*) with a little more specificity and precision.

Auditing for Windows Platforms

Starting with the earliest versions of Windows NT, all installations of the business-based Windows operating systems (NT, 2000, XP, and so forth—but not Windows 9*x*/ME) maintain three audit logs to track user and system activity. You can view these logs through the built-in Event Viewer utility:

- **Application log** Shows messages, status information, and events reported from applications and nonessential services on the Windows computer. (Note that some system services write to this log rather than to the System log.)

- **System log** Records errors, warnings, and information events generated by the Windows operating system itself and related core system services.

- **Security log** Displays success and failure records from audited activities. When you enable auditing and set specific auditing policies or settings in Windows, this is the log in which such items appear.

The last log is, of course, the most obviously important for our purposes, although investigators should not ignore the other two. Relevant information, such as the starting or stopping of a service or abnormal behavior of an application, can be obtained from the Application and System logs as well.

NOTE

There may be other logs displayed in the Event Viewer in addition to the standard Application, System, and Security logs, if certain services are running (such as Active Directory and DNS server services).

Launching the Event Viewer varies by platform but may generally be found under the Administrative Tools menu (Windows NT, 2000, XP, and .NET Server) or through the Computer Management MMC (the Microsoft Management Console, in Windows 2000, XP, and .NET Server). The Event Viewer is a good starting point when investigating abnormal or unusual system activity and to monitor system activity in general.

In Windows 2000, *group policy objects,* or *GPOs*, control the level of auditing performed by the operating system; in Windows NT, it's necessary to enable auditing in the Audit Policy menu in the User Manager for Domains administrative tool. Either way, only someone logged on with an account with administrative-level permissions can enable auditing or establish audit policies. By default, Windows does not enable security auditing; thus by default the Security event log contains no data. To enable auditing, simply create a GPO and configure it to monitor success and failure for one or more of various classes of defined events (Windows 2000 and newer) or use User Manager for Domains to enable auditing and set explicit audit policies. For Windows 2000, the following nine classes of events or activities may be audited:

- **Account logon events** Use this to monitor user account logon activity.

- **Account management** Use this to monitor administrative account management activities (creating, deleting, disabling, or changing account settings).

- **Directory service access** Use this to monitor use of Active Directory services and objects.

- **Logon events** Use this to monitor all logon events for system accounts, service accounts, and user accounts (a superset of account logon events, in other words).

- **Object access** Use this to enable auditing of individual files, folders, printers, or other computer resources (which must also be configured for auditing individually and separately).

- **Policy change** Use this to monitor GPO creation, deletion, or modification. This tracks important administrative activities on Windows systems.

- **Privilege use** Use this to monitor use of user and administrative privileges on a Windows system. This also tracks important administrative activities on Windows systems, as well as object owner/creator and user use of privileges.

- **Process tracking** Use this to monitor process creation, threads, and deletion. This is seldom used for security purposes (but may sometimes be helpful).

- **System events** Use this to monitor operating system activities. This is also seldom used for security purposes.

Figure 9.1 shows a Windows 2000 server's security log open in the Event Viewer. Note that successful and (one) failed logon events are audited.

The profound tradeoffs between auditing and system performance are manifested in at least two ways:

- The more objects and activities that are audited, the more impact that the collection and recording of such data will have on system performance and consumption of disk space (because all those logged activities are written to files on disk).

- The more objects and activities that are audited, the more data administrators and investigators will have to dig through to find items of interest among the routine or benign events or activities that will also be recorded.

If a large amount of data is collected, however, all is not lost. The Event Viewer can be configured to filter logged events so that only certain event types (for example, only failures) or only events that originate with specific sources, users, or computers are displayed in the log. Other options include displaying only events that occurred on a specified date and/or time or within a specified period, or events in a certain category or that are marked with a specific event ID. Figure 9.2 shows the dialog box that is used to configure display filtering.

Figure 9.1 The Windows 2000 Security log shows event types for which auditing is enabled.

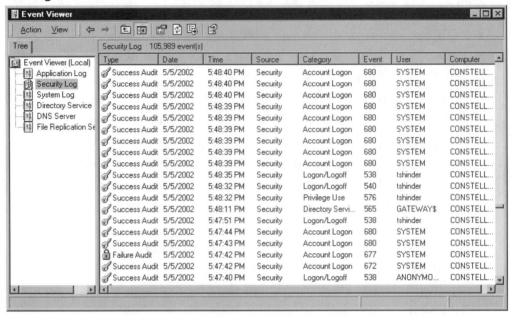

Figure 9.2 Event Viewer logs can be filtered to display only specified logged events.

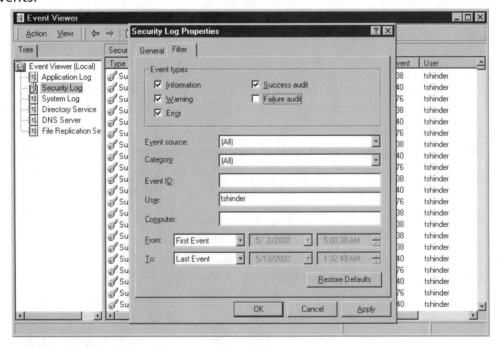

For an excellent overview on auditing Windows systems from a Windows XP perspective, consult the following TechNet reference: www.microsoft.com/ TechNet/prodtechnol/winxppro/proddocs/Audit_overview.asp (*Auditing Security Events Overview*). For information about capturing and analyzing logs from other Windows applications, see www.microsoft.com/TechNet/itsolutions/ecommerce/ maintain/monitor/logcanda.asp (*Log Capture and Analysis*).

On the Scene…

Designing Effective Audit Strategies

Ultimately, what the IT administrator chooses to audit depends on the kinds of activity that occur on the server or device in question, the kinds of attacks or intrusions that are anticipated, and the kinds of information or other assets the organization seeks to monitor (and protect). Thus, it might make sense to audit specific intrusion signatures at the periphery of the network (on firewalls, screening routers, application gateways, and so forth). But on those servers where sensitive files reside, it probably makes sense to audit access to such files, including attempted and successful accesses. In general, it's also a good idea to monitor administrative activities on all such devices (and to advertise that policy) so that IT professionals know they will be held accountable for all official (and unsanctioned) administrative activities they perform.

In some situations—perhaps when an account may be compromised—it may make sense to disable that account (and set up a new account for the old account's user), then audit subsequent attempts to use the old account. This practice permits administrators to determine if such activity originates inside or outside the local network boundary and can help establish an intruder's identity.

The general principle at work here is to audit for suspicious activities, to track administrative activity, and to monitor information or assets of known value or interest. By combining these activities into the auditing strategy, it's easier to strike the right balance between audit data volume and the amount of useful information that can be discerned from that data.

Auditing for UNIX and Linux Platforms

Every different distribution and version of UNIX and Linux logs critical audit information in its own unique way and stores the resulting log files in particular locations using specific platform-dependent formats. Nevertheless, most UNIX and Linux operating systems support extensive logging capabilities and share numerous common features.

The Syslog daemon (syslogd) is a clearinghouse for all kinds of log information on UNIX and Linux systems. The daemon is a process that diverts different system messages to different log files, depending on the type of message and how urgent or severe it is. For example, on a FreeBSD system, successful and failed FTP logins are shown in the ftp.log file, information about access to Apache Web sites is stored in access_log, and information about failed logins is found in secure.log.

Most networks that incorporate UNIX or Linux systems also set up special network drives to record logging data, so it can all reside in a single centralized location. In addition, the Syslog daemon receives event data from various operating system and user applications (listed in Table 9.1); it also stores all log data using a single standardized format for easy interpretation and analysis. (The same consistency, alas, is not found for all logs on Windows systems, where Event Viewer uses one format for its logs, but other applications and services use other formats.)

In fact, Syslog even prioritizes event or error messages according to a predefined scheme (listed in Table 9.2). Higher-priority messages appear at the top of this table, and lower-priority messages appear at the bottom of this table.

As mentioned previously, various specific UNIX or Linux log files store particular types of events or information. Thus, the *loginlog* records failed logon attempts, while the *sulog* records **su** (superuser) command activity on a specific system and identifies the user account where the activity originated. The *utmp* log identifies all users who are currently logged onto a system, and the *wtmp* log stores snapshots of *utmp* information at regular intervals. These are only some of the many log files you'll find on most Linux or UNIX systems; please consult your system documentation and *man* pages to obtain a complete listing of logging facilities, formats used, and (default) storage locations.

Table 9.1 Common Syslog facilities

Facility	Description
auth	Authorization systems (e.g., *login* and *su*).
cron	The *cron* daemon drives scheduled scripts and commands and executes them as scheduled.

Continued

Table 9.1 Continued

Facility	Description
daemon	Miscellaneous daemons not covered by other facilities.
kern	Abbreviation for *system kernel*—the operating system's memory-resident core code.
local0-local7	Reserved for local use (numbered 0 through 7).
lpr	Print spooling (line printer remote) system.
mark	A timestamp service that emits a timestamp for logging every 20 minutes (1200 seconds).
mail	E-mail system.
syslog	Internal *syslog* data.

Table 9.2 Syslog priorities

Priority	Description
Emerg	Panic conditions broadcast to all users.
Alert	Conditions requiring immediate intervention.
Crit	Critical errors, such as a device failure.
Err	Standard priority errors.
Warning	Warning messages.
Notice	Notifications that may require some action or response.
Info	Informational messages.
Debug	Shows messages written to Syslog when programs run in debug mode.

For an excellent basic overview of the UNIX Syslog facility, please see www.la.utexas.edu/lab/software/lib/gnu/glibc/libc_377.html#SEC380. In addition, the SANS Institute Reading Room offers numerous papers on Syslog and UNIX logging, including Ray McAlarnen's *Unix Security Logging* (April 18, 2001) paper. Use the site's search engine; an account and password are required to visit this repository of online security papers and resources, but there is no charge.

Macintosh OS X is a UNIX-based operating system and the Syslog daemon works as described previously. OS X makes it easy for administrators to access the UNIX log files through the Console application (found in the Utilities subfolder in the Applications folder on the Mac hard drive). The security and other important logs are found in the /private/var/log folder, which is hidden by default but can be accessed via the **Go to Folder** function in the **Go** menu (see Figure 9.3).

Figure 9.3 Security and other logs are stored in the /private/var/log folder in Mac OS X.

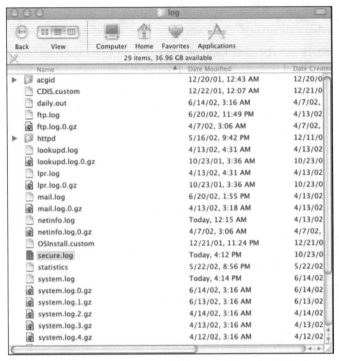

Firewall Logs, Reports, Alarms, and Alerts

In Chapter 7, we discussed the function of firewalls and the part they play in a network security plan. Because firewalls sit on the boundary between internal and external networks, they're ideally positioned to observe incoming (and outgoing) traffic. Thus, it should come as no surprise that firewalls not only represent a first and important line of defense to foil or deflect attack, but also that they can be configured to monitor and track activity that can point to incipient attacks as they commence. Unless attackers are savvy enough to erase log files (and alas, many are indeed smart enough to do this), firewall logs can also help document successful or attempted attacks after the fact. Most boundary devices, which include not only firewalls but also screening routers, application gateways, proxy servers, and so forth, can—and indeed should—log various kinds of activity routinely. Given that such logs can be very important sources of evidence in cases where strong evidence is needed, most such devices log a wide range of traffic and various types of activity.

Because so many such devices run in UNIX-based or UNIX-like environments, the good news here is that the same information covered in the preceding section about the Syslog facility and general Linux or UNIX logging techniques often applies to firewalls, routers, and other devices. For example, even though Cisco devices run a Cisco proprietary operating system, known as the *Internet Operating System* or *IOS*, this software environment uses a reasonably standard Syslog implementation to support its logging capabilities. With the proviso in mind that low-level details vary from system to system and implementation to implementation, our general coverage of logging facilities and operation remains applicable to many (if not most) boundary devices in wide use.

NOTE

Add-on software products that can monitor and analyze firewall logs are available. For example, *firelogd* is a daemon that monitors Linux firewall logs. *Fwanalog* is a shell script that parses and summarizes firewall log files on UNIX and Linux systems. *XP Firewall Reporter* is a commercial software package that analyzes the files created by Windows XP's built-in "personal" firewall. ZoneLog Analyzer imports the logs from the ZoneAlarm firewalls into an easily queried database. Web Trends makes a Firewall Suite that processes log files from Check Point, Cisco, Microsoft ISA Server firewalls, and others. (For more information about the Firewall Suite, see www.extralan.co.uk/products/Diagnostic-Tools/Webtrends/Webtrends.htm.)

For firewalls and other boundary devices, logging is only one of the ways in which they can provide information about activity and traffic they handle. Firewalls (and other boundary devices) do indeed create log files, where all kinds of data may be written and stored for the long term. But these devices also support various types of other outputs, some of which can be quite important:

- **Alarms** These systems can be instructed to issue high-priority messages in various formats should particularly suspicious activities or events occur. Many such systems can send e-mail messages to specific respondents and even page designated telephone numbers, in addition to logging information when specified events occur. This functionality permits these systems to provoke immediate responses from responsible individuals. Since routers, firewalls, and other boundary devices may be subjected to ping floods or other DoS attacks, and because they may witness repeated failed login attempts that can likewise signal that attacks have commenced, immediate action is sometimes essential in responding to such events.

- **Alerts** Some types of traffic activity are less obviously symptomatic of attack but should be looked into nonetheless. This explains why many boundary systems can also issue alerts when particular conditions occur. Although these alerts may also result in e-mail or pager calls, they are usually less urgent than outright alarms.

- **Reports** While reportable events fall into the more mundane category of cataloging and categorizing traffic, activity, errors, and failed login or other access attempts, most boundary devices can also report aggregate behavior and statistics over some specific period of time (daily, weekly, monthly, and so forth). Such reports are important indicators of overall system health and security and should be consulted regularly as part of the security monitoring and maintenance process.

In fact, most operating systems have some kind of alarm or alert facility as well. For example, Microsoft Windows NT/2000/XP/.NET support system alerts (configured via the System Monitor in the Performance administrative tool) to alert administrators of system performance- or error-related events. Although the Event Viewer provides no way to configure alerts when security events occur, some third-party software packages such as IPSentry (www.ipsentry.com) monitor the Windows event logs and send alerts when triggering events occur.

When it comes to working with firewall logs (or responding to related alarms or alerts), some of the most common types of information you'll encounter relate directly to attacks and exploits documented elsewhere in this book. Thus, it should come as no surprise that the following types of activities or traffic might be noteworthy from both an attack detection and a post-attack perspective:

- **ICMP traffic** Excessive pinging, ping scans, echo requests to broadcast address, ICMP time exceeded packets, distributed ICMP echo reply hits.

- **Regular, systematic scanning behavior** IP address range scanning, TCP/UDP port scans, NetBIOS name scans.

- **Attempts to access specific well-known port addresses** These include addresses associated with remote access software (pcAnywhere, Back Orifice, and so forth), instant messaging, or specific Trojan horse applications.

In fact, any type of traffic or activity pattern—otherwise known as an *attack signature*, or more simply as a *signature*—that can be directly associated with a specific type or method of attack represents events that should be logged if at all possible. Sometimes recognizing a signature can involve more intelligence than a typical boundary device such as a firewall or screening router might possess, however. For that reason, we return to this subject later in this chapter when we discuss a class of systems known as *intrusion detection systems,* or *IDS,* that are expressly built with this very kind of capability.

As to what kind of information occurs in a firewall log, it usually consists of fairly simple text records that document various aspects of network traffic underway. Though here again the details will vary to some extent, no log record is complete without including at least the following information (and usually more than appears in this deliberately brief list of common log entry fields):

- **Timestamp** Date and time at which event, activity, or communication occurred.

- **Source address** Reported IP address for traffic source.

- **Source domain name (if available)** Reported domain name for traffic source.

- **Destination address** Target delivery address for traffic.

- **Protocol** Name of IP protocol or service in use.

- **Message type or class (where applicable)** Type of message being sent.

- **Port address (where applicable)** TCP or UDP port to which the message is directed.

- **Socket address (where applicable)** Socket address to which the message is directed.

In some cases, log entries also include what's called a *reverse DNS lookup* or a *backtrace*. Some boundary devices can be configured to double-check the official IP address associated with domain names reported for inbound traffic against the actual IP address included in incoming traffic. When these two values differ, it can be a definite indicator of spoofing, which in turn may mean that suspicious activity (if not an outright attack) has ensued. This type of detection usually triggers an alert or alarm for that reason.

Some firewall products, such as Microsoft's ISA Server, provide a friendly GUI interface for configuring logging and alerts, as shown in Figure 9.4.

ISA Server makes it easy to configure security alerts. The New Alert Wizard is launched by right-clicking **Alerts** in the **Monitoring Configuration** node and selecting **New** from the context menu. The Wizard walks you through the steps involved in setting up alerts. Administrators can select to be alerted for all intrusion detections or choose specific detection types for which they want to be alerted, as shown in Figure 9.5.

Figure 9.4 The ISA Server firewall uses the Microsoft Management Console (MMC) interface.

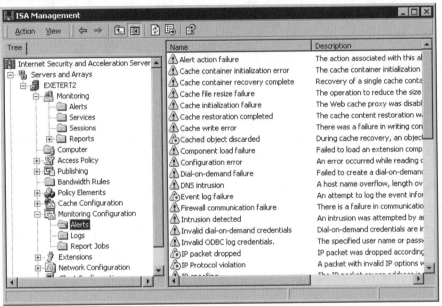

Configuring logging in ISA is just as easy. The logs are configured through the Monitoring Configuration node in the MMC (the Logs folder). You can configure and generate logs to be created on a daily, weekly, monthly, or yearly basis, and they can be saved to a file or logged directly to a specified database. By default, ISA log files are saved in a folder named ISALogs that is located in the ISA installation folder (named Microsoft ISA Server by default and located in the Program files directory on the partition where the Windows 2000/.NET operating files are stored).

The logs can be saved as comma-delimited text files, which can then be imported into a spreadsheet such as Excel or a database program such as Access. Figure 9.6 shows an example of an ISA Server log file.

Figure 9.5 It's easy to configure ISA Server alerts to notify of intrusions and other events.

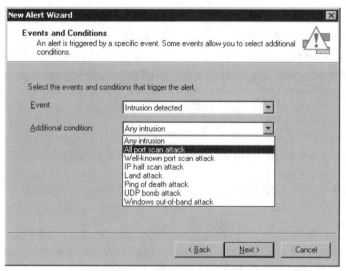

Figure 9.6 ISA Server can log events in comma-delimited text files.

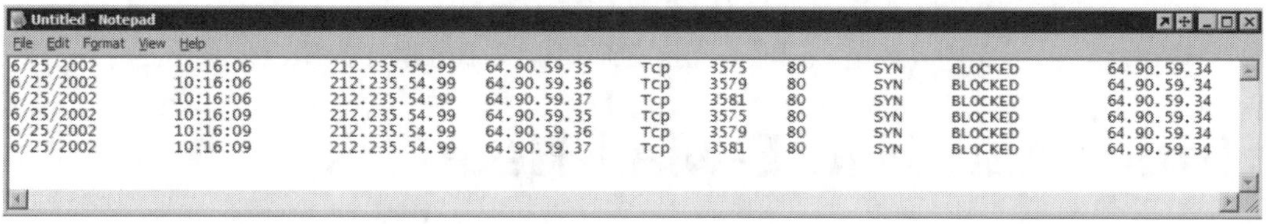

```
Untitled - Notepad
File  Edit  Format  View  Help
6/25/2002       10:16:06       212.235.54.99   64.90.59.35    Tcp    3575    80    SYN    BLOCKED    64.90.59.34
6/25/2002       10:16:06       212.235.54.99   64.90.59.36    Tcp    3579    80    SYN    BLOCKED    64.90.59.34
6/25/2002       10:16:06       212.235.54.99   64.90.59.37    Tcp    3581    80    SYN    BLOCKED    64.90.59.34
6/25/2002       10:16:09       212.235.54.99   64.90.59.35    Tcp    3575    80    SYN    BLOCKED    64.90.59.34
6/25/2002       10:16:09       212.235.54.99   64.90.59.36    Tcp    3579    80    SYN    BLOCKED    64.90.59.34
6/25/2002       10:16:09       212.235.54.99   64.90.59.37    Tcp    3581    80    SYN    BLOCKED    64.90.59.34
```

In the file shown in Figure 9.6, you see in the first three columns the date and times of the repeated attempted intrusions and the IP address of the intruder. The next column shows that the intruder tried different destination IP addresses in sequence (64.90.59.35, then 64.90.59.36, then 64.90.59.37) on TCP port 80, as shown in the fifth and seventh columns. (The sixth column shows the port used on the source computer.) The intruder sent a TCP SYN packet to try to establish a connection, as shown in column eight; however, port 80 was not "listening" (open and waiting for a connection) on any of these IP addresses (indicated by BLOCKED in column nine). The last field shows the primary IP address bound to the physical interface that was being probed. (This particular system has multiple IP addresses bound to a single network card, 64.90.59.34 through 64.90.59.37.)

Another ISA log file, shown in Figure 9.7, illustrates an intruder's attempt to gain access to files on the computer through the Web server, using its IP address (64.90.59.34). You'll note that all of these attempts originate from the same intruder who was trying to establish a connection in the previous log. The two logged Web accesses that use the www.tacteam.net URL are legitimate accesses. The attempts from IP address 212.235.54.99 were denied by ISA Server.

Figure 9.7 Another ISA Server log file indicates numerous attempts to access files on the computer.

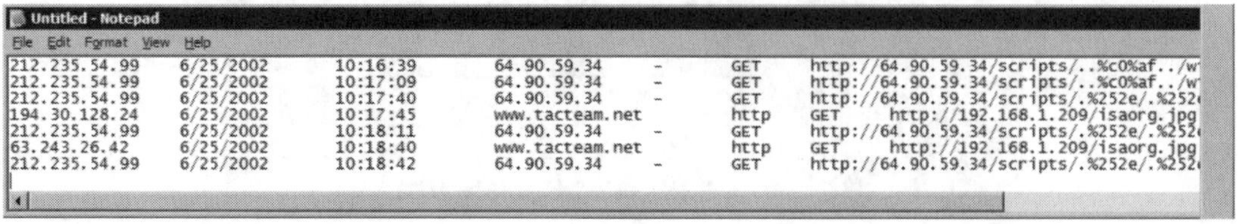

For an interesting walkthrough and analysis of typical firewall log data, visit Lenny Zeltser's traces and analysis listing in the SANS archives at www .incidents.org/archives/y2k/123199-1220.htm. Search on Zeltser's name to jump right to the portion of the file that contains the relevant listings and discussion. Matthew Tam also put together a nice PowerPoint presentation for the Professional Information Security Association (PISA) on configuring a Linux firewall that covers the details involved in filtering traffic through such a device; see www.pisa.org.hk/download/seminar20011117-fw/linux_firewall.ppt.

Understanding E-Mail Headers

There's more to managing information security than dealing with boundary devices and various types of logs. E-mail can open the doors for all kinds of attacks and infections into an organization. Besides making sure to install and use antivirus software that inspects all e-mail payloads (and hopefully, blocks all potential sources of such attack), it's also necessary for users and administrators to deal with unsolicited e-mail (also called *spam*) or with e-mail based DoS attacks (so-called *mail bombs*). To deal properly with spam and e-mail-based DoS attacks, it's absolutely essential to understand how to read e-mail headers. Such knowledge will not only permit administrators and investigators to determine at least a putative (if not the actual) source for the attack or spam, it also helps define a strategy for dealing with such behavior.

The ability to track e-mail messages is important in many different types of cybercrime cases. It is not unusual for criminals to use e-mail in the following ways:

- To harass victims (cyberstalking)
- To send extortion demands or threats

- To contact potential victims (pedophiles, serial rapists)

- To solicit "marks" for con games (Nigerian scam, pyramid schemes)

- To communicate with accomplices

In all these situations and others, e-mail may be one (or the only) clue to the criminal's identity and may become evidence at trial. Unless the criminal is kind enough to sign the message with a full (and accurate) name, address, and phone number, the only way to determine where a message originated is to examine the message "headers." E-mail generally goes through a number of different computers on the way from the sender to the intended recipient. Header information is added to the message at each machine along the way, until it reaches its destination. (The workstation on which the recipient reads the mail generally doesn't add header info.) It is important for investigators to know what information can—and can't—be discerned from e-mail headers and to understand that headers can be spoofed (forged).

Breaking down and understanding e-mail headers requires some knowledge of how to recognize and decode the fields in those headers. This level of structure is well documented and is primarily defined in RFC 822, which documents the layout and structure of Simple Mail Transfer Protocol (SMTP) message header fields. Although there are more fields than the ones we discuss here, Table 9.3 contains the most important fields as well as all fields you'll need to check to try to trace messages back to their origins and to identify the route they took from their putative original sender to reach the recipient's e-mail server.

Table 9.3 Important RFC 822 e-mail header fields

Field Name	Explanation
Source/Sender Header Fields	
From	Identifies e-mail sender, usually by name and e-mail address.
Sender	Identifies actual sender of e-mail (may differ from From field in some e-mail systems).
Reply-to	E-mail address to which replies should be sent.
Return-path	Path (address) back to sender.
Received	Except when users reside on the same server, known as a *message transfer agent,* or *MTA*, every e-mail goes through at least one intermediary server as it's routed from sender to receiver. Each such intermediary appears on its own Received line.

Continued

Table 9.3 Continued

Field Name	Explanation
Source/Sender Header Fields (Continued)	
Resent-*xxx*	Applies to resent messages, for from, sender, and reply-to fields.
Destination Header Fields	
To	Identifies name and/or e-mail address for recipient.
cc	Secondary message recipients.
bcc	Blind carbon-copy message recipients. (Message is delivered to all bcc designees, but no bcc designee information is included in the header itself.)
Resent-*xxx*	Applies to resent messages for to, cc, and bcc fields.
Date Headers	
Date	Date and time original message was sent.
Resent-date	Date and time resent message was sent.
Optional Headers	
Subject	Topic for message.
Message-ID	Unique message identifier (handled by MTA from originating system); also supplied for resent messages.
In-reply-to	Identifies message being replied to.
References	Identifies other messages to which this message applies.
Keywords	Keywords to help sort and organize message contents (seldom used).
Comments	Text comments about message (seldom used).
Encrypted	Indicates message content is encrypted.
X-xxx	Identifies user-defined fields.

The fields of greatest interest when dealing with malicious e-mail or spam are those that identify the putative sender (from, reply-to, sender, return-path, and so forth) and all the various *received* fields that indicate the mail servers that were involved in routing the message(s) from their sender to your server. Although those Received lines that don't include a From field do not actually identify a sender, users can report that spam is being routed through those servers to the ISPs or organizations that operate them. In many cases, the provider will be able to filter out the unwanted e-mail rather than forwarding it to the complaining user or some other hapless victim. In fact, it's best to concentrate on the IP address reported on these lines, because much of this information can be forged by clever e-mail attackers. For more information on dealing with unwanted e-mail, including detailed instructions on creating and issuing spam complaints to forwarding server operators, see the excellent article entitled *Reporting SPAM* at www.freelabs.com/~whitis/spam_reporting.html. (This site also contains a useful Links section with further pointers to spam investigation and reporting.)

Unfortunately, e-mail messages are far too easy to spoof, in the sense that knowledgeable individuals can either use software tools or construct entirely bogus RFC 822 e-mail headers by hand. Thus, not all reports of unwanted forwarding may produce the desired results of eliminating or reducing unwanted mail traffic. Some service providers operate special e-mail services known as *anonymous* or *pseudo remailers*. These so-called "anonymizer" services are deliberately designed to shield their users from outright or personal identification; many operate outside the United States.

Crimestoppers…

Dealing with Anonymizer Service Providers

In some cases, the companies or organizations that operate anonymizer services will respond favorably to requests for assistance from law enforcement professionals who seek to identify their customers who are using the service for criminal purposes. In other cases, a company may refuse to cooperate in any way at all; such noncooperation is more likely to occur when anonymizer service providers operate offshore. Nevertheless, some of the most notorious anonymizer services (for example, anon.penet.fi, originally based in Finland) have ceased operation, primarily in response to frequent repeated requests to identify their customers to law enforcement professionals all over the world. There's an old Internet saying that applies when seeking cooperation from anonymous remailers: YMMV ("your mileage may vary"). This is a polite euphemism for the very real situation in which things either do not work exactly as described or advertised or assistance with (or from) a service may simply not be available. It's worth a try (or a warrant, where one can be obtained), but seeking cooperation from these services may not always produce the desired results!

For more information about e-mail header fields and how to interpret them, consult the text for RFC 822 at www.faqs.org/rfcs/rfc822.html or the article titled *Reading Email Headers* on the StopSpam Web site at www.stopspam.org/email/headers/headers.html. You'll also find valuable e-mail resources online at http://everythingemail.net and through the Internet Mail Consortium at www.imc.org.

Here's an example of a somewhat truncated e-mail header, to help you identify the various fields mentioned earlier. This header was taken directly from a recent e-mail message:

```
Return-Path: <kate@syngress.com>
Received: from mail20.jump.net by serv1.jump.net (mail20.jump.net
   [206.196.91.20]) (8.9.3/jump.1.11)
        id NAA25382;  for <etittel@serv1.jump.net> Fri, 21 Jun 2002
   13:56:18 -0500 (CDT)
Received: from osmtp1.electric.net (osmtp2.electric.net [216.129.90.29])
        by deliverator.io.com (8.9.3/8.9.3) with ESMTP id NAA28104
        for <etittel@lanw.com>; Fri, 21 Jun 2002 13:56:15 -0500
Received: from [216.129.90.8] (helo=www1.electric.net)
        by osmtp1.electric.net with smtp (Exim 3.22 #1)
        id 17LTZu-000IHm-04
        for etittel@lanw.com; Fri, 21 Jun 2002 11:56:14 -0700
Received: (qmail 16354 invoked by uid 99); 21 Jun 2002 18:56:12 -0000
Message-ID: <1024685772.3d1376cc8b1b0@www.electricwebmail.com>
Date: Fri, 21 Jun 2002 14:56:12 -0400
To: Ed Tittel <etittel@lanw.com>
From: "kate@syngress.com" <kate@syngress.com>
Cc: Deb Shinder <deb@shinder.net>
Subject: Cybercrime ch 8
References: <NHEEJHCPPENDKBIKGHOEMECIGHAA.etittel@lanw.com>
In-Reply-To: <NHEEJHCPPENDKBIKGHOEMECIGHAA.etittel@lanw.com>
```

Some e-mail programs don't show the full e-mail headers by default, but you can view the headers if you drill down through the interface. For example, in Microsoft Outlook 2002, you need to open the message (not just preview it) and click **View | Options**. Figure 9.8 shows the "Internet headers" in the pane at the bottom of the Message Properties window. (You'll have to scroll through to see them all; you can also copy and paste the information into a text editor or word processing program.)

Figure 9.8 It may take a little digging to find the full e-mail headers in Outlook 2002 and other mail clients.

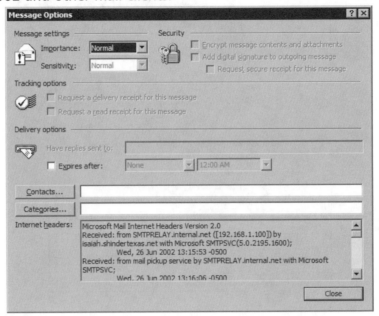

If this message were part of a mail bomb attack or spam, you'd want to contact the operators of the various servers identified in the Return-path, From, and inside the various Received fields in the header. But first, it would also be useful to employ the **whois** command at your command line to check the domain names reported against the IP addresses used. **Whois** allows you find out to whom a domain name is registered, as we discussed in Chapter 8.

Windows does not typically include built-in whois capabilities, but there are numerous sources for Windows–compatible whois utilities around, such as those at www.tatumweb.com/iptools.htm. Or you can use the services at www.samspade.org to perform the necessary lookups through its Web pages without using a whois tool on your Windows computer. Likewise, if you have access to a UNIX shell account, you should be able to use the **whois** command at the command line. Mac OS X has a useful graphical version of **whois**, as shown in Figure 9.9.

NOTE

Other useful commands include **nslookup** or **dig**, to map from domain names to IP addresses.

Figure 9.9 Macintosh OS X includes a graphical whois utility, along with several other network utilities.

Tracing a Domain Name or IP Address

The Domain Name System (DNS) is responsible for maintaining domain name to IP address mappings on the Internet. Numerous boundary devices, such as firewalls and screening routers, can perform reverse DNS lookups to make sure that reported domain names match actual IP destination addresses in inbound traffic. When these do not match up properly—that is, when looking up the domain name produces an IP address that is different from the one in the destination address—there's the probability that the sender is attempting to spoof a domain name without making sure the IP address matches. This is a sign of a less-than-savvy hacker. Hackers who know what they're doing generally make an effort to match the IP addresses from which they claim to originate with the domain names they use.

Nevertheless, the "reverse DNS lookup" technique permits a device to query the DNS server for an IP address to go along with a domain name, as well as to perform the more standard name-to-address translations that DNS typically provides whenever a computer attempts to connect to another machine using a "friendly" DNS name instead of the IP address. Most boundary equipment, and many IP servers, can be configured to perform a reverse DNS lookup before granting access even to anonymous users and to deny access to users whose reported domain names and IP addresses don't match up. Although this is not an entirely foolproof technique for blocking spoofed traffic completely, it is highly recommended for networks that permit traffic to enter from outside their local networks (especially from the Internet).

In general, DNS queries that use reverse lookup work backward through the IP address to the domain name, using a special file on the DNS server called *in-addr-arpa*. For example, if a Web server has an Internet address of 206.224.64.194, the lookup proceeds in reverse order into a file named 64.224.206-in-addr-arpa on some DNS server where individual addresses on that subnet can be resolved (such as the Web server named www.lanw.com at 206.224.65.194). Most network boundary devices and servers perform such lookups automatically and write them to their log files. Nevertheless, investigators should also know how to get from domain names to IP addresses and from IP addresses to domain names manually, if only to confirm the results they find in firewall, router, or server log files.

Table 9.4 summarizes key commands you can use to obtain domain name and IP address-related information. Rather than providing complete syntax information, we provide pointers to Windows and UNIX/Linux commands, with help files where such details and numerous examples may be found. Please note also that www.tatumweb.com/iptools.htm offers access to numerous Web-based lookup tools with the same functionality. The benefit of this latter approach is that you can simply enter a domain name or IP address and other arguments as needed and observe the results without mastering the underlying command syntax or details. Of these, the Elephant's Toolbox is particularly useful since it breaks up more complex **nslookup** requests into simple radio button activities.

Table 9.4 Domain name/IP address lookup utilities

Command	Explanation	Windows Help	UNIX/ Linux Help
Nslookup	Inspects contents of DNS server files, including forward and reverse lookups.	Enter **nslookup**, then type **help**.	man nslookup
DiG	Provides information from DNS servers about domain names and/or IP addresses.	Not available on Windows by default.	**man DiG**
Whois	Maps hostnames to IP addresses and vice versa.	Not available on Windows by default.	**man Whois**

A useful Web site for obtaining DNS information is at www.dnsreport.com. Administrators can use it to find out about problems and vulnerabilities with their DNS servers, as shown in Figure 9.10.

Figure 9.10 The DNS Report site is an excellent resource to obtain DNS information for a specific domain.

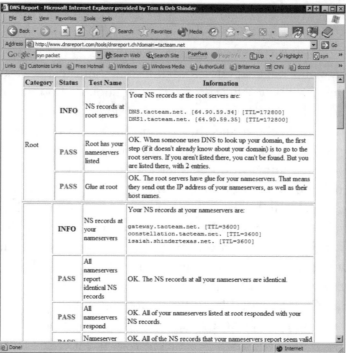

Commercial Intrusion Detection Systems

Earlier, we mentioned that firewalls and other simple boundary devices lack some degree of intelligence when it comes to observing, recognizing, and identifying attack signatures that may be present in the traffic they monitor and the log files they collect. Without sounding critical of such systems' capabilities, this deficiency explains why intrusion detection systems (often abbreviated *IDS*) are becoming increasingly important in helping to maintain proper network security. Whereas other boundary devices may collect all the information necessary to detect (and often, to foil) attacks that may be getting started or already underway, they haven't been programmed to inspect for and detect the kinds of traffic or network behavior patterns that match known attack signatures or that suggest potential unrecognized attacks may be incipient or in progress.

In a nutshell, the simplest way to define an IDS might be to describe it as a specialized tool that knows how to read and interpret the contents of log files from routers, firewalls, servers, and other network devices. Furthermore, an IDS often stores a database of known attack signatures and can compare patterns of activity, traffic, or behavior it sees in the logs it's monitoring against those signatures to recognize when a close match between a signature and current or recent behavior occurs. At that point, the IDS can issue alarms or alerts, take various kinds of automatic action ranging from shutting down Internet links or specific servers to launching backtraces, and make other active attempts to identify attackers and actively collect evidence of their nefarious activities.

By analogy, an IDS does for a network what an antivirus software package does for files that enter a system: It inspects the contents of network traffic to look for and deflect possible attacks, just as an antivirus software package inspects the contents of incoming files, e-mail attachments, active Web content, and so forth to look for virus signatures (patterns that match known malware) or for possible malicious actions (patterns of behavior that are at least suspicious, if not downright unacceptable).

To be more specific, intrusion detection means detecting unauthorized use of or attacks on a system or network. An IDS is designed and used to detect and then to deflect or deter (if possible) such attacks or unauthorized use of systems, networks, and related resources. Like firewalls, IDSs may be software-based or may combine hardware and software (in the form of preinstalled and preconfigured standalone IDS devices). Often, IDS software runs on the same devices or servers where firewalls, proxies, or other boundary services operate; an IDS *not* running on the same device or server where the firewall or other services are installed will monitor those devices closely and carefully. Although such devices tend to operate at network peripheries, IDS systems can detect and deal with insider attacks as well as external attacks.

Characterizing Intrusion Detection Systems

IDS systems vary according to a number of criteria. By explaining those criteria, we can explain what kinds of IDSs you're likely to encounter and how they do their jobs. First and foremost, it's possible to distinguish IDSs on the basis of the kinds of activities, traffic, transactions, or systems they monitor. In this case, IDSs may be divided into network-based, host-based, and application-based IDS types. IDSs that monitor network backbones and look for attack signatures are called *network-based IDSs*, whereas those that operate on hosts defend and monitor the operating and file systems for signs of intrusion and are called *host-based IDSs*.

Some IDSs monitor only specific applications and are called *application-based IDSs*. (This type of treatment is usually reserved for important applications such as database management systems, content management systems, accounting systems, and so forth.) Read on to learn more about these various types of IDS monitoring approaches:

- **Network-based IDS characteristics**

  Pros: Network-based IDSs can monitor an entire, large network with only a few well-situated nodes or devices and impose little overhead on a network. Network-based IDSs are mostly passive devices that monitor ongoing network activity without adding significant overhead or interfering with network operation. They are easy to secure against attack and may even be undetectable to attackers; they also require little effort to install and use on existing networks.

  Cons: Network-based IDSs may not be able to monitor and analyze all traffic on large, busy networks and may therefore overlook attacks launched during peak traffic periods. Network-based IDSs may not be able to monitor switch-based (high-speed) networks effectively, either. Typically, network-based IDSs cannot analyze encrypted data, nor do they report whether or not attempted attacks succeed or fail. Thus, network-based IDSs require a certain amount of active, manual involvement from network administrators to gauge the effects of reported attacks.

- **Host-based IDS characteristics**

  Pros: A host-based IDS can analyze activities on the host it monitors at a high level of detail; it can often determine which processes and/or users are involved in malicious activities. Though they may each focus on a single host, many host-based IDS systems use an agent-console model where agents run on (and monitor) individual hosts but report to a single centralized console (so that a single console can configure, manage, and consolidate data from numerous hosts). Host-based IDSs can detect attacks undetectable to the network-based IDS and can gauge attack effects quite accurately. Host-based IDSs can use host-based encryption services to examine encrypted traffic, data, storage, and activity. Host-based IDSs have no difficulties operating on switch-based networks, either.

  Cons: Data collection occurs on a per-host basis; writing to logs or reporting activity requires network traffic and can decrease network performance. Clever attackers who compromise a host can also attack and disable host-based IDSs. Host-based IDSs can be foiled by DoS attacks (since they may prevent any traffic from reaching the host where they're running or prevent reporting on such attacks to a console elsewhere on a network). Most significantly, a host-based IDS does consume processing time, storage, memory, and other resources on the hosts where such systems operate.

- **Application-based IDS characteristics**
  Pros: An application-based IDS concentrates on events occurring within some specific application. They often detect attacks through analysis of application log files and can usually identify many types of attack or suspicious activity. Sometimes an application-based IDS can even track unauthorized activity from individual users. They can also work with encrypted data, using application-based encryption/decryption services.
  Cons: Application-based IDSs are sometimes more vulnerable to attack than the host-based IDS. They can also consume significant application (and host) resources.

In practice, most commercial environments use some combination of network- and host- and/or application-based IDS systems to observe what's happening on the network while also monitoring key hosts and applications more closely.

IDSs may also be distinguished by their differing approaches to event analysis. Some IDSs primarily use a technique called *signature detection*. This resembles the way many antivirus programs use virus signatures to recognize and block infected files, programs, or active Web content from entering a computer system, except that it uses a database of traffic or activity patterns related to known attacks, called *attack signatures*. Indeed, signature detection is the most widely used approach in commercial IDS technology today. Another approach is called *anomaly detection*. It uses rules or predefined concepts about "normal" and "abnormal" system activity (called *heuristics*) to distinguish anomalies from normal system behavior and to monitor, report on, or block anomalies as they occur. Some IDSs support limited types of anomaly detection; most experts believe this kind of capability will become part of how more IDSs operate in the future. Read on for more information about these two kinds of event analysis techniques:

- **Signature-based IDS characteristics**
  Pros: A signature-based IDS examines ongoing traffic, activity, transactions, or behavior for matches with known patterns of events specific to known attacks. As with antivirus software, a signature-based IDS requires access to a current database of attack signatures and some way to actively

compare and match current behavior against a large collection of signatures. Except when entirely new, uncataloged attacks occur, this technique works extremely well.

Cons: Signature databases must be constantly updated, and IDSs must be able to compare and match activities against large collections of attack signatures. If signature definitions are too specific, a signature-based IDS may miss variations on known attacks. (A common technique for creating new attacks is to change existing, known attacks rather than to create entirely new ones from scratch.) Signature-based IDSs can also impose noticeable performance drags on systems when current behavior matches multiple (or numerous) attack signatures, either in whole or in part.

- **Anomaly-based IDS characteristics**

  Pros: An anomaly-based IDS examines ongoing traffic, activity, transactions, or behavior for anomalies on networks or systems that may indicate attack. The underlying principle is the notion that "attack behavior" differs enough from "normal user behavior" that it can be detected by cataloging and identifying the differences involved. By creating baselines of normal behavior, anomaly-based IDS systems can observe when current behavior deviates statistically from the norm. This capability theoretically gives anomaly-based IDSs abilities to detect new attacks that are neither known nor for which signatures have been created.

  Cons: Because normal behavior can change easily and readily, anomaly-based IDS systems are prone to false positives where attacks may be reported based on changes to the norm that are "normal," rather than representing real attacks. Their intensely analytical behavior can also impose sometimes-heavy processing overheads on systems where they're running. Furthermore, anomaly-based systems take a while to create statistically significant baselines (to separate normal behavior from anomalies); they're relatively open to attack during this period.

Today, many antivirus packages include both signature-based and anomaly-based detection characteristics, but only a few IDSs incorporate both approaches. Most experts expect anomaly-based detection to become more widespread in IDSs, but research and programming breakthroughs will be necessary to deliver the kind of capability that anomaly-based detection should be, but is currently not, able to deliver.

Finally, some IDSs are capable of responding to attacks when they occur. This behavior is desirable from two points of view. For one thing, a computer system can track behavior and activity in near-real time and respond much more quickly and decisively during early stages of an attack. Since automation helps hackers mount attacks, it stands to reason that it should also help security professionals fend them off as they occur. For another thing, IDSs run 24/7, but network administrators may not be able to respond as quickly during off hours as they can during peak hours (even if the IDS can page them with an alarm that an attack has begun). By automating a response to block incoming traffic from one or more addresses from which an attack originates, the IDS can halt an attack in process and block future attacks from the same address.

By implementing the following techniques, IDSs can fend off expert and novice hackers alike. Although experts are more difficult to block entirely, these techniques can slow them down considerably:

- Breaking TCP connections by injecting reset packets into attacker connections causes attacks to fall apart.

- Deploying automated packet filters to block routers or firewalls from forwarding attack packets to servers or hosts under attack stops most attacks cold—even DoS or DDoS attacks. This works for attacker addresses and for protocols or services under attack (by blocking traffic at different layers of the ARPA networking model, so to speak).

- Deploying automated disconnects for routers, firewalls, or servers can halt all activity when other measures fail to stop attackers (as in extreme DDoS attack situations, where filtering would only work effectively on the ISP side of an Internet link, if not higher up the ISP chain, as close to Internet backbones as possible).

- Actively pursuing reverse DNS lookups or other ways of attempting to establish hacker identity is a technique used by some IDSs, generating reports of malicious activity to all ISPs in the routes used between the attacker and the attackee. Because such responses may themselves raise legal issues, experts recommend obtaining legal advice before repaying hackers in kind.

For access to a great set of articles and resources on IDS technology, visit www.searchsecurity.techtarget.com and use the site's search engine to produce results on *intrusion detection* as a search string. We found Peter Mell's TechRepublic article *Intrusion Detection: A Guide to the Options* a particularly useful resource (see www.techrepublic.com/article_guest.jhtml?id=r00620011106ern01.htm&fromtm =e036), but there were lots of other good articles there as well.

Commercial IDS Players

Literally hundreds of vendors offer various forms of commercial IDS implementations. Most effective solutions combine network- and host-based IDS implementations. Likewise, most such implementations are primarily signature-based, with only limited anomaly-based detection capabilities present in certain specific products or solutions. Finally, most modern IDSs include some limited automatic response capabilities, but these usually concentrate on automated traffic filtering, blocking, or disconnects as a last resort. Although some systems claim to be able to launch counterstrikes against attacks, best practices indicate that automated identification and backtrace facilities are the most useful aspects that such facilities provide and are therefore those most likely to be used.

On the Scene...

Weighing IDS Options

In addition to the various IDS vendors mentioned in this section, judicious use of a good Internet search engine can help network administrators identify more additional potential IDS suppliers than they would ever have the time or inclination to investigate in detail. That's why we also urge administrators to consider an additional alternative: deferring some or all of the organization's network security technology decisions to a special type of outsourcing company. Known as managed security services providers, or MSSPs, these organizations can help their customers select, install, and maintain state-of-the-art security policies and technical infrastructures to match. For example, Guardent is an MSSP that includes comprehensive firewall and intrusion detection services among its various customer services; visit www.guardent.com for a description of the company's various service programs and offerings. Law enforcement professionals may find these organizations to be particularly knowledgeable sources for information, help, and support when tackling technology questions or teasing apart IT security puzzles.

A huge number of potential vendors can provide IDS products to companies and organizations. Without specifically endorsing any particular vendor, the following offer some of the most widely used and best-known solutions in this product space:

- **Cisco Systems** is perhaps best known for its switches and routers, but Cisco offers significant firewall and intrusion detection products as well (www.cisco.com).

- **GFI LANguard** is a family of monitoring, scanning, and file integrity check products that offer broad intrusion detection and response capabilities (www.gfi.com/languard).

- **Internet Security Systems (ISS)** offers a family of enterprise-class security products called RealSecure that includes comprehensive intrusion detection and response capabilities (www.iss.net).

- **Network-1 Security Solutions** offers various families of desktop and server (host-based) intrusion detection products, along with centralized security management facilities and firewalls (www.network-1.com).

- **TripWire** is perhaps the best known of all vendors of file integrity and signature-checking utilities (which are also known as TripWire). But TripWire also offers integrity check products for routers, switches, and servers, along with a centralized management console for its various products (www.tripwire.com).

A clearinghouse for Internet service providers known as ISP-Planet offers all kinds of interesting information online about MSSPs, plus related firewall, VPN, intrusion detection, security monitoring, antivirus, and other security services. For more information, visit any or all of the following URLs:

- ISP-Planet Survey: Managed Security Service Providers, participating providers chart
  www.isp-planet.com/technology/mssp/participants_chart.html.

- Managed firewall services chart
  www.isp-planet.com/technology/mssp/firewalls_chart.html.

- Managed virtual private networking chart
  www.isp-planet.com/technology/mssp/services_chart.html.

- Managed intrusion detection and security monitoring
  www.isp-planet.com/technology/mssp/monitoring_chart.html.

- Managed antivirus and managed content filtering and URL blocking
  www.isp-planet.com/technology/mssp/mssp_survey2.html.

- Managed vulnerability assessment and emergency response and forensics
  www.isp-planet.com/technology/mssp/mssp_survey3.html.

IP Spoofing and Other Antidetection Tactics

Despite your best efforts to backtrace unwanted e-mail or attack traffic, sometimes you will still be unable to determine its real source or conclusively identify the person or persons behind that activity. The primary reason for the phenomenon is that hackers typically generate network traffic or messages that contain fabricated data for the source address, port numbers, protocol IDs, and other information that normally permits such information to be conclusively associated with an originating IP address, if not also an originating process identifier (and by extension, the user or service responsible for creating that process). This is a deliberate and calculated technique to prevent identification of attackers and to deflect interest from the real source of such traffic to unwitting or uninvolved third parties.

The most common form of spoofing occurs when attackers try to insert fabricated traffic or messages that purport to originate inside a local network through an outside interface. That explains why the most common antispoofing rule enforced at most screening routers and firewalls is to drop any packets that arrive on an external interface that report an originating address that should only appear on an internal interface. Other forms of spoofing may be detected by using a backtrace or reverse DNS lookup to compare domain names and associated IP addresses (when that data is available) and dropping all packets where these two information items show no correlation (as when the reported IP address originates outside the range of addresses assigned to the organization from within which it claims to originate).

The real problem with spoofed traffic occurs when IDS or human administrators try to follow the traffic back to its source and hit various types of dead ends. Recall, for example, that various types of DoS or DDoS attacks rely on compromised intermediate computers, sometimes called zombies or agents, and you'll quickly understand why tracing attacks back to their source can't always identify attackers. When you determine where certain attacks originate, you may only be able to identify other victims rather than finding a "smoking gun" that points to an attacker. The more savvy and sophisticated the hacker who perpetrates an attack, the less likely it is that he or she will provide direct clues that lead directly to his or her primary presence on the Internet. Rather, you'll find your identification efforts will lead you down a trail of intermediaries, cut-outs, and anonymizer services, each of which must itself then be investigated to look for clues to the identity of the mastermind behind the cybercrimes you are pursuing.

This also explains why contacting service providers who may be forwarding attacks—and working with them not only to trace back the origination of attack traffic, but also to block it from going through unwitting intermediaries—is an important part of the process of handling security incidents and fending off future attacks. In addition, numerous Web sites and Internet services maintain lists of known IP addresses, domain names, and e-mail addresses from which attacks have originated in the past. By subscribing to such services and using them to configure packet and e-mail filters, administrators can fend off many potential sources of attack pre-emptively—as many ISPs themselves do—and avoid interacting with known sources of trouble.

Numerous sources for information about spammers and attackers are available online; we mention only a couple of examples here. To find more, use a good Internet search engine to search on strings such as *spam database, attacker database, spam prevention,* and so forth:

- DNS-Based Spam Databases: list of all known antispam databases www.declude.com/junkmail/support/ip4r.htm

- Lists of spammers, harassers, mail bombers, and other e-mail abusers www.sandes.dk/abusers/abusers.html

- *Intrusion Signatures and Analysis.* Stephen Northcutt, et al. New Riders, 2001, ISBN: 0735710635. This book documents hundreds of attack signatures, along with descriptions of remedies that often depend on blocking attacking IP addresses, subnets, or domain names. It covers many of the details involved in analyzing and responding to all kinds of attacks.

Honeypots, Honeynets, and Other "Cyberstings"

Although the strategy involved in luring hackers to spend time investigating attractive network devices or servers can cause its own problems, finding ways to lure intruders into a system or network improves the odds that you might be able to identify those intruders and pursue them more effectively. A *honeypot* is a computer system that is deliberately exposed to public access—usually on the Internet—for the express purpose of attracting and distracting attackers. Likewise, a *honeynet* is a network set up for the same purpose, where attackers will not only find vulnerable services or servers but will also find vulnerable routers, firewalls, and other network boundary devices, security applications, and so forth. In other words, these are the technical equivalent of the familiar police "sting" operation.

CyberLaw Review...

Walking the Line Between Opportunity and Entrapment

Most law enforcement officers are aware of the fine line that they must walk when setting up a "sting"—an operation in which police officers pretend to be victims or participants in crime with the goal of getting criminal suspects to commit an illegal act in their presence. Most states have laws that prohibit entrapment; that is, law enforcement officers are not allowed to *cause* a person to commit a crime and then arrest him or her for doing it. Entrapment is a defense to prosecution; if the accused person can show at trial that he or she was entrapped, the result must be an acquittal.

Courts have traditionally held, however, that providing a *mere opportunity* for a criminal to commit a crime does not constitute entrapment. To entrap involves using persuasion, duress, or other undue pressure to force someone to commit a crime that the person would not otherwise have committed. Under this holding, setting up a honeypot or honeynet would be like the (perfectly legitimate) police tactic of placing an abandoned automobile by the side of the road and watching it to see if anyone attempts to burglarize, vandalize, or steal it. It should also be noted that entrapment only applies to the actions of law enforcement or government personnel. A civilian cannot entrap, regardless of how much pressure is exerted on the target to commit the crime. (However, a civilian could be subject to other charges, such as criminal solicitation or criminal conspiracy, for causing someone else to commit a crime.)

The following characteristics are typical of honeypots or honeynets:

- Systems or devices used as lures are set up with only "out of the box" default installations so that they are deliberately made subject to all known vulnerabilities, exploits, and attacks.

- The systems or devices used as lures include no real sensitive information—such as passwords, data, applications, or services on which an organization must really depend or which it must absolutely protect—so these lures can be compromised, or even destroyed, without causing real damage, loss, or harm to the organization that presents them to be attacked.

- Systems or devices used as lures often also contain deliberately tantalizing objects or resources, such as files named *password.db,* folders named *Top Secret*, and so forth—often consisting only of encrypted garbage data or log files of no real significance or value—to attract and hold an attacker's interest long enough to give a backtrace a chance of identifying the attack's point of origin.

- Systems or devices used as lures also include or are monitored by passive applications that can detect and report on attacks or intrusions as soon as they start, so the process of backtracing and identification can begin as soon as possible.

Although this technique can certainly help identify the unwary or unsophisticated attacker, it also runs the risk of attracting additional attention or ire from savvier attackers. Honeypots or honeynets, once identified, are often publicized on hacker message boards or mailing lists and thus become *more* subject to attacks and hacker activity than they otherwise might. Likewise, if the organization that sets up a honeypot or honeynet is itself identified, its production systems and networks may also be subjected to more attacks than might otherwise be the case.

The honeypot technique is best reserved for use when a company or organization employs full-time IT security professionals who can monitor and deal with these lures on a regular basis, or when law enforcement operations seek to target specific suspects in a "virtual sting" operation. In such situations, the risks are sure to be well understood, and proper security precautions, processes, and procedures are far more likely to already be in place (and properly practiced). Nevertheless, for organizations that seek to identify and pursue attackers more proactively, honeypots and honeynets can provide valuable tools to aid in such activities.

Although numerous quality resources on honeypots and honeynets are available (try searching on either term at www.searchsecurity.techtarget.com), the following resources are particularly valuable for people seeking additional information on the topic. John McMullen's article *Enhance Intrusion Detection with a Honeypot* at www.techrepublic.com/article_guest.jhtml?id=r00220010412 mul01.htm&fromtm=e036 sheds additional light on this topic. The Honeynet Project at www.honeynet.org is probably the best overall resource on the topic online; it not only provides copious information on the project's work to define and document standard honeypots and honeynets, it also does a great job of exploring hacker mindsets, motivations, tools, and attack techniques.

Summary

Why is cybercrime detection important to investigators? Only by detecting that cybercrimes have occurred (or are occurring) will investigators be able to get a step ahead of the criminals and start the investigation while the trail is still "hot." Furthermore, only when suspicious activity is detected or observed do investigators know that they must take the steps necessary to obtain, secure, and prepare the evidence that will be necessary if any kind of legal charges are to stick. By following attack traffic from its targets back to its sources—even if those sources point only to other victims, not to the real attacker, as may often be the case—investigators can work with intermediate service providers to inform them about attacks and to help administrators and security personnel prevent such attacks from recurring. Even when prosecution isn't possible, or when those attacked decide not to pursue legal remedies, the information obtained and shared during the investigation can still have an overall positive impact on the security posture and awareness of the various parties investigators contact in the process.

One key element in obtaining evidence of cybercrimes may be found by enabling auditing of suspicious events in the boundary devices and operating systems that are likely to be subject to attack. IT professionals should understand how to instruct these systems and devices to log such data and should also be aware of what kinds and classes of events are most worth logging. These events include logon attempts, access to sensitive resources, use of administrative privileges, and monitoring of key system and data files. Likewise, law enforcement professionals should be aware not only that such logs exist, but that they often provide the most salient evidence of attempted or successful cybercrimes, and be aware of how to make appropriate efforts to secure and protect these logs before and during the investigation. Firewalls, routers, proxy servers, network servers, and intrusion detection systems can all contribute logs (plus related reports, alarms, and alerts) to substantiate allegations that unauthorized access, alteration, destruction, or denial of service occurred for information assets or services and, in some cases, to help track down the origin of the activity.

In the security model known as triple-A (authentication, authorization, and accounting), accounting is what makes auditing and logging of suspicious or illicit activity possible. IT and law enforcement professionals alike must understand this concept. Administrators must practice proper auditing and logging techniques to make sure they can detect cybercrimes (preferably before they succeed at compromising or damaging an organization's IT assets or infrastructure), obtain evidence that can help document illicit or unwanted activity, and assist in identifying the parties involved. Note also that boundary devices, Windows, and UNIX/ Linux systems all have their own methods for enabling and recording such data, but that evidence is readily obtainable to those who know what to ask for and where to find what they seek.

On the proactive, preventive side of system and network security, boundary systems and servers should be configured to prevent or deflect common known attacks while also auditing and logging any evidence that related activities may be occurring. Log data usually includes timestamps, putative source addresses and domain names, and other information that can be used to trace attacks to their systems of origin. E-mail messages include similar information so that unwanted e-mail can be tracked back through the systems that forwarded it from its sender to its ultimate receiver. All too often, however, such trails lead only to additional victims or to unwitting participants in cybercrimes rather than to the actual perpetrators.

When tracing the origin of cybercrimes and the paths their network activity takes from the point of origin to the point of attack, investigators will find numerous tools and utilities useful in obtaining information. Firewalls, screening routers, and IDSs can often seek out and obtain such information automatically, and numerous Windows and Linux or UNIX tools and commands also exist to reacquire or confirm such information manually. Both IT and law enforcement professionals should understand how to use such commands and utilities, particularly those that help map IP addresses to domain names, and vice versa, to help identify points along the path of attack as well as its ultimate origin.

Intrusion detection systems (IDS) not only help detect and actively foil cybercrimes, they also often help gather evidence about their patterns of attack, specific details about related activities, and so forth. Many IDSs operate on so-called attack signatures, which provide specific patterns of activity, network traffic, or behavior against which ongoing network activity may be compared to identify (and sometimes even foil) attacks as they occur. Like antivirus software and its signature databases, the IDS must also be constantly updated to keep its attack signatures up to date. Some IDSs also seek to identify anomalous behavior on systems or networks as a way to detect potential attacks for which signatures may not yet have been defined. In addition, IDSs can focus on individual hosts, applications, or networks to look for evidence of attacks or suspicious activity.

Despite investigators' real abilities to trace attacks and identify their points of origin, spoofing techniques can often foil their efforts to identify the real perpetrators of cybercrimes. Often, initial suspects in cybercrimes turn out to be themselves victims of cybercrimes that make them only intermediaries for real perpetrators, or they may only be unwitting participants in activities that originate elsewhere. That's why antispoofing techniques are important components when configuring firewalls, screening routers, and so forth to avoid potential attack and why investigators must be prepared to follow trails of attack further, rather than rely on what the initial available evidence reveals.

Some companies and organizations may choose to expose deliberate lures to attackers—sometimes known as honeypots (for individual systems that act as lures) or honeynets (for entire networks that act as lures)—as a way of attracting their attention, then distract them long enough to increase the odds of identifying the perpetrators involved. Although this strategy does incur some additional risks (much like those associated with what insurance professionals call an "attractive nuisance" or what law enforcement professionals can readily identify as "sting operations"), when properly implemented and practiced, it can produce definite, usable results.

In the final analysis, the proper practice of security includes planning for potential intrusion or compromise, with attendant tools and settings in place to gather evidence of the existence and operation of illicit or unwanted activities. Since such evidence is essential to detecting cybercrimes, preventing recurrence, and enabling successful prosecution, it's a key element of any proper security policy. This also explains why tracking and monitoring represents an essential "reality check" to make sure security is working properly and to be able to deal with unforeseen or unexpected attacks or vulnerabilities if and when they occur.

Frequently Asked Questions

The following Frequently Asked Questions, answered by the authors of this book, are designed to both measure your understanding of the concepts presented in this chapter and to assist you with real-life implementation of these concepts. To have your questions about this chapter answered by the author, browse to **www.syngress.com/solutions** and click on the **"Ask the Author"** form.

Q: What steps should IT or law enforcement professionals take to inventory logs, audit trails, and other potential sources of evidence or supporting data when investigating cybercrimes?

A: The short answer to this question is inventory, inspect, filter, document, and preserve. Let's expand on that a bit:

- **Inventory** Take stock of all firewalls, screening routers, IDS, systems and servers in use through which attack traffic may have passed or at which attack traffic or activity may have focused. Examine each element to identify related log files or audit trails, and take note of their names and locations.

- **Inspect** Examine the various log files or audit trails to determine if they contain records or entries that contain any traces of or evidence related to the incident under investigation. If so, add the name and location of each such audit trail to your list of evidence files.

- **Filter** Mathematics professionals call this step *data reduction* because it consists of ignoring entries that have no bearing on the incident you're investigating and collecting only those that are relevant to the matter at hand. Most log or event viewers include powerful data filtering tools; those that do not can usually be imported into a spreadsheet or database where those applications' built-in search tools can help you separate what's important from what's not. Make sure your notes include the name and location of the original source file and that you (or an expert witness) can attest that (a) data filtering is a common practice in log and event trace analysis and (b) you can demonstrate a direct relationship between the original file and the filtered file.

- **Document** Explain how the captured log entries, event listings, and so forth provide evidence of a cybercrime. In addition, document extensively the original sources for such data, including their locations; original filenames; current locations of original, unaltered files or drives; and how the data was handled since initial detection of the incident occurred.

- **Preserve** Take all steps necessary to preserve the original source of the log files or event data. This may require removing a hard drive from a system or even taking a system out of service so as to preserve the evidence in its most pristine possible state. See Chapter 10, "Collecting and Preserving Digital Evidence," for more information on handling evidence of cybercrimes.

Q: Given the need to interpret and explain the contents of some specific log file or event trace, how can an investigator obtain the information necessary to perform this task?

A: We've noted repeatedly that although the kinds of information recorded in logs and event traces is similar across multiple operating systems and boundary devices, the details vary according to each system and implementation. To document the layout and interpret the significance of log files and event traces, you will need to contact the vendor of the operating system, application, or device in question and ask the company to provide you with its documentation for those log files or event traces. In many cases, you'll be able to find this information for yourself if you use the vendor's search engine on its Web site or consult its technical support database or other information resources the vendor makes available online. If this doesn't produce the desired results, you may need to call the vendor's technical support operation and ask for assistance in identifying and obtaining the right information. In most cases, this should be an entirely routine matter and relatively easy to handle.

Q: How can an organization be sure that its IDS and other boundary devices are completely up to date and that they include the latest attack signatures, patches, fixes, and so forth?

A: In most cases, the system or software vendor that provides the IDS or other boundary device will also offer a notification service, online update information, and perhaps even tools you can use to assess the status of databases, patches, and fixes for such systems or services. Usually, a search on the vendor's Web site for the product in question will provide direct pointers to such information because the vendor understands the importance and urgency of that information as much as its customers do. When in doubt, contact the vendor's technical support operation. Here again, obtaining this information (or pointers to it) should be an entirely routine matter and easy to complete.

Q: If an organization becomes subject to an attack that appears to be unknown or for which no signatures appear to be available, how and to whom should this kind of information be reported?

A: The odds against falling prey to the first (or an early instance of an) attack are pretty low, but one unlucky organization must inevitably be the first victim of new vulnerabilities or be subjected to as yet undocumented attacks, as they occur. When this happens, it's important to notify all parties that might be concerned, including the following:

- Your upstream ISP and any other upstream ISPs that might sit between your network and the Internet.

- Any vendors whose products handle traffic related to such an attack, including firewall, proxy server, screening router, IDS, application, anti-virus (where applicable), and operating system vendors. Most companies have formal reporting mechanisms they provide to customers who want to report security incidents. It will help if you can identify these companies in advance so your response during an incident isn't slowed by researching this information.

- All the big general-incident clearinghouses should also be notified, including www.cert. org, www.nipc.org, and other more-focused security organizations that focus on your particular industry or market niche.

- In the United States, if your state has criminal laws that cover network attacks (such as unauthorized access or denial/disruption of network services), contact your local police or sheriff's office.

- In the United States, the FBI and Secret Service have developed guide-lines intended to encourage companies to report cyberattacks. See *CIO Cyberthreat Response & Reporting Guidelines* (in PDF format) at www.cio.com/research/security/incident_response.pdf for detailed information.

■ Outside the United States, contact the national or regional agency responsible for making and enforcing cybercrime laws. See the Appendix, "Fighting Cybercrime on a Global Scale," for more information.

Resources

■ *Auditing Security Events Overview*
www.microsoft.com/TechNet/prodtechnol/winxppro/proddocs/Audit_overview.asp

■ *Log Capture and Analysis*
www.microsoft.com/TechNet/itsolutions/ecommerce/maintain/monitor/logcanda.asp

■ *Overview of Syslog* (The GNU view of the UNIX Syslog facility)
www.la.utexas.edu/lab/software/lib/gnu/glibc/libc_377.html#SEC380

■ Use the SANS search engine to access SANS reading room articles, including Ray McAlarnen's *Unix Security Logging* paper
www.SANS.org

■ Lenny Zeltser's log traces and analysis archives
www.incidents.org/archives/y2k/123199-1220.htm

■ *Configuring a Linux Firewall,* by Matthew Tam
www.pisa.org.hk/download/seminar20011117-fw/linux_firewall.ppt

■ *Reporting Spam,* by Mark Whitis
www.freelabs.com/~whitis/spam_reporting.html

■ RFC 822 (RFC on SMTP e-mail header fields)
www.faqs.org/rfcs/rfc822.html

■ Everything E-mail
http://everythingemail.net

■ The Internet Mail Consortium
www.imc.org

- Sam Spade
  www.samspade.org

- Ad hoc IP Tools (Clearinghouse for online utilities to look up and attribute e-mail addresses, domain names, IP addresses, and more).
  www.tatumweb.com/iptools.htm

- *Intrusion Detection: A Guide to the Options,* by Peter Mell
  www.techrepublic.com/article_guest.jhtml?id=r00620011106ern01
  .htm&fromtm=e036

- Search Security (Search on "*IDS*" or "*intrusion detection system*" to locate great articles and resources on this subject)
  www.searchsecurity.techtarget.com

- Cisco Systems
  www.cisco.com

- GFI LANGuard
  www.gfi.com/languard

- Internet Security Systems
  www.iss.net

- Network-1 Security Solutions
  www.network-1.com

- TripWire
  www.tripwire.com

- ISP-Planet (Charts and surveys on MSSP providers)
  www.isp-planet.com/technology/mssp/participants_chart.html
  www.isp-planet.com/technology/mssp/firewalls_chart.html
  www.isp-planet.com/technology/mssp/services_chart.html
  www.isp-planet.com/technology/mssp/monitoring_chart.html
  www.isp-planet.com/technology/mssp/mssp_survey2.html
  www.isp-planet.com/technology/mssp/mssp_survey3.html

- Declude.com's DNS-based Spam Databases
  www.declude.com/junkmail/support/ip4r.htm

- Blocking Lists (Lists of spammers, harassers, mail bombers, and other e-mail abusers)
  www.sandes.dk/abusers/abusers.html

- *Intrusion Signatures and Analysis*, by Stephen Northcutt et al. New Riders, 2001, ISBN: 0735710635.

- *Enhance Intrusion Detection with a Honeypot,* by John F. McMullen www.techrepublic.com/article_guest.jhtml?id=r00220010412mul01.htm &fromtm=e036

- The Honeynet Project www.honeynet.org

Chapter 10

Collecting and Preserving Digital Evidence

Topics we'll investigate in this chapter:

- **Understanding the Role of Evidence in a Criminal Case**

- **Collecting Digital Evidence**

- **Preserving Digital Evidence**

- **Recovering Digital Evidence**

- **Documenting Evidence**

- **Computer Forensics Resources**

- **Understanding Legal Issues**

Introduction

In Chapter 9, we discussed methods of detecting that cybercrimes have occurred and tracking down the person(s) responsible. The next and perhaps most important step in prosecuting the offender is to collect the evidence that will be used to build the case to be presented at trial.

Forensics refers to the use of scientific or technological techniques to conduct an investigation or establish facts (evidence) in a criminal case. *Computer forensics* is defined as the application of computer investigation and analysis techniques in the interests of determining potential evidence, according to computer crime investigator Judd Robbins, quoted in *Computer Forensic Legal Standards and Equipment* on the SANS Institute Web site at http://rr.sans.org/incident/legal_standards.php. The field of computer forensics involves identifying, extracting, documenting, and preserving information that is stored or transmitted in electronic or magnetic form (that is, digital evidence). Like fingerprints, digital evidence can be visible (such as files stored on disk that can be accessed via the normal directory structure using standard file management tools such as Windows Explorer) or it can be latent (not readily visible or accessible, requiring some sort of processing—via special software or techniques—to locate and identify it). An important aspect of computer forensics involves finding and evaluating this "hidden data" for its evidentiary value.

Computer forensics standards have been developed that apply to the collection and preservation of digital evidence, which differs in nature from most other types of evidence and thus requires different methods of handling. Following procedures that are proper, accepted, and, in some cases, prescribed by law in dealing with evidence is vital to the successful prosecution of a cybercrime case. The proper handling of these procedures comes into play at two different points in a trial:

- If evidence is not collected and handled according to the proper standards, the judge may deem the evidence inadmissible when it is presented (usually based on the opposing attorney's *motion to suppress*) and the jury members will never get a chance to evaluate it or consider it in making their decision.

- If the evidence is admitted, the opposing attorney will attack its credibility during questioning of the witnesses who testify regarding it. Such an attack can create doubt in jury members' minds that will cause them to disregard the evidence in making their decision—and perhaps even taint the credibility of the entire case.

The entire investigation will be of little value if the evidence that shows the defendant's guilt is not allowed into the trial or if the jury gives it no weight. Thus proper handling of evidence is one of the most important issues facing all criminal investigators and, because of the intangible nature of digital evidence, cybercrime investigators in particular.

Because this is such an important topic—not only for investigators, but for prosecutors, judges, and justice system professionals involved in cybercrime cases—many organizations and publications are devoted solely to issues concerning digital evidence. The International Organization of Computer Evidence (IOCE) was established in 1995 to provide a forum for law enforcement agencies across the world to exchange information about computer forensics issues; its U.S. component is the Scientific Working Group on Digital Evidence (SWGDE). The International Association of Computer Investigative Specialists (IACIS; www.cops.org) is a nonprofit organization that is dedicated to educating law enforcement professionals in the area of computer forensics. The *International Journal of Digital Evidence* (www.ijde.org) is an online publication devoted to discussions of the theory and practice of handling digital evidence. *Computer Forensics Magazine* (www.forensic-computing.com) is published by DIBS, a maker of computer forensics equipment. *Computer Forensics Online* (www.shk-dplc.com/cfo) is a webzine that is run by attorneys and technical professionals specializing in computer law. Many other similar resources that focus on computer forensics are available, and more broad-based organizations such as the American Academy of Forensic Sciences (www.aafs.org) address computer crimes and digital evidence along with other forensics topics.

A glance at any of these resources will reveal that digital evidence handling is a huge topic that could easily fill several books (and already has). It is far beyond the scope of this chapter to cover every aspect of collecting and preserving digital evidence. This chapter provides an overview of the role evidence plays in a criminal case (particularly in a cybercrime case) and discusses standard procedures for dealing with digital evidence, as well as specific evidence location and examination techniques such as recovering supposedly deleted files, finding steganographic data, locating "forgotten" data, and decrypting encrypted data. We also outline procedures for documenting digital evidence and discuss some of the legal issues involved in evidence collection and handling. Finally, we provide many excellent online resources that furnish detailed instructions for performing the tasks described in this chapter and provide information about commercial services and equipment that can aid in the evidence recovery process.

Understanding the Role of Evidence in a Criminal Case

The process of collecting, examining, preserving, and presenting evidence is a legal process and is governed by the laws of the jurisdiction of the court in which the evidence will be introduced. Thus it is extremely important for investigators to become familiar with the applicable laws. These rules are adopted by statute and are usually codified into a document titled *Rules of Evidence*.

The rules of state courts may differ from those of the federal courts, and the rules for evidence in criminal trials may differ from those for civil trials. Generally, evidence must be *authenticated,* which in this context usually means that some witness must testify to its authenticity. In the case of digital evidence, this could be a witness who has personal knowledge of the evidence (for example, a person who shared the computer with the accused and observed the document or file in question on the computer). It could also be the first responder who saw the evidence on screen when responding to the incident or an expert who examined the computer and evidence after it was seized. One of the most important aspects of preparing to introduce evidence in court is determining which witnesses will testify as to its existence and validity, describe the circumstances of its discovery, and verify that it has not been tampered with.

CyberLaw Review…

When Authentication Is Not Required

Certain types of evidence are sometimes held by the Rules of Evidence to be self-authenticating. This means testimony as to authenticity isn't required and usually refers to such things as public documents under seal, certified copies of public records, official publications, and the like. It is also possible for both sides at trial to agree to *stipulate* as to the authenticity of a piece of evidence, in which case it does not have to be authenticated through testimony. When both sides agree to the stipulation of a fact (such as the fact that the evidence is authentic), the judge will advise the jury that they are to presume the fact is true and it is not a matter that has to be proved or disproved at trial.

Defining Evidence

Evidence can generally be defined as the means by which an alleged fact, the truth of which is subjected to scrutiny, is established or disproved. The legal significance of any given piece of evidence lies in its influence on the judge or jury at trial. There are three categories of evidence:

- **Physical evidence (sometimes called *real evidence*)** Consists of tangible objects that can be seen and touched.

- **Direct testamentary evidence** The testimony of a witness who can give an account of facts based on personal experience through the use of the five senses.

- **Circumstantial evidence** Not based on personal observation of the offense but on observation or knowledge of facts that tend to support a conclusion indirectly but do not prove it definitively.

CyberLaw Review...

It's "Only" Circumstantial

The news media and (via movies and novels) the entertainment industry—not to mention defense attorneys—often refer to evidence as "merely circumstantial," with the implication that circumstantial evidence does not really constitute evidence or that it is inherently inferior to direct evidence. In fact, circumstantial evidence is equally admissible in court, and most criminals are convicted based on circumstantial evidence. This is because in many cases criminals do not commit their offenses in front of witnesses, so there is no one to testify to having seen or heard the offense occur. It is the *totality of the evidence* in the minds of the jury members that matters—whether all that evidence, taken together, persuades them beyond a reasonable doubt that the defendant committed the crime.

Here is an example of direct evidence as compared to circumstantial evidence:

> **Direct evidence** John Smith testifies under oath that he was in the room with his friend, Joe Hacker, when Joe broke into the ABC Corporation's computer network and that John saw the break-in take place on Joe's computer screen.

Continued

> **Circumstantial evidence** The network administrator of ABC Corporation testifies that an intruder using the IP address *xxx.xxx.xxx.xxx* penetrated the network at 2:20 A.M. on December 12, 2001. ISP records show that the IP address in question was assigned via DHCP to Joe Hacker's computer at that time on that date. Joe's girlfriend testifies that Joe was in the study "doing something on the computer" between the hours of midnight and 4:00 A.M. on that date. No one actually saw Joe perform the intrusion, and none of the evidence definitively proves that he did, but taken together, the evidence supports the conclusion that Joe Hacker broke into the ABC Corporation network.

In a computer crime case, evidence tends to be one of the following types, as classified by the SWGDE/IOCE standards:

- **Digital evidence** Information of value to a criminal case that is stored or transmitted in digital form.

- **Data objects** Information of value to a criminal case that is associated with physical items.

- **Physical items** The physical media on which digital information is stored or through which it is transmitted or transferred.

Digital evidence can be classified as *original digital evidence* (that is, the physical items and data objects associated with those items at the time the evidence was seized) and *duplicate digital evidence* (referring to an accurate digital reproduction of all the data objects contained on an original physical item).

Another way in which "written" evidence is sometimes classified is as either demonstrative evidence or documentary evidence. *Demonstrative evidence* is that which reconstructs the scene or incident in question and allows jurors to view it, using visual aids such as graphs, charts, drawings, and models. *Documentary evidence* usually refers to written documents that constitute evidence. For example, a letter or photograph is generally considered documentary evidence. When documents are introduced as evidence, the entire document must generally be admitted even though only part of it might be read to the court. In some cases of digital evidence, there is debate among legal scholars as to whether it should be classified as documentary or demonstrative. Computer evidence is not quite like other documentary evidence (which is usually paper) for several reasons: A copy of a digital file is generally identical to the original, and a document can be copied without physically removing it from its location or leaving behind any indication that it has been copied. Many legal experts consider digital evidence to be more demonstrative than documentary, because the field of computer forensics basically concerns itself with reconstructing the crime scene. However, this view could vary depending on the type of digital evidence associated with a particular crime.

Under the *best-evidence rule*, the original document must be presented as evidence unless it has been destroyed or falls under other exceptions. However, the Federal Rules of Evidence recognize that computer evidence is different from other written evidence. Rule 1001-3 addresses this issue, saying, "If data are stored by computer or similar device, any printout or other output readable by sight, shown to reflect the data accurately, is an original." The burden is on the party introducing the evidence to show that it does indeed reflect the data accurately. It must be proven that the evidence is what it is claimed to be and that it hasn't been changed since it was taken into custody. Otherwise, the evidence will be deemed inadmissible.

Admissibility of Evidence

There are a number of requirements for evidence to be admissible in court. The evidence must be *competent* (that is, reliable and credible), it must be *relevant* (it tends to prove a fact of the case), and it must be *material* (it substantiates an issue that is in question in the case).

In addition, to be admissible in U.S. courts, evidence must be obtained legally. That is, it must be obtained in accordance with the laws governing search and seizure, including laws expressed in the U.S. and state constitutions. If evidence is obtained through an illegal search, even though it proves the guilt of the defendant, the evidence is considered to be "tainted." This is known as the "fruits of the poisonous tree" doctrine, or the *exclusionary rule*.

Case law in some jurisdictions sets special rules for the admissibility of scientific evidence. Under the Federal Rules of Evidence, Rule 402, all relevant evidence is admissible except as otherwise provided under the U.S. Constitution, by Act of Congress, or under the Federal Rules of Evidence themselves (for example, evidence obtained in violation of a suspect's constitutional rights). Rule 401 defines relevant evidence as "any evidence having a tendency to make the existence of any fact that is of consequence to the determination of the action more probable or less probable than it would be without the evidence." This is known as the *relevancy test*. Another standard sometimes applied to scientific evidence is the *general acceptance test*, also known as the *Frye standard*, which holds that a scientific technique must be generally accepted in the field before the results of the technique can be admitted as evidence.

Forensic Examination Standards

While the rules of evidence regarding digital data are not clear cut, it is always safest to exceed the minimum requirements for admissibility. When investigators take extra precautions to ensure the integrity of evidence, above and beyond what the court might find acceptable, not only will the possibility of having the evidence excluded by the judge be avoided, but the impression on the jury will be more favorable as well.

Organizations such as the IACIS provide standards governing forensic examination procedures for their members (see www.cops.org/forensic_examination_procedures.htm). Showing in court that you adhered to such high standards in conducting the investigation will enhance your case.

Most computer forensics organizations and experts agree on some basic standards regarding the handling of digital evidence, which can be summarized as follows:

- The original evidence should be preserved in a state as close as possible to the state it was in when found.

- If at all possible, an exact copy (image) of the original should be made to be used for examination so as not to damage the integrity of the original.

- Copies of data made for examination should be made on media that is *forensically sterile*—that is, there must be no pre-existing data on the disk or other media; it should be completely "clean" and checked for freedom from viruses and defects.

- All evidence should be properly tagged and documented and the chain of custody preserved, and each step of the forensic examination should be documented in detail.

Collecting Digital Evidence

As we discussed in Chapters 7 and 9, a network administrator will often be the first person to become aware of a cybercrime in a corporate setting, and the IT incident response team (if the company has one) will take the initial steps to stop the crime in progress and "freeze" the crime scene before law enforcement personnel take over. Even after the police are called in, the process of collecting digital evidence usually involves several people: the first responders (officers or official security personnel who arrive first at the crime scene), the investigator or investigative team, and the crime scene technicians and specialists who are called out to process the evidence. It is important that one person be designated in charge of the scene who has the authority to make final decisions as to how the scene will be secured, how the search will be conducted, and how the evidence will be handled. This is usually the role of the senior investigator. It is equally important that each member of this team understand his or her role and adhere to it. The ability of the team to work together is essential to the successful collection of evidence.

The Role of First Responders

First responders should follow the same edict to which aspiring physicians swear when they take the Hippocratic oath: *First, do no harm*. Unless specifically trained in computer forensics, people who are first on the scene should not attempt to do anything with or to the computers other than protect them from tampering or damage. It is very easy for technically astute criminals to plant Trojan horses or otherwise "rig" their computers to automatically destroy evidence when shut down or restarted by anyone other than themselves. The first responder should *not* attempt to shut down or unplug the computer or access it to look for evidence. The first responder *should* be concerned with the following tasks:

- **Identifying the crime scene** Officers who arrive first at the scene should identify the scope of the crime scene and establish a perimeter. This might include only one area of a room or it might include several rooms or even multiple buildings if the suspect is working with a complex setup of networked computers. First responders can begin compiling a list of systems that might have been involved in the criminal incident and from which evidence will be collected.

- **Protecting the crime scene** In a cybercrime case where digital evidence is sought, all computer systems—including those that appear to be powered off or nonfunctional—should be considered part of the crime scene, as should laptop, notebook, and other portable computers (including handheld computers and PDAs). The items subject to seizure may be limited by the wording of the applicable search warrant, but first responders should cordon off and protect as much of the computer and electronic equipment as possible and wait for the investigator in charge of the case to determine what equipment, if any, will be excluded.

- **Preserving temporary and fragile evidence** In the case of evidence that could disappear before investigators arrive (such as information that is on the monitor and changing), first responders should take any possible steps to preserve or record it. If a camera is available, photos of the screen will preserve a record of what was there. If no camera is available, officers should take detailed notes and be prepared to testify in court as to what they saw.

NOTE

Protecting the crime scene could also involve disconnecting the computers from the network so as to remove a way for the suspect or an accomplice to deliberately alter the evidence or for someone else to unintentionally do so.

The Role of Investigators

The IT incident response team might have already begun to collect evidence in some cases. If so, the best practice is to have one person from the IT team coordinate the hand-over (and explanation, if necessary) of that evidence with one person from the police investigative team. The investigator (or the investigative team) is generally responsible for coordinating the activities of all others at the scene and will be responsible for the following:

- **Establishing the chain of command** The investigator in charge of the scene should ensure that everyone else is aware of the chain of command and that important decisions are filtered through him or her. Computers and related equipment should not be accessed, moved, or removed without explicit instructions from the senior investigator. The investigators shape and control the investigation. If the investigator in charge has to leave the scene, he or she should designate a person remaining on the scene to be in charge of the scene and stay in close contact with that person until all evidence has been collected and moved to secure storage.

- **Conducting the crime scene search** An investigator should direct the search of the crime scene, which may be carried out by investigators or by other officers. If the search warrant allows, officers should look for all computer hardware, software, manuals, written notes, and logs related to the operation of the computers. This includes printers, scanners, and all storage media: diskettes, optical discs (CDs, DVDs, and so on), tapes,

Zip or Jaz and other removable disks, and any "extra" hard disks that might be lying around.

- **Maintaining integrity of the evidence** Investigators should continue to protect the evidence as preparations are made to preserve volatile evidence, duplicate the disks, and properly shut down the system. The investigator should oversee the actions of the crime scene technicians and convey any special considerations that should be taken based on the nature of case and knowledge of the suspect(s).

The Role of Crime Scene Technicians

Crime scene technicians responding to a cybercrime case should, if at all possible, be specifically trained in computer forensics. (See the "Computer Forensics Training and Certification" section later in this chapter.) Computer forensics specialists must have a strong background in computer technology with an understanding of how disks are structured, how file systems work, and how and where data is recorded. Generally, crime scene technicians will be responsible for the following tasks (although these may overlap with those of the investigators):

- **Preserving volatile evidence and duplicating disks** Volatile data is that which is in the computer's memory and consists of processes that are running. (See the "Preserving Volatile Data" section later in the chapter for instructions on how to deal with it.) Disks should be duplicated prior to shutdown, in case the system is rigged to wipe the disks on startup. (See the "Disk Imaging" section for information on how to duplicate disks.)

- **Shutting down the systems for transport** Proper shutdown is important to maintain the integrity of the original evidence. One school of thought says the computer should be shut down through the standard method (closing all programs and so on) to avoid corrupting files. Another says that after ensuring that no defragmentation or disk-checking program is running, you should shut down the computer by disconnecting the power cord, to prevent running of self-destruct programs that are set to run on shutdown. UNIX computers usually should not be abruptly shut down this way while the root user is logged on because doing so can damage data. Some forensics experts recommend that the technician change accounts using the **su** command or, if the root password is available, that the **sync;sync;halt** command be used before powering off.

NOTE

If the system is turned off, the investigative team generally should seize the computer and boot it in a controlled environment. When you do bring the system up, you should not boot from the computer's hard disk but instead boot from a controlled boot disk to prevent the operating system from writing to the hard disk, so that crucial data won't be over-written. Then you can create a bitstream image of the hard disk.

- **Tagging and logging the evidence** All evidence should be tagged and/or marked with the initials of the officer or technician, time and date collected, case number, and identifying information. The evidence on the tag or mark should also be entered in the evidence log. (See the "Documenting Evidence" section later in this chapter.)

- **Packaging the evidence** Computer evidence, especially any containing exposed circuit boards (such as hard disks), should be placed in antistatic bags for transport. Paper documentation such as manuals and books should be placed in plastic bags or otherwise protected from damage.

- **Transporting the evidence** All evidence should be transported as directly as possible to the secure evidence storage locker or room. During transport, the evidence should not be allowed to come into contact with any equipment that generates a magnetic field (including police radios and other electronic equipment in the squad car) nor left in the sun or in a vehicle or other place where the temperature rises above about 75 degrees Fahrenheit. The chain of custody must be meticulously maintained during transport.

- **Processing the evidence** When the duplicate disk is brought back to the lab, the disk image can be reconstructed and the data analyzed using special forensics software tools. (See the "Computer Forensics Equipment and Software" section later in this chapter.)

Computer Seizure Checklist

Every case is different, but some general guidelines should be followed when computer equipment is seized as evidence in a criminal case. Following these procedures will help protect the legal integrity of the evidence and, equally important, will help prevent loss of essential evidence. These procedures assume that the computer is turned on when you encounter it.

1. Photograph the monitor screen(s) to capture the data displayed there at the time of seizure. Be aware that more than one monitor can be connected to a single computer; modern operating systems such as Windows 2000/XP support spreading the display across as many as 10 monitors. Monitors attached to the computer but turned off could still be displaying parts of the desktop and open applications.

2. Take steps to preserve volatile data. (See the section "Preserving Volatile Data" later in this chapter.)

3. Make an image of the disk(s) to work with so that the integrity of the original can be preserved. This step should be taken *before* the system is shut down, in case the owner has installed a self-destruct program to activate on shutdown or startup. (See the "Disk Imaging" section of this chapter for information on different approaches to duplicating the disks.)

4. Check the integrity of the image to confirm that it is an exact duplicate, using a cyclic redundancy checker or other program that uses a checksum or hashing algorithm to verify that the image is accurate and reliable.

5. Shut down the system safely according to the procedures for the operating system that is running.

6. Photograph the system setup before moving anything, including back and front of the computer showing cables and wires attached.

7. Unplug the system and all peripherals, marking/tagging each piece as it is collected.

Continued

8. Use an antistatic wrist strap or other grounding method before handling equipment, especially circuit cards, disks, and other similar items.

9. Place circuit cards, disks, and the like in antistatic bags for transport. Keep all equipment away from heat sources and magnetic fields.

Preserving Digital Evidence

Digital evidence is, by its nature, fragile. Some data is *volatile*—that is, it is transient in nature and, unlike data stored on disk, will be lost when the computer is shut down. Data on a computer disk can be easily damaged, destroyed, or changed either deliberately or accidentally. The first step in handling such digital evidence is to protect it from any sort of manipulation or accident. The best way to do this is to immediately make a complete bitstream image of the media on which the evidence is stored.

NOTE

A *bitstream image* is a copy that records every data bit that was recorded to the original storage device, including all hidden files, temp files, corrupted files, file fragments and erased files that have not yet been overwritten. In other words, every binary digit is duplicated exactly onto the copy media. Bitstream copies (sometimes called *bitstream backups*) use CRC computations to validate that the copy is the same as the original source data. For more information, see *Bit Stream Backup—Defined* at www.forensics-intl.com/def2.html.

The "mirror image" should be an exact duplicate of the original, and the original should then be stored in a safe place where its integrity can be maintained. (See the "Environmental Factors" section later in the chapter.) The copy is made via a process called *disk imaging*. In some cases, evidence could be limited to a few data files that can be copied individually rather than creating a copy of the entire disk. In the following sections, we discuss both disk-imaging and file-copying techniques. We also look at the importance of ensuring the integrity of disks used for imaging or copying, and we consider environmental factors that can affect the integrity of evidence, as well as preservation concerns related to specific types of storage media.

Preserving Volatile Data

The data that is held in temporary storage in the system's memory (including random access memory, cache memory, and the onboard memory of system peripherals such as the video card or NIC) is called *volatile data* because the memory is dependent on electric power to hold its contents. When the system is powered off or if power is disrupted, the data disappears.

According to the IEEE Internet draft titled *Guidelines for Evidence Collection and Archiving,* the most volatile evidence should be collected first. This makes sense because the most volatile evidence is the most likely to disappear before it can be documented or collected. The draft lists the "order of volatility" as:

1. Registers and cache

2. Routing tables, ARP cache, process tables, and kernel statistics

3. Contents of system memory

4. Temporary file systems

5. Data on disk

Collecting volatile data presents a problem because doing so changes the state of the system (and the contents of the memory itself). Some experts recommend that investigators or crime scene technicians capture such data as running processes, the network status and connections, and a "dump" of the data in RAM, documenting each task or command they run to do so. Some of this work can be done by running such commands as **netstat** (on both Windows and UNIX systems) and **nbtstat** (on Windows only) to view current network connections. The **arp** command will tell you what addresses are in the ARP cache (and thus have recently connected to the system). The **dd** command can be used to create a snapshot of the contents of memory on UNIX machines, and the **ps** command can be used to view the currently running processes. On NT/2000 machines, the downloadable **pslist** utility can be used to list running processes, or they can be viewed in Task Manager. Other commands such as **ipconfig** (Windows) or **ifconfig** (UNIX) can be used to gather information about the state of the network. These programs should be run from a special forensics CD that you bring with you (instead of running the same commands from the hard disk of the suspect computer) and should not require any programs or libraries from the computer's hard disk to run.

Disk Imaging

Disk imaging refers to the process of making an exact copy of a disk. Imaging is sometimes also called *disk cloning* or *ghosting,* but the latter terms usually refer to images created for purposes other than evidence preservation. Disk imaging differs from just copying all the files on a disk in that the disk structure and relative location of data on the disk are preserved. When you copy all the data on a disk to another disk, that data will usually be stored on the new disk in contiguous clusters as there is room to store it. That way, all the data on the two disks will be identical, but the way that the data is distributed on the disks will not. When you create a disk image (a bitstream copy), each physical sector of the disk is copied so that the data is distributed in the same way, and then the image is compressed into a file called an *image file.* This image is exactly like the original, both physically and logically.

There are a number of different ways to create a bit-level duplicate of a disk, including:

- Removing the hard disk from the suspect computer and attaching it to another computer (preferably a forensic workstation) to make the copy

- Attaching another hard disk to the suspect computer and making the copy

- Using a standalone imaging device such as the DIBS Rapid Action Imaging Device (RAID)

- Using a network connection (Ethernet connection, crossover cable, null modem cable, USB, or the like) to transfer the contents of the disk to another computer or forensic workstation

Which of these methods you choose will usually depend on the equipment that you have at hand. A portable forensic workstation or standalone imaging device is probably the best solution, but it's also the most expensive.

A History of Disk Imaging

Disk imaging can serve a number of purposes and was initially used for purposes other than computer forensics and digital evidence collection. Computer virus researchers used disk imaging in the 1980s when studying new computer viruses, so they could execute the virus code without destroying or damaging the data on the original disk. Copying just the virus files didn't always work because some viruses had to be on specific parts of the disk to do what they were written to do. For this reason, a program was developed that would copy the data exactly as it was located on the disk, duplicating sector addresses and creating an exact duplication or disk "image."

According to *The History of Image Copying Technology* on the DIBS Computer Forensics Web site at www.forensic-computing.com/articles/imag.html, the usefulness of this program to computer crime investigators was first recognized by Detective Inspector John Austen at London's Scotland Yard, and the concept of computer forensics imaging equipment was born shortly thereafter.

Meanwhile, disk imaging has come to be used for creating backups that can be quickly and easily put into place if the original disk fails by simply swapping out the imaged disk for the original. Another popular use of imaging is to speed up the process of rolling out operating systems and software on a large number of computers simultaneously, with the same configuration. Norton Ghost is one of the most popular programs used for this purpose. There are several versions of Ghost; for more information, investigate the Product menus at www.symantec.com.

It is important for investigators to understand the differences between these imaging purposes and the products that are designed for the different purposes. Cloning products such as Ghost are not designed to preserve the user data on a disk; the purpose is to create a standard installation configuration that can be distributed to multiple computers. Although these products can be used on a disk with user data, there is another problem: The image they create is not an exact bit-by-bit copy of the original. According to the Symantec Knowledge Base, "Normally, Ghost does not create an exact duplicate of a disk. Instead, Ghost recreates the partition information as needed and copies the contents of the files." Thus a checksum of the image disk almost always results in a value that is different from the checksum value of the original disk. This could be reason for exclusion of the evidence in some courts, because Rules of Evidence generally require that when a duplicate is admitted as evidence in place of the original, it must be an *exact* duplicate of the original. Although investigators sometimes use Ghost to create a disk image, and some versions of Ghost have switches and options that can be used to force it to create a bitstream copy, it is usually best to use software specifically designed for forensics purposes. On the other hand, if Ghost is the only duplication program you have, a ghosted image is better than no image.

Imaging Software

A number of disk-imaging programs are popular with law enforcement computer forensics specialists. These programs were developed specifically for the purpose of creating duplicate disks to be used in processing computer evidence and analyzing that evidence. Here are some examples of these products:

- **SafeBack** SafeBack has been marketed to law enforcement agencies since 1990 and has been used by the FBI and the Criminal Investigation Division of the IRS to create image files for forensics examination and evidentiary purposes. It is capable of duplicating individual partitions or entire disks of virtually any size, and the image files can be transferred to SCSI tape units or almost any other magnetic storage media. The product contains CRC functions to check integrity of the copies and date and timestamps to maintain an audit trail of the software's operations. The vendor provides a three-day computer forensics course to train forensics specialists in the use of the software. (In fact, the company does not provide technical support to individuals who have not undergone this training.) SafeBack is DOS-based and can be used to copy DOS, Windows, and UNIX disks (including Windows NT/2000 RAID drives) on Intel-compatible systems. Images can be saved as multiple files for storage on CDs or other small-capacity media. To avoid legal concerns about possible alteration, no compression or translation is used in creating the image.

- **Encase** Unlike SafeBack, which is a character-based program, Encase has a friendly graphical interface that makes it easier for many forensics technicians to use. It provides for previewing evidence, copying targeted drives (creating a bitstream image), and searching and analyzing data. Documents, zipped files, and e-mail attachments can be automatically searched and analyzed, and Registry and graphics viewers are included. The software supports multiple platforms and file systems, including Windows NT with stripe sets and Palm OS devices. The software calls the bitstream drive image an Evidence File and mounts it as a virtual drive (a read-only file) that can be searched and examined using the GUI tools. Timestamps and other data remain unchanged during the examination. The "preview" mode allows the investigator to use a null modem cable or Ethernet connection to view data on the subject machine without changing anything; the vendor says it is impossible to make any alterations to the evidence during this process.

- **ProDiscover** This Windows-based application, designed by the Technology Pathways forensics team, creates bitstream copies saved as compressed image files on the forensics workstation. Its features include the ability to recover deleted files from slack space, analyze the Windows NT/2000 alternate datastreams for hidden data, and analyze images created with the UNIX *dd* utility and generate reports. The vendor hosts an e-mail discussion list for exchange of tips and techniques and peer support for users of computer forensics products (www.techpathways.com).

NOTE

The National Institute of Standards and Technology (NIST) developed a disk-imaging tool specification as part of its Computer Forensics Tool Testing Project, the objective of which was to provide for standardization of automated tools used in investigations involving computer forensics.

Standalone Imaging Tools

Standalone imaging tools such as the DIBS Portable Evidence Recovery Unit (PERU) and Rapid Action Imaging Device (RAID) eliminate the need for a second computer while maintaining the integrity of the suspect computer. These portable units can make duplicates of the suspect computer's disk(s) onto another clean hard disk or optical media without the need to remove the original disk from the suspect computer.

Role of Imaging in Computer Forensics

Disk imaging is accepted as standard practice in computer forensics to preserve the integrity of the original evidence. Disk imaging differs from creating a standard backup of a disk (for fault-tolerance purposes) in that ambient data is not copied to a backup; only active files are copied. Because a backup created with popular backup programs such as the Windows built-in backup utility, BackupExec, ARCserve, or the like is not an exact duplicate (in other words, a physical bit-stream image), these programs should not be used for disk imaging. Programs such as Norton Ghost include switches that allow you to make a bitstream copy, but these programs were not originally designed for forensics use and do not include the features and analysis tools that are included with imaging programs and standalone imaging systems designed especially for forensics examination.

"Snapshot" Tools and File Copying

Sometimes it is not possible or desirable to make a full bitstream image of a disk. This could be because the system is mission critical and management does not want to have it out of commission during an investigation or because the decision has already been made not to pursue prosecution. However, there are still

ways to collect data about the intrusion or other crime for the purpose of analyzing what happened and preventing it from happening again.

One set of software tools designed to allow administrators to create a "snapshot" of the state of a machine that has been compromised is the Coroner's
Toolkit, written by the authors of the popular UNIX utility called the System
Administrator Tools for Analyzing Networks (SATAN). Running these tools on a
UNIX system that has been breached is very helpful in performing a forensic
analysis, because it will provide information on running processes, the state of the
network, deleted files, user information, and much more. For more information
about the Toolkit, see http://rootprompt.org/article.php3?article=738.

In some cases, when evidence is documentary in nature, it might be possible
to introduce copies of individual files rather than copying the entire disk. This
method should be used only when you need specific identifiable documents and
there is no need to search for ambient data or other hidden data.

Special Considerations

Because certain kinds of digital evidence can be incredibly volatile, and all digital
evidence can be damaged or compromised by improper copying, storage, or handling, it's essential to exercise extreme care and diligence when gathering and
handling such evidence. Therefore, numerous special considerations can come
into play, including environmental factors, retention of time and datestamps, and
ways to preserve specific types of data. These concerns are discussed in the following sections.

Environmental Factors

Magnetically encoded data can be destroyed or damaged (scrambled) by exposure
to a magnet or an electromagnetic field generated by many types of electronic
equipment. Radio frequency (RF) transmissions can also damage digital data, as
can exposure to static electricity or extreme heat.

It is very important for investigators and crime scene technicians to be aware
of environmental factors that can affect the integrity of data. They must be sure
that digital evidence is packaged in such a way as to protect it from damage and
stored in an electromagnetically "clean" environment that is properly cooled.

When you're packaging magnetic or optical media (tapes, CDs, hard disks,
diskettes, Zip/Jaz disks), first place the media inside an antistatic bag, then place it
in a box that has enough extra room so that you can "pad" it with bubble wrap,
Styrofoam "peanuts," or other protective material. Try to anchor the media against
the bottom or side of the box so that it won't move around in transit. Be sure to

list the contents on the outside of the box and identify it as evidence (with case number). Labels warning carriers to handle the package carefully might also be appropriate. If you are shipping or mailing the package, use a method that allows tracking (registered mail when using the U.S. Postal Service).

Retaining Time and Datestamps

The time and date of creation or modification of a file can be an important issue in a criminal case. Remember that the time and datestamp on the files will be in accordance with the time and date set on the system clock. Some systems default to a particular time zone (usually Greenwich Mean Time, or GMT). If the user set up the system without configuring the proper time zone or if the user deliberately changed the date and time settings, the time and datestamps on the files might not correlate to "real-world" occurrences regarding when the files were created.

This can be a problem if, for example, the system records show that a file was created on a particular date and the suspect is able to prove that he or she was nowhere near the computer on that date. For this reason, you should note the system time and date settings before shutting down the computer and document them with a photograph, if possible; otherwise, with written notes.

Opening a file changes the file's time and date records. Thus it might be prudent to photograph the screen showing the file access or modification times prior to opening the file. You should be prepared to testify as to your actions and provide expert testimony that the actions you took changed the time and datestamps but did not modify the contents of the file in any way. When you do all your work on an image rather than the original, the original times and dates will be on the original disk. You can create a second copy of the original to illustrate this fact.

Preserving Data on PDAs and Handheld Computers

If evidence is contained on a personal digital assistant (PDA) or a palm-sized handheld computer (Palm OS or Pocket PC device), be aware that some of these models will lose data if their batteries die. Most come with recharger units, and it is prudent to seize the charger and keep the unit charged until the data can be extracted.

Research scientists at @Stake (www.atstake.com) created a forensics tool called Palm Disk Duplicator (PDD) that will duplicate the data on devices running the Palm OS, including the original Palm Pilots and devices marketed by Sony (Clio), Handspring (Visor), and other vendors. PDD creates a complete image of the device's memory, which includes all applications and user data and data that has been marked to be deleted. (These items are not actually removed until the next synchronization session.) The tool also gathers information about the device, such as OS version, processor and RAM/ROM information, and Flash ID. For more information about PDD, see the white paper at http://63.251 .138.38/atstake/acrobat/pdd_palm_forensics.pdf.

If you don't have such a tool available, another way to preserve data on a handheld is to copy the relevant files to a Compact Flash or Smart Media card. Most handhelds have a slot for using some sort of flash memory media.

NOTE

LCTechnology International conducts a 16-hour course in personal digital device forensics that focuses on retrieving evidence from Palm, Pocket PC, and other handheld devices. For more information, see www.lc-tech.com/Personal%20Digital%20Device%20Forensics.asp.

Recovering Digital Evidence

In some computer crimes cases, the evidence you need will be neatly stored on the hard disk (or on easily accessible removable media), with the files conveniently labeled to indicate their contents. In other cases, the investigator is not quite so lucky. Cybercriminals might get wind of the fact that they're about to be "busted" and delete incriminating data or even format and/or repartition the disk. Some particularly tech-savvy cybercriminals use sophisticated techniques to hide data in unlikely or nontraditional areas. Other times, the data that would be useful to the investigator is never stored on disk at all—at least, not to the computer user's knowledge. However, a great deal of *ambient data* is stored in locations such as cache files, swap/page files, and temporary (temp) files, as well as "leftover" data that occupies the "unallocated" space on the disk, the "slack" space in clusters that are larger than the files they hold, and the "gaps" between partitions or sectors. In the following sections, we look at how investigators can recover data that is not immediately apparent when browsing the file structure but that can prove critical to building a criminal case.

NOTE

Recovery of digital data, especially data that is partially destroyed or supposedly erased, is sometimes referred to as *electronic dumpster diving*.

Recovering "Deleted" and "Erased" Data

Many computer users—including cybercriminals—think that when they delete a file, it is erased from the hard disk. Even so-called computer experts have been heard to say on television and radio that once the Windows "trash" has been emptied, the files there are gone from the disk. This simply isn't true. Deleting a file does not remove the content of the file; it merely removes the pointer to that file from the file allocation table (FAT), master file table (MFT), or other scheme that the operating system uses to pinpoint the location of a particular file on the disk. Data is stored on the disk in *clusters,* which are units consisting of a set number of bits. Because parts of a file are not always stored in contiguous clusters on the physical disk, but instead parts of it could be spread across the disk in separate locations, removing the pointer makes it difficult for the file to be reconstructed—but *difficult* does not equal *impossible.*

When the file is deleted, the disk location in which it is stored is marked as *unallocated space,* which means that it is available when new data needs to be written. However, on a large disk it might be a long time before that particular part of the disk is used to write new data. In the meantime, the old data is still there and can be recovered if the investigator has the proper tools.

A brand-new disk is thought of as being "clean," or completely empty, but in reality it is full of *format characters,* which are repeated characters made by the test machine at the factory. When files and directories are created and saved to disk, they overwrite the format characters. When the files or directories are deleted, the clusters in which they are stored are not reallocated until new data is written there. Formatting the disk does not remove this data. Even if the disk is repartitioned using FDISK, Partition Magic, or a similar utility, the data is still there until those clusters are overwritten.

A number of software programs can be used to recover files in unallocated space. One example is the GetFree tool marketed by New Technologies Inc. (www.forensics-intl.com/getfree.html), the maker of SafeBack. NTI makes a variety of forensics software packages, and GetFree is designed specifically for law enforcement and forensics specialists to capture data in unallocated space on computers running Microsoft operating systems. This data can then be viewed using other utilities such as NTI's Filter I. WetStone Technologies (see the company Web site at www.wetstonetech.com) makes a program called Extractor (or SMART Extractor) that recovers deleted files in Red Hat Linux.

Supposedly erased data can be located in many places on a computer. For example, when a disk is repartitioned, it is possible for data from the previously configured partitions to end up in the space between partitions, called the *partition gap.* Disk search tools can locate this hidden data, which can then become a potential source of evidence for investigators.

Decrypting Encrypted Data

As you learned in Chapter 7, "Understanding Cybercrime Prevention," encryption is a method of scrambling data so that it can't be read by anyone who doesn't have the password or key to decrypt it. Cybercriminals often use encryption to conceal the criminal nature of their data. They could encrypt e-mail messages that include incriminating statements, or they could encrypt documents that could be used as evidence or pornographic pictures of children that constitute contraband.

Cryptanalysts specialize in "cracking" encryption algorithms. Strong encryption is difficult to break, but in many cases cybercriminals use relatively weak methods such as the password protection for Office documents that comes built into the applications. A number of "password recovery" programs exist ostensibly for use by legitimate users who protect documents and then forget their passwords. These programs can also be used to crack the passwords on Word or Excel documents. They are basically brute-force/dictionary attacks. An example is Advanced Office 2000 Password Recovery. Similar programs are designed to crack the passwords for the Outlook Express e-mail client, Internet Explorer passwords for protected Web sites, files created by Quicken and QuickBooks financial management programs, password-protected PDF files, protected documents created by Lotus 1-2-3 and other Lotus Office Suite programs, protected documents created by Corel WordPerfect, password-protected .zip files and other archives, and many more. For information about many of these password-cracking programs, see www.crackpassword.com.

Paraben (www.paraben-forensics.com) markets a "decryption collection" software suite as part of its line of forensic programs. The suite is designed to crack passwords for a large number of popular software programs and file types, including the Windows XP/2000/NT operating systems, Exchange, VBA Visual Basic modules, and many more.

Finding Hidden Data

In many instances, data hidden on the hard disk can be very useful to investigators in building a case against a cybercrime suspect. Some of this data might be ambient data that was left behind when files were deleted or disks were repartitioned. There are also a number of places where data can be deliberately hidden by technically savvy criminals using a disk editor, steganographic software, and other methods. Finding, retrieving, and reconstructing this hidden data can be an extremely tedious process, but it's worth the effort if it results in evidence that can make or break a case.

Where Data Hides

A *disk sector* is a unit of space of a fixed size (such as 512 bytes). Older hard disks could have some wasted storage space on the outside tracks because of the way the disks are divided into sectors that contain an equal number of sectors per track. The discrepancy in circumference between the inside and outside tracks causes this wasted space. It is possible in some cases to hide data in the space between sectors on the larger outside tracks. This space is called the *sector gap.* Some data recovery services might be able to locate and retrieve data that is hidden in this gap.

Another place that data can be hidden is in the *slack area* caused by file sizes that don't exactly match the size of the clusters in which they are stored. Cluster sizes can vary, but anytime a file or portion of a file is smaller than the cluster size, the "leftover" bits in that cluster go unused. In file systems such as FAT16, where cluster sizes increase based on the partition size, this can result in a very large amount of "empty" space, and that space can be used to covertly store other bits of data. Data can be hidden here, unbeknownst to the user. Clusters are made up of sectors. When the file is too small to fill up the last sector in a file, DOS and Windows use random data from the system's memory buffers to make up the difference. This is called *RAM slack* and can result in data from the work session (the time since the computer was last booted) being stored on the disk in this slack space to "pad" the final sector. All sorts of data dumped from memory can be lurking in the slack space and could prove useful to the investigator. Any kind of disk (diskette, hard disk, and removable disk) is subject to slack. Computer forensic analysis tools such as those marketed by NTI can recover data hidden in slack areas.

Shadow data is created because the vertical and horizontal alignment of the mechanical heads that write to the disk are not exactly the same each time a write operation is performed. This means that even when data is overwritten, remnants of the old data could still be there. It is sometimes possible (although very time consuming and expensive) to reconstruct the data from these remnants.

Detecting Steganographic Data

Steganography software hides files within other files, using empty space or the least significant bit to encode messages. For example, data can be hidden within an image file by slightly altering a single bit related to a particular pixel. If one pixel in the photo has a red component, represented by the binary number 10001100, the least significant bit (the last one) can be changed to a 1, making the binary 10001101. This will make that one pixel a tiny bit more red, which will not be noticeable to viewers. This creates one "hidden" bit, a 1. To create a 0, you would leave the least significant bit as it was. The entire file that you want to hide is broken up into its binary components, and these are then concealed in different parts of the photo image. Determining which pixels contain the hidden bits, and in what order, can be done by a random number generator that uses a key so that only someone who knows the key will be able to reconstruct the hidden message by retrieving the hidden bits in the correct order.

Several "antisteganography" programs on the market allow you to detect the presence of data that is hidden within other files using steganographic techniques. Examples of such software include StegoWatch, marketed by WetStone Technologies; for more information, see www.wetstonetech.com/stegowatchdatasheet.pdf.

Detecting the presence of steganographic data is much easier than extracting the message itself. This is usually done by software that checks the statistical profile of an image and looks for statistical artifacts left by steganographic software. *Steganalysis* is the process of detecting steganography in files and rendering the covert messages useless.

For more information on this topic, see *Steganalysis: The Investigation of Hidden Information* at www.jjtc.com/pub/it98a.htm.

Alternate Datastreams

Windows NT/2000 systems that use the NTFS file system support a feature called *alternate datastreams (ADS)*. Streams of any size can be created and linked to normal visible files (called the *parent files*), but the streams are invisible and special software is required to detect them. These streams provide another, legitimate function. They allow the NT/2000 operating systems to support Macintosh files, which consist of two *forks*: a data fork and a resource fork. The resource fork is stored in the hidden alternate datastream. In addition, some antivirus programs use the streams to store checksums for files. Streams can be attached to either files or directories (folders).

You can't directly delete an alternate datastream without deleting the parent file or directory. In fact, many file-wiping utilities delete only the parent files and do not get rid of the ADS. Trojans and viruses can hide themselves in streams, or technically savvy criminals can hide incriminating data there. Streams can be created in Notepad and other ADS-aware programs. The filename is in two parts, consisting of the parent file's name and the stream name, separated by a colon. For example, if the parent file is named *filename.txt,* the stream might be named *filename.txt:filestream.* The stream name does not have a file extension like a regular file. Editing the parent file doesn't change the contents of the stream file, and vice versa. For more information, see the ADS FAQ at www.heysoft.net/Frames/f_faq_ads_en.htm.

Methods for Hiding Files

There are a number of ways that files can be hidden on a system. On DOS/Windows file systems, setting the hidden attribute (**-h** at the command line, or set in the File Properties dialog box in the GUI) will prevent the file from showing up in response to the **DIR** command at the command line or in the files list in Explorer *if* the default settings are in place in Folder Options | View. However, if the Show Hidden Files and Folders option button is enabled, these hidden files will still be displayed. On UNIX systems, files and directories with names that begin with a dot are hidden and are not displayed in response to the **ls** command unless you use the **-a** switch.

On the Scene…

Hiding Files in Plain View

Another method for hiding files is known as *hiding in plain view*. Using this method, a cybercriminal gives a file a name that makes it appear to be something it isn't—and something that the investigator would not be interested in. For example, a graphic file containing child pornography could be renamed to something like window.sys and stored in the Windows system directory. To the casual observer, it looks like just another operating system file. When the criminal wants to access it, he merely has to change the file extension back to .jpg or .gif and open it in any graphics viewer program.

Utilities such as NT Rootkit allow you to hide files and directories (as well as processes and Registry entries) by renaming them with the prefix *_root.* This works only on the local machine; if the share is accessed remotely by mapping a drive to it, the _root files and directories will be visible. The NT Rootkit works on Windows NT/2000 machines; the concept comes from the original UNIX-based rootkits.

Linux systems using the ext2 file system provide several ways to hide data. One way to hide files on most UNIX file systems (including ext2) is to run a process that keeps the file open, then remove the file using the **/bin/rm** command. The data will remain on the disk and the space until it is overwritten by other files. You can find "unerase" utilities for Linux that will recover deleted ext2 files. It is also possible to manually recover these files using the debugfs utility. This process is described in the *Linux Ext2fs Undeletion mini-HOWTO* at www.tldp.org/HOWTO/mini/Ext2fs-Undeletion.html.

The ext2 file system stores data in *blocks* and creates slack space when files are smaller than the 1-, 2-, or 4KB blocks used by the file system. Data can be hidden in this slack space, just as in DOS/Windows file systems.

The Recycle Bin

Although it might seem obvious to technical experts that moving a file to the Recycle Bin or Trash does not even remove the file's pointers as deleting it does, many cybercriminals are *not* technical experts and could think that they have deleted evidence when in fact, it is still intact in the Recycle Bin. Of course, this is more likely to be true in the case of "nontechnical" cybercrimes such as child pornography or con-artist scams than network intrusions and other hacker activities. However, considering the level of technical knowledge required (or rather, *not* required) to launch attacks using the script- and click-kiddie methods, it never hurts to check. The evidence you need could be sitting right there waiting for you, easily restored with a single click of the mouse.

Locating Forgotten Evidence

A great deal of data is stored on computers automatically by application programs and/or the operating system. Some users are unaware of this stored data; others know about it but might forget to get rid of it when they are destroying evidence on a system. Depending on the nature of the offense, some of this data could be useful to the cybercrime investigator. Sources of forgotten evidence include Web caches, temporary (temp) files, swap/page files, and application logs. In the next sections, we look at how each of these sources can provide valuable evidentiary information in some cybercrime cases.

Web Caches and URL Histories

Web browsers are designed with performance in mind. Users want their Web pages to pop up in the browser as quickly as possible. One way to speed up access is to provide a way for the browser to get the file from the local computer's hard disk, rather than downloading it over a much slower Internet connection. For this reason, Web browsers by default *cache* the pages that a user visits, along with related graphics, sounds, and other embedded files. In other words, all this data is stored on the computer's hard disk so that if you visit the same page again, it can be quickly retrieved from the disk. These files are usually called *temporary Internet files* and are stored in a special folder, usually under the user's profile name, as shown in Figure 10.1. They provide a visual record of the sites that the user has visited recently. This information can be especially useful in child pornography cases or cases of terrorists who frequent certain Web sites.

Figure 10.1 Temporary Internet files (the Web cache) can provide clues to the Web sites a computer user has recently visited.

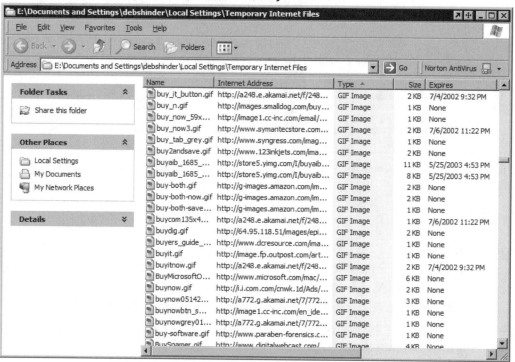

Another source of information about Web sites that have been visited is the History folder. Cybercriminals sometimes delete their temporary Internet files but forget to clear the history records. Unlike the Web cache, the History folder doesn't contain actual copies of the Web pages; instead, it contains a list of links (URLs) to those sites. On Windows machines using the Internet Explorer browser, these links are usually located in a folder named History under the user's profile name, as shown in Figure 10.2. (Separate Web caches and histories are maintained for every user who has a local account on the computer.)

Figure 10.2 The History folder contains URLs for recently visited Web sites.

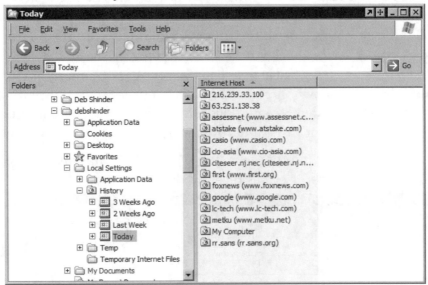

The Netscape browser stores its browsing history in a file named netscape.hst and another called fat.db, located in the Cache directory under the user's name in the Program Files\Netscape\Users subdirectory. These are binary files, so you'll need a utility to view the data in them.

Temp Files

Applications such as Microsoft Word create temporary (temp) files on a system. These files are used for tracking changes made to the original and for recovery if the program crashes. Working on a Word document can result in dozens of temp files, usually stored in the same directory as the original .doc file. In theory, when you close the document or application, these temporary files are deleted, but this doesn't always happen. Even when they are "deleted" by the system, they are still on the disk until overwritten, like other "deleted" files, and can be recovered using tools designed for that purpose.

Other temporary files include those that are downloaded from the Internet or e-mail attachments that have been opened and saved in a Temp directory, usually located in the system root directory (the directory where the operating system files are located, such as WINDOWS or WINNT). These temporary files can be deleted when the system shuts down or reboots, which is another reason to image the disk *before* shutting down the system if at all possible.

NOTE

Temporary files often have the .tmp extension. A search for files with this extension can turn up a wealth of forgotten data, some of which might be useful as evidence.

Swap and Page Files

Most modern operating systems utilize a feature called *virtual memory,* which allows the system to "fool" applications into thinking the computer has more RAM than is actually installed. A portion of the hard disk is used to emulate additional memory and data is "swapped" from real physical memory to this holding space on disk as it's needed by the processor. On Windows 9*x*, this data is held in a file called the *swap file.* On Windows NT/2000 systems, it is called the *page file* because data is swapped in units called *pages.* Linux systems create a swap partition on the disk for this same purpose. These files are generally created automatically by the operating system.

These files contain all sorts of data, including e-mail, Web pages, word-processing documents, and any other work that has been performed on the computer during the work session. Many computer users are either unaware of the existence of these files or don't really understand what they are, what they do, and what kind of data they contain. Some swap files are temporary and others are permanent, depending on the operating system in use and how it is configured. The files might be marked with the hidden attribute, which makes them invisible in the directory structure under default settings. Swap files are created by the operating system in a default location. Table 10.1 shows the swap filename and its default location for different Microsoft operating systems. Note that technically savvy users can change the location of the swap file or create additional swap/page files so that there are multiple virtual memory locations on a system.

Table 10.1 Swap filenames and locations

Operating System	Filename	Default Location
Windows 3.*x*	386SPART.PAR	Windows\System subdirectory or root directory of the drive designated in the virtual memory dialog box
Windows 9*x*	WIN386.SWP	Root directory of the drive designated in the virtual memory dialog box

Continued

Table 10.1 Continued

Operating System	Filename	Default Location
Windows NT/ 2000/XP	PAGEFILE.SYS	Root directory of the drive on which the system root directory (WINNT by default) is installed

To find the location of the swap or page file, open the Virtual Memory dialog box. (This is also where a user can change the file's location.) For example, in Windows XP Professional, open the **System** applet from **Control Panel**, click the **Advanced** tab, click the **Settings** button under **Performance**, then click the **Advanced** tab again, and click the **Change** button at the bottom of the page under **Virtual Memory**. This series of steps brings you to the Virtual Memory dialog box (at last!), and you can see the location of one or more page files, as shown in Figure 10.3.

Figure 10.3 To view the location, size, and status of the page file(s) on Windows XP, use the Virtual Memory dialog box.

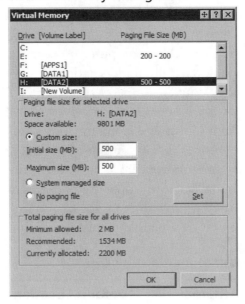

You can then navigate to the drive on which the file is stored and locate it there, as shown in Figure 10.4. Note, however, that the page file will not be visible unless you have unchecked the **Hide protected operating system files (recommended)** check box in the **Tools | Folder Options | View** advanced settings in Windows Explorer.

Figure 10.4 When protected operating system files are unhidden, the page file becomes visible in Windows Explorer.

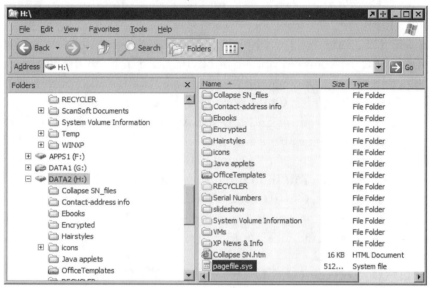

You can view the swap/page file with a utility such as DiskEdit, but much of the information is binary (0s and 1s) and not very usable. Special programs such as Net Threat Analyzer and the Filter I "intelligent forensic editor" are designed to read swap file data and other *ambient* computer data. Filter I uses a type of artificial intelligence (AI) to locate fragments of various types of files, including e-mail, chat conversations, newsgroup posts, and even network passwords and credit card and Social Security numbers. Net Threat Analyzer is provided free to law enforcement agencies by the vendor and is used to evaluate Internet browsing, download activity, and e-mail communications in ambient data for evidence related to terrorism and other illegal activities. Both of these software packages are marketed by NTI. The company also makes text search and disk search programs that can search storage devices at the physical level and locate data that is stored between allocated partitions or text strings that are in unallocated space.

Recovering Data from Backups

An often-overlooked source of data recovery can be especially useful in cases where the cybercriminal might have been savvy enough to destroy data completely (for example, using methods discussed in the next section, "Defeating Data Recovery Techniques"). This source is the backup(s) that the suspect or (if the suspect's computer is on a network) the systems administrator might have made for fault-tolerance purposes. In many cases in which suspects have destroyed incriminating files, copies of those files still existed on the backup media. This is especially true in a corporate situation, where system administrators often automatically back up user data to a server each day.

Even when the suspect uses a home computer, it's worth checking for the existence of backups. Many computer hobbyists, having been the victims of system failure in the past and having lost valuable data because of it, regularly back up their important files. Child pornographers often are emotionally attached to their kiddie porn collections and might have made extra copies in case of a disk failure. If there is a tape drive attached to the system, there's a good chance it's used for backups. If there is a CD or DVD writer installed, the suspect might have used it for archiving. You should request that the search warrant specify seizure of any tapes, disks, CD-ROMs, or other media commonly used to back up files, in addition to the computer equipment itself. Backups have saved the day in many cases when no evidence could be found on the computer's hard disk.

Defeating Data Recovery Techniques

At this point, some law enforcement officers might be wondering about the security of their own sensitive data, whether these same recovery techniques pose security threats to them, and whether and how they can protect against such threats. The bad news is that all this data lurking in unsuspected places can, indeed, pose a risk to the agency in the event that the wrong person gets control of law enforcement computers. The good news—in terms of protecting sensitive law enforcement data—is that there *are* ways to defeat data recovery methods. On the other hand, suspects can use the same techniques to cover their tracks and destroy evidence of their crimes. Thus for both reasons, investigators need to be aware of the ways that data *can* be removed from a disk "once and for all."

NOTE

If disks that have been used as target disks for making bitstream copies of suspect disks in forensics examinations are to be reused, it is very important to completely wipe the disk between uses to prevent remnants of data from prior cases "bleeding" through and appearing to be evidence in the current case.

Some of these data recovery techniques require physical access to the system, but others can be initiated over the network. In addition to the security methods that we discussed in Chapters 7 and 8, what can you do to ensure that confidential data doesn't remain on a disk after you're finished with it? In general, there are three ways to do this: overwriting, degaussing (demagnetizing), and physically destroying the disk.

Overwriting the Disk

The term *data remanence* refers to the residual physical manifestations of data that has supposedly been deleted or erased. Many "disk-wiping" utilities available commercially and as freeware or shareware on the Internet claim to remove this remanence, from which the data can be reconstructed. These utilities work by writing over the unallocated space on the disk. Windows XP Professional includes a command-line utility called CIPHER.EXE that, in addition to encrypting, decrypting, and managing encrypted files using EFS, has a switch that overwrites data in unallocated clusters. These utilities attempt to fill the unallocated space with random binary values and can overwrite several times (which is necessary to overwrite the shadow data).

> **NOTE**
>
> The best disk-wiping programs for FAT and NTFS file systems are DOS based (command-line programs); Windows-based programs cannot generally eliminate the ambient data in obscure areas of the storage space.

Tests of many of these utilities show that they often don't affect the data in file slack or alternate datastreams and can leave remnants of shadow data. To be effective, overwriting must be done many times, using alternating patterns, and still could leave some types of data behind. If you're serious about eliminating data remanence by the overwriting method, you should use a program that meets or exceeds the U.S. Department of Defense security standards. Under these standards, the overwrite process must undergo at least three passes: one pass overwrites data with a character, another overwrites that pass with the complement of the first character overwrite, and a third write uses a random character. The process must also be verified.

An example of a disk-wiping program that meets DoD standards is DiskScrub from NTI. Another NTI product, M-Sweep Pro Data Eliminator, was designed specifically for use on notebook systems but can also be used on desktop hard disks and removable disks. It overwrites the ambient data storage areas (file slack, unallocated file space, and so on). The sale of these products is restricted to law enforcement, U.S. medical facilities and hospitals, U.S. financial institutions, law and accounting firms, government agencies, and Fortune 1000 corporations.

Degaussing or Demagnetizing

Another way to get rid of the data remaining on a disk is to create a very strong magnetic field that is capable of reducing the magnetic state of the media to zero. This process is called *degaussing,* the device that generates the magnetic field is called a *degausser.* Degaussers work either by applying an alternating magnetic field using AC power or by applying a unidirectional field using DC power. Handheld permanent magnets can also be used to degauss some types of magnetic media (diskettes and hard disk platters; they are not usually used to degauss magnetic tapes). There are different types of magnetic tape, based on the coercivity of the media. It is important to have the proper type of degausser that matches the tape type, in order to purge all the data from the tape.

> **NOTE**
>
> When magnetic media is exposed to extreme temperatures or stored for long periods of time, it becomes more resistant to degaussing.

Physically Destroying the Disk

In cases where it is extremely important that there be no possibility that data remaining on a disk could ever be reconstructed—for example, in a national security situation in which classified data was stored on the disk—it might be preferable to physically destroy the disk. This can be done in several ways. The most effective include:

- Pulverization (completely crushing or grinding the disk down to powder)

- Incineration (burning the disk to ashes)

- Abrasion (using a sander or emery wheel to completely remove the surface of the disk)

- Acid (applying a concentrated solution of hydriodic acid to the surface of the disk)

Documenting Evidence

According to *Digital Evidence Standards and Principles,* developed by the SWGDE and IOCE in 1999 and published in the April 2000 issue of *Forensic Science and Communications* (a publication of the FBI), "[C]ase notes and observations must be in ink, not pencil, although pencil (including color) may be appropriate for diagrams or making tracings. Any corrections to notes must be made by an initialed, single strikeout; nothing in the handwritten information should be obliterated or erased. Notes and records should be authenticated by handwritten signatures, initials, digital signatures or other marking systems."

In the following sections, we discuss the evidence documentation procedure in a cybercrime investigation. We look first at how evidentiary items should be tagged or marked and the practice of keeping an evidence log. Then we discuss how the analysis of evidence should be documented by the person(s) performing the forensics examination. Finally, we discuss the chain of custody and the importance of documentation to preserving the integrity of the chain.

Evidence Tagging and Marking

Evidence is tagged and/or marked by the person who originally takes it into custody. That person places his or her initials or name on the item, along with the date and time and the case number. Physically marking the evidence is preferable when possible, because tags can become separated from items, thus damaging the chain of custody. Items that can't be physically inscribed can be placed in a bag or contained and sealed, and then the container can be marked. The mark should be made using a permanent ink or marker.

> **NOTE**
>
> In some cases involving digital evidence, a cryptographic (digital) signature can be used if this can be done without modifying the evidence.

Evidence Logs

The *evidence log* is a document that lists all evidence collected in a criminal case, with a description of each piece of evidence, who discovered and collected it, the date and time of collection, and the disposition of the evidence. The description should be detailed enough to differentiate the item from others like it and should include serial numbers and other identifying numbers when possible. The log should show all transfers of custody of the evidence from one person to another. This process of logging the transfer of evidence is tangible proof of the preservation of the chain of custody.

Documenting Evidence Analysis

Another type of log should be kept by the person(s) who analyze the bitstream image of the suspect computer's disk(s). This log should show each step of the analysis process, including who was present, what was done (for example, running a software utility to remove binary data from a swap file), the result of the procedure, and the time and date.

As the data on the disk is assessed for its evidentiary value, you should document all potential evidence that is found. For example, if you open a .jpg that appears to be a pornographic photo of a child, document the filename, where on the disk it was located, date and timestamps, and other file properties. In addition to the volatile data and obscure areas on the disk where data hides that we discussed earlier (slack space, unallocated space, partition gaps, and so forth), some of the data that should be examined for evidence, depending on the type of cybercrime offense, includes:

- List of URLs recently visited (obtained from the temporary Internet files or Web cache and History folders)

- E-mail messages and list of e-mail addresses stored in the suspect's address book; the filename depends on the e-mail program in use—for example, the .pst file for Outlook (In some cases, this information will be stored on an e-mail server, such as an Exchange server)

- Word-processing documents; the file extension is dependent on the program used to create them—common extensions are .doc, .wpd, .wps, .rtf, and txt

- Spreadsheet documents; the file extension is dependent on the program used to create them—examples include .xls, .wg1, and .wk1

- Graphics, in the case of child pornography cases; the file extensions include .jpg, .gif, .bmp, .tif, and others

- Chat logs; the filename depends on the chat program

- The Windows Registry (where applicable)

- Event viewer logs

- Application logs
- Print spool files

Documenting the Chain of Custody

The term *chain of custody* refers to continuity of the evidence. That is, you must be able to trace the route that the evidence has taken from the moment it was collected until the time it is presented in court, every person whose hands it has passed through, and when and where it was transferred from one person to another. Documentation of the chain of custody is one of the most important purposes of the evidence log.

Any break in the chain of custody opens the prosecution to allegations that the evidence has been tampered with or other evidence substituted for it. Proof of chain of custody is provided by testimony of the person who collected the evidence, establishing that the item presented in court is in fact the same evidence that was collected (or is an exact representation of that evidence), that the evidence was not tampered with while in his or her custody, and when and where custody of the evidence was transferred to the next person in the chain. This same process can be followed with each person who had custody of the evidence.

Obviously, the fewer people who handle the evidence, the easier it will be to preserve the integrity of the chain. It is a best practice to designate one person as the custodian of the evidence. Sometimes computer evidence must be delivered to a lab or data recovery/forensics service, however. If the designated custodian is unable to stay with the evidence (keeping it within his or her sight) while it is processed, the lab or technician should provide a receipt when the evidence is delivered, and the evidence should be examined by the custodian when it is retrieved, to ensure that it is the same evidence. The lab technicians will also need to testify as to what happened to the evidence while it was in their custody and how it was stored and protected at the lab.

Computer Forensics Resources

Computer forensics is a relatively young field. However, standards are quickly evolving and a large number of resources are available to aspiring computer forensics experts. Cybercrime investigators who want to expand their knowledge, corporate IT personnel who are interested in specializing in this area, and crime scene technicians who want to learn to deal with digital evidence will all find a plethora of available training programs, equipment, and software available.

Investigators who prefer to "farm out" the technical aspects of digital evidence examination will find many commercial services that do imaging, data recovery, and related tasks. Many of these services employ people qualified to testify as expert witnesses in court. Several associations and organizations provide white papers, articles, and other information sources to keep computer forensics personnel updated on the latest developments in the field. The following sections provide an overview of some of these resources.

Computer Forensics Training and Certification

Training programs are available through private companies that make forensics software and equipment, such as NTI (www.forensics-intl.com/training.html) and DIBS (www.dibsusa.com/training/training.html), through community colleges and universities, through some law enforcement in-service academies, and through computer crime/forensics associations and organizations.

There are at least a couple of recognized certification programs in computer forensics:

- IACIS provides a Certified Forensic Computer Examiner (CFCE) certification for individuals, both in law enforcement and outside law enforcement, who submit an application demonstrating extensive knowledge, training, and/or experience in the computer forensics field, along with an understanding of forensic procedures, standards, ethics, and legal and privacy issues. Candidates must have technical knowledge and skills and have the equipment necessary to conduct forensic examinations. In order to earn the certification, candidates undergo a rigorous testing process in which they must complete a number of hands-on problem-solving exercises, prepare reports and present the evidence obtained, and then pass a written examination. For more information about the CFCE certification, see www.cops.org/External%20Certification.htm.

- The High Tech Crime Network (HTCN) offers basic and advanced Certified Computer Forensic Technician and Certified Computer Crime Investigator certifications. To obtain the certifications, applicants must demonstrate a minimal level of combined education and experience (in either law enforcement or corporate environment) and submit documentation derived from at least 10 cases. For more information, see www.htcn.org/certification.htm.

A good computer forensics training course should cover theory, process, and methodology and include hands-on practice in techniques and tools.

Computer Forensics Equipment and Software

Special equipment to aid in forensics examinations is marketed by a number of companies, such as DIBS (www.dibsusa.com). The following types of equipment can be useful to investigators and forensics technicians:

- **Imaging equipment** These devices allow you to rapidly make bitstream copies of hard disks onto another hard disk, an optical cartridge, or a tape. Portable units that fit into a suitcase are available and can be easily transported to the crime scene to make disk copies on site before the computer is shut down. The target media include write-protection features to ensure that data cannot be tampered with after the copies are made.

- **Forensic workstations** These are complete computer workstations set up for easy reconstruction and analysis of copied drives, usually with removable drive racks that allow booting of the "working copies" of suspect disks. Analysis software is installed to assist in searching for particular types of data using AI techniques or fuzzy logic to conduct searches when the investigator isn't sure of the text strings or file types he or she is looking for. Data recovery software is installed to locate data from "deleted" or "erased" files. Mobile workstations set up on portable computers are also available. Examples include the DIBS forensic workstations and F.R.E.D., the Forensic Recovery of Evidence Device, which is made by Digital Intelligence (www.digitalintel.com/fred.htm).

- **Forensic software** Packages provided by companies such as NTI and DIBS include imaging software, "undelete" programs, comprehensive file and text string search programs, programs that can verify the accuracy of bitstream copies, programs that can remove binary characters from data to make analysis of the data easier, programs that quickly document lists of files and directories, programs that can capture the data in unallocated space or file slack space, programs that can rebuild cache, uncompression tools, system-checking utilities, steganography detection software, password recovery programs, and much more. For a list of some of the best computer forensics software programs, see the Timberline Technologies Web site at www.timberlinetechnologies.com/products/forensics.html. NTI provides several free forensics tools at www.forensics-intl.com/download.html.

On the Scene...

Building a Forensic Workstation

You can build your own forensic workstation using either a portable or desktop computer instead of buying the prepackaged hardware/software combination. The system should be powerful enough to run forensics application software; we recommend a processor of at least 800MHz and a minimum of 512MB of RAM. The workstation should run an operating system compatible with your forensics application software.

You might find it useful to set up a dual-boot configuration so you can boot into either Windows or Linux, or you can run VMWare (www.vmware.com) virtual machines to allow you to view an NTFS formatted disk, for example, from within the Linux operating system using a Windows 2000 VM.

Another handy utility for your workstation is NTFSDOS, which allows you to view the files on an NTFS-formatted disk from within MS-DOS or Windows 9x. Another advantage is that it is read-only, so you don't have to worry about accidentally writing to and changing the original files. NTFSDOS is available for download from www.sysinternals.com.

Computer Forensics Services

A huge number of companies offer data recovery and other computer forensics services. Many of these services work on a consultant basis and provide expert witnesses for court testimony. Services might bill by the hour or by the job, and some services offer discounts or even free services to law enforcement agencies. Full-service companies might also rent forensics equipment to investigators who want to do their own forensics work, and they might provide training in computer forensics.

Most medium-sized to large U.S. cities have one or more local firms specializing in computer forensics or offering these services as part of their businesses. A Web search on the term *computer forensic service* using Google turns up numerous hits. From one-person operations to large, well-known companies such as Ernst & Young, this hot field is expected to expand even more in the next few years as computer crime awareness grows. This is particularly true in the wake of the September 11, 2001, terrorist attacks and subsequent information that the terrorist network uses the Internet and might be planning future attacks on critical IT infrastructures.

We recommend that when you consider employing a computer forensics service or expert, you inquire about his or her training and certification, professional association memberships, and past experience and ask for references from past clients. Law enforcement agencies should also keep in mind that in many cases, other law enforcement agencies will provide forensic services, either as a courtesy or for a fee, to smaller agencies that don't have the equipment or personnel to do their own computer forensics work. Check with larger municipal and county agencies in your area, the state police or department of public safety, and, in cases of high-profile or important cases, the FBI and other federal agencies for assistance.

Computer Forensics Information

Computer forensics is a field that is not only growing fast but changing fast as well. New techniques and technologies are being developed and proven all the time, and it's important that investigators keep up with the latest news in the field. There are several ways to stay current, including:

- Reading computer forensics and general forensics periodicals, both print publications and webzines such as *Computer Forensics Online* (www.shk-dplc.com/cfo) and *Computer Forensics Magazine* (www.forensic-computing.com).

- Attending seminars and conferences that focus on computer crime and cybercrime, such as Foundstone's Incident Response and Computer Forensics, the Techno-Security Conference sponsored by Guidance Software (information on the 2003 event is located at www.thetrainingco.com/html/Techno2003.html), Cybercrime 2003 (www.cybercrime2002.com/2003.html), and many others.

- Joining associations of computer forensics and cybercrime investigation professionals, such as IACIS (www.iacis.com), the High Technology Crime Investigators Association (http://htcia.org), the High Tech Crime Consortium (www.hightechcrimecops.org), and others.

Understanding Legal Issues

Computer forensics is concerned as much with complying with the law and following prescribed procedures for evidence collection as with the technical aspects of collecting digital evidence. Evidence that is inadmissible in court is worse than useless; not only can illegal search and seizure damage or destroy the prosecution's case and result in a cybercriminal going free, it can also result in administrative or even criminal actions against officers who violate the rules.

Thus it is imperative that law enforcement officers and others who will be involved in the collection and preservation of evidence understand the legal issues under which they operate. The laws vary from one jurisdiction to another and change on a regular basis, so all cybercrime investigators should make it a practice to stay up to date on passage of statutes and court decisions that apply to their jurisdictions.

This chapter does not purport to give legal advice. The following sections are intended only to provide an overview of some of the laws and court cases that pertain to search and seizure of computers and digital evidence in the United States at the time of this writing. These issues are constantly being debated; new laws are passed and courts hand down rulings regularly. For example, the U.S. Patriot Act, passed in the wake of the September 11, 2001, terrorist attacks, gave greater leeway to the federal government to monitor electronic communications and made it easier to get a search warrant to seize digital evidence.

Searching and Seizing Digital Evidence

A *search* was legally defined by the courts in *State vs Woodall* as "an examination of a man's house or other buildings or premises, or of his person, or of his vehicle, aircraft, etc., with a view to the discovery of contraband or illicit or stolen property, or some evidence of guilt to be used in the prosecution of a criminal action for some crime or offense with which he is charged" (according to *Black's Law Dictionary*). A *seizure* was defined in *Molina vs State* as "the act of taking possession of property, e.g., for a violation of law or by virtue of an execution" [of a warrant].

Traditional ideas of search and seizure did not take into account the ways in which computers are used today as a repository of information (and potential evidence). The courts have had to develop interpretations of the law to apply to the unique aspects of these digital "places" and the types of evidence that can be found there. For example, the laws generally restrict entering a person's private premises to conduct a search without a warrant, except under certain restricted circumstances. Courts have generally held that a person has a reasonable expectation of privacy when information is stored in a computer, similarly to the contents of a closed container.

On the other hand, when evidence is in plain view in a public place, the law allows officers to seize it. Attempting to apply these same rules to today's networked world brings up interesting questions. Is data on a person's private computer that is connected to the public Internet and accessible to the public considered to be on private premises or in a public place? The answers are still evolving as the courts address cases that hinge on such issues.

Some general principles govern search and seizure in the United States based on the federal laws and the U.S. Constitution. Be aware, however, that states can impose further restrictions on police powers within their boundaries, so understanding federal guidelines is only the starting point. In the following sections, we discuss these general principles with these caveats in mind.

U.S. Constitutional Issues

The Bill of Rights of the U.S. Constitution consists of 10 amendments designed to protect the citizenry from government oppression and guarantee certain basic human rights to the people of the United States. One of the most important amendments in terms of its impact on law enforcement is the fourth, violation of which is common grounds for suppression of evidence in criminal trials.

Understanding the Fourth Amendment

The Fourth Amendment to the U.S. Constitution prohibits "unreasonable" searches and seizures. Specifically, it states: "The right of the people to be secure in their persons, houses, papers, and effects, against unreasonable searches and seizures, shall not be violated, and no warrants shall issue, but upon probable cause, supported by oath or affirmation, and particularly describing the place to be searched, and the persons or things to be seized."

Perhaps one of the most important things to understand about the Fourth Amendment is that its restrictions apply only to agents of the government such as the police and other public employees or public officials. A private party cannot violate a suspect's Fourth Amendment rights unless acting at the direction of the police or another government agency. In other words, if a landlord searches a tenant's home or an employer searches an employee's office, it is not a Fourth Amendment violation. However, such a search could be a violation of privacy and a basis for a civil suit in some cases and not in others; for example, courts have held that an employee generally does not have an expectation of privacy in an office owned by the employer.

How does this interpretation apply to search and seizure of computers? Again, only an agent of the government is prohibited by the Fourth Amendment from searching a computer's hard disk. In *United States vs Hall,* a case involving a computer repair person who found child pornography on a client's computer, the court held that "the Fourth Amendment does not apply to searches conducted by private parties who are not acting as agents of the government," and in *United*

States vs Jacobsen, the court held that "the Fourth Amendment is wholly inapplicable to a search or seizure, even an unreasonable one, effected by a private individual not acting as an agent of the Government or with the participation or knowledge of any governmental official."

Thus if a private party searches a computer and finds evidence of a crime, then contacts law enforcement authorities, who obtain a search warrant based on the private party's information, this does not constitute a violation of the computer owner's constitutional rights.

In fact, the Supreme Court has held (*United States vs Jacobsen*) that law enforcement agents can reenact the original private search without a warrant and that this does not constitute a violation of reasonable expectation of privacy. However, if officers exceed the scope of the original search, evidence can be suppressed as it was in *United States vs Barth,* when a computer repair technician found child pornography on a customer's computer and agents looked at additional files that the technician had not viewed in his original search. The evidence originally viewed by the technician should have been used to obtain a search warrant to seize and view the additional files.

NOTE

Whether or not a search or seizure is permissible under the Fourth Amendment is only one aspect of its legality. Privacy acts and other statutes could apply in particular cases.

Case Law Governing Search and Seizure

We can look to many court cases for guidance in regard to search and seizure in general and search and seizure regarding computer equipment and electronic evidence in particular. *Katz vs United States* held that a search is considered to be constitutional if it doesn't violate a person's reasonable or legitimate expectation of privacy. Circumstances under which a person does or does not have a reasonable expectation of privacy are open to debate and generally must be decided by the courts in a particular case, although there is case law that establishes certain premises:

- In *Payton vs New York,* the Supreme Court held that there is a reasonable expectation of privacy when a person is inside his or her own home.

- In *United States vs Ross,* the Supreme Court held that there is a reasonable expectation of privacy regarding the contents of closed opaque containers.

There have been court cases that establish that a person has a reasonable expectation of privacy in the data stored on the hard disk of a computer (*United States vs Barth* and *United States vs Blas*). On the other hand, courts have ruled that when a person makes computer information publicly available, the reasonable expectation of privacy is lost. *Katz vs United States* held that "what a person knowingly exposes to the public, even in his own home and office, is not a subject of Fourth Amendment protection." Posting information on a Web site open to the public would obviously eliminate the expectation. Generally, information in transit (such as a message sent across the Internet) has been held not to constitute public exposure or sacrifice the expectation of privacy. However, the expectation might be lost when the message reaches the recipient. It has also been generally held that a person relinquishes the expectation of privacy if he or she turns information over to someone else whose use of it he or she cannot reasonably expect to control. Other cases have found that "mere information" revealed to third parties does not fall under reasonable expectation of control or privacy.

When there is no reasonable expectation of privacy, such as when property is abandoned or when evidence of a crime is displayed in plain view in a public place, officers generally can search and seize without a warrant. When circumstances create a reasonable expectation of privacy, a search warrant is required.

Search Warrant Requirements

A *search warrant* is a document signed by a magistrate giving law enforcement officers the authority to search a specified place for specific items that are particularly described in the warrant. A warrant must be based on another document called an *affidavit,* which is signed under oath by some person (a police officer or any other person) expressing the belief that certain items will be found at the location to be searched and giving facts that support the belief. Those facts must constitute *probable cause* that the objects of the search will be found at the described location. Only those items specifically named in the warrant can be searched for. A warrant can authorize the search and seizure of computer hardware, digital information, or both. Overly broad language (such as authorization to seize "all records" or "all computers") can result in the warrant being invalidated; the warrant must specify the crime(s) to which the evidence pertains.

On the Scene...

Affidavit Checklist

The affidavit for a search warrant should articulate probable cause that:

1. An offense has been committed (specify by name and penal code number).
2. Digital evidence is located at the named location.
3. The digital evidence is associated with the crime (tell how).
4. The digital evidence is associated with a particular person/suspect (name or describe).

The affidavit should be specific enough to satisfy the legal requirements but remain as general as possible so as not to exclude any evidence that might be found.

Search warrants can be obtained to search for specific types of property or for a person. State laws usually define exactly for what things a search can be issued. For example, under the Texas Code of Criminal Procedures, section 18.02, search warrants can be issued to search for any of the following:

- Property that was acquired illegally (through theft, fraud, etc.)
- Property that was made, designed, or adapted for use to commit an offense and implements or instruments that were used in committing a crime (the tools of the crime, such as a computer used to launch a network attack)
- Contraband (property that is illegal to own; this would include child pornography intended for the suspect's own use)
- Illegal drugs, prohibited weapons, and illegal gambling equipment
- Obscene material for commercial distribution (this would include child pornography intended for commercial distribution as well as other materials deemed "obscene" that are intended for commercial distribution)
- Evidence of a crime
- A person

Search warrants and the supporting affidavits must follow strict guidelines as to form and content, and the reliability of the affiant (the person signing the affidavit) must be established to the satisfaction of the magistrate who issues the warrant. From the officer's point of view, it is always preferable to have a search warrant rather than searching without a warrant, because a warrant relieves the officer of the responsibility of showing that probable cause and/or applicable exceptions to the search warrant requirements existed.

NOTE

Generally, a copy of the search warrant must be served on the person in control of the premises being searched or left or posted in a prominent place if there is no one there to accept service. In some cases, courts have authorized so-called "sneak and peek" warrants that do not require officers to provide notification that a search has been conducted. Some changes to federal law following the September 11, 2001, terrorist attacks make broader exceptions to the notification requirement in the case of searches for evidence of terrorist activities.

A related matter is the "no-knock" warrant. Generally, officers are required to announce their presence when they serve a search warrant and identify themselves as law enforcement officers. However, courts have held that the announcement is not required if it would result in danger to the life of some person or destruction of evidence. Because computer evidence can be so easily and quickly destroyed, officers with search warrants for digital evidence are often held to be justified in foregoing the announcement.

Special problems can arise in constructing search warrants for electronic evidence, because of the intangible nature of the evidence. For example, a suspect can move or destroy computer data quickly and easily without leaving the premises. A person with technical expertise should advise the officers and magistrate regarding the technical aspects of searching for and collecting digital evidence based on the facts of a particular case. It is just as important, if not more important, to gather all the information possible about the object of the warrant in a computer-related case as in one involving the search of a physical location. This includes the hardware platforms, operating system environment, and software applications in use, as well as the network connections and configuration. This specificity will help pinpoint the types of files to look for in the search and possible locations where they might be stored.

Search Without Warrant

In some circumstances, Fourth Amendment protections don't apply because the action is deemed *not* to be a search. If police take a vehicle into custody (for example, because they have arrested the person who was driving it), they are allowed to *inventory* the contents of the vehicle as a standard procedure. This does not constitute a search because it is not done for the purpose of looking for evidence of a crime but for the purpose of protecting the owner's property (and protecting the agency against claims of theft). However, this exception does not allow police to open locked containers, such as a briefcase, as part of the inventory process. To do so, they would generally need a warrant (unless some other exception, such as exigent circumstances, applies). A laptop or other computer that is in the vehicle when it is seized would generally be treated like a closed container in that in most cases law enforcement agents should obtain a warrant to open it and view the data on it.

There are a number of other exceptions to the requirement for a search warrant, as established by statutes and court cases. These include:

- Consent searches
- Abandoned property
- Exigent circumstances
- Plain view
- Search incident to arrest

Consent Searches

If the party who has control over the premises or thing to be searched gives voluntary consent to the search, officers don't need a warrant. This is called a *consent search*. Officers don't even need to show probable cause of a crime; they can legally search with consent even if there is no reason whatsoever to believe that a criminal offense has occurred. The key element here is that the consent must be voluntary. If consent is obtained under duress, threat, or intimidation, it is not voluntary and thus is not valid.

Furthermore, the person giving consent must have the authority to do so. For example, courts have held that a landlord cannot give consent for officers to search a tenant's home. On the other hand, courts have also held that employers can give consent to search employees' offices and school administrators can give consent to search students' lockers. In determining the legality of a search, courts consider the authority of the person giving consent and the scope of the consent. That is, if a person gives consent to search his house, does that include searching the contents of his computer's hard disk?

On the Scene...

The Joint Ownership Dilemma

Generally, if two or more people have joint ownership of a computer (for example, two roommates), consent has to be obtained from only one of the owners in order to conduct a legal search. The computer is then considered to be a "common area," much like the shared areas of a home. However, one party does not have the authority to give consent to search the other's "private areas" such as a bedroom used exclusively by one roommate. Likewise, the roommate could not legally give consent to search a computer solely owned by the other roommate. Even on a commonly owned computer, the use of password protection or file encryption by one roommate can establish that those files are part of a "private area" on the computer, and if the other roommate has not been given the password or key, he or she does not have authority to consent to search those files.

Generally, a spouse can give valid consent to search the property of the other spouse, and parents can give consent to search the property of their children who are under 18 years old. In the case of adult children who live with their parents and pay rent, the situation becomes more like that of roommates, in that parents can consent to searches of common areas but not private areas where the children have demonstrated expectation of privacy (for example, by putting locks on the doors or encrypting files).

In most cases, systems administrators have been held to have the authority to give consent to search files stored on a network, if network users have no reasonable expectation of privacy in files stored on the network (as in the case in which the files are created in the course of an employee's job and stored on the employer's network). In other cases, such as those where a person purchases disk space to store data on a remote server, this issue is not as clear-cut.

NOTE

Although a verbal consent to search can be legal, it is always best practice for law enforcement officials to get a signed consent form. Officers should carry a supply of preprinted Consent to Search forms for this purpose.

Abandoned Property

Law enforcement officers are generally allowed to search property that has clearly been abandoned without obtaining a warrant. For example, if a suspect is carrying a diskette and, upon observing that police are in the area, throws the diskette in a public trash can, officers can lawfully retrieve it.

Exigent Circumstances

Another situation in which searches can be conducted without a warrant is the case of *exigent circumstances*—that is, an emergency in which there is not time to get a warrant and the search is required immediately to save a life or prevent physical injury to some person, to keep the suspect from escaping, or to prevent evidence from being destroyed. This last situation is most applicable to digital evidence because of its fragile nature. It is very easy to destroy evidence that consists of computer data. In *United States vs David* and *United States vs Romero-Garcia,* the courts have held that seizure of electronic evidence without a warrant was legal because the evidence was about to be destroyed.

An important tenet regarding the exigent circumstances exception is that law enforcement officers cannot create the exigency. In *United States vs Reyes,* the court ruled against the government when the argument was made that incoming messages or battery failure could destroy the evidence in a pager, because the officers created the exigency by turning the pager on.

Plain-View Searches

The concept of *plain view* (sometimes also referred to as the *open fields doctrine*) rests on the premise that the law enforcement officer is legally in a particularly place where he or she can see obvious evidence of a crime in plain view. Because the contents of a file stored on a computer are usually not in plain view (unless the officer lawfully entered the room where the suspect had the file open on the screen), this doctrine is not often applied to electronic evidence.

This issue has come into play when officers had a warrant to search for evidence of one crime (for example, child pornography) and during that legal search came across evidence of a different crime (for example, a photo indicating that the suspect had committed a murder). Courts have generally held that the plain-view doctrine applies, but upon finding the evidence of the second offense, officers should return with that evidence to the magistrate to establish probable cause for issuance of a search warrant to search for further evidence of the second crime.

Search Incident to Arrest

Officers may search a person and his or her immediate surroundings when making an arrest, without obtaining a search warrant. This has been interpreted by the courts to mean that officers can go through a person's wallet or purse, address books, and the like. The courts have held that information stored in a pager may be accessed when arresting the person wearing the pager. A number of cases that support this ruling, including *United States vs Reyes, United States vs Thomas,* and *United States vs Lynch.* Whether this ruling would also apply to PDAs and handheld or laptop computers is not clear.

> **NOTE**
>
> Yet another exception to the requirement for a search warrant is the border inspection. Routine searches of persons entering or leaving the United States are allowed without probable cause or any indication of criminal activity. This was held to apply in a case where a computer disk was seized and accessed as part of a "routine export search" of a man who was leaving the country (*United States vs Roberts*).

Seizure of Digital Evidence

There are several different ways digital evidence can be seized when it is located. Early computer crime investigators often printed incriminating files or made digital copies (on floppy disks or other removable media) of the files in question. Another option is to seize all the computer equipment and go through the data stored on it at another location. As we mentioned previously, the best accepted practice today is to first make a complete exact bitstream copy of the hard disk(s) before shutting down the computer. These copies can be used to reconstruct the suspect disk and analyze it at another location later. After making the copies, investigators should seize the equipment and original disk, mark it as evidence, and store it in a secure location.

The search and seizure process should be well planned in advance. Determine the best day and time of day for the process, and estimate the number of officers and technicians and levels of expertise that will be needed on site when the search and seizure are conducted.

Forfeiture Laws

Computer equipment used as a tool or instrumentality of certain crimes (for example, illegal drug trafficking) can be subject to state and federal asset forfeiture laws. This means that the ownership of the equipment is transferred to the state or the law enforcement agency making the seizure and can be converted to their own use or sold.

Privacy Laws

The U.S. Privacy Protection Act (PPA) covers search and seizure of items that fall under the First Amendment (freedom of speech and freedom of the press) protections. The Privacy Act was intended to protect journalists, publishers, and other such people who might have evidence of criminal activity but are not suspected of having committed any criminal act. This law applies to materials that are created for the purpose of disseminating information to the public (which could apply to writings intended to be posted to Web sites, because this is a form of publishing to a public forum).

If there is reason to suspect that the person who has the materials is committing the crime that the materials pertain to or if there is a danger to some person of physical injury or death that could be prevented by seizing the evidence, the search and seizure is not a violation of the Privacy Act. Violation of the act is a civil rather than a criminal matter. Violators of the act are subject to civil lawsuit, but a violation does not mean that the evidence will be thrown out of court, as is the case with a violation of constitutional rights.

NOTE

Some states have their own privacy statutes that can be applicable in specific cases in addition to the federal Privacy Protection Act. Furthermore, special rules under both federal and state laws govern information held to be confidential or privileged by statute, such as that arising from the physician/patient, attorney/client, or clergy/parishioner relationships. These are called *legally privileged documents*.

The Electronic Communications Privacy Act (ECPA) was passed to protect the privacy rights of customers of ISPs when their personal information is disclosed. Penalties for violation include civil damages and, in some cases, criminal charges. The ECPA provisions are laid out in Title 18 of the U.S. Code. However, the passage of the U.S. Patriot Act made changes to some of the provisions of the ECPA, which we discuss in the next section.

The Effects of the U.S. Patriot Act

The U.S. Patriot Act went into effect in October 2001, in response to the continued threat of terrorism in the United States. Its passage resulted in several changes to federal law regarding computers and digital data as evidence. For example:

- Previously, under the Computer Fraud and Abuse Act, government investigators were not allowed to intercept voice wire communications as evidence in cases. The Patriot Act adds U.S. Code Title 18, Section 1030 (Computer Fraud and Abuse Act), as one of the offenses for which a wiretap order can be obtained.

- Previously, investigators had to get a wiretap order to seize and listen to unopened voicemail messages stored with a third-party provider. The Patriot Act rewords the definition of *wire communication* so that stored messages are not included and investigators can obtain voicemail evidence under a search warrant rather than undergoing the more difficult process of obtaining a wiretap order.

- Previously, investigators could not subpoena certain records such as credit card numbers of customers from ISPs. The Patriot Act added to the types of records that could be subpoenaed such items as credit card numbers and other payment information, temporarily assigned network (IP) addresses, and records of session times and durations.

- Previously, records could not be subpoenaed or obtained by search warrant from cable companies. Notice had to be given to the customer if the government wanted to examine the records, and the customer had to be given the opportunity to appear in court for a hearing to determine whether the government was justified in examining the records. The Patriot Act changed this stance so that these requirements apply only to records regarding cable TV programming, not Internet services provided by cable companies.

- Previously, ISPs were not authorized to disclose information about customers in emergency situations (for example, when the customer was suspected of planning a terrorist attack), nor was there any provision that permitted ISPs to voluntarily disclose noncontent information (for example, login records) when their networks were attacked. The Patriot Act permits ISPs to disclose both content and noncontent information in emergency situations where there is an immediate risk of death or serious bodily injury or to protect their own property and rights. (ISPs are not required by the act to review records for dangers nor required to disclose records in these situations.) The act also provides a defense against civil lawsuits for ISPs and others who provide information relying in good faith on the request of a government agent to preserve evidence.

- The Patriot Act expanded the scope of pen register and "trap and trace" devices to apply to information used in processing and routing electronic communications, such as e-mail header information, IP addresses, and port numbers. (Pen/trap orders can't be used to intercept the contents of a message—only the routing, addressing, and signaling information can be used.) The authority of the federal courts was expanded to allow issuance of pen/trap orders anywhere in the United States (previously limited to the court's particular district or jurisdiction).

- Previously, law enforcement officers were limited in their legal ability to assist owners of computers and networks in monitoring activity to protect against and detect intrusions and attacks. The Patriot Act specifically authorizes victims of network attacks to allow law enforcement officers to monitor their systems as part of an ongoing investigation (civil or criminal).

- The Patriot Act extends the scope of search warrants for e-mail communications to a nationwide basis so that such warrants can apply to records that are not in the district in which the issuing court is located.

- The Patriot Act increases penalties and modifies sentencing guidelines for offenses that involve intentionally damaging protected computers (under Title 18, Section 1030) and extends the scope of the law to apply to computers that are located in other countries, if U.S. interstate or foreign commerce is affected. The act also clarifies the culpable mental state (*mens rea*) required to charge a hacker under Section 1030; only intent to cause damage must be proven, rather than intent to cause a specified dollar amount of damage. Enhanced penalties are provided when the damage is to computers that are used for national security or criminal justice purposes.

NOTE

For a detailed discussion of the changes made by the U.S. Patriot Act pertaining to computer crime and electronic evidence, as outlined in the Department of Justice Computer Crime and Intellectual Property Section (CCIPS) field guidance memo, see www.usdoj.gov/criminal/cybercrime/PatriotAct.htm.

Summary

Evidence is the foundation of every criminal case, including those involving cybercrimes. The collection and preservation of digital evidence differs in many ways from the methods law enforcement officers are used to using for traditional types of evidence. Digital evidence is intangible, a magnetic or electronic representation of information. Its physical form does not readily reveal its nature. In addition, digital evidence is fragile. It is very easy for a criminal to deliberately delete crucial evidence in an instant or for an officer or technician to unintentionally damage or destroy it.

Fortunately, in many cases, evidence that appears to be gone is still on the disk or other media and can be recovered. A number of data recovery software packages are on the market, several of which are designed specifically for computer forensics work and marketed with law enforcement use in mind. There are also many commercial data recovery services that will perform the recover operation for a fee, using sophisticated equipment that might be beyond the budget of many law enforcement agencies.

Computer forensics is a relatively new field, but standards are rapidly being established. To ensure that digital evidence is admissible in court, it is best to adhere to accepted current standards and practices and use software that has been tried and tested. The primary objective in conducting an examination of a suspect computer's data is to leave the original in the same condition in which it was found. This means that, whenever possible, disk-imaging technology should be used to create an exact duplicate of the suspect hard disk, and this duplicate alone should be used for examination. In order to recover data that might be hidden in obscure areas of the disk or left behind after deletion or erasure, the copy must be a bitstream image, in which every bit is copied, sector by sector, from the original disk to the duplicate. This duplicate ideally should be made on site when the computer is seized, before the computer is shut down. At the same time, steps should be taken to record or preserve volatile data that will be lost when the computer's power is turned off.

Once one or more duplicates have been made, the original can be locked up securely in an evidence locker or evidence room until needed. Chain of custody must be maintained throughout the entire process. The duplicate disk can be examined for evidence of criminal activity. This examination should address not only those files that are visible in the file system but also should include a search for ambient data that is not obvious and that the user of the computer might not know still exists on the disk. For this task, you will need special forensics software, which can be installed on a forensic workstation set up for this purpose.

Collection of evidence involves not just technical know-how; it also requires knowledge of the laws pertaining to evidence. Violation of those laws can result in the evidence being thrown out of court, regardless of its technical quality and regardless of how definitively it proves the guilt of the defendant. In the United States, admissibility of evidence often hinges on the Fourth Amendment to the Constitution, which protects citizens against unreasonable search and seizure. If the search and seizure of computer equipment and/or digital data violates the suspect's constitutional rights, the evidence will be suppressed by the judge and will never be seen by the jury. Other federal laws and state laws govern the admissibility of evidence in criminal trials as well. These laws are generally collected in codifications called *Rules of Evidence*, and every investigator should be intimately familiar with the laws in his or her jurisdiction.

In the next chapter, "Building the Cybercrime Case," you will learn how the evidence is used in conjunction with the basic criminal justice process to put together a winnable case for the prosecution and what happens when that case finally goes to court.

Frequently Asked Questions

The following Frequently Asked Questions, answered by the authors of this book, are designed to both measure your understanding of the concepts presented in this chapter and to assist you with real-life implementation of these concepts. To have your questions about this chapter answered by the author, browse to **www.syngress.com/solutions** and click on the **"Ask the Author"** form.

Q: How can investigators view the time attributes on files in UNIX/Linux?

A: On UNIX-based systems, the time attributes are displayed in the file list when you use the **ls** command. The time attributes you'll see are *atime* (the time the file was last accessed), *mtime* (the time the file was last modified), *ctime* (the time of the last status change), and, on some Linux systems, *dtime* (the time the file was deleted). Whenever someone reads the file, the *atime* attribute will be updated, or, if the file is an executable, the *atime* is updated when the program is run. When you make any changes to a file, the *mtime* value is updated. The *ctime* attribute is updated whenever changes are made to the file's properties—for example, if permissions are changed. For more information about the UNIX time attributes (as well as NTFS time attributes) and how they can be used in an investigation, see www.ddj.com/documents/s=880/ddj0010f/0010f.htm.

Q: Why is documentation so important? Doesn't the evidence speak for itself?

A: In many computer-related criminal cases, the evidence speaks a language that most of the members of the jury (and often the judge, prosecutor, and law enforcement officers) don't understand. At one time, juries were likely to accept the testimony of expert witnesses without question, but as the public has become more technically sophisticated and expert testimony has been called into question in high-profile cases such as the O. J. Simpson case, juries have become more skeptical of experts' infallibility and more likely to accept the opposing attorney's challenges that raise doubts about evidence-processing methods and forensics techniques. This is the reason it is so important to document the actions of law enforcement officers and technicians every step of the way. Documentation is also important to refresh the memories of people who must testify in the case. Often trials are delayed for months or even years, and by the time an officer or technician is required to take the stand, he or she has handled many other cases.

Q: Why is it important that all the software used by law enforcement officers be licensed and registered? Law enforcement budgets are often tight; why not use freeware as much as possible?

A: Some freeware and shareware tools that are available on the Internet are good tools, and the price is certainly right. However, there are some dangers in using these programs for forensic purposes. First, you never know exactly what you're getting when you download a free program (and you certainly can't ask for your money back if it doesn't work properly). Downloads can be infected with viruses or Trojans that can damage the systems on which you use them. Using unlicensed software (illegal copies) is even worse. The opposing attorney(s) will have a field day if they discover that the police used pirated or "borrowed" software in the investigation. This behavior can destroy the credibility of the people who conducted the forensic examination and even result in losing the case. In addition, with properly purchased and registered software, you will be able to get technical support from the vendor if necessary. Makers of computer forensics software often offer discounts to law enforcement agencies, making it easier to afford the proper tools for the job. After all, officers and agencies probably wouldn't suggest saving money by buying their duty weapons from a pawnshop; that's because these are essential tools of the trade and must be as reliable as possible. For the cybercrime investigator or technician, the same is true of the forensics software that is used to collect and preserve evidence that can make or break a criminal case.

Resources

- IACIS Forensics Procedures Standards
www.cops.org/forensic_examination_procedures.htm

- *International Journal of Digital Evidence*
www.ijde.org

- *Digital Evidence Collection and Handling*
http://faculty.ncwc.edu/toconnor/495/495lect06.htm

- Federal Rules of Evidence
www.law.cornell.edu/rules/fre/overview.html#403

- *Computer Forensics Legal Standards and Equipment,* by Damian Tsoutsouris
http://rr.sans.org/incident/legal_standards.php

- New Technologies, Inc.: SafeBack Mirror Image Backup Software
www.forensics-intl.com/safeback.html

- High Technology Crime Investigation Association (HTCIA)
http://htcia.org

- Computer Forensics Online
www.shk-dplc.com/cfo

- High Tech Crime Network
www.htcn.org

- SANS Institute: *Incident Handling/Forensics*
http://rr.sans.org/incident/incident_list.php

- *Computer Forensics Magazine*
www.forensic-computing.com

- American Academy of Forensic Sciences
www.aafs.org

- DIBS*: History of Image Copying Technology*
www.forensic-computing.com/articles/welcome.html

- *Forensic Computer Analysis: An Introduction,*
by Dan Farmer and Wietse Venema
www.ddj.com/documents/s=881/ddj0009f/0009f.htm

- *An Explanation of Computer Forensics,* by Judd Robbins
  www.computerforensics.net/forensics.htm

- New Technologies, Inc. (NTI)
  www.forensics-intl.com/intro.html

- Timberline Technologies Forensics Products
  www.timberlinetechnologies.com/products/forensics.html

- *Linux Data Hiding and Recovery,* by Anton Chuvakin, Ph.D.
  www.linuxsecurity.com/feature_stories/data-hiding-forensics.html

- SANS: *What You Don't See on Your Hard Drive,* by Brian Kupper
  http://rr.sans.org/incident/dont_see.php

- *Windows Wipe Utilities Fail to Shift Stubborn Data Stains,* by John Leyden
  www.theregister.co.uk/content/55/23759.html

- *Secure Deletion of Data from Magnetic and Solid-State Memory,*
  by Peter Gutmann
  www.cs.auckland.ac.nz/~pgut001/pubs/secure_del.html

- *Memory Imaging and Forensic Analysis of Palm OS Devices,* by Joseph Grand
  http://63.251.138.38/atstake/acrobat/pdd_palm_forensics.pdf

- *Computer Evidence Processing: Good Documentation is Essential,*
  by Michael R. Anderson
  www.forensics-intl.com/art10.html

- DoJ Computer Crime and Intellectual Property Section*:
  Searching and Seizing Computers and Obtaining Electronic Evidence in
  Criminal Investigations*
  www.cybercrime.gov/searchmanual.htm

- *Admissibility of Electronic Evidence,* by Michael R. Overly
  www.forensics.com/resources/admiss.htm

Chapter 11

Building the Cybercrime Case

Topics we'll investigate in this chapter:

- Major Factors Complicating Prosecution
- Overcoming Obstacles to Effective Prosecution
- The Investigative Process
- Testifying in a Cybercrime Case

☑ Summary

☑ Frequently Asked Questions

☑ Resources

Introduction

Experienced investigators know that, contrary to the philosophy of the modern murder mystery, discovering "who dun it" is not the end of an investigation—it's only the beginning. In the previous chapter, we discussed how to collect and preserve evidence. Although in a cybercrime case this can be one of the most difficult aspects of the investigation, it's still not the final step. A criminal investigation, in order to result in prosecution of the offender, must culminate in the building of a solid *case file* containing documentation of all the evidence that can be used to obtain a conviction in court.

Constructing a criminal case is a long, often complex process. The more technical the facts of the case, the more difficult it is to build a good case that presents the evidence in a way that can be thoroughly understood by the following key players:

- The prosecuting attorney or a grand jury (one of which, depending on the level of the offense and the governing code of criminal procedure, will make the decision as to whether to bring the case to trial)

- The trial jury (which ultimately decides guilt or innocence in a felony case and sometimes sets the penalty)

- The judge (who may decide guilt or innocence in a misdemeanor case and who often is responsible for setting the penalty even in cases where guilt or innocence is decided by a jury)

The investigator is not the only person involved in constructing the case, but he or she usually plays the most important role and often coordinates the tasks of others who are involved. These others can include first-response law enforcement officers, crime scene technicians, crime lab personnel, and members of assisting agencies (for example, when local law enforcement agencies send digital evidence to the state police or FBI for enhancement or interpretation). Because of the technical nature of some cybercrimes, it is also common to call on private sector specialists or experts to provide assistance during the investigation. The criminal investigator in charge of the case will need to work closely with such outside experts to help them understand their roles and provide the type of documentation necessary for the case file.

Investigative techniques, tools, and processes are basically the same in a cybercrime case as in any other criminal case, but special considerations apply and several factors complicate the prosecution of these types of crimes. In this chapter, we discuss such complicating factors as the difficulty of defining the crime, jurisdictional issues, and special problems related to the nature of some of the evidence. We also take a brief look at how the authoritarian attitudes of many law enforcement officers, the elitist and anti-authority attitudes of many IT people, and the natural adversarial relationship that often exists between the two can complicate an investigation. Then we provide an overview of the investigative process as it applies to the typical cybercrime case, including discussion of investigative tools, the steps involved in an investigation, and the importance of defining areas of responsibility and preserving the chain of custody. Finally, we look at the trial process and offer tips on testifying in a cybercrime case, either as an evidentiary witness providing direct evidence or as an expert witness offering conclusions and opinions.

Major Factors Complicating Prosecution

Few criminal prosecutions are as simple as they seem at first glance. Even a lowly, seemingly straightforward speeding ticket can turn into a complex matter if it goes to trial. Officers can be required to prove that they have been adequately trained in the use of radar equipment, and the veracity of that equipment can be brought into question based on a myriad of theoretical technical possibilities. Prosecuting more serious offenses requires even more preparation on the parts of all who will testify, as well as people who won't be called to the stand but who are involved in handling evidence or putting together the documentation for the case file.

Cybercrimes are inherently complex by their very nature. Computers—which are complicated machines, the operation of which is really understood by very few people—always play a key role in every cybercrime case. Cybercrimes are often poorly defined in the statutes that govern them. This is partly because the legislators who make those laws don't understand the technology. It is also in part because the theories on which the criminal justice system is based were formulated long before computers existed and did not anticipate the changes they would bring to criminality. Jurisdictional ambiguities create nightmares for investigators and prosecutors alike. As if that weren't enough, much of the evidence in a cybercrime case might be both intangible and circumstantial. In the following sections, we address each of these obstacles to prosecution and then discuss some ways to overcome them.

Difficulty of Defining the Crime

The first step in investigating a reported crime is to determine that a crime has in fact been committed. Many people who don't work in the legal field—including tech people—have only a vague understanding of the law and what constitutes a crime. We've all heard (and most of us have said) the phrase "There ought to be a law," but unless there *is* a law—one that specifically describes the act that was committed—we can't prosecute no matter how "wrong" that act seems to be.

Not everything that's immoral or unethical is against the law, and we should be thankful for that. The justice system is already overcrowded, and the more laws there are on the books, the more potential there is for two conflicting but equally undesirable developments:

- There is more potential for abuse of the laws, resulting in innocent people being punished.
- There is more potential for the laws to be ignored, resulting in guilty people going unpunished.

A society that tries to regulate everything and protect its citizens from every possible unpleasantness (even from themselves) soon finds that it has also stifled the spirit and creativity of those people and created a police state in which the oppression is not worth the illusion of security. On the other hand, a society that seeks to make no rules and accepts the premise that "it's all good" and that everyone should be free to do his or her own thing soon descends into anarchy and chaos. The challenge of finding a sensible balance between these two extremes is a job for the legislative branch of government, and it is a challenge that is currently facing those legislators in regard to the formerly largely unregulated regions of cyberspace. Crime in the context of cyberspace is being defined and redefined regularly as governmental bodies seek to provide adequate—but not overly oppressive—legislation that balances our desire for control and order with the rights to free speech and the benefits of free flow of ideas.

In the following sections, we look at how criminality is defined in terms of bodies of law and basic criminal justice theory, and we discuss the concepts of elements of the offense and burden and level of proof on which the criminal justice system rests.

Bodies of Law

Computers, networks, and the data that passes through them are, like other aspects of our lives, subject to a confusing number of laws that have been enacted by legislative bodies at different levels of government (local, state, national, and international), created by courts in the form of case law, or set down through administrative orders or regulatory bodies. Because the law is such a maze of complicated and ever-changing rules, many non-lawyers don't even try to understand how the legal system works, the differences between different bodies and types of law, and how all these different laws interact with one another.

> **NOTE**
>
> In the United States, individual laws are passed by a legislative body, and then groups of related laws are gathered into collections called *codifications* or *codes*. For example, a penal code contains criminal laws; a motor vehicle code contains laws pertaining to driving, traffic offenses, and the operation and maintenance of vehicles; a family code contains laws related to child custody, adoption, marriage and divorce, and other family matters.

Generally, laws can be divided into three different "bodies." Each of these bodies of law has its own rules of procedure, different penalties for violation, and different enforcement agencies and courts that have jurisdiction. The burden of proof and the level of proof required to win a case are different, depending on the applicable body of law. The three bodies of law are:

- Criminal law
- Civil law
- Administrative/regulatory law

In the following sections, we discuss each of these bodies of law and how they differ.

> **NOTE**
>
> The information in this chapter pertains directly to the U.S. legal system. Other countries have similar divisions of law, but these might differ. For more information about international issues, see the resources listed in the Appendix, "Fighting Cybercrime on a Global Scale."

Criminal Law

When we hear or use the term *illegal*, we generally think of a violation of criminal law. We consider something that is "against the law" to be an act for which a person can be jailed or at least fined by the state. However, many acts that violate the law are not *crimes* but rather civil infractions or breaches of civil contract. For example, in the tech industry you often hear it said that "it's illegal" to give away a copy of software that you purchased. Although software *piracy* (which involves making and distributing copies of copyrighted software without the authorization of the copyright holder) is a criminal offense in some circumstances and jurisdictions, giving away a copy you purchased legally is not. However, doing so might be a breach of contract—the end-user licensing agreement (EULA) that a person "signs" when he or she installs the software. This means the software vendor could file a lawsuit against you in civil court asking for monetary damages, but you could not be put in jail for it.

A *criminal offense* must be specifically defined as such by a locality's, state's, or country's written statutes. (We discuss statutory law a little later in this chapter.) Criminal laws are designed to protect society, as well as individual persons, from harmful acts. They are also designed to punish offenders as a deterrence both to the offender and to others, and in some cases they are intended to ensure that the offenders are unable to pose a further risk to society by placing them in jail or prison or even, in extreme cases, taking their lives.

Criminal complaints can be filed by the individual(s) who are harmed or by law enforcement officers or citizens who observe the offense. However, the charges are prosecuted not on behalf of the victim but on behalf of the governmental entity having jurisdiction. That is, a crime defined in the state penal code is prosecuted by the state, and a federal crime is prosecuted by the federal government. The *style of the case* is the term used to describe the language at the top of all court documents identifying a case. If the case is brought under criminal law, the style will read something like this: *The State of Texas vs. John Smith* or *The United States of America vs. Jane Doe.* In a criminal case, the person or entity that files the charges is referred to as the *complainant,* and the person (or company) against whom the charges are brought is called the *defendant.*

Penalties for violating a criminal law can include monetary payment or loss of liberty and range from light to severe, including:

- A warning citation (usually in the case of traffic laws or other lowest-level misdemeanors)

- A citation that imposes a fine (monetary payment that goes to the state)

- Compensation or restitution (monetary payment that goes to the victim)

- Community service (mandatory "volunteer" work for some charitable organization or governmental body)

- Probation (supervision or oversight by the government for a specified period of time in lieu of confinement, which can include court-order restrictions on behavior such as no use of computers or required attendance at counseling sessions)

- Confinement in jail (usually for a limited time, such as a few days to a year)

- Confinement in prison (usually for a more extended time, ranging from a few months to life)

- The death penalty (in some jurisdictions; usually limited to people convicted of murder)

CyberLaw Review...

Defining the Law

Generally, in the United States each state adopts a code of criminal procedure and a penal code that define, respectively, how criminal laws are enforced and the criminal offenses themselves. The penal code generally sets forth the way in which offenses are classified (violations, misdemeanors, and felonies), *penalty grades* within each classification (such as Class A, B, and C misdemeanors and first-, second-, and third-degree felonies), and the penalty range for each grade of offense.

Criminal offenses are generally classified according to the seriousness of the crime and the severity of the penalty. These classifications can include the following, depending on the jurisdiction: *violations,* the least serious offenses, the penalty for which is only a fine, *misdemeanors,* more serious than violations with a penalty of fine or jail term, and *felonies,* the most serious offenses, which carry a penalty of imprisonment (and in some jurisdictions, the death penalty for the most serious cases). Cybercrimes span the range of classifications and penalty grades. In many jurisdictions, offenses such as theft, property damage, and others that cause monetary loss are classified according to the dollar amount of the loss or damage. That is, a network intrusion that causes little loss is a misdemeanor, whereas an attack that results in large monetary losses to the victim is a felony.

In the United States, the Constitution gives persons accused of serious crimes (felonies) the right to trial by jury. The accused can waive the right if desired and have the case decided by a judge.

Civil Law

The objective of civil law is to settle disagreements between persons or entities (*parties* to the suit or action). Thus the style of the case will usually name two private parties (such as *John Smith vs. Joe Jones* or *Jane Doe vs. BrandX Corporation*), although governmental entities can be parties to civil suits as well. Civil wrongs are not crimes; they are called *torts*, and civil litigation is the legal process of petitioning a court for compensation or correction of these wrongs. In a civil suit, the party who initiates the lawsuit is called the *plaintiff*, and the person against whom the suit is brought is called the *respondent*. (Although you might hear the respondent referred to as the *defendant*, that term is not technically correct in these cases.)

The losing party in a civil suit does not generally go to jail or prison unless also convicted of a criminal offense such as contempt of court. Instead, he or she is subject to one of two types of court orders:

- An order requiring that the respondent pay monetary damages. These damages can include *compensatory damages* for the actual and anticipated losses suffered by the plaintiff—both tangible and intangible—and *punitive damages* beyond the actual losses, designed to punish the party who committed the wrong.

- An injunction requiring that the respondent do some specified act or *not* do some specified act. For example, an injunction could order that the party stop sending e-mail to the plaintiff. An injunction is a legally binding order, and ignoring it can result in criminal charges.

An act can be both a crime and a civil wrong. Thus, cybercrime investigators may find that the evidence in their cases is also evidence in a civil lawsuit. When a company's network is invaded, in addition to filing criminal charges against the hacker, the company can also file a civil suit that seeks to directly collect monetary compensation for damages such as loss of worker productivity and lost sales due to the hacker's actions.

Another important concept in civil law is that of *vicarious liability*. This is the legal responsibility that one person or entity has for someone else's actions. Vicarious liability is usually created by some sort of "oversight" relationship. That is, a person or entity that has oversight or control over another person can be held civilly liable for wrongs committed by that person. This means a parent can be held liable for a child's acts, and an employer can be held responsible for an employee's acts. Thus if a hacker uses company equipment and time to illegally break into other networks, to send child pornography, or to commit other cyber-crimes, the employing company could be sued for allowing it to happen.

NOTE

It is important to understand that vicarious liability generally applies only to civil law. There are limited circumstances in criminal law (such as criminal conspiracy) in which a person can be charged for an offense actually committed by someone else, but in general, criminal responsibility requires *culpability* (overt involvement in commission of the prohibited act) before a charge can be brought.

Administrative/Regulatory Law

A third body of law, often overlooked in discussions of criminal and civil law, is *administrative law*, also called *regulatory law*. This body of law consists of rules and regulations that are enacted by a governmental agency under authority given to it by the legislative body and that apply to a particular occupational field or govern a particular area of life. Examples include Environmental Protection Agency regulations as well as rules that govern the practice of medicine, law, engineering, and the like.

Administrative laws are neither criminal nor civil but have the authority of law within their areas of jurisdiction. For example, an administrative action can be brought against a doctor or lawyer who violates the state regulatory agency's rules. If found guilty, the accused person might be censured, fined, or have his or her license revoked. (If the latter occurs, and the person continues to practice, criminal charges of practicing without a license could be brought.) Administrative actions are usually conducted according to procedures set out by law that are similar to those of a court, but the councils or other bodies that hear the cases are not officers of the court. Thus the proceedings are called *quasijudicial*.

NOTE

In some cases, one act can be subject to more than one body of law. For example, killing a person could result in both a murder charge (under criminal law) and a wrongful death lawsuit (under civil law). Likewise, a cybercriminal working in the finance industry who discovers and misuses insider information in a stock trade might be subject to both criminal charges and administrative sanctions.

Types of Law

Laws of all three types—criminal, civil, and administrative/regulatory—come into being in one of three ways: They're passed by a legislative body, they're created through court decisions, or they arise out of tradition and practice. The origin of a law determines whether it is considered to be statutory law, case law, or common law.

Statutory Law

Statutory law carries the most weight of the three types of law and is what we usually think of when we think of "the law." Statutory laws are created through a formal process known as *legislation*. They are introduced as proposed laws, or *bills,* debated, sometimes amended, voted upon, and passed by one or more legislative bodies and signed into law by an executive officer of the jurisdiction. In most cases, both the members of the legislative body and the executive officer are elected by popular vote of the citizens. Statutory laws are written and published as statutes, then *codified* (collected into codes) and enforced by police and other law enforcement agencies.

Case Law

Case law is based on judicial interpretation of laws that have been enacted by legislative bodies (statutory law) and governing documents (for example, the U.S. or state constitution or the city charter). Case law doesn't carry the same weight as statutory law because different courts can issue drastically different interpretations, and court decisions are subject to the appeals process.

Nonetheless, even though case law is not binding as is statutory law, the judicial opinions that form the basis of case law do establish *precedent,* which means case law is given weight by other judges making decisions in subsequent cases. In both criminal and civil court, an attorney cites previous case decisions to back up his or her case, and this forms an important part of the basis for a judge's decision.

Often the principles set down by judges in case law find their way later into statutory law. For example, in the famous case *Miranda vs. Arizona,* the U.S. Supreme Court held that law enforcement officers must inform suspects in criminal cases of their constitutional rights before questioning them in relation to a crime. This decision was not based on any statute but on the justices' interpretation of the due process guarantees in the U.S. Bill of Rights. However, after this landmark case, legislative bodies in many states passed statutory laws requiring that officers *Mirandize* (read the rights to) criminal suspects.

NOTE

Case law is important in cybercrime enforcement because many of these offenses haven't been on the books for a long period of time and thus their interpretations haven't been clearly defined in court. In ambiguous areas such as jurisdiction, in particular, it is important for investigators and prosecutors to stay up to date on applicable case law, because it can determine whether or not a case is prosecutable.

Common Law

Common law has grown less prominent over the years as more and more formal laws have been passed governing matters that once were ruled by tradition and custom. In the early days of the United States, common law (based on the English common law system) was an important way of governing society in a time when far fewer laws were formally enacted. Common law is based on practice, or "the way we've always done it."

A good example of common law still in existence is common law marriage, which is legal in many U.S. states. Two persons can become legally married without obtaining a marriage license from the state by meeting the common law requirements, which usually include a public declaration that they are married and living together, co-mingling funds, and otherwise acting as a married couple.

Because common law is open to ambiguity (for example, in the case of common law marriage, if one party denies that the marital relationship exists, it can be difficult for the other to prove that it does), in the United States and other countries more and more matters that were once subject to common law are being formally legislated.

One might say that in the early days of the Internet, a form of common law governed. Although there were no governmentally imposed laws that directly pertained to online activity, "netizens" set their own rules based on consensus. For example, "flamers" (people who launched verbal and personal attacks on others) and spammers (those who deluged lists and individuals with unsolicited advertising) were often shunned and even kept out of IRC channels and mailing lists. There was even a sort of "profiling" that took place, as people with certain e-mail addresses (for example, those ending with @aol.com) were immediately suspect. As in earlier societies, traditions were quickly established defining what was and wasn't acceptable behavior. These traditions still persist in many areas of the Net today and influence online behavior. As with common law in earlier societies, these rules are now finding their way into formal legislation as governing bodies introduce bills aimed at criminalizing spam and other such activities.

Levels of Law

Statutory laws are enacted at different levels of government. Often these laws overlap so that one act might be both a state and federal crime, for example. Generally, the *scope* of law falls into one of four categories:

- Local laws
- State laws
- Federal laws
- International laws

The processes of enacting these laws are very similar; the differences are the legislative body that enacts them, the executive officer who signs them, and the geographic jurisdiction within which they can be enforced.

Local Laws

In the United States, *local law* generally refers to laws enacted by a city or town council or by a county commission, signed into law by the mayor or a county judge. Some cities and counties give the executive officer the power to veto laws; in others, the signing is a mere formality. Local laws are usually called *ordinances*.

Cities and counties can enact ordinances making certain acts criminal offenses, but generally only at the lowest levels. For example, in Texas a criminal offense under city law is a Class C misdemeanor, the lowest level of criminal offense. Local laws can be enforced only within the boundaries of the city or county that enacts them.

People accused of violations of ordinances are tried in municipal or county courts. These courts often are not *courts of record*—that is, no court reporter records the proceedings. A guilty verdict in these lower courts can be appealed to a higher court of record. Cities and counties could pass laws regarding computer and network usage, but this generally isn't done at the local level.

NOTE

Local law is subject to state and federal law. A locality cannot pass a law that would violate the U.S. or state constitution or specific laws that grant sole control over certain behaviors to the state. For example, some states have laws that prohibit cities and counties from passing gun control laws, reserving that right for the state. On the other hand, in many states you'll find that some cities have laws imposing curfews on juveniles or requiring helmets for bicyclists, whereas other cities in the same state do not.

State Laws

Most penal laws (criminal offenses) enforced by police—including municipal police and county sheriff's offices—are *state laws*, passed by a state legislature and signed into law by the state's governor. Many states have a bicameral legislature patterned after the U.S. Congress, so the laws must be passed by both houses. In some states, the governor has veto power.

States can pass criminal laws at all offense grades (misdemeanors and felonies), with penalties ranging from fines to the death penalty (in states that allow it). States have wide latitude in the types of behaviors that can be outlawed. In general, unless the U.S. Constitution or federal law prohibits a state from regulating a particular behavior, the state is free to do so. Many U.S. states now have some laws regarding computer crime, but these laws vary widely from state to state.

Federal Laws

The U.S. Constitution grants all federal legislative powers to Congress, which consists of two branches: the Senate and the House of Representatives. Federal laws are introduced as bills in either the House or the Senate (designated by *HR* or *S* before the bill number to identify its origin) and are generally debated and amended in committee, where public hearings may be held to obtain citizen input, before being brought to the full body for a vote. After passage by one branch, the bill must go to the other. If changes are made there, it comes back to the originating body for approval, and it goes back and forth until agreement is reached. Alternately, a conference committee with members from both the House and Senate may be appointed to resolve the differences. Once a law has been passed by both bodies, it goes to the President, who can sign it, veto it, or let it pass into law without signature. A presidential veto can be overridden by vote of two-thirds majority of both the House and Senate.

Federal criminal laws are enforced by the FBI and other enforcement agencies that specialize in particular areas of law, such as the Drug Enforcement Administration (DEA); the Bureau of Alcohol, Tobacco, and Firearms; and the Criminal Investigation Division of the Internal Revenue Service. The FBI investigates federal cybercrime offenses, and the Computer Crime and Intellectual Property Section (CCIPS) of the Criminal Division of the Department of Justice provides legal expertise to federal prosecutors. The Federal Rules of Criminal Procedure govern the proceedings in these cases. Most federal criminal laws are contained in Title 18 of the U.S. Code (the federal equivalent of a state's penal code).

The federal government doesn't have general police powers within the states. That is, the FBI cannot arrest people for violations of state laws. The federal government does have general criminal jurisdiction over U.S. locations that are not within state boundaries, such as federal land, U.S. territories, and the District of Columbia.

International Laws

Laws can also originate through treaties, which are agreements entered into between countries. For example, Congress enacted the infamous Digital Millennium Copyright Act (DMCA) in 1998 to implement the World Intellectual Property Organization (WIPO) copyright treaty concluded at Geneva, Switzerland, in 1996. WIPO is an agency of the United Nations that has 179 member states. For more information about international laws, see the Appendix, "Fighting Cybercrime on a Global Scale."

Basic Criminal Justice Theory

Investigating and prosecuting crimes of any type requires a basic understanding of criminal justice theory. Even experienced criminal justice theorists are challenged by the need to fit a type of criminality that didn't exist when these theories were established into a system designed to deal with less complex crimes that involve tangible property and evidence. In this section, we discuss some of the concepts on which the U.S. criminal justice system is based and the ways in which cybercrimes fit into these concepts.

Mala Prohibita and Mala in Se

Crimes can be divided into two groups based on whether they are considered to be acts that are inherently evil or acts that are "wrong" only because a legislative body made them illegal:

- Historically, acts that are considered to be *true crimes* under the laws of nature or God are described as *mala in se*, meaning "bad in itself." Acts such as murder, stealing, rape, robbery, and so forth are examples of this type of crime.

- Offenses that are not universally considered to be criminal but are made so by act of legislature are described as *mala prohibita* crimes. Examples include driving faster than the posted speed, possessing a gun without a permit in a state where that's required, or drinking alcohol when under a certain age.

The classification of some cybercrimes is a matter of debate. Is copying data from someone else's network without permission more akin to picking flowers on state property (*mala prohibita*) or stealing tangible goods that belong to another (*mala in se*)? The distinction between *mala in se* and *mala prohibita* offenses is not very important from a legal standpoint—the two types of law are enforced identically—but is interesting from a philosophical point of view.

Corpus Delicti: The Body of the Crime

The concept of *corpus delicti,* which literally means *the body of the crime,* is another important criminal law concept. This term describes the essence of the crime, or material evidence showing that a crime has been committed. It derives from the historical rule in a murder case that a dead body is necessary to prove that a murder has been committed. This rule has evolved over time to allow the *corpus delicti* to be established through *presumptive evidence*—that is, conclusive evidence that would lead a reasonable person to presume that a person has been murdered, even though the body is never found. For example, large amounts of blood established by DNA testing to be that of the presumed victim, along with the disappearance of the victim, would constitute presumptive evidence.

One factor that makes prosecution of cybercrimes difficult is the absence of a concrete *corpus delicti*. That is, there might be no tangible evidence of a crime at all.

Actus Reus and Mens Rea

Before a criminal offense can be charged, two essential elements must exist:

- *Actus reus* **(Latin for *guilty act*)** This is the act or omission that is prohibited by the criminal law. For example, the act of taking an item from a store shelf and removing it from the store without paying for it is the prohibited act for the offense of shoplifting (theft). The act of accessing a file on a network that you don't have permission to enter is a prohibited act under the offense of unauthorized access. In addition to overt acts or omissions, criminal laws might also prohibit mere possession, as with drug laws and some weapons offenses.

- *Mens rea* **(Latin for *guilty mind*)** This term refers to the state of mind that the prosecution must prove to convict the defendant in a criminal case. This is also sometimes referred to as the *culpable mental state*. The particular mental state required to constitute an offense is defined in the statute for that crime and differs depending on the crime.

The U.S. criminal justice system is based on the principle of *actus reus non facit reum nisi mens sit rea*. This is Latin for "An act does not make a person guilty of a crime unless his mind be also guilty." In other words, in order to convict, the prosecution must prove not only that the accused committed the prohibited act but also that the accused possessed the culpable mental state at the time of the offense.

Most penal codes define the culpable mental states as follows:

- **Intent** It is the deliberate desire of the person to obtain the outcome of the act (such as the death of a person).

- **Knowledge** The person is aware that the act will result in the outcome.

- **Recklessness** The person knows there is a substantial risk that if he or she engages in the act, it will result in the outcome.

- **Negligence** The person *ought to have known* that there was a substantial risk that if he or she engaged in the act, it would result in the outcome.

CyberLaw Review...

Understanding Criminal Culpability

Generally, criminal culpability includes one of four mental states: intentional, knowing, reckless, or negligent. Often a single act can be interpreted as different offenses depending on the perpetrator's mental state. Here's an extreme example—the act of killing a person by running over him with a motor vehicle:

1. If a person sees a pedestrian crossing the street in front of him, notices that it is his archrival whom he has long wished dead, and deliberately aims the car at the pedestrian and accelerates, killing him, the mental state is *intentional* and the crime is murder.

2. Even if he doesn't have the intent to kill, if the driver sees the pedestrian, simply doesn't feel like slowing down, and runs him over, the mental state is *knowing*. The crime is still murder in most jurisdictions because the murder statutes generally specify "intentionally or knowingly" as the required level of culpability for that offense.

3. If a person is driving much too fast for conditions, breezing through stop signs and paying no attention to the road as he "bops to the tunes" on his car stereo and in so doing he runs over a pedestrian at a crossing and kills him, the mental state is *reckless* and the crime is manslaughter.

4. If a person knows that his brakes are bad, has had them go out several times but continues to keep driving the car without having them fixed, sees the pedestrian crossing the street in front of him and tries to stop but is unable to do so and kills the pedestrian, the mental state is *negligent* and the crime is criminally negligent homicide.

On the other hand, if a person is driving down the street, obeying the speed limit and traffic signs and otherwise taking care, and a pedestrian suddenly darts into the road from between two parked cars right into the path of the car and is hit and killed, there is no culpable mental state and there is no crime; the incident is an accident.

How do these definitions apply to cybercrimes? It is important for cyber-crime investigators to realize that as with other criminal offenses, there must be evidence to prove *mens rea* as well as *actus reus*. That is, a person who "stumbles into" a network without intent to do so (for example, by running some program or script a hacker left on the computer, without knowing what that program or script will do) or who accidentally deletes critical files on a system does not have the intent or knowledge that is necessary under some statutes to obtain a criminal conviction.

Elements of the Offense

The prohibited act and the culpable mental state are the two most important of the *elements of the offense*. The elements are those things that must be proven by the prosecution to obtain a conviction. Most penal codes define additional elements, such as:

- **Required result** Some offenses require a specific result of the act before that offense can be charged. For example, murder cannot be charged unless a death occurs as a result of the accused person's act. (Most jurisdictions also provide for an offense called *criminal attempt* that can be charged when an offense is attempted but is unsuccessful.)

- **Negation of exceptions** Some offenses provide in the statute for *exceptions* to prosecution. An exception differs from a defense to prosecution in that if the exception applies, the offense can't be charged. A person can still be charged with the crime even if there is an applicable statutory defense; it's up to the defendant to prove the defense (at trial), but it's up to the prosecution to prove the negation of exceptions.

On the Scene...

Analyzing the Elements of an Offense

Texas Penal Code Section 33.02 defines the offense of Breach of Computer Security:

> (a) A person commits an offense if the person knowingly accesses a computer, computer network, or computer system without the effective consent of the owner.
>
> (b) [defines penalty grades]

Continued

> Section 33.03 defines defenses:
>
>> It is an affirmative defense to prosecution under Section 33.02 that the actor was an officer, employee, or agent of a communications common carrier or electric utility and committed the proscribed act or acts in the course of employment while engaged in an activity that is a necessary incident to the rendition of service or to the protection of the rights or property of the communications common carrier or electric utility.
>
> If we analyze the statute, we find that the prohibited act is "accessing a computer, computer network, or computer system without the effective consent of the owner." The culpable mental state (*mens rea*) is "knowingly." The defense to prosecution can be argued in court, if applicable. If the defendant can prove that the defense applies, he or she will be acquitted. If this were an exception instead of a defense, the law enforcement officers would have to ensure that it didn't apply before they could make a lawful arrest. This particular offense does not have a required result other than "access." It is not necessary that damage or loss occur in order to bring charges.

All elements of an offense that are laid out in the statute must be present before a suspect can be arrested. Cybercrime investigators must be familiar with the statutes under which they plan to bring charges and ensure that each and every required element is present before making the arrest.

Level and Burden of Proof

Two important differences between criminal and civil law are the *level of proof* required to find a person legally accountable for an act and the side on which the *burden of proof* lies—that is, which side must prove its case to win at trial.

In a criminal case, the burden is on the prosecution to prove its case; if it does not, the defendant will be acquitted without having to provide any case at all. This is based on the presumption of innocence until proven guilty that is the basis of U.S. criminal law. The level of proof required in criminal cases is very high: Guilt must be proven *beyond a reasonable doubt,* and in a jury trial, all jurors must agree on the verdict.

Some countries' criminal justice systems operate on the opposite presumption; under the Napoleonic Code, which forms the basis of the criminal laws of France and other European countries, a person accused of a crime is presumed guilty and the burden is on the accused to prove his or her innocence.

In a civil case, the burden is generally on the respondent who is accused of a civil wrong to prove that he or she isn't liable. The level of proof required is much lower than in a criminal trial; the party that proves its case by a *preponderance of the evidence* (that is, there is slightly more evidence supporting that side than the other) wins the case. In many civil cases, only a majority of the jurors must be convinced; the decision doesn't have to be unanimous.

Cybercrimes investigators must always be cognizant of the fact that criminal cases work toward two different levels of proof at different points in the investigation. *Probable cause* (facts and circumstances that would cause a reasonable and prudent person to believe that the accused person committed the crime) is the first level and is required to make a lawful arrest. Conviction requires much more evidence—enough to constitute proof beyond a reasonable doubt in the minds of an entire jury. This is the reason that followup investigations are so important, even after enough evidence has been gathered to arrest the suspect.

Jurisdictional Issues

Cybercrime cases, more than most others, often involve complex jurisdictional issues that can present both legal and practical obstacles to prosecution. To understand why jurisdiction presents such a problem in enforcing cybercrime laws, we have to look at how jurisdiction is defined, including the different types of jurisdictional authority, levels of jurisdiction, and statutory and case law pertaining to jurisdiction. In the following sections, we discuss these issues and explore the complications that arise when multijurisdictional cases take on an international flavor. We also examine the practical considerations that make it difficult to prosecute cases that span jurisdictional lines.

Defining Jurisdiction

Legal jurisdiction refers to the scope of authority given to a law enforcement agency to enforce laws or to a court to pronounce legal judgments. All governmental powers are jurisdictional in nature. That is, they are applicable only in regard to specific places or subject matter. A law passed in France does not apply to Americans unless they travel to France. At least, that's the way it used to be. Cyberspace complicates matters because a person can now—via computer—commit an act in France (or any other country accessible through the Internet) without physically being there. Does this mean that the American who has never set foot in France can be charged with a crime under French law? Later in this chapter we look at an actual case that addresses that very question. First, however, we need to discuss the different types and levels of jurisdictional authority.

Types of Jurisdictional Authority

The jurisdiction of an enforcement agency or of a court can be based on several things. These include:

- **The legal system under which the law falls** Police agencies have jurisdiction over criminal cases but no jurisdiction over civil matters. Citizens often ask police officers to intervene in civil disputes, but police are legally unable to do so. This must be done by agencies of the civil system. In some states, for example, county constables' deputies have the authority to enforce civil orders such as evictions and seizure of property to satisfy civil judgments. Regulatory agencies may have enforcement arms that have jurisdiction over their specific scope of responsibility. Courts likewise have jurisdiction over either civil or criminal cases; some courts have jurisdiction over both.

- **The case type** Municipal and state police have jurisdiction over all state criminal offenses, but some enforcement agencies have jurisdiction over only certain types of cases. For example, the state alcoholic beverage commission has jurisdiction over crimes pertaining to the sale, use, and transport of alcoholic beverages; the state racing commission has jurisdiction over criminal acts related to horse racing, and the state pharmacy board can enforce criminal laws related to controlled substances. Courts sometimes are limited to jurisdiction over specific types of cases (for example, family courts that hear only child custody and juvenile cases).

- **Offense grade** Courts often hear cases related to particular grades of offense. Thus in Texas, municipal courts hear cases related to Class C misdemeanor offenses, county courts hear cases related to Class A and B misdemeanors, and district courts hear cases related to felony offenses.

- **Monetary damages** Some civil courts hear cases based on limits on the amount of monetary damages claimed. The most common example is small claims court, in which damages are limited to no more than a few thousand dollars. This court is often presided over by a justice of the peace, an elected judicial officer who, unlike judges of higher courts, often is not required to be a licensed attorney.

- **Government level** Both enforcement agencies and courts are assigned jurisdiction based on level of government. Courts, too, operate at the municipal, county, state, and federal levels.

- **Geographic area** *Geographic jurisdiction* refers to the physical area over which an agency or court has jurisdiction. Municipal police officers have jurisdiction within their city limits, state police have statewide jurisdiction, and so on. In many states, however, police officers have legal jurisdiction throughout an entire state, although their agency policies often restrict them to making arrests only within the limits of the city or county for which they work. Courts likewise have jurisdiction within specified geographic areas. For example, a municipal court in the City of Houston has jurisdiction over Class C misdemeanors—but only those that occur within the city limits.

Geographic jurisdiction is what most of us think of when we hear the term *jurisdiction*. However, it's important to realize that the scope of jurisdictional authority can be based on many things other than geographic area.

On the Scene...

Multijurisdictional Task Forces

One way that enforcement agencies at different jurisdictional levels can cooperate to address special crime problems such as cybercrime is through a *multijurisdictional task force*. The U.S. Secret Service has assisted agencies by forming these types of task forces composed of members from local, state, and federal law enforcement agencies. The model for this type of task force was the New York Electronic Crimes Task Force (NYECTF) that was located in the World Trade Center in New York City prior to the September 11, 2001, terrorist attack that destroyed the Trade Center buildings.

Level of Jurisdiction

Levels of jurisdiction correspond to the levels of law. Jurisdiction of enforcement agencies and courts can be local (city or county), statewide, federal, or international. Jurisdictional levels can overlap. Most U.S. citizens are familiar with the concept of *double jeopardy*. Based on the Sixth Amendment to the U.S. Constitution, this principle states that no one can be subject to being tried twice for the same offense. What many people don't understand is that a person can indeed be charged and tried twice for the same act if those charges are brought at different jurisdictional levels. This is what occurred when Sgt. Stacy Koon and other Los Angeles Police Department officers were tried and acquitted at the state level for police brutality in the Rodney King case in the 1990s, then tried again and convicted at the federal level. This is *not* considered to be double jeopardy.

Likewise, a cybercriminal could be charged with unauthorized network access under a state's computer crimes laws and also be charged at the federal level for the same act if the offense involved matters that come under federal jurisdiction (for example, if the computer belongs to a financial institution).

The Problem with Cyberspace

Jurisdiction presents a special problem in cybercrime cases because the offenses are by definition committed in cyberspace, which is not a physical "place." The criminal and the victim are often miles apart, and the criminal might never set foot in the state or country where the harm occurs.

Another complicating factor is the cyberspace culture. Many believe that the Internet should remain a "free zone" where no governmental regulation or laws apply. Others believe that existing laws are sufficient and can be effectively applied to the cyberspace environment. Still others think we should have special "cybercops" whose jurisdiction *is* the Internet. The latter solution, while intriguing, brings up more questions: For whom would these cybercops be employed—an international entity such as the U.N.? If so, would they have jurisdiction only in member nations? Would an international body have authority to pass laws regulating behavior on the Internet? What would happen if or when those laws conflicted with laws in the states or nations that belong to the international body?

Statutory Law Pertaining to Jurisdiction

Most U.S. states have laws that address the jurisdiction of the states' laws and courts. For example, the Texas Penal Code, section 1.04, titled Territorial Jurisdiction, says:

> "(a) This state has jurisdiction over an offense that a person commits by his own conduct or the conduct of another for which he is criminally responsible if:
> (1) either the conduct or a result that is an element of the offense occurs inside this state;
> (2) the conduct outside this state constitutes an attempt to commit an offense inside this state;
> (3) the conduct outside this state constitutes a conspiracy to

> commit an offense inside this state, and an act in furtherance of
> the conspiracy occurs inside this state; or
> (4) the conduct inside this state constitutes an attempt, solicita-
> tion, or conspiracy to commit, or establishes criminal responsi-
> bility for the commission of, an offense in another jurisdiction
> that is also an offense under the laws of this state."

This code gives the state broad authority to bring charges in a wide range of
cases and would cover most cybercrimes that originated within the state or when
a "result" (such as loss of intangible property) occurs within the state even though
the perpetrator might be in another state or even another country. Legally, then,
Texas could bring charges against citizens of other states or countries who had
never been inside Texas. Practically, this would require extradition, which might
or might not be granted by the state or country where the accused is physically
located. Later in this chapter, we look more closely at how practical considerations can complicate prosecution.

Case Law Pertaining to Jurisdiction

We mentioned the case of *Tennessee vs. Robert and Carleen Thomas* earlier in this
book. In the Thomas case, the long arm of the law reached approximately 2000
miles from a Tennessee court to California, where the Thomases lived and
worked. The grand jury in Tennessee handed down an indictment against the
Thomases for violating the Tennessee obscenity statutes, even though their adult
BBS had already been declared legal in Santa Clara County, California, where
they were located, and the Thomases were tried and convicted in Tennessee and
sent to prison. This was a landmark case in the matter of jurisdiction as it applies
to acts committed in cyberspace.

Another case that promises to be important in terms of international jurisdiction is unfolding during the writing of this book. In May 2000, a court in France
ordered Yahoo!, the U.S.-based Web service, to remove all Nazi paraphernalia
that was offered for sale on its site (which is hosted in the United States). Yahoo!
refused, and in November 2000 the French court threatened to fine Yahoo!
$13,000 per day if the company didn't comply. The next month, Yahoo! filed in
U.S. court for a declaration that the French order couldn't be enforced by the
U.S. government, and in November 2001, the U.S. District Court issued a decision that enforcement of the French order would violate Yahoo!'s constitutional
right to freedom of speech. Then in February 2002, the French court countered
that it would take Yahoo! to trial in France for condoning war crimes! This case
isn't over yet, and it will be interesting to see how it plays out. As with the
Thomas case, the act committed is not a crime in the jurisdiction where the

accused is located, but it is considered a crime in another location where the "criminal" items can be accessed over the Net.

The potential for many similar jurisdictional sparring matches exists now that it's so easy for a criminal to use the Internet to "reach out and touch someone" in a state or country other than the one in which the criminal is located.

International Complications

In international law, the concept of *territoriality* is based on the principle that nations should not exercise their jurisdiction outside their own territory (*Dictionary of Law,* Oxford University Press). However, nations are allowed to exercise jurisdiction inside their territory over acts committed by their own citizens when outside their territory. Furthermore, they generally are permitted to exercise jurisdiction over a criminal act in which part of the act occurred within their territory (that is, the offense either originated in their territory and was completed outside or originated outside their territory but was completed inside it).

How does this concept affect cybercrime cases? Can a nation apply its laws to persons who reside outside its territory who, for example, operate Web sites that violate the laws of that nation? All these questions must be answered before cybercrime can be addressed on a global scale. Proposed international treaties such as the International Convention to Combat Cyber Crime and Cyber Terrorism always end up highlighting the fact that there is a great deal of disagreement among and within nations as to what constitutes cybercrime. It is unlikely that the problems associated with international enforcement will be solved easily or soon.

Practical Considerations

Legalities aside, for a number of practical reasons law enforcement agencies and prosecutors choose not to pursue cybercrime cases that take them outside their normal jurisdictions. These reasons include the following:

- The cost of travel to investigate leads in distant cities, states, or countries

- The difficulty of bringing in witnesses and records from far away for the trial

- The difficulty of extraditing a suspect who is located in another jurisdiction

- The political reality that citizens generally want their police agencies to address local crime first

- The lack of technical understanding and expertise within the enforcement agency and prosecutor's office

- The paperwork and "red tape" that are often involved in obtaining the cooperation of agencies in other jurisdictions, especially in other countries

- The language barriers that often make it difficult to communicate with agencies and witnesses in other countries

The fact that an agency has the legal authority to bring criminal charges in a particular case doesn't mean that it will necessarily do so, especially if it is deemed more cost effective or more politically expedient not to do so. In this, cybercrimes are no different from other types of offenses. However, there might be more reasons *not* to prosecute in a cybercrime case than in the typical criminal case.

The Nature of the Evidence

In addition to the difficulty of defining the offense and the jurisdictional issues that complicate prosecution, another obstacle that stands in the way of building and winning a case against a cybercriminal is the nature of much of the evidence. The law generally recognizes three types of evidence:

- **Physical evidence**   Tangible items that provide proof of the commission of an offense and/or the identity of the offender (for example, the "smoking gun" that was used to commit a murder).

- **Direct evidence**   The testimony of witnesses who saw the offense occur, observed the accused taking preparatory steps toward committing the offense, or otherwise have direct knowledge of the crime.

- **Circumstantial evidence**   Facts and circumstances that tend to support the theory that the accused person committed the offense but that do not offer definitive proof.

Much of the evidence in cybercrime cases is digital; this means that it is not tangible evidence but rather is made up of electronic or magnetic pulses that are stored in the form of electromagnetic charges on the media of a disk or tape. Not only is this evidence largely intangible, but it is also fragile, much like evidence consisting of a footprint in the snow. A record of the evidence's existence must be captured before it "melts away." As with the footprint, it might be impossible to preserve the original cybercrime evidence for presentation in court, and the inability to produce the original evidence tends to weaken the prosecution's case.

Hackers with technical expertise can destroy the evidence by going through multiple servers to get to their targets and then, once they've accomplished their objective, deleting the log files on each server to cover their tracks. According to fraud investigator Dan Clements, quoted at http://news.com.com/2009-1017-912708.html, this is the digital equivalent of "vacuuming up the crime scene."

Because digital evidence is intangible, fragile, and easily destroyed (either deliberately or accidentally), proper evidence handling is even more important in cybercrime cases than in other types of crimes. As we discussed in Chapter 10, "Collecting and Preserving Digital Evidence," investigators should immediately make copies of disks that might contain evidentiary material and work only on the copies, preserving the integrity of the original evidence. In addition, all such evidence should be documented carefully.

Human Factors

The obstacles to prosecution of cybercrime cases that we have discussed thus far pertain to legal or technical issues. However, other factors make it difficult to build a cybercrime case; these might be thought of as *human factors*. These factors pertain to the necessity that law enforcement officers and IT professionals work together to most effectively put together a prosecutable case and the difficulties that both sides often encounter in doing so.

Law Enforcement "Attitude"

Law enforcement officers have a saying: *Nobody understands a cop except another cop.* In many ways, it's true. Police officers are put on the streets and given an incredibly difficult job to do, saddled with a tremendous responsibility and burdened with impossible expectations. Often with too little training, they are given positions of authority but placed under close public scrutiny, restricted by law and departmental policies and tasked with making split-second decisions in life-threatening situations. Later their decisions will be critiqued at leisure by people with no street experience who hold the officers' careers in their hands.

Law enforcement agencies are, by and large, paramilitary organizations—with the emphasis on *para*. Military personnel generally have a clearly defined mission. Police agencies often operate at the whim of politicians and bureaucrats and are expected to be all things to all people—"tough on crime" yet unfailingly nice to citizens, heroes who save the day from the bad guys yet sensitive enough to never offend anyone. Officers are often undertrained, underpaid, overworked, and over-stressed. Salaries are low, hours are long, and divorce, alcoholism, and suicide rates are high.

It's no wonder that many police officers have "an attitude." Most eager young police recruits really do join the force because they want to help people and make the world a better, safer place to live. Because officers see the worst side of humanity day after day, they can slowly become cynical and suspicious, developing an "us versus them" mentality that excludes everyone who's not a cop (including, all too often, their own families).

This is the law enforcement culture. People on the other side of the "thin blue line" must understand it in order to work effectively with law enforcement officers. Investigators generally must have several years of experience on the streets before they're eligible for promotion to detective, so the "attitude" is often firmly engrained. IT professionals who want to be part of the investigative team need to learn to think like cops, just as the police investigator needs to learn to think like hackers to penetrate their culture and understand what they do and how they do it. Understanding law enforcement types isn't really difficult, if you keep in mind a few basic facts:

- **Most police officers are not as confident as they seem** "Command presence" is a job requirement, and officers get good at "bluffing," but those who come off as most authoritarian are often the least confident in themselves.

- **Most police officers don't understand technology** There are exceptions, of course. However, the majority of officers are not technically savvy. They often know a lot about radios, light bars, and other traditional police paraphernalia but think computers are for "nerds." This attitude is changing as computers become more ubiquitous within departments, but the changes come slowly.

- **Most police officers don't like not understanding** They are suspicious, and perhaps a bit envious, of people who do know about computers. IT professionals generally make a lot more money than cops do, without having to put their lives on the line. For that reason, a little resentment on the part of the police officer is understandable.

- **Many police officers feel pretty powerless** Despite the "police power" myth, many officers feel weighted down by the highly structured agency environment, where the slightest misstep results in disciplinary measures, and by the weight of the law, policies, political factors, and public relations requirements.

All of this leads to a touch of police paranoia about working with "outsiders"—those who aren't sworn police officers. This attitude must be overcome if the police are to work effectively with IT professionals, corporate management, and the general citizenry to fight cybercrime. For officers and investigators, the first step in overcoming negative attitudes is to recognize the problem. For IT professionals, the first step is to recognize how the sharp contrast between the highly structured police environment and the more relaxed high-tech lifestyle widens the chasm.

The High-Tech Lifestyle

Now that the dot-com bubble has burst and many high-tech companies have disappeared off the map, the high-tech lifestyle has moved down a notch, from the ridiculous to the merely sublime. At least, it seems that way when the average police officer compares his or her earnings to the salaries and perks that come with many technology industry jobs. The lifestyle differences, however, are about much more than just money.

Police officers, who work in a highly structured environment, tend to live structured lives outside the job as well. The typical cop is straitlaced and punctual and believes in doing things "by the book," according to the rules. The typical techie takes a more relaxed approach to life, living on Jolt and pizza and often admiring of those who are smart enough to bend or get around the rules. The majority of police officers are political conservatives, whereas high-tech workers tend to be politically liberal. Police officers tend to stay with one job, often retiring from the agency where they went to work at an early age. Officers tend to grow "roots," staying in the same community all or most of their lives. Tech workers tend to jump from job to job, often moving from one geographic location to another for bigger salaries and better opportunities. It's no wonder cops and techies don't understand one another.

Natural-Born Adversaries?

At first glance, police officers and IT professionals don't mix at all. In addition to their differences, it's not unusual to find an elitist mentality on both sides. Police officers feel superior by virtue of their governmental authority, whereas tech people feel superior based on their positions in the business world. There is a mutual mystique at work. Cops carry guns, something many techies have no experience with and of which they're more than a little fearful. Techies can make computers do their bidding, and many police officers are a little afraid of those mysterious machines.

Many IT professionals support—or at least understand—hackers, who the police see as criminals. Many IT professionals see nothing wrong with trading software or downloading music through file-sharing services patterned after Napster, while the police see this as breaking the law. Many police officers don't understand or appreciate the difference between black-hat and white-hat hacking, nor do they recognize that the same skills used by cybercriminals can also be used for legitimate purposes. Furthermore, many IT professionals blame the police for laws with which they disagree (such as those against software piracy) and don't understand that the police don't make the laws, they only enforce them.

As far apart as the two careers may seem, you don't have to look far to find common ground. Police officers and IT professionals actually have many things in common:

- Both work long, odd hours. Who can you often find hard at work at 3:00 on a Sunday morning when the rest of the world is sound asleep? Police officers and programmers.

- Both generally are dedicated to their jobs and would not want to do anything else.

- Both suffer from caffeine addiction, although they might argue the merits of Jolt Cola versus thick black police station coffee.

- Both want things (law, code) to "make sense" and get frustrated when they don't.

- Both are problem solvers by nature.

In this last commonality lies the key to overcoming all the differences and working together as part of a team. Both jobs involve identifying problems or potential problems and taking action to solve them. Police officers and IT professionals who are able to see beyond the surface will find that they're really not so different after all, at least not in the ways that count when it comes to fighting cybercrime together.

Overcoming Obstacles to Effective Prosecution

Despite the many obstacles that stand in the way of effectively prosecuting cybercrime cases—including the difficulty of even defining the crime in the first place, the jurisdictional nightmares that arise when suspect and victim are in different geographic locations, and the attitudes and lifestyle differences that make it difficult for police and IT professionals to work together—it *is* possible to overcome all these challenges and put together a case that will stand up in court.

Law enforcement agencies can work with prosecutors to clarify definitions and ensure that they understand the elements that must be proven to arrest and convict in a cybercrime case. IT personnel who anticipate working with law enforcement on cybercrime cases must learn the basics of how the criminal justice system operates, and both must know how civil, criminal, and regulatory laws differ and which specific acts fall under which bodies of law in their jurisdiction.

Speaking of jurisdiction, investigators must be prepared for legal complications when cybercrimes cross state or national boundaries—as they so often do. Investigators must also be realistic enough to understand that even when they legally have jurisdiction, many practical factors can prevent successful prosecution of multijurisdictional cybercrime cases.

Law enforcement officers and IT professionals can learn to work together on cybercrime cases, resulting in much more effective investigations than either could conduct alone. An important part of building the bridge is learning to "talk the talk." Police officers need to learn technical terminology, and IT personnel need to become comfortable with the language of law and police jargon so the two can better understand one another. A successful prosecution is based on the work of many people and on many factors. An important element in building a solid case hinges on proper implementation of the investigative process.

The Investigative Process

Cybercrime investigators must be familiar with the process of gathering data, materials, and information that might be related to the commission of an offense; this is, in fact, the definition of *criminal investigation*. IT professionals who work with law enforcement officers to facilitate the process might be intimidated by the word *investigation* and its official implications, but it's easier to understand if you realize that we all conduct investigations, all the time. Whenever we meet a new person, make a major purchase such as a home or automobile, or make a major life decision such as changing jobs or getting married, we *investigate*—the gist of which is simply gathering information. Certainly a network administrator often has reason to investigate; he or she investigates when a server goes down, when a user is unable to access a network resource, when a software application doesn't work properly, and so forth.

The only differences between the sort of investigations that are a normal part of everyday life and a police investigation are the formality and the ultimate goals of the investigation. In both cases, the primary objective is to gather information. In a criminal investigation, that information is ultimately used to prove the guilt of the accused person in court. Thus the process must be formalized to provide a standard structure that ensures compliance with the laws that govern evidence collection.

However, it is important for investigators to remember that even evidence that's not admissible in court can still be useful during the course of the investigation because it can help the investigator reconstruct the circumstances of the illegal act or omission and lead to other, admissible evidence. For presentation in court, evidence must be evaluated in light of the following questions:

- **Is it relevant?** In other words, does it relate to this case? If you are investigating a hacker suspected of launching a DoS attack on a computer network, the discovery that this hacker was once arrested for using a blue box to make illegal long distance calls has no bearing on the current case and probably won't be admissible as evidence (although such information *can* be introduced, in many jurisdictions, during the sentencing phase of the trial, after the defendant is found guilty).

- **Is it material?** In other words, does it prove one of the essential elements of the case? Does the evidence provide proof that the suspect committed the prohibited act, show the suspect's culpable mental state, support the fact that a required result occurred, or negate the existence of statutory exceptions?

- **Is it competent?** Is the evidence believable? If the evidence is witness testimony, is that witness credible? If the evidence is digital, is its meaning clear, and can you show that it hasn't been tampered with?

An investigation should be objective; after all, the purpose of an investigation is not to indict a particular person but to determine the truth. Investigators should put aside personal feelings and approach the investigation in the same way a good journalist approaches a story. In fact, it is useful for the investigator to use the rule of thumb journalists are taught to use in collecting information for publication: Find out *who, what, when, where, why* ,and *how*, also known as the *5WH method*. These are the questions that must be asked and answered before you—as a writer or as an investigator—can rest assured that you have the whole story. Table 11.1 shows a breakdown of the objectives of a criminal investigation and how the journalistic approach can be used to accomplish them.

Table 11.1 Investigative objectives and the 5WH approach

Objective	Questions to Answer
Determine if a crime has been committed	*What* happened? *Who* was involved?

Continued

Table 11.1 Continued

Objective	Questions to Answer
Protect the crime scene	*Where* did the illegal act occur? *When* did it happen?
Identify the suspect	*Who* had motive, means, and opportunity?
Identify the M.O.	*How* was the act committed?
Prove that the suspect did it	*Who* observed the crime or its results? *Where* was the suspect when the crime occurred? *What* records/documents/logs identify the suspect?

When these questions have been answered, the next step in the process is to effect a lawful arrest. This doesn't mean the investigation is over. At the time of arrest, you must have collected enough evidence to constitute probable cause, but that's not enough to convict—proof beyond a reasonable doubt is required—so the investigation continues as you prepare an effective case for prosecution.

NOTE

Probable cause is required in two situations: to obtain a search or arrest warrant or to make an arrest without a warrant. Evidence does not have to be admissible at trial to be used as a building block of probable cause.

In a cybercrime case, as in any other criminal case, the investigator might need to revisit witnesses, and new evidence may be discovered at any time up to the start of the trial. Under the U.S. system of justice, the existence of evidence must be made known to the defense attorneys under the rules of *pretrial discovery*.

Investigative Tools

An investigator builds a case using standard investigative tools. The "Three Is" that form the nexus of the investigator's toolkit are:

- Information
- Interview and interrogation
- Instrumentation

In the following sections, we look at each of these tools in detail and discuss their applicability to a typical cybercrime case.

Information

Information, the foundation of the case, can be obtained in many different ways. Here we refer to the information that an investigator can gather through observation, examination of documents or electronic data, and examination of physical evidence. One important means of obtaining this information is through the *crime scene search*. In the case of a cybercrime, much of the evidence might be on the computer—stored on its hard disk or even still in memory. However, it's important for investigators to resist tunnel vision that leads them to focus solely on the computer, because the crime scene can encompass the area around the computer as well.

If there is evidence on the system showing that a particular computer was used to commit a cybercrime, you still must establish a link between the computer and the suspect. Then traditional crime scene techniques are appropriate, such as dusting for fingerprints and conducting a thorough area search that can turn up such evidence as printouts of computer data, notes jotted by the suspect that pertain to the offense, backup diskettes or tapes containing evidentiary information, and so forth. It is also important to remember that evidence can be stored off site where it has been uploaded over the Internet or physically transported on removable media.

Interview and Interrogation

Interview and interrogation refer to the questioning of persons involved in the cybercrime in some way. The difference lies in the person's role in the crime and in the manner of questioning. An *interview* involves questioning witnesses, victims, and other people who might have information relevant to solving the crime. These people could include technical experts who can explain how the crime was committed and who may also testify as expert witnesses at trial or who may merely provide background information to help the investigator understand the technicalities of the offense. An interview is basically a conversation (recorded or documented by the interviewer) with the objective of obtaining facts that will help identify the perpetrator of a crime and build a case against that person.

An *interrogation* involves questioning persons suspected of committing or aiding in the commission of the offense. The interrogation is generally recorded, and it is important to document that the suspect has been advised of his or her rights before questioning, either by recording the advisement or by obtaining a written waiver of rights from the suspect, or both. The objective of an interrogation is to obtain incriminating statements and/or a confession.

> **NOTE**
>
> Although witness interviews should be recorded or documented, in most cases the witness in a criminal case will need to personally testify to the facts in court. The U.S. justice system in most cases gives the accused the right to face his or her accuser(s), and hearsay evidence (third-party evidence) is generally not admissible. There are exceptions, including child abuse cases (including child pornography and child rape cases that might be cybercrimes), dying declarations, and other cases in which the witness is emotionally or physically unable to personally testify.

An interrogation is often adversarial in nature, but it doesn't have to be. One of the best ways to get useful information from a suspect is to gain his or her confidence, make the suspect think that you're sympathetic to his or her cause. In cybercrimes involving hacking and technical exploits, it can be useful to have an officer who is technically savvy interrogate the suspect, because someone who "speaks the same language" might be able to draw the suspect into bragging about the technical prowess necessary to pull off the job. The old familiar "good cop, bad cop" routine might also work, especially if you set up a team that features a young, "techie" type good cop playing against an older, apparently technophobic bad cop. There are many different interrogation techniques, and the investigator should use those that work best for and come most naturally to him or her. Some tried and true techniques, in addition to the sympathetic approach, include:

- **Logical approach** Use reasoning to convince the suspect that it's in his or her best interest to confess.

- **Indifference** Pretend you don't need a confession because you already have enough evidence without it. This can work well with multiple suspects when you can imply to each that the other(s) has already "spilled the beans."

- **Facing-saving approach** Allow the suspect to provide excuses for the behavior and show understanding of why he or she committed the crime.

On the Scene...

Confession Is Good for the Soul— and for the Prosecution's Case

To be admissible in court, a confession must be voluntary; that is, it must be given without duress, bribery, or other undue influence. Some jurisdictions hold that a confession cannot be admitted unless there is independent *corroboration* of some sort. For example, if a person admits to being the one who sent threatening e-mail to another party, this could be corroborated by his knowledge of the specific contents of the e-mail, which had not been made public and would not be known by anyone other than the recipient, law enforcement officers, and the sender of the e-mail.

Investigators must always be on guard for the possibility of *false confessions.* Why would someone confess to a crime he or she didn't commit? Most such confessors do it to get attention, and many high-profile crimes attract a number of people who line up to claim "credit." This can be a problem in the case of a "popular" crime, such as a Web site defacement that expresses a popular political idea or a network attack against a corporation that has a bad reputation with the public. This is one reason investigators don't publicize all the facts of a case or even sometimes "leak" false or misleading information about the case to the media. Confessions can then be measured against the true facts of the case, which would be known to only a few people, one of whom is the person who actually committed the offense.

NOTE

In certain circumstances, statements may be used against a suspect without that suspect first being advised of and waiving the Miranda rights, including *res gestae* statements (statements made suddenly and not in response to questioning—"blurted out").

For both interviews and interrogations, the same basic guidelines apply to cybercrime witnesses and suspects as in other types of cases:

- Separate the persons being interviewed or interrogated. Even in the case of witnesses who are not innocent of any crime, witnesses can be influenced by one another's statements. Suspects can reveal their guilt by telling conflicting stories.

- Use *kinesic interview techniques;* note body language, voice tone, facial expression, and other nonlinguistic communication that provides clues to whether or not a person is telling the truth. Use *mirroring,* in which the investigator subtly emulates the other person's body language to create a sense of rapport with the person.

- Have a tactical plan for the interview or interrogation; be aware of all the available facts about the case and know exactly what information you're seeking going in.

- Ensure that standard procedures are followed for recording and/or obtaining written statements.

Once you've obtained information in the course of an interview or interrogation, that information should be analyzed to determine its value and admissibility. This analysis can be based on the answers to the following questions:

- Does the information substantiate one or more elements of the offense (is it material?)

- Could the information negate a suspect's defense or alibi?

- Does the information corroborate a suspect's confession?

Investigators often use a "two-pronged test" to evaluate the credibility of witness information. This test consists of separately evaluating both the witness giving the information and the information itself, as shown in Table 11.2.

Table 11.2 The two-pronged test for evaluating the credibility of witness information

Evaluating Witness Credibility	Evaluating Information Credibility
Has the witness given information in the past that proved to be true?	Does the information fit with the facts observed or obtained from other sources?
Is the witness an "upstanding" member of the community, considered honest, etc.?	Does the information make sense?

Continued

Table 11.2 Continued

Evaluating Witness Credibility	Evaluating Information Credibility
Is the witness objective (in other words, does he or she have a personal stake in the investigation or personal relationship with the victim or suspect)?	Is the information something that the witness would be in a position to know?

Instrumentation

Instrumentation refers to the use of technology to obtain evidence. In cybercrime cases, use of data recovery techniques to recover "deleted" and "erased" information on disks is a type of instrumentation. Other, more traditional examples include forensics techniques for collecting and analyzing trace evidence, DNA analysis, and the like.

On the Scene...

Bad Luck, Good Investigation, or Both?

Contributed by Dr. Bernard H. Levin, professor, Blue Ridge (VA) Community College and commander, Waynesboro Police Department, and Robert S. Baldygo, vice president, Blue Ridge Community College. The names of the victim and cybercriminal as well as the college involved have been changed.

Sometimes the bad guys have a run of bad luck, making investigators' lives easier. The following report summarizes some of the cyber-related elements of a recent arrest, made after the suspect's an attempt to extort funds by means of the Internet. The alleged perpetrator, "James Palmer" has been arrested and has pled guilty to federal charges. Palmer also has been charged with several state offenses.

The case came to the attention of local and federal authorities when an individual, "Timothy Vaughan," reported to Major Eastern University police the receipt of e-mail messages that threatened injury to Vaughan's family if money were not paid to the sender of the e-mail

Continued

message. Over a two-week period, the messages built in severity of threatened actions and in specificity of details about the recipient's personal life. It later turned out that an acquaintance of Palmer was a coworker of Vaughan's wife. A key feature in this extortion attempt was Palmer's perceived ability to maintain his anonymity throughout the series of communications. That perception on his part turned out to be incorrect.

Palmer sent Vaughan a large number of messages, generally during the late afternoons. After Vaughan filed a complaint, the university police department queried the public e-mail service Palmer used. The service allows users to establish e-mail addresses anonymously, and thus the service was unable to provide direct information about the sender's identity. However, the service was able to provide the IP addresses used. The IP addresses of the PCs Palmer used were traced to various PCs at another, nearby college. Unlike the computers on many networks, the computers Palmer used had fixed IP addresses. This was Palmer's first bit of bad luck. As a result, the college IT personnel were able to provide the investigators with a complete listing and location diagram of each Internet-enabled PC on campus. Palmer's second piece of bad luck was to choose a college with IT staff members who were eager to put some energy into the investigation, and they identified Palmer rather quickly.

On the day that Palmer had established as the deadline for meeting his payment demand, the investigators had real-time telephone contact with Vaughan and the e-mail service provider. The investigators were also on site at the sending college. They were quickly able to establish the location of the sending PC, in a temporarily unused computer laboratory. Palmer was sitting at a PC with his back to a glass panel that separated him from the hallway. The investigators watched him for about an hour as he continued to send a long series of e-mails to Vaughan. These e-mails were confirmed as emanating from the observed PC at that location.

Palmer was arrested in mid-message, and the PC he used was seized as evidence. Unfortunately for Palmer, even more bad luck was coming his way. The third piece of bad luck involved Palmer's meticulousness in using the e-mail service's spell-check function. The e-mail service Palmer chose saves, in temporary Internet files, screen shots of spelling checks. A final piece of bad luck: When Palmer was arrested, he was in possession of printouts of many of the e-mails he had sent.

Steps in an Investigation

Investigators should follow the same step-by-step process each time they conduct investigations. This will help avoid the possibility of skipping steps or neglecting important tasks. These steps should be documented in a procedure manual that can be part of the agency's policies and procedures. A suggested set of steps follows:

1. Analyze the complaint.
2. Collect physical evidence.
3. Seek expert advice, if necessary.
4. Interview witnesses and interrogate suspects.
5. Construct the case file.
6. Analyze the case.
7. Follow up investigations.
8. Decide whether to prosecute.

Analyzing the Complaint

Upon receiving a complaint or notification that a cybercrime has occurred, the investigator first must analyze the complaint to determine:

- If a crime was committed
- If so, what crime was committed

The analysis includes evaluating the plausibility of allegations that a violation of the law has occurred, considering the nature and seriousness of the crime, and considering other factors that might complicate the crime's prosecution. In an ideal world, all complaints would be thoroughly investigated and all criminal actions would be prosecuted. In our less than ideal world, manpower limitations and other considerations can prevent pursuing less serious cases. If the analysis of the complaint determines that a crime was committed and warrants a preliminary investigation, the next step is to start collecting evidence.

Collecting Physical Evidence

Physical evidence in this context refers to tangible items that can be gathered, marked or tagged, and stored in a secure location until trial. Although the evidence itself may be digital in a cybercrime case, the disk on which it is stored is a tangible item. There might be other physical evidence in addition to digital information, including fingerprints, documents, and so forth. These should be preserved in accordance with standard crime scene practices.

Traditional crime scene techniques such as making crime scene sketches, photographs, and videotapes can be useful. This is especially true if, when investigators seize the computer, there is information on the screen that is not saved on disk. There might be information in memory and status information (network connections that are open, applications and processes that are running, and the like) that is useful as evidence but will be lost when the computer is powered down. Saving the contents of memory or other information or dumping the contents of memory to a file changes the system so that you've altered it and can no longer testify that it is exactly as you found it. One way to avoid this problem is to use photography to record the displayed information. Another is to transfer the data to another computer. Remember that every time you perform a task on a computer, even something as simple as saving a file, you change it in some way. See Chapter 10, "Collecting and Preserving Digital Evidence," for more information on how to handle digital evidence so that no changes are made and what to do if changes have already been made (for example, if IT personnel took preliminary investigative steps before law enforcement investigators became involved in the case).

NOTE

Crime scene sketches, photographs, and videotapes all serve separate purposes in documenting the crime scene; none of these takes the place of another. The sketch shows perspective, while the videotape provides an overview of the scene. Still photographs are used to document specific items or information. None of these is admissible as evidence unless accompanied by a witness (usually the sketch artist, photographer, or videographer) who can testify under oath to the circumstances in which they were made and that they represent the scene as he or she remembers seeing it.

Seeking Expert Advice

When a crime involves technical details that are beyond the knowledge of the investigator and/or prosecutor, it is often necessary as part of the investigation to seek advice and help from an expert in the field, much as you would seek the services of an interpreter if all the witnesses at a crime scene spoke a language with which you weren't familiar. The ideal situation is to have technically savvy law enforcement officers on board or available on loan from other agencies. Because this is often not the case, investigators might have to seek outside help.

When investigating a cybercrime in which a corporate network is the victim, why not just use the IT personnel there as your experts? Although this might save the agency some time and effort, it might not be the best idea. The expert you consult for technical advice should be objective, and it is often difficult to obtain objective opinions from people whose own networks have been victimized. Even if the company IT professionals *are* completely objective, there could be a perception that they are otherwise, and this perception could be exploited if defense attorneys discover that they provided you with technical guidance. Agencies might be able to find IT experts within the community who are willing to volunteer their expertise for a good cause. One good place to look is the academic world; computer science and computer security instructors at local colleges are often happy to help with technical questions in cybercrime cases. Associations of computer professionals might also be able to point you in the right direction.

Interviewing and Interrogating

Interviewing witnesses and interrogating suspects can be an ongoing process throughout the investigation. As more information is gathered, new witnesses might be discovered and new suspects come to light. Followup interviews with witnesses who have already been interviewed might be necessary as the case develops.

Investigators should be sure to get contact information from all witnesses, even those who might not need to be interviewed at the time. This information includes work addresses and phone numbers *and* home addresses and phone numbers. It is not unusual for witnesses to leave a company or to move during the course of an investigation, making them difficult to locate if you have only one set of contact information. It is also a good idea, in today's mobile, connected world, to get witnesses' e-mail addresses. Many people retain the same e-mail address when they move and/or leave a job, so this could be the only contact information that remains constant.

Case Construction

After physical evidence has been gathered and documented and interviews and interrogations have been conducted, the next step is to start putting together the physical case file. This is an important element in *case preparation. Black's Law Dictionary* defines a *case* as "an aggregate collection of facts which furnishes occasion for the exercise of the jurisdiction of a court." *Preparation,* according to *Webster's New Collegiate Dictionary,* is "the action or process of making something ready." From these definitions, we can extrapolate that a simple definition of *case preparation* is "a compilation of information made ready for court presentation."

The case file will contain all documentation of the case, including (but not limited to):

- Initial incident report from the officers or investigator who responded to the complaint

- Followup reports

- Documentation of evidence collection by crime scene technicians

- Lab reports by forensics lab personnel

- Written statements of witnesses, suspects, and experts

- Crime scene sketches, photographs, and videotapes

- Printouts of digital evidence, where applicable

The case file is used to organize information and evidence in one place and will be used by the prosecutor in making a decision as to whether to prosecute the case and at trial. The case file *must* contain documentation of proof of the elements of the offense, the legality of the entry/search/seizure/arrest, and the preservation of the chain of custody.

Case Analysis

When the case file has been constructed and all documentation included, the next step is to analyze the legal significance of the information and the evidence it contains. This step should usually be done in conjunction with the prosecutor, who might be able to provide the investigator with guidance as to the weaknesses of the case and what additional information or evidence needs to be obtained to strengthen it. This could be the first of several *pretrial conferences* between members of the prosecution team and the investigator(s).

Followup

After the case analysis, you might need to obtain additional evidence or clarify facts and information. Reinterviewing witnesses at this point can serve several purposes. In addition to obtaining specific additional information, the second interview will help refresh their memories about the case, refresh the investigator's memory about the case, and prepare the witnesses for the courtroom process if and when the case goes to trial.

Decision to Prosecute

After all additional information has been collected and the case file is considered complete, the prosecutor will make the decision to prosecute (or refer the case to a grand jury, depending on the jurisdiction and its procedures). At this time, the selection of the charge will also take place. In some cases, several different offenses could be charged. The prosecutor will select based on the provability of the elements and the difficulty of obtaining a conviction as well as the severity of the punishment. For example, a suspect's actions might contain the elements of two different offenses—for example, unauthorized access and theft of trade secrets. If the latter charge is a felony and the former is a misdemeanor, the prosecutor may choose to charge only the more serious offense. In other cases, both charges would be brought. Generally, if one offense is a *lesser included offense* of another, the jury can find the defendant guilty of the lesser charge even though only the higher charge was filed.

Defining Areas of Responsibility

Rarely will a complex investigation be conducted by one person. The investigative team might consist of one or more detectives, crime scene technicians, crime scene photographers and videographers, evidence recorders and custodians, and specialists such as computer forensics team members.

It is important that there be one person who is designated to be in charge of the investigation. This is the team leader and is often a senior investigator. The team leader should assign each team member a specific *area of responsibility*. Team members should be accountable for their designated areas of responsibility (for example, collecting, tagging, documenting, and securing the physical evidence) and should not overstep their bounds and perform tasks that fall under other members' areas of responsibility, unless approved by the team leader.

Testifying in a Cybercrime Case

The entire investigation and building of the case file is aimed toward one end result: obtaining a conviction of the cybercriminal in a court of law. No matter how good the evidence you obtain—log files showing unauthorized access to the network, hard disks seized from the suspect's computer containing clear-cut indications of the criminal activity, network records tracking the intruder back through Internet servers to his or her computer—none of this evidence can stand alone.

Under most criminal justice systems, physical and intangible evidence must be supported by testimony. Someone must testify as to when, where, and how the evidence was obtained and verify that it is the same when it is presented in court as it was when it was collected. When evidence is technical in nature and difficult for laypersons to understand, experts may be required to testify to explain the nature of the evidence and what it means to the jury and judge. Police investigators and IT personnel may both be required to take the witness stand in a cybercrime case. In the following sections, we discuss the criminal trial process, the two types of witnesses that can be called to testify in criminal actions, and some tips on how to prepare for and give testimony as either an evidentiary or an expert witness.

The Trial Process

The trial process actually begins when a suspect is arrested or a warrant is issued for a suspect's arrest. After the arrest, the defendant is taken before a magistrate (a judge or, in some cases, the mayor of a city or town) within a specified time period—usually within 48 hours—and *arraigned*. This arraignment is an informal process whereby the magistrate tells the defendant what charges have been filed against him or her, Mirandizes the defendant, and sets or denies bail.

A preliminary hearing usually takes place within a few days. In this hearing, the prosecution must present enough evidence to convince the judge that the defendant should go to trial. In some cases, the defendant goes before a grand jury instead of a judge. This is a secret proceeding in which the grand jury decides whether to hand down an *indictment*. Next a formal arraignment may be held, at which the defendant can enter a plea for the charges against him or her.

Before the actual trial, there is usually a pretrial conference or hearing at which motions can be filed (for example, asking for a change of venue). Finally, the case goes to trial. If the defendant pleads not guilty to the charges, a jury is selected through the *voir dire* process, during which each side gets to question potential jurors and *strike,* or exclude, a certain number. The judge instructs the jury on the applicable law, and then the attorneys each give an opening statement.

Because the burden of proof is on the prosecution, the prosecuting attorney gets to go first with an opening statement. After the defense attorney's opening statement, the prosecution calls witnesses. With each of the witnesses, the prosecution asks questions; this process is called *direct examination*. Then the defense attorney is allowed to question the witness about the matters that were brought up during direct examination. Afterward, the prosecution can *redirect,* after which the defense can *recross.* This process occurs with each witness until both attorneys are finished questioning that witness.

When the prosecution has presented all its witnesses and evidence, the defense attorney usually makes a motion to dismiss the case due to lack of evidence. If this motion is granted, the trial is over and the defendant goes free. If not, the defense presents its case, calling witnesses to testify. These witnesses are cross-examined by the prosecutor, and so forth, in the same manner as the prosecution witnesses. After the defense has presented its case, the prosecution is allowed to call rebuttal witnesses, and the defense can rebut those witnesses.

Finally, when all the rebuttals are done, the attorneys make their closing statements (which side goes first depends on the court) and the judge gives more instructions to the jurors, who are then sent out to reach a verdict.

An investigator or IT professional testifying as to personal knowledge of the evidence in the case (an evidentiary witness) will be testifying as a prosecution witness and thus will be directly examined by the prosecutor and cross-examined by the defense attorney. Expert witnesses may testify for either side.

Testifying as an Evidentiary Witness

An evidentiary witness is someone who has direct knowledge of the case. For example, a network administrator might be called to testify as to what he or she observed during an attack on the network, or an investigator might be called to testify as to the evidence that he or she observed on a computer that was seized pursuant to a search warrant. An evidentiary witness can only testify as to facts (what he or she saw or heard) but cannot give opinions or draw conclusions.

Testifying as an Expert Witness

An expert witness has no direct involvement in the case but has special technical knowledge or expertise that qualifies him or her to give professional opinions on technical matters. Expert witnesses sometimes prepare reports that outline their opinions and give reasons for each opinion. In some countries, expert witnesses must be registered as experts in a particular field. In the United States, experts must generally prove their expertise by presenting their credentials in court.

Qualifying as an Expert

The expert witness will generally be asked a series of questions by the attorney calling him or her. These questions are designed to show the person's credentials as an expert. Such questions might include:

- What degrees do you have?

- What positions have you held in the field?

- What courses have you taught in this field?

- What books or papers have you written pertaining to the field?

- What is your past experience as an expert witness in this field?

The opposing attorney may challenge the expert witness's credentials to attempt to have the expert's testimony thrown out.

Employing Experts

In many cases, expert witnesses are paid to testify. Payment is usually on a *per diem* basis and may include travel expenses and accommodations during the trial. Many people hire themselves out as expert witnesses, specializing in many different technical or scientific fields, including computer forensics. Many such expert witnesses advertise their services on the Internet. For example, The Expert Pages (http://expertpages.com/experts/computers.htm) is a database listing expert witnesses in many fields, available throughout the United States.

Giving Direct Testimony

The first rule for giving direct testimony (or any sworn testimony) is to always tell the truth. Witnesses should not be afraid to say "I don't know" or "I don't remember" when that's the truth. Beyond that, there are a number of best practices for testifying in court. If you are a law enforcement officer or technical expert required to testify in court, remember that the jury will evaluate the credibility of each witness and decide whether to believe the testimony based on that evaluation. Here are some ways to enhance your credibility as a witness:

- **Be on time or slightly early for court** This allows you time to prepare and scope out the layout of the courtroom, the route you'll walk from your seat in the courtroom to the witness stand, and so on. Arriving late makes a bad impression on the jury and detracts from your credibility.

- **Don't appear to be nervous** Juries expect people to act nervous when they're lying. You might not be able to control how you *feel,* but with practice you can control any visible manifestations of nervousness, such as repetitive gestures.

- **Remain calm and don't get angry** The opposing attorney might try to make you lose your temper; doing so will damage your credibility with the jury. Witnesses should never argue or be sarcastic in response to an attorney's questions. Remaining calm and professional will strengthen the case.

- **Don't volunteer extra information** Answer the questions you are asked, but don't provide more information or veer off the topic. Don't provide hearsay evidence (what other people said to you), because it's generally inadmissible.

- **Dress professionally** Appearance does count, and your credibility will be enhanced by conservative business attire.

- **Consider the question carefully before you answer** Be sure you understand the question, and if you don't, ask the attorney to repeat it. Don't start answering until you're sure that the attorney is finished asking the question.

- **Speak clearly and confidently** An effective witness doesn't shout but speaks loudly enough to be heard by the judge, jury, and attorneys.

Testimony as an evidentiary witness should be limited to "just the facts, ma'am, just the facts." Don't offer opinion or speculation; in an impartial, objective manner, simply tell what you did or observed.

Cross-Examination Tactics

It is the job of the cross-examining attorney to discredit the opposing side's witness. Attorneys may use psychological techniques to attempt to discredit witnesses. When testifying in a cybercrimes case, be careful not to fall into their traps. Be prepared for and ready to avoid such cross-examination tactics as:

- Rapid-fire questions with no time to answer between questions

- Leading questions ("Isn't it true that what you saw was …?")

- Repeating your words with a twist that changes their meaning

- Pretending to be friendly, then turning against you suddenly

- Feigning bewilderment, outrage, or shock at what you've said

- Prolonged silence designed to cause discomfort in hopes you'll say more

The most important thing for you to remember when subjected to these tactics is this: Don't take the attorney's tactics personally; he or she is just doing a job. Our advice to the witness is, just do *your* job; keep your cool and state the facts.

Using Notes and Visual Aids

What if you're required to testify as a witness, but your memory isn't so great? What if you're afraid of forgetting important facts, especially difficult-to-remember information such as numbers? Is it legal for you as a witness to take notes along to use as a reference when testifying?

Police officers use notes as a memory aid during court testimony all the time. There are advantages and disadvantages in doing so. Some jurors might be impressed by the fact that you're reading from notes, because they might trust the written word more than someone who relies on memory alone. On the other hand, others might think you're being coached or prompted if you refer to notes; they believe that if what you're saying is the truth, you would remember it without notes. A very important consideration in deciding whether to use notes is the fact that if a witness does so, the notes will be entered into evidence and taken into the custody of the court for the duration of the trial. If you do choose to use notes, therefore, it's important to be sure that the notebook or paper on which they're written doesn't have other notes that refer to matters not related to the case, because the opposing attorney can question you about anything in the notes.

Summary

Building a cybercrime case is a complicated process, more so than is true for some other types of criminal cases. This is because special factors that present obstacles to prosecution must be considered and dealt with if the investigator is to successfully put together a winning case. Because many of the offenses under which cybercrimes are prosecuted are relatively new, the elements are not always clearly defined, and often there has not yet been time to clarify and interpret the statutes through the process of case law. It is important for cybercrime investigators to keep up to date on relevant court cases that might affect the applicability of the local, state, and federal laws that pertain to cybercrime.

Understanding the complex system of laws that govern our lives and how they interact with one another is essential to building a criminal case. Investigators and those who work with them should be aware of the function of various bodies of law, understand the differences between different types of law, be aware of the existence of different levels of law, and learn the legal terminology necessary to communicate intelligently within the system.

Jurisdictional issues are one of the biggest challenges to the cybercrime investigator and to prosecutors who attempt to bring cybercriminals to justice. It is important to acquaint yourself with just what jurisdictional authority means and the practical issues affecting multijurisdictional cases. The intangible nature of much of the evidence in a cybercrime case creates yet another obstacle.

Law enforcement officers and IT personnel must work together as a team to prosecute cybercrimes effectively, because each plays an essential role in building the case. IT professionals understand the hacker mindset, know where to look for digital evidence, and understand what can and can't be done with the technology. Law enforcement personnel know the law and investigative procedures that must be followed to preserve the integrity of evidence. Together, the two can fight cybercrime effectively, but they must overcome the natural distrust and adversarial relationship that often hamper the cooperative process.

The investigative process is basically the same in a cybercrime case as in any other criminal case, but investigators must be cognizant of the importance of defining the roles of everyone on the investigative team and ensuring that each team member has an assigned area of responsibility. A good case file is the result of hard work on the parts of many different people, but the ultimate goal is to bring the case to trial—and win. Toward that end, both law enforcement investigators and IT personnel with direct knowledge of the crime may be called to testify in court as evidentiary witnesses. IT pros may also be qualified to testify as expert witnesses, who are allowed to analyze evidence, give opinions and draw conclusions, and/or explain the technical aspects of the case to the court and jury.

Frequently Asked Questions

The following Frequently Asked Questions, answered by the authors of this book, are designed to both measure your understanding of the concepts presented in this chapter and to assist you with real-life implementation of these concepts. To have your questions about this chapter answered by the author, browse to **www.syngress.com/solutions** and click on the **"Ask the Author"** form.

Q: Should cyberspace be treated as a distinct "place" for purposes of jurisdictional issues?

A: Some legal experts think that's the most logical approach. David R. Johnson and David G. Post, writing in the *Stanford Law Review* in 1996, posited that geographic boundaries are irrelevant when considering legal issues in the online world and that treating the Internet as merely a "transmission medium" confuses the issue and has ultimately unsatisfying results. They propose that when engaged in online activity, a person should be considered to be in a distinct "place" or jurisdiction that has its own laws, just as a geographic jurisdiction does. They argue that cyberspace has distinct boundaries in that you are either online or not at a given time, and thus there is no ambiguity about whether and when your actions would fall under that jurisdiction. Furthermore, they argue that treating the process of going online as crossing a border would greatly simplify the ability to set and enforce laws regulating behavior in the online "space." For a complete discussion of their ideas, see the paper *Law and Borders: The Rise of Law in Cyberspace* at the Cyberspace Law Institute's Web site at www.cli.org/X0025_LBFIN.html# II.%20%20A%20New%20Boundary%20for%20Cyberspace.

Q: There appear to be thousands of computer forensics expert witnesses advertising on the Internet. How can an investigator determine which one to use?

A: Many companies and individuals do provide this service. Some are highly qualified, and others have little experience or expertise. In the United States, there is no regulation of fields such as computer forensics. "Experts" don't have to meet any particular educational or experience standards, and there are no standard certifications or training programs. Basically, anyone can hang out a shingle and call him- or herself a computer forensics expert. In selecting from among the many self-proclaimed experts, then, you'll need to put your investigative skills to work. Find out what the expert's background is: Does he or she have a degree(s) in computer science and/or forensics studies? How about actual job experience in addition to academic experience? At how many trials has the expert testified, and what was the outcome of those trials? In other words, ask all the same questions that the court will want answered in qualifying this person to testify as an expert witness. Ask for references (from previous clients) and check them out. Ensure that you get someone who is experienced in testifying in *criminal* matters, because the rules of procedure and other aspects of testifying in civil trials are different.

Resources

- Criminal Justice Resource Center
  www.wadsworth.com/criminaljustice_d

- Cornell Law School: *Criminal Law: An Overview*
  www.law.cornell.edu/topics/criminal.html

- *How Our Laws Are Made,* revised and updated by Charles W. Johnson
  http://thomas.loc.gov/home/lawsmade.toc.html

- Federal Rules of Criminal Procedure
  www.law.ukans.edu/research/frcrimI.htm

- Original Intent: *The Law*
  www.originalintent.org/thelaw.shtml

- ZDNet, June 26, 2002: *How the Secret Service Became Cybercops*
  http://zdnet.com.com/2100-1107-939425.html

- OAS: *Cybercrime and Jurisdiction,* by Jack Goldsmith
  www.oas.org/juridico/english/cybercrime_and_jurisdiction.htm

- Nedbank ISS Crime Index*:*
  Intangible Evidence? Policing in the Information Age
  www.iss.co.za/PUBS/CRIMEINDEX/01VOL5NO4/Intangible.html

- Capsule Summary*: Criminal Procedure*
  http://lawschool.lexis.com/emanuel/web/crimpro/tocfull.htm

- The Expert Pages
  http://expertpages.com/experts/computers.htm

Afterword

In this book, we've examined the historical background of cybercrime, and discussed how Internet-related offenders can be defended against and brought to justice today. What does the future hold for us in terms of online lawbreaking? Surely we can expect both the cybercriminals and the methods used to combat them to grow more sophisticated. We also can expect more and more legislation regulating Internet behavior. Cybercrime today ranges from the seemingly trivial to the deadly serious and it's likely that in the years to come we'll see more of it, at both ends of the spectrum.

As this book goes to press, United States officials are cracking down on Americans' increasingly popular practice of buying Cuban cigars over the Internet. Since the 1960s, the United States trade embargo against Cuba has prohibited United States citizens from purchasing goods made in Cuba, even when traveling outside the country. For years, cigar aficionados have journeyed to Canada and other countries to buy the highly coveted Havana cigars, but in recent years the Internet has made it much easier and less expensive for Americans to break this law.

At the same time, cyberterrorism (a topic we only touched on briefly here) has been in the news more and more, especially during the past few weeks as I've put the finishing touches on this book. On June 27, 2002, it was reported in the *Washington Post* that authorities were investigating suspicious patterns of surveillance originating in the Middle East and South Asia, against the computer systems of public utility and government facilities in the San Francisco area. There is a growing fear that al Qa'ida and other terrorist organizations may be planning to attempt takeovers of critical infrastructure components via the computers that run them. Dams, electrical power plants, telephone companies, air traffic control, and nuclear and gas facilities are just a few of the systems that could be vulnerable. The damage done by the typical hacker attack pales in comparison to the possibilities.

The newly created Office of Homeland Security is ramping up to deal with these threats, along with other agencies. President George W. Bush appointed the first special adviser to the president for cyberspace security, and government officials seem to be aware now just how dependent the American and world economies are on computer networks and electronic communications.

Meanwhile, legislators at the state and federal levels, in the United States and abroad, struggle with more mundane cybercrime-related issues as well. Spam (junk e-mail) is a matter of concern to lawmakers all over the world. In May 2002, the European Parliament adopted a directive that makes it illegal to send unsolicited e-mail advertisements to persons with whom a company doesn't already have an existing business relationship. In the United States, the first attempts by state legislatures in California and Washington to pass anti-spam laws were thwarted by judges who ruled the laws unconstitutional—held to be violations of the dormant commerce clause of the Constitution that prohibits states from placing undue burdens on interstate commerce. The federal government has taken up the cause, however. Beginning with the Inbox Privacy Act of 1999, a number of bills were introduced in the U.S. Congress, but these bills generally didn't make it into law. At the time of this writing, yet another anti-spam measure had been introduced by U.S. Senators Conrad Burns, Ron Wyden and Ted Stevens, and approved by the Senate Commerce Committee.

Debates continue to rage over the issue of pornography (and the filtering software designed to keep it out) in regards to its access at public libraries. Lawsuits have been filed and/or threatened against libraries in several parts of the country, both for allowing access to pornography and for violating free speech tenets by blocking access. Legislators in many states have grappled with the issue of whether libraries have a legal obligation to protect children from obscene or offensive material available on the Internet, and how such an obligation can be reconciled with the First Amendment. Some states (including Virginia and Arizona) have passed legislation that requires filtering on computers in libraries and schools; Congress passed a federal law called the Children's Internet Protection Act (CIPA) that requires Web filtering in public libraries. Lawsuits have been filed challenging those laws on constitutional grounds. Just before this book went to press, a three-judge panel in the Third U.S. Circuit Court of Appeals struck down the CIPA as unconstitutional; the next appeal will go to the Supreme Court. A final decision remains to be seen.

The Internet is also being used with increasing frequency to publish and disseminate information about accused and convicted criminals. Many localities are using the Internet to notify the public about registered sex offenders' residence locations. Most states require those convicted of certain sex crimes to register with the state after their release from prison, maintaining updated information about where they live. This information is, in turn, made available to the community. Sex offender databases are a popular feature of state and municipal Web sites. There are other sites that allow users to search criminal history databases to obtain public information about all types of crimes (usually for a fee). One site in Maricopa County, Arizona, for a while even provided a live webcam that let site visitors watch the prisoners in the county jail's intake and holding areas. In December 2001, the site reported receiving 3 million visitors per week. The "jailcam" sparked controversy, and eventually a lawsuit. A retired judge filed the suit accusing the county sheriff of violating prisoners' privacy rights. The site that hosted the live look at life behind bars has been removed, although the notice posted there states only that the jailcam is "temporarily" unavailable.

Hackers continue to make the news, and sentiment regarding high-tech law breakers continues to be mixed. Kevin Mitnick, convicted of numerous high profile hacks in the late 1980s and 1990s, is out of prison and making the rounds of tech-oriented talk shows such as Tech TV's Screen Savers. His book, *The Art of Deception,* due out in the fall of 2002, was already highly ranked at number 925 on Amazon.com's sales list three months prior to its announced publication date. The government is arresting hackers, and cadets are being dishonorably discharged from the military when caught hacking. At the same time, government and military personnel frequent popular hacker conventions like Def Con, sponsoring "Meet the Fed" events there, and attempting to recruit talented hackers to put their skills to work legally. Large corporations are also hiring hackers to man their security teams.

These and many other issues complicate the already complex world of cyberspace law at the beginning of the twenty-first century. As we look toward the future, it seems likely that things will get even more confusing. As a result of the hybridization of mobile phone and wireless Internet technologies, soon we will literally be able to take the Internet with us wherever we go. It becomes more and more apparent that in tomorrow's world, he (or she) who controls the Net will control our lives. Online demographics are changing all the time and the "digital divide" is narrowing. Already the idea of high-speed Internet access as something available only to the elite or wealthy is fading fast. Soon Net-connected computers will be as commonplace as color television sets even in low income areas in the United States and other first-world nations. Will our IP addresses one day replace our Social Security numbers and driver's license numbers as our primary identifiers?

Scientists are working now to develop machines based on quantum mechanics called *quantum computers*, which would, in theory, be able to do computations on many different numbers simultaneously using quantum bits, or *qubits,* as the basis of processing instead of bits. A qubit can exist in more than one state at the same time, unlike regular bits which can represent only a 1 or a 0 at any given time. Most experts agree that if working quantum computing becomes a reality, it will turn today's computer security measures on their heads. Quantum machines would be able to break our strong encryption algorithms quickly and easily. A quantum algorithm for efficient factoring of large numbers has already been developed by Peter Shor of AT&T Laboratories; a computer that can use such algorithms will be able to perform in a short time tasks that would require hundreds of years using ordinary computers. The times, they are a-changin'—and each change (and anticipated change) holds the potential for expanding the virtual universe to a degree never dreamed of a few years ago. One thing is certain, based on history: The larger a community grows, the more crime it experiences. And with every technological advance, the online community grows by leaps and bounds.

We all have a vested interest in helping to lower the rate of cybercrime. The online world is quickly becoming our "home away from home." I don't want the Internet to become such a high crime area that we must all be afraid to let our children go there to play and study and learn. Over the past several years, police in many areas of the United States and in other countries have been successful in reducing the overall incidence of crime in their communities by getting the citizens of the community involved in crime fighting. I believe the same techniques can be applied to the online world, as well.

In writing this book, I wanted to bring together the people who have the skills and the authority to do what it takes to make cyberspace a safer, more pleasant place for all of us. That includes the technical personnel who will often be the first to see the results of the cybercriminal's work, and who have the expertise to help track them down. It includes the law enforcement officers who will be tasked with collecting the evidence to build the case against the cybercriminal, and who must work closely with technical experts to ensure that all avenues have been exhausted in hunting down that evidence and presenting it properly. But it also includes the legislators who make the laws those police officers will have to enforce, as well as the judges who will oversee the trials, and the juries who will ultimately make the decisions regarding guilt or innocence of those accused of cybercrimes. Finally, it includes we, the people—the citizens in good standing of the online community and all those whose lives are affected by it, to whatever degree.

Cybercrime is not just an interesting subtopic of criminal law. It is a very real problem, and the problem will continue to grow until all those involved work together to take back the networks from the criminals, just as those in many formerly high crime neighborhoods have taken back their streets.

There is much more to the subject of cybercrime than could fit into this book. Even as the book was being written, new developments in cybercrime have continued to occur. In one sense, it will always be an unfinished project. I invite questions, comments, and suggestions on how I can make the next book better. Please e-mail me at debshinder@sceneofthecybercrime.com. For updates on topics in the book and other cybercrime news, visit my Web site at www.sceneofthecybercrime.com and the publisher's Web site at www.syngress.com/solutions.

Fighting Cybercrime on a Global Scale

Topics we'll investigate in this Appendix:

- **How Nations Are Updating Their Cybercrime Legislation**
- **Comparing International Cybercrime Laws**
- **Investigating an International Cybercrime**

☑ **Summary**

☑ **Resources**

Introduction

Cybercrime is a global plague that is combated by law enforcement throughout the world. Countries have suffered estimated billions in damages and been forced to update their legal structure to address this new form of crime. Cybercrime has led to the creation of new positions within law enforcement, new units in police departments, and new specialties for lawyers.

With traditional forms of crime, a person generally violates a law within a single jurisdiction. Cybercrime is different from other crime because a single offense can cross multiple jurisdictions—even cross the globe itself. This scope has created legal and logistical problems that need to be addressed, forced cooperation between law enforcement throughout the world, and made obvious the need for governments to work together. Unfortunately, although the need is there, many governments have failed or fallen short of the objective to effectively deal with cybercrime.

In this appendix, we look at the special issues involved with international investigations and the problems that relate to them. We'll see how laws differ from one nation to another, the cooperative efforts between countries to combat cybercrime, and how jurisdictional and other obstacles can prevent cybercrimes from ever being prosecuted.

This appendix also provides the Web site addresses for reference material available on the Internet. The Web sites provide information on laws governing other countries, law enforcement Web sites, and background materials that are useful when investigating computer-related crimes on an international scale.

How Nations Are Updating Their Cybercrime Legislation

Because cybercrimes are committed throughout the world, many people in the United States assume that legislation similar to that found in North America exists throughout the world. This couldn't be further from the truth. Many countries rely on existing laws to deal with cybercrime and might update those laws only after it becomes apparent that they fail to apply to cybercrimes (just as U.S. state laws often were not updated—and in some cases still haven't been—until the need became obvious). Ineffective law is as bad as no law whatsoever, and when the legal elements of an offense don't quite fit the actual crime, the law is ineffective—at least, for the purposes of prosecuting that particular crime.

In some countries, no laws whatsoever apply to crimes commonly associated with computers and the Internet, making it legal "by default" to perform actions that would subject a person to arrest in North America. However, the international attitude toward cybercrime is changing, and new laws are appearing throughout the world. Keeping up with all these changes presents a challenge to people who must work with the laws of different jurisdictions.

In comparing the laws of nations throughout the world, the overwhelming conclusion is that many countries are failing to address the problem of cybercrime because they don't have legislation that deals with it specifically, whereas others have been more aggressive than the United States in addressing these issues. As we've seen throughout this book, many computer-related crimes are variations on old themes. For example, a country can have child pornography laws on the books and make no distinction as to whether the illegal materials are distributed in a paper or digital format. The fact that the crime is now being committed over the Internet is merely a new way to do something that's already illegal. In these cases, existing statutes might apply to someone committing the crime, regardless of whether a computer is involved.

On the other hand, they might *not*. If the legislation is too vague, it can be interpreted in a way that disqualifies any cyber-based variation. An example of this situation is the Love Bug virus that attacked systems throughout the world and resulted in estimated billions of dollars in damages. Investigation found that the author of the virus was located in the Philippines, and a suspect named Onel de Guzman was arrested under the Philippine Access Devices Act of 1994, which is also known as Republic Act 8484. This Act, traditionally applied to cases involving credit card theft, dealt with the illegal use of account numbers and passwords. Unfortunately, after determining that the law wasn't applicable to this case and didn't address virus dissemination or the havoc it created, the charges were dropped. Even if the Act could have been used to prosecute this crime, it imposes a penalty of only six months to six years in prison. The same crime, if committed in the United States, could be prosecuted under laws that carry a penalty of up to 20 years' imprisonment.

Because the existing laws of the time were inadequate to prosecute the Love Bug author (and other cybercriminals), the Philippine government found itself in the position of having to create new laws that dealt with cybercrime effectively. The creation of legislation that addresses computer and Internet-related crime is often a similar reactive approach to inadequate legislation. In fact, few countries have taken *proactive* measures against cybercrime. Even when existing laws are changed to contend with cybercrime, they often fail to address the full range of possible offenses. For example, while the Czech Republic has updated its laws to address such issues as unauthorized access and data modification, no laws deal with virus dissemination. In other words, the same problem that the Philippines experienced is being repeated in another part of the world.

Until countries throughout the world update antiquated laws and create new laws that directly deal with cybercrime, the problem of not being able to prosecute cybercriminals effectively will continue. A survey conducted by McConnell International in December 2000 (www.mcconnellinternational.com/services/CyberCrime.htm) showed that surprisingly few laws currently protect citizens throughout the world from cybercrime. Of 52 countries surveyed, nine had laws addressing five or fewer types of cybercrime, 10 had laws addressing six to 10 types of cybercrime, and 33 hadn't upgraded their laws to deal with *any* type of cybercrime. If cybercriminals commit crimes within these countries, a government's ability to prosecute them is limited.

Reaping the Benefits of International Influence

As nations cooperate with one another in various endeavors, a global vision of what is considered right and wrong has been established on a variety of subjects. Because numerous countries don't have laws or adequate legislation dealing with child pornography, cyberterrorism, and other activities related to cybercrime, international consortiums saw a need to provide a legal framework for updating the laws of these countries. International organizations and political coalitions have influenced legal changes in many countries, pressuring some countries to create new laws or revise existing ones to deal with crimes that the majority of the world considers abhorrent or potentially devastating.

With the intervention of the United Nations (U.N.) and the International Labor Organization (ILO), many countries that previously didn't have laws dealing with child pornography have changed existing legislation or created new laws criminalizing this offense. In doing so, they have made it illegal to distribute or obtain child pornography through such sources as the Internet, allowing law enforcement to shut down pedophile Web sites, arrest owners of these sites, and arrest Internet users acquiring such digital images and movies. For example, in the summer of 2002, Europol (the European Union's police agency) reported that European police conducted child porn raids as part of Operation Twins in seven countries, seizing equipment and arresting suspects in Belgium, Britain, Germany, Italy, the Netherlands, Spain, and Sweden. Twelve countries were involved in the operation, including the United States and Canada.

The U.N. Convention on the Rights of the Child (CRC), which includes an Optional Protocol on child prostitution and child pornography, has been ratified by almost 200 countries, and over 100 of them have signed the Protocol. (For more information, see www.unicef.org/crc/crc.htm.) The ILO has been fighting child pornography since the 1930s and, at the International Labor Conference of 1997, extended its pressure on member nations to pass strong laws against child pornography "whatever the technical method used," thus ensuring that such activities using the Internet (or other, future technologies) would be addressed. In 1999, the European Parliament and the Council of the European Union adopted a multiannual action plan devoted to promoting safer use of the Internet by combating illegal and harmful content on global networks. The plan, managed by the European Commission (EC), runs through December 2002 and provides 25 million euros in funding.

The impact of such agreements between countries has significantly changed laws throughout the world. For example, child pornography laws are a recent addition to Mexico's legal framework. In January 1999, the Mexican Congress amended the country's criminal code to categorize child pornography and child prostitution as "grievous crimes." Before this time, no law dealt with such activity.

In the wake of the events of September 11, 2001, the North American public has become more concerned with the potential for disasters caused by cyberterrorism. Cyberterrorism involves using common hacking methods (such as unauthorized access to computers, viruses, e-mail bombs, and so forth) for the purpose of causing damage, especially to critical national infrastructure (water supplies, electrical grids, telephone switches) or national security and military defense systems. As with other forms of terrorism, cyberterrorism is generally politically motivated and is directed against noncombatant targets (civilians). An act of cyberterrorism can result in damage to a country's economy and infrastructure as well as loss of life. We can only imagine the devastation that could be caused by a hacker taking down an air traffic control system, a government computer system that controls nuclear missile targeting, or a 911 emergency system. The threat is exacerbated by the fact that traditional counterterrorism tactics are useless against an enemy who can use technology to strike from thousands of miles away.

The more dependent a society becomes on its computer systems, the more vulnerable it becomes to cyberterrorists. Food-processing and pharmaceutical plants, electrical and natural gas utilities, traffic control systems, medical facilities, and military, public safety, and civilian communications systems are all areas of great vulnerability. The terrorist generally aims for destruction on a large scale, and that is certainly possible for someone who manages to take control of one or more of these crucial systems. For discussion of possible scenarios involving cyberterrorism, see http://afgen.com/terrorism1.html.

Cyberterrorism is an issue that has been a concern for law enforcement agencies in many countries over the last several years. Computer and network security has been a major focus for both IT departments and police management throughout the world. Regulations and internal policies dealing with connectivity to the Internet and securing information have become commonplace. IT specialists in corporations and small business networks have shown increased diligence by implementing firewalls and applying security updates, antivirus software, and numerous other measures.

The threat of cyberterrorism isn't new. On October 1, 1997, Arnaud de Borchgrave, director of the Global Organized Crime Project of the Center for Strategic and International Studies, testified before the U.S. House of Representatives Committee on International Relations. During this testimony, he stated that "there are already eight hostile or potentially hostile nations that have developed the required technology and skills to wage information warfare by means of electronic sabotage and lethal destruction and 120 nations have developed computer attack capabilities." *Information warfare* could include not only acts of cyberterrorism but also espionage and intelligence gathering. Further information on this testimony can be found at the Web site for the Center for Strategic and International Studies (CSIS) at www.csis.org/hill/ts100197.html.

Although many countries have laws dealing with terrorism, a number have updated existing laws or created new ones to specifically address the threat of cyberterrorism. For example, in December 2001, the Canadian government passed the Anti-Terrorism Act, which, among other things, addressed issues dealing with different forms of terrorism, including activities affecting computers and data. Through such legislation, countries are able to deal with cybercrime in a way that reflects national ideals of freedom and security.

The difficulties with imposing legislation dealing with cyberterrorism and its impact on citizens are in many ways similar to the problems of imposing security measures within an organization. For years, companies have had to balance security with accessibility when new policies were used to limit staff members' activities. With every new policy, members of an organization would find that their ability to access certain information was reduced. Too much security could result in people being unable to do their jobs, whereas too little resulted in vulnerabilities that left the company at risk. The impact of cyberterrorism and other cybercrime legislation can pose similar risks, affecting the freedom of people to access certain information or perform actions that are commonplace to their online activities. Freedom and security are, by definition, on opposite ends of a continuum. The more you have of one, the less you have of the other. Balancing the need for governmental control to provide protection of its citizenry with that citizenry's desire to be free from oppressive overregulation is a political dilemma faced by democratic countries founded on the principles of liberty and human rights.

Another category of cybercrime related to but different from cyberterrorism is "hacktivism," which generally involves damage to property without risk of injury to people. During the Kosovo conflict, many "hacktivists" used the Internet to spread propaganda, taking over Web sites of government agencies and changing them to reflect the hackers' political views. Hacktivism shouldn't be confused with simple political activism that involves using the Internet. The latter includes such activities as constructing a Web site of your own and posting your political opinions there. Hacktivism is a criminal activity in that it involves hacking into someone else's site without permission or disrupting the network activities of organizations or governments whose policies you dislike. Hacktivists use e-mail bombs, DoS attacks, viruses and worms, and other common hacker ploys for political purposes. However, when hacktivist attacks cross over the line to disrupt services (such as those of medical facilities or utility companies) in a way that poses a threat to human life or livelihood, they become cyberterrorists.

To address the issues of all these computer and Internet-related crimes, numerous countries have joined together and signed the Council of Europe (COE) Convention on Cybercrime that requires members to criminalize activities related to cyberterrorism and other forms of cybercrime. Nonmember states such as the United States, Canada, Japan, and South Africa have also signed. Through this cooperative effort, activities such as hacking, interference with computer systems, fraud, forgery, and other related offenses are made illegal in each country that signs the Convention. The Convention also supports cooperation between countries to detect, investigate, and prosecute such crimes and to collect evidence through electronic methods of offenses related to terrorism, organized crime, and other crimes that are carried out on a global scale using computers and networks. The Convention itself can be viewed on the COE's Web site at http://conventions.coe.int/Treaty/EN/projets/FinalCybercrime.htm. The current status of the Convention, showing which countries have signed, can be viewed online at http://conventions.coe.int/Treaty/EN/searchsig.asp?NT= 185&CM=&DF=.

Law enforcement groups in various countries are also working together to attack the threat of Internet-related criminal activity. Because such activities can cross international jurisdictions, such cooperation is vital to combating cybercrime.

In December 2000, a joint effort between Russia's Moscow City Police and the United States Customs CyberSmuggling Center resulted in the shutdown of the Blue Orchid, a Russian Web site that featured images and videos of children being physically and sexually abused. As a result of this and other operations, many hundreds of videocassettes and DVDs and over 1000 pornographic pictures were seized. Arrests in both countries resulted from the operations.

Even corporations can assist in combating international computer crimes, as seen in the case that culminated in nearly 1500 arrests in 2000. Italian police sought the assistance of Microsoft to create a fake pedophile Web site called *amantideibambini* ("Lovers of Children"). This site specifically stated that the content was illegal, but despite the warnings, 1032 people subscribed to the site. Italian police raided 600 residences, arrested 831 Italians, and attempted to extradite another 660 from various other countries.

Comparing International Cybercrime Laws

When investigating crimes that span multiple countries, it is important to recognize that the laws of one country might be inconsistent with those of other countries. Each nation has its own views on justice, freedoms, and civil liberties. When your investigation leads you into the jurisdiction of another country, you might be surprised at how different that country's laws are from yours. In some cases, you might be surprised that laws dealing with particular offenses are nonexistent.

It is beyond the scope of this book (or any other) to cover every law in every country dealing with computer and Internet-related crime, and laws in all jurisdictions are constantly changing. However, it is useful for the investigator to have a list of resources that outline some of the cybercrime-related laws in various countries and provide general information on global aspects of cybercrime investigation and prosecution. When looking at these laws, remember that the justice system of any country is complex and involves much more than just its penal statutes. Procedures and rules of court and of evidence vary widely. For example, under the Napoleonic Code of France, accused criminals are presumed guilty— the opposite of the presumption of innocence that is the foundation of U.S.

criminal law. If you need more information about the laws of a particular nation, contact a member of that country's government or law enforcement community or an attorney specializing in criminal law in that jurisdiction.

A good resource for any investigator is to first contact Interpol and determine whether an activity is illegal in a specific country. If possible, contact an embassy for a particular country or a law enforcement agency within the country itself to determine whether specific legislation exists (and is enforced) within that country. By doing so, you will be able to determine whether your investigation can continue beyond jurisdictional boundaries.

Argentina

Argentina has no special laws dealing with cybercrime. However, the country's penal code does have other laws that can be applied to certain crimes regardless of whether they are committed using computers and the Internet. For example, Articles 128 and 129, which deal with child pornography, make it illegal to publish, make, reproduce, or distribute obscene images.

The ability to deal with computer crimes other than child pornography in Argentina has been very limited. Take, for example, an Argentinian court ruling that occurred in April 2002 involving a group of hackers called the X-Team. This group hacked the Supreme Court's Web page in 1998 and defaced the site. This was the first hacking case that Argentina had prosecuted, but the judge in this case ruled that Argentinian law covered crimes on "people, things and animals," not digital attacks.

Australia

Federal legislation under the Commonwealth Laws of Australia deals with issues related to computer crime. The Crimes Act of 1914, Part VIA, sections 76B and 76D (see the Act at http://courses.cs.vt.edu/~cs3604/lib/Crime/Australia .law.html) deal with unlawful access to data and make it illegal to intentionally obtain unauthorized access to data in a Commonwealth computer or data stored on behalf of the Commonwealth in another computer. In other words, much like U.S. Title 18, this law only addresses data residing on government systems, not those of companies or personal computers. The penalty under this law is six months in jail. The punishment is more severe if the person performs these actions with the intent to defraud someone or knows or has reasonable knowledge that the data relates to certain sensitive information. This includes data dealing with Australian security, defense, international relations, law enforcement, protection of public safety, the personal affairs of a person, financial records, trade secrets, or commercial information. In such cases, the offense carries a penalty of two years' imprisonment.

The federal legislation of the Commonwealth is limited to powers that are specified in Australia's constitution. In addition, the six states and two territories of Australia also have unrestricted powers, which are superseded by Commonwealth law in the case of a conflict. Crimes not covered by the federal laws (such as unauthorized access to nongovernment computers) are prosecuted under the laws of the individual states and territories. For example, in 1998, Victoria enacted the first state computer crimes laws, and the rest of the states and territories have done so since (although the laws are *not* uniform across state and territorial borders).

In Australia, laws dealing with child pornography are mainly handled at the state level. Australian law defines child pornography as involving a subject who appears to be under the age of 16 years. By qualifying child pornography in this way, law enforcement is relieved of the burden of proving the exact age of a subject during the time when the pornography was produced. If the person looks to be underage, the material is considered kiddie porn.

The states of Victoria and Queensland use the Classification of Films and Publications Act as a source of legislation to deal with child pornography. Under this Act, procuring a child to be part of an "objectionable film" (such as that involving sexual penetration) could result in up to five years' imprisonment. Possession of child pornography could result in up to a year in prison. Each state has additional laws to deal with this crime.

For more information on computer crimes laws in Australia, see the Web site of Baker & McKenzie at www.bmck.com/Australia/australia_crime.htm.

Brazil

In 2000, Brazil changed a number of its laws addressing cybercrime. Article 313-A of the Penal Code deals with entering false data or excluding the entry of correct data into a computer system or data bank of the public administration. If a person does this for the purpose of achieving improper advantage for himself or another person or causing damages to another, that person can be imprisoned from two to 12 years and face a fine. If a person modifies or alters data without authorization, that person may be charged under Article 313-B and be imprisoned three months to two years and face a fine. Penalties under either of these articles can be increased by a third to one-half if damage occurs to public administration systems (in other words, government computer systems) or individuals whose records are stored under these systems.

Brazil's Penal Code has two articles dealing specifically with the production of child pornography but no laws dealing with possession. Article 240 of the Brazilian Statute of the Child and the Adolescent states that an offender can receive one to four years' imprisonment and a fine for producing or directing a theater performance, television show, or movie with scenes of explicit sex or pornography involving a child or adolescent. Article 241 of this statute goes on to provide the same punishment for people taking pictures or making public sexually explicit and pornographic scenes involving a child or adolescent. In Brazil, a child is defined as someone under 12 years of age; an adolescent is defined as someone between 12 and 18 years of age.

Canada

Under Canada's Criminal Code, a number of sections directly deal with cybercrime. Section 342.1 deals with the unauthorized use of a computer and (unlike the laws at the national level in many countries) applies to any computer service, including private systems. This law addresses issues dealing with hackers, who can crack their way into a computer system with various programs or Trojans or by using another person's passwords. It also deals with interception of data and virus dissemination. Violating this law can result in imprisonment for up to 10 years.

Section 342.1 deals with the act of unauthorized computer use; Section 342.2 takes the law a step further, making it illegal to possess, sell, offer for sale, or distribute instruments and devices that could be used to commit the crimes mentioned in Section 342.1. Even if the offender didn't actually break into a system but merely offered the tools to do so, he or she could be sentenced to up to two years in jail.

Privacy is also addressed in the Criminal Code, and Section 184 focuses on interception of communications. By intercepting private communications, a person can be subject to imprisonment of up to five years.

Section 380 deals with fraudulent transactions in relation to contracts and trade and addresses computer-related fraud. A person who commits such a crime can face up to two years in jail if the fraud is less than Can$2000 and can be imprisoned for up to 10 years if the fraud exceeds Can$5000.

Section 430.1 deals with *mischief*, and Section 430(1.1) specifically addresses mischief in relation to cybercrime. It deals with data modification, network interference, network sabotage, and dissemination of viruses. Anyone who causes damage to property in this manner can face up to two years in prison, but if damages exceed Can$5000 or data is involved (such as when data is modified or destroyed), the offender can face a prison term of up to 10 years. If the commission of the crime causes a danger to life, the person can be imprisoned for life.

Section 163.1 deals with child pornography. This law makes no distinction between formats in which child pornography might exist. In other words, it doesn't matter if the pornography is in an electronic format, photographic, film, video, or other visual representations. Kiddie porn is kiddie porn, regardless of the medium in which it is presented.

In Canada, child pornography exists when the subject of the pornographic material is under the age of 18 or is depicted as such. This is an intelligent definition, because it can be difficult if not impossible to track down every model or actress in a pornographic film to determine his or her exact age. As such, if the person appears to be a child, the material is deemed child pornography. If someone makes, distributes, or sells such pornography, they are liable to receive up to 10 years in prison. If someone simply possesses it, they are risking up to five years' imprisonment.

On the Scene…

What's the Difference Between Summary Conviction and Indictment?

Under Canadian law, there are two basic types of criminal offenses. Minor offenses are known as *summary conviction offenses* and carry a penalty of a fine of up to Can$2000 or six months in jail (unless a larger fine is specified in the statute for the particular offense). In addition, those who are convicted of summary conviction offenses are not fingerprinted and are eligible for pardon after three years.

Offenses deemed to be more serious are classified as *indictable*. Because the penalties are greater (large fines and/or imprisonment), those accused of most indictable offenses have the right to trial by jury. An offender is not eligible for pardon until five years after conviction.

Offenses that can be prosecuted as either summary conviction or indictable offenses are known as *hybrid offenses* or "Crown option" because the Crown (equivalent to the State in the United States) has the option of choosing which way to prosecute.

The Copyright Act is another piece of legislation that addresses computer piracy. Anyone who sells, rents, or distributes copyrighted software can face fines and imprisonment. On summary conviction, offenders can face a fine of up to 25,000 Canadian dollars and/or six months in jail. On conviction of indictment, they can face a fine of up to 1 million Canadian dollars and/or five years' imprisonment.

European Nations

As mentioned earlier, many of the members of the European Union have signed the COE Convention on Cybercrime. These countries include the United Kingdom, Spain, Portugal, Italy, Ireland, Germany, Poland, Hungary, France, Greece, Switzerland, and most of the Scandinavian nations. However, the treaty is not self-enforcing; in other words, when a member nation adopts and ratifies the treaty, that country still has to pass legislation to actually implement its terms.

The EU treaty is similar to the U.S. Computer Fraud and Abuse Act (Title 18, section 1030 of the U.S. Code) in terms of the activities that it outlaws. However, it does contain provisions that go beyond the U.S. laws, such as the prohibition on so-called "burglar tools" (hacker tools) that can be used to gain unauthorized access to computers and networks. There were attempts to include a similar provision in the U.S. Digital Millennium Copyright Act (DMCA), but Congress rejected them.

Some European countries already had their own cybercrime laws prior to the convention. For example, the Computer Misuse Act in the United Kingdom, originally instituted in 1990, addresses several specific activities, including:

- Unauthorized access to computer material
- Unauthorized access with intent to commit or facilitate commission of further offenses
- Unauthorized modification of computer material

For the full text of the Act, see www.ja.net/CERT/JANET-CERT/law/cma.html.

The French Penal Code has had computer crime provisions in since 1993. Articles 323-1 through 323-4 address fraudulently gaining access to, hindering or distorting the function of, or fraudulently introducing data into automated data-processing systems. Penalties range from one year to three years' imprisonment and fines of up to 300.000 FF. The German Penal Code contains sections dealing with data espionage, alteration of data, and computer sabotage (Penal Code

Sections 202a, 303a, and 303b). Italian law, Penal Code Article 615, prohibits unauthorized access to computers and telecommunications systems, illegal possession and diffusion of access codes to computers or telecommunications systems, and diffusion of programs aimed at damaging or interrupting a computer system. On the other hand, some countries such as Spain have no specific Penal Code provisions dealing with computer crimes, although other laws regulating privacy, fraud, and the like could be applicable to cybercrimes.

People's Republic of China

The People's Republic of China (PRC) has legislation that protects computer information in Decree No. 147. Article 23 of the Decree states that it is illegal to deliberately input a computer virus or other harmful data that would endanger a computer information system or sell special safety protection products for computer systems without permission. In such cases, public security organizations can give warnings or impose a fine of 5000 Yuan on individuals or 15000 Yuan on organizations. Illegal income resulting from the crimes is confiscated, and a fine can be imposed that is one to three times the amount of the illegal income.

Legislation in the PRC addresses the production, sale, and distribution of any type of pornography, with the punishments varying. If the crime is committed for profit, offenders can receive three years' imprisonment, forced labor, or surveillance, along with a fine. "Serious" offenders can receive between three and 10 years' imprisonment and a fine, whereas the "gravest" offenders can receive between 10 years and life imprisonment and either a fine or confiscation of property. In cases involving the distribution of pornographic literature, film, video, or images, the culprit can receive two years in prison, detention, or surveillance.

Many acts are regarded as criminal in the PRC that would not be elsewhere. For example, the Ministry of Public Security's Computer Information Network and Internet Security, Protection and Management Regulations (Article 5) states that "no unit or individual may use the Internet to create, replicate, retrieve, or transmit the following kinds of information" and goes on to list such things as:

- Inciting division of the country, harming national unification

- Making falsehoods or distorting the truth, spreading rumors, destroying the order of society

- Promoting feudal superstitions, sexually suggestive material, gambling, violence, murder

- Engaging in terrorism or inciting others to criminal activity; openly insulting other people or distorting the truth to slander people

- Injuring the reputation of state organs

This is only a partial list of prohibited activities. There are many regulations on use of the Internet in business, and all Internet users are required to register with their local police agency within 30 days after they obtain an account with an ISP. Some other relevant Chinese laws include the following:

- PRC Regulations for the Safety Protection of Computer Information Systems

- Computer Information Network and Internet Security, Protection and Management Regulations

- Telecommunications Regulations of the PRC

- State Secrets Protection Regulations for Computer Information Systems on the Internet

Penalties for violation of some of these laws can be severe. Users can receive the death penalty for posting material of which the government disapproves.

On the Scene...

Crime and Punishment in the PRC

In April 2000, a writer named Guo Qinghai was sentenced to four years in prison at a trial where he had no lawyer. His crime was posting articles from a Hong Kong magazine that called for political reform. In September 2000, author Qi Yanchen was sentenced to four years in prison for posting excerpts from his book, *The Collapse of China,* on the Internet. In May 2001, Jiang Shihua, a teacher, was sentenced to two years in prison for posting articles on an Internet bulletin board that criticized the Chinese government. Numerous other Chinese have been detained, arrested, and convicted for crimes such as downloading articles with political or religious content from foreign Web sites. See www.hrw.org/backgrounder/asia/china-bck-0701.htm for more information.

Mexico

The Federal Criminal Code of Mexico addresses cybercrime in several sections, with other laws (such as those dealing with fraud) being applicable regardless of the medium (whether conducted through the Internet or by other means). Articles 211 bis 1 and Articles 211 bis 2 of the Code are provisions protecting unauthorized access on private computers that are protected by security devices; Articles 211 bis 3, bis 4 and bis 5 deal with unauthorized access to computers of the Mexican government and the Mexican financial system. These articles of law deal with hacking, virus decimation, and other criminal actions that pertain to computers and data. If a person copies or views content that's protected by any security device, the offender can be imprisoned for anywhere from three months to a year and be fined from US$150 to US$450. Unauthorized use of a computer where data is modified, destroyed, or lost can result in imprisonment ranging from six months to two years and a fine of US$300 to US$900.

At the time of this writing, changes are underway in Mexico to modify existing laws to address the problem of child pornography. The Commission for Attention to Vulnerable Groups of the Chamber of Deputies of the Mexican Federal Congress made changes to Article 201 of the Federal Criminal Code and Organized Crime Law. Article 201 makes it illegal to create, reproduce, or transmit child pornography over the Internet. Anyone who commits this crime can be imprisoned from 10 to 14 years and face a fine equivalent to 500 to 3000 days of the legal minimum wage. If three or more people are involved together in the crime of child pornography or involved in stealing and trafficking in children, they can be charged under the Second Article of the Organized Crime Law.

Russian Federation

The Russian Federation has three articles in its Criminal Code that specifically address various types of cybercrime. Violating these articles can result in fines, imprisonment, or both. The Russian Federation also has other articles in its Criminal Code that can be applied to computer and Internet-related crimes, even though they don't directly address the technologies used to commit the crimes.

Article 272 of the Criminal Code deals with unauthorized access and the modification or blockage of information. Breaking this law can result in a fine and/or incarceration of up to two years in prison. If the crime involves a conspiracy, in which a group plans and carries out the crime, the sentence can result in up to five years' imprisonment.

Article 273 of the Criminal Code deals with malicious programs. If a person is found guilty of producing and distributing a dangerous computer program, he or she can receive up to seven years' imprisonment.

Article 274 is the final article that directly addresses cybercrime and the exploitation of computer networks. Violating this law can result in up to four years' imprisonment.

The Russian Federation has no specific legislation dealing with child pornography, but it does have laws dealing with pornography in general. Article 242 of the Russian Federation's Criminal Code states that it is illegal to distribute or advertise pornographic materials or objects (not specifically related to children). The punishment is a fine of 500 to 800 times the minimum wage or other income of the convicted person for a period of five to eight months or imprisonment of up to two years. Although new legislation and revamping of existing laws are being considered at the time of this writing, the Russian Federation has no definition of child pornography, what the legal age is to be a subject of such material, nor any definitive legislation dealing with such crime. At present, there is no set legal age for sexual consent in Russia, although legislation addresses sexual acts as illegal with a child under 14 years of age.

NOTE

For an excellent discussion of computer crime laws in 43 countries, updated regularly, see www.mossbyrett.of.no/info/legal.html.

Investigating an International Cybercrime

The ability to perform investigations that go outside of jurisdictional boundaries almost always relies on cooperation with law enforcement entities in those areas. Police in one country generally have no official jurisdiction in other countries. However, when police in different countries work together, the impact on crime can be significant. This impact is seen in a number of collaborative efforts between police and other law enforcement agencies in various countries.

A major achievement in international policing was seen in the British-led Operation Cathedral, which focused on the pedophile network called

Wonderland that provided kiddie porn to its members over the Internet. To become a member of Wonderland and participate in the exchange of child porn, a person had to show that he or she possessed at least 10,000 images depicting child pornography. In September 1998, 100 raids in Britain, Australia, Austria, Belgium, Finland, France, Germany, Italy, Norway, Portugal, Sweden, and the United States were carried out. The cooperation of police in all these countries resulted in effectively shutting down this massive cybercrime operation.

In some cases, dealing with law enforcement agencies in other countries won't be necessary until you've already built a solid case. If you're investigating a suspect within your own country and find out that this person is using Internet resources provided through servers and services in other countries, you might be tempted to go through the police in that jurisdiction to gather more evidence. As you'll see in the sections that follow, bringing additional law enforcement into your case during the early investigative stage isn't always required. Although you will need cooperation to prosecute a case, gathering evidence can often be done without involving additional agencies.

Gathering Evidence

Free e-mail services are commonly used to commit crimes. For example, a suspect might use a free e-mail service to entice victims into a fraud scheme, send death threats, or commit some other crime. Upon discovering this crime and tracking down the origin of the e-mail (using the techniques discussed in Chapter 9, "Implementing Cybercrime Detection Techniques"), you might find that the free e-mail service is located in another country.

Since you will probably need the ISP's account information to ascertain the person's identity, you should first contact the company providing this service. Visit the Web site of the company and look for an e-mail address for account abuse. If no other contact information is available, you might be able to use the e-mail address that is used for reporting spam and other abuse to the service as a starting point. This e-mail address will usually be abuse@*domainname*. For example, Hotmail's e-mail address for account abuse is abuse@hotmail.com. You can contact the company via this address to request more specific contact information and to inform them that an investigation is underway involving their service. In many cases, these companies will have a policy dealing with the release of customer information. The provider's Web page will often provide a phone number to contact the company, which is useful in discovering what documentation they require to release account information. In some cases, the company will require a subpoena, warrant, or some other court order. This is especially true in the United States and other countries that have strong privacy laws. In other cases, all the company will ask for is a letter on police letterhead officially asking for the information.

After contacting the provider, you can then draft an official letter or contact the district attorney's office, crown attorney, or whatever the prosecutorial office is called in your particular jurisdiction. Once you have the documentation the provider requires, you can then fax or courier it and acquire the evidence you need.

The same method can be used if a suspect in your country is running an illegal operation from a server in another country. In many cases, a Web site will be run on a server provided by an ISP or a company that sells server space (called a *Web hosting company*). The domain name belongs to your suspect and might be designed and maintained by this person, but the files actually sit on a server that belongs to another company. This company provides technical and/or administrative services, relieving customers of the technical burdens of maintaining a Web server. In some cases the suspect makes it easy for you by putting a hyperlink to the hosting company's Web site on the suspect's Web page, or some other contact information might be displayed. In such cases, you merely need to go to the Web hosting company's site and look for an e-mail address or phone number to contact the provider of this server space. In other cases, you might need to use NSLookup or Whois to obtain this information.

Using Lookup Tools

NSLookup is a tool that can be run from computers running Windows NT and 2000, but Web-based versions of this tool are also available on the Internet. NSLookup can provide you with an IP address for a specified domain name or with a domain name for a specified IP address. Whois is a Web-based tool that can provide a bit more information, including contact information (mailing address and phone number) for the person who registered the site. When these tools are used, they will query DNS servers that store information about a particular Web site. A good Web site to use for determining information on a Web site is *name.space*. The name.space site can be visited at http://swhois.net and allows you to seek out information using either of these tools. By entering the Web site address into the **Whois** field and clicking the **Search** button, you can perform a search of the holder of this particular address. The screen shown in Figure A.1 reveals a great deal of information about a site.

Figure A.1 Results of a Whois search on the name.space Web site.

In Figure A.1, we have performed a Whois search on tacteam.net (one of many Web sites registered by the author of this book). On this screen, we can see that the "Registrant" section has different information from the "Technical Contact" section. The name of the person who registered the site appears in the "Registrant" section; this field probably contains the name of the person who paid for the site's registration or the name of a person who designed the site. For some sites, you'll see a name and street address here. Other, more careful registrants (like the author), aware that anyone can get this information easily, provide only a company name and post office box. The information might or might not be accurate, since there is no verification of this information and no requirement that it be updated if the registrant moves or changes phone numbers. The

"Technical Contact" section could contain the same information as the "Registrant" section, but in this case, another company is used to take care of the site's technical issues. The results often provide phone numbers, fax numbers, and e-mail addresses to contact both. Using this information, you can obtain valuable contact information and data about where additional information about the site's owner can be obtained.

At least, that's the way it works in an ideal world. In reality, you might find that the information you obtain through a Whois search is not as useful as you'd like. Cybercriminals who know they're engaging in illegal activity through their Web sites, as well as ordinary citizens concerned about privacy, usually won't be so accommodating as to provide street addresses and valid telephone numbers. You could end up with little more than a post office box number (which might no longer be valid) and an out-of-service telephone number. When suspects run their own Web servers on their own premises and use their own DNS servers, it becomes considerably more difficult to track down information.

Interpreting Domain Names

When looking at domain names, you will notice that they end with a top-level domain name, which is used to show the domain's purpose or country of origin. Common top-level domains and their general uses are as follows:

- **.com** Sites for commercial business use.
- **.edu** Sites belonging to an educational institution.
- **.gov** Sites belonging to U.S. government agencies.
- **.int** Organizations and databases established through international treaties.
- **.mil** American military sites.
- **.net** Network providers.
- **.org** Organizations (nonprofits).

You might have noticed when browsing the Internet that many of these domains are no longer reserved for their original purpose. Some sites ending in .com might not be business-related sites; they might be personal sites or Web sites with nonprofit-related purposes. This is also seen with .net sites; companies and people who aren't network providers use them. Therefore, you shouldn't accept the top-level domain as firm evidence of the purpose of a site.

Recently, the number of top-level domains has been expanded to include of the following additional ones:

- **.aero** Aviation-related companies.
- **.biz** Business-related sites (replaces intended use of .com).
- **.coop** Cooperative businesses.
- **.info** Information-related companies.
- **.museum** Museums.
- **.name** Personal sites.
- **.pro** Professionals (e.g., doctors, attorneys).

Two other popular top-level domains are .cc and .tv, which were originally country codes. Country codes are domain names that specify the country in which a site is registered and end in designations like .cc, tv, and others shown in Table A.1. Although many of the country code domains are restricted to companies and individuals within the associated country, .cc and .tv are exceptions to the rule. Tuvalu (a small Pacific island) has the .tv extension but entered into an agreement with a California company, and the .tv domain is now commonly used by television and Internet TV Web sites. Similarly, .cc belongs to the Cocos (Keeling) Islands, which is a small territory of Australia, but anyone willing to pay for this extension to their domain name can purchase it.

The information in Table A.1 is particularly useful when you are investigating e-mail addresses or Web sites with unfamiliar domains. If you were looking at a site or e-mail with a domain ending in .zw, would you really know it's registered in Zimbabwe? Knowing where a site is registered by looking at a table such as this one can provide a head start in determining where e-mail originates, where a site is located, and which Whois search engine should be used to acquire additional information. When looking at this table, however, remember that some information could change over time. In addition, remember that just because a site is registered in a particular country, that doesn't mean the person running the site currently lives there. Criminals can use false identification to register a site in another country, and even if the registrant lived in the country at the time the site was registered, there is generally no requirement that he or she give up the site after moving out of the country.

To obtain additional information through Whois search engines, you need to use a search engine that queries the country codes you're looking for. Common Whois search engines you'd use to obtain information about such sites are:

- ARIN for U.S. registry: www.arin.net
- CIRA for Canadian registry: www.registry.ca
- RIPE NCC for European registry: www.ripe.net
- APNIC for Asian Pacific registry: www.apnic.net
- Registro.br for Brazilian registry: http://registro.br
- NIC–Mexico for Mexican registry: www.nic.mx

Table A.1 Country codes of Web sites and e-mail addresses

Internet Country Code	Country Associated With Code
ad	Andorra
ae	United Arab Emirates
af	Afghanistan
ag	Antigua and Barbuda
ai	Anguilla
al	Albania
am	Armenia
an	Netherlands Antilles
ao	Angola
ar	Argentina
as	American Samoa
aq	Antarctica
at	Austria
au	Australia
aw	Aruba
az	Azerbaijan
ba	Bosnia and Herzegovina
bb	Barbados
bd	Bangladesh

Continued

Table A.1 Continued

Internet Country Code	Country Associated With Code
be	Belgium
bf	Burkina Faso
bg	Bulgaria
bh	Bahrain
bi	Burundi
bj	Benin
bm	Bermuda
bn	Brunei Darussalam
bo	Bolivia
br	Brazil
bs	Bahamas
bt	Bhutan
bv	Bouvet Island
bw	Botswana
by	Belarus
bz	Belize
ca	Canada
cc	Cocos (Keeling) Islands
cd	Democratic Republic of the Congo (formerly Zaire)
cf	Central African Republic
cg	Republic of the Congo (formerly French Middle Congo)
ch	Switzerland
ci	Cote d'Ivoire (Ivory Coast)
ck	Cook Islands
cl	Chile
cm	Cameroon
cn	China
co	Colombia
cr	Costa Rica
cs	Czechoslovakia (Former)
cu	Cuba

Continued

Table A.1 Continued

Internet Country Code	Country Associated With Code
cv	Cape Verde
cx	Christmas Islands
cy	Cyprus
cz	Czech Republic
de	Germany
dj	Djibouti
dk	Denmark
dm	Dominica
do	Dominican Republic
dz	Algeria
ec	Ecuador
ee	Estonia
eg	Egypt
eh	Western Sahara
er	Eritrea
es	Spain
et	Ethiopia
fi	Finland
fj	Fiji
fk	Falkland Islands (Islas Malvinas)
fm	Micronesia
fo	Faroe Islands
fr	France
fx	France (Metropolitan)
ga	Gabon
gb	Great Britain (United Kingdom)
gd	Grenada
ge	Georgia
gf	French Guyana
gh	Ghana
gi	Gibraltar

Continued

Table A.1 Continued

Internet Country Code	Country Associated With Code
gl	Greenland
gm	The Gambia
gn	Guinea
gp	Guadeloupe
gq	Equatorial Guinea
gr	Greece
gs	South Georgia and the South Sandwich Islands
gt	Guatemala
gu	Guam
gw	Guinea-Bissau
gy	Guyana
kh	Cambodia
hk	Hong Kong
hm	Heard Island and McDonald Islands
hn	Honduras
hr	Croatia (Hrvatsaka)
ht	Haiti
hu	Hungary
id	Indonesia
ie	Ireland
il	Israel
in	India
io	British Indian Ocean Territory
iq	Iraq
ir	Iran
is	Iceland
it	Italy
jm	Jamaica
jp	Japan
jo	Jordan
ke	Kenya

Continued

Table A.1 Continued

Internet Country Code	Country Associated With Code
ki	Kiribati
km	Comoros
kn	Saint Kitts and Nevis
kp	North Korea
kg	Kyrgyzstan
kr	South Korea
kw	Kuwait
ky	Cayman Islands
kz	Kazakhstan
la	Laos
lb	Lebanon
lc	Saint Lucia
li	Liechtenstein
ls	Lesotho
lr	Liberia
lt	Lithuania
lu	Luxembourg
lv	Latvia
ly	Libyan Arab Jamahiriya
ma	Morocco
mc	Monaco
md	Moldova
mg	Madagascar
mh	Marshall Islands
mk	Macedonia
ml	Mali
mm	Myanmar
mn	Mongolia
mo	Macau
mp	Northern Mariana Islands
mq	Martinique

Continued

Table A.1 Continued

Internet Country Code	Country Associated With Code
mr	Mauritania
ms	Montserrat
mt	Malta
mu	Mauritius
mv	Maldives
mw	Malawi
mx	Mexico
my	Malaysia
mz	Mozambique
na	Namibia
nc	New Caledonia
ne	Niger
nf	Norfolk Island
ng	Nigeria
ni	Nicaragua
nl	Netherlands
no	Norway
np	Nepal
nr	Nauru
nu	Niue
nz	New Zealand (Aotearoa)
om	Oman
pa	Panama
pf	French Polynesia
pe	Peru
pg	Papua New Guinea
ph	Philippines
pk	Pakistan
pl	Poland
pm	Saint Pierre and Miquelon
pn	Pitcairn Islands

Continued

Table A.1 Continued

Internet Country Code	Country Associated With Code
pr	Puerto Rico
ps	Palestinian Territory
pt	Portugal
pw	Palau
py	Paraguay
qa	Qatar
re	Reunion
ro	Romania
ru	Russian Federation
rw	Rwanda
sa	Saudi Arabia
sb	Solomon Islands
sc	Seychelles
sd	Sudan
se	Sweden
sg	Singapore
sh	Saint Helena
si	Slovenia
sj	Svalbard and Jan Mayan Islands
sk	Sri Lanka
sk	Slovakia
sl	Sierra Leone
sm	San Marino
sn	Senegal
so	Somalia
sr	Suriname
st	Sao Tome and Principe
su	Russia (former Soviet Union)
sv	El Salvador
sy	Syrian Arab Republic
sz	Swaziland

Continued

Table A.1 Continued

Internet Country Code	Country Associated With Code
tc	Turks and Caicos Islands
td	Chad
tf	French Southern Territories and Antarctic Lands
tg	Togo
th	Thailand
tj	Tajikistan
tk	Tokelau
tm	Turkmenistan
tn	Tunisia
to	Tonga
tp	East Timor
tr	Turkey
tt	Trinidad and Tobago
tv	Tuvalu
tw	Taiwan
tz	Tanzania
ua	Ukraine
ug	Uganda
um	United States Minor Outlying Islands
us	United States
uy	Uruguay
uz	Uzbekistan
va	Vatican City
vc	Saint Vincent and the Grenadines
ve	Venezuela
vi	Virgin Islands (British)
vn	Vietnam
vq	Virgin Islands (U.S.)
vu	Vanuatu
wf	Wallis and Futuna Islands
ws	Samoa

Continued

Table A.1 Continued

Internet Country Code	Country Associated With Code
ye	Yemen
yt	Mayotte
yu	Yugoslavia
za	South Africa
zr	Zaire (Former)
zm	Zambia
zw	Zimbabwe

Extraditing and Prosecuting

The ability to investigate and prosecute cybercrimes can become complicated when a single crime crosses one or more international borders. Although a suspect might be physically sitting at a machine in one country, the information he or she taps into could go across many jurisdictions as it flows from another computer in a foreign land. In some cases, the cybercriminal might use anonymous e-mail addresses or technologies that make him appear to be working in a different country than the one he is actually in. By attacking a system in this way, the crime becomes more difficult to detect and even more difficult to prosecute. Other difficulties inherent in prosecuting international cybercrimes include:

- **The language barrier** Difficulty of communicating with law enforcement and others in countries where you don't speak the language.

- **Time factors** Any cybercrime investigation can stretch out over months or even years. Keeping the investigation alive is difficult enough when all the parties involved are in the same geographic area, but it becomes even more difficult across national boundaries.

- **Cost** Traveling to a foreign country or countries could be necessary to pursue an international case. Few police agencies have budgets that cover such expenses, except in the most heinous and high-profile crimes.

- **Political factors** Even when law enforcement agencies in different jurisdictions want to cooperate, they might be restricted by political factions above them.

In many cases, the source of a crime might originate in one country where legislation differs from that of your own country or where the act is not a crime at all. For example, although child pornography might be defined as pornographic images of persons under 18 years of age in North America, the legal age to pose for such images in other countries might be considerably younger. This difference can cause a dilemma for law enforcement officers, since it is legal for a Web site in one country to distribute the images but illegal for people in other countries to download them. Investigators can arrest people in possession of the pornographic files, but they might be powerless to shut down the Web site distributing the pornography.

If a crime is committed in one country and the offender is located in another country, there is sometimes a need to extradite the offender. However, this isn't always possible. Extradition requires the cooperation of the country in which the offender resides. In the case of the person who allegedly authored the Love Bug virus, U.S. law enforcement officers tried to have the culprit extradited to the United States from the Philippines. As has been the case with numerous crimes committed on one nation's soil when the offender is located in another nation, the request for extradition was denied by the Philippine government. Many countries have laws and punishments that differ from those in the United States, and they might refuse extradition if they feel the punishment that the offender would be subject to in the United States for a particular crime is unjust under their law. In other cases, they could feel it is bad precedent to turn their citizens over into the hands of a foreign nation anytime they're asked to do so. Although the person who allegedly wrote the Love Bug virus was charged in the Philippines, as we noted, it was found that he couldn't be prosecuted there because no laws existed that explicitly dealt with the dissemination of viruses.

NOTE

Under international law, there is no obligation for a country to extradite unless a treaty between the countries creates such an obligation. This situation gives nations a lot of leeway in granting or refusing extradition. The extradition treaties that the United States has signed generally require that evidence be provided showing the accused person has violated both U.S. law and the law of the country requesting extradition. Often, extradition treaties specify the particular offenses for which a person can be extradited. Unlike the United States, some European nations try their own citizens for crimes committed in other countries.

Once a suspect is extradited to your jurisdiction, additional international cooperation is usually needed. Witnesses might need to be flown in from the other countries. If they choose not to come voluntarily, a subpoena can be issued. Ignoring the subpoena can be declared contempt of court by the judge, who can then have a warrant issued for the witness's arrest. However, since the witness is in another country and might never set foot in yours, the warrant can't be served and is effectively useless. The criminal suspect might have been extradited, but it is doubtful that an extradition request will be granted for a witness who failed to show at trial. If the witness does comply, he or she will need to be transported to the location of the court and provided with proper accommodations and food during the trial. It might be necessary to hire interpreters if the witness speaks a foreign language. All these factors increase the cost of prosecuting the offender, which may lead the prosecutor to drop charges or never file them to begin with.

Summary

In this appendix, we discussed the problems that arise when cybercrime crosses international boundaries. When investigating a cybercrime, you might find that the person who committed the crime has traveled through cyberspace across numerous jurisdictions and committed crimes using computers in foreign countries, often in a deliberate attempt to remain elusive. When crimes are committed in this way, you might need to consider the laws of other nations when you attempt to arrest and prosecute a suspect.

Although many nations lack laws that specifically deal with cybercrime, this situation is improving as countries modify existing laws and create new ones that address this growing threat. In some cases, however, you might find that the perpetrator of a crime cannot be arrested or extradited due to legislation or custom in the country in which the offender resides. In other situations, cooperation could be possible and even welcomed by police and the governments in other countries. It is important to contact officials in those countries to determine the level of cooperation available before pursuing the case.

The Internet can be a powerful tool for acquiring information about another country's legislation and the law enforcement agencies you might deal with. Many police and law enforcement agencies throughout the world have Web sites and e-mail addresses, allowing you to contact a representative and form a cooperative relationship that will be invaluable in proceeding against an international cybercriminal.

Resources

- U.S. Department of Justice's Computer Crime and Intellectual Property Section: Information on cybercrimes committed around the world
  www.cybercrime.gov

- Canadian Department of Justice: Provides a search engine for determining which Canadian laws apply to a particular crime
  http://laws.justice.gc.ca/en/index.html

- Canadian Security Intelligence Service (CSIS)
  www.csis–scrs.gc.ca

- Communications Security Establishment (CSE) of Canada: Provides IT security to the government
  www.cse.dnd.ca

- Royal Canadian Mounted Police (RCMP): Information on investigating computer crime and assisting local police services with crimes related to computers, networks, and the Internet
www.rcmp-grc.gc.ca/scams/cpu-cri.htm

- The London Metropolitan Police in England: Information dealing with cybercrime; site provides crime prevention tips and other information
www.met.police.uk/computercrime

- The Police Services of the UK: Links to law enforcement organizations throughout the United Kingdom
www.police.uk

- International Criminal Police Organization (Interpol): Reference guide dealing with child sexual offences in member countries. This guide provides a country-by-country listing of member countries' laws. When viewing this information, it is important to remember that these laws might have changed since the last update, and contacting representatives of the country you're researching could be required
www.interpol.int/Public/Children/SexualAbuse/NationalLaws

- Europol: European law enforcement organization
www.europol.eu.int

- The International Association of Chiefs of Police: Police organization with members from over 100 countries
www.theiacp.org

- Officer.com: Provides resources for law enforcement officers
www.officer.com

- The Information Warfare Site
www.iwar.org.uk/law/index.htm

- The Center for Democracy and Technology
www.cdt.org/international/cybercrime

- Investigative Resources International: Links to information that might be useful in investigations
www.factfind.com/database.htm

- The Internet Watch Foundation (IWF): Users report child pornography located on any Web server in the world and racist material residing on servers in the United Kingdom. Once a report of child pornography is made, the IWF will view the material to determine if it is illegal and then contact the ISP hosting the site and the police www.internetwatch.org.uk

- Cyber Criminals Most Wanted
www.ccmostwanted.com

- FindLaw: Search for legislation for a wide number of nations http://findlaw.com/12international/countries

- Pritchard Law Webs: Searchable Internet Law Library www.priweb.com/internetlawlib/52.htm

- Center for Strategic and International Studies: Articles dealing with a variety of cybercrime and security issues, including cyberterrorism www.csis.org

- Moss tingrett (Moss District Court): Norwegian site that provides information on cybercrime legislation for 43 countries www.mossbyrett.of.no/info/legal.html

- Privacy International's cybercrime section www.privacyinternational.org/issues/cybercrime

Index

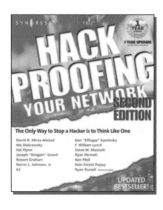